THE LOST TRAVELLER'S DREAM

KELLY CHERRY

P9-EEL-720

Morový sloup   The Plague Monument

by Jaroslav Seifert   translated by Lyn Coffin

POEMS BY
Philip Appleman

DARWIN'S ARK

ILLUSTRATIONS BY
Rudy Pozzatti

He found giants
in the earth: Mastodon,
Mylodon, thigh-bones
like tree-trunks, Megatherium skulls

FANATIC HEART
SELECTED STORIES OF
EDNA O'BRIEN

FOREWORD BY PHI

Dictionary of Literary Biography
Yearbook: 1984

Dictionary of Literary Biography

Documentary Series

Yearbooks

Dictionary of Literary Biography
Yearbook: 1984

6232

Edited by
Jean W. Ross

A Bruccoli Clark Book
Gale Research Company • Book Tower • Detroit Michigan 48226

Manufactured by Edwards Brothers, Inc.
Ann Arbor, Michgan
Printed in the United States of America

Copyright © 1985
GALE RESEARCH COMPANY

Library of Congress Catalog Card Number 82-645185
ISBN 0-8103-1628-5
ISSN 0731-7867

Contents

Obituaries

Updated Entry

New Entries

Plan of the Series

. . . Almost the most prodigious asset of a country, and perhaps its most precious possession, is its native literary product—when that product is fine and noble and enduring.

Mark Twain*

The advisory board, the editors, and the publisher of the *Dictionary of Literary Biography* are joined in endorsing Mark Twain's declaration. The literature of a nation provides an inexhaustible resource of permanent worth. It is our expectation that this endeavor will make literature and its creators better understood and more accessible to students and the literate public, while satisfying the standards of teachers and scholars.

To meet these requirements, *literary biography* has been construed in terms of the author's achievement. The most important thing about a writer is his writing. Accordingly, the entries in *DLB* are career biographies, tracing the development of the author's canon and the evolution of his reputation.

The publication plan for *DLB* resulted from two years of preparation. The project was proposed to Bruccoli Clark by Frederick G. Ruffner, president of the Gale Research Company, in November 1975. After specimen entries were prepared and typeset, an advisory board was formed to refine the entry format and develop the series rationale. In meetings held during 1976, the publisher, series editors, and advisory board approved the scheme for a comprehensive biographical dictionary of persons who contributed to North American literature. Editorial work on the first volume began in January 1977, and it was published in 1978.

In order to make *DLB* more than a reference tool and to compile volumes that individually have claim to status as literary history, it was decided to organize volumes by topic or period or genre. Each of these freestanding volumes provides a biographical-bibliographical guide and overview for a particular area of literature. We are convinced that this organization—as opposed to a single alphabet method—constitutes a valuable innovation in the presentation of reference material. The volume plan necessarily requires many decisions for the placement and treatment of authors who might properly be included in two or three volumes. In some instances a major figure will be included in separate volumes, but with different entries emphasizing the aspect of his career appropriate to each volume. Ernest Hemingway, for example, is represented in *American Writers in Paris, 1920-1939* by an entry focusing on his expatriate apprenticeship; he is also in *American Novelists, 1910-1945* with an entry surveying his entire career. Each volume includes a cumulative index of subject authors. The final *DLB* volume will be a comprehensive index to the entire series.

With volume ten in 1982 it was decided to enlarge the scope of *DLB* beyond the literature of the United States. By the end of 1984 fourteen volumes treating British literature had been published, and volumes for Commonwealth and Modern European literature were in progress. The series has been further augmented by the *DLB Yearbooks* (since 1981) which update published entries and add new entries to keep the *DLB* current with contemporary activity. There have also been occasional *DLB Documentary Series* volumes which provide biographical and critical background source materials for figures whose work is judged to have particular interest for students. One of these companion volumes is entirely devoted to Tennessee Williams.

The purpose of *DLB* is not only to provide reliable information in a convenient format but also to place the figures in the larger perspective of literary history and to offer appraisals of their accomplishments by qualified scholars.

We define literature as the *intellectual commerce of a nation:* not merely as belles lettres, but as that ample and complex process by which ideas are generated, shaped, and transmitted. *DLB* entries are not limited to "creative writers" but extend to other figures who in this time and in this way influenced the mind of a people. Thus the series encompasses historians, journalists, publishers, and screenwriters. By this means readers of *DLB* may be aided to perceive literature not as cult scripture in the keeping of cultural high priests, but as at the center of a nation's life.

*From an unpublished section of Mark Twain's autobiography, copyright © by the Mark Twain Company.

DLB includes the major writers appropriate to each volume and those standing in the ranks immediately behind them. Scholarly and critical counsel has been sought in deciding which minor figures to include and how full their entries should be. Wherever possible, useful references will be made to figures who do not warrant separate entries.

Each *DLB* volume has a volume editor responsible for planning the volume, selecting the figures for inclusion, and assigning the entries. Volume editors are also responsible for preparing, where appropriate, appendices surveying the major periodicals and literary and intellectual movements for their volumes, as well as lists of further readings. Work on the series as a whole is coordinated at the Bruccoli Clark editorial center in Columbia, South Carolina, where the editorial staff is responsible for the accuracy of the published volumes.

One feature that distinguishes *DLB* is the illustration policy—its concern with the iconography of literature. Just as an author is influenced by his surroundings, so is the reader's understanding of the author enhanced by a knowledge of his environment. Therefore *DLB* volumes include not only drawings, paintings, and photographs of authors, often depicting them at various stages in their careers, but also illustrations of their families and places where they lived. Title pages are regularly reproduced in facsimile along with dust jackets for modern authors. The dust jackets are a special feature of *DLB* because they often document better than anything else the way in which an author's work was launched in its own time. Specimens of the writers' manuscripts are included when feasible.

A supplement to *DLB*—tentatively titled *A Guide, Chronology, and Glossary for American Literature*—will outline the history of literature in North America and trace the influences that shaped it. This volume will provide a framework for the study of American literature by means of chronological tables, literary affiliation charts, glossarial entries, and concise surveys of the major movements. It has been planned to stand on its own as a vade mecum, providing a ready-reference guide to the study of American literature as well as a companion to the *DLB* volumes for American literature.

Samuel Johnson rightly decreed that "The chief glory of every people arises from its authors." The purpose of the *Dictionary of Literary Biography* is to compile literary history in the surest way available to us—by accurate and comprehensive treatment of the lives and work of those who contributed to it.

The *DLB* Advisory Board

Foreword

The *Dictionary of Literary Biography Yearbook* is guided by the same principles that have provided the basic rationale for the entire *DLB* series: 1) the literature of a nation represents an inexhaustible resource of permanent worth; 2) the surest way to trace the outlines of literary history is by a comprehensive treatment of the lives and works of those who contributed to it; and 3) the greatest service the series can provide is to make literary achievement better understood and more accessible to students and the literate public, while serving the needs of scholars. In keeping with those principles, the *Yearbook* has been planned to augment *DLB* by reflecting the vitality of contemporary literature and summarizing current literary activity. The librarian, scholar, or student attempting to stay informed of literary developments is faced with an endless task. The purpose of *DLB Yearbook* is to serve these readers while at the same time enlarging the scope of *DLB*.

DLB Yearbook is divided into four sections: articles about the past year's literary events or topics; obituaries and tributes; updates of published *DLB* entries; and new author entries. The articles section features essays which discuss the year's work in literary biography, fiction, poetry, and drama. The *Yearbook* also endeavors to cover major awards and prizes. This volume covers the 1984 Nobel Prize in Literature (including the Swedish Academy's announcement, three of Jaroslav Seifert's poems in translation, and an appreciation of his work) and the Ingersoll Prizes. Each year a literary research archive is described; the 1984 *Yearbook*'s subject is the Lilly Library. In a new feature, "Biographical Documents," the *Yearbook* presents the revised *Who's Who in America* questionnaires of fifteen writers. Literary topics of current interest are explored: in this *Yearbook* there are reports on Chicano literature, the new edition of James Joyce's *Ulysses*, and the Orwell year; an opinion poll on Anthony Burgess's *99 Novels;* and an assessment of the bestseller lists. In addition, there is a report on the Modern Language Association of America, which celebrated its centennial in 1983 and 1984. A special feature of the first section is an interview with a distinguished practicing biographer—this year Humphrey Carpenter—and an article on the Jargon Society is the first in a new series on small presses.

The death of a literary figure prompts an assessment of his achievement and reputation. The Obituaries section marks the passing of ten authors and the publisher Alfred A. Knopf in 1984. Comments from the authors' and publisher's contemporaries have also been solicited.

The third section, Updated Entries, is designed to supplement the *DLB* series with current information about the literary activities of authors who have entries in previously published *DLB* volumes. An Updated Entry takes as its point of departure an already published *DLB* entry, augmenting primary and secondary bibliographical information, providing descriptions and assessments of new works, and, when necessary, reassessing an author's reputation. The form of entry is similar to that in the standard *DLB* series, and an Updated Entry is preceded by a reference to the *DLB* volume in which the basic entry on the subject appears. Readers seeking information about an author's entire career should consult the basic entry along with the Updated Entry for complete biographical and bibliographical information.

The fourth section is devoted to New Entries on figures not previously included in *DLB*. These entries follow the established format for the series: emphasis is placed on biography and summaries of the critical reception of the author's works; primary bibliographies precede each entry, and a list of references follows the entry.

Each *Yearbook* includes a list of literary prizes and awards, a necrology, and a checklist of books about literary history and biography published during the year.

From the outset, the *DLB* series has undertaken to compile literary history as it is revealed in the lives and works of authors. The *Yearbook* supports that commitment, providing a useful and necessary current record. The march of literature does not halt.

Acknowledgments

This book was produced by BC Research. Karen L. Rood is senior editor for the *Dictionary of Literary Biography* series.

Art supervisor is Claudia Ericson. Copyediting supervisor is Joycelyn R. Smith. Typesetting supervisor is Laura Ingram. The production staff includes Rowena Betts, Kimberly Casey, Patricia Coate, Kathleen M. Flanagan, Joyce Fowler, Pamela Haynes, Judith K. Ingle, Victoria Jakes, Vickie Lowers, Judith McCray, and Alice Parsons. Joseph Caldwell, photography editor, did photographic copy work for the volume.

Walter W. Ross did the library research with the assistance of the staff at the Thomas Cooper Library of the University of South Carolina: Lynn Barron, Daniel Boice, Sue Collins, Michael Freeman, Gary Geer, Alexander M. Gilchrist, David L. Haggard, Jens Holley, David Lincove, Marcia Martin, Jean Rhyne, Karen Rissling, Paula Swope, and Ellen Tillett. Valuable help was given also by staff members of the Richland County Public Library in Columbia, South Carolina.

Random House and Harcourt Brace Jovanovich kindly provided photographs for the volume, as did the Ingersoll Foundation, the Modern Language Association of America, Center for Book Research, and the International Order of E.A.R.S., Inc.

Special thanks are due to the Swedish Embassy in Washington, D.C., and the Swedish Academy; and to the Berg Collection, New York Public Library.

Dictionary of Literary Biography Yearbook: 1984

Dictionary of Literary Biography

The 1984 Nobel Prize in Literature

ANNOUNCEMENT BY THE SWEDISH ACADEMY

In October 1984 the Swedish Academy awarded the Nobel Prize in Literature to Jaroslav Seifert for his poetry, "which, endowed with freshness, sensuality, and rich inventiveness, provides a liberating image of the indomitable spirit and versatility of man."

Born on 23 September 1901 in a working-class district on the outskirts of Prague, Seifert made his debut as a poet in 1920 with *City in Tears.* His travels brought him into contact with French modernism and dadaism. On his return to Czechoslovakia he joined the "poetists," who while remaining political radicals hailed freedom and imagination and art as play, and rejected the idea that art should have a social and moral mission. A trip to the Soviet Union in 1925 left Seifert critical of the revolution and led to his break with the Communist Party in 1929.

In the late 1930s Seifert developed patriotic themes in his poetry. The poems *Eight Days,* written in 1937 upon the death of Masaryk, are an address to the founder of Czechoslovakia and were published in six editions the same year. Later books contain resistance poems and deal with the Prague rebellion and the liberation of Czechoslovakia.

After the Communist takeover in 1948, Seifert wrote poetry that was considered disloyal, bourgeois, and escapist. Because of his refusal to conform to the slogans of social realism, he was felt to be a traitor to his class. A speech he gave at the Czechoslovakian Writers' Association in Congress in 1956, in which he criticized the cultural policies of the state, resulted in a ban on publication of his new works, though his previous works continued to be published. When the political climate changed in 1964, Seifert was awarded the title of National Artist. His poetry between 1964 and 1968 took a

new direction with his abandonment of regular verse forms.

During 1968 Seifert worked for the rehabilitation of persecuted authors and condemned the Soviet invasion. In 1969 he was elected chairman of the Czechoslovakian Writers' Association, but was deposed by the Husák regime. After a period of suppression, his works began to be published again by 1979, though, according to some of his American translators, they were recently not stocked by any of Prague's two hundred bookshops.

Seifert, now in his eighties, is bedridden with a heart condition. His daughter attended the awards ceremony in Sweden to accept his prize. In its press release, the Swedish Academy praised Seifert as a writer who "conjures up for us another world than that of tyranny and desolation—a world that exists both here and now, although it may be hidden from our view and borne in chains, and one that exists in our indomitable spirit. His poetry is," the Academy concludes, "an act of deliverance."

JAROSLAV SEIFERT THROUGH THE EYES OF THE ENGLISH-SPEAKING READER

George Gibian

Since Jaroslav Seifert was awarded the Nobel Prize in October 1984, Czechs living in English-speaking countries have become accustomed to being asked, who is Seifert, and what is his poetry like? Does he deserve the Nobel Prize? To understand something of Seifert's appeal, the reader

Jaroslav Seifert

should consider certain qualities that make his work outstanding.

First, his poetry, particularly in the last two decades, is utterly simple and understated. Seifert is unrhetorical, transparent. He has such a light touch that the translator can easily fall into bathos or flat banality. His ordinariness is very deceptive, however; within his prose-like narrative, which reads sometimes like a plain letter to a close friend, there is a strange tension, and he can suddenly leap out with a very poignant word, phrase, or line that seems all the more powerful for its contrast with the deceptively light touch surrounding it.

A second quality is a frequently recurring sensuality. Seifert's eroticism is not exhibitionistic, but rather accepting and natural.

Third, Seifert is very unpretentious. One has to explain to people in the United States that on the whole, poetry is much more widely read in Czechoslovakia than in the United States; poets (Seifert as a signal example) are revered and sometimes even become famous personages, national heroes. The Czech people regard Seifert as very much one of them, both popular and populist. His poetry is not

intellectual, but comfortable.

Fourth, Seifert's verse is haunting and lyrical. He can sing, and particularly in his poetry of the 1920s and 1930s, he often rises into haunting heights of lyricism. Sometimes there is great charm and even magic in his poetry. One strain which occurs often is melancholy.

Fifth, Seifert occasionally rises into high pathos, which produces a poignancy all the more powerful for its rarity. This is especially true in his poems about Prague, Czechoslovakia, and historical tragedies such as the death of Thomas Masaryk, the disaster of the Munich agreement, the German occupation, and the killing of the Jews in World War II.

One must admit to the English-speaking public that, for the non-Czech reader, there are difficulties in the way of appreciating Seifert. His poetry is very allusive: his references to Czech culture range from historical anniversaries to wildflowers, sometimes including the sculptures and other architectural landmarks of Prague. The emotional resonances these cause in Czech readers are lost in explanatory footnotes. Seifert's memoirs especially can seem local and parochial to a non-Czech. An American academic will take notice if he reads Seifert's pages on Roman Jakobson, who went on to become a famous scholar in the United States after he left Prague, but most of Seifert's memoirs (and many passages in his poems) will seem to be confined to an alien, private milieu.

On still another level, Seifert is difficult to translate for the English reader. Much of his poetry plays on the sound resources of the Czech language. Not only is Seifert a genius at finding surprising, original rhymes, but he mingles meters and rhythms with patterns of vowels and consonants, assonances, internal rhymes, and half rhymes. Particularly untranslatable are his harmonies based on long vowels, which in Czech are independent of stress and carry phonological meaning (unlike those in English or Russian).

Some of the Czech attitudes expressed in Seifert's poetry might present difficulties to the English reader. A literal translation can be misleading.

One of the two Seifert books published in the United States (Iowa City: The Spirit That Moves Us Press, 1983)

The word *bydli*, for example, is difficult to translate. The English "to live" is too general (it also carries the meaning of the Czech *zije*, with which *bydli* contrasts); the meaning of "to live" as "to exist" is exactly what Seifert is avoiding in the line *"To se to pekne na tom svete bydli."*

Seifert often refers to smells: in English these references must be translated as perfume, odor, or fragrance, because *smell* connotes unpleasantness in English. Particularly Seifert's lines about the odor of someone's mouth easily become in translation inaccurate, ludicrous, or offensive.

One final difficulty of Seifert's work is that he wrote a great deal, and some of his poems—especially some early, shrill, political ones—are not very good. An English translation of these would cause the reader to have a low opinion of Seifert. He benefits from a careful selection. An anthology of perhaps one hundred poems would demonstrate best to the English-speaking world how and why this modest poet, who is very Czech in language, feeling, and attitude, richly deserved the Nobel Prize—on his own behalf and on behalf of the ten or twelve Czech poets of his generation—including Halas, Nezval, and Holan—whose appearance in twentieth-century Czech literature seems almost a miracle, and whose excellence non-Czech readers unfortunately have to take on faith.

THREE POEMS BY
JAROSLAV SEIFERT

Translated by George Gibian

Paradise Lost

The old Jewish cemetery
Is all a bouquet of grey stones
that time stepped on.
I wandered among the graves
and thought of my mother.
She used to read the bible.

Letters in two columns
spouted before her eyes
like blood out of a wound.
The lamp crackled and smoked
and my mother put on her glasses.
She had to blow it out at times
and straighten the glowing wick
with a hairpin.

But when she half shut her tired eyes
she dreamed of Paradise

before God had occupied it
with his armed cherubs.
Often she fell asleep and the book
slipped into her lap.

I was still young
when I discovered in the Old Testament
gripping verses about love
and eagerly looked up places
where it talks about incest.
I did not have an inkling then
how much tenderness hides in the names
of Old Testament women.

Ada is Ornament and Orpha
is Doe,
Naomi is Sweet One
and Mikol, Rivulet.

Abigail is Spring of Comfort.
But when I remember
How helplessly we watched
while they dragged the Jews
with crying children
even today terror shakes me
and a chill runs down my back.

Jemima is Dove and Tamar
is Palm.
Tersu is Charming
and Zelpha, Raindrop.
My God, how beautiful it is.

Hell more or less was here already,
and still nobody dared
to tear the weapons away from those murderers.
As if we did not have in us
even a little human pity!

The name Jeholia means
The Lord is powerful.
But their frowning god
looked past the barbed wire
and did not move a finger.

Delilah is Delicious, Rachel
is Little Lamb.
Debora is Bee
and Esther, Bright Star.

I had just come back from the cemetery
when the June evening with its perfumes
leaned against the windows.
But out of the quiet distance from time to time thun-
    dered
the future war!
There is no time without murdering.

But I almost forgot,

Rhoda is Rose.
And this blossom may be the only thing
that is left in our world
from the old Paradise.

A Conversation

/She/:

Were you kissing my forehead or my mouth,
I don't know
I only caught the sound of a sweet voice
and thick darkness
Encircled my frightened eyelashes.

/He/:

I kissed you hastily on your forehead,
because I was benumbed
by the fragrance of your streaming breath,
but I don't know
—I only caught the sound of a sweet voice
and thick darkness
encircled my frightened eyelashes,
were you kissing my forehead or my mouth?

The Poets' Mistress

Foolish moments of first loves!
At that time I still believed
that to die amidst blossoms,
when one is in love
head over heels,
or to die in Venice during the carnival
can be more beautiful
than at home in one's bed.

Death, though, is the mistress of all pains
known to the world.
Her train is woven
with the rattle of the dying
and embroidered with stars of tears.

Death is the flute of laments,
the torch of burning blood,
the urn of beauty
and the gate to nowhere.

Sometimes she is even the mistress of poets.
Let them court her
in the smell of dead blossoms,
if they aren't bothered
by the tolling of gloomy bells,
which have started to march
and step in bloody mud.

Death slips her long slender hand
into the bodies of women
and chokes the infants under their hearts.
They will go to paradise
but all covered with blood.

She is the empress of all murdering
and her scepter
has commanded since the beginning of the world
the horrors of the wars.

Death is the little sister of rot,
the messenger of vanity and nothing,
and her hands
push down on everybody's breast
the load of the grave.

But death is also only the moment,
a scratch of the pen
and no more.

A Contemporary Flourescence of Chicano Literature

Carl R. Shirley
University of South Carolina

Chicano literature is at once as old as the Spanish presence in the New World and as new as today's *Los Angeles Times*. Generally, Chicanos, or Mexican Americans, as they are also called, are citizens of the United States whose ancestors were Spanish until 1821, the year of Mexico's independence from Spain, or Mexican. Some families have been here since the early seventeenth century, while others are newcomers. They all share, to a greater or lesser degree, language, culture, history, religion, traditions, and values that make them unique. Chicano literature is but one artistic manifestation of their increasingly significant place in modern America.

A glance at a map of North America from around 1600 will reveal that Spain controlled, albeit rather loosely, the area which today comprises the states of Texas, Arizona, New Mexico, California, Nevada, Utah, and Colorado. In addition to autochthonous peoples, the region was populated by Spaniards, Creoles (Spaniards born in the New World), and Mestizos (a mixture of Spanish and Native American), all moving north from what is now Mexico. They established towns, built missions and roads; they brought with them the Spanish language, the Catholic church, Spanish laws, new methods of agriculture, food, livestock, art, architecture, literature, and a literary tradition. In 1848 Mexico signed the Treaty of Guadalupe Hidalgo, by which this vast territory was added to the United States. After one year, all people who chose to remain in the region automatically became United States citizens. From that date to the present, Anglo-American culture, language, traditions, and values have been combined with or superim-

posed on the Hispanic ones to form the Chicano. Immigration, both legal and illegal, and the proximity to Mexico have continued to reinforce the Hispanic ways so that the majority of Chicanos have never been fully "Americanized" in quite the same way as most other ethnic groups. Rather, they are an adaptive and creative people who have assimilated elements from three cultures to form a separate, very distinct one. They are by no means a homogenous group, but they do share a history, values, and traditions. Population estimates vary greatly, but most sources agree that there are at least 14 million Chicanos. While the majority live in the Southwest, there are large concentrations in other places, notably the Midwestern states of Illinois, Indiana, Ohio, Minnesota, and Wisconsin. Chicanos presently live in every state in the union.

There are several theories concerning the origin of the word *Chicano*, the most prominent being that it is a derivative of *mexicano*, which is in turn derivative of *mexica* (pronounced "meshica"). No matter what its origin, the term was in widespread use by the 1950s, supplanting the old designation of *Mexican* or the sociological sounding *Mexican-American*. Some people today resent the word, viewing it as pejorative, but it has gained in use and popularity to the point that for many it is a symbol of pride, especially among politically and socially active groups.

The languages of the Chicanos are an intriguing combination. Many people are perfectly bilingual in standard Spanish and standard English, while some speak only English and others only Spanish. Most speak and understand a third lan-

Cover for the best-known Chicano novel and winner of the Premio Quinto Sol National Chicano literary award

guage, variously called "Caló," "Pocho," or "Pachuco." This is a mixture of English and Spanish vocabularies, grammars, and structures which is more than a hybrid in that it is greater than the sum of its parts. It is a new language which combines borrowings from each of its ancestors with additions of new words and unique structures. Contemporary Chicano literature is written in all three languages in varying combinations. While the blend may pose difficulties for the person who does not speak Spanish, it is a source of literary strength for a Chicano writer because it enables him to reflect three sometimes distinct realities: Anglo, Mexican, and Chicano.

The Chicano's literary heritage, like his cultural heritage, is tripartite: 1) The Indian past, called *Aztlán,* after the name of the mythical home of the Aztecs (the period prior to 1519, the date of the Cortéz invasion); *Aztlán* generally refers to the entire Southwest but has also become a symbol for a homeland of a spiritual nation of Chicanos; 2) The

Spanish and Mexican heritage, from 1519 to 1848, with reinforcement continuing to the present; 3) The Anglo overlay dating from the early and mid-nineteenth century. Chicano literature can be said to extend as far back as 1598, when the troops of Spanish explorer Juan de Oñate first performed a play in what is now the United States. There is a rich history and tradition of folklore, poetry, prose, and theater from that time to the present. It is with the writings following World War II, however, that Chicano literature really began to draw attention to itself from outside its own circle.

Historically, the themes and subjects are the ones common to all literatures. In contemporary writing, there are some special ones which appear frequently in all genres. Among them are social protest and exploitation, the migratory experience, self-exploration or definition (which includes the exploration of myths and legends), and life in the "barrio," the Chicano district of a city or town. There is also "La Raza," or the Race, which, like Aztlán, has a spiritual connotation that joins all peoples of Spanish-speaking America. Beginning in the mid-1960s, much Chicano literature became a reflection of a social and political movement, with attitudes ranging from the advocation of complete separation from the Anglo society to a stance calling for a Mexican-American cultural identification within the framework of the larger society.

The history of prose written by Chicanos can be traced to the chronicles of the earliest explorers. These, combined with letters from government officials and the clergy, provide not only valuable historical information but also entertaining reading. In the first half of the nineteenth century, there was a flourishing of histories, diaries, and memoirs; short narrative pieces were published in countless newspapers, and novels began to appear toward the end of the century. Contemporary prose can be dated from 1947 with the short stories of Mario Suárez in the *Arizona Quarterly.* His characters live in Tucson in a barrio called "El Hoyo" (The Hole) and represent a variety of Mexican-American traits, customs, and values. Suárez's work is wryly humorous and his figures are rather cynical, in marked contrast to most of the romanticized and precious characters in prose prior to World War II. Although he is frequently dismissed as merely another local colorist, Suárez has been called the first truly Chicano writer because he was not uncomfortable with the term, as many were in his day. Moreover, his characters are not treated as comical, colorful, or eccentric members of a cultural minority, performing for the amusement of Anglos (see, for example, John

Steinbeck's *Tortilla Flat*). They are proud, successful people, capable of coping and existing comfortably in either the majority culture or in their own world.

The first modern Chicano novel, according to most critics, is *Pocho* (New York: Doubleday, 1959) by José Antonio Villarreal. This book, a variation on the British example of the German Bildungsroman, or novel of self-discovery, is a sensitive portrayal of a young man, Richard Rubio, and his growing up in Santa Clara, California, during the 1930s. He is introspective, a reader, yet with a wide range of friends—Japanese, Portuguese, Italian, Mexican, and Anglo—and thus in contact with a spectrum of cultural and philosophical perspectives. The novel chronicles the disintegration of Richard's family: his sisters become completely Americanized, while his parents separate, torn by opposite cultural influences from Mexico and the United States. At the conclusion of the work, Richard escapes to military service, thus avoiding, at least for a time, identification with any culture. Villarreal has also written *The Fifth Horseman* (New York: Doubleday, 1974), noteworthy because it takes place prior to the Mexican Revolution of 1910, and *Clemente Chacón* (Binghamton, N.Y.: Bilingual Press, 1984), in which the protagonist, unlike Richard in *Pocho*, finally asserts his Chicano cultural identity.

The best-known Chicano novel is *Bless Me, Ultima* (Berkeley, Ca.: Quinto Sol, 1972), by Rudolfo A. Anaya. This book, which won the prestigious Premio Quinto Sol national Chicano literary award, is about the coming of age of a New Mexico boy, Antonio Márez. He learns about life through a series of telling experiences which are placed in perspective for him by the wisdom of Ultima, a *curandera*, or faith healer. It is an exceptional novel which has sold over 170,000 copies and generated a great deal of scholarly criticism both in the United States and in Europe. By means of a flashback narrated from a child's viewpoint and including highly significant dream and nightmare sequences, Anaya portrays Tony's religious awakening, his first encounters with death, and his learning about the rich mythology and legends of his past. Through Ultima he gains an appreciation for magic, the sanctity of life, and the landscape surrounding him. The author blends Christianity and ancient Indian myth, realism and mysticism, and presents a concept of mythic versus linear time to create a novel which demands much of its reader. *Bless Me, Ultima*, combined with two other books by Anaya, *Heart of Aztlán* (Berkeley: Editorial Justa Publications, 1976) and *Tortuga* (Berkeley: Editorial Justa Publications,

1979), form a loose trilogy which presents the Anglo reader a new reality which reflects that of the Chicano peoples. *The Silence of the Llano*, a collection of short stories, was published in 1982 (Berkeley: Tonatiuh-Quinto Sol).

The novel is the genre which has attracted the most critical attention, especially outside the Chicano community. Another outstanding novelist is Rolando Hinojosa-Smith, whose *Klail City y sus alrededores*, [Klail City and its surroundings] (La Habana, Cuba: Casa de las Américas, 1976) won the important Premio Casa de las Américas literary award and has been widely disseminated in the Spanish-speaking world. (It was published in 1977 in the United States by Editorial Justa Publications under the title *Generaciones y Semblanzas* [Generations and sketches].)Employing a style which imitates the teller/listener technique of oral literature, Hinojosa portrays the history of a region in south Texas. His novels, all loosely connected, present tales, poems, anecdotes, gossip, and images of a time and place which are rapidly fading into memory. Other highly acclaimed novels include Tomás Rivera's "*. . . y no se lo tragó la tierra*"/"*. . . and the earth did not part*," published in a bilingual edition in 1971 (Berkeley: Quinta Sol), and *Peregrinos de Aztlán* [Pilgrims from Aztlán] (Tucson: Editorial Peregrinos, 1974), by Miguel Méndez M. *The Road to Tamazunchale* (Reno: West Coast Poetry Review, 1975), by Ron Arias, was nominated for the National Book Award and has been called "one of the least known Chicano works outside its ethnic readership, and thus one of the most unjustifiably ignored pieces of superior fiction in the United States."

Contemporary Chicano drama has a unique history. There is ample evidence of a flourishing theater in the Southwest, consisting principally of religious or folk presentations, dating back to colonial times. Most critics, however, give the date 1965 as the beginning of Chicano theater. This is the year of the founding of El Teatro Campesino, generally translated as "the Farmworkers' Theatre." Luis Valdéz, a drama student and son of migrant laborers, approached César Chávez, leader of the fledgling United Farm Workers' Union, and suggested the use of theater as a means of entertaining and educating strikers during the Delano grape strikes in California's San Joaquin Valley. Drawing on his experience with the San Francisco Mime Troupe, his knowledge of the Italian commedia dell'arte form and slapstick style, and the agitprop theater of Germany's Bertolt Brecht, Valdéz developed the "acto." As he defined it, the acto is short—ten to fifteen minutes—and improvised, with an inten-

Covers for a highly acclaimed Chicano novel published in 1971

tion of inspiring the viewers to social action or to educate them concerning social problems. It is bilingual and always treats subjects and themes of the farmworker and his world. Frequently the early actos were collective efforts, with nightly revisions, thus reflecting their evolutionary and revolutionary nature. The scenery, costumes, and props were kept to a minimum, with the focus on the message and not the theatrical trappings.

As the Teatro Campesino grew and moved to Del Rey and later San Juan Bautista, it also evolved and developed other forms, broadening its themes to include all aspects of Chicano existence. El Centro Campesino Cultural, or the Workers' Cultural Center, emerged in 1967 as an outgrowth of the theater. This complex, located in San Juan Bautista, became a significant center for dissemination not only of theater but also music, art, and other manifestations of Chicano culture.

One of the most popular of the actos is "Los

Vendidos" [The Sellouts], written by Valdéz and first performed in 1967 (published in *Contemporary Chicano Theatre*, ed. Robert J. Garza, Notre Dame, Ind.: University of Notre Dame Press). This piece takes place at Honest Sancho's Used Mexican Lot, where Miss Jímenez (she pronounces it "Jimmy-nez," a distinctly "American-sounding" name) arrives in search of a token Mexican to work in the governor's office. Sancho demonstrates several models, including the Farmworker, the Pachuco or urban gangster, the Revolutionary, and finally, the much-desired middle-class Mexican-American. She rejects the first three, finding the last the only acceptable one because he has embraced Anglo-American values so completely that he has denied his heritage, thus becoming a vendido. It is a humorous play treating the serious problem of cultural assimilation, the abuse of workers, and racial and ethnic stereotypes.

While El Teatro Campesino was and still is the

largest and best-known Chicano theater group, it by no means stands alone. There were many small groups in communities throughout the Southwest in the 1960s, so many in fact that El Teatro Campesino decided to hold a national theater festival in 1970. This led, in 1971, to the founding of TENAZ, an acronym for El Teatro Nacional de Aztlán, or the National Theater of Aztlán. TENAZ was responsible for coordination and communication of theater activities; it also established a series of summer workshops for members. There have been summer festivals held most years since, and membership has grown to over fifty groups.

Among the most prominent Chicano playwrights is Carlos Morton, author of "The Many Deaths of Danny Rosales" and "El Jardin," translated as "The Garden." The former is concerned with the double standard of justice faced by minorities and the latter is a farcical Chicano version of the Fall of Man. (Both plays are published in *The Many Deaths of Danny Rosales and Other Plays*, Houston: Arte Publico Press, 1983.)

While Morton and many other Chicano dramatists have focused on contemporary social and political themes, a few have also treated other subjects. Estela Portillo Trambley, poet and short-story writer as well as playwright, wrote *The Day of the Swallows* (1971), a full-length play in three acts (published in *Contemporary Chicano Theatre*). Josefa, the protagonist, maintains a lesbian relationship with a younger woman, an ex-prostitute. She is a bitter woman who has suffered because of her treatment by men. In order to keep her relationship secret, she mutilates a young male witness to her affair, an act which eventually leads to her suicide. The play is realistic, with rich imagery, fine language, and a homosexual theme rarely treated in Chicano literature and one which has caused it to be seldom performed. Portillo, one of the few women playwrights to see her work in printed form, has also published *Sun Images* (in *Nuevos Pasos: Chicano and Puerto Rican Drama*, ed. Nicolás Kanellos and Jorge A. Huerta, *Revista Chicano-Rigueã*, 7, Winter 1979) and a collection, *Sor Juana and Other Plays* (Ypsilanti, Mich.: Bilingual Press, 1983). In 1973 she received the Quinto Sol Literary Prize.

A musical play, *Zoot Suit*, by Luis Valdéz, after a long and successful California run, has the distinction of being the first by a Chicano to be performed on Broadway (Winter Garden Theatre, March 1979). The author portrays the incidents surrounding the Los Angeles Sleepy Lagoon Murder of 1942. It is the story of the pachucos or zoot-suiters who were tried and convicted of the crime and later released. Although it did not enjoy a lengthy Broadway run, *Zoot Suit* is significant because it is a social and political play, founded in the acto form, which has been performed outside Chicano or academic circles, before all of America. It was also made into a commercial film (1981), directed by Valdéz and starring Edward James Olmos, Daniel Valdéz (Luis's brother), and Tyne Daly.

Contemporary Chicano poetry also originated in the 1960s. This is not to say that poetry does not have deep roots. There is a large and significant body of verse dating from the Spanish colonial and Mexican periods prior to 1848. Virtually all of these poems are in the Spanish language, reflecting the Spanish poetic traditions and forms. During the last half of the nineteenth century, works written in English began to appear, and after 1900 it became common for many poets to write either completely or predominantly in English. The majority of Chicano verse prior to the 1960s appeared in newspapers or magazines and reflected themes following either the American or Spanish (principally peninsular) tradition, depending on the language in which it was written.

With the beginning of the social and political movements around 1960, many groups began to publish newspapers, in both languages, as a means of reporting their activities. Along with news and information, these periodicals included literature, chiefly poetry. So much poetry was written during the decade that it has been called the "Chicano Renaissance." It is a period marked not only by the quantity of material printed but also by a noticeable change in thematic concerns. In an effort to assert a new cultural and political identity, the Renaissance Chicano poet looked not to Anglo America or European Spain; instead he turned to Aztec pre-Columbian Mexico (Aztlán) or identified with modern Mexico, usually from the period following the important Revolution of 1910. Common subjects were of course political, but also included cultural identity, Chicano life (either migratory or in the barrio), and "carnalismo," or brotherhood.

The most immediately striking characteristic of contemporary poetry is its language. It is written in a mixture of English and Spanish, frequently in the same line, along with Caló. An example is provided by Alurista (Alberto Urista), in his short "address" which presents, through two languages, the values of two different worlds in sharp contrast:

address
occupation
age

Theater poster for the first Chicano play to be performed on Broadway, a portrayal of the incidents surrounding the Los Angeles Sleepy Lagoon Murder of 1942

marital status

—perdone . . .   [pardon me . . .
    yo me llamo pedro   my name is pedro]

telephone

height

hobbies

previous employers

—perdone . . .   [pardon me . . .
    yo me llamo pedro   my name is pedro
    pedro ortega   pedro ortega]

zip code

i.d. number

classification

rank

—perdone . . .   [pardon me . . .
    mi padre era   my father was
    el señor ortega   señor ortega
    (a veces don José)   (sometimes don José)]

race

Alurista is one of the most prolific and among the best of Chicano poets; his experiments with bilingualism and his use of indigenous themes have made him a major influence. His published collections include *Floricanto en Aztlán* [Flower and song in Aztlán] (Los Angeles: University of California, 1971), *Nationchild Plumaroja* [Nationchild redfeather] (San Diego: Toltecas en Aztlán, 1972); and *Timespace Huracan* [Timespace hurricane] (Albuquerque, N.M.: Pajarito Publications, 1976). He also composed the proclamation "El Plan Espiritual de Aztlán," which means the Spiritual Plan of Aztlán, written for the first Chicano Youth Liberation Conference held at the Crusade for Justice in Denver in 1969. This document served as a catalyst for discussions on the role of the artist in the Chicano movement.

Another important poet, Rodolfo "Corky" González, was the organizer of the Crusade for Justice. His major work is *I Am Joaquin/Yo Soy Joaquin* (Crusade for Justice, 1967; New York: Bantam, 1972), an epic poem presenting a Chicano Everyman who resists assimilation and subjugation. González, an ex-boxer, wrote in his introduction that his poem "was a journey back through history, a painful self-evaluation, a wandering search for my peoples and, most of all, for my own identity. The totality of all social inequities and injustice had to come to the surface. All the while, the truth about our own flaws—the villains and the heroes had to ride together—in order to draw an honest, clear conclusion of who we were, who we are, and where we are going." He concludes that there is "no inspiration without identifiable images, there is no conscience without the sharp knife of truthful ex-

posure, and ultimately, there are no revolutions without poets." Poetry continues to be the most popular mode of artistic expression by the Chicanos, perhaps because of the relative simplicity with which a poem can be disseminated.

Francisco A. Lomelí and Donaldo W. Urioste compiled a useful bibliography of Chicano literature in 1976, *Chicano Perspectives in Literature* (Albuquerque: Pajarito). In their introduction they defined their subject as literature written by Chicanos and added that "due to a diverse cultural experience, Chicanos are capable of portraying non-Chicano topics." They take the position, however, that non-Chicanos rarely capture the uniqueness of Chicano reality and propose that literary works written about Chicanos by others be termed "literatura chicanesca" because the authors have the appearance of being Chicano. They argue that the perspective "is from the outside looking in. This perspective loses the spontaneity of a natural outpouring of a people's subconscious through the writer's creativity; instead it becomes a calculated object of study which is valued from a relative distance, that is, not lived."

Lomelí and Urioste coined the term in response to an increasingly common phenomenon which has also moved one step further: presently, non-Chicanos are not only writing about Chicano subjects and exploring Chicano themes, they are also disguising their identities by altering their names or using pseudonyms and actually pretending to be Chicanos.

The most popular and successful author of literatura chicanesca who makes no attempt to disguise his Anglo identity is John Nichols. He was already an established author (*The Sterile Cuckoo*, New York: McKay, 1965), when he published his New Mexico Trilogy, composed of *The Milagro Beanfield War* (New York: Holt, Rinehart & Winston, 1974), *The Magic Journey* (Holt, Rinehart & Winston, 1978), and *The Nirvana Blues* (Holt, Rinehart & Winston, 1981). Nichols is a longtime resident of Taos, New Mexico, and has been heavily involved in social and political causes. His tragicomic trilogy presents a large number of Chicanos and depicts their lives and problems in a realistic manner. Lomelí and Urioste praise his work and state that *The Milagro Beanfield War* is "the most convincing *chicanesca* novel," with the conclusion that it "makes entertaining reading and proposes a good example for non-Chicanos to follow."

Two authors writing under assumed names have received high praise from literary critics. Chester Seltzer, an Anglo newspaperman, wrote short fiction under a variation of his wife's maiden name (Amado Muro) and has his work published in such places as the *Arizona Quarterly* and the *Southwest Review*. His Chicano disguise was not an attempt to deceive so much as it was a ploy to avoid personal attention. Critics had no trouble finding his writing, however, with at least seven of his pieces appearing in *The Best American Short Stories*. One anthology which published his "Cecilia Rosas" states in the introduction that Muro "seems to have written more good short fiction than any other young Mexican American." Seltzer died in 1971; his work has been published in *The Collected Stories of Amado Muro* (Austin, Texas: Thorp Springs Press, 1979).

Danny Santiago and his novel, *Famous All Over Town* (New York: Simon & Schuster, 1983), made the front page of the *New York Times* in 1984 when it was revealed that the author is not the young Chica-

no writer he had pretended to be. He is Daniel James, a 73-year-old Yale graduate who spent twenty years in the Los Angeles barrio as a volunteer worker. James claims that he chose to assume a Chicano identity not to deceive but because he believed that he was blacklisted after he was named as a member of the Communist party in 1951 by the House Un-American Activities Committee. In spite of the problem of the author's identity, *Famous All Over Town* has been hailed as a classic of the Chicano urban experience.

Much of Chicano literature is intensely personal. Some writers have personalized their work so much that they have created fictionalized autobiographies. Ernesto Galarza's *Barrio Boy* (Notre Dame, Ind.: University of Notre Dame Press, 1971) traces the migration of his family from Mexico to the United States during the Revolution of 1910, a

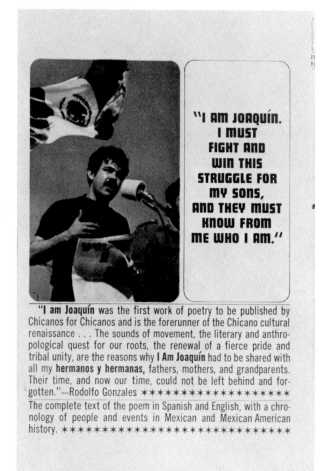

"**I am Joaquín** was the first work of poetry to be published by Chicanos for Chicanos and is the forerunner of the Chicano cultural renaissance . . . The sounds of movement, the literary and anthropological quest for our roots, the renewal of a fierce pride and tribal unity, are the reasons why **I Am Joaquín** had to be shared with all my **hermanos y hermanas**, fathers, mothers, and grandparents. Their time, and now our time, could not be left behind and forgotten."—Rodolfo Gonzales ★★★★★★★★★★★★★★★★★★★ The complete text of the poem in Spanish and English, with a chronology of people and events in Mexican and Mexican American history. ★★★★★★★★★★★★★★★★★★★★★★★★★★★

Covers for the epic poem that presents a Chicano Everyman who strives to define and preserve his own identity

common experience for large numbers of Chicanos. It is significant in that it recounts the painful process of assimilation in the first half of this century and includes some bitter memories of growing up with a dual heritage. Galarza became an outstanding authority on Mexican emigrants, publishing the classic study *Merchants of Labor: The Mexican Bracero Story* (Charlotte/Santa Barbara: McNally & Loftin, 1964).

Oscar "Zeta" Acosta has written two highly autobiographical novels, *The Autobiography of a Brown Buffalo* (San Francisco: Straight Arrow, 1972) and *The Revolt of the Cockroach People* (Straight Arrow, 1973), in which he explores his relationship to his cultural history. Both contain characters bearing strong resemblance to prominent social and political figures who participated in many of the militant activities in the late 1960s and early 1970s.

The most outstanding example of autobiography is Richard Rodriguez's highly sensitive and controversial *Hunger of Memory,* published in 1981 (Boston: Godine). In a clear, riveting style, the author tells his tale of maturing in a society alien to his ethnic background. As the subtitle, "The Education of Richard Rodriguez," confirms, he writes about his school years, focusing on language: "Language has been the great subject of my life. In college and in graduate school I was registered as an 'English Major.' But well before then, from my first day of school, I was a student of language. Obsessed by the way it determined my public identity. The way it permits me here to describe myself, writing. . . ." He relates the pain of separation that takes place in a Chicano Spanish-speaking family as the children gradually learn English, and, by so doing, grow distant and different from their parents. Although the work got mixed reviews from the Chicano community, most Anglo critics agree with Walter J. Ong's assessment that "few have presented with such skill the indestructible intimacy of family love and its resilience under the stress of change." Rodriguez's book has done much to draw attention to the educated Chicano and the frequently painful dilemma of his position in today's society.

Since the 1960s Chicanos have been reading their own literature or attending their theater more than ever before. A great need for publishing outlets for writers has begun to be filled; among the outstanding firms are Tonatiuh-Quinto Sol in California and Bilingual Press in Michigan. Major older houses are beginning to issue works by Chicanos. Increased academic recognition has led many colleges and universities to establish undergraduate majors as well as graduate programs in Chicano

Cover for twenty-three tales set in the Hispanic villages of New Mexico and southern Colorado, telling of witchcraft and magic and the events of everyday life

Studies, all of which include literature courses in their curricula. These developments have drawn much deserved attention from critics, not only in established literary journals but also in new ones whose focus is completely or partially on Chicano literature. In addition, full-length critical studies are being published by major university presses. Previously, most aspects of Chicano culture were foreign or unknown to the majority of non-Chicanos. Like other ethnic American literatures, that of the Chicanos was relegated to second-class status. As the limits of American literature expand and as the vitality and excitement of Chicano literature are increasingly felt, it is taking its rightful place in the field of American letters.

Recommended Readings:
Juan Bruce-Novoa, *Chicano Authors: Inquiry by Interview* (Austin: University of Texas Press, 1980);

Ernestina Eger, *A Bibliography of Criticism of Chicano Literature* (Berkeley: Chicano Studies Library, 1982);

Joel Hancock, "The Emergence of Chicano Poetry: A survey of Sources, Themes and Techniques," *Arizona Quarterly,* 29 (Spring 1975): 57-73;

Jorge A. Huerta, *Chicano Theatre: Themes and Forms* (Ypsilanti: Bilingual Press, 1982);

Luis Leal, Fernando de Necochea, Francisco Lomeli, and Roberto G. Trujillo, *A Decade of Chicano Literature (1970-1979) Critical Essays and Bibliography* (Santa Barbara: Editorial La Causa, 1982);

Carey McWilliams, *North From Mexico: The Spanish Speaking People of the United States* (New York: Greenwood Press, 1968);

Matt S. Meier and Feliciano Rivera, *The Chicanos: A History of Mexican Americans* (New York: Hill & Wang, 1972);

Raymond A. Paredes, "The Evolution of Chicano Literature," *MELUS,* 5 (Summer 1978): 71-110;

Joseph Sommers and Tomás Ybarro-Frausto, *Modern Chicano Writers* (Englewood Cliffs, N.J.: Prentice-Hall, 1979);

Charles M. Tatum, *Chicano Literature* (Boston: Twayne, 1982).

Biographical Documents I

The original *Who's Who in America* questionnaires provide an overlooked resource for biographical evidence—showing how the respondents revised their entries before publication. This material is particularly useful for the study of writers because it may reveal how a writer wanted to be presented to posterity.

Many of these forms have been scattered or have disappeared over the years. The Berg Collection at the New York Public Library has had the foresight to acquire valuable examples of these specimens of autobiography. They are reproduced here with the generous cooperation of Dr. Lola L. Szladits, Curator of the Berg Collection of English and American literature.

NOTE—The following personal sketch appears in the 1912-13 edition (Vol. VII) of Who's Who in America (issued about May 1, 1912), and will be printed in the 1914-15 edition (Vol. VIII) after being revised.

Please read and revise with particular care, supplying such additional facts as may be necessary, if any, to bring the sketch down to date.

It is not desired that these personal data be rewritten or rearranged, nor that minor and unimportant matter be introduced. The aim is simply to verify the printed facts, correct typographical errors and other mistakes, if any, and bring the sketch down to date by adding anything of importance that has occured since the last volume of Who's Who in America was issued.

Please revise this sketch and return by mail with as little delay as possible. It is essential that the sketch be returned even if no corrections or additions be made.

Return to A. N. MARQUIS & COMPANY, CHICAGO, ILL.

ORDER

565

BAUM, L(yman) Frank, author; b. Chittenango, N.Y., May 15, 1856; s. Benjamin Ward and Cynthia (Stanton) B.; acad. edn., at Syracuse, N.Y.; m. Maud, d. Matilda Joslyn Gage, of Fayetteville, N.Y., Nov. 9, 1882. Began newspaper work, 1880; edited Dakota Pioneer, Aberdeen, S.D., 1888-90; The Show Window, Chicago, 1897-1902. *Clubs:* Press, Chicago Athletic, Colonist (Chicago), Players (New York). *Author:* Mother Goose in Prose, 1897, 1902; By the Candelabra's Glare (poems), 1898; Father Goose—His Book, 1899; The Wonderful Wizard of Oz, 1900; A New Wonderland, 1900; The Songs of Father Goose, 1900; The Army Alphabet, 1900; The Navy Alphabet, 1900; American Fairy Tales, 1901; Dot and Tot of Merryland, 1901; The Art of Decorating (technical), 1900; The Master Key, 1901; The Life and Adventures of Santa Claus, 1902; Enchanted Isle of Yew, 1903; The Magical Monarch of Mo, 1903; The Marvelous Land of Oz, 1904; The Woggle-Bug Book, 1905; Queen Zixi of Ix, 1905; Animal Fairy Tales, 1905; John Dough and the Cherub, 1906; Ozma of Oz, 1907; Dorothy and the Wizard, 1907; Baum's Fairy Tales, 1908; The Road to Oz, 1908; The Emerald City of Oz, 1909; Baum's Juvenile Speaker, 1909; The Sea Fairies, 1910; The Daring Twins, 1910; Phoebe Daring, Conspirator, 1911; Sky Island, 1912. *Plays:* The Maid of Arran, prod. New York, 1881; Matches, prod. New York, 1882; Kilmorne, prod. Syracuse, 1884; The Queen of Killarney, prod. Rochester, 1885; The Wizard of Oz (musical extravaganza), prod. Chicago, 1902; The Woggle-Bug (musical extravaganza), prod. Chicago, 1905; The Radio-Play (motion pictures of Baum's Fairy Tales), prod. Chicago and New York, 1908-9. Has for 20 yrs. written children's and other stories for Youth's Companion, Harper's, St. Nicholas and other periodicals. *Home:* "Ozcot," Hollywood, Cal.

the

; and

(Los Angeles, Cal.),

insert 3 lines

"The Little Wizard Series, (6 titles), 1913;
"The Patchwork Girl of Oz," 1913;
"Tik-Tok Man of Oz," 1914.

insert 2 lines

"The Tik-Tok Man of Oz," prod. Los Angeles, 1913.

Attention is especially called to the importance of indicating any change that may have occurred in your position or business or professional occupation since the last edition of Who's Who in America was issued.

Please furnish here both home and business address, if not already correctly given above.

Home Address (legal residence) _____

Business Address _____

This sketch returned by *L. Frank Baum*

Date *Dec 14* 1913

839   V N .K   ORDER.   969

NOTE. The following personal sketch has been prepared for insertion in the 1910–1911 edition of Who's Who in America (Vol. VI).

In preparing the sketches for this edition, rearrangement of data has been made with a view to securing a better chronological statement than in any previous edition.

Spaces for dates and other data, tending to make the sketch complete in detail, have been provided. Kindly fill in these blank spaces as indicated. Both Christian and Surnames should be given in full.

The importance of securing absolute accuracy will be apparent when it is understood that Who's Who in America is in constant use, as a recognized authority, in leading libraries, colleges, government offices, editorial rooms, and in many homes and business offices in all parts of the world. The greatest pains should be taken to write perfectly plain.

Please return this sketch by mail at your earliest convenience. IT IS ESSENTIAL THAT THE SKETCH BE RETURNED, EVEN IF THERE ARE NO CORRECTIONS OR ADDITIONS TO BE MADE.

Return to A. N. MARQUIS & COMPANY, CHICAGO, ILL.

IN REVISING THIS SKETCH PLEASE COMPARE WITH THE DATA IN THE 1908–1909 EDITION (VOL. V) OR WITH EARLIER EDITIONS.

BIERCE, Ambrose, author, journalist; born ~~at~~ *in*

~~Ohio~~, ~~(date)~~ *June 24,*

1842; ~~son of~~   ~~and~~

~~educated at~~

served as line officer during Civil War; bvtd. maj. for

distinguished services ~~married Miss~~

~~of~~   , ~~(date)~~

~~to~~   ; went to Calif., 1866, ~~went to~~ London, 1872, contributing to Fun fables, purporting to be translations from Zambri, the Parsee (published in vol. Cobwebs from an Empty Skull, 1874); returned to Calif., and contributed to Overland Monthly, edited Argonaut and Wasp for many yrs. contributed Prattle columns in San Francisco Examiner. *Author:* Cobwebs from an Empty Skull, 1874 &1; The Monk and the Hangman's Daughter (with Dr. A. Danziger), 1892, new edit., 1907 N2; Black Beetles in Amber, 1892 &1; Can Such Things Be? 1893, 2d, 1903 N2; In the Midst of Life (former title, Tales of Soldiers and Civilians), 1898 P2; Fantastic Fables, 1899 P2; Shapes of Clay, 1903; The Cynic's Word Book, 1906; *Address:* Army and Navy Club, Washington.

1877–1884;

The Shadow on The Dial and Other Essays, 1909; R10; Write It Right, 1909, N3; Collected Works in course of publication N3.

(50)

KINDLY FILL OUT BLANK SPACES AND MARK SUCH OTHER EXTENSIONS AS MAY BE NECESSARY TO COMPLETE THE SKETCH.

Attention is especially called to the importance of indicating any change that may have occurred in your position or business or professional occupation since the last edition of Who's Who in America was issued, and not accounted for in the above sketch.

Please furnish here both home and business address, if not already correctly given above.

Began my present occupation of

Date

Home Address

Business Address

This sketch returned (Date) *August 28,* 1909, by *Ambrose Bierce*

6

CABELL, James Branch, author ~~and~~ _genealogist_; b. Richmond, Va., Apr. 14, 1879; s. Robert Gamble and Anne (Branch) C.; A.B., William and Mary, 1898; married ~~~~ _Priscilla, d. of William Joseph Bradley,_ of "Auburn", Chas. City Co, Vª _~~~~ November 8_ , 1913. _Richmond (Vª) Times, 1898,_ On staff New York Herald, 1899-01, Richmond (Va.) News, 1901; writer for mags. since 1902, ~~Societies~~ _mem._ Kappa Alpha.

~~Politics:~~ ~~Religious denomination:~~ _Episcopal._

Author: The Eagle's Shadow, 1904; The Line of Love, 1905; Branchiana, a Record of the Branch Family in Virginia, 1906; Gallantry, 1907; The Cords of Vanity, 1909; Chivalry, 1909; ~~~~

Branch of Abingdon, a Record of the Branch Family in Engl 1911; The Soul of Melicent, 1913; The Rivet in Grandfather Neck, 1915; The Majors and Their Marriages, 1915. ~~Address~~ _home_ Dumbarton Grange, Dumbarton, Vª.

(35)

having contributed over 100 short stories, considerable verse, translations, and numerous papers upon hist. and biog. subjects; has personally _conducted much geneal._ work and original _research in America, France and England_

Please furnish here both home and business address, if not correctly given above. { Home Address _Dumbarton Grange, Dumbarton, Vª_
{ Business Address _____ " _____

Returned (Date) _January 22nd_ 1916   by _James Branch Cabell_

For WHO'S WHO IN AMERICA (Vol. 11, 1920-21).   559

The following personal sketch appears in the last edition of WHO'S WHO IN AMERICA, issued about two years ago, and will be printed in the next edition after being revised and editorially approved.
Please read the sketch with particular care, making necessary alterations or additions, and promptly return by mail.
It is not desired that these personal data be rewritten or rearranged, nor that MINOR AND UNIMPORTANT matter be introduced. The aim is simply to verify the printed facts, correct typographical errors and other mistakes, if any, and bring the sketch down to date by adding anything of importance that has occurred since the last volume of WHO'S WHO IN AMERICA was issued.
The sketch should be returned even if no change be made. This is very important, as it will obviate the necessity of sending out another proof, and it will be taken as assurance that the printed address is correct.   A. N. MARQUIS & COMPANY, Chicago, Ill., U. S. A.

My Antonia, 1918   6   *Litt. D., 1917;*

CATHER, Willa Sibert, author; b. Winchester, Va., Dec. 7, 1876; d. Charles F. and Mary Virginia (Boak), C.; B.A., U. of Neb., 1895 un-married. On staff of Pittsburgh Daily Leader, 1897-01; asso. editor McClure's Magazine, 1906-1912.; *Author:* April Twilight, 1903; The Troll Garden, 1905; Alexander's Bridge, 1912; O Pioneers, 1913; The Bohemian Girl, 1912; The Song of the Lark, 1915; Also mag. writer. *Home:* 5 Bank St., New York.

, N.Y. also

Gentlemen;

        If you wish to use this sketch, please correct the date of
my birth, which have had wrong in several issues, and add the later
University degree and also the title of my last book.

                                Very truly yours

                                Willa Sibert Cather

Attention is especially called to the importance of indicating any change that may have occurred in your position or business or professional occupation since the last edition of Who's Who in America was issued.

Please furnish here both home and business address, if not already correctly given above.   Home Address (legal residence)_____

        Business Address_____

This sketch returned by_____

        Date_____191___

1913

NOTE—The following personal sketch appears in the 1912-13 edition (Vol. VII) of Who's Who in America (issued about May 1, 1912), and will be printed in the 1914-15 edition (Vol. VIII) after being revised.

Please read and revise with particular care, supplying such additional facts as may be necessary, if any, to bring the sketch down to date.

It is not desired that these personal data be rewritten or rearranged, nor that minor and unimportant matter be introduced. The aim is simply to verify the printed facts, correct typographical errors and other mistakes, if any, and bring the sketch down to date by adding anything of importance that has occured since the last volume of Who's Who in America was issued.

Please revise this sketch and return by mail with as little delay as possible. It is essential that the sketch be returned even if no corrections or additions be made.

Return to A. N. MARQUIS & COMPANY, CHICAGO, ILL.

COBB, Irvin Shrewsbury, writer; b. at Paducah, Ky., June 23, 1876; s. Joshua Clark and Manie (Saunders) C.; ed. pub. and pvt. schs.; m. Laura Spencer Baker, of Savannah, Ga., June 12, 1900. Shorthand reporter, contbr. to comic weeklies, reporter on local paper up to 17; editor Paducah Daily News at 19; staff corr. and writer "Sour Mash" column, Louisville (Ky.) Evening Post, 1898-1901; mng. editor Paducah News-Democrat, 1901-4; spl. writer and editor humor section, New York Evening Sun, 1904-5; staff humorist and spl. writer New York Evening World and Sunday World, 1905-11; staff contbr. to Saturday Evening Post since 1911. Democrat. Mem. Ky. Soc. of New York, Sons Confed. Vets. Clubs: Friars, Park Hill Country, National Press. Author: (plays) The Campaign, produced 1907; Mr. Busybody (musical skit), 1908. Wrote: New York Through Funny Glasses series; The Hotel Clerk series; Live Talks with Dead Ones; The Escape of Mr. Trimm; Making Peace at Portsmouth; Speeches Up to Date; The Good News, etc. Contbr. to mags. and syndicates. Home: Park Hill, Yonkers, N.Y.

[Handwritten annotations:]

Dunwoodie

; Back Home (comedy) with Bayard Veiller, produced 1913, Sergeant Bagby (one-act play) with Bozeman Bulger, produced 191

Billed Buzzard,

Books:— Back Home, 1912; Cobb's Anatomy, 1912; The Escape of Mr. Trimm, 1913; Cobb's Bill of Fare, 1913; Roughing It De Luxe, 1914; Cobb's Baedeker, 1914.

1036

(15)

[Stamp:] RECEIVED SEP 23 1913

Attention is especially called to the importance of indicating any change that may have occurred in your position or business or professional occupation since the last edition of Who's Who in America was issued.

Please furnish here both home and business address, if not already correctly given above.

Home Address (legal residence) Park Hill, Yonkers, N.Y

Business Address Curtis Publishing Company

This sketch returned by Irvin S. Cobb

Date Sept 22 1913

For WHO'S WHO IN AMERICA (Vol. 13, 1924-25)

The following personal sketch appears in the last edition of WHO'S WHO IN AMERICA, issued about two years ago, and will be printed in the next edition after being revised and editorially approved.

Please read the sketch with particular care, making necessary alterations or additions, and promptly return by mail.

It is not desired that these personal data be rewritten or rearranged, nor that MINOR AND UNIMPORTANT matter be introduced. The aim is simply to verify the printed facts, correct typographical errors and other mistakes, if any, and bring the sketch down to date by adding anything of importance that has occurred since the last volume of WHO'S WHO IN AMERICA was issued.

The sketch should be returned even if no change be made. This is very important, as it will obviate the necessity of sending out another proof, and it will be taken as assurance that the printed address is correct.

A. N. MARQUIS & COMPANY, Chicago, Ill., U. S. A.

HECHT, Ben, author; b. N.Y. City, Feb. 28, 1893; s. Joseph and Sarah (Swernofsky) H.; ed. high sch., Racine, Wis.; m. Marie Armstrong, writer and dramatic critic, of Chicago, Nov. 30, 1915. Began with Chicago Journal, 1910; with Daily News since 1914; corr. in charge Berlin office of News, Dec. 1918-Dec. 1919. *Author:* Erik Dorn (novel), 1921; also short stories in mags. *Home:* 1414 E. 53d St., Chicago, Ill.

The above is still authentic. Additional items are—

Author: Erik Dorn (novel); Gargoyles (novel), 1922; Fantazius Mallare (novel), 1922; The Florentine Dagger (novel), 1923; 1001 Afternoons (vol. short stories), 1923; The Egotist (drama played 1923; also short stories in mags performed by Leo Ditrichstein); founded Chicago Literary Times, 1923. Home

5210 Kenwood avenue, Chicago, Ill.

The leading essentials of every sketch are: Full name, place and date of birth, full names of parents, education, college degrees, (including dates), marriage (including full name and date).

Attention is especially called to the importance of indicating any change that may have occurred in your position or business or professional occupation since the last edition of Who's Who in America was issued.

{ Editor and part owner of The Chicago Literary Times

Please furnish here both home and business address, if not already correctly given above.

Home Address (legal residence) 5210 Kenwood

Business Address 644 S. Clark st Chicago

This sketch returned by Ben Hecht

Date Jan 4 1924

RECEIVED OCT 24 1911

OCT 13 1918 — 12 1910

PLEASE RETURN BY MAIL

Kindly furnish on this sheet the necessary data for a concise personal sketch of yourself, and return it at your early convenience. The facts will be arranged in proper form and sent for revision before they are put into print.

WHO'S WHO IN AMERICA

Published by A. N. MARQUIS & COMPANY, Chicago, Ill.

Name in full .... *Joyce Kilmer, author,*

Chief Occupation or Profession .... *Writer*

Date and Place of beginning it ....

Residence Address .... *Pinehurst Apartments, 180th St. & Fort Washington Ave., New York.*

Business Address .... *10 Bank of Virginia Bldg., 44 E. 23d St., N.Y.*

Place of Birth .... *New Brunswick, N.J.*

Date of Birth, etc .... *Dec. 6, 1886*

If born abroad when did you come to America? ....

Father's Name in full .... *Frederick Barnett Kilmer*

Mother's Maiden Name in full .... *Annie Elene Kilburn*

Education, when and where, in detail: Name and location of Schools, Colleges and Universities attended (including business and technical schools), with dates of graduation (if a graduate), and degrees conferred.

Rutgers Preparatory School (graduated 1904)
Rutgers College, New Brunswick, N.J. (1904-1906,
A.B. Columbia University, N.Y. (1906-1908,
A.B. 1908,

1908,

Are you Married? .... *Yes*

(50)

If Married, to whom? .... *Aline Murray*

of .... *Norfolk, Virginia*

Date of Marriage .... *June 9, 1908*

For WHO'S WHO IN AMERICA (Vol. 14, 1926-1927)

09494

The following personal sketch appeared in the last edition of WHO'S WHO IN AMERICA, issued about two years ago, and will be printed in the next edition after being revised and editorially approved.

Please read the sketch with particular care, making necessary alterations or additions, and promptly return by mail.

It is not desired that these personal data be rewritten or rearranged, nor that MINOR AND UNIMPORTANT matter be introduced. The aim is simply to verify the printed facts, correct typographical errors and other mistakes, if any, and bring the sketch down to date by adding anything of importance that has occurred since the last volume of WHO'S WHO IN AMERICA was issued.

The sketch should be returned even if no change be made. This is very important, as it will obviate the necessity of sending out another proof, and it will be taken as assurance that the printed address is correct.

A. N. MARQUIS & COMPANY, Chicago, Ill., U. S. A.

LEWIS, Sinclair, author; b. Sauk Center, Minn., Feb. 7, 1885; s. Edwin J. (M.D.) and Emma (Kermott) L.; A.B., Yale, 1907; m. Grace Livingstone Hegger, of N.Y. City, Apr. 15, 1914. Reporter New Haven Journal and Courier, San Francisco Bulletin, Associated Press, etc.; successively asst. editor or editor Transatlantic Tales, Volta Review, Frederick A. Stokes Co., Adventure, Publishers' Newspaper Syndicate, and editor George H. Doran Co., to 1916. Author: (novels) Our Mr. Wrenn, 1914; The Trail of the Hawk, 1915; The Job, 1917; The Innocents, 1917; Free Air, 1919; Main Street, 1920; Babbitt, 1922; also play, Hobohemia, prod. New York, 1919. Contbr. short stories to Century, Saturday Evening Post, etc. Address: Care of Alfred Harcourt, 383 Madison Av., New York, N.Y.

; Arrowsmith, 1925 ;

CHILDREN:—List here all of your children (if any) in order of birth, giving Christian names in full, and indicating deaths; also designate whether by first or second marriage.

Wells L., 6-1917.

Please Write or Print Names Plainly

The above is quite O.K. with addition of novel "Arrowsmith" Feb. 1925. Lewis

50

The leading essentials of every sketch are: Full name, place and date of birth, full names of parents, education, college degrees, (including dates), marriage (including full name and date).

Attention is especially called to the importance of indicating any change that may have occurred in your position or business or professional occupation since the last edition of Who's Who in America was issued.

Please furnish here both home and business address, if not already correctly given above.

Home Address (legal residence)

Business Address

This sketch returned by Sinclair Lewis

Date Oct. 17, 1925

For WHO'S WHO IN AMERICA (Vol. 12, 1922-23).

The following personal sketch appears in the last edition of WHO'S WHO IN AMERICA, issued about two years ago, and will be printed in the next edition after being revised and editorially approved.

Please read the sketch with particular care, making necessary alterations or additions, and promptly return by mail.

It is not desired that these personal data be rewritten or rearranged, nor that MINOR AND UNIMPORTANT matter be introduced. The aim is simply to verify the printed facts, correct typographical errors and other mistakes, if any, and bring the sketch down to date by adding anything of importance that has occurred since the last volume of WHO'S WHO IN AMERICA was issued.

The sketch should be returned even if no change be made. This is very important, as it will obviate the necessity of sending out another proof, and it will be taken as assurance that the printed address is correct.

A. N. MARQUIS & COMPANY, Chicago, Ill., U. S. A.

HAS DONE A GREAT DEAL OF LECTURING ON THE HISTORY OF ART AND ISSUED MANY PRIVATE PAMPHLETS # ILLUSTRATED BY HIMSELF

on the History of Art

LINDSAY, Nicholas Vachel; writer; b. at Springfield, Ill., Nov. 10, 1879; s. Vachel Thomas and Catharine (Frazee) L.; grad. Springfield High Sch., 1897; student Hiram Coll., Ohio, 1897-1900; Art Inst. Chicago, 1900-3; New York Sch. of Art, under Chase and Henri, 1904-5; unmarried. Lectured for West Side Y.M.C.A., New York, winters, 1905-6, 1906-7, 1907-8, Springfield (Ill.) Y.M.C.A., winter, 1908-9; lecturer for Anti-Saloon League, throughout Central Ill., 1909-10; walked from Ill. to New Mexico, summer of 1912, distributing "rhymes" and speaking in behalf of "The Gospel of Beauty." Mem. Christian (Disciples) Ch. Club: Cliff Dwellers (Chicago). Mem. Poetry Soc. Am. *Author:* A Handy Guide for Beggars, 1916; General William Booth Enters Heaven, and Other Poems, 1913; Adventures While Preaching the Gospel of Beauty, 1914; The Congo and Other Poems, 1914; The Art of the Moving Picture, 1915; The Chinese Nightingale and Other Poems, 1917. Has recited his poems before the English depts. of many schs. and univs. Pen name "Vachel Lindsay." *Address:* 603 S. 5th St. Springfield, Ill.

VACHEL LINDSAY

recited in Oxford England, and London, Oct. 1920

SUMMER OF 1921 CLIMBED ON A LONG EXPEDITION AWAY FROM THE TRAILS THROUGH THE AMERICAN AND CANADIAN ROCKIES WITH STEPHEN
STEPHEN GRAHAM ENGLISH TRAVELLER

THE GOLDEN WHALES OF CALIFORNIA AND OTHER POEMS 1920.
THE GOLDEN BOOK OF SPRINGFIELD

THE GOLDEN BOOK OF SPRINGFIELD, (A SEALED BOOK OF PROPHECY -) 1920

35

Attention is especially called to the importance of indicating any change that may have occurred in your position or business or professional occupation since the last edition of Who's Who in America was issued.

Please furnish here both home and business address, if not already correctly given above.

Home Address (legal residence) _____

Business Address _____

This sketch returned by _____ Nicholas Vachel _____ Lindsay _____ NOV 21 1921.

Date _____ November 19, 1921

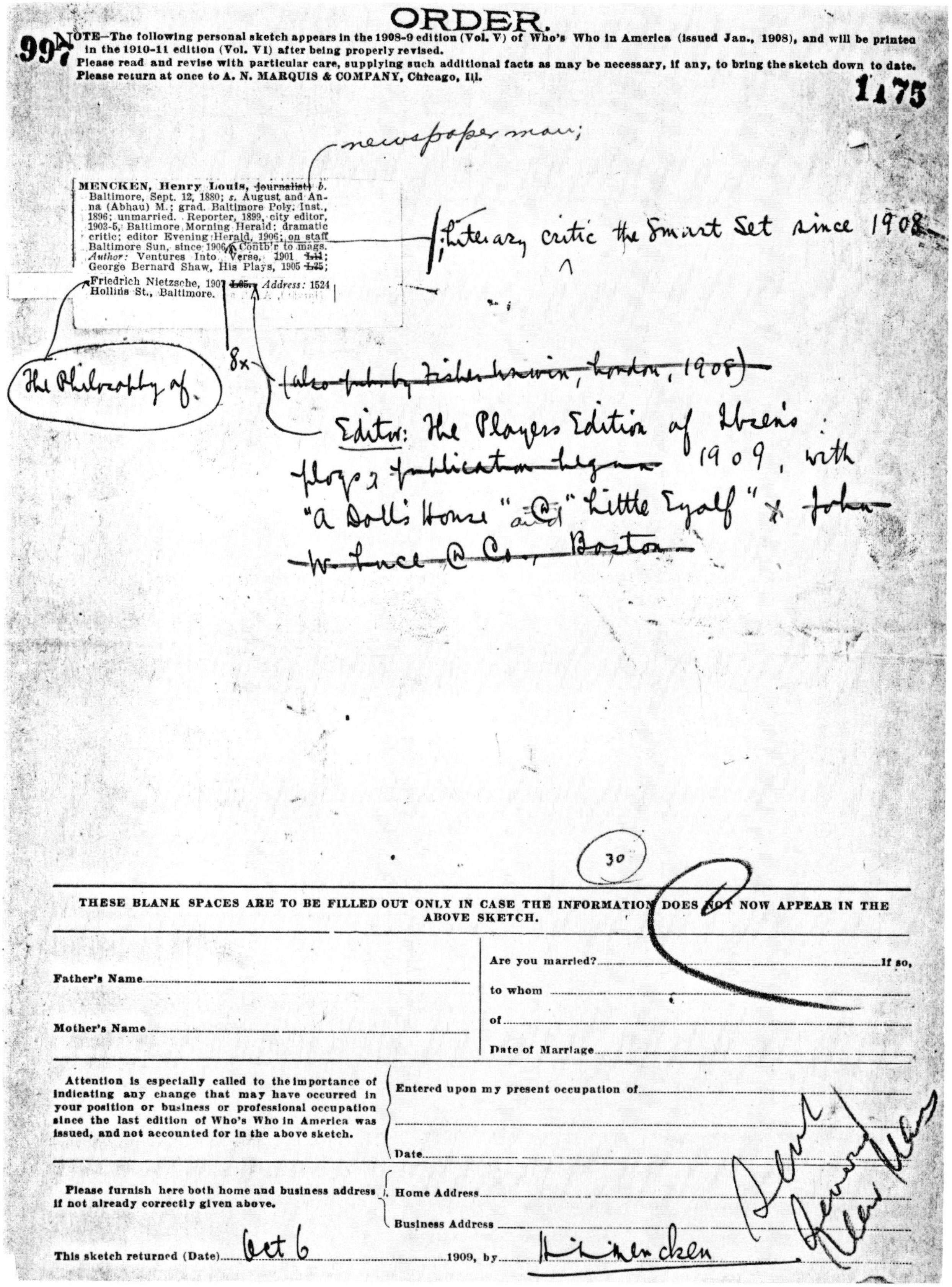

ORDER.

997 NOTE—The following personal sketch appears in the 1908-9 edition (Vol. V) of Who's Who in America (issued Jan., 1908), and will be printed in the 1910-11 edition (Vol. VI) after being properly revised.
Please read and revise with particular care, supplying such additional facts as may be necessary, if any, to bring the sketch down to date.
Please return at once to A. N. MARQUIS & COMPANY, Chicago, Ill.

1175

newspaper man;

MENCKEN, Henry Louis, journalist; b. Baltimore, Sept. 12, 1880; s. August and Anna (Abhau) M.; grad. Baltimore Poly. Inst., 1896; unmarried. Reporter, 1899, city editor, 1903-5, Baltimore Morning Herald; dramatic critic; editor Evening Herald, 1906; on staff Baltimore Sun, since 1906. Contb'r to mags. *Author:* Ventures Into Verse, 1901 1.11; George Bernard Shaw, His Plays, 1905 1.25; Friedrich Nietzsche, 1907 1.65; *Address:* 1524 Hollins St., Baltimore.

literary critic the Smart Set since 1908.

The Philosophy of

8×

(also pub. by Fisher Unwin, London, 1908)

Editor: The Players Edition of Ibsen's plays & publication begun 1909, with "A Doll's House" and "Little Eyolf" & John W. Luce & Co., Boston—

30

THESE BLANK SPACES ARE TO BE FILLED OUT ONLY IN CASE THE INFORMATION DOES NOT NOW APPEAR IN THE ABOVE SKETCH.

Father's Name...

Are you married?...If so,

to whom...

Mother's Name...

of...

Date of Marriage...

Attention is especially called to the importance of indicating any change that may have occurred in your position or business or professional occupation since the last edition of Who's Who in America was issued, and not accounted for in the above sketch.

Entered upon my present occupation of...

Date...

Please furnish here both home and business address if not already correctly given above.

Home Address...

Business Address...

This sketch returned (Date) Oct 6 ....1909, by H L Mencken

PRINTER'S COPY No. ___ **W T 1**

This sheet is printer's copy for the new edition. Please return promptly to The Editors, Who's Who in America, A. N. Marquis Company, Marquis Publications Building, Chicago—11, Illinois, U. S. A.) whether or not changes are indicated, as the accuracy of the necessary alphabetization depends on each numbered sheet being in hand. You will be sent a printer's proof before publication in order that any succeeding current changes may be noted.

1731

WHO'S WHO IN AMERICA

VOLUME 25—1948-49

FIFTIETH ANNIVERSARY EDITION

NOTE: Your sketch as it appeared in the last edition is below. The Fiftieth Anniversary Edition—Volume Twenty-Five (1948-49) —is to be a printing involving extensive revision, planning and preparation, and accordingly it is now actively in compilation.

Therefore please promptly note below—on this sheet, beside the proof—any necessary alterations or additions. To obviate the necessity of sending out another printer's copy sheet, please return this one at once, regardless of whether or not changes are suggested.

Whenever possible, future events now known— including coming publications and changes in appointments or offices—should be anticipated and added to this printer's copy sheet, as so doing conserves critical composing room time and material. Such information will remain entirely confidential until publication, while the printer's proof which is sent before then assures an opportunity to recheck it.

DO N   volume of verse. Address: care Brandt & Brandt, 101 lready been set in type as shown. Since scattered minor
         Park Av., New York, N.Y.
alterations may involve complete resetting, the editors, because of the continuingly difficult production situation, will additionally appreciate cooperation in minimizing them for the duration.

Should the biographee involved not be living, the editors will appreciate this sheet being returned to them by the person into whose hands it may fall, with a notation of the date of death. Such cooperation will assure transfer of the sketch to the next edition of "Who Was Who in America."

Please give particular attention to the accuracy of the indication of the pronunciation of your surname, if it is at all unusual—see notations overleaf.

Proof of Your Sketch
As Published in "Volume 24"

Deadline for corrections in this proof:

Within U.S.A. — 6 days from receipt hereof to assure insertion.

Outside U.S.A. — As promptly after receipt as practicable —air mail suggested.

MILLAY, Edna St. Vincent (mĭl-lāʹ), author; b. Rockland, Me., Feb. 22, 1892; d. Henry Tolman and Cora (Buzzelle) Millay; A.B., Vassar Coll., 1917; Litt.D., Tufts, Russell Sage Foundation Coll., Colby Coll., U. of Wis., 1923. L.H.D., New York U.; m. Eugen Jan Boissevain, 1923. Mem. Am. Acad. Arts and Letters, Am. Soc. Composers, Authors and Pubs. Author: Renascence and Other Poems, 1917; Figs from Thistles, 1920; Second April, 1921; Aria da Capo, 1921; The Lamp and the Bell, 1921; Two Slatterns and a King, 1921; The Harp-Weaver and Other Poems, 1923; The King's Henchman, 1927; The Buck in the Snow, 1928; Fatal Interview, 1931; Wine from These Grapes, 1934; Flowers of Evil (from the French of Charles Baudelaire, in collaboration with George Dillon), 1936; Conversation at Midnight, 1937; Huntsman, What Quarry?, 1939; Make Bright the Arrows (poems), 1940; There Are No Islands, Any More (poems), 1940; Collected Sonnets, 1941. Collected Lyrics, 1943. Winner Pulitzer prize, 1922, for best volume of verse. Address: care Harper Bros., New York, N.Y.

Brandt & Brandt, 101 Park av., New York, N.Y.

YOUR SIGNATURE (or an authorized one)—so that the editors may be assured personal data has been checked at first hand.

DEC 23

If a sketch does not include an address, proofs can not be sent for revision necessary to current publication and avoidance of transfer to the non-current classification. Therefore, if not already correctly given above, please note below both home and business addresses, including any postal zone. If you do not wish the addresses published, and to be available only to The A. N. Marquis Co., check this square ☐

HOME ADDRESS: *Edna St. Vincent Millay*

PROFESSIONAL or BUSINESS ADDRESS: *Brandt & Brandt*
                                    101 Park av., N.Y.C.

25

BY WAY OF RECIPROCATION

By way of reciprocating somewhat for the cooperation which must be asked of biographees in checking listing manuscripts and bringing published sketches down to date every two years, for many years those listed in "Who's Who" have been extended a ten percent discount—such as is also allowed libraries and educational institutions—on ordering in advance of publication. Every effort will be made to continue this practice despite the currently increasing costs, and a blank validating it for Volume 25, the Fiftieth Anniversary Edition, is pinned hereto. Additionally, under present conditions pre-publication orders amount to a priority, as current postwar production retardations, as well as supply conditions in respect to certain materials, affect press runs, and consequently the increased demand has resulted in pre-publication orders practically exhausting the last four editions before publication.

Please write very plainly—preferably printing out or having typewritten. See overleaf for essential details in connection with publication of the above sketch.

PRINTED IN U. S. A.

HC 1092

NOTE. This brief personal sketch will appear under your name in the next edition of WHO'S WHO IN AMERICA. If any important fact (conformatory to the plan of the book) has been omitted it is because the information has not been furnished to the editor, and it should be supplied herewith. All blank spaces should be properly filled in. Please be sure to see that the name is given in full and correctly spelled. Kindly revise and return at once.

Return to A. N. MARQUIS & COMPANY, 440-2 Dearborn St. South, Chicago, Ill.

O'NEILL, Eugene Gladstone, playwright;
b. N.Y.City, Oct. 16, 1888; s. James and
Ella (Quinlan) O.; student Princeton,
1906-7, Harvard (English and technique of
drama), 1914-15; m. Agnes Boulton Burton,
of London, Eng., Apr. 12, 1918. Successively
engaged in *Successively in* various lines of business in U.S.,
Central and S. America, 6 yrs. at sea *2 yrs.*, actor
in vaudeville version of "Monte Cristo", and
reporter on New London(Conn.) Telegraph; has
devoted attention to play writing since 1914.
Mem. Authors' League America. Author: Thirst,
and Other One-Act Plays, 1914; The Moon of the
Caribbees, and Other Plays of the Sea, 1918; *9*
Beyond the Horizon (play in 3 acts), 1918; *9*
Wrote 11 one-act plays which have been prod. in
New York. Home: Provincetown, Mass.

Thirst and Other One Act Plays, 1914.

Home; Provincetown Mass.

50

Please furnish here both home and business address, if not correctly given above.

Home Address *Provincetown, Mass.*

Business Address " "

Returned (Date) *Jan. 2 1920* by *Eugene G. O'Neill.*

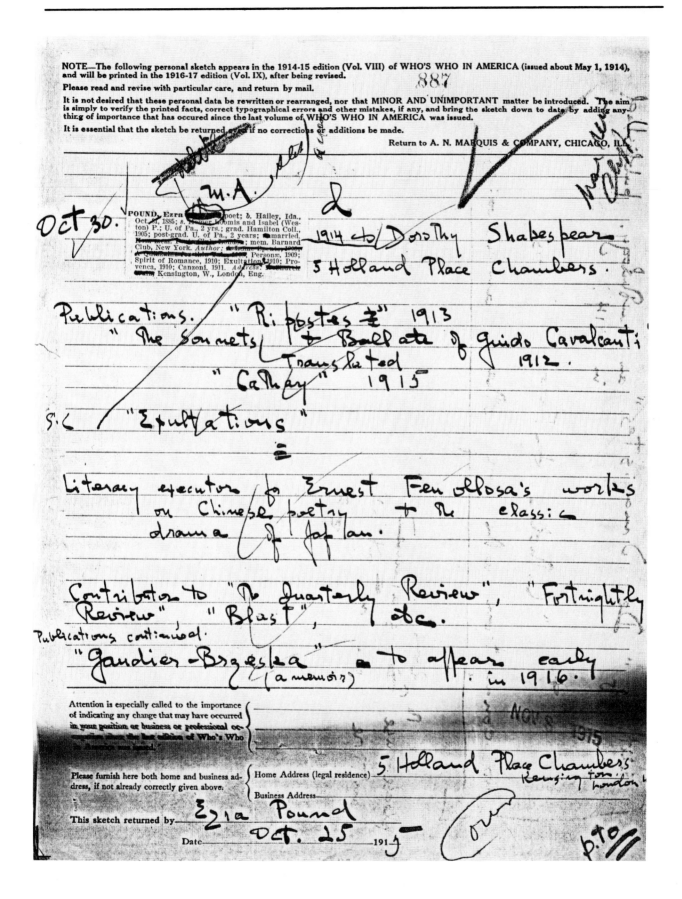

NOTE—The following personal sketch appears in the 1914-15 edition (Vol. VIII) of WHO'S WHO IN AMERICA (issued about May 1, 1914), and will be printed in the 1916-17 edition (Vol. IX), after being revised.

Please read and revise with particular care, and return by mail.   *887*

It is not desired that these personal data be rewritten or rearranged, nor that MINOR AND UNIMPORTANT matter be introduced. The aim is simply to verify the printed facts, correct typographical errors and other mistakes, if any, and bring the sketch down to date by adding anything of importance that has occured since the last volume of WHO'S WHO IN AMERICA was issued.

It is essential that the sketch be returned even if no corrections or additions be made.

Return to A. N. MARQUIS & COMPANY, CHICAGO, ILL.

Oct 30.   **M.A.**

POUND, Ezra ... poet; b. Hailey, Ida., Oct. 31, 1885; s. Homer Loomis and Isabel (Weston) P.; U. of Pa., 2 yrs.; grad. Hamilton Coll., 1905; post-grad. U. of Pa., 2 years; married. mem. ... Club, New York. *Author:* ... 1909; ... Personæ, 1909; Spirit of Romance, 1910; Exultations 1910; Provenca, 1910; Canzoni, 1911. *Address:* ... Kensington, W., London, Eng.

1914 — Dorothy Shakespear
5 Holland Place Chambers.

Publications.   "Ripostes £" 1913
" The Sonnets + Ballata of Guido Cavalcanti
Translated   1912.
" Cathay " 1915

S.C   " Exultations "

Literary executor to Ernest Fenollosa's works on Chinese poetry + the classic drama of Japan.

Contributor to " The Quarterly Review", " Fortnightly Review", " Blast", etc.

Publications continued.
" Gaudier-Brzeska " to appear early (a memoir) in 1916.

Attention is especially called to the importance of indicating any change that may have occurred in your position or business or professional oc...

NOV 8 1915

Please furnish here both home and business address, if not already correctly given above.

Home Address (legal residence) *5 Holland Place Chambers Kensington London*

Business Address

This sketch returned by *Ezra Pound*

Date *Oct. 25* 191*5*

For WHO'S WHO IN AMERICA (Vol. 12, 1922-23).

The following personal sketch appears in the last edition of WHO'S WHO IN AMERICA, issued about two years ago, and will be printed in the next edition after being revised and editorially approved.

Please read the sketch with particular care, making necessary alterations or additions, and promptly return by mail.

It is not desired that these personal data be rewritten or rearranged, nor that MINOR AND UNIMPORTANT matter be introduced. The aim is simply to verify the printed facts, correct typographical errors and other mistakes, if any, and bring the sketch down to date by adding anything of importance that has occurred since the last volume of WHO'S WHO IN AMERICA was issued.

The sketch should be returned even if no change be made. This is very important, as it will obviate the necessity of sending out another proof, and it will be taken as assurance that the printed address is correct.

A. N. MARQUIS & COMPANY, Chicago, Ill., U. S. A.

SANDBURG, Carl, writer; b. Galesburg, Ill., Jan. 6, 1878; s. August and Clara (Anderson) S.; student Lombard Coll., Galesburg, 1898-02; m. Lillian Steichen, of Milwaukee, Wis., June 15, 1908. Sec. to mayor of Milwaukee, Wis., 1910-12; asso. editor System Magazine, Chicago, 1913; Newspaper Enterprise Assn., Stockholm corr., 1918; editorial writer, Chicago Daily News. Awarded Levinson's Prize, Poetry Magazine, 1914; shared half Poetry Soc. of America prize award, 1919. Pvt. Co. C, 6th Ill. Vols., 1898, active service in Porto Rico. Mem. editorial bd. Nat. Labor Defense Council. *Author:* Chicago Poems, 1915; Corn Huskers, 1918; *Home:* Elmhurst, Ill.

The Chicago Race Riots, 1919; Smoke and Steel, 1920. *Am. folk song recitalist.*

American folk song recitalist.

Attention is especially called to the importance of indicating any change that may have occurred in your position or business or professional occupation since the last edition of Who's Who in America was issued.

{ Data on "American folk song recitalist" is sent by this mail under separate cover.

Please furnish here both home and business address, if not already correctly given above.

Home Address (legal residence) Elmhurst, Ill.

Business Address Chicago Daily News, Chicago, Ill.

This sketch returned by Carl Sandburg

Date Oct. 29 19 2

25

NOTE—The following personal sketch appears in the 1914-15 edition (Vol. VIII) of WHO'S WHO IN AMERICA (issued about May 1, 1914), and will be printed in the 1916-17 edition (Vol. IX), after being revised.

Please read and revise with particular care, and return by mail.

It is not desired that these personal data be rewritten or rearranged, nor that MINOR AND UNIMPORTANT matter be introduced. The aim is simply to verify the printed facts, correct typographical errors and other mistakes, if any, and bring the sketch down to date by adding anything of importance that has occured since the last volume of WHO'S WHO IN AMERICA was issued.

It is essential that the sketch be returned even if no corrections or additions be made.

Return to A. N. MARQUIS & COMPANY, CHICAGO, ILL.

see VOL. VIII (1914-1915).   151

SANTAYANA, George, author; b. at Madrid, Spain, Dec. 16, 1863; came to U.S., 1872; A.B., Harvard, 1886; A.M., Ph.D., 1889; (Litt.D., U. of Wis., 1911). Instr. philosophy, 1889-98, asst. prof., 1898-07, prof., 1907-12, Harvard. Hyde lecturer in France, 1905. Mem. Nat. Inst. Arts and Letters. Author: Sonnets and Other Poems, 1894; The Sense of Beauty, 1896; Lucifer—A Theological Tragedy, 1899; Interpretations of Poetry and Religion, 1900; The Hermit of Carmel and Other Poems, 1901; The Life of Reason, 1905; Three Philosophical Poets, 1910; Winds of Doctrine, 1913. Home: Paris, France. Address: care Brown, Shipley & Co., London.

I am not aware of either of these facts. G.S.

Attention is especially called to the importance of indicating any change that may have occurred in your position or business or professional occupation since the last edition of Who's Who in America was issued.

Please furnish here both home and business address, if not already correctly given above.

Home Address (legal residence) *none*

Business Address *as above*

This sketch returned by *G. Santayana*

Date *Oct. 26, 1915* —191—

NOV 9 1915

Anthony Burgess's *99 Novels:* An Opinion Poll

Anthony Burgess's *99 Novels* nominates the 99 best novels published between 1939 and 1983. His choices have generated disagreement—which is what such lists are intended for.

Dictionary of Literary Biography has invited critics and novelists to react to the Burgess 99.

1939
Party Going Henry Green
After Many a Summer Aldous Huxley
Finnegans Wake James Joyce
At Swim-Two-Birds Flann O'Brian

1940
The Power and the Glory Graham Greene
For Whom the Bell Tolls Ernest Hemingway
Strangers and Brothers (to 1970) C. P. Snow

1941
The Aerodrome Rex Warner

1944
The Horse's Mouth Joyce Cary
The Razor's Edge Somerset Maugham

1945
Brideshead Revisited Evelyn Waugh

1946
Titus Groan Mervyn Peake

1947
The Victim Saul Bellow
Under the Volcano Malcolm Lowry

1948
The Heart of the Matter Graham Greene
Ape and Essence Aldous Huxley
The Naked and the Dead Norman Mailer
No Highway Nevil Shute

1949
The Heat of the Day Elizabeth Bowen
Nineteen Eighty-four George Orwell
The Body William Sansom

1950
Scenes from Provincial Life William Cooper
The Disenchanted Budd Schulberg

Anthony Burgess

1951
A Dance to the Music of Time (to 1975) Anthony Powell
The Catcher in the Rye J. D. Salinger
A Chronicle of Ancient Sunlight (to 1969) Henry Williamson
The Caine Mutiny Herman Wouk

1952
Invisible Man Ralph Ellison
The Old Man and the Sea Ernest Hemingway
The Groves of Academe Mary McCarthy
Wise Blood Flannery O'Connor
Sword of Honour (to 1961) Evelyn Waugh

1953
The Long Goodbye Raymond Chandler

1954
Lucky Jim Kingsley Amis

1957
Room at the Top John Braine
The Alexandria Quartet (to 1960) Lawrence Durrell
The London Novels (to 1960) Colin MacInnes
The Assistant Bernard Malamud

1958
The Bell Iris Murdoch
Saturday Night and Sunday Morning Alan Sillitoe
The Once and Future King T. H. White

1959
The Mansion William Faulkner
Goldfinger Ian Fleming

1960
Facial Justice L. P. Hartley
The Balkans Trilogy (to 1965) Olivia Manning

1961
The Mighty and Their Fall Ivy Compton-Burnett
Catch-22 Joseph Heller
The Fox in the Attic Richard Hughes
Riders in the Chariot Patrick White
The Old Men at the Zoo Angus Wilson

1962
Another Country James Baldwin
An Error of Judgement Pamela Hansford Johnson
Island Aldous Huxley
The Golden Notebook Doris Lessing
Pale Fire Vladimir Nabokov

1963
The Girls of Slender Means Muriel Spark

1964
The Spire William Golding
Heartland Wilson Harris
A Single Man Christopher Isherwood
The Defence Vladimir Nabokov
Late Call Angus Wilson

1965
The Lockwood Concern John O'Hara
The Mandelbaum Gate Muriel Spark

1966
A Man of the People Chinua Achebe
The Anti-Death League Kingsley Amis
Giles Goat-Boy John Barth
The Late Bourgeois World Nadine Gordimer
The Last Gentleman Walker Percy

1967
The Vendor of Sweets R. K. Narayan

1968
The Image Men J. B. Priestley
Cocksure Mordecai Richler
Pavane Keith Roberts

1969
The French Lieutenant's Woman John Fowles
Portnoy's Complaint Philip Roth

1970
Bomber Len Deighton

1973
Sweet Dreams Michael Frayn
Gravity's Rainbow Thomas Pynchon

1975
Humboldt's Gift Saul Bellow
The History Man Malcolm Bradbury

1976
The Doctor's Wife Brian Moore
Falstaff Robert Nye

1977
How to Save Your Own Life Erica Jong
Farewell Companions James Plunkett
Staying On Paul Scott

1978
The Coup John Updike

1979
The Unlimited Dream Company J. G. Ballard
Dubin's Lives Bernard Malamud
A Bend in the River V. S. Naipaul
Sophie's Choice William Styron

1980
Life in the West Brian Aldiss
Riddley Walker Russell Hoban
How Far Can You Go? David Lodge
A Confederacy of Dunces John Kennedy Toole

1981
Lanark Alasdair Gray
Darconville's Cat Alexander Theroux
The Mosquito Coast Paul Theroux
Creation Gore Vidal

1982
The Rebel Angels Robertson Davies

1983
Ancient Evenings Norman Mailer

BRIAN W. ALDISS

I would venture a suggestion that the comments of those excluded from Anthony Burgess's distinguished list will be more waspish than the comments of those included. As one of the writers included, I will point to some of the sterling virtues of the list.

For a start, Burgess cheats—a cheerful indication that we are not to become too ponderous; literature is not the thinking man's equivalent of a horse race. So we should approve when he directs our attention as readers to whole series, of which it would be otiose to single out one particular volume for praise. It is proper that we should be reminded of such series, which have spanned a good part of our reading lifetimes and enhanced it, as have the Anthony Powell or the C. P. Snow novels—though there is perhaps less virtue in including the multitudinous volumes of Henry Williamson's *Chronicles of Ancient Sunlight*, despite those chronicles' telling pictures of the First World War.

What is most admirable about Burgess's bold list is the inclusion of so many novels which have not been generally considered as worthy of shelf space by a cultured reading public. There are in particular novels which would be dismissed as generic fiction by critics who love prescriptive boundaries more than writers do; such as the Raymond Chandler—a very good choice—White's *Once and Future King*, Keith Roberts's haunting *Pavanne*, and Len Deighton's *Bomber*. But the keynote of the list is adventurousness. It bears the imprint of Burgess's omnivorous appetite, and his impatience with the small novel, the tidily observed, the merely perfect. He is on the side of Henry James's baggy monster, on the side of generosity rather than parsimony.

Nor does fashion blind him. That's worth a special cheer. Many much touted names fail to put in an appearance: Margaret Drabble, Edna O'Brien, Fay Weldon, and Eric Ambler (whose marvellous *Passage of Arms* I would have substituted for Ian Fleming's silly *Goldfinger*). On the other hand, what better shows Burgess's independence of mind than to include three Aldous Huxley novels? Huxley scores highest with three; and one hopes that, as

a result, more attention is paid to *Ape and Essence* and *Island* than has so far been the case.

Burgess has plainly gone for novels which attempt to capture something of the zeitgeist without being trendy. There are some dull things on his list (I speak as one who failed to weather more than fifty pages of *Ancient Evenings*); one might consider, for instance, that the Australian novelist Patrick White would be better represented by the exemplary *A Fringe of Leaves* than by *Riders in the Chariot*. But it really is an exciting list, untainted by classroom, which should be genially accepted as a whole, rather than have reductive minor bones picked over it.

The one major bone, of course, is that the list excludes *The Malayan Trilogy*, *Beard's Roman Women*, and *Earthly Powers*.

CARLOS BAKER

De gustibus non est disputandum—One man's Mede is another man's Persian. The Roman apothegm and the American pun mean roughly the same thing, and both fit the problem of choosing the 99 best American and British and Irish novels from the past forty-five years. It is easy to cut Burgess's list from 99 to forty-nine by the expedient of crossing out those that in someone else's judgment are *not* the best. For examples, *The Coup* is one of Updike's weakest (why not the second of the Rabbit series?); *The Victim* is very early Bellow, good but not best; *Dubin's Lives* is not vintage Malamud; *Wise Blood* is probably the better of Flannery O'Connor's novels, but she really excelled only in short fiction, where she triumphed repeatedly; Golding's *The Spire* is superb, but how can one rightly ignore such others in the Golding canon as *Lord of the Flies* and *The Pyramid*? And so on, almost ad infinitum.

Burgess's list is heavily weighted towards the United Kingdom. This is understandable, not so much for jingoistic reasons as for the probability that a man of letters and practicing novelist like Burgess gets many books from publishers for comment, reviews many, and clearly feels more matey with the work of his native confreres. So he misses many equally good novels, or even better novels, from the U.S.A. There is something adventitious about what a man reads out of the vast annual eruption, and something arbitrary about his choices. It cannot be otherwise unless a busy writer takes time to read everything, which is simply impossible even if he does nothing but read. If 99 other novelists chose 99 novels each as the best of

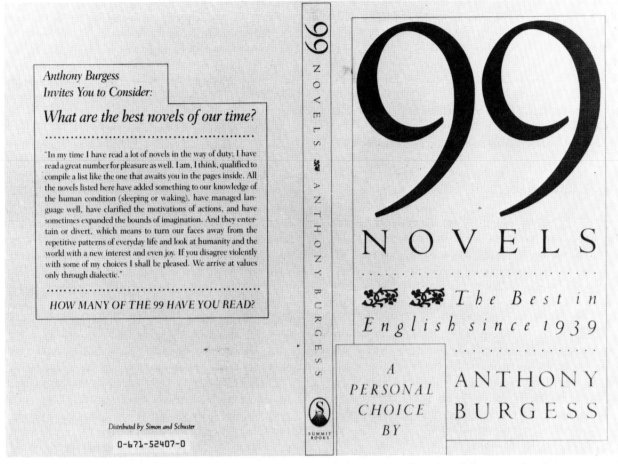

Dust jacket for the book containing Anthony Burgess's choices and a discussion of the merits of each

half a century, each list would differ widely from all the others. The overlap might be ten to twenty percent, but not much more.

Among the notable omissions from Anthony Burgess's list would be Cozzens's *Guard of Honor* (1948), the best novel about World War II; two novels of 1955 (the year that Burgess skipped)— *Andersonville* (Kantor) and *Ten North Frederick* (O'Hara); *When She Was Good,* the valuable novel of 1967 in which Roth for once escaped the strait-jacket fixation that led to *Portnoy's Complaint* and the more recent trilogy. I miss the names of Eudora Welty (*Losing Battles* and *The Optimist's Daughter*), Anne Tyler's *Earthly Possessions* (1977). Where is Elizabeth Spencer (*The Voice at the Back Door*)? Where is Jessamyn West? Only ten women appear on the list, and ten percent of 99 doesn't adequately represent the achievement of women in fiction for the period in question. Other notable omissions: Faulkner's *The Hamlet, The Town, Intruder in the Dust,* and *The Reivers;* Bellow's *Augie March* (1953) and *The Dean's December* (1982); Anthony West's *Heri-*

tage, a first-rate job; Michael Shaara's *The Killer Angels* (1974 Pulitzer); two from 1977 that are much better than Burgess's selections for that year: Jon Hassler's *Staggerford* and Don Robertson's tenth novel, *Miss Margaret Ridpath and the Dismantling of the Universe;* and a recent discovery of mine, William Wiser's *Disappearances* (1980).

I suppose the chief value of lists like Burgess's is to stimulate disagreement and to enable others to bring forward their choices in lieu of his. If I had more time, patience, and belief, the foregoing could be much extended. But I will spare you such a tour de force.

[Professor Baker challenged the following titles: *At Swim-Two-Birds, The Razor's Edge, Titus Groan, Under the Volcano, Ape and Essence, The Naked and the Dead, The Body, The Disenchanted, Invisible Man, The Groves of Academe, The Long Goodbye, Lucky Jim, The Alexandria Quartet, The Bell, Goldfinger, The Balkans Trilogy, Catch-22, Riders in the Chariot, Another Country, An Error of Judgement, Island, The Golden Notebook, Heartland, A Single Man, The Lock-*

wood Concern, The Mandelbaum Gate, A Man of the People, The Anti-Death League, Giles Goat Boy, The Late Bourgeois World, The Last Gentleman, The Image Men, Cocksure, Pavane, Portnoy's Complaint, Bomber, Sweet Dreams, Gravity's Rainbow, The History Man, Falstaff, How To Save Your Own Life, Farewell Companions, Staying On, The Coup, The Unlimited Dream Company, Life in the West, Riddley Walker, How Far Can You Go?, A Confederacy of Dunces, Lanark, Darconville's Cat, Creation, The Rebel Angels, and *Ancient Evenings.*]

BRIGID BROPHY

"De gustibus non est disputandum" is true in the sense that you can't by argument prove your taste right or mine wrong; but as social observation, which it is often mistaken for, it's rubbish. A great deal of civilized social intercourse takes the form: "I have a great fondness for black currants." "I hate them but adore red currants."

In such an exchange, the interlocutors, unless they're in love, don't heed one another's taste. Each treats the other's as a mere stimulus to or pretext for the always agreeable activity of declaring his own. Anthony Burgess's list of "best" post-1939 novels will serve that purpose, though someone else's quite different 99 would do equally well.

The year that marks "Go," 1939, represents the beginning of World War II for British readers but not for readers in the U.S.A. Yet one of the most suspect things about the list is the "even-handed" (or saleable?) balance it maintains between titles to which a U.S. readership can be expected to react and titles to which British readers can. Still more suspect is the distribution of titles through the forty-four years concerned. It is implausible that excellent works of literature emerged at a steadyish rate averaging, on the model of the "average family," two point something per year. I should not be grossly surprised if it turned out that all 99 of the truly best novels of the period were first published in, say, 1964.

MALCOLM COWLEY

Anthony Burgess's *99 Novels* made me realize how many presumably good books I haven't read. Especially I haven't tried hard to follow the course of English fiction during the last forty-odd years. There were some curious omissions toward the beginning of his list. *The Grapes of Wrath* (1939) is one of them. Two others are books by William Faulk-

ner, *The Hamlet* (1940) and *Go Down, Moses* (1942), which are the last publications of his great period. For Saul Bellow, *The Adventures of Augie March* (1953) marked a new stage in his career and is still good reading. But I haven't energy now in dog days, to go through his whole list and make comments.

R. W. H. DILLARD

The game of listing best books is a grand game to play, for both the lister and argumentative reader of the list. As long as we remember that the list is an expression of personal taste and not of objective fact, it can be an instructive game as well. Anthony Burgess has played it with skill, and his readers can learn a great deal about him and about some fine novels. I was especially pleased to find that he hadn't forgotten Henry Green or Joyce Cary at a time when too many literary folk appear to have done so. I was also pleased to see—in addition to all the obvious choices, those hallowed by received opinion—books that deserve greater attention such as J. G. Ballard's *The Unlimited Dream Company* and Alexander Theroux's *Darconville's Cat.* And among his choices within the works of particular authors, I was happy to see Huxley's *Ape and Essence,* Golding's *The Spire,* and Nabokov's *Pale Fire.*

My only serious complaints with inclusions in Burgess's list have to do with his placing Erica Jong's tawdry *How to Save Your Own Life* and William Styron's clumsy *Sophie's Choice* on such a distinguished list.

There are, to my mind and taste, some notable omissions on Burgess's list. I was surprised that the author of *Nothing Like the Sun* omitted the brilliant Elizabethan novels of George Garrett, *Death of the Fox* (1971) and *The Succession* (1983); and, although I agree that Ian Fleming deserves a place on the list for historical as much as literary reasons, I was also surprised that J. R. R. Tolkien's *Lord of the Rings* (1954-1955) did not earn a place on similar grounds.

Some other books I would draw Burgess' attention to are these:
1939 *Tropic of Capricorn* by Henry Miller
1940 *Owen Clendower* by John Cowper Powys
1941 *Ida* by Gertrude Stein
1945 *All Hallows' Eve* by Charles Williams
1948 *Guard of Honor* by James Gould Cozzens
1962 *Ship of Fools* by Katherine Anne Porter
1964 *Little Big Man* by Thomas Berger
1965 *One Day* by Wright Morris

1968 *Dagon* by Fred Chappell
  The Universal Baseball Association, J. Henry Waugh, Prop. by Robert Coover
  Morning Noon and Night by James Gould Cozzens
  Night Climber by Jon Manchip White
1969 *The Philosopher's Stone* by Colin Wilson
1974 *The Dispossessed* by Ursula K. LeGuin
  The Death of the Detective by Mark Smith
  And I would add *A Clockwork Orange* (1962) or *The End of the World News* (1983), both, of course, by Anthony Burgess.

IHAB HASSAN

Professor Hassan challenged the following titles: *Strangers and Brothers, Titus Groan, No Highway, The Body, The Disenchanted, A Chronicle of Ancient Sunlight, The Caine Mutiny, The Long Mutiny, The Long Goodbye, The London Novel, Goldfinger, Facial Justice, The Balkans Trilogy, An Error of Judgement, Heartland, A Single Man, The Lockwood Concern, The Mandelbaum Gate, Pavane, Bomber, Sweet Dreams, The Doctor's Wife, Falstaff, How To Save Your Own Life, Farewell Companions, Staying On, The Coup, Life in the West, Riddley Walker, How Far Can You Go?, A Confederacy of Dunces, Lanark, The Mosquito Coast, Creation,* and *The Rebel Angels.*

"I would also add to the list," he writes, "Saul Bellow's *The Adventures of Augie March* and *Henderson the Rain King,* Norman Mailer's *Why Are We in Vietnam?,* John Updike's *Rabbit Run,* Don de Lillo's *Ratner's Star,* J. P. Donleavy's *The Ginger Man,* Nathanael West's *Miss Lonelyhearts* and *The Day of the Locust.* Robert Penn Warren's *All the King's Men,* Nelson Algren's *The Man With the Golden Arm,* Paul Bowles's *The Sheltering Sky,* John Hawkes's *The Cannibal,* John Cheever's *The Wapshot Chronicles,* Jerzy Kozinski's *The Painted Bird,* Donald Barthelme's *The Dead Father,* James Jones's *From Here to Eternity,* Thomas Berger's *Crazy in Berlin,* Stanley Elkin's *A Bad Man.*" But he adds, "I have the strongest reservations against this kind of list."

CHRISTOPHER ISHERWOOD

I would nominate *In the Thirties* by Edward Upward, published by Heinemann in 1962.

ORVILLE PRESCOTT

Lists of best books, of course, are highly personal, subjective and emotional. So not to be taken seriously. Nevertheless, they are fun and provocative.

Anthony Burgess has listed many novels of which I have no knowledge. But he has not mentioned eight outstanding American novels which he may not know or of which he thinks little. I think they are superb and should be on any such list. They are: *The Just and The Unjust* (1942) and *Guard of Honor* (1948) by James Gould Cozzens; *H. M. Pulham* (1941) and *Point of No Return* (1949) by John P. Marquand; *The Trees* (1940), *The Fields* (1946) and *The Town* (1950) by Conrad Richter; and *The Big Sky* (1947) by A. B. Guthrie, Jr.

There are six novels on Mr. Burgess's list to which I strenuously object. They are: *Finnegans Wake,* which is not a novel, only a monstrous puzzle for pundits; *Titus Groan* by Mervyn Peake, a pretentious, wretchedly written and stupifying dull fantasy; *Goldfinger,* perhaps amusing but preposterous trash; *The Lockwood Concern,* a late and tired work by an author who never wrote anything worthy of a best list; *Portnoy's Complaint,* a cheap novel made popular because of its indecency; and *Gravity's Rainbow,* which I understand is a cult book among the young, but which is considered unreadable by the few people I know who have ever sampled it.

PETER S. PRESCOTT

The best one can say for this rather sorry enterprise is that it's no worse than anyone else's desert-island compendium. It represents Burgess trying to pick up a little easy money in a way that's not wholly disreputable. The purpose of such a list is to be idiosyncratic, provocative. The unspoken message of all such lists is: See, here's a great book and you haven't even heard of it! Fair enough, I guess.

We all know that Burgess is widely read—at least in English letters. Some of his selections are intriguing (Raymond Chandler's *The Long Goodbye,* for instance); those that are clearly ill-advised probably result from Burgess's relative unfamiliarity with American literature. No reader of taste or judgment, for instance, would include either Herman Wouk's *The Caine Mutiny* or John O'Hara's *The Lockwood Concern*(!) in such a list. But then he shouldn't have included Maugham's *The Razor's*

Edge or Amis's *The Anti-Death League* either. With Maugham, and with Flannery O'Connor, he confronted a dilemma: both were masters of the short story, yet he wants to send a friendly nod in their direction.

I think the list itself is of little use unless it is read with the defenses that Burgess provided in his brief book, "99 Novels." There we find conclusive proof of how Burgess approached this matter with

his left hand. *The Mansion*, he tells us in his magisterial way, is "the last book that Faulkner wrote"—which will come as news to readers of *The Reivers*. Stingo, the hero of Styron's *Sophie's Choice*, is given to us as "Ringo"—indeed! He must have been a rock star, not a novelist. There, too, Burgess employs a phrase, "the general consensus," that he's far too good a writer ever to use—that is, if he's really thinking about what he's doing.

The Bestseller Lists: An Assessment

The first American bestseller list appeared in the February 1895 issue of the *Bookman*. It contained sixteen books:

Trilby, by George du Maurier;
The Prisoner of Zenda, by Anthony Hope;
The Manxman, by Hall Caine;
The Dolly Dialogues, by Anthony Hope;
Slum Stories of London, by H. W. Nevinson;
Beside the Bonnie Brier Bush, by Ian Maclaren;
The Good Ship Mohock, by W. Clark Russell;
The Ralstons, by F. Marion Crawford;
The American Commonwealth, by James Bryce;
Peter Ibbetson, by George du Maurier;
Barabbas, Marie Corelli;
The Adventures of Sherlock Holmes, by A. Conan Doyle;
Coffee and Repartee, by J. K. Bangs;
The Green Carnation;
The Ascent of Man, by Henry Drummond;
Social Evolution, by Benjamin Kidd.

That only two or three of these titles would be recognized by a moderately well read reader today and that only one continues to be generally read raises the question of what purpose bestseller lists serve.

"A bestseller," according to Daniel J. Boorstin, Librarian of Congress, "is known primarily (sometimes exclusively) for its well-knowness." Even if bestseller lists are reliable, they indicate only the number of copies purportedly sold. These figures are of great interest to the author, the publisher, the booktrade, the IRS, and cultural historians. That they are also deemed necessary information for

outsiders reveals that the bestseller lists are regarded as ought-to-read lists—or, at least, ought-to-buy lists. As such, they are pernicious but no doubt useful to the celebrated common reader who finds it difficult to "keep up" with books. The formation of literary taste and the rewards of reading should be intensely personal activities. (The circumstance that sex manuals frequently turn up on the bestseller lists may well indicate that the people who consult the lists are incapable of developing any personal skills.) One of the rewards of literature is the joy of discovery; but this experience is vitiated by the shopping-list approach to books. The newspapers and magazines do not publish weekly lists of bestselling toothpastes, laxatives, or deodorants because people know what they want: that is, advertising has told them what they want. The selection of books requires aesthetic judgment or mere intelligence. The need for bestseller lists indicates that book buyers and book borrowers expect help. A 1984 *Publishers Weekly* article revealed that most book buyers do not select books on the basis of author recognition. This discovery goes counter to a commandment of publishing: If people liked the author's last book, they'll buy his next one. Most people buy a book because they've heard about it. Where they hear about it is usually on the bestseller list or in book-club promotional material—which is much the same thing. A book on the bestseller lists sells better because it is on the bestseller lists.

The influence of the lists points up the need for more and better book news. How many newspapers have a daily book review? How many have a weekly book page? How much advertising space is devoted to books? (It isn't profitable to advertise books unless they are bestsellers, and publishers are convinced that advertising does not create bestsellers.)

A familiar criticism is that publishers are good at everything having to do with books except publishing them—that is, making them public. Publishers contend that printing books now is not their responsibility. They sell books to bookstores, not readers. The two dominant bookstore chains, Twiddlewald and Twiddledalt, stock bestsellers because that is what their customers come to buy.

It would be misleading to claim that bestseller lists do direct harm. They sell books, and anything that sells books is good. Perhaps the greatest service they perform is in calling attention to the need for other and better ways to disseminate book news. Unless, of course, it really is the case that most readers want to read the books that most readers are reading.

The *Yearbook* has assembled comments on the bestseller lists showing how the lists are compiled and how they are regarded by those who live off them.

—*M. J. B.*

JOHN BAKER
Publishers Weekly

We compile our lists by a large number of calls to individual independent bookstores across the country, which includes stores in both large and small towns, university bookstores, regional chains; and of course we also have access to the computerized sales results of the two major chains. Walden and Dalton. From these various sources we work up the list each week. In our phone calls to the stores, we ask them what is selling best, to rate them in order as to how they're selling in the store. When we've got all these reports in, we weigh them essentially according to what we know of the size of the store. We then construct a sequence each week of the order in which the books seem to appear.

As I'm sure other people may have told you, the bestseller lists don't necessarily reflect the long-term sales of any individual book; all they really reflect is the rate of sale within a given week. In other words, a book that may become a major bestseller in the course of the year simply because it sells steadily week after week and never rises above four or five may end up as the year's major seller. That's because it sells more copies over the long haul than a book that appears at the top of the list for a couple of weeks and by degrees drops off the list, all within the course of a few weeks. A lot of people, I think, don't seem to realize that the lists only reflect the rate of sale in any one given week. They say, well, our book has sold 200,000 copies already. To which the answer is, it has sold 200,000 copies over the course of ten months whereas the book that's at the top this week has sold fifteen or twenty thousand copies in a single week, which is an extraordinary sale. That faster book doesn't maintain that speed, in which case it will soon drop off the list. That's the method whereby we compile the lists.

We have four categories essentially. We haven't played around as the *Times* has, attempting in effect to make value judgments as to what are serious books and what aren't. We have hardcover and paperback lists divided into both fiction and nonfiction in each case—with the paperback list between mass-market and trade. We occasionally list what we call candidates, which means new books and authors that are just off the bottom of the list, sort of hanging around there, that with another few votes would get on. Sometimes they get on the following week; sometimes they never do. They simply hang around as also-rans. The method is as scientific as we know how to make it. It is not, however, apart from the computerized sales reports from the chains, computerized at our end. It's done essentially by putting down the lists of books and putting down the points which we assign to them on the basis of the size of the source.

I'm not sure philosophically that bestseller lists are good for the industry except to the extent that they do inspire a lot of consumer interest in the books on them. As we all know, lots of books hang around the fringe of the list and in fact may in the course of a given year sell more copies than some of the books that make it to the list in any given week. On the other hand, it is newsy; people compete vigorously to get their books on the list. All sorts of important extras come to publisher and author as a result of the placing on the list: prime location in the bookstores, better terms in subsidiary rights deals of various kinds—including serial and movie rights and escalators that give the author a greater share of the proceeds and eventual sales to TV or the movies. All those sorts of things accrue from the position of a book on the bestseller list and therefore it's an important business element, whatever you may think of it philosophically or psychologically. It can't really be neglected by an organ that is at the center of the book trade.

ART SEIDENBAUM
Los Angeles Times

We contact more than fifteen sources each Tuesday for our bestseller lists of the following Sunday. Since those sources include major chains, our lists reflect rankings from hundreds of bookstores, from San Diego up to Santa Barbara. In most cases, the reports are relative standings, not numbers of copies sold. We weigh those reports based on gross sales for each outlet.

I do not like bestseller lists much and I don't much trust them either. There is always a fear that a bookstore may report a title because it has overstocked that title, hoping a place on the lists will spur sales. There is also a fear that a bookstore may not have time/energy to compile an accurate report each week. I wish readers would use reviews, word-of-mouth, personal browsing as better recommendations than any bestseller list.

We run the lists because readers seem to want them, publishers want them, and booksellers want them. We are as accurate as we can be, as accurate as telephone surveying allows.

THE NEW YORK TIMES BOOK REVIEW

Hardcover List: Based on reports from 2,000 nationwide bookstores, "adjusted to represent sales in all bookstores." Once a month these stores receive a list of thirty-six titles with additional blank spaces for write-in titles or newer titles, and every Monday the dealers are phoned for their sales figures.

Paperback List: Based on reports from 2,000 nationwide bookstores and representative wholesalers with more than 40,000 retail outlets (including newsstands, supermarkets, and other stores). "These figures are statistically adjusted to represent sales in all such outlets. . . ."

The large chains—Dalton, Walden, Doubleday—prepare their own weekly reports for the *Times.*

SIMON MICHAEL BESSIE
Joshua Town Publishing Associates

As a publisher of books for approximately forty years, I feel that bestseller lists are:

1. *Inevitable,* in a culture which likes (needs?) to know what other people think, or value.

2. *Interesting,* whether or not you believe them to be accurate.

3. *Indicative,* if not always so, of which books people are buying and, probably, reading.

4. *Responsible,* in part, for the increasing emphasis on blockbusters. So are movies, TV in general, and talk shows in particular.

5. *Irritating,* when you get the feeling they are not just to your books of the moment.

6. *Pleasant,* when the opposite is the case.

In sum, they are a *fact.*

GEORGE A. HALL
Little, Brown

Although a bestseller list can be inaccurate and often a misleading indicator, it seems to me that they do provide some guidance to the reader and vitality to the industry. Every time a reader enjoys a book, it helps every other book, bookseller and publisher.

JOHN JAKES

No denying it: to hit a major bestseller list is an unparalleled thrill. For me, though, the thrill has nothing to do with computation of royalty cash; it's joyful validation that a book has found a big audience.

Making of the lists has improved, it would appear. Gone is some of the imprecise, not to say downright suspicious, methodology of the past: What's selling? Quickly cast the old eyeball across the counter to the stacks of stock. Computer-generated reports have helped clear some of the murk of doubt about compilation techniques.

Even so—beware. It's hardly a revelation that popularity isn't the only yardstick in the closet. The acknowledged masterpieces of Dickens, for example, are mostly the dark, dense, later novels, not the lighter and more popular ones of his youth.

I suppose the wisest thing to add to any consideration of lists is that familiar pinch of salt. The author's attitude probably should be this. Savor the success—store it fondly in memory—but meanwhile, on to the next piece of work. To shorten an anecdote often told about Sir Laurence Olivier, the career actor must not only try to ignore the bad notices, but the good ones, too.

ALLAN KELLOCK
Viking Penguin

I think that bestseller lists are a positive factor for the book industry. They help sell more copies of those books they list to a segment of the book-buying public that probably does not otherwise stay very abreast with the enormous number of new books being published, nor buy a significant portion of them. But to blame bestseller lists for the poor sales performance of other books is both fallacious and an exercise in scapegoating. With 40,000 new books published every year, only a small proportion are destined to achieve respectable sales. Sometimes the publisher can be faulted for an inadequate job of bringing a new book to the public's attention. More often, the real problem is the book itself, particularly the small size of the audience to which it appeals.

I find the notion of abolishing bestseller lists highly elitist. But even if it could be accomplished, I fail to see how the lot of marginally saleable books would therefore improve.

PETER S. PRESCOTT
Newsweek

Of bestseller lists, virtually all that can be said has been said—many times. There's nothing really wrong with unimaginative or unadventurous readers wanting to keep up with what everyone else is reading. That's what these lists help them to do. And it can't be denied that the news of what people

are reading is of at least minor interest.

The real problem is that these lists determine to large degree which books a store will stock. The room it takes to house a bin full of Billy Graham's book on angels is room that can't be used to shelter a modest supply of my collected works.

What we greatly need is a method by which to bring to the attention of potential book buyers the news of all those so-called "midlist" books that readers might really enjoy—if only they knew about them. The all-too-brief "recommended" lists that publications tack on at the end of bestseller lists are pathetic, yet an acknowledgement that somehow there's something disgraceful going on in the marketplace of ideas when success is measured only in commercial terms.

BUDD SCHULBERG

There is not the slightest doubt in my mind that the featuring of bestseller lists tends to discourage the sales of books not on them. I would like to refer you to my book *Writers In America: The Four Seasons of Success*, in which I deal with this problem. We are very much a Top Ten and Top Twenty country. The buyers get lazy and unless they have a very special interest, they tend to want to buy what everyone else is buying. Bookstores all over America feature the *New York Times* bestseller list at the entrance, and all too often customers go no further than the glamorous bestseller rack.

Freedom of speech and print may forbid us from actually abolishing the publication of the bestseller list, but I have always maintained that their effect should be played down, and that booksellers make a conscious effort not to take the easy way but to broaden the range of choice to deserving but sometimes unrecognized books as much as possible.

WILLIAM W. STARR
Columbia (South Carolina) *State*

I'm not one of those book editors who is dogmatic on the subject. I look at such lists with a lighter spirit than some, I suspect. No, I don't believe they discourage sales of books not on the list, but in fact they may serve as a lure to get people into some bookstores. And after all, so few people read

Best Sellers

SOUTHERN CALIFORNIA
Placement on national list is noted in parentheses.

FICTION

1 The Sicilian by Mario Puzo (Linden) (3)
2 If Tomorrow Comes by Sidney Sheldon (Morrow) (1)
3 The Talisman by Stephen King and Peter Straub (Viking) (2)
4 So Long, and Thanks for All the Fish by Douglas Adams (Harmony) (4)
5 Love and War by John Jakes (Harcourt Brace Jovanovich) (7)
6 Illusions of Love by Cynthia Freeman (Putnam's) (6)
7 Life Its Ownself: The Semi-Tough Adventures of Billy Clyde Puckett by Dan Jenkins (Simon & Schuster) (10)
8 Moscow Rules by Robert Moss (Villard)
9 The Life and Hard Times of Heidi Abromowitz by Joan Rivers (Delacorte) (5)
10 The Fourth Protocol by Frederick Forsyth (Viking) (8)
11 The Raj Quartet by Paul Scott (Morrow)
12 . . . And Ladies of the Club by Helen Hooven Santmyer (Putnam's) (9)
13 Dream of Orchids by Phyllis A. Whitney (Doubleday) (13)
14 Glitz by Elmore Leonard (Arbor House)
15 Stones for Ibarra by Harriet Doerr (Viking)

GENERAL

1 Iacocca by Lee Iacocca with William Novak (Bantam) (1)
2 Loving Each Other by Leo Buscaglia (Slack/Holt, Rinehart & Winston) (3)
3 What They Don't Teach You at Harvard Business School by Mark H. McCormack (Bantam) (2)
4 The Bridge Across Forever by Richard Bach (Morrow) (8)
5 Nothing Down by Robert G. Allen (Simon & Schuster) (5)
6 Women Coming of Age by Jane Fonda with Mignon McCarthy (Simon & Schuster) (4)
7 "The Good War": An Oral History of World War Two by Studs Terkel (Pantheon) (10)
8 The One Minute Salesperson by Spencer Johnson and Larry Wilson (Morrow) (7)
9 Citizen Hughes by Michael Drosnin (Holt, Rinehart & Winston)
10 Weight Watchers Quick Start Program Cookbook by Jean Nidetch (NAL Books) (6)
11 Son of the Morning Star: Custer and the Little Bighorn by Evan S. Connell (North Point) (13)
12 Distant Neighbors: Portrait of the Mexicans by Alan Riding (Knopf)
13 Pieces of My Mind by Andrew A. Rooney (Atheneum) (5)
14 Chef Paul Prudhomme's Louisiana Kitchen by Paul Prudhomme (Morrow)
15 Cats, Dogs, and Other Strangers at My Door by Jack Smith (Watts)

AND THE CRITICS COMMEND

Sitting in Darkness: Americans in the Philippines, David Haward Bain (Houghton Mifflin). Gripping historical account of antagonism between two cultures.
Sexual Choice: A Woman's Decision, Heather Trexler Remoff, Ph.D. (Dutton/Lewis). Anthropological study charmingly reveals who chooses whom.
The Art of the Knock, Philip Graham (Morrow). Funny, fragmented fantasies; people relate to each other's symptoms but not to each other.
Neville Chamberlain, David Dilks (Cambridge University). First of a two-volume biography revealing much about the former British Prime Minister.

Feb. 3, 1985   THE NEW YORK TIMES BOOK REVIEW

Best Sellers

This Week	Fiction	Last Week	Weeks On List
1	IF TOMORROW COMES, by Sidney Sheldon. (Morrow, $16.95.) A young woman contrives to destroy the crime lords who got her an undeserved prison term.	7	2
2	THE SICILIAN, by Mario Puzo. (Linden Press/Simon & Schuster, $17.95.) A fictionalized life of Salvatore Giuliano, the Sicilian bandit-hero of the 1940's.	1	12
3	THE TALISMAN, by Stephen King and Peter Straub. (Viking, $18.95.) Two parallel worlds and a young boy who can travel between them.	2	15
4	SO LONG, AND THANKS FOR ALL THE FISH, by Douglas Adams. (Harmony, $12.95.) Suddenly returned to Earth, the hero of the "Hitchhiker's Trilogy" science fantasy is confronted with new riddles to answer.	3	8
5	THE LIFE AND HARD TIMES OF HEIDI ABROMOWITZ, by Joan Rivers. (Delacorte, $6.95.) The comedienne tells the "true story" of her high school "friend," a notorious tramp.	4	12
6	LOVE AND WAR, by John Jakes. (Harcourt Brace Jovanovich, $19.95.) The Civil War rages in this saga of a Pennsylvania family and a South Carolina family, begun in "North and South."	5	16
7	ILLUSIONS OF LOVE, by Cynthia Freeman. (Putnam, $15.95.) A romantic triangle that spans a quarter of a century, from an Italian village to Manhattan to San Francisco.	6	10
8	THE FOURTH PROTOCOL, by Frederick Forsyth. (Viking, $17.95.) A London jewel robbery leads to plots and counterplots behind the Iron Curtain.	8	25
9	". . . AND LADIES OF THE CLUB," by Helen Hooven Santmyer. (Putnam, $19.95.) Life in an Ohio town, 1868 to 1932.	11	34
10 *	LIFE ITS OWNSELF, by Dan Jenkins. (Simon & Schuster, $15.95.) The adventures of a Giants halfback turned television commentator.	9	12
11 *	JITTERBUG PERFUME, by Tom Robbins. (Bantam, $15.95.) Reflections on the olfactory senses and the tyranny of growing old, presented in an idiosyncratic fictional style.	10	8
12	STRONG MEDICINE, by Arthur Hailey. (Doubleday, $16.95.) A strong woman rises in the pharmaceutical industry.	12	19
13	STILLWATCH, by Mary Higgins Clark. (Simon & Schuster, $14.95.) A woman's search for her past puts her life in peril.	14	11
14	DREAM OF ORCHIDS, by Phyllis A. Whitney. (Doubleday, $15.95.) A young woman's quest for her long-lost father leads to romance in Key West.		1
15 *	FIRST AMONG EQUALS, by Jeffrey Archer. (Linden Press/Simon & Schuster, $16.95.) Three young men vie to be chosen Prime Minister of Britain.		18

And Bear in Mind
(Editors' choices of other recent books of particular interest)

GERMAN BIG BUSINESS AND THE RISE OF HITLER, by Henry Ashby Turner Jr. (Oxford, $25.) This richly documented history argues that big-business support for the early stages of Nazism was modest compared both to business gifts to other parties and Nazi fund-raising within its own dedicated membership.

PSYCHOTHERAPY IN THE THIRD REICH, by Geoffrey Cocks. (Oxford, $24.95.) A fascinating account of the survival of the "Jewish science" of psychoanalysis during the Nazi regime, under the wing of a psychiatrist who was Hermann Göring's cousin.

AMERICAN SURVIVORS: Cities and Other Scenes, by Karen Gerard. The economist and former Deputy Mayor of New York wittily examines the irrationalities that drive policy makers and the limits of government power for good or ill in urban areas.

THE FINISHING SCHOOL, by Gail Godwin. The relationship between an insecure adolescent girl and her middle-aged woman mentor, a small-town sophisticate, is the ground of this compassionate psychological novel of growing up.

SOLSTICE, by Joyce Carol Oates. (Dutton, $15.95.) Through the friendship of Sheila, a natural aristocrat, and Monica, a born victim, this blackly funny novel examines and rejects some comfortable notions about feminine benignity and sisterly love.

THE FACT OF A DOORFRAME: Poems Selected and New 1950-1984, by Adrienne Rich. (Norton, $18.95; paper, $9.95.) A register of the poet's development from an imitator of Yeats and Auden to the impassioned partisan of a new literature for women.

EXODUS AND REVOLUTION, by Michael Walzer. (Basic Books, $15.95.) A clear and careful study, by a distinguished political philosopher, of the Exodus story as a continuing metaphor in subsequent revolutions, including this country's.

This Week	Nonfiction	Last Week	Weeks On List
1	IACOCCA: An Autobiography, by Lee Iacocca with William Novak. (Bantam, $17.95.) The rise of the automobile executive from immigrants' son to top jobs at Ford and Chrysler.	1	14
2	LOVING EACH OTHER, by Leo Buscaglia. (Slack/Holt, Rinehart & Winston, $13.95.) Suggestions for "setting our priorities right in order to enjoy life to the fullest."	2	23
3	THE BRIDGE ACROSS FOREVER, by Richard Bach. (Morrow, $16.95.) The author of "Jonathan Livingston Seagull" recounts his search for a true love.	3	22
4	"THE GOOD WAR," by Studs Terkel. (Pantheon, $19.95.) World War II as remembered by men and women who lived through it.	6	16
5 *	PIECES OF MY MIND, by Andrew A. Rooney. (Atheneum, $12.95.) More essays by the journalist and television commentator.	4	21
6	MOSES THE KITTEN, by James Herriot. (St. Martin's, $9.95.) A waif kitten is adopted by a pig; illustrated.	8	17
7	HEY, WAIT A MINUTE, I WROTE A BOOK! by John Madden with Dave Anderson. (Villard Books, $14.95.) An anecdotal autobiography of the popular television sports announcer.	5	20
8 *	A LIGHT IN THE ATTIC, by Shel Silverstein. (Harper & Row, $13.50.) Light verse and drawings by the author.	10	115
9	DR. BURNS' PRESCRIPTION FOR HAPPINESS, by George Burns. (Putnam, $11.95.) The octogenarian comedian provides a regimen of laughs.	7	13
10	SON OF THE MORNING STAR, by Evan S. Connell. (North Point Press, $20.) A biography of George Armstrong Custer that is also a history of the Plains Indian wars.	9	8
11	ELVIS IS DEAD AND I DON'T FEEL SO GOOD MYSELF, by Lewis Grizzard. (Peachtree Publishers, $11.95.) Humorous observations on music, morals, food, fashion and other contemporary matters.	12	11
12	THE BRAIN, by Richard M. Restak. (Bantam, $24.95.) A companion volume to the PBS television series.	13	8
13	HERITAGE, by Abba Eban. (Summit, $35.) An account of Jewish history by the Israeli diplomat who hosted the PBS show of the same name.	11	16
14	THE WEAKER VESSEL, by Antonia Fraser. (Knopf, $19.95.) Woman's lot in 17th-century England.	14	16
15	ONE WRITER'S BEGINNINGS, by Eudora Welty. (Harvard, $10.) The novelist recalls her childhood in Mississippi.	15	45

Advice, How-to and Miscellaneous

#		Last Week	Weeks On List
1	WHAT THEY DON'T TEACH YOU AT HARVARD BUSINESS SCHOOL, by Mark H. McCormack. (Bantam, $15.95.) Notes and tips of a "street-smart executive."	1	20
2	NOTHING DOWN, by Robert G. Allen. (Simon & Schuster, $16.95.) How to buy real estate with little or no money; revised edition of a 1980 book.	3	9
3	WOMEN COMING OF AGE, by Jane Fonda with Mignon McCarthy. (Simon & Schuster, $19.95.) Advice for middle-aged women on fitness, health and nutrition.	4	9
4	THE ONE MINUTE SALES PERSON, by Spencer Johnson and Larry Wilson. (Morrow, $15.) Advice on increasing selling skills.	5	11
5	WEIGHT WATCHERS QUICK START PROGRAM COOKBOOK, by Jean Nidetch. (NAL Books, $17.95.) A cuisine that slims.	2	3

The listings above are based on computer-processed sales figures from 2,000 bookstores in every region of the United States, statistically adjusted to represent sales in all bookstores. In Advice and How-to, five titles are listed because, beyond that point, sales in this category are not generally large enough to make a longer list statistically reliable.

*An asterisk before a book's title indicates that its sales, weighted to reflect the bookselling industry nationally, are barely distinguishable from those of the book above.

Left, Los Angeles Times Book Review, *3 February 1985*

PW HARDCOVER BESTSELLERS

Compiled from data from large-city bookstores, bookstore chains and local bestseller lists across the U.S.

February 8, 1985

Fiction

1. **If Tomorrow Comes.** Sidney Sheldon. Morrow. $17.95. ISBN 0-688-04217-1. A new fiction leader.
2. **The Talisman.** Stephen King and Peter Straub. Viking. $18.95. ISBN 0-670-69199-2
3. **The Sicilian.** Mario Puzo. Linden Press/Simon & Schuster. $17.95. ISBN 0-671-43564-7
4. **So Long, and Thanks for All the Fish.** Douglas Adams. Harmony Books. $12.95. ISBN 0-517-554439-9
5. **The Life and Hard Times of Heidi Abromowitz.** Joan Rivers. Delacorte. $8.95. ISBN 0-385-29359-3
6. **Illusions of Love.** Cynthia Freeman. Putnam. $16.95. ISBN 0-399-13009-8
7. **Love and War.** John Jakes. Harcourt Brace Jovanovich. $19.95. ISBN 0-15-154496-4
8. **The Fourth Protocol.** Frederick Forsyth. Viking. $17.95. ISBN 0-670-32637-2
9. **". . . And Ladies of the Club."** Helen Hooven Santmyer. Putnam. $19.95. ISBN 0-399-12965-0
10. **Life Its Ownself: The Semi-Tougher Adventures of Billy Clyde Puckett.** Dan Jenkins. Simon & Schuster. $15.95. ISBN 0-671-46024-2
11. **Jitterbug Perfume.** Tom Robbins. Bantam. $16.95. ISBN 0-553-05068-0
12. **Stillwatch.** Mary Higgins Clark. Simon & Schuster. $14.95. ISBN 0-671-46952-5
13. **Dream of Orchids.** Phyllis A. Whitney. Doubleday. $15.95. ISBN 0-385-19601-6
14. **Strong Medicine.** Arthur Hailey. Doubleday. $16.95. ISBN 0-385-18014-4
15. **Lincoln: A Novel.** Gore Vidal. Random House. $19.95. ISBN 0-394-52895-6

Nonfiction

1. **Iacocca: An Autobiography.** Lee Iacocca with William Novak. Bantam. $19.95. ISBN 0-553-05067-2
2. **What They Don't Teach You at Harvard Business School: Notes from a Street-Smart Executive.** Mark H. McCormack. Bantam. $16.95. ISBN 0-553-05061-3
3. **Loving Each Other.** Leo Buscaglia. Slack/Holt, Rinehart and Winston. $13.95. ISBN 0-03-000083-1
4. **Women Coming of Age.** Jane Fonda with Mignon McCarthy. Simon & Schuster. $19.95. ISBN 0-671-46997-5
5. **Nothing Down: How to Buy Real Estate with Little or No Money.** Robert G. Allen. Simon & Schuster. $16.95. ISBN 0-671-50469-X
6. **Weight Watchers Quick Start Program Cookbook.** Jean Nidetch. NAL Books. $17.95. ISBN 0-453-01010-5
7. **The One Minute Salesperson.** Spencer Johnson and Larry Wilson. Morrow. $14.95. ISBN 0-688-03946-4
8. **The Bridge Across Forever.** Richard Bach. Morrow. $16.95. ISBN 0-688-03917-0
9. **Pieces of My Mind.** Andrew A. Rooney. Atheneum. $12.95. ISBN 0-689-11492-3
10. **"The Good War": An Oral History of World War II.** Studs Terkel. Pantheon. $19.95. ISBN 0-394-53103-5
11. **Hey, Wait a Minute, I Wrote a Book!** John Madden with Dave Anderson. Villard Books. $14.95. ISBN 0-394-53109-4
12. **Eat to Win: The Sports Nutrition Bible.** Dr. Robert Haas. Rawson Associates (dist. by Scribners). $14.95. ISBN 0-892-56228-5
13. **Son of the Morning Star.** Evan S. Connell. North Point Press. $20. ISBN 0-86547-160-6
14. **Moses the Kitten.** James Herriot. St. Martin's. $9.95. ISBN 0-312-54905-9
15. **Heritage: Civilization and the Jews.** Abba Eban. Summit Books/Simon & Schuster. $32.95. ISBN 0-671-44103-5

anything these days that it's gratifying to know there are some who will read something—even if it's Harold Robbins and his ilk.

I put little stock in lists as barometers of public taste (they are easily manipulated by publishers and some media), but I don't feel they do any harm. Just about any publicity for books is helpful, especially in our society, which seems more and more passive when it comes to reading. I run a list in the *State* because many of our readers ask us to, but maybe the useful part of it is the local paperback bestseller list; perhaps it tells us what a lot of Columbians are really reading, a more accurate reflection of local preferences than a nationally compiled bestseller list.

WILLIAM TARG

Yes, I'd like to see bestseller lists abolished; then the shame of America's reading taste would be concealed.

Also, I don't believe the lists are accurate except in an occasional instance where a Ludlum or Michener is involved. I think the chain stores tend to affect the lists by sheer weight. There are many first-rate books published each year—read the *New York Review of Books* and see what is being published. These books rarely get attention, not to mention

bestseller status. I'd like to see a bestseller list of the month's best books chosen by a committee of librarians and true *critics* (not reviewers).

ROBERT TOWNSEND

Don't like 'em, and don't like people who do. (*Pace* Clarence Darrow)

JOHN E. WOODS
Harcourt Brace Jovanovich

Bestseller lists do not represent a measure of enduring literary merit, but neither do they necessarily exclude it. They are a barometer of reading tastes and marketing emphases. As such, they serve their function well. Although some publishers may be tempted to trim their books solely on the demands of bestseller lists, reputable houses concerned with books and their place in society—as well as commercial success—will see the market as broader and deeper than that represented by such lists. They want bestsellers, and they want good books, and, if they do their jobs right, they will have both.

What's Really Wrong With Bestseller Lists

Judith Appelbaum

Truman Capote's *Answered Prayers* was a bestseller.

"Impossible," you say, for we now know, of course, that no one could find the manuscript of that novel after Capote's death, and it seems pretty clear at this point that it never got written.

Nevertheless, *Answered Prayers* was reported as a bestseller a while back when *Esquire* magazine was publishing excerpts from the work in progress.

Examining the phenomenon of phantom bestsellers in a cogent 1976 *Los Angeles Times* article, David Shaw noted: "Capote's reputation—both as brilliant literary stylist and as a provocative social

gadfly—seemed to guarantee instant bestsellerdom for [the book], and sure enough, inquiries and orders . . . flooded a number of bookstores as soon as the second Esquire excerpt was published."

"At least two bookstores—one in Ohio and one in Washington—reported *Answered Prayers* to their respective local newspapers on that week's best-seller list," the *L.A. Times* piece went on to reveal.

"Why did two stores report an unwritten, unpublished unavailable book as a best seller?" Shaw asked. Because, he explained, the compilation of newspaper and magazine bestseller lists is often haphazard, slipshod, imprecise, and—at times—dishonest. Unfortunately, and despite certain improvements effected in the years since Shaw published his exposé, bestseller lists still purvey a good deal of misinformation.

Here, in brief, are a dozen reasons ratings tend to be wrong.

1. *The Ignorance Factor.* As I discovered in the course of calls to bookstores that provide data for major bestseller lists, some booksellers don't know the basic facts of their business. "How many titles do you stock?" I'd ask, trying to provide a context for information about specific books I'd be discussing in an article. Or, "What's the mix of fiction and nonfiction in your store?" Or, "Which subject categories are your customers most interested in?"

"Gee," more than one independent bookseller said, "I guess I should know that stuff, but I really don't have the faintest idea."

Thanks to the computer, abysmal ignorance is on the wane among booksellers, but it's not entirely gone yet.

2. *Incentives to Guess.* In bookstores that haven't computerized their records, ranking top sellers is a chore. Faced on the one hand with customers waiting to be served, and confronted on the other with a reporter asking for facts and figures, a bookseller may elect to get rid of the reporter fast by guessing which titles have sold in what numbers, instead of taking the time to tot up the relevant sales.

3. *The Effects of Ulterior Motives.* Every so often, bookstores load up on a much-touted title only to find that readers don't want it. Given the need to pique the public's interest, some booksellers may decide to cite a loser as a winner; the label "bestseller" will serve to boost sales, so the theory goes, and experience bears it out.

4. *The Duplication Dilemma.* Bestseller lists derive only in part from data that book retailers supply. Book wholesalers report to the lists too, and may fabricate facts just as retailers do, for the same reasons. But the figures they provide pose another problem. Because wholesalers report sales to retailers rather than to readers, it's reasonable to imagine a scenario something like this:

A wholesaler sells certain retailers fifty copies of one of its top sellers and reports that figure to the bestseller lists. The retailers then manage to sell thirty copies of the book and duly report those sales when they occur, some time later. Eventually persuaded that the remaining twenty copies will never sell, the retailers return them to the wholesaler, who resells them or destroys them or returns them to the

publisher, in which case the publisher may resell them or not. And so on.

Since any number of books may follow similarly tortuous routes through many wholesale and retail outlets, some questions seem worth raising. For instance: Is it possible to figure out (A) how many copies of the book in the example really sold; (B) which sales would have been reflected on bestseller lists; and (C) what rational relationship, if any, exists between those two figures?

5. *The Selective Perception Syndrome.* If a publisher heralds a book's publication with big ads in the trade publications, glossy promotional materials, and a press release that promises a huge first printing, an author tour and a hefty ad/promotion budget, booksellers know right away that the book is slated for bestsellerdom. When the listmakers call, that's one title they'll be sure to check on.

Conversely, when a publisher releases a book with little fanfare or none, booksellers may well assume the title is headed for oblivion and fail to focus on its sales when they compile their top sellers tallies.

M. Scott Peck's *The Road Less Traveled* illustrates the crippling effects of small expectations. In its trade paperback edition, Dr. Peck's *New Psychology of Love, Traditional Values and Spiritual Growth* sold 176,000 copies in less than two years, according to Simon & Schuster's records, but the publisher had to fight to get booksellers to notice it. "It has been selling at legitimate best seller levels . . . sales on this book have actually doubled yearly. . . . Yet it has never made the lists. Make the extra effort to keep this title a part of your bestseller displays and if genuine, report it to the lists," S&S's marketing director said in an August 1982 letter to the firm's bookselling accounts.

The letter, along with an energetic push for publicity, paid off before too long, and *The Road Less Traveled* became a fixture on trade paperback bestseller rosters, but many other sleepers never get noticed.

6. *Omissions of Significant Sales.* Bestseller lists are designed to reflect one week's worth of sales by selected retailers and wholesalers, which means they ignore books sold through book clubs and other mail-order operations, books sold to libraries, and, for the most part, books sold through health food or sporting goods stores or other so-called nontraditional outlets—even though mail-order and institutional and nontraditional sales on certain titles can be huge.

7. *Too-tight Time Frames.* Because bestseller lists are based on sales figures for one week, they high-

light books that move fast and fail to recognize books that reach a great many readers over extended periods. "*I'm OK, You're OK* by Thomas Harris still hadn't made a bestseller list by the time it sold a million copies in hardcover. It just blew my mind," a publisher's publicity manager remembers. And plenty of other titles—including *A Portrait of the Artist as a Young Man, Baby and Child Care, The Exorcist, Take Care of Yourself,* and *Sons and Lovers*—have also sold far better over the years than many, most, or all of the bestsellers on any given week's list.

8. *Tardiness.* Forget the sleepers and the books that really reach the biggest audiences through the years. Assume for the moment that one week's sales are a reasonable measure of success, and time remains a problem. Consider the provenance of "this week's" rankings. A bestseller list in a weekly magazine or a major Sunday newspaper is apt to go to press about a week and a half before the cover date on the issue it will be part of. As a result, the information it's based on will be two to three weeks old by the time the list appears.

9. *Changeable Competition.* It's relatively easy to get on bestseller lists in some weeks and relatively hard in others, depending on the general level of book sales. In fact, an executive at the *New York Times* declared, "If a book comes out in a period of the year when sales are generally low, it can sell so many copies in one place that it makes up for selling hardly any copies anywhere else."

The executive who advanced this theory was trying to explain to *Publishers Weekly* how Mayor Edward I. Koch's *Mayor* happened to appear on the *Times* bestseller list at a time when the publisher had shipped out only 27,000 copies of the book, all of them to booksellers in the New York metropolitan area, and how *Mayor* made it to the #1 position before the book had full-scale national distribution. Tom Peters, coauthor of *In Search of Excellence,* proffered a different explanation. "Ah, the obvious is finally confirmed," he asserted in a letter to the editor; "the *New York Times* bestseller list is a local, not a national list."

But whatever you believe about the implications of the Koch case in particular or the breadth of the *Times* bestseller survey in general, the fact remains that some books make bestseller lists during the weeks when business is slow while others which rack up considerably higher sales during prime selling seasons don't manage to get on.

10. *Tie Scores.* Some of the bookstores that report to the lists may be able to move six or eight or a dozen copies a week of the titles toward the top of their bestseller rosters but manage to sell only one copy each of the titles toward the bottom, in which case rankings are obviously pretty arbitrary.

11. *Inconsistent Criteria.* People who compile weekly bestseller lists aren't eager to talk about how many copies a book ordinarily has to sell to earn a slot, but *Publishers Weekly* does reveal its ground rules when it gets up its lists of the year's bestselling titles. (These lists, it should be noted, are based on figures reported by publishers, who, like booksellers, have reasons to be less than accurate.)

The fifteen books that qualified as nonfiction bestsellers in hardcover in 1983 generally performed better than the fifteen that qualified as bestselling hardcover fiction that year. *In Search of Excellence,* the top nonfiction title, sold well over a million copies; each of the other top ten nonfiction titles sold more than 300,000 copies, and at least ten works of nonfiction with sales "well over" six figures couldn't make it into the ranks of the top twenty-five, let alone the top fifteen. The bestselling hardcover fiction titles, however, had 1983 sales ranging from highs well under a million (882,124 for *Return of the Jedi Storybook* and 786,235 for *Poland*) down to lows between 151,000 and 158,000 for *August, Ancient Evenings,* and *Moreta: Dragonlady of Pern,* and only "a few" works of fiction with "sales just into the six-figure area" got shut out.

Although six-figure sales didn't suffice to make bestsellers of several hardcover books, five-figure sales assured bestsellerhood for similarly shaped volumes with soft covers; trade paperbacks that sold 50,000 copies or more were listed as 1983 bestsellers.

By contrast, books known as mass-market paperbacks weren't considered bestsellers unless they'd racked up seven-figure totals for copies in print. (Mass-market publishers maintain that they can't give out sales figures; the number of copies in print is the only statistic they're generally willing to divulge.) Obviously, therefore, there are bestsellers and bestsellers, and a bestseller at the low end of one category may be quite a bit better seller than a bestseller at the high end of another.

Also, of course, a bestseller according to one periodical may not be a bestseller according to another. The weekly and the annual *Publishers Weekly* and *New York Times Book Review* lists don't jibe, and neither the *PW* list nor the *Times* list is the same as lists in other magazines and newspapers, lists compiled by bookstore chains, or lists prepared by publishers' and booksellers' associations for any particular period.

12. *The Division-by-Format Distortion.* Because

major media divide bestsellers into format categories (ranking hardcovers separately from paperbacks and sometimes also segregating books known as trade paperbacks from books known as mass-market paperbacks) the same book can appear on two or more lists in the same publication at the same time. When that happens—when, say, a book like *Megatrends* shows up both on the trade paperback list and on the hardcover list of the very same periodical in the very same week—then in all likelihood the reported sales of that book that week were greater than the reported sales of any other title on the periodical's lists.

Why, then, is this best of the bestsellers outranked by the #1 hardcover and the #1 paperback titles?

Is this any way to run a popularity contest?

Judith Appelbaum is associate director of the Center for Book Research at the University of Scranton and managing director of Sensible Solutions, Inc., a consulting firm that serves publishers and authors and specializes in attracting readers to books that are not being groomed for bestsellerdom. Formerly an editor of the *New York Times Book Review* and managing editor of *Publishers Weekly*, she is coauthor of *How to Get Happily Published* (New American Library), a member of the faculty at the University of Denver's Publishing Institute, and book review editor of *Book Research Quarterly*.

The New *Ulysses*

Ira B. Nadel
University of British Columbia

James Joyce, *Ulysses, A Critical and Synoptic Edition,* edited by Hans Walter Gabler, Wolfhard Steppe, and Claus Melchior (New York: Garland, 1984), is in three volumes and runs to almost two thousand pages. It is actually the eleventh edition of the novel. But significantly, it is the first to incorporate more than five thousand corrections in the text. Why should there have been so many errors? Why has it taken sixty-two years to issue this corrected form of the work? And what, finally, are the major textual changes? To answer these questions is not only to recognize the achievements of this new *Ulysses,* but to understand the challenges of literary history and textual criticism.

Physical causes were the major reason for the errors in the first edition of *Ulysses.* Joyce's handwriting was difficult to read, and to the eyes of the compositors of Darantière, the French firm which printed the book in Dijon for Sylvia Beach, it was nearly illegible. Their inability to understand English did not help, and they continuously deciphered Joyce's manuscript incorrectly. "Weekly Freeman" appeared as "Wattly Freeman" while

"Hackney Cars" became "Stackney Cars." Joyce's eyesight was also beginning to deteriorate and his own ability to recognize what he wrote became impaired. The pressure on Sylvia Beach to publish the book on Joyce's fortieth birthday (2 February 1922) also meant that she had only a few months to produce the completed work from a diffuse and disorganized manuscript.

Joyce's eagerness to revise and correct proof did not simplify the process. In June 1921 he began to receive proof which he started to work on in July, while completing other sections of the novel; by August he told Harriet Shaw Weaver, "I write and revise and correct with one or two eyes about twelve hours a day I should say, stopping for intervals of five minutes or so when I can't see any more" (*Letters* I: 168). By November 1921 he explained to Miss Weaver that "I am extremely irritated by all those printer's errors. Working as I do amid piles of notes at a table in a hotel I cannot possibly do this mechanical part with my wretched eye and a half. Are these to be perpetuated in future editions?" (*Letters,* I: 176).

Photo of James Joyce, inscribed to American collector John Quinn

The revisions made by Joyce were not minor. The "Hades" episode was greatly augmented while he added an extended scene to "Circe" which he completed that summer. The initial request by Joyce for only one set of galleys and one set of page proofs soon became inadequate; before publication he required up to four sets of *placards* (eight unnumbered pages printed on one side of a large sheet, four pages wide by two high) and up to five sets of page proofs (printed on both sides of a sheet) for every page of the book. This of course increased the percentage of possible errors with the continual resetting of type. Between August and October 1921, the printers worked with renewed intensity, often setting type for more than one episode at the same time with the expected confusions. Ironically, on 7 October 1921, Joyce optimistically thought the novel would be published the next month "if the French printers don't all leap into the Rhone in despair at the mosaics I send them back" (*Letters,* I: 172). But in January 1922, over two hundred pages remained to be set in page proof, including the "Ithaca" and "Penelope" sections, which Joyce returned with an extraordinary number of additions and corrections. Darantière received these "mosaics" and incorporated the changes a mere two days before publication. Remarkably, the book met its 2 February deadline with two copies sent by express train to Paris to be greeted by an anxious Sylvia Beach on the platform of the Gare de Lyon. With the book growing nearly a third in size through the corrections and Joyce working on the text up to two days before it appeared, one can understand why several critics have remarked that only Joyce's desire to see the novel published halted his revisions and additions to the work.

Joyce himself prepared a list of corrections from the first edition, later supplemented by Stuart A. Gilbert when he prepared a 1932 French translation. Joyce expanded the list when he read the novel through in 1936 for publication in London by the Bodley Head Press. Not all the original errors, however, were Darantiere's; the amateur typists hired by Joyce and who first read his manuscript did not miss the opportunity to correct what they thought to be errors—including the addition of hundreds of commas inserted in the "Eumaeus" episode Joyce did not want. Later editions perpetuated such mistakes, one of the most famous the deletion of the final dot at the end of the "Ithaca" section which was assumed to be a fly speck. It was in fact Joyce's obscure answer to the question "Where?" and correctly appears in Volume III: 1633 of the new edition.

The editors of the "Critical and Synoptic Edition" of *Ulysses* compared holograph drafts, fair copies, typescripts, galleys, and proofs of the first edition plus additions and corrections to establish what the general editor, Hans Walter Gabler, describes as his twofold goal: the establishment of the corrected text of the novel and the analysis and process of composition and revision of the published novel. Citing an average of seven errors per page, although many are "accidentals," matters of punctuation or spelling, the editors, with the aid of a computer, have corrected words, phrases, part sentences, and paragraphs as well as spelling and punctuation. Text has also been recovered, although it was once lost, forgotten, or misplaced as in a single five-line passage given to Stephen in the "Scylla and Charybdis" episode. The lost final working draft was fair-copied, further revised, and then typed, but the typescript lacked the crucial answer when Stephen, talking about Shakespeare's affection for his granddaughter, suddenly thinks to himself, "Do you know what you are talking about? Love, yes. Word known to all men." This and the following sentence disappeared from the text because the typist's eye probably skipped over it, since in typing from the final working draft two phrases end on ellipses and are underlined as well as closely following one another. The typist picked up the text not after "*L'art d'être grand*—. . . . " but after "*Amor—concupiscimus*. . . ."(see in the Garland *Ulysses*, I: 418-419 and III: 1738). The importance of the passage confirms Stephen's question to his mother in the "Circe" episode, "Tell me the word, mother, if you know now. The word known to all men" (II: 1269). This recovery of text solves a critical debate as to the exact word Stephen sought, which we now know to be "love."

But how is such information presented to the reader? The answer is in the printing of parallel texts, the left-hand page containing a continuous manuscript text with symbols indicating the various changes and/or deletions (the Synoptic text), while the right-hand page prints the finished, reading text (the Critical text), incorporating those changes. The symbols accompanying the manuscript text, indicating intra- and inter-document changes, are not difficult to follow, while sigla which supplement the original symbols outline the sequence of emendations. The result is a complete, although not complex, set of guides to the Synoptic text, also doubling as the copytext. The right-hand text incorporates the major emendations while textual notes printed at the end of the third volume explain the nature and importance of the changes. A list in the final volume collates departures from the critical edition and the first as well as all subsequent editions. Emendation, however, is limited to the established copytext of the Critical edition.

The use of diacritical marks in the emended continuous manuscript text makes it possible to follow in detail the compositional history of *Ulysses*. This Synoptic text on the left side of the edition incorporates these changes, putting every variant or revision in relation to others to show the nature and place of the changes at successive levels of text completion. The presentation of text is dynamic since the diacritical marks illustrate the stage and frequency of change. The reading text on the right is the emended continuous manuscript text at its ultimate level of compositional development, but without the diacritical marks. The new edition arranges the texts in parallel sequence so that a reader can glance across the page to uncover the level of textual development. However, this arrangement necessitates irregular page lengths; hence, line numbering by episodes has been introduced. But this interactive edition now makes it possible to locate and trace the origin of major and minor alterations and emendations. Another useful feature of the edition is the restoration of Joyce's practice of not indenting direct discourse. This follows his manuscript practice of indicating the opening of direct speech by dashes without indentation and by deeply indenting paragraphs to emphasize the contrast. Dialogue thus appears integrated with narrative paragraphs. This restores a feature of layout fundamental to Joyce's original intention and essential to the critical understanding of the novel.

The generation of the Synoptic text of *Ulysses* resulted from the establishment of a copytext based on recovering the ideal state of development achieved by traceable acts of composition. This involved the analysis of manuscripts, typescripts, proofs, revisions, additions, and corrections. According to the editors, Joyce's autograph nota-

Announcement of the three-volume, eleventh edition of the 1922 novel. As originally published, the novel contained more than 5,000 departures from Joyce's text.

Stately,° plump Buck Mulligan came from the stairhead, bearing a bowl of lather on which a mirror and a razor lay crossed. A yellow dressinggown, ungirdled, was sustained gently behind him ⌐(B)⌐[by] on°(B)⌐ the mild morning air. He held the bowl aloft and intoned:

5   —*Introibo ad altare Dei.*

Halted, he peered down the dark winding stairs and called out° coarsely:

—Come up, Kinch⟨.⟩!° Come up, you fearful jesuit!°

Solemnly he came forward and mounted the round gunrest. He faced

10 about and blessed gravely thrice the tower, the surrounding land° and the awaking mountains. Then, catching sight of Stephen Dedalus, he bent towards him and made rapid crosses in the air, gurgling in his throat and shaking his head. Stephen Dedalus, displeased and sleepy, leaned his arms on the top of the staircase and looked coldly at the shaking gurgling face

15 that blessed him, equine in its length, and at the light untonsured hair, grained and hued like pale oak.

Buck Mulligan peeped an instant under the mirror and then covered the bowl smartly.

—Back to barracks⟨,⟩! he said sternly.

20 He added in a preacher's tone:

—For this, O dearly beloved, is the genuine ^⟨☒⟩ christine^: body and soul and blood and ouns. Slow music, please. Shut your eyes, gents. One moment. A little trouble about those white corpuscles. Silence, all.

He peered sideways up and gave a long slow° whistle of call,° then

25 paused awhile in rapt attention, his even white teeth glistening here and there with gold points. Chrysostomos. ⌐⁵⁵[Three] Two⁵⌐ strong shrill whistles answered through the calm.⌐

—Thanks, old chap, he cried briskly. That will do nicely. Switch off the current, will you?

PRECEDING PAGE I] *CF* Faire préceder par une page vide marquée au milieu ainsi I al *GENERAL NOTE* →TN   1 Stately,] (tB); *NOT INDENTED* aR   3 on] LR,Eg; by (aC) *PCU*; *CF* §92.23   6 out] *STET* aR; *TD:* up (tB) (*ANTICIPATION*)   8 Kinch!] *STET* aR; *TD:* Kinch (tB);

2

First pages of text of the Garland Ulysses, A Critical and Synoptic Edition, *with reading text right and manuscript text left, indicating changes*

Stately, plump Buck Mulligan came from the stairhead, bearing a
bowl of lather on which a mirror and a razor lay crossed. A yellow
dressinggown, ungirdled, was sustained gently behind him on the mild
morning air. He held the bowl aloft and intoned:

—*Introibo ad altare Dei.*

Halted, he peered down the dark winding stairs and called out
coarsely:

—Come up, Kinch! Come up, you fearful jesuit!

Solemnly he came forward and mounted the round gunrest. He faced
about and blessed gravely thrice the tower, the surrounding land and the
awaking mountains. Then, catching sight of Stephen Dedalus, he bent
towards him and made rapid crosses in the air, gurgling in his throat and
shaking his head. Stephen Dedalus, displeased and sleepy, leaned his arms
on the top of the staircase and looked coldly at the shaking gurgling face
that blessed him, equine in its length, and at the light untonsured hair,
grained and hued like pale oak.

Buck Mulligan peeped an instant under the mirror and then covered
the bowl smartly.

—Back to barracks! he said sternly.

He added in a preacher's tone:

—For this, O dearly beloved, is the genuine christine: body and soul and
blood and ouns. Slow music, please. Shut your eyes, gents. One moment. A
little trouble about those white corpuscles. Silence, all.

He peered sideways up and gave a long slow whistle of call, then
paused awhile in rapt attention, his even white teeth glistening here and
there with gold points. Chrysostomos. Two strong shrill whistles answered
through the calm.

—Thanks, old chap, he cried briskly. That will do nicely. Switch off the
current, will you?

Kinch. LR,a4   8 jesuit!] *STET* aR; *TD:* jesuit. (tB); Jesuit. 1; jesuit. aE   10 land] *STET* aR; *TD:*
country (tB)   24 slow] *STET* aR; *TD:* low (tB)   24 call,] *STET* aR,aE; call a4

EPISODE 1

3

tions found in his typescripts and proofs provided the best authority for a critical edition of *Ulysses*. The means for obtaining the emended continuous manuscript text began with the editing of an early-version text, in actuality episodes 1 to 14 of the novel serialized in the *Little Review* (New York) March 1918 to December 1920. The foundation text of the remaining four episodes became the critically edited equivalent of the printer's copy of the first edition. This intermediately edited text of the entire novel was then augmented by edited segments of autograph overlay from typescripts and proofs. A special computer program for text data processing developed at the University of Tübingen assisted in this work, using as input the Rosenbach manuscript (the only comprehensive holograph manuscript of *Ulysses*), chapter typescripts, other serializations, the first edition of 1922, and the second edition of 1926. Machine collation at various stages established and confirmed variants which were added to the computer file. The edition text resulted from the grafting of the early-version

text incorporating lists of typescript and proof changes, with a computer file copy of the first edition. After final collation and proofing, the new text was computer typeset. For historical collation, the editions of 1932, 1936, and 1961 were added to a second computer text file of the first edition.

The triumph of seven years work, the new Garland *Ulysses* presents the novel for the first time in its definitive form. The clarity of print, choice of acid-free paper, and sewn binding make the three volumes a readable as well as durable edition. But more important, the new *Ulysses* establishes a textual purity for the novel unmatched by previous editions. The old seaman's outburst to the elderly reader at the cabman's stand in the "Eumaeus" episode, "Give us a squint at that literature, grandfather, the ancient mariner put in, manifesting some natural impatience" (III: 1439), has been met with a blazing, eye-opening, three-volume text that gives us Bloom defined, Molly restored, Stephen recovered, and Dublin renewed.

The Orwell Year

Peter Stansky
Stanford University

Nineteen eighty-four is clearly George Orwell's year. What is less clear, however, is the nature of the relation between this calendar year 1984 to the novel of the same name (and, indeed, to the author of the novel). Except it is not quite the same name. What is frequently ignored is that the title of the novel is spelled out—that is, it is given in words rather than in numbers: *Nineteen Eighty Four*. It is tantalizing to speculate on what the difference means. One wonders if there is buried in the archives of Secker and Warburg, the English publisher of the book, any correspondence about this issue. I have been unable to discover much about the title in published material. In a letter of 22 October 1948 to his publisher Frederic Warburg, Orwell wrote that he expected, "DV," to finish the book early the next month, and he added, "I am not pleased with the book but I am not absolutely dissatisfied. I first thought of it in 1943. I think it is a good idea but the execution would have been better if I had not written it under the influence of TB. I

haven't definitely fixed on the title but I am hesitating between 'Nineteen Eighty-Four' and 'The Last Man in Europe'." Though Orwell evidently decided on the title of the book as *Nineteen Eighty-Four* spelled out, it would seem that he hadn't made that completely clear to the publisher. In a recent bookseller's catalogue, an uncorrected proof copy of the book is recorded, sent out by Secker and Warburg in advance of publication, with *1984* on the title page. (One proof copy was sold at auction for £1,265 in the summer of 1984.) In the recently published draft of part of the novel, the year is given as 1980 and then 1982 before 1984 is settled upon. Perhaps I am making too much of the title and the importance of the exact way it is given, but I think not. That happy choice on Orwell's part has resulted in a lot of words and thoughts being expended in 1983 and 1984.

By spelling out the date Orwell intended to remind us—something consistently ignored by many of the commentators on the book and the

George Orwell (International Portrait Gallery)

year—that he was writing a satire or fantasy of "things as they are" at the time he was writing, or at most a warning of how existing tendencies might eventuate, but not a prediction of what was likely to happen in 1984. His appreciation for technological likelihoods in the future shaped much of what he put into the book; and, at another level, so much of the political structure of the world as he imagined it has turned out to be correct. Even so, it can be argued that his accuracy about both the technical and political shape of the world we find ourselves in today is almost coincidental to the main purposes of the book. Admittedly, that aspect has captured the world's attention and is a precipitating factor in all the many public gatherings inspired by the book. By spelling out the title, Orwell was, in effect, telling us that we were not to take the novel too literally as a document; that we were to remember the ways in which it was a work of imagination. Yet there is an unmistakable power in the book that removes it from the literary genre to which it belongs—a novel of fantasy—an intensity that sears it into the minds of its readers. Even those who have not read the novel but are familiar with the terms Orwell has given the language—"Big Brother," "Newspeak," "doublethink," among others—are affected by it.

There is an irony here, for these phrases—such brilliant examples of Orwell's fecundity and imagination—have almost become the sort of jargon which he, as a critic of language, so detested: they call up images in an automatic and easy way, and are shortcuts to thinking.

I do believe that the title he finally chose is important—but it was also a whimsical stroke of genius that has clearly captured the Western world's imagination. Only the future will tell whether *Nineteen Eighty-Four* will lose its astonishing popularity now that 1984 has become a part of the past. But the title has acted as a magnetic force, attracting people to read the book; and then, once within its pages, they are carried into a world that somehow terrifies and convinces.

Whether or not books about Orwell have sold well, *Nineteen Eighty-Four* itself has done so extraordinarily, to the extent that bookstores were caught short as the year began. The Signet mass-market paperback in the United States appeared with a gold label printed on its cover stating it was the "commemorative edition" with a special preface by that antithesis of Big Brother, Walter Cronkite. There, he combined both the predictive and warning aspects of the book: "Critics and scholars may argue quite legitimately about the particular literary merits of *1984*. But none can deny its power, its hold on the imaginations of whole generations, nor the power of its admonitions . . . a power that seems to grow rather than lessen with the passage of time. It has been said . . . that Orwell's terrible vision has been averted. Well, that kind of self-congratulation is, to say the least, premature. 1984 may not arrive on time, but there's always 1985. Still, the warning has been effective; and every time we use one of those catch phrases, . . . recognize Big Brother in someone, see a 1984 in the future, . . . notice something Orwellian, . . . we are listening to that warning again." Late in 1983 Cronkite and others participated in a television program striking the note that would be heard too often as time passed: to what degree was the real 1984 similar to the world depicted in the novel. (The film of the program, *1984 Revisited*, is available for rental from Kent State University.) At the beginning of the year the American paperback was in its seventieth printing, and probably more were called for as the year progressed.

I am attempting here to serve, to the best of my knowledge, as something of a historian of the Orwell year, although I am sure that there are many events, publications, television and radio presentations of which I am unaware. On 1 January 1984

Public Television in America greeted the year with a somewhat avant-garde, quite irrelevant and disappointing revue program produced in New York and Paris entitled "Goodmorning Mr. Orwell/Bonjour M. Orwell." It was directed by Nam June Paik; among the participants were Allen Ginsberg, John Cage, and Merce Cunningham; but it was questionable how much it had to do with Orwell. The extremely popular morning program in the United States "The Today Show" had four spots in the first week in January dealing with Orwell: the first with the man and the book, the rest with the novel's implications. Although there were various programs on American television that considered the relationship between the novel and reality, the more ambitious television productions were British. One, done by BBC2, was factual, consisting of five hours of interviews with Nigel Williams, the producer, doing Orwell's voice at appropriate locations in Orwell's life. In connection with that series, Audrey Coppard and Bernard Crick edited *Orwell Remembered* (Ariel Books, British Broadcasting Corporation), which consisted of excerpts from the program as well as quotations from earlier programs, articles, and books. Also, BBC1 did a ninety-minute dramatization of the last three years of his life, "Orwell on Jura: The Crystal Spirit," with Ronald Pickup as Orwell. Britain's Channel 4 did another docudrama about Orwell, "The Road to 1984," starring James Fox as Orwell. The two BBC productions were shown by the Arts and Entertainment Network in America in October 1984. TV Ontario in its Realities series had an interview with Irving Howe, broadcast on 23 February 1984. The Canadian Broadcasting Corporation prepared a five-hour program on Orwell with interviews with those who knew him. Two hundred and forty-five American Public Radio stations, as well as Canadian ones, broadcast it, either as a five-hour marathon on 1 January or over the first five Sundays of the year. A 1984 Orwell calendar was issued in conjunction with the broadcasts. There were surely many media events in many other countries in the West about Orwell. As a single example, I note that in the spring of 1983 there were two discussion programs on Spanish television, one dealing with Orwell in Spain and the other with *Nineteen Eighty-Four*.

Charles Schulz in "Peanuts" greeted the year in his Sunday strip of 1 January 1984 with Charlie Brown talking to Snoopy: "You look terrible. Drank too much root beer last night, huh?" "Not really." "And then you ate too many pizzas. Is that right?" "Not really." "And then you stayed up all night dancing." "No, that wasn't it. That wasn't it at all. It wasn't the root beer, the pizza or the dancing. It's thinking about all the George Orwell jokes we're going to have to listen to in 1984." Jules Feiffer, too, had several of his series mentioning Orwell, and the strip "Bloom County" on 2 January had Big Brother watching its characters.

There had been a dramatization of *Nineteen Eighty-Four* on the BBC in 1953, and a film three years later with Michael Redgrave. Now there was a new version of the film, with Richard Burton—his last movie performance—as O'Brien and John Hurt as Winston, directed by Michael Radford. There was a not-particularly-successful version of *Animal Farm* performed at the Cottesloe, the experimental theater of the National Theatre in London. Another play, designed to be performed for schools and colleges, done by the National Theatre in the autumn of 1984, is *Orwell's England*, dealing "with the literature, politics and social history of the first half of the century, seen through the eyes of George Orwell." The New Vic performed *George Orwell's 1984* Off-Off Broadway. At the Barbican in London, "Thoughtcrimes at the Barbican," organized by the Royal Shakespeare Company for the first two weeks in January, included films, news plays, and discussions, the most notable being the Public Writers' Day, a symposium organized by the Writers' Guild and Capital Radio, at which Salman Rushdie, Michael Foot, Angus Wilson, Raymond Williams, Hugh Thomas, David Caute, and others spoke. On 18 September 1984 in Niagara-on-the-Lake, Ontario, from 6:30 to midnight, a presentation by the Shaw Festival Theatre company converted the town into Airstrip One, with the audience dressed in coveralls, climaxing as the theater itself became Room 101. In Minneapolis, a revue, *Orwell That Ends Well*, was staged. I know of two tapes available, one, from National Public Radio, "1984: Are Orwell's Predictions Coming True?" broadcast on National Public Radio's "All Things Considered" in 1983 and scenes from the novel, starring David Niven, issued by the Nostalgia Broadcasting Corporation (oddly copyrighted 1948 and 1977).

Let us consider the numerous publications of the year. In England Penguin published an omnibus edition of the novels, as well as a new edition of *Nineteen Eighty-Four*: "As the countdown begins, a new edition of Orwell's legendary novel. The book of the year—the year of the book." The Clarendon Press brought out an edition with a long critical introduction and annotations by Bernard Crick. Irving Howe also edited *1984 Revisited: Totalitarianism in Our Century* (Harper and Row, 1983), which

included essays by Michael Walzer, Leszek Kola-
kowski, Milovan Djilas, Robert Nisbet, and Richard
Lowenthal. Perhaps the grandest and most important publication of the year is *George Orwell, Nineteen
Eighty-Four, the Facsimile*, a reproduction of 143
leaves, about half of the original manuscript, all that
is known to survive, with a preface by Daniel G.
Siegel, the owner of the manuscript since 1969, and
an introduction by Peter Davison (Harcourt Brace
Jovanovich and M and S Press, and by Secker and
Warburg in Britain). The book is quite magnificent
with each page reproduced, and an exact replica-
tion—in print—for those sheets that are handwrit-
ten. One can see Orwell at work, rewriting, revising,
polishing his book. For instance, the first version of
the famous first sentence was "It was a cold, blowy
day in early April, and a million radios were striking
thirteen." "[A] million radios" becomes "innumerable clocks" and then there is the final tight version:
"It was a bright cold day in April, and the clocks
were striking thirteen."

In both England and the United States there
was announced for publication during the year a
new nine-volume edition of the novels (apparently
with emendations because of changes imposed
upon first publication by the publishers) and books
of reportage, and a nine-volume edition of the *Collected Essays, Journalism, and Letters*, now to be published in 1986, under the editorship of Peter Davison. Perhaps the most exciting discovery of the
year, largely by William J. West, were 250 Orwell
letters and 62 radio scripts in the files of the BBC,
unnoticed before because they were filed under the
names of the announcers, from the time that Orwell
worked for the BBC during the war. They are
scheduled for publication in two volumes edited by
West, *Orwell: The War Broadcasts* and *Orwell: The
War Commentaries*, before the year ends by the BBC
and Duckworth of London and Arbor House in the
United States.

There have been many other publications on
Orwell during the year, and here I will attempt to
give as complete a list as possible. I've edited a
collection of essays, *On Nineteen Eighty-Four* (Portable Stanford and W. H. Freeman), where I attempted, with varying degrees of success, to keep
the contributors, including Martin Esslin, Alex
Comfort, Gordon Craig, Sidney Drell, Ian Watt,
Alexander Dallin, and Paul Robinson, on a fairly
narrow path in discussing the book. Inevitably, and
perhaps desirably, as there may not be that many
readers exclusively interested in Orwell, some of
the essays tend to concentrate on the particular area
of expertise of the writer and seem to forget about

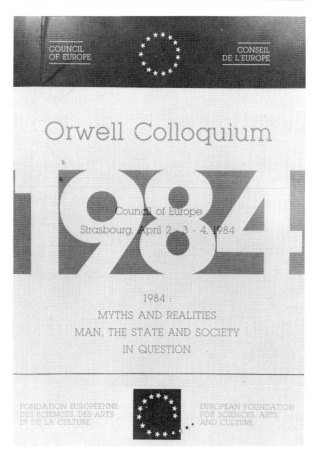

*Announcement of one of the many conferences spawned by the
Orwell year*

Orwell. This is true too of *The Future of Nineteen
Eighty-Four*, edited by Ejner J. Jensen (University of
Michigan Press), papers from the spring 1983 symposium at the University of Michigan, which includes an essay by Eugene McCarthy. The best
essays in the collection, such as those by Leslie Tent-
ler and Alex Zwerdling, are those which keep
closest to the text, even though all the pieces are
ostensibly on the man and/or the book. I've heard
of several special Orwell calendars for the year
1984, three in America and one in Germany: *The
1984 Calendar: An American History* (Point Blank
Press), *The Sign and Sound of Eighty-Four* (Perry Vas-
quez), and *The 1984 Big Brother Calendar* (Price/
Stern/Sloan). Also published is *The Big Brother Book
of Lists: including notes, quotes and anecdotes that reveal
we already live in the Orwellian Nightmare* (Price/
Stern/Sloan).

There were quite a few other books inspired
by the year and Orwell. Raymond Williams continued his disillusionment with Orwell (to be discussed among other aspects of Orwell's reputation

in John Rodden's forthcoming book) in a reissue of his *Orwell* with a new chapter on *Nineteen Eighty-Four* (Penguin). Other titles to be mentioned are Gyorgy Dalos, *1985: What Happens after Big Brother Dies* (Pantheon); Tom Winnifrith and William V. Whitehead, *1984 and All's Well* (London: Macmillan); Lynette Hunter's literary discussion, *George Orwell: the Search for a Voice* (Open University Press); Sandy Craig and Chris Schwarz, *Down and Out: Orwell's Paris and London Revisited* with photographs from today; the not-particularly-well-received W. F. Bolton, *Orwell's English and Ours* (University of Tennessee Press); a rather heavy-handed comic book by David Smith and Michale Mosher, *Orwell for Beginners* (W. W. Norton); and an unsuccessful thriller, deriving its title from the first line of the novel, *Thirteen O'Clock* by Thurston Clarke (Doubleday) that takes place on Jura, where Orwell wrote his novel, with flashbacks to Orwell's visit to Paris in 1945 and aspects of the Spanish Civil War, all in an unbelievable potpourri.

Undoubtedly there were quite a few special issues of journals. One particularly worth mentioning was the September-December 1983 issue of *Cogito* published at the University of the Philippines, with an introduction and an essay by guest editor Dennis Rohatyn, a philosopher at the University of San Diego, who has appeared at many of the Orwell conferences of the year. Rohatyn also moderated five half-hour videotapes discussing the novel and its implications. Two very interesting negative views of Orwell have appeared during the year: *Orwell: Views from the Left*, ed. Christopher Norris (Lawrence and Wishart) and Beatrix Campbell's *Wigan Pier Revisited: Poverty and Politics in the 1980s* (Virago).

Perhaps the most exciting book of this group is Daphne Patai, *The Orwell Mystique: a Study in Male Ideology* (University of Massachusetts Press), an angry feminist critique of Orwell that suffers from an ahistorical point of view but nevertheless makes for very lively and stimulating reading. In the course of her research, Patai discovered a group of almost a hundred letters in the Lilly Library of Indiana University from Orwell to his literary agent, Leonard Moore. The discovery was reported and discussed by Michael Shelden in the *Times Literary Supplement* (6 January 1984). Probably the best introduction to Orwell to be published during the year is Ian Slater, *The Road to Airstrip One* (W. W. Norton).

Undoubtedly there are quite a few recent foreign publications on Orwell, but the only ones I have run across are Jean-Daniel Jurgenson, *Orwell*

ou La Route de 1984 (Robert Laffont); a special issue of *Revista de Occidente* (Numbers 33-34), "Orwell y 1984: de la Utopia a La Libertad"; *Orwell's Jahr. Is die Zukunft von genstern die Gegenwart von heute?* (Ullstein, 1983), ed. Dieter Hasselblatt; Gerd E. Hoffman, *Im Jahrzehnt der Grosses Bruder: Orwell's "1984" und unsere Wirklichkeit* (Fischer); and Robert Plank, *Orwell's "1984": Eine psychologische Studie* (Suhrkamp).

Needless to say, there have already been innumerable articles about Orwell in all sorts of publications. Let me name just a few. To begin with, the novelist E. L. Doctorow wrote a piece in the February 1983 issue of *Playboy*: "On the brink of *1984*." Orwell has appeared on the cover of the *New Republic* with an excerpt from Irving Howe's essay in the book he edited and on the cover of *Harper's* with an essay by Norman Podhoretz claiming, quite wrongly in my opinion, that if Orwell were alive today he would be a neoconservative. (It is always a risky business to predict what a figure of the past would think in the present. I think that it is a further act of audacity that the Committee for the Free World, a group with which Podhoretz is affiliated, calls its publishing arm the Orwell Press, drawing the mantle of the great man about its opinions.) In the following issue there was a debate between Norman Podhoretz and Christopher Hitchens about Orwell, both demonstrating the richness of Orwell's text and the possibility of finding appropriate quotations in it. Podhoretz gave a version of his argument in the January 1984 issue of the *Reader's Digest*. Hitchens also wrote "For George Orwell" in the Winter 1984 issue of *Grand Street*. Gordon Beadle effectively attacked the neoconservative case in "George Orwell and the Neoconservatives" in *Dissent* (Winter 1984) and in talks, among quite a few he gave during the year, at an Orwell conference at Pullman, Washington, and an Orwell session at the meeting of the North American Conference on British Studies in Toronto. Orwell appeared on the cover of *Time* (28 November 1983), with the story written by Paul Gray. The illustrations for the piece, by Eugene Mihaesco, were put on sale by the Galerie St. Etienne of New York. "1984: Orwell's World: How Close?" was the cover story with five pieces in the *Radcliffe Quarterly* for December 1983.

There are other publications that should be mentioned, although here particularly I should point out that undoubtedly there are many more which I am not aware of. As early as 1 February 1983 the *Village Voice* had an issue largely devoted to the novel; in conjunction with that there was an exhibition of relevant contemporary art at Ronald

Feldman Fine Art in New York, and a catalogue, *The 1984 Show* (Ronald Feldman Fine Arts Inc. and the *Village Voice*). Here I would now like to give a more or less miscellaneous listing that may provide a sense of the wide variety of the year: Christopher

The influence of the Orwell year extended into advertising.

Lasch, "1984: Are We There?," *Salmagundi* (Fall 1984); Irene Collins, President of the Historical Association, Great Britain, "Freedom and History," *History* (Spring 1984); Michael Sherman and others, "Nineteen Eighty-Four in 1984," *Perspectives* (Autumn 1983 and Winter 1984); Alfred Kazin, "Not One of Us," *New York Review of Books* (14 July 1984); Leopold Labedz, "Will George Orwell Survive 1984?," *Encounter* (June 1984); three articles in *Index on Censorship* (August 1984); two articles in *Survey* (Spring 1984); Raymond G. McInnis and Michael Turner, "A Reader's Guide to George Orwell's 1984" in the *Reference Services Review* (Spring 1984); and "According to Six-National Surveys, Few of Orwell's '1984' Predictions Have Come True," *Gallup Report* (January/February 1984).

Perhaps a sampling of newspaper and other articles might be mentioned: Kay Ekevall, "British road to anti-socialism" in *Artery* (vol. 8, nos. 1-2); various articles in *Cultura* section of *O Estado de S. Paulo* (1 January 1984); Robert W. Kastenmeier, "On the Road to Orwell's 1984," *Computers and People* (March-April 1984); George Steiner, "Killing Time," *The New Yorker* (12 December 1983); Conor Cruise O'Brien, "Stranger than Fiction," *The Observer* (18 December 1983). And finally *W* announced in its issue of 13-20 January 1984 that "Since this is 1984, George Orwell is very OUT, as are any references to his futuristic novel."

It was clearly also the year of the conference and the lecture series on Orwell and the implications of his book. Perhaps the grandest was at the Council of Europe at Strasbourg on 2-4 April: "Orwell 1984: Myths and Realities: Man, the State and Society in Question." When the members of the conference arrived they were greeted with a huge tome containing sixty papers. The Council issued its proceedings with parts of the discussion but not the papers themselves. There were three days of extraordinarily wide-ranging discussion. The call to come to Strasbourg revealed both the strengths and weaknesses of the use of Orwell. It was assumed in the summons that the book is a prophecy: "We are in 1984, well within the time span of the universe whose birth George Orwell foretold, his prophecies overtaking us: a society in which men are brainwashed, caught up within the cogs of a machine that governs their every movement, their every thought from the cradle to the grave. A planet torn into two bitterly hostile camps." (Actually, in the world and in the book it would be more accurate to say three hostile camps.)

These questions can be construed out of Orwell's book and have captured the world's attention. But in some fundamental sense they are a misunderstanding of the book. Orwell was writing about what *might* happen, not what *would* happen. It is not, to my mind, correct to ask the question "Was he mistaken or had he correctly interpreted the history of his time?" To the degree that his book has proven to be wrong, to that extent it will have served its purpose. What he attempted to do was take to a logical conclusion the destructive elements inherent in Nazism and Stalinism. Sometimes he was correct in crucial guesses; sometimes not. Was Orwell unusual in foreseeing two central developments of the postwar world: first, the extraordinary growth of technology that would permit a degree of mechanical manipulation of our lives and potential supervision of them not known in the 1940s; and second, the political future of three superstates which never fight each other directly? The heart of the book is not so much the technological nor the political situation, but, rather, the question of whether we have internalized a set of conformities to the needs of the state. Presumably it might be argued, rather arcanely, that if this had happened we would not be aware of it. I suspect that this has not happened: Orwell's direst warning of what the future might hold has not yet been fulfilled.

Other European conferences dealt with Orwell. On 11-13 November 1983, the OrwellCon met at Antwerp, sponsored by the Belgian Science Fiction and Fantasy Association, with Anthony Burgess as the guest of honor. The announced papers for Antwerp sound as if they were planned to stay fairly close to the text, although the conference as a whole looked as if it might have wandered away from the hard world of political facts into the universe of fantasy. In Autumn 1984 there was announced a seminar in Milan: "1984: Labyrinth of Fear" with Kurt Vonnegut, Alvin Toffler, and Stanley Hoffmann. In Paris, on 7-9 November 1984, the International Sociological Association Research Committee on Sociolinguistics sponsored "1984: Orwell and the Language Question."

The United States appeared to be the home of the Orwell Conference. On 7-10 December 1983, at the Smithsonian Institution in Washington, D.C., there was "The Road after 1984: High Technology and Human Freedom. A Tribute to George Orwell." T. R. Fyvel was at the meeting and acted as a living link with Orwell. The conference took its theme from two quotations from William Steinhoff's *George Orwell and the Origins of 1984* (1976) emphasizing Orwell's commitment to fight totalitarian ideas in the minds of intellectuals and the dangers of a totalitarian society. The first session was

devoted to Orwell, but from then on the symposium paid little attention to its honoree, although the basic theme of the freedom of human expression is certainly a central concern of *Nineteen Eighty-Four*. There was an associated art exhibition, "Dreams and Nightmares: Utopian Visions in Modern Art," 136 works at the Hirshhorn Museum, "casting a sidelong glance at George Orwell's *1984* as we actually enter that year." The press release cited as one of the themes of the exhibition the following quotations:

> In the early 20th century the vision of a future society unbelievably rich, leisured, orderly and efficient—a glittering antiseptic world of glass and steel and snow-white concrete—was part of the consciousness of nearly every literate person.

> The idea set up by the Party was something huge, terrible, and glittering—a world of steel and concrete, of monstrous machines and terrifying weapons—a nation of warriors and fanatics, marching forward in perfect unity, all thinking the same thoughts and shouting the same slogans, perpetually working, fighting, triumphing, persecuting—300 million people all with the same face.

The pictures in the exhibition presented both the art deco neo-Wellsian sort of utopia so popular through the first half of this century, as well as the dreary and grim world of Orwell's book. The alienated world of the painter George Tooker seems to suggest to many the Orwellian world, and three of Tooker's most famous paintings of the 1950s and 1960s were on display: "Government Bureau," "The Waiting Room," and "Landscape with Figures." In the framework of the exhibition, utopian visions were located before the Second World War: Italian Futurism, Russian Avant-Garde, German Expressionism, the Bauhaus, Dutch De Stijl, French Purism, and American Precisionism and Architecture. Dystopia, as with Orwell, comes to prominence *after* the war. A handsome catalogue was issued for the exhibition.

A general pattern for many of the conferences and series of lectures of the year is a tendency to use Orwell as a jumping-off point, such as that at the University of Delaware, called *1984*, with eight lectures given in the fall of 1983. Nearby at West Chester State College in Pennsylvania there was "George Orwell: A Literary Symposium," and there was a special connected issue of *College Literature* (January 1984) with nine articles. At Rosemont College on 23-25 March there was "An Orwell Symposium" with an imposing list of speakers. Other universities that had Orwell lectures included Syracuse, Sonoma State, and California Polytechnic at San Luis Obispo. At the University of Akron, Ohio, there was in January 1984 a very successful conference sponsored by the Institute for Future Studies and Research, entitled "On the Way to 2019, After 1984, What Futures for Personal Freedom, Political Authority and the Civic Culture?" On March 1-3 in Milwaukee a conference took place on "Premonitions and Perspectives from 1984: Has the Orwellian World Arrived?" It included a talk by Frances Fitzgerald, "Rewriting History." Later in March, Brigham Young University devoted its History Day to George Orwell. On 23-24 March at Northern Illinois University there was a conference titled "George Orwell: Unresolved Contradictions." On 25 March Congressman Ted Weiss of New York arranged a conference, "Orwell's *1984:* Fact or Fiction?," with various panels and Vartan Gregorian, Director of the New York Public Library, as the keynote speaker. On 26 and 27 March there was a conference on Orwell sponsored by the Tennessee Committee for the Humanities and Austin Peay State University in Clarksville, Tennessee. With the spring, and the closeness of the opening day of the novel, the pace increased, with "Orwell's 1984: The Text and its Transformation and Legacy" at the University of Minnesota on 5-7 April, which appeared to attempt to keep quite close to the man and his book. Its topics were "Orwell and His Sources," "*1984* and Other Media," "Critical Responses to *1984*," "Changing Student Perceptions of *1984*," "*1984* and the Dystopian Literary Tradition," and "Orwell's Politics and the Ideology of *1984*." The outstanding talk was "Who Speaks Doublespeak in 1984" by William Lutz, the editor of the *Quarterly Review of Doublespeak.* (The National Council of Teachers of English, the sponsors of the journal, have given its Doublespeak Award to the State Department for its use of "unlawful or arbitrary deprivation of life" for "killing." The George Orwell Award for Distinguished Contribution to Honesty and Clarity in Public Language went to Ted Koppel.) At Cornell University on 13-14 April there was "Utopia and its Discontents: Zamyatin, Orwell & Mayakovsky: the View from 1984," in which one of the six sessions was devoted to Orwell. The Library of Congress devoted two days to Orwell: 30 April to Orwell the man, with talks by Peter Davison, Jenni Calder, and Peter Stansky; and 1 May to the book, with talks by Denis Donoghue, Alfred Kazin, Jeffrey Meyers, Bernard

Crick, and Nathan Scott, Jr. The Library will publish the proceedings. On May 4 to 6, Ohio State University held the conference "1984: Vision & Reality." The topics were "Theories of Power," "Control and Authority," "Language and Orthodoxy," "Control of the Past as Control of the Future," "Hegemony and its Enemies," and "Orwell the Man and his Works." On 24-25 August the International Christian Studies Association sponsored at its First World Congress in Pasadena a conference on Christian Alternatives to Huxley's Brave New World and Orwell's 1984. At Washington State University in Pullman there was a three-day conference on "George Orwell's 1984: Myth, Reality and Legend" organized by Allan Kachelmeier. On 10-11 October the University of Louisville had talks by Irving Howe, Bernard Bergonzi, and Douglas Hofstadter; and on the 11th, 12th and 13th Hofstra University had a conference with nine panels and a keynote address on the book as a novel of the 1930s. The next weekend Fayettesville State University sponsored "1984: Then and Now." Finally, on 23-24 November, Simon Fraser University, the University of British Columbia, and the University of Victoria sponsored a conference in Vancouver with six panels and an address by Bernard Crick on "Orwell and English Socialism." An entire academic program was devoted to the book at the experimental Evergreen State College in Washington State.

One pales at the thought of how many courses were given with the book in their title or on their reading list, not to mention how often graduating seniors in America heard the book and the author evoked in commencement addresses. How deep Orwell must be in the American consciousness.

On the island of Jura, where the novel was written, four week-long seminars were scheduled. Orwell received the immortality of being installed at Mme. Tussaud's waxwork museum in London, writing while being watched by a member of the Thought Police. There was also an Orwell summer school at the University of London with talks by Barbara Hardy and John Wain, among others. Three million dollars is being spent to restore the pier at Wigan itself—which is a nice ironic touch, for the title, *The Road to Wigan Pier*, was derived from a music-hall joke, that the poor, rather than going to the pleasure piers at Blackpool, have to make do with a coal chute at Wigan. The town is also contemplating erecting a statue to the writer.

There are various miscellaneous happenings that deserve to be recorded: Amnesty International issued a press release entitled "1984: Has Orwell's

1.

the/ clocks/
innumerable clocks[1]

bright,
—‖It was a/cold, blowy day in early April, and a million radios /
his chin nuzzled into his breast
were striking thirteen. Winston Smith, pushed open the glass door of
in an effort to escape the vile ᴇᴇ[2] wind. slipped quickly through the glass
Victory Mansions, turned to the right down the passage-way and press-
doors of Victory Mansions, though not quickly enough to prevent a swirl of
ed the button of the lift. Nothing happened. He had just pressed a
cold air &> gritty dirt dust from entering along with him.‖ NP.
second time when a door at the end of the passage opened, letting out
ᴇᴇ[3]‖ The hallway smelt permanently of boiled cabbage & old rag
a smell of boiled greens and old rag mats, and the aged prole who
mats. At one end of it, completely dominating it> a coloured poster, too
acted as porter and caretaker thrust out a grey, seamed face and stood
large for indoor display, had been tacked to the wall. It depicted
for a moment sucking his teeth and watching Winston malignantly.

more
than
simply an enormous face, ⟍ at least a metre across/wide — the face of a man
"Lift ain't working," he announced at last.
of about forty-five. with ruggedly handsome features,> thick black hair, a
"Why isn't it working?" ruggedly handsome features.‖
heavy moustache, & an expression at once benevolent & vaguely menacing.‖
"No lifts ain't working. The currents is cut orf at the main.
‖Winston made for the stairs. It was no use trying the lift. Even

the all[4]
electric
current
The 'eat ain't working neither. All currents to be cut orf during
at the best of times it was seldom working, & at present all electrical power
daylight hours. Orders!" he barked in military style, and slammed the
was cut off during the daylight hours. It was part of the economy drive in
door again, leaving it uncertain whether the grievance he evidently
preparation for Hate Week. The flat was seven flights up, & Winston, who
felt was against Winston, or against the authorities who had cut off
was thirty-nine & had a varicose ulcer above his right ankle, went slowly,
the current.
opposite/
resting several times on the way. On each landing, facing/the lift shaft,
Winston remembered now. It was part of the economy drive in
the poster with the enormous face gazed from the wall. NP.
preparation for Hate Week. The flat was seven flights up, and Winston,

conscious of his thirty-nine years and of the varicose ulcer above

his right ankle, rested at each landing to avoid putting himself out

of breath. On every landing the same poster was gummed to the wall —

a huge coloured poster, too large for indoor display. It depicted

simply an enormous face, the face of a man of about forty-five, with

ruggedly handsome features, thick black hair, a heavy moustache and> an

Typed in black and written in blue ink on unlined paper

CW: 3
HBJ: 3
S&W: 1/5

[1] 's' of 'clocks' very indistinct and
uncertain
[2] False start for 'wind'?

[3] Obscured: possibly 'O.P.' first
written with 'NP.' written over and
then scored out
[4] 'all' added later

wm 1

*Two pages from the facsimile edition of the 1984 manuscript (HBJ/M & S Press, 1984). Left, transcription of the text; right
Orwell's revised typescript.*

It was a cold, blowy day in early April, and a million radios
were striking thirteen. Winston Smith pushed open the glass door of
Victory Mansions, turned to the right down the passage-way and pressed the button of the lift. Nothing happened. He had just pressed a
second time when a door at the end of the passage opened, letting out
a smell of boiled greens and old rag mats, and the aged prole who
acted as porter and caretaker thrust out a grey, seamed face and stood
for a moment sucking his teeth and watching Winston malignantly.

"Lift ain't working," he announced at last.

"Why isn't it working?"

"The lifts ain't working. The currents is cut orf at the main.
The 'eat ain't working neither. All currents to be cut orf during
daylight hours. Orders!" he barked in military style, and slammed the
door again, leaving it uncertain whether the grievance he evidently
felt was against Winston, or against the authorities who had cut-off
the current.

Winston remembered now. It was part of the economy drive in
preparation for Hate Week. The flat was seven flights up, and Winston,
conscious of his thirty-nine years and of the varicose ulcer above
his right ankle, rested at each landing to avoid putting himself out
of breath. On every landing the same poster was gummed to the wall —
a huge coloured poster, too large for indoor display. It depicted
simply an enormous face, the face of a man of about forty-five, with
ruggedly handsome features, thick black hair, a heavy moustache and

Nightmare Come True?" The Frankfurt Book Fair announced as its theme "Orwell 2000." There were undoubtedly small exhibitions at many libraries and elsewhere, but only a few came to my notice. There was one at University College, London, where the Orwell archive is located. At the British Library from 17 August to 18 November there was a display of "The Works of George Orwell in the Languages of Eastern Europe." As the press release states, "Though such activities carry heavy penalties, Orwell's works are smuggled in from the West, copied out by hand and reproduced in various forms in Eastern Europe. In Poland, enthusiasm for Orwell is fed by the most sophisticated clandestine publishing industry in Eastern Europe. Print runs of 10,000 or more are not unusual and the arrival of 'Orwell year' has inspired Orwell calendars, stamps and wall stickers." Orwell is not available legally in the East, but an article appeared in the Soviet *New Times* claiming that Orwell's vision was a reality in the United States. (See the *New York Times*, 8 January 1984, p. 8.) The Russian émigré sculptor Alex Shagin struck a medal in honor of Orwell. The Camden Arts Centre in London had an exhibition, *1984*, which a leading art critic, Marina Vaizey, found "peculiarly tame." At the London Barbican Centre during the summer there was an exhibition called "The Best of British Naive Painters in the Year of Orwell," which included a painting by Margaret Loxton for the Battles of the Cowshed from *Animal Farm*, by Ditz of a scene from *A Clergyman's Daughter*, and by Jean Stockdale of Orwell on a country railway station platform. In Vienna there were paintings, graphics, and environments by Guttuso, Kienholz, Lichenstein, and Vedova in a show titled "Nineteen Eight-Four: Orwell and the Present" at the Museum of the 20th Century.

But what does all this activity mean, and how much does George Orwell really matter to it? One might say that to many readers and commentators the title *1984* in numerals has more significance than the actual title of the book, *Nineteen Eighty-Four*. Many of us prefer to take Orwell as a political commentator rather than a novelist and to consider the degree to which he has been accurate and insightful about the present state of the world.

Perhaps on the deepest level that is correct. Orwell has transformed his own nightmares and our half-conscious apprehensions into realistic fiction that asks us how we live and what are our primary political concerns. Are we free? Individual liberty and equality are the cornerstones of our values, and our aim is to make untrue that powerful phrase in *Animal Farm*: "some are more equal than others." With so much activity, and with so much of it being concerned, at least in a preliminary way, with the man and his book, with so many serious individuals reconsidering the book and the world that it presents, the questions being raised by Orwell are receiving serious attention. So inevitably all through the year, and even before, many have been reminded of Orwell's particular concerns. If in their thoughts, triggered by the book, they dwell on the political and technological state of our present world, that is quite legitimate. But the most important part of *Nineteen Eighty-Four* is its cry that we must maintain individual freedom; that we must be free to think what we believe to be true; and that we must resist those, most frequently to be found in the ranks of government, who wish us to behave, not to cause trouble, to conform, and to allow *them* to preserve their power. Yes, George Orwell does matter, and the activities of "his" year, no matter how many may be distracted and lose sight of him in the millions of words expended on the topic, provide testimony to a truth that will survive—indeed, must survive—beyond 1984.

(The author is deeply grateful to Jane Sommerich, Dennis Rohatyn, Gordon Beadle, Willy Reimer, Mark Jarrett, and Raymond G. McInnis for their assistance in drawing items for this article to his attention.)

The Modern Language Association of America Celebrates Its Centennial

English Showalter

In 1983 and 1984 the Modern Language Association of America, usually called the MLA, celebrated its hundredth year of existence. The MLA is a learned and professional society, which seeks to promote study, criticism, and research in modern languages and their literatures and to further the common interests of teachers of those subjects. Although membership is generally open to anyone, most of the members are college and university professors of English or of foreign languages; a significant number, however, are graduate students in those fields, and there are many others who hold jobs outside the academic world or who teach in other fields. With a total membership of about 26,000, the MLA is one of America's largest associations of academic humanists.

The MLA publishes several periodicals, of which the best known is *PMLA,* originally called *Publications of the Modern Language Association.* Each year, it holds a convention at which members meet, deliver papers, and discuss problems and policies. Since 1921 the MLA has published an annual bibliography of scholarship and criticism in its fields. It also publishes books on teaching and scholarship in modern languages and literatures. It provides a large number of services and sponsors a variety of activities, all designed to serve the study of modern languages and literatures.

The MLA headquarters is located at 62 Fifth Avenue, New York; the full-time staff now number around eighty, headed by an executive director, a deputy executive director, and eight divisional directors. Responsibility for policy is lodged with an executive council, composed of twelve members elected on a rotating basis for four-year terms, plus the three association officers, the president, first vice-president, and second vice-president. A new second vice-president is elected annually and automatically moves up a rank in successive years. In addition, the members elect a delegate assembly, which meets during the convention, makes general recommendations to the council, and has control over certain aspects of the budget. Finally, a score of committees participate in governing the association or directing its activities and formulating its policies.

The MLA was founded in 1883 by forty professors, led by A. Marshall Elliott, professor of Romance languages at Johns Hopkins University. They met on 27 and 28 December at Columbia University. In the early days, the members concentrated their efforts on winning recognition for their field as worthy of inclusion in the curriculum of higher education; previously, only classical languages and literatures had been widely accepted. As a result, the early convention papers and articles included a high proportion devoted to pedagogy. By the early 1900s, however, the status of modern language studies in the curriculum had been secured, and the association abandoned its pedagogical orientation in favor of a more exclusive attention to scholarship, so as to compete with the prestigious research universities of Europe.

Higher education was expanding rapidly in the United States at that time. Increasing enrollments in English and modern foreign language courses led to growth in those faculties, and the MLA attracted more and more members. In 1884, its first full year, there were 126; by 1911, the number passed 1,000. In 1922 it stood at 2,095; in 1930, at 4,055. The rise stopped and the membership even dropped a little during the Depression and World War II, but in the post-war years the rate of expansion accelerated dramatically. In 1945 there were 4,173 members; by 1950 there were 6,515; by 1960 there were 11,800; and in 1970 the membership reached its all-time peak of 31,356.

The years of rapid growth in the 1950s and 1960s brought many changes in the orientation of the association. The definition of the fields became more flexible; convention sessions soon began appearing regularly on new subjects like film, children's literature, science fiction, area studies, ethnic studies, women's studies, gay studies, and relations between literature and other disciplines. The training of large numbers of new faculty members posed problems of pedagogical method and professional organization; members turned to the MLA to work out guidelines and solutions. The development of new technologies in audiovisual equipment, microforms, copying, and computers, for example, required that information and advice be made

Eudora Welty, winner of the 1984 Common Wealth Award in Literature, at the presentation ceremony (MLA)

available; again, the MLA seemed the natural agency to investigate applications and make the results known to members. The MLA developed computer programs for operating scholarly associations, which it now shares through a consortium with about twenty other organizations; and it devised a bibliographical and indexing program, which is used for the MLA *Bibliography* and increasingly by other bibliographies.

For many members the annual convention is the principal function of the MLA; when they say, "I am going to MLA," they mean "to the convention." The convention has been held between Christmas and New Year's Day almost every year since the founding of the association. The site alternates among major cities, returning most often to New York and Chicago; since 1970 it has also been held in San Francisco, Houston, and Los Angeles. Since the early 1960s attendance has ranged between 6,000 and 14,000; New York meetings, such as the Centennial Convention in 1983, tend to draw the higher numbers.

The convention program lists around 700 sessions of various sorts. A typical session lasts one hour and fifteen minutes. One person, who often solicits the papers and selects the speakers, chairs the meeting; three or four participants deliver short papers; usually the audience is invited to ask questions and join in discussion at the end.

MLA members belong to divisions that reflect their scholarly or professional interests; typical of the seventy-six divisions are such topics as poetry, religious approaches to literature, black American literature and culture, methods of literary research, teaching of writing, Shakespeare, French literature outside Europe, and twentieth-century Latin American literature. Another twenty-eight topics are represented by discussion groups, which may become divisions after a trial period. Each division has an elected executive committee, whose principal function is to organize up to three sessions at the convention.

Besides the division programs, individual members may propose special sessions on any topic. Proposals are reviewed by a program committee in April and those that are deemed most interesting and best prepared are given a place on the program. Normally there are more than 200 special sessions; examples from the Centennial Convention include Patterns of American Jewish Writing; Wordsworth and Autobiography; The Writing Center as a Context for Composition Research; Medical Metaphors of Cultural Crisis in German Literature after 1890; Female Poets of the Italian Cinquecento; How Publishers Sell Your Books; Ellison's *Invisible Man* Reconsidered; Margaret Drabble; and so forth. Nearly one hundred smaller associations hold their own annual meetings as a part of the MLA convention; they are called allied organizations and may organize two sessions each. In 1983 they included groups like the American Dialect Society, the Association for Computers and the Humanities, the Conference of Editors of Learned Journals, the Modern Humanities Research Association, and a large number of societies devoted to the study of a particular author. Finally, at each convention about five forums are presented, with a topic and speakers expected to appeal to a very wide range of listeners; in 1983, there were forums on the centennial of Kafka's birth, with an appearance by Jorge Luis Borges; on women's writing in 1883 and 1983, with Joyce Carol Oates, Paule Marshall, and Sally Miller Gearhart; on literature by American ethnic minority groups; and on the MLA's own history, with Ralph Ellison, John William Ward (president of the American Council of Learned Societies), and Geoffrey Marshall (deputy chairman of the National Endowment for the Humanities). These various kinds of sessions provide the principal intellectual exchanges of the convention.

At the same time, several other important activities are taking place. The program includes a significant number of social events, either receptions with cocktails or meals, bringing together current faculty, students, and graduates of certain universities, or members of a division or allied organization, or simply people sharing a particular interest. The association conducts some of its business during the convention, notably the meeting of the delegate assembly. A major focus of attention at the convention is the exhibit hall, where about 150 publishers, manufacturers, and vendors display their latest books, audiovisual equipment, teaching aids, computers, and software.

For many convention-goers, however, the job information service is the most important function. Department chairs from all over the country arrange to interview candidates for jobs during the convention, and almost everyone looking for a job

in a college English or foreign language department plans to attend the convention so as to be available for interviews. The MLA, working with two organizations it sponsors, the Association of Departments of English (ADE) and the Association of Departments of Foreign Languages (ADFL), provides services to both chairs and candidates, taking messages, keeping records on file, and setting up interviews. Furthermore, special workshops and advisory sessions for job candidates are scheduled early in the convention to assist job seekers.

PMLA began in 1884 as a journal containing the proceedings of the annual meetings. Soon, however, it began accepting additional articles. Over the years, it has established a solid reputation as a vehicle for essays representing the best of American scholarship and criticism in modern languages and literatures. It also publishes information on matters of interest to members, such as conferences, journals, and fellowships, and carries significant advertising as well.

The editorial procedures at *PMLA* are among the most rigorous in the profession. Every article submitted must be read by a specially selected expert reader and by a specialist in the field from the *PMLA* advisory committee. These readers are selected because they are qualified to judge the article's accuracy, originality, and importance within its own field. If they both give it favorable recommendations, it must then be approved by the editorial board, with seven members from different fields who consider its broad interest and significance. The entire evaluation is conducted anonymously, that is, without the editorial readers knowing the author's name. This procedure guarantees that each submission is judged on its own merits.

Besides the issues containing articles, which appear in January, March, May, and October each year, *PMLA* publishes the directory of MLA members in September and the convention program in November. The directory issue contains the constitution, lists of committee members, department chairs, useful addresses, and a good deal of other important information about the MLA and about the profession.

The *Bibliography* was originally part of *PMLA*. From the founding of the association, the members dreamed of producing an annual bibliography of American scholarship in their fields. The dream was realized for the first time in 1922, when the "American Bibliography for 1921" appeared, in the form of an essay on work published in America; a significant part of its purpose was to advertise the quality of American scholarship to the rest of the world. In 1927 the essay was abandoned and the bibliography took the form of a list, but descriptive comments were still included. In 1948, even these one- or two-line comments were eliminated.

In 1956 the title was changed to *MLA International Bibliography,* and the coverage was extended to include all significant scholarly work in modern languages and literatures. During the 1960s, the volume of material to be surveyed rose dramatically; the first international edition contained 12,925 items, and the 1968 edition contained a barely manageable 24,126. The next year, therefore, the *Bibliography* ceased to be part of *PMLA* and was published separately in four volumes devoted respectively to General, English, American, Medieval and Neo-Latin, and Celtic Literatures; European, Asian, African, and Latin American Literatures; Linguistics; and Pedagogy in Modern Foreign Languages.

In the 1970s the MLA undertook another major revision of the *Bibliography,* with the aid of a grant from the Research Tools Program of the National Endowment for the Humanities. The principal result was the development of the Contextual Indexing and Faceted Taxonomic System (CIFT), which allowed the bibliography to be compiled and indexed with the aid of a computer. Beginning with the 1981 edition, the *Bibliography* appeared in five volumes: English and American literature; Foreign literature; Linguistics; General

literature; and Folklore. The volume on pedagogy had been dropped in 1973, as its sponsor, the American Council of Teachers of Foreign Languages, became an independent organization.

With computerization, the *Bibliography* became available for on-line use; the years 1969 through 1983 are currently accessible through Dialog Information Services. Earlier years are being added to the data base; the complete bibliography from the beginning will eventually be included, and of course the current year is added regularly. For students, critics, and scholars working on subjects in any of the modern languages or literatures, the *MLA International Bibliography* is an indispensable research tool.

Most students are likely to know of the MLA first through another of its publications, the *MLA Handbook for Writers of Research Papers.* This guide explains in simple terms with abundant examples the most widely accepted conventions for presenting in written form the results of research on literary topics. The first edition was printed in 1977; a new and significantly revised version was issued in 1984. Together they have sold almost a million copies. The *Handbook* is frequently used as a textbook in writing courses but can equally well be used as a reference book for writers.

The *Handbook* is the best known but is by no means the only book published by the MLA. Some other important works include a series of volumes

Ralph Ellison, speaking on the MLA's history (MLA)

called Approaches to Teaching Masterpieces of World Literature, containing essays describing various practical methods teachers have used to present books like *Don Quixote, Beowulf,* and *David Copperfield*; another series called Technology and the Humanities, describing computer applications; specialized bibliographies; reviews of research; publications on women in literature and in the profession; publications on literature and ethnic minorities; a series on Options for Teaching; a series on Introductions to Older Languages; works on employment and careers, on scholarly publication, and on general questions of concern to teachers of language and literature. The MLA also sponsors the New Variorum Edition of Shakespeare, and its Committee on Scholarly Editions examines volumes submitted to it and issues a seal of approval to those that meet high editing standards.

In 1969 the MLA began publishing a *Newsletter* to supplement *PMLA* as a way of keeping the members informed; the *Newsletter* now appears four times a year. *Profession,* a volume of essays on questions of broad professional interest, is published annually. The *Directory of Periodicals,* a listing of the 3,000 periodicals covered in the *Bibliography,* with information about editorial policies, is issued every two years.

The Association of Departments of English (ADE) and the Association of Departments of Foreign Languages (ADFL) bring together administrators of college departments. The associations conduct seminars each summer where members exchange information and hear expert advice about running academic departments and about facing general problems in the profession. Each association publishes a *Bulletin* three times a year, with articles on similar matters. Together they operate the job information service to assist departments in recruiting new faculty and to assist job seekers in finding appropriate openings. Besides its functions at the convention, the job information service publishes the quarterly *Job Information Lists,* in which departments advertise vacancies.

The MLA has several committees that monitor aspects of the profession and recommend policy or action. For example, the committee on academic freedom keeps members informed about situations where academic freedom is threatened and inter-

venes when appropriate. The committee on careers sponsors programs to assist members of the profession, especially new Ph.D. recipients, find jobs. The committees on research activities and on teaching and related activities advise the MLA on book publications and sponsor programs to further both research and teaching. For special situations, the MLA may appoint a commission to collect data and recommend actions. A recent commission reported on the future of the profession, recommending actions in twenty areas to prepare for anticipated conditions in the 1980s. Current commissions are those on the status of women in the profession, on the literatures and languages of America, on writing and literature, and on foreign languages, literatures, and linguistics.

As one of the largest professional associations, the MLA articulates the concerns of its members and exerts an influence on the policies of the federal government, foundations, and other agencies. One of its major functions is to collect data on the study of modern languages and literatures, so as to provide clear documentation of trends in enrollments, curriculum, and so forth. The MLA's positions on professional ethics and policy are often adopted by other associations and cited by local academic administrators. The MLA is a leading sponsor of the Joint National Committee for Languages and the National Humanities Alliance, two organizations in Washington which work closely with Congress and federal agencies and make sure that the concerns of MLA members are expressed.

Finally, the MLA awards several prizes for outstanding scholarly and creative work, including annual recognition of the best article in *PMLA*, of the best book by a member, of an outstanding work by an independent scholar, and of outstanding research publications both in English teaching and in foreign language teaching. Every two years an award is made in Italian studies. The MLA also provides a jury for the prestigious Common Wealth Award in Literature, an annual prize given to an outstanding living writer of any nationality. The 1984 award of $23,500 was presented to Eudora Welty at a ceremony held at the New York Public Library. Previous winners have been Christopher Isherwood (1983), Wright Morris (1982), Nadine Gordimer and Milan Kundera (1981), and Robert Penn Warren and Gabriel García Marquéz (1980).

Center For Book Research

John P. Dessauer

The Center for Book Research was founded by the University of Scranton on 1 March 1983 to "devote itself to examining the past, present and future role of the book in our culture." In creating the Center, the University was mindful of an urgent need, long recognized and paradoxically neglected in the book field, for factual information on the creation, publication, and use of books in modern society. As first conceived, the Center was to "place particular emphasis on the use of books in education, scholarship and the professions, and on their relationship with the emerging electronic media."

Within the University the Center was placed under the jurisdiction of the Academic Vice-President, with book-industry analyst and statistician John P. Dessauer named Director of the Center. The following were appointed to serve on the Center's Policy Board: Henrik Edelman, University Librarian, Rutgers—The State University of New Jersey, Chair; Howard Aksen, Vice-President and Publisher, College Division, Harper and Row; Henry M. Amato, Dean, School of Management, University of Scranton; Judith Appelbaum, Managing Director, Sensible Solutions, Inc.; DeWitt C. Baker, President, Zipsan Systems; James H. Clark, Director, University of California Press; Mark Carroll, Chief, Branch of Professional Publications, United States National Park Service; Richard B. Gladstone, Executive Vice-President and Publisher, Houghton Mifflin; Karen Hunter, Planning Officer, Elsevier Science Publishers; Kenneth T. Hurst, formerly President, Prentice-Hall International; B. Carl Jones, President, Haddon Craftsmen; Jerome Kagan, Professor of Developmental Psychology, Harvard University; Richard Koffler, President, Associated Faculty Press; William S. Lofquist, Industry Specialist, International Trade Administration, U.S. Department of Commerce; John McInerney, Chairman, Department of English, University of Scranton; Kenneth J. Oberembt, Director, Library and Media Resources, University of Scranton; and Richard R. Rowe, President, F. W. Faxon. In 1984, David R. Godine, President of David R. Godine, Publisher, replaced Mr. Aksen, and Robert J. R. Follett, Chairman, Follett Corporation, was added to the board.

In keeping with the Center's objective first to

John P. Dessauer, Director, Center for Book Research
(Terry Connors)

examine the future relationship of books and the electronic media, it was proposed that the Center's initial project be a major, in-depth, two-year study exploring the prospects for books and potentially rival technologies in educational, scholarly, and professional settings. This approach soon proved impractical. Conservative estimates placed the cost of the Center's proposed program at one million dollars. In many of its facets, the Center's effort would overlap with other studies in progress or being launched. Furthermore, given its protracted approach to a fast-moving field, it was likely that the Center's findings, when finally released, would probably prove to be out of date.

Accordingly, the massive study approach was abandoned. In its place the Center developed a research strategy capable of attacking several issues simultaneously, in more manageable proportions. The scope of the Center's concerns was broadened to include all areas touching the book, particularly those involving the public interest. A program was formulated featuring three categories of activity: public conferences, publication of a research journal, and sponsored research.

The conference program is designed to illumine major research topics by allowing leading experts and researchers to address and interact with a select audience on various aspects of a chosen theme. The occasion receives maximum exposure through publication of the proceedings in the Center's research journal. The conferences are scheduled at eighteen-month intervals.

The first such event, the "International Conference on the Book in the Electronic Age," was held on the campus of the University of Scranton on 16 and 17 March 1984. The event was attended by one hundred individuals, mostly book professionals, who were addressed by seventeen internationally known speakers. Funding for the occasion was provided by Haddon Craftsmen and sixteen other book industry firms, as well as by Northeastern Bank of Pennsylvania and the Scranton Area Foundation. The second conference, "Copyright—New Perceptions and Solutions," is scheduled to be held in Washington, D.C., in October 1985.

Book Research Quarterly provides the principal vehicle for realizing the research objectives of the Center. Devoted mainly to thematic issues on book-related topics of major public interest, the journal also carries government and industry statistical data, and book reviews. The premier (January 1985) issue contains the expanded proceedings of the "International Conference on the Book in the Electronic Age." Themes of subsequent issues—covered largely through case studies conducted especially for the quarterly—will treat the effects of the school adoption process on the quality of textbooks; the cultural implications of concentration in the publishing and bookselling industries; the problem of "forgotten" midlist books; editorial responsibilities in a culturally pluralistic society; research tools of the 1990s; and the significance of the growing internationalization of publishing and book marketing.

The quarterly is published for the Center by the Transaction Periodicals Consortium at Rutgers—The State University of New Jersey. John P.

Dessauer is editor of the journal; Leigh Estabrook of Syracuse University, William S. Lofquist of the U.S. Department of Commerce, and Frederick C. Lynden of Brown University Library are associate editors. Judith Appelbaum is book review editor.

The quarterly's editorial board includes Judith Appelbaum; Mark Carroll; John Y. Cole, Center for the Book, the Library of Congress; Hendrik Edelman; Jack G. Goellner, the Johns Hopkins University Press; Irving Louis Horowitz, Transaction—Rutgers University; Jerome Kagan; Dan Lacy, McGraw-Hill; A. J. Meadows, Primary Communications Research Centre, University of Leicester; and James R. Squire, Ginn and Company.

The Center undertakes selected research projects sponsored by professional and industry groups or firms. Principal among these assignments is *Book Industry Trends*, an annual estimate and forecast of industry sales, supplemented by monthly Updates, which Dessauer has been compiling for the Book Industry Study Group since 1977. Currently the Center has also been requested by the Professional and Scholarly Publishing Division of the Association of American Publishers to conduct a

First issue of the Center for Book Research's new journal

survey of library acquisition practices of professional and scholarly books and journals.

Funding for the Center has come from a variety of sources, with the University furnishing the bulk of the required capital. The Scranton Area Foundation awarded a grant to support start-up activities for the Center. Other donors have included Arcata Graphics, Banta, Book Manufacturers' Institute, The Book Press, R. R. Bowker, R. R. Donnelley and Sons, P. H. Glatfelter, Haddon Craftsmen, Harris Graphics, Joanna Western Mills, W. A. Krueger, Lindenmeyr Paper, the Maple-Vail Book Manufacturing Group, Murray Printing, New England Book Components, the New York Times Foundation, Northeastern Bank of Pennsylvania, Perkins and Squier, Rand McNally, and the Transaction-Wiley Fund.

The Ingersoll Prizes

Bryce J. Christensen

Beginning in 1983 The Ingersoll Foundation, with the cooperation of The Rockford Institute, has annually awarded two prizes, each in the amount of $15,000, for notable achievement in literature and the humanities: The T. S. Eliot Award for Creative Writing, and The Richard M. Weaver Award for Scholarly Letters.

The Ingersoll Foundation, sponsor of the prizes, is the philanthropic division of Ingersoll Milling Machine Company of Rockford, Illinois. The Rockford Institute, under contract to assist in the administration of the prizes, is an independent study center, also headquartered in Rockford, devoted to advancing a public philosophy for supporting the American experiment in free society. In 1982, the trustees of The Ingersoll Foundation decided to focus the Foundation's efforts upon the reinforcement of fundamental cultural values and attitudes. These include lawfulness and integrity; ethical commitment to the traditional family unit; truthfulness and rationality in resolving public issues; and the Judeo-Christian ideals summarized in the Ten Commandments. The trustees recognized that among formative activities influencing the beliefs and behavior of American citizens, literature and scholarly studies in the humanities play a powerful role as they interpret the meaning of human existence and render judgment on social institutions.

The trustees' decision to initiate the Ingersoll Prizes was guided by the perception that over the last twenty-five years insufficient recognition has been given to talented writers and scholars who affirm the principles essential to a moral and free civilization. As Dr. John A. Howard, president of both The Ingersoll Foundation and The Rockford Institute, explained at the inception of the awards:

> Each civilization is built upon a specific vision of order and virtue. . . . In our era the cultural leadership of the West has been blind to this requirement and has enthroned as its models and mentors, scholars and artists and writers of an iconoclastic bent. . . .
>
> Our purpose in establishing the prizes, then, is both to provide a symbol of abiding public gratitude to authors who address the themes of order and virtue, and to stimulate an ever-larger readership for the wisdom which they have made available by their life's labors.

Mr. Leopold Tyrmand, vice-president of The Rockford Institute and permanent secretary of the Ingersoll Prizes, further explained the reason for the prizes in these words:

> In recent decades, we . . . were troubled by a suspicion that in literature and the humanities there has been a diminishing endeavor to understand humanness as both destiny and spiritual substance; that writers have, by and large, abandoned their mission. . . . The fundamental worth of ethical norm, grace, and dignity had become, in our view, endangered. . . . As our attempt to restore to prominence those standards of intellectual integrity and moral elegance . . . we therefore called the Ingersoll Prizes into being.

The prizes are named for two outstanding exemplars in the two categories in which the awards

Prizewinners James Birnham, left, and Jorge Luis Borges, center, with Ingersoll Foundation Chairman Clayton Gayford
(Robert H. Bradford)

are made. The T. S. Eliot Award for Creative Writing honors one of the greatest poets, critics, and dramatists of this century, and one of the most profound interpreters of the modern conservative impulse.

The Richard M. Weaver Award for Scholarly Letters is named for a former distinguished professor of English at the University of Chicago, whose *Ideas Have Consequences* (1948) is widely regarded as a starting point of the intellectual renaissance of American conservatism. With Eliot, Weaver (1910-1963) was deeply disturbed by the disappearance of the sense of the transcendent and by the consequent decline in communal integrity. Seeking to rescue the ancient conception of rhetoric as a humane art, Weaver established himself as a leading scholar in the field with his landmark study *The*

Ethics of Rhetoric (1953). In the essays collected in *Visions of Order* (1965) and *Life Without Prejudice* (1966), he demonstrated his own mastery of rhetoric as he eloquently defended the "world of substantial things" against the "dogmatic utilitarian, essentially contumacious doctrines of liberalism and scientism."

The T. S. Eliot prize is awarded for works in literature, including fiction, drama, poetry, essays, and literary criticism. The Richard M. Weaver prize is awarded for scholarly achievements in the humanities, including philosophy, history, ethics, and social and political science. The basis for selection may be a body of work produced over a period of years, an oeuvre, or it may be a single exceptional volume. Laureates will be designated on the basis of cultural, intellectual, and scholarly merit, without

Anthony Powell, author of the twelve-novel sequence A Dance to the Music of Time *and second winner of the T. S. Eliot Award in Creative Writing*

regard for race, creed, sex, nationality, or citizenship, provided their literary or scholarly works are available in English. The prizes may be awarded posthumously.

All procedures governing the awarding of the prizes are controlled and implemented by an Executive Council. This Council consists of (1) a representative of the Ingersoll Milling Machine Company; (2) the president of The Ingersoll Foundation; and (3) the permanent executive secretary of the prizes, who is an officer of The Rockford Institute.

Annually, the Executive Council designates an Ingersoll Prizes Review Panel consisting of three or more members. Panel members are chosen for their scholarly, literary, or intellectual eminence. Panel members serve for one year but may be reappointed for one or two additional consecutive terms. Members of the Review Panel provide evaluations of each name accepted by the Executive Council for consideration and may submit nominations for consideration. Final selection is made by the Executive Council.

Public announcement of winners is made each year near Labor Day, and presentation of the prizes is made at an awards banquet in Chicago in the late fall. Essays about the laureates are published each year in the December issue of *Chronicles of Culture*, a publication of The Rockford Institute edited by Mr. Tyrmand, and the acceptance essays by the recipients are published in the March and April issues of *Chronicles*.

The first recipient of the T. S. Eliot Award in

Creative Writing was Jorge Luis Borges (b. 1899), Argentine poet, critic, and short-story writer. Widely regarded as Latin America's most brilliant writer, Borges, many commentators believe, would long ago have received the Nobel Prize were his political vision left-of-center. He is best known for metaphysical fictions of the sort collected in *Ficciones* (1956) and *El Aleph* (1957). In such fictions, Borges, as Mr. Tyrmand observes, "became a tireless wanderer through the spiritual territory where the enigmas of destiny intertwine with moral concerns. As such, he came to symbolize the complexity and depth of Western intellectual tradition."

The second recipient of the Eliot Award was Anthony Powell (b. 1905). One of England's greatest living novelists, Powell is best known for his *A Dance to the Music of Time* (1951-1975), a twelve-novel sequence examining the changes in attitudes and mores among the upper and educated classes in Britain in the middle decades of this century. Combining an elegiac resignation with gentle satire, this Proustian sequence ranks among the highest achievements of English fiction. As *Chronicles*

Russell Kirk, second winner of the Richard M. Weaver Award for Scholarly Letters, in his library at Mecosta, Michigan

observed, "Powell's novels . . . are marked by painstaking observation and understated irony and constitute a valuable chronicle of life in the mid-20th century."

The first recipient of the Richard M. Weaver Award for Scholarly Letters was James Burnham (b. 1905). Philosopher, political analyst, journalist, and author, Burnham began his career as a leading Trotskyite. But he came to be one of the most perceptive and articulate foes of collectivist thought. In his internationally acclaimed book *The Managerial Revolution* (1941), he presciently analyzed the forces undermining capitalism and threatening to sweep the world into totalitarianism. George Orwell was among those powerfully influenced by this work. In such later works as *The Struggle for the World* (1947) and *Containment or Liberation?* (1952) Burnham cogently evaluated international communism and the American response.

The second winner of the Weaver Award was Russell Amos Kirk (b. 1918), author, critic, and educator. Professor Kirk's widely translated and acclaimed *The Conservative Mind* (1952) signaled the emergence of a newly vital conservative intellectual movement in America. Kirk has been a leader of that movement ever since. Among the major scholarly works he has written are *Decadence and Renewal in Higher Learning* (1979), *Eliot and His Age* (1972), *Enemies of the Permanent Things* (1969), *Edmund Burke* (1967), and *John Randolph of Roanoke* (1951). A creative writer as well as a scholar, Kirk is perhaps the greatest living practitioner of the supernatural tale. His most recent collections are *The Princess of All Lands* (1979) and *Watchers at the Strait Gate* (1984).

The Bread Loaf Writers' Conference 1983

David Haward Bain

The fifty-eighth session of the Bread Loaf Writers' Conference convened 16-28 August 1983 at its upland valley campus in the Green Mountains of Vermont, some ten miles south of Middlebury College, under whose auspices the Conference has run since 1926.

Under the direction of poet and Middlebury professor Robert Pack (*Faces in a Single Tree*), who has headed the Conference since 1973, when he took over from John Ciardi, the faculty included names both new and familiar to Bread Loaf. Robert Stone (*Dog Soldiers* and *A Flag for Sunrise*) appeared for his first session, while Galway Kinnell (*Mortal Acts, Mortal Words*), creative writing director at New York University, returned after a twelve-year absence. Two faculty members with prominent work behind them and currently deeply involved with new novels were John Irving (*The World According to Garp* and *The Hotel New Hampshire*) and Tim O'Brien (National Book Award-winning *Going After Cacciato*). Both have taught at the Conference more or less constantly since the mid-1970s. Other longtime staff members made appearances: poets Marvin Bell (University of Iowa), Howard Nemerov (Washington University), William Matthews (Columbia), Nancy Willard (Vassar), and Linda Pastan

(*PM/AM: New and Selected Poems*); novelist Hilma Wolitzer (*In the Palomar Arms* and *Hearts*), and Ron Powers, writer of fiction and nonfiction (*Super Tube: The Rise of Television Sports*), who is also media critic for CBS network. Novelist Jerome Charyn (*Darlin' Bill*), of Princeton, returned for a second year.

This faculty was assisted by twelve staff associates, all of whom have had at least two books published: Pamela Hadas, Ron Hansen, Carolyn Forché, Mary Morris, Bob Reiss, Page Edwards, Robert Finch, Sydney Lea, Wyatt Prunty, Carole Oles, David Huddle, and David Bain.

The Bread Loaf campus owes its existence to a Vermont eccentric, Joseph Battell (1839-1915), who in 1865 journeyed up the stagecoach road from his home in Middlebury, past the hamlet of Ripton, until he arrived at a farmhouse hard by the 3,823-foot Bread Loaf Mountain. Being a young man of means, and liking what he saw, Battell bought the building and its land. Eventually he constructed a mansard-roofed Victorian inn, which came to be attended by some twenty outbuildings, including a massive dairy barn. All buildings, most of their shingled and gingerbread-laden exteriors painted in a uniform yellow trimmed with forest green, are intact today—furnished with battered

Some of the faculty for the Bread Loaf Writers' Conference, 1983. Front: Hilma Wolitzer, Marvin Bell, Nancy Willard, Robert Pack, Linda Pastan, Page Edwards, Robert Finch, David Bain. Back: Jerome Charyn, Wyatt Prunty, Ron Hansen, John Irving, David Huddle, William Matthews, Bob Reiss, Ron Powers, Pamela Hadas, Mary Morris, Carole Oles, Carolyn Forché (© 1984 David Haward Bain).

but nonetheless picturesque antiques from the Battell era.

Battell advertised his establishment as a retreat for refined ladies and gentlemen—a place where hunting, fishing, hiking, and riding in the thousands of acres of surrounding forestland could be leavened by a genteel croquet match or a more strenuous game of bowling. Battell not only was an innkeeper; he published the *Middlebury Register* and several unreadable books of his philosophies, enthusiastically bred Morgan horses, donated a fortune to local institutions, and presided over a one-man crusade against the horseless carriage.

Following his death in 1915, the inn and all its surrounding lands were bequeathed to Middlebury College; within a few years, the college, unequipped to deal with such a business venture, all but put the lot up for sale. The college was dissuaded, however, by several members of its faculty who desired to establish a summer school for the study of English. In 1921, under the direction of Charles Baker Wright and Wilfred Davison, the Bread Loaf School of English commenced. It has operated ever since, with a distinguished faculty drawn from all over the country, offering masters' degrees after four intensive summer sessions.

In 1925, faculty members laid plans for a two-week "extension" of the summer session, during which time creative writing would be taught. The first Conference in 1926 was directed by John Farrar, editor of the *Bookman* and soon to be cofounder of the publishing firm Farrar and Rinehart. Farrar was succeeded in 1929 by R. M. Gay, a Middlebury English professor, who in turn was replaced in 1932 by the poet Theodore Morrison, then at the beginning of his long tenure at Harvard.

It was under Morrison's direction that the Writers' Conference bloomed, for he attracted during his twenty-three-year directorship such writers/ teachers as Robert Frost, Bernard DeVoto, Wallace Stegner, Edith Mirrielees, Louis Untermeyer, Catherine Drinker Bowen, and John Mason Brown. Visiting lecturers included Sinclair Lewis, Archibald MacLeish, James T. Farrell, W.H. Auden, William Carlos Williams, Richard Wright, and Katherine Anne Porter. And under Morrison a fellowship program was established to give recognition to writers at the beginning of their careers; some who benefited from it were Howard Fast (1935); John Ciardi, Carson McCullers, and Eudora Welty (1940); Theodore Roethke (1941); A. B. Guthrie, Jr. (1945); Mae Swenson (1957); Anne Sexton (1959); and Joan Didion (1963). This program was gradually expanded as John Ciardi assumed the directorship in 1956, followed by Robert Pack in 1973; by then the Conference granted scholarships to contributors to periodicals, and working scholarships to students with promising work.

Continuing this tradition, the 1983 Conference distributed forty-two working scholarships to writers in exchange for duties in the dining room or administration. Seventeen authors of periodical poetry and prose, including essayist Fay Moskowitz (whose columns often appear in the *New York Times*), Michael Cunningham (his novel, *Golden States*, was published with good notices later in 1983), and short-story writers Bob Shacochis and Sharon Stark, received partial scholarships in recognition of their work. And The Bread Loaf Fellowship program honored eighteen writers in 1983, including poets Edward Hirsch, Ursula Hegi, and Terry Hummer, and novelist Jim Shepard, all of whose first book-length efforts drew critical praise in the press. Another Bread Loaf fellow, memoirist Joyce Johnson, was the author of *Minor Characters*, a book about coming of age in the orbit of Jack Kerouac and the Beat Generation. It later received a National Book Critics Circle Award.

The first John Gardner Fellowship was awarded in 1983 (to Johnson), an indication of the affection and esteem felt toward Gardner, who had served on the Bread Loaf faculty every year but one since 1974, and who died in 1982. "He was committed to the goals of the Conference—to bring new and established writers together for their mutual benefit," wrote Robert Pack and his administrative director, Stanley Bates, soon after the motorcycle accident that killed Gardner. "John was a generous

Poet Wyatt Prunty and Bread Loaf director Robert Pack conferring outside the Bread Loaf Inn's Little Theater (© 1984 David Haward Bain)

Poet Howard Nemerov, winner of the National Book Award, Pulitzer Prize, and Bollingen Prize, at Bread Loaf, 1983
(© 1984 David Haward Bain)

colleague, a genuine friend who helped and provoked us with his thought, pleased and moved us with his art, inspired us by the example of his humanity. We [could] think of no better way to honor his service to Bread Loaf than to offer a fellowship in his name."

If there was a sense of loss during the 1983 Conference because of Gardner's death, the tradition of hard work and sometimes frantic conviviality forced participants' attention on the matter at hand: talking about the craft and the art of writing. There were some seventeen lectures, five panels, and workshops and discussion groups; participants were given the opportunity to attend readings given

by thirty-seven staff members and fellows and some fifty others given by working scholars.

Not all was hard work. The Conference hosted a series of afternoon cocktail parties on the grounds around the inn and lunchtime picnics. An ad hoc madrigal singers' group formed around Conference secretary Carol Knauss and Stanley Bates, giving a performance during the second weekend. Participants availed themselves of the surrounding national parkland—the Long Trail passes nearby, and there are several small lakes and streams for those hardy enough to stand Vermont's chilly spring-fed water in the waning summer days. Pilgrims headed down the mountain about a mile to tramp around Robert Frost's farm, where he spent his summers from the late 1930s until his death in 1963. Others formed carpools to investigate the antique stores which line Vermont Route 7. The inn's two clay tennis courts, which once thudded under the sneakers of Louis Untermeyer, Robert Frost, and Theodore Roethke, were in demand.

Following the evening readings, many participants headed for the social nerve center of the campus, Battell's old dairy barn, which was converted many years ago. With a fire roaring in the massive fieldstone fireplace, and with dimmed lights throwing the three-story-high raftered ceiling into shadows, revelers gathered around an old Steinway grand to sing rock tunes and, as the evenings would wear on, to harmonize on hoary maudlin ballads—all a great release of pent-up energy. Musical interludes in the barn are a tradition— square dances were held in the 1930s and 1940s; Wallace Stegner used to sing cowboy ditties at the top of his lungs; and Catherine Drinker Bowen gave yearly violin recitals—and those at the Conference in 1983 were typically energetic. George Murphy, editor of the literary magazine *Tendril* and possessor of an encyclopedic memory for arcane lyrics, harmonized with teaching associate David

Bain, who played piano; poet Sydney Lea (coeditor of the *New England Review/Bread Loaf Quarterly*) contributed raucous blues songs as fellow Terry Hummer attempted to keep up on flute; Robert Stone, contributing several gospel-based renditions, shook off the vocal assistance of novelist Robert Houston by attempting to clamber atop the Steinway, a task he was persuaded to abandon.

On the evening of the first Saturday of the Conference, a band appeared to play at a barn dance that lasted until a little closer to dawn than many participants would have liked when they struggled awake in late morning on Sunday. By then it was time for the third annual Writers Cramp Run, a long-distance race across the campus. Quipped New York novelist John Gillespie, "Any writer who can't run 3.5 miles with a hangover doesn't belong here."

In his biography of Bernard DeVoto, Wallace Stegner writes of how the conference produced in him and many others "a kind of frenzy, a heightening of every perception, capacity, and emotion. It combined a frantic amount of business with an equally frantic amount of fraternizing, revel, and emotional release." This tradition continues into the 1980s. Since all of the Conference members are

Novelist John Irving (right) answers questions outside the Little Theater at Bread Loaf, 1983 (© 1984 David Howard Bain)

77

writers, conversations—even the most casual— usually touched on literary matters both artistic and commercial, often stimulated by the many speakers. Linda Pastan lectured on writing about dreams, and Nancy Willard on fables; William Matthews discussed "Richard Hugo and Detective Fiction"; John Irving, "Narrative Momentum and Comic Relief"; Howard Nemerov, "The Nature of Poetry." Visiting literary agents and editors talked on their concerns and wants. Poet Paul Mariani (*Crossing Cocytis* and a work on William Carlos Williams) appeared briefly to lecture on the art of biography. And though the Conference is physically isolated, with radios and televisions banned ("walls are thin," explains a brochure) and newspapers often unread because there is not time, news of the assassination of Philippine opposition leader Benigno Aquino, and of continuing troubles in Central America, gave resonance to a number of nonfiction and poetry readings delivered by staff associates.

Critic Ron Powers delivered a stirring talk on the media threat to the printed word: that television "is no less appalling to writers for the fact that it has no particular political or pedagogic axe to grind against print. It has no value system of its own, and it is in fact infuriatingly neutral. It colonizes indifferently—almost independently of human passion."

Television will not make people illiterate, Powers said, but its effects were extremely subtle. A growing number of people committed to the printed word were giving in to the temptation to imitate broadcasting: "to somehow transfer its kinetic, immediate, and visceral impact to the page of linear type." Still others, seemingly "the most sensitive and gifted" young writers, "cast a very cold and measured eye across the battlefield of electronics and print, and then they lift their gaze to take in the society that seems to have rushed out drunkenly to embrace the invader—and then these writers turn away. They reject this fickle culture as having grown too profane, too promiscuous to be worthy of a serious literary investment, or offering. They begin to write in a narrow and increasingly codified language for what they imagine as a small surviving garrison of kindred spirits: academics and fellow writers." This could open, said Powers, a "gulf of ideas" in the middle of our society. "The language atrophies, and along with it, people's capacity to analyze, to make distinctions, to intervene in a life beyond the personal life—even the capacity to become indignant about continually being had."

This lecture, and that of Tim O'Brien, who exhorted his audience to write with a commitment to something beyond their immediate world and concerns, caught and reflected the spirit of the 1983 Conference—which, after all, had its roots in an era when movies were silent and subtitled, and when radios were at their beginning of mass appeal. The world, as well as the world of writing, is a vastly different place now, and for at least twelve days in that Victorian community in the Green Mountains of Vermont, some 250 writers seemed imbued with a desire, in Powers's words, "to conquer both their deference to the colonizers from the broadcast world, and their contempt for the mass culture that has been its victim."

Author David Haward Bain solicits recollections and memorabilia from all past Conference participants, care of the *DLB Yearbook*.

Storytelling: A Contemporary Renaissance

Jean W. Ross

For as long as man has had the words, he has been telling stories—to explain nature's quirks, to perpetuate his traditions, to hold an audience, to calm the young. "Storytelling," says present-day practitioner of the art Lee Pennington, "is to the common culture, the oral culture, what literature is to the written culture." Swept along on the recent wave of renewed interest in the folk arts, it is enjoying a renaissance that has brought it to national attention and continues to swell the ranks of enthusiasts, both tellers and listeners. Once in danger of extinction as the old storytellers died off and the younger generation turned to the mass media for entertainment, it is now practiced at more than 400 organized events across the country.

The oldest and largest of these is the National Storytelling Festival at Jonesborough, Tennessee. Held annually since 1973, always on the first full weekend of October, the Jonesborough festival was begun by local restaurant owner Jimmy Neil Smith, with support from the Jonesborough Civic Trust, to preserve the Appalachian storytelling heritage. True to its name, however, it attracts storytellers from as far away as Utah and Texas.

The Jonesborough festival is sponsored by the National Association for the Preservation and Perpetuation of Storytelling (NAPPS), founded in Jonesborough after the 1975 festival. Today NAPPS is headquartered in the Old Slemons House in the restoration area of town, where it operates the National Storytelling Resource Center and publishes a monthly newsletter (the *Yarnspinner*), the *National Directory of Storytellers*, and the *National Catalog of Storytelling Resources*, a listing of materials available from NAPPS. In addition to the National Storytelling Festival, it sponsors each June the

A storyteller and his audience on the front lawn of Locust Grove, Louisville, 1984 (Courier-Journal *and* Louisville Times)

National Conference on Storytelling, a workshop for learning storytelling skills.

An offshoot of the National Storytelling Festival in Jonesborough, and running it a lively second, is the Corn Island Storytelling Festival in Louisville, Kentucky, which began at the instigation of Lee Pennington with the sponsorship of Louisville's Jefferson Community College in 1976 when NAPPS encouraged the formation of regional events. Though the first Corn Island Festival attracted only twenty people (the price of admission was a dollar or a story), the 1984 festival saw a gathering of more than 7000 at its closing event, the ghost-tales session at historic Long Run Cemetery, with another 3000 turned away.

The Corn Island Storytelling Festival's growing success seemed a mixed blessing after the 1983 meeting, when Jefferson Community College decided it had become too big a job to maintain its sponsorship. At that point Pennington and his wife Joy, both of whom teach English at JCC, rallied other supporters and formed the International Order of E.A.R.S., Inc. (an acronym whose meaning remains a secret except to its members) to raise funds and take up the festival's sponsorship. Thanks to their own energy and to enthusiastic help at all levels, they ended the 1984 festival well in the black.

The Louisville festival is held each year on the third full weekend of September. In addition to Long Run Cemetery, sites for its events include Locust Grove, a 1790 Georgian home where pioneer George Rogers Clark lived for nine years; the Louisville water tower, an architectural gem on the Ohio River; and the Belle of Louisville, the city's old stern-wheel paddleboat.

Of the 1984 festival's twenty-six professional storytellers, one of the most popular was "Story Lady" Jackie Torrence from Granite Quarry, North Carolina, who tells Uncle Remus stories, ghost stories, and "Jack" tales—Appalachian stories that derive from such Anglo-Saxon tales as "Jack and the Beanstalk." The subject of a 1984 article in the *Christian Science Monitor*, Torrence claims that she can "work for at least twenty-nine days, three hours per day, averaging three stories per hour, and not tell the same one twice." Other full-time storytellers included Michael Parent, of French Canadian origins, who likes "Pourquoi"—how-and-why—stories and incorporates some fancy juggling into his tales. Torrence and Parent are among the few who make their living exclusively as storytellers.

The most unusual participants at the 1984

The governor's proclamation of Storytelling Week in Kentucky, 16-22 September 1984

Corn Island Storytelling Festival were centenarians Frank Smith, who says he was born "two years behind the Civil War," and Quint T. Guier, who turned 102 in December 1984. Both men are Kentuckians. Guier draws his stories from his own experiences as a child and the stories he heard from his relatives, who told of the family's early settlement near Daniel Boone's family. After his wife died in 1971, Guier went back to Valparaiso University in Indiana and took courses in journalism, the Bible, and creative writing. He has written "about 600 pages" of his life story and plans to finish the job.

For Quint Guier, telling stories was a way around loneliness after the death of his wife. New England storyteller Jay O'Callahan, whose material is mostly original, likes "the drama in storytelling. It allows you to be the writer, producer and director. . . ." As one of eleven children in his Eastern Kentucky mountain family, Lee Pennington grew up with storytelling and sees it as an antidote to twentieth-century media blight. "Storytelling puts back the senses," he says.

Jean Smith, of the National Storytelling Resource Center in Jonesborough, told a *Washington Post* writer in 1982, "We are still struggling to have it defined as an art." To the 7000 spellbound in Long Run Cemetery on a starlit September night, the magic was definition enough.

AN INTERVIEW
with MICHAEL PARENT

When Michael Parent tells a story, every muscle in his face seems to be at work. His eyes evoke surprise, terror, and delight. On the rolling lawn of Locust Grove, at the 1984 Corn Island Storytelling Festival, he so thoroughly enchanted an audience of all ages that he had to break the spell in order to disperse his followers and talk with *DLB* about his life as a storyteller.

DLB: How long have you been telling stories?

PARENT: In the sense that stories are being told all the time whenever we tell what happened, I've been telling stories ever since I learned to talk—and so have all of us. I like to think of stories that way, as whenever we communicate in the narrative form. But doing it this way, as a way to make a living, as a way to entertain people, I'm in my eighth year now.

DLB: Is it hard to get to the point of making a living at it?

PARENT: Well, it took me four years, maybe five, before I began to make as much as I did as a teacher. Now I make more than I did as a teacher, but it took that time. I learned to live on very little fairly early on, though, so that wasn't a big deal. I don't *like* being broke, and I didn't particularly enjoy being poor, but I think to everything there's a price and a payoff. The price was that I had to really scale down my life-style for a few years, but the payoff was that here I was doing this thing that I really loved doing. I always weigh things in that fashion rather than by the idea that I'm supposed to make $25,000 or whatever a year because that's the American standard. To hell with the American standard; I don't care about it.

DLB: Where do you get most of your stories?

PARENT: More and more I just get them from my own experience. As a matter of fact, this morning in my hour session I told three stories, and two of them were just personal stories about things that happened. The other was something I got from a book. It's breaking down pretty much that way now, whereas when I first started it was probably eighty or ninety percent things I got from books, kind of literary stuff or folk tales. Now it's a half to two-thirds things that people have told me. That's folkloric in the real sense, stories that I get from *folks*—either folks I've been in contact with or folks I've heard about or the person that *I* have been, walking through the world. There's definitely been a shift in the last two or three years toward more of that sort of personal stuff. Not personal in the sense of intimate, but personal like here's what happened at this time, that I hope people can relate to on another level.

DLB: What are the ethics of taking another person's story and using it yourself?

PARENT: Suppose you tell me a story right now and I like it so much that I want to use it. The simple thing to say is, "I love that story. I'd love to tell it. Can I?" If you say yes, fine. Or you might say, "Yes, but I want fifty bucks every time you tell it." So OK; that's pretty straightforward. If you want to tell a story from a folk tale collection, that stuff is pretty much public domain. They belong to everybody. I think credit should be given to the collector of the stories. But things come in different versions. There are certain folk tales I heard from my folks that I've found versions of in a book, and I feel there isn't really any imperative in that case for me to give anybody credit. But if I use a story that's in a book, I feel the first thing is to give the author credit, and the second thing is to give the author money if that's appropriate. Copyright can get to be a ticklish subject, but basically, with the stuff I'm using now, I have to deal with that less and less. I also make up stories, like "The Wicked Wizard of Wellington Woods," that I just told. That's one of my own, so I don't need to ask anybody about that. And of course anybody can tell personal experience kinds of stories. It really isn't much of a problem, especially in the direction I'm going now.

DLB: If you take a folk story, say, or a family story, do you try to embellish it in some way?

PARENT: I think you have to have a balance. What

"Story lady" Jackie Torrence on the grounds of Locust Grove in Louisville (International Order of E.A.R.S., Inc.)

you're trying to do is communicate a story. I think there are ways to desecrate a story. There are stories that have a certain amount of pathos and sadness and tragedy in them. If the tone of a story is completely mishandled, I think that's a desecration—for example, if everything is played for a laugh. There are different kinds of stories, and different kinds of appropriateness. I like the stories that have elements of all sorts of emotions in them. But some people play everything for a laugh, and I don't like that.

What I generally do is try to stick fairly close to the source that I take a story from, but not feel as though I have to do it word-for-word, because the writing down, or the putting into literary form, is an interruption of a process in a sense. Here is a story that developed to the point where this person wrote it down. Does that mean it stopped developing? There's that angle.

I used to do things that I don't want to do anymore. For example, I used to do Indian folk tales, and I'd throw an anachronism in, like somebody wearing a watch. Of course that would get a laugh, but then I realized that that's all I was doing

with that, just getting a laugh. So I try to stay away from that. I might slip into it once in a while, but I'm conscious of it and I really don't want to do it.

DLB: What makes an audience for you? Can it be one other person? Does it have to be a group called together?

PARENT: Once I went to the geriatric ward of a mental hospital. There were forty people in the room, and they were all totally gone. It was the most depressing thing I'd ever seen in my life. For twenty minutes I tried everything. Nothing worked. Finally I just started singing every song I could remember, and somewhere in the middle of "Down by the Riverside" I saw the first movement I'd seen in that room. It was one of the women tapping her foot. I sang to her, played to her, for the next ten minutes. I realized that she was my audience. Every notion I'd ever had about what success and failure mean was turned on its head. We have these notions about what it means to be successful—"He's a successful businessman," or "She's a successful writer"—what

Michael Parent at work

does it mean? Does it really mean that they're doing what their heart bids them? That experience made me look at all audiences in a completely different light. I said to myself, forget about looking in people's faces and trying to figure out what's going on, because there is no way to tell. Some things are helpful: it's nice to look and see people smiling or see people really enraptured. But some people sit there expressionless the whole time, and they may be the ones who come up to you later and say, "Oh, that was wonderful!"

There are times when you're definitely in hostile situations. I've gone to prisons. What makes it for me in a situation like that is whatever transformation takes place. You walk in and you feel hostility, but there are other things going on there. They're sizing you up—"What the hell is this guy doing?" When you treat them like people, maybe

things change. I've been in situations where there was nothing but hostility when I walked in, and fifteen minutes later they were a devoted band of followers. It doesn't happen that way every time— sometimes the transformations are a little more muted than that kind of drama.

To give you a more specific answer, I really am enjoying doing more things for grownups, because I have a bunch of songs and stories that grownups can appreciate more. I can't tell the story of the mental hospital to a group of kids; they don't know what that's all about. I can't tell them "The Cow Tail Switch," which is a folk tale about death. I'm trying to do more grownup audiences. I like it where you have these grownups thinking, "Oh, storytelling. What the hell am I doing here?" and then you see the transformation.

A Conversation with Chaim Potok
(19 February 1929-   )

S. Lillian Kremer

See also the Potok entry in *DLB 28, Twentieth-Century American-Jewish Fiction Writers.*

Chaim Potok is a scholar-novelist: a Ph.D. in Western Philosophy, biblical translator and commentator, university instructor, and ordained rabbi. His major contribution to American fiction is his authentic portrayal of Orthodox Jews, Jews who know Torah, Talmud, the commentaries, and Kabbalah. According to Potok, the central subject of his fiction is "the interplay of the Jewish tradition with the secular twentieth century." He writes of Jews "who are at the very heart of their Judaism and at the same time . . . encountering elements that are at the very heart of the umbrella civilization." The tension in Potok's novels springs from the drama of ideas, from his Orthodox characters' encounters with scientific biblical criticism, Freudian concepts, Western art, and Marxism. The underpinning of Potok's work is an affirmative vision which posits a pervasive striving for meaning in the midst of chaos, for good in the face of evil, a celebration of the enduring decency of humanity, revealing a vital counterpoint to the dominant twentieth-century mode of despair and alienation.

In addition to writing fiction, Potok has served as an editor for *Conservative Judaism* (1964-1965) and editor for the Jewish Publication Society (1965-1975). Recently he has taught in the philosophy department at the University of Pennsylvania.

Potok lives with his wife and children in a gracious rambling Tudor house set in a heavily wooded site north of Philadelphia. On the second floor are his writing and painting studios, one which evidences his wide-ranging intellectual interests and the other, the place where he works at the first creative art he practiced, painting. His extensive library suggests Potok's broad interests in the human intellect and imagination.

A CONVERSATION
with CHAIM POTOK

DLB: Please comment on your writing method and the reflection process for a novel.

POTOK: Almost always, it starts with a problem. It takes me about a year or a year and a half to think a problem through, and what comes out of the think-

Chaim Potok

I'm not too far into it, and read up to the point where I'm going to start writing again. As I read, I revise. If I get beyond page forty or fifty, I will then start at the previous major break and read up to the point where I start again, so that revision is constantly going on. What I'm looking for when I revise are rhythms and removal of the baroque because it is all too easy, especially when you are writing about ideas that you are translating into fictional terms, to get sloppy with ideas and to hide the sloppiness with the pyrotechnics of language. Whenever I sense that in my writing, I always know that I haven't thought something through and I will very quickly remove the baroque, unless I need it for stylistic effect. That's why the novels have the fairly simple tonality that they have. In addition is the fact that the people I'm handling are so exotic in themselves that my fear was and remains that if the style is exotic in addition to the people, the novel will just be leaden.

DLB: What aspects of writing are most difficult for you?

POTOK: All of them; all of them. I really mean that. I don't find that it's getting easier either as the years go by. With each book I create, the greater the aesthetic mountains that I have to climb; otherwise, it's dull. I couldn't imagine repeating a book. *The Chosen* is fairly simple technically. The difference in structure between *The Chosen* and *The Book of Lights* is enormous and that is very deliberate.

DLB: Is there a topic that you have wanted to treat, but have been unable to?

POTOK: Yes, and I think I'm going to take it up after the book I'm doing now. That is the topic of power and what people do with it, empire building for good purposes and how it corrupts, even for good purposes.

DLB: Writers often say that in the process of writing, a book takes on a life of its own. Has that ever been your experience?

POTOK: Oh yes. As a matter of fact, you look for that. After a number of pages have been written the material itself begins to generate its own aesthetic requirements. Things are suddenly made necessary for you by what it is that you put on the paper already, that you didn't anticipate. You know you need a certain conversation in order to move it in a certain direction and you didn't anticipate needing

ing process is only remotely related to what started the thinking process. To be concrete, as I started to concern myself with the problem of the artist in the closed society which has no value for art, it never occurred to me that I would be writing about a Jew, from the heart of things Jewish, painting a crucifixion. While on the surface of things it appears a simple and obvious dilemma for a religious Jew who enters the mainstream of Western art, it clearly was neither simple nor obvious to me when I started to think about what ultimately became *My Name Is Asher Lev*. It's a problem of confrontation of ideas which sparks a novel, the people caught up in the confrontation, and then an attempt to take what is essentially abstract thought and translate it in terms of action, flesh, and blood. I revise every day as I go along. I will write in the mornings and break for lunch; write in the afternoons and break for dinner and then stop. At night, I'll either read for the next day's writing or go out or just relax and let the energies restore themselves. The next morning I will reread. Depending upon where I am in the book, I may start from the beginning of the book, if that conversation. You have to explore in a certain direction that you never thought you would have to explore and you suddenly start researching something you never thought you would get to. That is a tip-off that what you created is a living thing. If by around page sixty or seventy this is not happening to me, I stop and I start all over again—and I have done this repeatedly. Every novel that I have written has had an equivalent of three or four novels that have never been published and have been thrown away. I have about eleven hundred pages of typescript for *The Promise* upstairs that I set aside before I actually started to write *The Promise*. That is one of the gauges that helps me ascertain whether or not the thing is alive. It's never the situation, or it ought never to be the situation, that a novel takes over and you don't know what you're doing anymore. That's a romanticized version of writing. The writer is always in control of his material. What you want is the living quality of the material, the pulsing quality of the material.

DLB: Would you comment on your interests in painting and music and how those art forms have affected your writing?

POTOK: Well, the painting has probably affected the writing stylistically in the sense that people tell me I am a very visual writer and that I have a sense of the color of a scene and where things are located. I started to paint when I was very young, when I was about nine or ten, and stopped because it became a serious problem in my house. I grew up in an Orthodox Jewish home and there's not much hospitality toward the fine arts or the graphic arts in a setting of that kind. When I was about fifteen, I diverted the hunger to create into writing, which is much more acceptable in the Orthodox Jewish tradition. Judaism is essentially a word-oriented religion and so if you sit at a desk and write, it somehow seems to fit in better with the tradition than standing in front of an easel flinging paint onto a canvas. Although I must say that writing stories was not terribly acceptable.

DLB: Did your father finally accept creative writing as your profession?

POTOK: I don't think he ever made his peace with my writing. He did not live to see *The Chosen* published, but I suspect he would not have known what to make of all the fuss. The notion that the Western man utilizes an aesthetic form and the imagination in order to somehow get configurations of human experience, to think through what it is we're trying to do on this planet, was utterly foreign to the traditional Orthodox mentality. What you do in the world is what God told you to do. The configuration of reality is very clearly spelled out. "What do you mean you've got to explore reality all over again through fiction?" I think that would have been my father's reaction.

DLB: I wonder whether your method of character construction was influenced by Evelyn Waugh's method in *Brideshead Revisited*, namely the juxtaposition of two men from socially and religiously divergent backgrounds?

POTOK: I don't sense it as a conscious influence. As far as I know the conscious influence for that structure was from something that actually did occur to me. In a confrontation of cultures, it's going to be almost a one-on-one kind of situation and in my situation it was a boy and boy, not boy and girl. It may be that I was taken with the Evelyn Waugh model because it resonated to my specific cultural situation rather than the Evelyn Waugh model shaping my cultural situation. That novel gave configuration to what I was experiencing. It shaped what I was going through myself. I was in a specific world and I was caught up in ideas from the world outside. And this was going on in that book. I kept having confrontations in summer camp, in college, and in Korea, over and over again. I would come from my traditional Jewish world and encounter individuals like me from secular worlds. It would be one set of ideas encountering another set of ideas and it was always boy and boy, man and man. I suppose a good case might be made out for almost all writers having a certain model of reality which they then play with in various ways throughout all their books. Hemingway's *The Sun Also Rises*, Jake Barnes and Lady Brett; *A Farewell to Arms*, Frederic Henry and Catherine Barkley; *For Whom the Bell Tolls*, Robert Jordan and Maria; and it's the same dynamic in different settings with somewhat different problems. In the same way that in Bellow's novels the victim victimized by women appears over and over again. The victim is a college professor, or an editor, or an actor. In Dickens's novels there seems to be a measure of patterning and I rather suspect that the patterning comes at a certain point in an individual's development. The chaos of experience achieves a serious measure of configuration. That's the writer's model to his life; that is what he is going to take through life and he is going to see the world through that model. It is very difficult to alter fundamental models that we bring into the chaos of reality.

DLB: I think another model that is both yours and Bellow's and probably has its source in the Jewish tradition is the character construct based on the student-teacher relationship.

POTOK: Absolutely, Bellow has that all the way through and I have that too. And it would seem to me to be inconceivable that somebody coming from deep inside the Jewish tradition could not stumble across this model and integrate it into his art. What's of interest to me is the variations you play on the model, to take that model and do with it what Beethoven does—to play with it; to see how far you can stretch it without breaking your universe entirely. Someone who writes seriously has a vision of the world, a model that is going to be the infrastructure or the scaffolding for that individual's writing. I have a very specific way of looking at my world and much of it is shaped by the way I was raised. A writer can't write outside his own vision of things. It is like trying to think the world outside of categories like time and space, quality, quantity. I can't think outside my model of reality and my model involves human interactions as a result of confrontations with ideas.

DLB: To what extent have your characters been based on real people and how do you transform the fictional from his real model?

POTOK: Well, I don't think that for the most part real people are multidimensional enough to afford the kind of richness that you need on paper. Most of my characters have some beginning in reality and then are invented. Asher Lev is pure invention, although so many people have told me they're Asher Lev. Jacob Kahn is based to some extent on Jacques Lipchitz, but then I just took off and did with him what I needed to do. The mothers are all invented; the women are all invented. This girl that I'm writing about now is pure invention and she's really very much alive. It's the invention part of writing that I really love. It's fairly easy to find a person you know and just report that person. For the most part there may be a kernel in most of the characters and the rest of it is pure invention. Danny Saunders is pure invention, though there is a kernel of Danny Saunders that is someone I knew in Korea, a very dear friend of mine. The model for David Malter in *The Chosen* is my father-in-law, but the Talmud part of David Malter was somebody

else. My father-in-law was a very beautiful and enlightened Jew and a very lovely human being. It is true to some extent Danny Saunder's father, Reb Saunders, is my father. The closest to my father I've come is Max Lurie in *In the Beginning*. Arthur Leiden in *The Book of Lights* is pure invention, from beginning to end, although people have told me that they know an Arthur Leiden, which is marvelous to me. (I did know someone) and to some measure, I myself served for Gershon Loran.

DLB: Do you read what has been written about your work, and if so, how much has the criticism affected your subsequent writing?

POTOK: I read everything that my publisher sends me about my work and things that friends send me. For the most part people seem to know what I'm talking about, and there's a good deal that's being done now in academic circles about the work, which is pleasing. There seem to be some professionally nasty people around writing which in some strange way is also pleasing because you sort of get into this crowd of writers who have been nastified by places like *Commentary* and I suppose that's a measure of a certain stage in your career when *Commentary* does a number on you and on John Updike and on Mailer and on all the people it does a number on, but for the most part, it seems to me that people are taking the writing seriously. What's of interest to me is, no one quite knows how to categorize my work. I'm trying to take essentially good people caught up in conflicts of ideas and not treat them necessarily ironically, which is the going mode in modern fiction, but in a way that doesn't make the novel sound like *Ann of Green Gables* or *A Tree Grows in Brooklyn* or *Uncle Tom's Cabin*. To deal with good people in a serious way that doesn't turn the world off and make it say it is just sentimental twaddle is, I think, very difficult to do, especially in the twentieth century. I'm not interested in writing abstruse fiction and I'm not interested in playing with words for their own sake, although I could do that. I'm interested in communicating on my terms. I want people to read what I write but I don't want them to forget it. What I've developed for myself is a way of handling a story line that keeps the reader interested in the people and at the same time digging deeply into the people and into their ideas. Now, I'm fully aware of the fact that at this point in twentieth-century writing story lines per se are suspect and, therefore, my contention is that a story line is a necessary but insufficient ingredient in a serious novel. The serious novel without it has a serious lack and the novel that is only story line is simply not serious fiction. Somewhere between these two requirements, story line and probes in depth, there has got to be a way of handling the serious novel so that it continues to be read and taken seriously and is not just another product.

DLB: Do you feel that critics who misunderstand your work do so because of their limited knowledge of the ideas and cultural references you use?

POTOK: Absolutely. They don't quite know how to handle it. There are a number of things that put critics off. One is the style. One of the things I look for when I start a book is the voice of the individual whose book it is. I'm a vehicle for that voice and it takes me months and sometimes more than a year before I get the right sounds for that voice and very often what I do is create the fiction on a page that isn't mine but is the voice's fiction. The style in *The Chosen* is quite different in quality from the style in which *The Book of Lights* is written. The trick is not to write all of the books in the same style and not to make somebody like Rabbit Angstrom sound like he's read James Joyce's *Ulysses*. The trick is to get inside the head and being the individual whose story you are telling, or who is telling the story, and to be inept if you have to be because he's inept and, at the same time, retain the integrity of the prose. So, some critics were put off by that, because the style seems somehow shapeless. Another problem critics have with the books is their ethnicity. There is a tendency in American criticism to take a book about Jews and immediately slot it in a lower echelon. Now, my contention in this regard is that I am writing about my world in precisely the same way Faulkner wrote about Yoknapatawpha County. And nobody in a million years will convince me that Yoknapatawpha County is more American than the world I am writing about. The world that I am writing about is as fundamental to the way Americans structure reality as Yoknapatawpha County and its rednecks and its rapists and its beautiful people and its lawyers, and its Snopses. That's num-

ber two. Number three: there has been a tendency in modern fiction since about the middle of the last century generally to deal with the antihero, the individual who doesn't quite make it in the world and isn't caught up with ideas. It's very unusual to have somebody who is a thinking person at the core of major fiction. That's Joyce's extraordinary accomplishment, and I'm not altogether sure that Stephen Dedalus is a successful writer. Joyce was a great writer, but not Stephen Dedalus. I'm writing about people who are serious, who are bright, who are capable, who are caught up with ideas, and who are, therefore, not in the antihero mainstream, with the exception of the chap in *The Book of Lights*. And the same thing is going to be the situation with this woman writer whom I'm writing about now, who is going to be caught up by some of the major ideas of the twentieth century. All of them will disappoint her. I think these and probably one or two other reasons account for some of the confusion that some of the critics have shown when they read my work. Although there are those who really have caught on, really understand it and, once making the assumption that the works are serious, they then proceed to go ahead and look at the work.

DLB: Some readers expect writers on religious subjects to hold didactic intentions. Do you intend your work to be read as an epistle from the Hebrews?

POTOK: No, that's the last thing in the world I think a novelist ought to do. Essentially what I do is deal with this or that individual, caught in this or that particular set of problems, and working out this or that particular set of responses; and in no way at all are those novels meant to proselytize or to be an epistle to anybody, certainly not in the Pauline sense. The purpose of the novel is to tell a story in configurations that will somehow leave the reader more knowledgeable, more excited about living, more concerned about living, more interested in the possibility of words, and more interested in the possibility of the human imagination that he or she was before he or she came to that particular novel.

Small Presses I: Jargon Society

JONATHAN C. WILLIAMS INTERVIEWS J. CHAMBERLAIN WILLIAMS

JCW: Basic stuff for starters. How long has the Jargon Society been operating? And why the name?

jcw: The first publication was a poem of mine with an absolutely hideous title in the Kenneth Patchen mode: "Garbage Litters the Iron Face of the Sun's Child." Good golly, Miss Molly! Kenneth could (sometimes) get away with such words — let his sycophants beware. The engraver, Dave Ruff, whom I had known at Bill Hayter's Atelier 17 in Greenwich Village, printed one of his copper plates intaglio on this little folded yellow sheet. We made the piece in June 1951. It was dedicated to Kenneth Rexroth, in honor of a fine Chinese meal in North Beach, San Francisco, we all enjoyed.

Why Jargon Society? The word is suggested by the painter Paul Ellsworth, whom I'd become friendly with at the Institute of Design in Chicago earlier that year. The irony of the word appealed. And in French it means "a twittering of birds." It has certainly been that. And, too, a French diminutive, *jargonelle,* refers to a variety of spring pear. Nice to think about.

By the way, J. M. Edelstein (the Librarian of the National Gallery of Art in Washington, D.C.) is just now completing his bibliography of the Jargon Society. Jordan Davies, publisher (356 Bowery, New York City 10012) hopes to publish it in 1986.

JCW: A lot of people think Jargon began at Black Mountain College.

jcw: Not true, as I have just indicated; but, it *continued* at Black Mountain in July 1951. I went there to study photography with Harry Callahan and Aaron Siskind. Emerson Woelffer had told me in Colorado Springs, in June, to watch out for his large friend, Charles Olson, at Black Mountain College. Charles had written a very interesting Melville study, *Call Me Ishmael,* and was quite a guy. I'd never heard of him, but from the moment I spied him having lunch with Ben Shahn in the dining room at the college, he became the energizer, the man who taught me the importance of the writer's press, a self-initiating process that could let you do what you wanted to in literary life. "EACH MAN IS HIS OWN INSTRUMENT," Olson said.

Jonathan Williams (John Menapace)

JCW: What was it with Olson? His size? His blarney?

jcw: I don't know, but whatever it was, I found him an enchanting 6'10" citizen, a person capable of enkindling others like no one I had ever known. His thinking was a stew-pot of everything: Pound, Dewey, Whitehead. He preached MAKE IT NEW! DO IT YOURSELF! BE ROMANTIC, BE PASSIONATE, BE IMAGINATIVE, AND NEVER BE RUSHED! No one had ever told me things like that at docile Princeton.

JCW: From Princeton University to Black Mountain College must be one of the stranger moves in American literary doings. How did it come about?

jcw: Too long a tale to tell, and I am merely the person living the life — I probably don't have the clarity to see what "really" happened. My Georgia/ North Carolina parents, like all parents from decent working backgrounds and modest educations, wanted me to have better than that. I spent six years at a good prep school (St. Albans at the National Cathedral in Washington, D.C.) and was particularly lucky in having one amazing teacher (John Claiborne Davis) who knew what kindling to use to fire the imaginations of those few of his charges who had imaginations. What worked for me was: Sibelius, Delius, Aldous Huxley, C. S. Lewis, Sorokin, H. P. Lovecraft, Henry Miller, Kenneth Patchen, Redon, Courbet. By the time I got to Princeton, Blake and Rouault had joined this pantheon. Word and image, how to put them together, how to print and publish—it all began to heat slowly on some back burner. Then I met Patchen, Rexroth, and Miller. I read the anarchist/pacifist literature. And I turned away from the Establishment World of Princeton. I clearly did not want to become a Byzantinist in the basement of the Morgan Library; or an art critic for the *New Yorker;* nor did I want to live in the world of competitive business. A great blow to my baffled, conservative, helpful, Southern parents. (More blows were to follow: becoming a poet, becoming a conscientious objector, having male companions in life. "Oi veh, oi veh, that's all I need," sayeth the Despairing Parents. Can you blame them?)

JCW: So, with Olson's precepts ringing in the air of Buncombe County, North Carolina, you began producing artists' books.

jcw: Yes. Summer 1951 at Black Mountain found people like Fielding Dawson, Joel Oppenheimer, Francine du Plessix, Mary Fitton, Victor Kalos, Nick Cernovich, Edward Dorn, Robert Rauschenberg, Cy Twombly, and me on the premises. Jargon #2 was a poem of Oppenheimer's, "The Dancer," with a drawing by Rauschenberg. It was dedicated to Katherine Litz, who was there that summer teaching. Next, *Red/Gray,* poems of mine, drawings by Paul Ellsworth; next, *The Double-Backed Beast,* Victor Kalos's poems, Dan Rice's drawings. Then two things happened: I went into the Medical Corps (Army) and off to Stuttgart for eighteen months; and I was left $1500 in the will of a friend from Demorest, Georgia, named Charles Neal. In my mind, I had three choices: (1) buy a Porsche automobile; (2) buy a Max Beckmann portrait; (3) start publishing books. Idiotic from the beginning, I opted for #3 and have been an aristocratic, cranky beggar ever since.

JCW: Now came actual books instead of pamphlets and broadsides, right?

jcw: Yes. *The Maximus Poems*/1-10, by Charles Olson; *Fables & Other Little Tales,* by Kenneth Patch-

en; *The Immoral Proposition,* by Robert Creeley; *Four Stoppages,* poems by myself. The Olson was marvelously printed by the printshop of Dr. Walter Cantz. I had seen examples of their work for *New Directions,* especially *Sleep in a Nest of Flame,* by Charles Henri Ford. The offices were within a ten-minute walk of the Fifth General Hospital I was stationed at in Bad Cannstatt. The Patchen was printed in Karlsruhe/Durlach by Tron Brothers, another excellent firm of craftsmen. I learned a lot in a hurry from these two printers. The Creeley (also Tron Brothers) was designed as a little "Japanese" book for the table, with string binding and drawings in the Sumi manner by the Frenchman René Laubies, painter and translator of Ezra Pound. My poems (Ernst Klett, printer) were also done in an oriental style as a four-part folding paper screen, for the table or to be pinned on the wall. The drawings were by Charles Oscar (the husband of Katherine Litz), who was later murdered on a New York rooftop by some lethal hustler. I remember that there were 200 copies of *Four Stoppages.* It came in a white envelope with my military address imprinted. The price was 50 cents a copy. At a book auction in New York City last spring, James Jaffe of Haverford, Pennsylvania, paid $1400 for the copy that had belonged to Kenneth Patchen. Since I gave that copy to Patchen in the first place and had to pay the airmail postage to the States, my return on the investment is even less than it might seem. Which is not to snarl at dealers and collectors. They play different games in that ball park than I do, but it's comforting to recognize the existence of new fans. Just yesterday, out of the blue came catalog nine from Origin Books (Steven Clay, Merce Dostale, 821 West 43 Street, Minneapolis, Minnesota 55409), 473 items by Jargon Society and writers published by us. A complete surprise.

JCW: Is there any "why" you have published what you have?

jcw: For *pleasure,* surely. I am a stubborn, mountaineer Celt with an orphic, priapic, sybaritic streak that must have come to me, along with H. P. Lovecraft, from Outer Cosmic Infinity. Or maybe Flash Gordon brought it from Mongo? Jargon has allowed me to fill my shelves with books I cared for as passionately as I cared for the beloved books of childhood—which I still have: *Oz, The Hobbit, The Wind in the Willows, Dr. Dolittle,* Ransome, Kipling, et al.

Let me quote some of a statement I wrote for Jargon's catalog in 1983: "THE JARGON SOCI-

Some Jargon Society publications (Alex Harris)

ETY has been 'at it' for thirty-two years. Jonathan Williams is director and Thomas Meyer is his assistant. Despite the fact that we edit at Highlands, North Carolina (winter/spring), and Dentdale, Cumbria (summer/autumn), we are not ruralist or retreatist by nature. We are elitist in the tradition of James Laughlin's New Directions. We publish the best we know to please ourselves and our friends and to confound our enemies. Our board includes distinguished Americans: R. Buckminster Fuller, Donald B. Anderson, J. M. Edelstein, and R. Philip Hanes, Jr. Among our friends and advisors are Guy Davenport, Basil Bunting, R. B. Kitaj, Theodore Wilentz, W. H. Ferry, Lou Harrison, and John Russell.

"Publication costs for the Jargon Society are underwritten by foundations, corporations, and individuals who support our efforts to publish work by poets, writers, photographers, and artists who have the goods to put on the table when the establishment world seems long out to lunch. For yearly contributions of $100 or more, contributors will receive Jargon Society titles as they are published.

For contributions of $1000 or more, contributors will be deemed National Patrons and recognized by name on the colophons of forthcoming publications. Contributors of less than $100 may select one current or forthcoming title as a token of our appreciation. For further details, contact: F. Whitney Jones, President, The Jargon Society, 100 West Fifth Street, Winston-Salem, North Carolina 27101. Telephone: (919) 722-2371.

"The Republic has never been teeming with readers of real books, *Readers Digest* and *Penthouse Forum* to the contrary. Our sales indicate we reach about five out of every one million souls! Still, the *New York Times Book Review* has said: 'The Jargon Society had come to occupy a special place in our cultural life as patron of the American imagination. But however attractive the books are to look at, and they are justly collector's items, the chief pleasure they afford is the intellectual shock of recognizing an original voice ignored by sanctioned critical opinion.' Hugh Kenner has said that Jargon is the 'Custodian of Snowflakes,' and that Jonathan Williams is 'America's truffle-hound of Poetry.' "

JCW: You seem to have a flawless instinct for spending your time and money on what cannot be "sold."

jcw: Like the man says, I couldn't sell ice to an Eskimo. We have taken such an adversary position for so long that we are stuck in some amber-like limbo. A few persons respect this. Most keep silence and ignore the books sedulously. Flaubert once made this comment: "I'm frankly a bourgeois living in seclusion in the country, busy with literature and asking nothing of anyone, not consideration, nor honor, nor esteem. I'd jump into the water to save a good line of poetry or a good sentence of prose from anyone. But, I don't believe, on that account, that humanity has need of me, any more than I have need of it." Still, the trick is: getting the printers paid quickly and fully.

JCW: The list is now nearly one of a hundred titles. Some of the most notable would include Robert Duncan's *Letters;* Louis Zukofsky's *Some Time;* Michael McClure's *Passage* (his first book); Ronald Johnson's *A Line of Poetry, A Row of Trees* (his first book); Paul Metcalf's *Genoa* (and four other prose narratives); Bucky Fuller's *Untitled Epic Poem on the History of Industrialization;* Thomas Meyer's *The Bang Book* (his first book); *The Appalachian Photographs of Doris Ulmann;* Ralph Eugene Meatyard's *The Family Album of Lucybelle Crater;* the Art Sinsabaugh/Sherwood Anderson book of Midwestern photographs and chants; Mina Loy's *The Last Lunar Baedeker;* and the complete writings of Lorine Niedecker, *From This Condensery,* in press at the moment. Many other titles seem marginal and of the Village-Idiot School. How do you justify them?

jcw: I've always followed Pound's old saw: "I now divide poetry into what I can read and what I cannot." People like Simon Cutts and Thomas A. Clark and Russell Edson and Bob Brown have offered tremendous pleasure. I am as little interested in coterie as I can possibly manage to be. I do not have lunch with Richard Howard four times a week in Manhattan to hear who's hot, who the latest cupcake is, who will win the Bollingen, or be buried alive in the vaults of the American Academy and Institute of Arts & Letters. Princeton was one club, and Black Mountain was another. I made distance from each as quickly as possible. Most of the people we've published despise ninety-five percent of the others we've done—that's probably a very healthy thing. Remember, you're dealing with a hillbilly oligarch, a crank. Whether it's poetry or photography or visionary folk-art or persons themselves, I

love things that are "bright-eyed, non-uppity, autochthonous, wacko, private, isolate, unconventional, unpaved, non-commercial, non-nice, naive, outside, fantastic, sub-aesthetic, home-style and bushy-tailed." I am delighted to have published Alfred Starr Hamilton and not Robert Lowell. The gentleman members of the Century Club will take care of Mr. Lowell. Mr. Hamilton's fate is much more fragile.

JCW: The Southern visionaries seem to occupy more and more of your time.

jcw: True. After thirty-four years I have published *most* of what I want to in poetry. The Niedecker, finally coming, will be one of our finest books. Beyond that, I still want to do the *Selected Poems of Mason Jordan Mason.* They have seemed worthy and bizarre and idiosyncratic for all of thirty years. We want to do *Drawings of Truth & Beauty* by Bill Anthony. Robert Hughes sees what they're about—can't 5000 other zany citizens do likewise? We want to do Richard Craven's *Notches Along the Bible-Belt.* He's been at it long enough not to be such a well-kept Tarheel secret. There needs to be a superbly produced, huge book of Art Sinsabaugh's banquet-camera photographs. And perhaps another book or two by Simon Cutts. I do not keep up properly with the younger generations. Some of them are nice to look at, as Petronius might say, but they seem to have little to offer but youth. The writing seems untalented. Which cannot be entirely true. It is up to young publishers to convince us otherwise. Anyway, now I write books about weirds, and long walks, and still enough poems to keep my hand in. People don't really like fifty-five-year-old poets any more than they like to drive cars with 55,000 miles. The voice of the bulldozer, not the turtle, is loud upon the land.

JCW: You sound like the aging scold very far from the gadfly-bitten hunkers of the madding crowd.

jcw: As far as I can get, but that's not all that far these days. Our place, near Highlands, North Carolina, is halfway between Sky Valley, Eastern America's most Southern artificial ski-slope, and a new development called Wild River Townhouses. In simpler times, Sky Valley was just Mud Creek; and the water below the townhouses was Middle Creek. (Observe, please, the poetry of top-dollar land-over-use-cum-ruination.)

I live in hiding from the Cornbelt Metaphysicals, the Ally-Oopists, the Language Poets, the

*The poet Charles Olson at Black Mountain College, 1954
(Jonathan Williams)*

Great Unwashed, the Jewish Princes, the Ivy-League Heavies, the International Homosexual Conspiracy, the Heap-Big He-Men, the Hem & Haw Femmes, the Primal-Scream Minorities, and the Tireless Untalented—there are thousands and thousands of these people ready to push you into a tar pit. Like I said before, there are only about 1420 people in these United States who celebrate what we do—and what anybody else does. We are trying to do a decent job for one and all of these folk. From the rest I hide, like any good hyperliterate rattle-snake. And I beg: DON'T TREAD ON ME!

JCW: Does the fact of being "Southern" make any difference?

jcw: I "have no idea" how to answer questions like that. It says on a piece of paper in the courthouse that I was born 8 March 1929 in Asheville, Buncombe County, North Carolina. That means whatever I, and others, make of it. The South produces Jerry and Jesse and Strom; and Thelonious Sphere Monk and Doc Watson, and Clarence John Laughlin (R.I.P.).

It occurs to me that a blurb I recently wrote (not used) for Duke University Press's new edition of my *Blues & Roots/Rue & Bluets* might just give a new reader a fairly clear picture of what J. Williams, Loco Logodaedalist, is really about. It reads: "Guy Davenport remarks that 'JW is in himself a kind of polytechnic institute, trained to write poems as spare, functional, and alive as a blade of grass.' Ba goom, I bloody hope so, sez I in my non-Appalachian voice. Professor D. says a lot about my work that makes sense. He tells us that the poems are *peripatetic, cathectic, and paratactic.* He's dead right. But let me put such matters, one hopes, in simpler terms.

"Consider this: four men are hiking the Appalachian Trail. The mycologist is the one who knows to look for oaks and apple trees on a north slope and, hence, for morels. The archaeologist won't have to stub his toe to spot the arrowhead or the pot shard. The ornithologist will laugh like a pileated woodpecker if he thinks he's heard Sutton's Warbler in a place it couldn't be. The poet (the guy who knows how to put all the right syllables in their proper places) is the one who wants to stop with the local boy who is digging ramps on the side of Big Bald Mountain and hear what kind of talk he has in his head.

"Poets are forever seeing things, whether Angels in trees, or just things written on the sides of buses like 'Jesus Saves & Satisfies. Are You?' Poets are forever hearing things—'always the deathless music!' I like to catch people speaking 'poems' who never heard of the word *poet* in their lives. It has been my business, along with others (W. C. Williams, Louis Zukofsky, Lorine Niedecker) to try to raise 'the common' to grace; to pay very close attention to the *earthy.* I no more write for 'nice' people than I do for 'common' ones. I make poems for the people who want them. 'He was Southern, and he was a gentleman, but he was not a Southern Gentleman'—which is Allen Tate talking about Edgar-Allan-Poe-White-Trash. I sense a tradition there.

"*Blues & Roots/Rue & Bluets* is a hoard: the best of what the mountains and I have found out about each other, so far. And a little of the worst as well. The tone ranges from the blade of grass (or hot-shot banjo string) picked by the likes of Mr. Earl Scruggs, to the cello sonorities of Frederick Delius, to occasional glorifications and organ points in the manner of another mountaineer, Uncle Tony Bruckner. For those rare souls who wish to look inside, I counsel: TAKE CHAIRS, DIGEST YOUR DINNER, SIP THE JUG!"

Conversations with Publishers I

AN INTERVIEW ——————————
with PATRICK O'CONNOR

Patrick O'Connor is a leading figure in paperback publishing, as well as a poet and dance critic. He has served in editorial capacities at New American Library, Curtis Books, Popular Library, Pinnacle Books, and Washington Square Press. O'Connor is now Senior Editor at Warner Books.

Born in Braddock, Pennsylvania and educated at Catholic University, he served as president of the National Tap Dance Foundation and founded the Dance Library of Israel. O'Connor's ability to combine the requirements of mass-market publishing with literary quality has been recognized by the Carey-Thomas Award. He is also one of the best talkers in American publishing.

DLB: You've spent your professional life as a paperback editor. Have you ever been tempted to switch your allegiance to cloth publishing?

O'CONNOR: Bore-ing. It's like graduate school. I always had a horror of graduate school. I say, when you die God is going to tell you, "For your sins you have to go to graduate school."

DLB: Don't you want to be Max Perkins?

O'CONNOR: Cloth is slow. It could take two or three years. There's no action; there's no money; there are no numbers; there's no trash; there's no pizzazz. It's just endlessly boring. If I see a manuscript that I really am nuts about, I can always nurse it along and put it in the hands of a good hardcover editor who will publish it. It is, I must say, a labor of Hercules these days to take a manuscript which comes to you that you're crazy about and get it published in hardcover. But it can be done. It's done. Sometimes it's done.

DLB: In a case like that you retain paperback rights.

O'CONNOR: Yes, you retain paperback rights.

DLB: How many books a year do you point at the hardcover people?

O'CONNOR: Oh, I point thousands. I throw a lot

Patrick O'Connor

against the wall and almost none stick. Everybody knows this: the hardcover business is in the business of collecting paperback royalties—or has been for years. It seems to be changing because of the sinking of the paperback industry and the lack of those big advances. I always said that the hardcover people didn't publish books; they collected paperback royalties. But that changed. And now they're back in the business again of publishing books.

DLB: When did that start?

O'CONNOR: It started about a year or two ago.

They really decided to get down to business and go back to publishing books, which, of course, is the way they really make money. And now that they all have their own trade paperbacks, they are competing with us for the paperback rights to very good books, and they're paying. The trade paperback line of the hardcover publisher has become a competitor.

DLB: They don't have the rack exposure.

O'CONNOR: No, they don't have the rack exposure. Well, the wholesale business for quality fiction and quality books is so difficult. Selling quality books through the wholesaler is so difficult that selling only direct can perhaps one day be the answer. Direct is where the salesman goes to the store and sells the book. There are variations. The salesman is sophisticated about what he is selling, and the store buyer, more important than that, is more sophisticated about what he's buying—*she*, it's always a she; I don't know why we say he—what she is buying. So the returns are lower. And we're not in the book business at all. We're in the returns business. We only care about how many we get back. We don't care how many we sell.

DLB: The returns on mass market now run about one-third?

O'CONNOR: Dreamer. One-third! Well, it depends. I'm not gonna give a figure: wholesale returns are one thing and direct returns are another. Direct returns went up in the last four or five years, too, but they may be leveling off, I hope.

DLB: Your reputation in publishing is that you're the chap who manages somehow to fill the category racks and sneak in literature. Would you agree with that?

O'CONNOR: Well, I like it put better that way than people who say, "Oh, you only publish good books." People in the book business. That is pretty naive. I have been publishing trash for twenty-six years, some of the best-selling trash of all time—Helen van Slyke. And I shouldn't use the word *trash*, either. I've been publishing commercial fiction for years. And that allowed me, from time to time, to publish truly quality work. And the truly quality work eventually sells. Eventually. If you make a connection with the reader, they'll buy every book. I mean, there are Anne Tyler readers and they buy every Anne Tyler book, and there are Margaret

Drabble readers, and so forth. And Barbara Pym, for God's sake. Who would've thought Barbara Pym? By the way, an English lady said to me, a woman in the book business but who is an English aristocrat, said, "Well, I don't know how Americans can read those books. Those people are all dreary. We wouldn't have them to dinner, any of the people in those novels."

So let me tell you the Lucia story, about the books called "Lucia books." They are six novels by E. F. Benson. They have always been my favorite novels. I wish my favorite novels were *The Idiot* and *War and Peace.* But my favorite novels have been these six books by Benson. And for many years there was in New York a bookstore called O'Malley's. Run by two Irish brothers. They had a list and it said at the top, printed in crude letters, "Will pay anything for Lucia books." And on that list was Noel Coward, Gertrude Lawrence, Bella Spewack, Cyril Ritchard, John Van Druten, and Patrick O'Connor. I was the only name on it that I didn't recognize. The O'Malley's were very democratic. They just gave out the Lucia books as they came in. And if the one you got was a four-volume omnibus called *All About Lucia,* then you were in heaven because it was the one you really wanted. And for years I wanted to do these. I read them before I got into the book business. I got in the book business late. I was thirty-five when I got in the book business. And I wanted to do these. It was not an easy task—English novels about English pastoral life. This was long before "Masterpiece Theatre" and so forth. So, I noticed that at New American Library, in the summertime, occasionally the executives that constituted the "management committee," which approved books to be published, would have a cool cup or three at lunch if the meeting went over to the afternoon. And often on a hot summer afternoon you could get a book through that you otherwise might not be able to because certain executives were nodding at the switch. So I carried these books around with me, six of them—they became like an extension of my body—for weeks waiting for just the right afternoon and the right level of lack of sobriety, and I pushed them through one afternoon. And the next day, the president—wonderful man, Herb Small— said to me, "Who did these damn books? Where did these books come from?" I said, "Well, they went through the management committee." He growled at me. So we did them. I bought them for a thousand dollars apiece. We published them. *Never* has there been such a disaster. We got more copies back than we put out. The covers were lovely; they were really beautiful. They weren't exactly right for the books, but they were sweet and nice. It was a total disaster. And I thought, well, chalk that one up. But I never give up. I've done books as often as four times. I just never give up. I knew there was an audience for these books, because my passion for them is so strong—and I read them every time I have a cold. So I thought, well, another time. I kept my eye on them. They were such a failure for NAL that they let the rights go immediately, and I was then at Popular Library.

I picked up the rights quickly, including the hardcover rights. So, I look around New York for a patsy to do it in hardcover. I romanced every hardcover editor I knew. And I finally found a wonderful fellow at T. Y. Crowell named Nick Ellison. I took him to many expensive lunches and fed him a lot of booze at CBS's expense. He was having me on, pretending, although he liked the books. Finally he said to me, at the last lunch at the Four Seasons, which cost a lot of money, "You know, Pat, I work for this tough guy named Lou Gillinson, and if you think he's gonna let me publish a six-volume novel"—I wanted them to do 'em in one volume—"by the faggot son of the Archbishop of Canterbury about English country life, you're crazy." Then I lied—and I don't lie because it's bad for the digestion and my analyst told me it was bad for everything—I said, "But what are you going to do when these books appear on 'Masterpiece Theatre'?" He said, "Masterpiece Theatre!"—the magic words in the paperback book industry—"Jesus Christ!"

He went back to his meeting, and of course they said, "Yes! yes! Stop the presses!" The book was published, I think for $16.95, and was called *Make Way for Lucia*—a title I stole from a John Van Druten play; John Van Druten had written a play once with Isabel Jeans and Cyril Ritchard—and got front page in the *New York Times Book Review*. Mr. Ellison's first front page. Lead review *Time, Newsweek*, and so forth. One person, Bill Cole at *Saturday Review*, said, "Well, the only reason these terrible books are being published is because they're going to be on 'Masterpiece Theatre.'" And everybody mentioned "Masterpiece Theatre" and every time I saw "Masterpiece Theatre" I crawled under the desk. I just couldn't bear that this lie was following me around. So I owned the paperback rights for no money. And it was a big smash. And I'm sitting at my desk one day in a meeting and my secretary, Mary Ployard—wonderful woman, hip to everything—called and said, "Well, Patrick, it's 'Masterpiece Theatre' on the air for you." The woman said, "Mr. O'Connor, we have traced this lie to you." She was right about that, and you know how people are

when they get caught in a lie. They tell another lie. I was so embarrassed, felt so awful about it. I just mumbled something. She gave it to me pretty good for a while, and then after about ten minutes, she let me off the hook and laughed. She said, "Well, Mr. O'Connor, now that these books have been brought to our attention, we're quite interested." That was a long time ago. At any rate, the books were a success—so successful at that time I called up the agent to see if I could do them again. This would make, like, the fourth time. And she said, no, that T. Y. Crowell had kept the rights and they were now at Harper, and Harper was doing them.

I have this wonderful letter from Auden that says, see there . . .

DLB: "Dear Mr. O'Connor: As a devoted Lucia fan for many years, you can imagine how delighted I am to see that they are now going to be available at a cheap price. Thank you so much. Yours sincerely, W. H. Auden." The letter is dated 30 November 1976.

O'CONNOR: Yes. So that's why I left being a television producer. And that's why I love the paperback book industry. I don't know if that explains why I like it. But I love it. I was born for paperback. I like those numbers. When I do books I like, I like to think of them out there at all those airports.

DLB: You're a literary populist.

O'CONNOR: I think I am a populist. Yes, I am a populist. I worked for a woman of limited imagination who said, "Everybody knows the reason we're in the book business, so that we get paid to read." I thought, "Nope. I am in the book business so I can give books away." And that's the truth of it. That's how I feel. My real aim is to get people to read. I am not a proselytizer or a propagandist. I'm not out to get them to read things that will be good for them, politically and so forth. I want to get them to read things that give them pleasure. And I make that distinction. I am very clear about what I am doing. There are pleasures on all levels. There's Henry James and there's Helen van Slyke.

DLB: As far as the great world is concerned, the folks out there, you're perfectly happy to practice segregation. For the people who read schlock and only schlock, you publish schlock.

O'CONNOR: Not anymore. But for many years, lots. Lots.

DLB: For better readers, you publish better books.

O'CONNOR: Yeah, right.

DLB: And you don't regard these as overlapping markets?

O'CONNOR: I guess I really don't. I once did and I don't. I don't see that there is an overlapping market. In my own personal experience with the people I know—my family, etc.—who are readers, I know almost no one who moves from what I consider one to the other. My own experience is that I am able to read women's fiction with absolute ease because that is what I grew up on. Those were the books in our house; that's what I read. And I moved—theoretically, I hate that kind of elitist talk—from Faith Baldwin to Djuna Barnes, Henry James, whatever you want. I moved myself. I started with Hemingway and Fitzgerald and Wolfe. For someone from my generation, that's it. Those were the three. And then the Russians. I went right through the Russians. And then you begin to branch out. Then once that foundation was laid—Americans and Russians—I read all the others. Four years in the army, that's what did it. I guess I am a populist—what I resent is black women on the subway with nothing to read. They're reading Harold Robbins. Nothing wrong with reading Harold Robbins. It just makes me crazy when I see them reading these books, and I know that there's nothing for them to read. Because black writers do not write—for the most part—commercial fiction. Black writers have didactic messages. And there's this black woman on the subway, and what is she reading? There should be something for her to read. Really. And I don't mean Jimmy Baldwin or John Williams.

DLB: You'd be happy then, to provide them with a black Helen van Slyke novel?

O'CONNOR: You bet I would. It would be a dream of my life come true. I don't know what that says about me at all. But I see them every day on the subway, and I say, "Ah, there must be somebody to write a book for these women." The whole process is so complicated it boggles the mind. It has to be written. It has to be published. It has to be placed where they can buy it. All of those things are just too complicated to even think about. But we do it with white women. I've tried, by the way. I did a black nurse series. It didn't succeed. Why shouldn't little twelve-year-old black girls have books with role models in them? Why not? I don't know what that's all about, but that's how I feel.

DLB: Let's go back to the roll call of the "class" authors you have published and republished?

O'CONNOR: Yeah. Anne Tyler. Benson. P. D. James I think is a very classy one. Dorothy Richardson. Doris Lessing. Margaret Atwood. Anne Beattie was one of our big enthusiasms. I first read her in the *New Yorker.* I thought she was possibly going to be the voice of the 1970s, of the '80s. It seemed a distinctive new voice. The kids, the young editors in the shop liked her. It wasn't a big deal. We bought her cheaply. Anne Tyler was a personal favorite of mine. Margaret Atwood I started publishing in 1970. One of the best books I ever did was *Willo,* by Karen Snow. Judith Rossner. I published two of her books before she achieved any notability. Margaret Drabble I've always liked. I'm very proud of having published the three novels by Stevie Smith. They were published at Pinnacle for the first time in paperback. P. D. James was a project of Sheila Levine at Popular Library. Sheila thought she was a superior mystery writer. She brought them in. We all read them. We all liked them. There were no secrets involved. Instead of concentrating on what we would sell in big quantities, we all there at Popular—Sheila Levine, Dudley Frazier, Karen Solem, Kate Duffy—we all read books to our own tastes. That is to say, books that we might buy for ourselves. And occasionally, once or twice a month, we would do these books. It seems like a big deal now, because these books are still in print. Warner Books has bought Popular Library, and the books keep coming up for reprint. They found their market. That's all.

The most outrageous series for books which I did with Sheila Levine was *Pilgrimage* by Dorothy Richardson. I mean that really was an outrageous piece of mass-market paperback. Joyce Johnson said to me, "Boy, I knew you did good books, but when I saw you were doing Dorothy Richardson I thought, well, that man has really lost his mind." There are many mass markets. I have all kinds of friends and all kinds of relatives. They have all kinds of tastes. There is Helen van Slyke to Dorothy Richardson. And I would think that I have sense enough to fill those needs. You can't do it by being an elitist. You can't do it by being commercial. You have to be wider, broader. Also your own tastes have to enter into it. You must be one of that audience. Otherwise it doesn't work. Otherwise the fire goes out. And you might as well be manufacturing wickets.

DLB: So far, with the exception of Benson, they were all women. Is that the effect of your early reading of women's fiction?

O'CONNOR: That's right, the early reading of Kathleen Norris, Faith Baldwin, Ursula Parrott, Margaret Culkin Banning, and I could just reel them right off. My Aunt Rosella was a shop girl. She brought five books a week from the library, and I read everything in the children's section at Braddock Public Library, oldest library in the country. That's what I read, from about seven to fourteen. That's not so odd. I've met one or two who've had the same experience. I read the books that came into the house. And there were no books available in that town, in the Depression. There were no books. There was the juvenile section of the library and there was Faith Baldwin. Olive Higgins Prouty. I think I thwarted my psychological development. But that's OK.

DLB: Speaking of getting books to the people, there are many people in the book world who feel that the Walden and Dalton chains are the worst thing that's happened to American publishing and American literature in a long, long time.

O'CONNOR: Well, you know, it's good and bad. There are stores where there were never stores before. There are bookstores where there were never bookstores before.

DLB: People who never set foot in a bookstore before in their lives now set foot in one because it's in the shopping mall.

O'CONNOR: That's right.

DLB: But when they get in there . . .

O'CONNOR: You can get anything you want there. You have to be a little aggressive about it, that's all.

DLB: You feel, then, that because they make books available where books were not available, they're performing a valuable service.

O'CONNOR: That's their service. The romantic idea of the mom and pop bookshop, the cute little mom and pop bookshop—Parnassus-on-Wheels—is a myth. There was no little bookshop in my town or any town of the fifty towns that I knew surrounding Pittsburgh. There are booksellers, but if people think there are bookshops in every town in America, they're wrong. There just aren't. I never saw

Award given to Patrick O'Connor in recognition of literary quality in mass-market publishing

one. I never saw a bookshop until I was fourteen years old and could go downtown on a streetcar to Kaufmann's Department Store. Kaufmann's, Hornes, Gimbels had book departments. That's where I spent Saturdays, all day. I still know those ladies. I used to go there early in the morning and they let me hang out there when I was fourteen. They let me sit in corners and read books. It was wonderful. And I still know those ladies. I see them at the American Booksellers Association Meetings.

I'm not knocking booksellers either. I just mean that the idea that there's one everywhere is wrong. It's that whole problem of elitism. I never resolved that for myself, in my head. I have such a strong esthetic bias in other arts—in the theater, in dance, in music, and so forth. What do you call it? Antididactic? I don't object to Jane Fonda's politics. The fact that she's an actress and telling me what to do! I don't even listen to George Keenan, for Christ's sake.

I don't want anybody telling me what to do. So, I don't think that I have the right to tell people what to read. I think I have the right to try to get it out there. And this isn't true because I'm always saying, "You must read this." My whole life. "You must read this or I'll never speak to you again." Or, "We can't be friends unless you've read this book."

DLB: Who were some of your author discoveries?

O'CONNOR: Well, I really feel that I discovered Helen van Slyke. There was a joint effort with a guy named Larry Ashmead at Harper. *He* discovered her and I really put her on the map, through my faith in her ability to write this kind of Fannie Hurst novel. Which she did happen to do better than anybody else.

DLB: Who have you pulled out of the slush pile?

O'CONNOR: When I went to work for Pinnacle Books the previous Editor in Chief Andy Ettinger had neglected the slush pile—the unsolicited manuscripts—for about a year, so there was a room full of them. I mean an absolute bloody room full. What you do when you are confronted with hundreds of manuscripts is hire a recent graduate student or a current graduate student or a recent graduate to come in and work for slave wages, read through and look for anything that might be likely. I hired a young man, and he came in and read through a lot of stuff. What we do in a case like this is, if there is anything worthwhile the reader will write a report and give it to an editor or an editor in chief or in this case me, the editorial director; and I take it home and have a look at it. To see, number one, if it's a new reader, to see if he's right and I agree with him. We're always looking for material. After a few days of going through the stuff, he brought me three manuscripts with three reports, and I took them home that night and I read all of the reports. One of the reports was a bad report, which seemed odd, but I read the manuscript anyway, and I was crazy about it. It was an homage to Hammett, the way so many first novels are. Why shouldn't first novelists write homages to Hammett? But I liked it. It was tough. The writer obviously knew what he was talking about. It was a good book. The next day I brought the report and the manuscript to the kid. I shouldn't call him a kid, but he was young. I said, "Look, I don't understand your report, but I like the manuscript. I want to buy it." There was a lot of hemming and hawing, pulling at his hair, blushing, and so forth. Then I realized that it was his manuscript that he had submitted, his novel. And I thought that I had been had, but I had been had in a charming way, so I agreed to publish his book. It was called *Tough Luck LA.* His name was Murray Sinclair, and eventually it went on to be

nominated for one of the best first paperback mysteries of the year.

At any rate, three days later he's still reading through this slush, and he comes to my office, very much as I did when I was a young editor and as I still do, waving this manuscript at me, "Oh, Mr. O'Connor, this is the best thing I've read in years." "Wait a minute, kid, I already have one of your books. One a year is plenty." "No, no, it is really wonderful." That day I was taking him out to lunch to celebrate the fact that we were doing his book. All during the lunch, uncharacteristically, for an author, he talked about this other book. I said I would read it that night. That night I had a very important business late meeting, ten o'clock in the evening, with an important writer. I took this manuscript home and started to read it. After about forty pages I thought I was being had because what happens in the book business is that often prisoners will type a published book—that is, they will type *Gone With the Wind* or a novel by Jersey Kozinsky. They type it and send it to you as an original work. Here I was reading this manuscript and I thought, somebody has discovered a novel by James M. Cain that I didn't know, and they typed it up and they sent it to me. Then I realized that this was an original piece because it was quite up-to-date, and there were some things in it that convinced me that it was genuine. In addition to which, I thought it was not only the best book I had ever read from the slush pile, but one of the best books I had read in years. The first page of the typescript was the name of the author. You remember from *Catcher in the Rye* when Holden Caufield read a book that he liked he wanted to call up the writer. I had the same feeling. I wanted to call up the writer; besides, it was a local call. It's a very unprofessional thing to do because if you are going to buy a book on Monday morning you shouldn't be calling the writer at eight o'clock on Friday night telling him what a wonderful book he's written. You should be cool. But I couldn't resist and I made the phone call. I said, "Mr. Petievich?" He said, "Yes." "My name is Pat O'Connor, the editor in chief of Pinnacle Books. I've just read your novel. Terrific." I could hear the hand going over the receiver, the guy shouting at somebody, "Hey, the guy really likes my book!" I said, "May I ask what you do for a living?" He said, "I'm a Secret Service man." I said, "Should you be telling me that?" He said, "Yeah." I said, "May I ask you where you learned to write, Mr. Petievich?" "I took every creative writing course in Southern California. It's all bullshit." I said, "Mr. Petievich, are you Serbian?" He got very defensive, "How do you know I'm Serbian?" he asked. I said,

"I happen to know a lot about the Serbs." He said, "Does this mean you want to buy the book?" I said, "Yeah." He said, "I'll be in your office seven o'clock Monday morning." I said, "Try nine."

I went off to meet Don Pendleton, the author of *The Executioner*. Monday morning at nine o'clock I get a call from Mr. Petievich, who said, "I'm bringing my agent." Now, in the course of thinking about this book, Mr. Petievich's book, I was really profoundly excited at the prospect of publishing this great new writer. I had also said to myself—I don't cheat people and I don't double-deal and I'm not dishonest. We really must treat this man with the utmost delicacy and respect. I must make sure that he gets everything that's coming to him. I went through all these things in my head, just to keep myself honest. I said, I want to have a long and satisfying business relationship with this man. I thought that I would behave as though he had quite a good agent, so that in later years he wouldn't say to me, you cheated me or you did this or you did that. I

One of publisher O'Connor's favorites, from the "Lucia books"

was going to treat him as straight as I could. At nine o'clock in the morning the phone rings. Mr. Petievich on the line says, "I'm bringing my agent." Friday night he not only hadn't mentioned an agent, I didn't think he knew what an agent was. In my head I figured, I bet he called up a friend at the Los Angeles Police Department and asked for Joseph Wambaugh's agent, and he showed up on Monday morning with Wambaugh's lawyer. I really got mad. I got mad because I had psyched myself up to treat this man with great respect, and then he brings a lawyer along with him. But in the end we bought not only the book I had read, but two more. I did the impossible: I sold two of the books to Harcourt Brace Jovanovich for hardcover publication before paperback. And Petievich has gone on to get wonderful reviews. His first book is now being filmed. It's taken a while, three or four years, but he's going to make his mark as an important writer of American fiction.

DLB: Where is paperback publishing going?

O'CONNOR: Diverse. The commercial fiction is going to be done in trade paperback, as trade paperback originals. There's going to be a whole range of paper. It's all going to be paper. I think the hardcover is going to go back to doing what they're doing best—important publishing. I really do. They needed sort of a goose and they seem to have gotten it. Lots of wonderful books being published. Let me tell you a story. My assistant, as assistants do, fell in love with this book called *Our House in the Last World* by Oscar Hijuelos. I took the book home and it was on my night table for three weeks. And then all over New York I began to see these ads in the subways and the buses for this book, *Our House in the Last World* published by Persea Books. A distinguished novel, literary novel. The first Cuban immigrant novel. Terrific. Persea Books is a company that's barely meeting its payroll. Nice, really nice people, idealistic, terrific, but how can they afford a $100,000 New York bus and subway campaign? As soon as I saw it, I started to read the book. I was crazy about it. I bought it for a small price which would not have paid for one subway ad. The author wanted to have lunch, so somebody arranged it. He was a nice Cuban from 106th Street and Broadway. Wonderful writer and seemed to be OK, but I thought, "I wonder what this guy does for a living?" Because you can't make any money on a $1,000 advance. So I finally said to him—it was getting towards the end of the lunch, and I always want to know what people do for a living because then I want to tell them not to give up their daytime job—I said, "Mr. Hijuelos, what do you do for a living?" He said, "I work for Transit Ads." What a sweetheart. So, we're going to get another $200,000 worth of free advertising when his paperback comes out.

DLB: Tell me about the list of books you still want to publish.

O'CONNOR: I want to publish *Nightwood* by Djuna Barnes in mass-market paperback. That is a very important book for me. I think it's a great novel and one of the great novels of the twentieth century. And she'd never allow it to be in paperback. Ever. She was a very strange and difficult woman. I don't know whether the T. S. Eliot introduction would still help it or not. Yeah, that I'd really like to do.

DLB: What else is on your list?

O'CONNOR: Anthony Powell. I'd like to do *A Dance to the Music of Time.*

DLB: The whole cycle?

O'CONNOR: Yeah, well, I did it once at Popular and now I'd like to do it again.

DLB: How did it do?

O'CONNOR: It didn't do badly. And I did all the Peter De Vries books at Popular, too. That was nice. Wonderful books. And I'd like to do a mass-market paperback of the collected Cavafy. C. P. Cavafy was an Alexandrian Greek poet who died in the 1930s, one of the most important poets of the twentieth century. Premodern, one might say. Pre-Wallace Stevens. E. M. Forster has translated some of his poetry. A chapter in one of his books is about Cavafy. And Cavafy is a character in Lawrence Durrell's *Alexandria Quartet.* Cavafy is a figure called "the poet."
    I'm proudest of doing the Denby books. I've done them twice, for the good of the republic and certainly not for the good of the company. Edwin Denby, the great art critic—the dance critic too, but a great art critic. I don't believe in critics much, but he was an exception to the rule. *Looking at the Dance* and *Dancers, Buildings and People in the Street.* I did them twice in paperback and now I've lost the rights.

DLB: What about the ones who got away? The books that you had a chance to do, didn't, and wish you had?

O'CONNOR: Le Carré was the one that I missed. And then I became a fan later. I don't know how that happens. I read *The Spy Who Came In From the Cold* and I said, "Nobody's gonna understand this book. I mean *nobody.* And certainly no American is going to read it." Then I became a fan later and went back and read it again and I thought, "How could you have been such an idiot? You must have been hungover or crazy." It does happen sometimes.

DLB: What are the rewards in publishing?

O'CONNOR: Seeing those books on the stands. The rewards are giving books away—meaning, making them available. People came up to me in tears and said, "I understand that you were responsible for the Lucia books." The Lucia books are silly books, you know; you must understand that—but there's something so powerful about them. I gave them to a friend named Alec Wilder, a composer, in 1968. After he read them for the first time, he said, "Well, I really don't know how to thank you because I never have to read another book as long as I live. All of life's wisdom is contained in these books, like the Bible." So he read them; he never stopped reading them. He read them until he died, for the next twelve, fifteen years.

DLB: What do you spend most of your days doing? People think you spend most of your time reading.

O'CONNOR: I spend most of my time on the phone, talking to subsidiary rights people.

DLB: You've been in publishing how many years?

O'CONNOR: Twenty-four.

DLB: How many titles have you published in twenty-four years?

O'CONNOR: Five thousand? Hard to say. Once at Pinnacle I was doing twenty-five a month. Once at Popular twenty-two a month. Once at Curtis eight a month. It's hard to say.

DLB: What is the big difference between a paperback editor and a cloth editor?

O'CONNOR: A paperback editor is a merchandiser.

He is somebody who sees in a hardcover book, mostly hardcover books, the market value of the book and how it should be done and why it will do well. It's a merchandising job. I once met a woman at a party and she asked me what I did. And I told her *specifically*. She said, "I want to know specifics," and I told her. She said, "You're not an editor at all. You're a merchandiser. You're like a buyer at a department store. You buy and sell." I said, "That's right. Don't tell anybody." She said, "Why do you call yourself an editor?" I said, "Sounds better." We're merchandisers. We're merchandisers who deal with books. So I'm a merchandiser who deals with that product with which I want to deal, I could've made a lot more money merchandising almost anything else, but I choose to do books because every month a box comes in and I'm responsible in some way—sometimes a small way, sometimes a big way—for this book.

DLB: Who are the other good merchandisers?

O'CONNOR: Don Fine was one of the best. And Jim Bryans at Popular Library was good. There's a whole generation of ex-paperback people. Knox Burger was a great paperback editor. He was really an editor because he did a line of original books called Gold Medal. The first generation of paperback editors came out of men's action/adventure magazines. They came from *True* and *Argosy.* And the subsidiary rights directors of the hardcover houses, the first ones, those ladies—there was a whole group of them—who were the secretaries of the presidents of companies and went on to prove a point about women's liberation, went on to be powerful women in the book industry, who thought that they were going to spend their lives being secretaries. And how it happened—I make this up, but I know that it would happen this way—is when Herb Alexander called up the president of whoever published *Lost Horizon* in hardcover and said, "We would like the paperback rights to *Lost Horizon.*" The president of that company said to his secretary, "Sweetheart, honey, you handle that." And all those women then became important executives. A whole group of them. I remember them well. I got in the paperback industry just as that first generation was peaking. It was '60.

DLB: What about the prices of paperbacks—$3.50, $3.95?

O'CONNOR: They're outrageous and that's because of paper and printing prices. Writers aren't getting

all the money. Editors aren't getting any more money.

DLB: The writers are getting more money. They're getting a percentage based on $3.50 instead of a percentage based on fifty cents.

O'CONNOR: The writers aren't getting any more. Many people are still paying the same advances they were paying in 1960.

DLB: It's all printing and paper?

O'CONNOR: I think so. Printing and paper and transportation.

DLB: A lot of people are saying that paperbacks are going to price themselves right out of business. That the kinds of people who buy paperbacks for, let's just call it recreational reading, aren't going to buy their five, six romances a week at $3.50 and $4.00.

O'CONNOR: Maybe not. I had friends who would buy three, four, five mysteries for the weekend. And I know they don't do that every week. That's probably right. That's sad, but they don't. I don't know what is going to be done about it.

DLB: Prices can't come down?

O'CONNOR: No, prices can't come down. I don't think so.

DLB: And that price for most paperbacks doesn't include a cushion factor for all the wrong guesses at auctions?

O'CONNOR: No, I don't think so. No. It's too close to the edge of loss for there to be any cushion.

DLB: What about the paperback originals, which rarely get reviewed? How do they reach a readership?

O'CONNOR: This is what happened to a book that was very close to my heart. I'm from a small town outside of Pittsburgh, Braddock, Pennsylvania. About ten years ago, or maybe fifteen, I started getting some short stories, poems, and fragments from a steel worker in Braddock. Because he was from my hometown I wrote little notes on the side—this is good, this is bad, try this, try that—just to encourage him. This is a steel worker—not a student, a

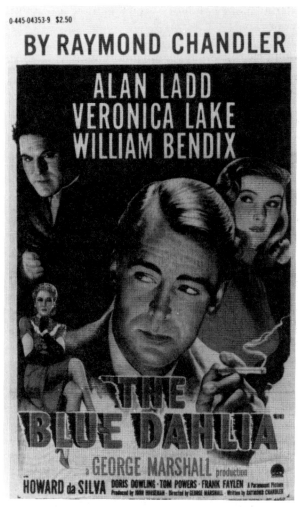

0-445-04353-9 $2.50

BY RAYMOND CHANDLER

ALAN LADD
VERONICA LAKE
WILLIAM BENDIX

THE BLUE DAHLIA

a GEORGE MARSHALL production

HOWARD da SILVA · DORIS DOWLING · TOM POWERS · FRANK FAYLEN A Paramount Picture
Produced by JOHN HOUSEMAN · Directed by GEORGE MARSHALL · Written by RAYMOND CHANDLER

Front cover for Raymond Chandler screenplay published by Patrick O'Connor as part of the Popular Library Screenplay Series

steel worker. Over the years we had never met. I didn't know who he was. Never talked on the phone. Finally, this gentleman wrote a novel. I liked it. It was primitive. It was unsophisticated, but I liked it. It had a certain raw power. I decided to do it. I found a title for it, *No Place to Go But Home*. Put Al Pacino's picture on the cover. There was a galley. The guy was happy; his book was being published. Everything was fine.

Then the president of Pinnacle books said, "We're canceling this book. We don't have any orders." I said, "You can't cancel that book. This guy has worked his whole life." "We're canceling it. There are no orders for this book." He wasn't being hostile. He regretted as much as I did that the book was being canceled. But there were no orders from the salesmen. They took the cover out to the local buyers, and the buyers didn't buy it. The writer's name was Carmen Caratazzo. I put off calling him for a number of days, as you can guess. And finally he was on the phone. I said, "Carmen, they've canceled your book." Notice I said "they." He said, "What do you mean, they've canceled my book?" I said, "They're not going to publish your book here They've canceled it." "No, they ain't. They ain't canceling my book. They're not making an asshole of me. I've been writing this book for years. I told the guys in the mill. I told the guys in the bar. The guys in the street. I told my family. I told the priest—I don't even go to church—I told the priest I'm going to be published. No New York publisher's going to make an asshole out of me. They'll call me a liar. They'll think I'm a bullshitter. You ain't doing that to me." I said, "I don't know what to say, Carmen. I'm afraid that's what's going to happen." He said, "What's the name of the president of your company." I said, "Stanley Reisner." He said, "Tell him I'm going to come to New York on Friday. I'm going to kill him." He said something else. I've heard it three different times in my life, but I can never get it quite right. It's when an Italian tells you that he's going to perform an act of violence, and that he's doing it alone—that he's not connected with a group of any kind. That's what Carmen said at that point. Then he said, "If you think I'm bullshitting you, then you ain't from this town, and you don't know where my head is." Well, I'm from that town and I know where his head is. I go into Mr. Reisner's office. I said "Stanley, Carmen Caratazzo is coming to New York on Friday, and he's going to kill you." Stanley's reaction was the reaction of every middle-class Jew to every situation. He said, "I think I'll go to Miami."

I get on the stick, on the phone, and I call in my western Pennsylvania markers. Now, I don't have any. I left there when I was eighteen, so I don't know anybody there. But I called. Kaufmann's, Gimbels, Hornes, the local wholesaler in Mckeesport. I just combed the area. I said, "Please buy this book. You don't have to sell it, you can return it. But please buy it." After a day of hard selling on the phone, I run down to the president's office, and I say, "Look, I have 15,000 orders." Fifteen thousand orders doesn't mean anything, and it's certainly peanuts in the paperback business. He said, "Okay. I don't want to hear about this book again. We'll do the book." I called Mr. Caratazzo up and told him that we were going to do the book. He was quite happy. When I came back from lunch on Friday, sitting in my secretary's office was Mr. Caratazzo. Mr. Caratazzo is not a tall man, but he is a tough man. And he looks like a bull, with hands that could strangle a bull. I walk in and he puts his arms around me in the wonderful Italian way, crushes me to his bosom; and, of course, I could feel the gun that he was going to use to kill Mr. Reisner.

The *Publishers Weekly* review came in, and it was terrific. So we were all quite happy. Mr. Caratazzo became a celebrity in Pittsburgh for about fifteen minutes. He was front page, second section, above the centerfold. Television. The book was on sale. Two months later Mr. Caratazzo called with the usual question, "Hey, Patrick, there are no books in the stores?" I said, "That's it, sweetheart. There won't be any more. You had your best shot. You had my best shot. We did the best we could." But I got Mr. Carmen Caratazzo's book published.

The Practice of Biography III

AN INTERVIEW
with HUMPHREY CARPENTER

Humphrey Carpenter became a biographer after working for seven years as a producer and broadcaster for the BBC. His books include *A Thames Companion* (with his wife, Mari Pritchard, 1975); *Tolkien: A Biography* (1977); *The Inklings: C. S. Lewis, J. R. R. Tolkien, Charles Williams, and Their Friends* (1978); *Jesus* (1980); *W. H. Auden: A Biography* (1981); and *The Oxford Companion to Children's Literature* (with Mari Pritchard, 1984). He has also edited, with Christopher Tolkien, *The Letters of J. R. R. Tolkien* (1981) and has written several books for young readers.

DLB: The same kind of curiosity that got you into trouble as a child for peeking into other people's bureaus and letters has served you in a positive way as a biographer. Besides curiosity, what do you consider the major requisites for writing about other people's lives?

CARPENTER: I suppose *empathy* is the best word for what I consider the most important quality for a biographer, though it's an overworked term these days. I mean one's got to have almost a sixth sense about them and their character. Or at least you've got to *believe* that you've got it. I think I first realized that when I read Lord David Cecil's brilliant life of Cowper, *The Stricken Deer*, published about fifty-five years ago, because it was the first biography I'd ever come across in which the author simply assumed that he knew what was going on in his subject's head. One can't know that, of course. And it can easily become an affectation to pretend that one does. But when researching for a biography you've got to soak yourself in the writings and other relics of your subject to the extent that you really feel you know what he would have done in any given circumstance, you really feel you're inside his head.

That's not the only way to write a biography, and it has its dangers. There's a lot to be said for the cool, objective, critical stance. But it's not one that I myself find I can take. I have to be *mimetic* rather than critical. I have to play the part of my subject, like an actor taking on a role. I think, incidentally, that this was how Dickens created his characters. He just got up on a kind of private, interior stage and performed the parts to himself. And I find myself playing at being Auden, or Tolkien, or Pound, or whoever it is.

DLB: Your subjects have come mostly from the same time period, beginning with J. R. R. Tolkien and going on to W. H. Auden, Christopher Isherwood, Stephen Spender, C. S. Lewis, Charles Williams, and now Ezra Pound. Were you especially interested in the twentieth-century British writers or was it happenstance?

CARPENTER: The time period thing was accidental at first. I wrote the Tolkien life because I'd known him, and I was brought up in Oxford where he lives, and I knew many of his friends. And after that it was natural to write about Lewis. Only when it came to the Auden book did I realize that I was "specializing" in twentieth-century literary figures, particularly around the 1930s. It really could have worked out quite differently. My first piece of biography was a play about Father Ignatius, a Victorian would-be monk who set up a cranky monastery in South Wales, and Victoriana was an early love

Humphrey Carpenter (© Tara Heinemann)

with me. But in fact I suppose I have certain qualifications for the 1930s and the decades surrounding it. I was brought up just a little after it—the 1950s—and close enough to it to be aware of its tone and character. Particularly I feel I know what the 1930s were like in Oxford. (It hadn't changed much there in the '50s!) And it's not a long step from that to feeling one understands the decade as a whole. I love almost all '30s fiction, and most of its poetry, and really I'd like to have lived then, on that odd ridge between the peaks of the two world wars. A wonderful decade. I adore '30s jazz and dance music too.

DLB: How do you know when a subject is right for you?

CARPENTER: A subject feels "right" if, for a start, you're convinced people are going to want to read and buy the book! I am after all first and foremost somebody trying to make a living out of full-time authorship, and that really is the primary concern. It's astonishing how often publishers suggest lives of people who really command very little public attention. After that, I suppose a major consideration is that one should be able to make oneself enjoy one's subject's writing. But really, you know, I'd rather work on a life of someone thoroughly *difficult* like Pound, for whom I have no particular feel-

ing at the outset, than an author I'm really already wildly enthusiastic about. Somehow I feel that to write about one of my own favorites would be a soft option.

DLB: What do you feel the biographer owes his readers? And is there ever a conflict between his obligation to his readers and his obligation to the subject?

CARPENTER: The chief thing the biographer owes his reader is what any writer owes readers—to keep them stimulated all the time. Too many biographies are too boring too often. A biography is primarily a piece of writing, and must be treated as such. After that, I don't think there are any other considerations. I certainly don't feel the biographer "owes" his readers any particular revelations about his subject. Biography these days is such a mass industry that it seems to be accepted, even by an outstanding practitioner like Michael Holroyd, that the reading public has the right to know this or that about the subject. I don't think anyone has any right to know anything. The whole thing is in the end a fairly inexcusable trampling on the subject's privacy. The only thing that can excuse it is the skill of the book. If you've produced a biography that is "true" in the sense that great novels or poems are, then the whole thing has been justified. Of course most of the time one doesn't manage that. Only occasionally, or in flashes.

I don't, on the other hand, think the biographer has any particular obligation to his subject. I think there *are* obligations to living people—children, wives, mistresses—though that rather depends on how they behave to you! If they help you, then you incur an obligation to try and write something acceptable to them. Which can hamstring you a lot. On the other hand if they are obstructive, or just take no part in the whole thing, you perhaps don't feel so obliged to them. But really I hate all this aspect of it. It reveals that, at its lowest, biography is really just gutter journalism tarted up between hard covers. As I've just said, a biography really has to be extremely good to justify the dubious morality of the whole thing.

DLB: You came to biography from a seven-year stint as a producer and broadcaster for BBC. Did that work in any way shape your approach to writing biography?

CARPENTER: My years as a broadcaster and producer were immensely valuable. They taught me how to communicate clearly and to the point, and entertainingly. Writing for radio is quite an art—short sentences, quite a lot of repetition, quite slangy expressions. Everything you're taught not to do at school or university. And really you *should* do it if you're going to keep your reader's attention. The writer who really taught me this was C. S. Lewis. He says all these things somewhere. And you can see them exemplified in his own books, particularly his broadcast talks. So radio work was a far more useful training for me than I think academic life would have been.

DLB: What have you found to be the greatest problems in writing biography?

CARPENTER: I don't actually find any great problems in *writing* biography. The writing is the fun part. You spend months assembling huge amounts of information, and then just to sit back at the typewriter and let it all sort itself out onto the paper is gorgeous. If I've done my preparatory work properly I find it almost as effortless as reading someone else's book. The problems come at the research stage, when you can't find an answer to some problem, or certain papers prove to be inaccessible. Mind you, that kind of thing worries me less and less now. There are always lacunae, always some things you can't answer. They don't mar the

book providing you make a clean breast of your ignorance to the reader.

DLB: Are biographers treated fairly by reviewers?

CARPENTER: No, reviewers usually do a naughty thing, which is to write a potted life of the subject themselves, and then devote their final line and a half for praising or damning the actual biography—from which, of course, they've plundered all their information! Very few reviews of biographies actually review the book rather than its subject.

DLB: In *The Inklings* you did a collective biography, dealing primarily with C. S. Lewis, J. R. R. Tolkien, and Charles Williams. What are the advantages of writing that kind of book over writing the sort that concentrates on one figure?

CARPENTER: Collective biographies are fun, but you've got to have a shape, a framework for them. *The Inklings* was fairly easy; I've sometimes considered other "collective" subjects, groups of writers and so on, but have realized that the story would have no obvious dramatic shape. I am going to tackle another soon—an attempt (by no means the first!) to portray the various generations of American literary exiles in Paris, particularly, of course, the Lost Generation of the 1920s. Shape and pace of narrative will certainly be a problem there.

DLB: The exception so far to your having twentieth-century British writers as subjects (not to argue the point of whether Lewis is to be considered British or American) is in the little "biography" of Jesus you wrote for Hill and Wang's Past Masters series. How did that book come about, and how did you deal with the obvious difficulties?

CARPENTER: The Jesus book was done at the invitation of Henry Hardy of Oxford University Press, who created the Past Masters series. I found it immensely exciting, as I was brought up in a Church of England family (my father was a bishop) and then had recently exposed myself to the fundamentalist dogmatism of C. S. Lewis and the seductive theology of Charles Williams. This was the chance to look at the raw material for myself! The book that came out was, I suppose, in fact a fairly representative specimen of twentieth-century skepticism, but it had many excitements for me— not least the discovery that modern biography and the Gospels have in common a very shaky grasp on truth. By which I mean that you find the same degree of variation in the Gospels, between one account of an incident and another, as you will find if you compare (say) two present-day biographies of the same subject.

DLB: How do you feel about doing an authorized biography?

CARPENTER: The Tolkien life was an authorized biography. In a sense it's marvelous: you have a free run of the papers, and everyone feels they ought to help you. On the other hand, you incur obligations, as I've already said. You really have to toe the party line. Not that there's anything in the Tolkien book which was censored by the family, but I think I could have been more detached, and perhaps more objective, if I hadn't felt under some obligation to his family. The ideal was the Auden book, where Ed Mendelson, Auden's literary executor, gave me a complete *imprimatur* without in any way trying to dictate what I ought to write. With Pound I feel more of an outsider, partly because there's no one person who holds the key to all Pound's life and works, no one who can act as a mentor. There are lots of Pound experts, some of them in his family, but the subject is so vast that no one pretends to complete expertise. And I feel rather an outsider looking in. But this may be to the benefit of the biography, which certainly requires a good deal of detachment.

DLB: In *Dictionary of Literary Biography Yearbook 1982*, biographer Stanley Weintraub spoke of the involvement he sometimes experiences with his subject, so that "killing him off becomes like a death in one's family." How emotionally involved do you become with your subjects?

CARPENTER: I don't get involved in the way Weintraub suggests—though I admit to being moved by the death of Charles Williams in *The Inklings*, because it was so perfectly timed dramatically. No, in my experience one has to be careful not to become irritated with one's subject, having to live with him (so to speak) for so many months. I admit to having turned against Tolkien and Lewis at various stages in the books. Auden I thought was marvelous company from start to finish, despite all his awful habits or perhaps because of them. Pound is a bit different. He's intellectual company rather than emotional. And after many months of research I still don't feel I know what it would have been like to meet him. I don't think he engaged with people on the same level that one usually does. I think his rela-

tionships only occupied certain areas of the personality.

DLB: Sometimes these days we read more than we really want to know about public figures. Maybe that's why there are so few heroes. Are there areas of life that should be off limits to the biographer?

CARPENTER: If you're going to write a life there's no point in setting arbitrary bounds about propriety and what-have-you. As I've already said, the whole exercise is in a sense improper anyway. And of course you're going to reveal warts. Masses of them. But I think the strengths actually come out of the warts. Auden was essentially a *good* man—in a way that I think C. S. Lewis wasn't—though he was made up of masses of oddities, and rather nasty habits, and selfishness. He's rather like a great statue built out of bits of kitchen garbage, solidified. And he knew this. He knew he was flawed, knew he was sinful (he became a practicing Christian, remember). And somehow, at least at the best stages of his life, he managed to produce great things out of this. (Though I suppose his best poetry really comes in the early period when he was simply a creature of unguilty appetites.) So I don't think we destroy heroes by examining their warts.

DLB: You have written several books for children. How do you feel about biography written especially for children?

CARPENTER: I can't see the point of biography for children. It seems to me a fake genre. Intelligent children soon come to discover and enjoy adult biography, so they might as well wait. Watering the thing down for kids either produces irritating hagiography or reduces the subject to pure trivia. But it's not a genre I've read much in, and there may be some honorable exceptions.

DLB: What's your biggest quibble with the current practice of biography?

CARPENTER: Length. Far too many biographies are too long. We've got back to Victorian lengths again. Someone recently published an eight-hundred-page life of Edward Elgar, a composer who's scarcely been heard of outside England. The trouble is that half the readership for biographies tends to be professional academics, hungry for small details that they can use in their own research. With Pound, for example, I maybe ought to have written a terse, quite short book. On the other hand

- 5 -

remark to ▨ one of his sons: 'Most doctors are either fools or mere "doctors":
tinkerers with machinery. Havard at any rate is a Catholic who thinks of people

ib, 28/4/41 as people, not as collections of "works".'

When the light has been switched on, Warnie Lewis puts some coal on the
fire, and grumbles to Havard about the shortage of beer in Oxford - it is in

low
▨▨ supply thanks to the war, and the Bird & Baby frequently has a <u>No Beer</u> sign
on the door. 'My idea of an ideal life,' says Warnie, 'would be to buy a pub,
put up one of those <u>No Beer</u> notices, lock the customers out, and drink the stuff

Havard now myself.' The two men talk about beer for a few minutes more, Warnie referring
contemptuously to an inferior brew that he and Havard have just been drinking
at a hotel down the road - he describes it as 'varnish', the term that he and Jack
always use for bad beer.

                 fixed   **at which the Inklings meet on Thursdays**
There is no ▨▨▨ hour ▨▨▨▨▨▨▨▨▨▨▨▨▨▨▨▨▨▨, but
by general agreement people turn up any time between nine and ten-thirty. Nor is
there any formal system of membership or election, and in theory it is only
                                               particularly
necessary for one Inkling to obtain the approval of the others (▨▨▨▨ of Lewis)
before introducing somebody new. But in practice this does not happen very often,
and on most Thursdays the company consists solely of the Lewis brothers,
~~Havard has turned up regularly on Thursdays since the beginning of 1940, Williams~~
Tolkien, Havard and Williams, sometimes with the addition of Hugo
~~(of course) since he arrived in Oxford late in 1939, Jack and Warnie Lewis and~~
Dyson (who still teaches at Reading University but is often in
~~Tolkien since the Inklings began (its origins are already lost in the mists of~~
Oxford).
~~time).~~ ~~There are other who come along. Hugo Dyson turns up~~ ~~if he happens to be in Oxford~~
~~(he still lectures at~~
~~the University of Reading University),~~ ▨▨▨ Nevill Coghill used
                                         he
to be quite a regular member of the group, ~~but~~ ▨▨▨ is in great demand as a
producer of plays for the university dramatic society and other local groups,
and he is now rarely seen in Lewis's rooms on Thursday nights. He is not the only
earlier Inkling to have dropped out: Adam Fox, the Magdalen chaplain who (thanks
to the influence of Lewis and Tolkien) was elected Professor of Poetry in 1938
rarely comes now, ▨▨▨▨▨▨▨▨▨▨▨▨▨▨▨▨▨▨▨▨▨▨▨▨▨▨▨
~~There are occasional guests, ▨▨▨ once or twice Williams has~~
~~brought his Press friend Gerry ▨▨▨▨~~ Owen Barfield **very** occasionally turns up
on his visits from London, where he is still working as a solicitor, and sometimes
Charles Wrenn looks in. But for the most part *this Thursday party* ~~it~~ is a small group. A direct

Revised page from the typescript for The Inklings *(the author)*

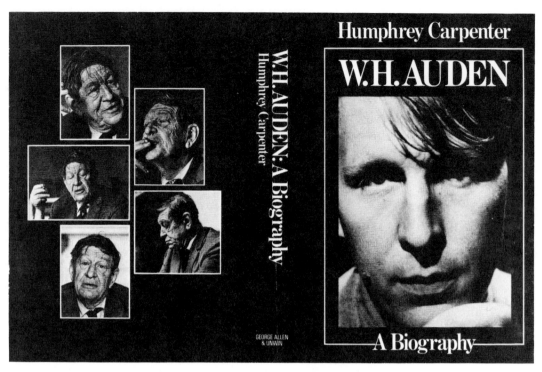

Dust jacket for biography by Humphrey Carpenter

I've gathered and collated so much sheer information that I know I shall be letting down a certain section of my readers if I don't let them have a pretty full account.

DLB: What are your all-time favorite biographies?

CARPENTER: Boswell's *Life of Johnson* is the only indisputably great biography, though there are masses of others that one finds splendidly entertaining. But something I go back to again and again is Henry James's *The Aspern Papers,* a novella *about* biography. It's amazing how James, writing in the era before the modern literary biographer had hatched himself from the egg, could anticipate a whole industry of vultures like the story's narrator, who's trying to prize some crucial papers out of the former mistress of a great poet. It's a situation that I recognize completely! Even to the Venetian setting, where Ezra Pound is concerned! And, of course, the story shows how utterly amoral the whole enterprise is.

—Jean W. Ross

Literary Research Archives III: The Lilly Library

David Warrington
Indiana University

The Lilly Library, named for the family that founded the Indianapolis pharmaceutical firm, has from its beginnings collected extensively in the fields of British and American literature. When it first opened its doors in June 1960 it housed both the private library of J. K. Lilly, Jr., which had been presented to Indiana University in 1956, and the books and manuscripts of the Indiana University Libraries Department of Special Collections, established in the 1940s by Dr. Robert A. Miller, director of the University Libraries. When the Lilly Library was formally dedicated on 3 October 1960, the collections numbered more than 75,000 books and 1,500,000 manuscripts. Since then, with the combined support of Indiana University and the Lilly Endowment, Inc. of Indianapolis, the Library has more than quadrupled the number of its books and more than tripled the number of its manuscripts.

Special collections at Indiana University date from 1914, when Librarian William E. Jenkins bought several hundred duplicates from the collection of William P. Trent of Columbia University, consisting of English history and literature published from 1689 to 1731. This purchase formed the nucleus of what was soon known as the Augustan Collection. The Library steadily added to its holdings in this field throughout the 1920s and 1930s, and in the spring of 1942 it purchased the Defoe collection, formerly owned by the Right Honourable Algernon William Stephen, fifth Earl Temple—117 bound volumes, containing 421 items, of which 128 were by Defoe and 293 were by his contemporaries. At this point, the Library found itself in possession of a first-rate collection of more than 9,000 volumes in British history and literature beginning with the events leading to the Civil War (1642-1649) and continuing through the end of Walpole's administration (1745). A serious effort to strengthen the Library's holdings for the period between the death of Defoe (1731) and the pamphlet war just prior to the American Revolution (another area of special interest) resulted in steady buying over a period of at least ten years and the acquisition of a total of approximately 7,500 more pieces printed prior to 1800. The Lilly gift and subsequent purchases, including nearly 250 pre-1750 plays, added substantially to this collection.

Josiah K. Lilly, Jr., whose 1956 gift of his personal library made the Department of Special Collections a major rare book library (The Lilly Library)

The Lilly Library has reported more than 20,000 titles to the Eighteenth Century Short-Title Catalogue, and the Defoe collection, one of the strongest in the country, figures prominently in John Robert Moore's *A Checklist of the Writings of Daniel Defoe* (Hamden, Conn: Shoe String Press, 1971).

In 1943 the Department of Special Collections acquired the William Wordsworth collection formed by Oscar L. Watkins of Indianapolis. The most important portion of this acquisition included a virtually complete collection of first editions and first appearances of poems that were published during the poet's own lifetime. Among its notable rarities are *Evening Walk* (1793), *Descriptive Sketches* (1793), and two copies of the *Lyrical Ballads* of 1798 (a third copy with the Bristol imprint was added later). Mr. Watkins sought to include everything in printed form that would be of value to the scholar's understanding of Wordsworth; because of Wordsworth's close association with Coleridge, therefore, the nucleus of a collection on Coleridge was formed containing nearly all the contemporary editions of his poetry and prose. There were likewise a large number of works of other early-nineteenth-century writers of associational interest, such as Robert Southey, Joseph Cottle, Leigh Hunt, Charles Lamb, and Walter Savage Landor. Among other contemporary volumes in the collection of special value to the scholar are the parodies and burlesques that followed in the wake of Wordsworth's publications, including Reynolds's *Peter Bell, a Lyrical Ballad* (1819) and the anonymous *Dead Asses* of the same year (a pamphlet so rare that Watkins searched forty years or more before finding it). Mr. Watkins made it a point to acquire all these pieces because of their associative interest and because of the light they throw on the contemporary reception of Wordsworth's poetry. The entire collection is described in Russell Noyes's *The Indiana Wordsworth Collection: A Catalogue* (Boston: G. K. Hall, 1978).

The gift in 1956 of the personal library of Josiah K. Lilly, Jr., transformed the Department of Special Collections almost overnight into a major rare book library. Rich in British and American literature, the Lilly gift consisted of more than 20,000 volumes and 17,000 manuscripts. Throughout his career as a book collector, Mr. Lilly attempted to gather complete collections of first editions of major authors, and although he eventually collected in other fields, most notably science and medicine, his collection of English and American literature remained the cornerstone of his library. He avoided buying author collections en bloc, preferring instead to acquire his books one by one in original condition whenever possible. Thus, his copies of the *Spectator*, Pope's *Essay on Criticism, Rape of the Lock*, and the four parts of the *Essay on Man* are all in original state, uncut, as issued, and a high proportion of his books are in the form in which they first appeared to contemporary readers.

Mr. Lilly began collecting about 1925 when he endeavored to put together complete collections of first editions of such Hoosier authors as Booth Tarkington, George Ade, Theodore Dreiser, Lew Wallace, and James Whitcomb Riley. In 1927 he decided to form a collection of Edgar Allen Poe, and by 1934, having acquired all of Poe's books in first editions, including *Tamerlane* (1827) and a presentation copy of *Tales* (1845) in original wrappers, he had brought together one of the finest Poe collections ever assembled. Meanwhile, using the Grolier Club and the A. Edward Newton "Hundred" lists as guides, he began to collect English authors. By the time his collection came to Indiana University, he had purchased all but five of the Grolier and all but one of the Newton "Hundred" (the single absentee in the latter collection being the 1865 *Alice in Wonderland*, which the Library later acquired). Mr. Lilly collected more than just "highspots," however; he formed notable collections of the works of J. M. Barrie, Robert Burns, Charles Dickens, A. Conan Doyle, John Galsworthy, Rudyard Kipling, and Walter Scott. Moreover, his continued interest in American literature led to his amassing a collection in that field that ran into thousands of volumes, including complete sets of first editions for many first-rank writers. Among the strongest of these author collections, many of which included presentation copies, manuscripts, and letters, were those for Theodore Dreiser, Ralph Waldo Emerson, Henry Wadsworth Longfellow, Edgar Allan Poe, James Whitcomb Riley, Mark Twain, Lew Wallace, and Walt Whitman. Because of Mr. Lilly's eclectic tastes (he also formed a fine collection of nineteenth-century French "firsts" in original condition), his gift brought to Indiana University one of the last of the truly great collections of American and European literature in private hands.

Shortly after the arrival of the Lilly gift, David A. Randall, manager of Scribners's Rare Book Department in New York and purveyor of many of Mr. Lilly's books, was named the first Lilly Librarian. With his broad knowledge of books, his consummate understanding of the antiquarian book trade, and his wide acquaintance with contemporary collectors, he instituted an aggressive acquisitions policy that led to a phenomenal growth in the collections.

Mr. Randall had a clear understanding of the nature of the scholarly enterprise; he realized the researcher's need to examine not only printed books but also prepublication materials—notes, drafts, proofs, and correspondence. With this in mind, he placed top priority on the acquisition of collections containing such materials, either those formed by collectors or, better yet, archives assembled by writers themselves. An example of the latter was secured shortly after Mr. Randall's arrival in Bloomington. In early 1957, he acquired the mas-

David A. Randall, first Lilly Librarian (The Lilly Library)

sive archives that Upton Sinclair had created over his sixty-year career as an author, politician, humanist, and reformer. This collection, which weighed eight tons when it was received, contained Sinclair's complete files, records, and manuscripts from 1909 on, as well as his personal library. The correspondence consisted of more than sixty thousand items, including letters from such twentieth-century figures as Eugene V. Debs, Theodore Dreiser, Albert Einstein, D. H. Lawrence, Thomas Mann, H. L. Mencken, Ezra Pound, George Bernard Shaw, Rabindranath Tagore, Leon Trotsky, and H. G. Wells. The printed materials in the collection have been described in Ronald Gottesman's *Upton Sinclair: An Annotated Checklist* (Kent, Ohio: Kent State University Press, 1973); the manuscripts in Ronald Gottesman and Charles L. P. Silet's *The Literary Manuscripts of Upton Sinclair* (Columbus: Ohio State University Press, 1972).

The Sinclair collection, which is the largest and most frequently consulted of all the Library's literary archives, has continued to grow. Mr. Randall himself added a dozen more collections of Sinclair correspondence, the most important of these containing 2,500 letters received from Viking Press and a large group of letters and documents con-

cerning his marriage to his first wife, Meta. More recently, Mr. Randall's successor and current Lilly Librarian, William R. Cagle, has added the complete correspondence of Sinclair and his publishers Charles and Albert Boni, composed of 631 letters written between 1926 and 1939.

Mr. Randall's tenure as librarian lasted nineteen years until his death in 1975. Other notable acquisitions in literature during those years included the H. Bacon Collamore collection of the works of A. E. Houseman, including books, letters, manuscripts, and proofs; the Valentine collection of Victorian fiction, especially rich in early works by Ainsworth, Borrow, Carlyle, Edgeworth, Gaskell, Hardy, Hunt, Kingsley, Bulwer-Lytton, Mary Shelley, Albert Smith, and Trollope; the collection of William Butler Yeats formed by his bibliographer, Alan Wade; the Ian Fleming collection of nineteenth-century science and thought, together with the manuscripts and the author's personal copies of the James Bond books; the Fred Bates Johnson collection of the works of Joseph Conrad (now probably the most complete collection anywhere of Conrad's printed works in bibliographical depth); and the Pete Martin collection of the works of George A. Henty, complete with all the English and American editions in their variant issues and pictorial bindings. Another important addition to the Library's nineteenth-century English literature holdings was a sizable collection of the papers of Frederick Tennyson, older brother of the laureate Alfred Tennyson and a poet in his own right. The collection included not only all known manuscripts of the elder Tennyson's poems and over 850 letters written by and to him but also editions and proof sheets of his poetry and books from his library.

This emphasis on the acquisition of large collections and archives continues. In 1977, William Cagle secured for the Library an extensive collection of Sylvia Plath's papers. Acquired from Aurelia Plath, the poet's mother, the collection includes more than 2,000 letters to and from Plath, nearly 300 poetry manuscripts, more than 50 stories and 30 articles in manuscript, her diaries, scrapbooks, drawings, and childhood memorabilia. Covering her career from youth and early efforts at publication, through high school and Smith College, to her later work, the collection also includes more than 200 books from Plath's library, many containing her own annotations.

In 1977 and 1982 the Library acquired two major collections of papers of Ezra Pound. The earlier of these acquisitions, material dating from the early 1920s obtained from the heirs of publisher

William R. Cagle, current Lilly Librarian (The Lilly Library)

William A. Bird, included Pound's translations of stories of French author Paul Morand, the publisher's file copies of Pound's *Draft of Sixteen Cantos,* and nearly two hundred letters to Pound and Bird from such major literary figures as T. S. Eliot, Ernest Hemingway, William Carlos Williams, James Joyce, George Bernard Shaw, and Nancy Cunard. The more recent addition to the Library's Pound holdings encompasses more than 11,000 letters from the estate of Pound's widow, Dorothy Shakespear Pound. The letters span the years from 1900 (a letter from William Butler Yeats to Dorothy's mother, Olivia Shakespear) to 1973, the year of Dorothy's death. They are predominantly from the period between 1946 and 1958, the years of Pound's confinement at St. Elizabeths Hospital, and the period least well documented in his biographies, but also include many letters both earlier and later. There are large numbers of letters from Basil Bunting, E. E. Cummings, Ronald Duncan, T. S. Eliot, Marianne Moore, and William Carlos Williams, as well as smaller lots from Richard

Aldington, Sylvia Beach, Paul Blackburn, Robert Creeley, Nancy Cunard, Hilda Doolittle, Ford Madox Ford, Ernest Hemingway, James Joyce, T. E. Lawrence, Wyndham Lewis, H. L. Mencken, Katherine Anne Porter, Kathleen Raine, William Butler Yeats, Louis Zukofsky, and many others. Meanwhile, the Library completed its collection of early editions of Pound's work with the acquisition of his first book, *A Lume Spento* (1908), and his even more elusive second book, *A Quinzaine for this Yule* (1908).

Scholars have pointed out the importance of publishers' records for such fields of literary research as textual study, attribution of authorship, and the appraisal of an author's reputation and influence. The Library has been fortunate to acquire over the years the records of several publishers, both British and American.

The files of Bobbs-Merrill Company, Indianapolis, were presented to the Lilly Library by the firm in the spring of 1964. These records are among the most substantial and complete of those of any major American publishing house. The files are presently arranged alphabetically by author, and most contain the following types of material:

(1) Authors' correspondence from about 1903 to 1940. Bobbs-Merrill's longtime editor Laurance Chambers was a formidable correspondent, and there are approximately 50,000 letters, most accompanied by a carbon copy of the reply.

(2) Autobiographical questionnaires sent to all authors published by the House. There are approximately 500, dealing with the subject's background, ancestry, education, previous publications, etc. Many of the writers supplied additional information not covered by the questionnaire, with long letters amounting sometimes to autobiographical essays.

(3) Readers' opinions, about 5,000, many favorable reports being accompanied by the readers' suggestions for revisions, corrections, etc. Many famous authors, such as Sinclair Lewis, were readers.

(4) Promotional material used by the House during the years 1903-1940 in what has been considered the first and most successful book advertising campaign in the United States. Every bit of promotional material used in the sale, advertising, and distribution of the books issued by the Company seems to have been saved: general and special announcements addressed to the trade; special announcements to buyers; samples of

prospectuses and order blanks; copies of advertisements, national and foreign; original drawings for the dust jackets and proofs as they developed; "reviews" (often prepared by the House and sent for syndication); photographs, broadsides, poster advertisements, and other selling aids. Included are many photographs of authors and some original art work.

(5) Contracts for more than 4,000 titles issued by the House, together with, in each case, the Library of Congress copyright records as well as those of foreign publications, movie, theater, and serial rights.

Also present is an extensive file of the firm's ledgers, stock and minute books, as well as royalty checks, dating from 1850, together with many records and documents relating to the early history and establishment of the company. Of considerable interest are materials and documentation on various libel suits.

Another substantial publisher's file acquired was that of the Appleton-Century Company. Though not as large or as diversified as that of Bobbs-Merrill, it is very extensive for the first half of the twentieth century. Earlier material is included back to 1848, with letters and contracts by William Cullen Bryant, General Ulysses S. Grant, Thomas Huxley, Henry William Herbert ("Frank Forester"), and General Sherman.

The files consist of contracts with authors for the publication of their works and for dramatizations, motion picture rights, foreign editions and translations; correspondence with authors; royalty statements; and other business papers. Papers relating to more than 300 authors, ranging from Zoe Akins to Israel Zangwill, number well over 6,000 letters and documents. Among a number of great interest are, for example, the original contract for the publication of Stephen Crane's *The Red Badge of Courage*, dated 17 June 1895; letters of U. S. Grant regarding his *Personal Memoirs*, published by Century in 1895; letters from John Foster Dulles regarding infringement of copyright on Joel Chandler Harris's *Tar Baby*; and galley proofs of Edith Wharton's *The Age of Innocence*, with correspondence about its dramatization by Lee Shubert.

Other important publishers' archives now in the Lilly Library include those of Samuel Sidney McClure's publishing and newspaper enterprises (21,000 items dating from 1865 to 1949); the stock ledgers, 1892-1944, of Methuen and Company, publishers, London; the publishing records of Noel Young's Capra Press, Santa Barbara, California

(9,600 items from 1955 to 1983); manuscripts and files of correspondence of authors published by S. Fischer Verlag (5,162 items from 1887 to 1965); and the records, 1950-1975, of London publishers Calder and Boyars.

The Library's strong holdings in little magazines further support literary scholarship. The Lilly houses nearly 600 runs of little magazines, 187 of which are listed in Hoffman, Allen, and Ulrich's *The Little Magazine: A History and a Bibliography* (1947). Among the prominent ones in complete or nearly complete runs are Harriet Monroe's *Poetry, A Magazine of Verse* (1912-   ); Dora Marsden and Harriet Shaw Weaver's *Egoist* (1914-1919); Margaret Anderson's *Little Review* (1914-1929); Wyndham Lewis's *Blast* (1914-1915); James Oppenheim's *Seven Arts* (1916-1917); Robert Graves's *Owl* (1919-1923); W. C. Williams's *Contact* (1920-1923); Harold Loeb, Slater Brown, and Malcolm Cowley's *Broom* (1921-1924); Ford Madox Ford's *transatlantic review* (1924-1925); Ezra Pound's *Exile* (1927-1928); Lincoln Kirstein, Allen Tate, and Yvor Winters's *Hound and Horn* (1927-1934); Eugene Jolas and Elliot Paul's *Transition* (1927-1938); James Angleton and Reed Whittemore's *Furioso* (1939-1953); Ruth and John Stephan's *Tiger's Eye* (1947-1949); Stephen Spender and Melvin Lasky's *Encounter* (1953-1959); Paul Carroll's *Big Table* (1959-1960); and the *Evergreen Review* (1957-1973).

In addition to the magazines themselves, the Library owns the files of *Poetry* from 1954, when Henry Rago assumed editorship of the magazine, to 1982 as it continues to receive, in annual installments, the retired files of this important publication. Other magazine archives obtained by the Library include LeRoi Jones and Hettie Cohen's *Yugen* (1958-1962); Diane Di Prima and LeRoi Jones's *The Floating Bear* (1961-1969); Cid Corman's *Origin* (1960-1962); David Wright and Patrick Swift's *X: A Quarterly Review* (1959-1962); and the English Carmelites' *Aylesford Review* (1955-1968).

It is only in the past few decades that literary scholars have turned their attention to the serious study of early children's literature and just as recently that research libraries have recognized their obligation to acquire and preserve materials in this field. The Lilly Library got an early start in collecting children's books because of Mr. Lilly's collection of the works of a boys' author he particularly admired, Harry Castlemon. Children's literature remained a special interest throughout his collecting career and, using such bibliographies as Blanck's *Peter Parley to Penrod*, he collected the clas-

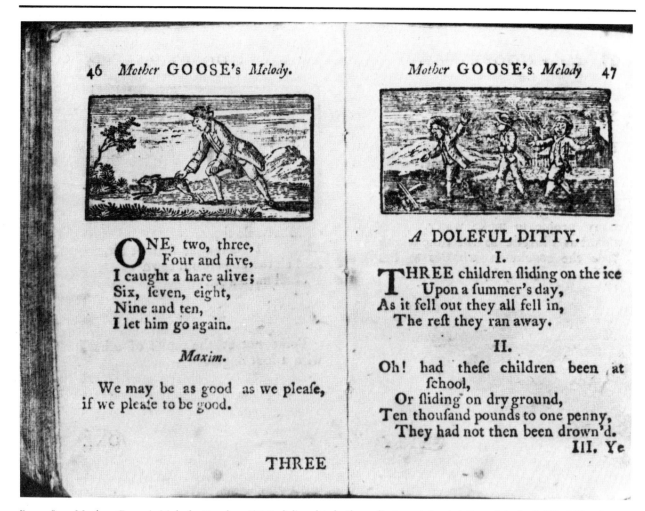

Pages from Mother Goose's Melody *(London, 1791), believed to be the earliest surviving printing of the book (The Lilly Library)*

sics. By the time his books came to Indiana University, he had gathered a notable collection rich in English, American, and European first editions.

In August 1983, the Board of the George and Frances Ball Foundation presented the Library with the superb collection of early children's literature formed by Elisabeth W. Ball of Muncie, Indiana. Led by his curiosity about books that had influenced his favorite authors, George A. Ball, Miss Ball's father, had begun the collection in the 1920s. In 1930 Mr. Ball acquired en bloc six thousand children's books offered for sale by the Parisian bookselling firm of Kirkor Gumuchian. Some years later he supplemented this acquisition by the purchase of the C. T. Owen Collection. Mr. Ball enjoyed sharing his books with others, and, frequently after dinner, guests in his Muncie home were treated to a showing of some of his treasures. On one such evening, after the guests had left and he and Elisabeth were returning the books to their shelves,

he told her that she should now consider the collection her own. She took the responsibility seriously and continued to add to the collection throughout her lifetime. As the Elisabeth W. Ball Collection it was consulted by scholars, cited by bibliographers, and achieved stature as a world-famous library of children's books.

During the later years of her life, Miss Ball began the dispersal of her extensive holdings. Several libraries were recipients of her gifts, among them Indiana University, Vassar College, the Philadelphia Free Library, the American Antiquarian Society, and the magnificent donation to the Pierpont Morgan Library, featured extensively in their handsome exhibition catalog *Early Children's Books and Their Illustration* (Boston: Godine, 1975), which is dedicated to Miss Ball. Yet, in spite of these many and generous gifts, the majority of her books remained in her possession at the time of her death in April 1982. The library, along with most of her

Catalogue for a 1975 exhibit (The Lilly Library)

sixteenth through the twentieth centuries, the books date primarily from the late eighteenth and early nineteenth centuries, a critical period in the history of children's literature.

Research libraries have a responsibility to inform the scholarly community of their holdings. The Lilly Library catalogues its monograph holdings in reports to the OCLC data base and its manuscript holdings to the *National Union Catalog of Manuscript Collections.* Many of its books are recorded in the *National Union Catalog: Pre-1956 Imprints,* and cataloging data of its eighteenth-century English language holdings have been sent to the *Eighteenth Century Short Title Catalogue* and the *North American Imprints Project.* Most of the Library's major collections are recorded in such reference works as *Subject Collections* and *American Literary Manuscripts.*

The Library itself has an ambitious publication program. It stages four major exhibitions a year, and many exhibitions are described in catalogs. Several exhibits in recent years have been devoted to literary topics, and some of the accompanying catalogs are still in print. Included among these are: *An Exhibit of Seventeenth-Century Editions of Writings by John Milton* (1969); *American Literature Honoring the Completion of the Editorial Work in its 100th Volume Approved by the Center for Editions of American Authors* (1973); *Science Fiction and Fantasy* (1975); *Twentieth-Century Literary Manuscripts* (1977); *American Poetry 1950-1980* (1980); and *A Baker's Dozen, Being a Selection of Books and Manuscripts by One English and Thirteen American Authors from the Library of Keith H. Baker of Oshkosh, Wisconsin* (1984). The Library also publishes *The Indiana University Bookman,* which describes various collections and frequently presents papers based on them. Recent issues have been devoted to the Library's collections in Victorian popular culture, the S. Fischer Verlag, and film studies.

In his letter to President Herman B. Wells offering his collection to Indiana University, Mr. Lilly wrote that "it is my hope that at Bloomington, Indiana there may be assembled ultimately in the custody of Indiana University the most outstanding institutional general collection of rare historical and literary material in the Middle West." As the Library nears its twenty-fifth anniversary, most observers acknowledge that Mr. Lilly's vision has been realized.

estate, was left to the George and Frances Ball Foundation. Justin G. Schiller, the specialist book dealer in children's literature, who appraised the collection for the estate, wrote in his appraisal: "As it currently stands, the library of the late Elisabeth Ball is composed chiefly of her collection of historical children's literature, original drawings and related manuscripts, hornbooks, juvenile card games, board games, &c. and as such is the finest assemblage of its kind still in private hands—rivaling or surpassing many of the greatly acclaimed collections in research libraries both here and abroad."

Consisting of approximately 8,500 titles and important manuscripts, the collection is particularly strong in English language imprints. Nearly 700 of the titles are in French, about 200 are in German, and there is a sampling of books in other languages. Although the collection includes items from the

The Year in Literary Biography

Anthony M. Friedson
University of Hawaii

Is the genius inevitably a social pariah? George Barker's old question comes up again as we look at this year's literary biography. More important, and less hackneyed for the biographer: how does the lifewriter make the "difficult" subject interesting and sympathetic? The reader is likely to read so much in the way of impossible behavior and ultimately to snort with impatience, boredom, or both. And there is always the chance that the reader may confuse conduct and craft so that he or she will allow the response to the writer's genius to be modified accidentally by the folly of the writer's behavior.

This problem of biographical craft was raised dramatically this year by A. N. Wilson's *Hilaire Belloc* (Atheneum)—a biography which, in readability and reach, is worthy of its subject. It has become, by now, commonplace to see Belloc as the unlikable, if talented, literary cad. The judgment has been raised too often—in his own time and since. Wilson's account conveys perforce, but incidentally and without gloating malice, the sad machinery of innocent boorishness which alienated many in Belloc's lifetime. More lately, H. B. was a top nominee in a recent *New York Times* contest for the least likable writer of our time. And this judgment has been confirmed by reviewers of Wilson's book. Graham Greene describes it as "an excellent biography of the most unlikable man of letters of our time," and Robert Martin is stung out of charity to describe Belloc as "a ramshackle monster" who is high on the list of famous men he is glad he never met.

One would have thought that a figure who inspires such staunch dislike would have discouraged biographers, especially good biographers. Yet there is nothing corpse-pounding about Wilson's definitive life of this Anglo-French wit. In the course of a long life (1870-1953) Belloc's raging energy took him from his father's native France to England. There he excelled and appalled at Oxford; sat twice in parliament; wrote voluminous poetry, fiction, biography, history, casual prose— 150 books of anything and everything; befriended literary men of the caliber of G. K. Chesterton (and his awful brother Cecil); and was a household name among innumerable members of the social and political elite. Wilson rehearses conscientiously the grounds for Belloc's unpopularity then and now. He was a forthright and dogmatic conservative, even when he was in parliament as a liberal M.P.; a jingoistic monarchist; a party-line Roman Catholic who embarrassed members of his own church; a professional Jew-baiter who raised eyebrows even in an age when many of the upper crust were given to fashionable anti-Semitism; an almost comic sexist who opposed women's suffrage because he thought that "the bringing of one's women, one's mothers and sisters and wives into the political arena, disturbs the relations between the sexes"; and an archaic and caustic idealist in most of his attitudes.

So much for the nays. But Wilson also conveys the qualities which make Belloc's life a fascinating and instructive paradox—a paradox which simplicists like to ignore. He shows how Belloc's conservatism, for example, was moved by his idealism. He did not think of himself as a greedy timeserver, but as a Christian egalitarian equally suspicious of tycoons and union leaders; and if there was some naiveté and self-deceit there, he adhered to this position with parliamentary integrity. His monarchism and Catholicism were also held critically. The book is full of stories in which his devotion was modified by the iconoclasm which only the true believer can afford. His male chauvinism was not moved by shabby sexual opportunism and was sufficiently complex that he was befriended to the end by outstanding women who were, like his mother, suffragists—most, not some, of his best friends were intelligent women. His anti-Semitism is a more complex matter. Wilson says that he was not a Jew-baiter. Belloc's constant slurs and downright insults, wincingly recorded by Wilson, argue that, within any meaning of the word, he *was*. It can be pointed out that he "baited" everyone; that some of his best friends were Jews; and—convincingly— that he was as appalled at Nazi persecution as at what he saw to be Jewish power play. And the whole matter is sufficiently complex that it takes Wilson at his best to sort some sense out of the nonsense. It is remarkable that Belloc did not think of himself as anti-Semitic, and that Jewish friends such as Max Beerbohm and his caring secretary, Ruby Goldsmith, must have had to take his racism into account.

Possibly much of Belloc's appeal to his many friends derived from his promiscuous energy. Wilson gives as an example the years 1911-1912 during which he wrote seventeen books, founded and ran the important periodical *The Eye Witness,* and lectured widely. Wilson conveys Belloc's bumptious verve with an urbane skeptical detachment and a wit as sharp as his subject's. He does not try to upstage Belloc, which would be an embarrassing attempt. His more English wit complements Belloc's and, fortified by an excellent sense of phrase, makes for a compelling account. And this complementarity is a general trait. Wilson avoids what Leon Edel feels to be a major biographical error—a "transference" whereby he would recreate Belloc in his own image—and yet retains a sympathy for his difficult subject.

Hilaire Belloc merits its description as a "definitive biography." Wilson is rigorous. He has used his sources—untapped material as well as previous biographical material from family memoirs to Robert W. Speaight's *The Life of Hilaire Belloc* (Farrar, Straus, 1957)—with discretion and skill. He is deft with the unobtrusive quotation, and his novelist's way with narrative makes this a most readable biography.

The same paradox of the awful and the fascinating is shown in Margot Peters's *Mrs. Pat,* (Knopf). Her study raises the question of the relationship between genius and impossibility, with gold-leaved insistence. Those who think in sexual dichotomies may pose once more the question implicit in David Plante's *Difficult Women* (Dutton, 1983): are there special ways in which "difficulty" emerges in talented women? Previous biographical material on Mrs. Patrick Campbell has been restrained in bringing out the flaky side of this celebrated actress whose genius was matched by her eccentric, almost schizoid, mixture of the generous and the petty. Alan Dent (*Mrs. Patrick Campbell,* Museum Press, 1961) certainly suggests the qualities which made directors, producers, fellow actors, friends, and family suck their breaths with alarm and pity. But his work is, as Peters points out, directed at the career rather than the life. *Mrs. Pat* manages to fuse the study of Mrs. Pat's personality with that of her considerable achievement as an actor.

And the extent to which that achievement was remarkable is made clear as Peters describes the problems which faced Stella Tanner (Mrs. Pat) as she forced her way from genteel poverty, through a mendicant marriage and motherhood, to become one of the most celebrated actors of her time.

Peters's organization is chronological—the pages are headed with the years involved—but the account never degenerates into the plod which can result from mere sequence. Much of this has to do with Peters's addressing detail to convey atmosphere and emotion. Here her subject helps her. Mrs. Pat is still alive in the minds of contemporaries to whom Peters had access; and in letters, reviews, and memoirs by the actor herself and by such intimates as John Gielgud, James Agate, and Bernard Shaw. She was, furthermore, a woman as dramatic offstage as onstage. The curl was electric in her forehead. When she was good she was very, very good; and even when she was bad, her appalling behavior avoided the banality which so often goes with prolonged childhood.

Peters's assessment of the secondary material is punctilious and intelligent. She uses the obviously crucial writings mentioned above as carefully as the equally important if less known recollections by friends such as Agnes Claudius who served the star through her decline and death. The early chapters dealing with Mrs. Pat's childhood and marriage derive much from unpublished sources such as the letters to her sister in the Tanner Collection, and from Mrs. Pat's own *My Life and Some Letters.* Peters makes dramatically clear the meaning of the much bandied phrase "shabby genteel." The horrifying squalor of the dispossessed middle class is seen in the families of both Stella and her first husband, Patrick Campbell. It is tellingly conveyed in desperate letters and empty coal scuttles.

The bulk of the biography is given to the more prosperous years of Mrs. Pat's triumph. Both words, *prosperous* and *triumph,* are hyperbolic. Mrs. Pat was incapable of managing money. The extent of her profligacy and generosity is itemized in the account of the years which followed her legendary success as Paula Tanqueray in 1893. She was never *prosperous;* she had bursts of wealth which she promptly dispelled. And the *triumph,* too, was periodic and fragile. Peters shows us frankly the qualities which made all reluctant to work with her—and, ultimately, to associate with her: baiting directors and producers; chattering, even giggling, at fellow performers such as George Alexander; and submitting all and sundry to a wit and whimsy which were often irresponsible and sometimes overtly malicious. But the book also contains astute comments by Mrs. Pat on her stage roles and several of her delightful "Pattigrams" so that we are able to understand the power as well as the silliness. And there is no doubting the power. Gerald du Maurier's verdict on the horrors of her love—that

*Dust jacket for new biography of the celebrated actress
Mrs. Patrick Campbell*

it was a mixture of heaven and hell—was true of her theatrical association. She often undid herself and alienated the critics who might have rewarded her excellence, but she was not given to pretense or affectation. Peters describes the change from domestic to career woman and, as she relates Mrs. Pat's journey to fame, examines the theatrical world in which that fame was set. More important in terms of biography, we finally credit Mrs. Pat's special genius. She emerges as a sensitive plant in a rough garden; a lyric talent, not an epic one. And Peters's sometimes over-thorough, but theatrically aware, accounts of her performances bring to life the "embodied poem" which Shaw says he found so refreshing an alternative to mere "actors." An incidental achievement which Peters leaves largely implicit: we have some idea of the special problem of the woman as star in a society which was not used to allowing the fair sex certain sorts of dignity on which Mrs. Pat insisted until she was sometimes as silly as the opposition. One can understand from Peters's account the behavior which led to the

breakup with, and breakdown of, her lover and colleague, Ian Forbes-Robertson—even if one's sympathies are with him.

By the time Mrs. Pat gets to her American tour, the myth of her stardom is established. Peters's account of Mrs. Pat in New York, Hollywood, and other theatrical points brings out the vulgarity of the media which pandered to her silliest side, as well as those traits in Mrs. Pat which made such pandering inevitable. She could finish a dullard with a phrase, and the press delighted in the maleficent wit of the idol they could use as a plaything.

The larger social accomplishment of *Mrs. Pat* derives from the comparison between the English and the American experiences as they bear on the narrative of a life which spanned the decline of British dominion and the ascent of the U.S. For the biography transcends its subject. Mrs. Pat was that most bright and frail of entities, the shooting "star." And the course of that star is traced through the dark skies of three wars, from the Boer War to World War II. These conflicts cost Mrs. Pat her husband and her son, Beo. But the wars, along with economic and political developments which accompanied them, cost Britain her Empire. And, as the actress is seen more and more beleaguered by the sickness and malaise which punctuated even her youth, both her dignity and her pathetic obsolescence image her times.

Until recently, H. D., one of the more critically esteemed of the imagist poets, has had too little attention from biographers. Janice Robinson's comprehensive biography, published two years ago, was the first well-documented attempt to assess Hilda Doolittle's confused and confusing life and to relate that life to her art. In her introduction, Robinson remarks that "we are only just beginning to know H. D." Barbara Guest's *Herself Defined* (Doubleday) assesses fully the personality and writing of this dryad who wandered nimbly out of a Moravian family in Bethlehem, Pennsylvania; consorted with Ezra Pound and D. H. Lawrence, among others— male and female; married Richard Aldington (who, however, was not the father of her only daughter, Perdita); formed a lesbian marriage with Annie "Bryher" Ellerman; and produced poetry, fiction and nonfiction and even a film, which works emerge as the most responsible factors in an eyebrow-raising life.

Guest deals concisely with H. D.'s childhood and her strange habitual debt to her astronomer father—a congenially earnest, tall, bearded professor at the University of Pennsylvania. She conveys enough of H. D.'s position as the Pennsylvania princess to indicate why a teacher's kid would revolt against the academic life at Bryn Mawr and leave with little except her friendship with Frances Gregg—a "twigs" and "flower" private sorority they dubbed "the wee witches," which foreshadowed H. D.'s later sexual ambivalence.

The narrative winds in nicely H. D.'s literary debts to these formative years. But the literary importance of the life begins with Guest's treatment of H. D. as an imagist poet. At first the songs of the "pagan mystic," as Harriet Monroe termed H. D., were out of tune with much of Pound's credo—cited by Guest: "Objectivity and again objectivity, and no expression, no hindsight beforeness . . . *nothing* that you couldn't in some circumstance . . . *actually say.*" H. D.'s poems at this stage often violate the party line. Punctuated by the artificial exclamations of the would-be faun, they pipe a forced poignancy clad in fay neoclassicism; the very "literaryism" Pound said violated sincerity. These traits would be modified as H. D. matured, but they were always there, and Guest is faced with the task of conveying the genius as well as the ridiculousness of one whose personal and artistic life mingle excellence with self-centered affectation.

Guest's accomplishment is considerable. She shows the fabric of H. D.'s genius without ducking the problems of the pained poseur which often detracted from her work. In the same way, she treats the lesbian marriage with the Napoleonic heiress, Bryher Ellerman, with the dignity it ultimately warrants while at the same time allowing the reader to gather the sometimes comic sides of these two eccentrics. It is, in fact, the paradoxical achievement of this biography that we see the dignity of H. D. and Bryher—and the extent to which it is reflected in H. D.'s work—most strongly as her life runs into time's customary damage. The dryad begins to crumble as dryads will. She goes through disappointments in love and art; confused motherhood and bewildered divorce; ill health; nervous collapse; clinical treatment which includes urinating on Havelock Ellis and pandering to Freud's fragile ego; and, ultimately, of course, death. These miseries are conveyed in the chapter titles which read like headings to a soap opera. But the power of her poetry, which, as Guest reveals, reflected and transcended these negative experiences, depended on certain virtues connected with that discrimination and persistence which endure.

Guest has invoked previously unpublished material by H. D., by her daughter, Perdita, by Richard Aldington, and by Ezra Pound. She has,

moreover, read and interviewed assiduously. The thorough biography is, unfortunately, sometimes marred by whimsies of form and syntax. The events of her narrative are insufficiently governed by what she may consider enslaving notions about H. D.'s rationale. And this diffuseness, which often loses the reader, is accompanied by the frequent absence of mere transitions. These qualities may be apt to the subject—they parody the form of H. D.'s poetry—but they don't make for an easy read.

H. D.'s life and *ton* raise the accusatory question: did the imagists have strong human emotions to express, or was their passion just "hair-tearing?" This question was posed in a 1915 letter to May Sinclair by the English poet Charlotte Mew, cited in Penelope Fitzgerald's *Charlotte Mew and Her Friends* (Collins). Mew's life, lived tortuously a generation prior to H. D.'s, may not answer the question as far as the imagists are concerned, but it does show a woman who, if she lost her hair, did so by fair wear and genuine passion.

The two women had many qualities in common. Both came from middle-class backgrounds; both were eccentric but bright students who wrote good poetry early and continued strong; both emerge from their correspondence, behavior, and writing as sensitive creatures divided between the shy and the outrageous; and both formed strong lesbian attachments important to their life and writing.

There were, though, some important differences. "Lotti" Mew typified her age. She was, in Fitzgerald's words, a "Yellow Book Woman." H. D.'s start came from Pound to the imagists, and from post-World War I writers such as Lawrence and the establishment which dismissed the Georgians and their contemporaries as dilettantes. Mew, in life and art, has a strong smell of British dinge. H. D., whose background was more prosperous and who was as physically beautiful as Lotti was plain, seems a postwar princess by comparison. It is difficult to think of H. D.'s life as that of a winner, in the superficial sense, but it is impossible to think of Mew in that light. She seems to have started out as a creature of moderate privilege whose London schooling saved her from an isolated life in the Isle of Wight, and she was helped in her career by patrons who ignored her mixture of arrogant iconoclasm and distressing shyness. Mrs. "Sappho" Dawson Scott included her in her Southall set after her work had been published in the *Yellow Book*, *Temple Bar*, and, when that folded, the *Nation*. Harold Monro pushed her work at the Poetry Bookshop. And Sidney Cockerell assured some ultimate success by touting her to the Hardys and persuading them, John Masefield and Walter de la Mare, to recommend her for a civil list pension. But the background of neurotic Bloomsbury gentility which Fitzgerald conveys with carpet-smelling skill smothered the life outside her poems. Unlike H. D., who was innocently selfish, Charlotte Mew's life was given to caring for a difficult mother and keeping the sister she loved in respectable surroundings. But her special qualities of iconoclastic perversity, her laziness, and the accidents of family confinement, which Fitzgerald documents with charitable honesty, made for a life which seems appropriately ended by her swallowing Lysol.

Fitzgerald's biography is aptly designed. She reveals Mew's life and literary development as it is dramatized by the poet's interaction with those who influenced it most. Fortunately, Lotti's English fussiness made her attract interesting people—and an interesting biographer. Fitzgerald's style is as shyly firm as Mew's writing. She tells with wit and sympathy of Mew's lesbianism and provides the possible rationale for this persuasion—the ineffectual father; the dominating mother supported by a warrant officer nanny; the powerful lesbian model teacher; and the imposition of worthy and powerful patrons who made a husband unessential. But there is no pat attempt to form a case history. In fact, Fitzgerald errs toward the oblique. This pertains more to her comments on the fiction and the poetry than to those on the life. She says of "The Farmer's Bride," for example, that "anyone who could say what prompted her to write it, at the age of forty two, would be able to understand the nature of the poetic impulse itself." To many readers this poem, recounting a newlywed's shrinking from the sexual imposition marriage has laid on her, must seem clearly vicarious. Perhaps such comment seems too palpable to Fitzgerald, but throughout the book she resists systematic assessment of the ways in which Mew's life and art reveal the complex patterns of her lesbianism. Lotti's inappropriate attempts at the seduction of unwilling women, such as May Sinclair, whom she chased five times around the bed, are presented with a clear sympathy; but although the reader can infer the reasons for Mew's failure to find a Bryher Ellerman or an H. D., Fitzgerald is little given to such speculation. She may feel that the secretive subject must not be harried by the cataloguing author. And she may be right. But there is that bed chase.

The impact of the public on the private life has been especially (and usually destructively) clear as the media have pervaded modern life. "Celebrity status" must have annoyed Nell Gwynn; it obviously annoyed—and flattered—Mrs. Pat. And it probably made an impact on her personality. But that impact may have been less dramatic because it was more controllable. The tyranny of the impersonal press, for example, is less organic than the gossip of immediate friends and enemies.

John Raeburn's study of Hemingway as public writer, *Fame Became of Him* (Indiana), makes clear how the interaction between a certain cast of soul and the ascent to stardom can bear strongly on a writer's life and work. Raeburn's book has the advantage of an angle. His study of Hemingway's life does not attempt the full-scope, birth-to-death coverage of Carlos Baker's authorized *Ernest Hemingway: A Life Story* (Scribners, 1969), nor even of Hotchner's Boswellian *Papa Hemingway* (Random House, 1966). Rather it centers on Hemingway's love-hate relationship with the media of his time.

Raeburn begins with a useful discussion of past writers with public images—writers such as the New England wits. He points out that these managed to preserve some privacy in their lives, even when their work was a matter of public notoriety. Hemingway suffered from sensationalistic journalists who catered to a much larger public than that of Holmes and Longfellow, say; or even than that of more recent "public" writers such as Dreiser, Anderson, or Lewis. And, whereas there have always been some writers who managed to preserve a "private" image, Hemingway was not one of these. In fact, Raeburn shows, whether writing the early fiction such as the stories in *Death in the Afternoon;* his novels from *A Farewell to Arms* to *The Old Man and the Sea;* his journalistic reports on the Spanish Civil War or World War II; or testy rebuttals to the critics, he was busy forming, enjoying, resenting, and, ultimately, suffering from the public image which he created in collusion with the media.

This image was one which, even nearly thirty years after his death, most of us know only too well: the macho, pugilistic, high-living adventurer who claimed to be as interested in landing the largest marlin as he was in writing the best novel. Raeburn pulls no punches. He brings out the fatuous side of Hemingway's behavior: the sophomoric boxing bouts; the self-aggrandizing contentions with anyone who threatened his status; the heroic posing—all the traits which made him a model for some and anathema to others. Fortunately for Raeburn's biographical distance, he also points out the sides of

Hemingway which counteracted (and maybe prompted) the bluster: the industriousness; the genuine courage; and even at times, especially in relation to his children, the affection.

Raeburn's work is right out of American studies. His main strengths are humane rather than literary. The analyses of the fiction are adroit, but there is a thinness as he shows how the public image determined, and was evidenced in, the major characters. This is partially rectified in the "Afterword," which contains a searching literary analysis that should pervade the entire work.

Biography is sometimes assessed as mere classy gossip. And it is the fate of the literary biographers to be more liable to this charge than, say, historians or philosophers. Literature is a primary outpouring of the soul. It is intimately related to the life of the writer, who usually makes little effort to hide the relationship. History, on the other hand, is concerned with the impact of men on their times and on a world which may involve them, mostly on the secondary level. A good biographer will transcend his pigeonhole, of course. He or she will fuse the study of a personality with the analysis of the subject's significance in a given field. Michael Holroyd (*New Directions in Biography*, University of Hawaii Press, 1981) sees a growing reconciliation between the historians and the literary biographers.

There is too little evidence of this fusion in Peter Marshall's *William Godwin* (Yale). Marshall's approach is, as one would expect from a philosopher, primarily ideological. Certainly, he brings out the impact of Godwin's father, a dissenting minister; and the way in which the bullying Samuel Newton modified Godwin's arrogance and imposed the Sandemanarian creed which formed the basis of Godwin's early thought. He shows, too, how Godwin reacted to Newton's tutorial bludgeoning with an anarchistic resistance to tyranny and brute force, and that this resistance informed major works such as *Caleb Williams* and *Political Justice* and pervaded Godwin's service to the radical movement of his time. But, especially in the chapters dealing with Godwin's early years, the emphasis is on the doctrine rather than the man.

The doctrine is important, of course; and Marshall's treatment of Godwin's development from a Calvinist Tory to an atheistic radical is traced thoroughly. Marshall discusses the influence of the tutors at Hoxton—"one of the most liberal centers of higher education in Britain"—and shows how the belated impact of that liberal regimen converted him to a radicalism which was to inspire poets and

political activists from his own time to the present. But one reads through the exegeses of Godwin's works, and through Marshall's summation of the way in which Godwin's ethics formed the basis for positions later propounded by John Stuart Mill, Henry Sidgwick, and others, with a growing feeling that something is missing. The abstractions are there and the "reflections," as Godwin would term them, are telling enough. But the specifics and narrative detail which are essential to vital biography are spare. It is as though Marshall had bought completely Godwin's conviction that the understanding is "a faculty distinct from sensation" and that physical impressions sink into nothing when compared with the "inexpressible operations of reflection." However tenable this dichotomy may be for the writer on political justice, it is not conducive to great biography. One yearns for vulgar exemplification; even for cheap anecdotes which would support the expensive generalities. "He seems," says Marshall of the young Godwin, "to have suffered deeply from the persecution of his fellow students and found it necessary to defend his beliefs as a means of upholding the integrity of his personality." How did he suffer? When? What persecution? What beliefs, and how and when did he defend them? So pants the reader.

Fortunately, Marshall is as human as Godwin. As the life and the radical movement make more demands on the man who became the mentor for Robert Southey, Samuel Taylor Coleridge, and William Wordsworth among others, the description becomes more balanced. Marriage and ill health—neither of which Godwin believed in, but both of which he suffered—push Marshall into the concrete. We are at last relieved to know from Godwin's daughter that the great emancipator depended on an old char to do his housework, and we savor with the writer of *Political Justice* the mutton chop in the Dutch oven. Ironically, Marshall becomes more compelling as Godwin endures the loss of his first wife in childbirth; his two daughters' involvement with Shelley; the cold dominion of his second wife; political and financial persecutions culminating in legal action and bankruptcy; the antagonism of conservatives and even of some of his close friends; and, above all, the decline of the creative verve which made him the grandfather of modern radicalism. In spite of the abstractions in style and substance, the biography is valuable in several ways. It provides a systematic analysis of Godwin's work and thought, and an aware examination of his sources and influence. The passages dealing with Jonathan

Edwards and Tom Paine, for example, are especially original and enlightening. Edwards's interaction with his British contemporaries are insufficiently acknowledged, and in the ideological arena, Marshall swings a good net.

Many of this year's biographies will annoy the discriminating reader because they do not descry any significance in the life concerned. This accusation certainly does not apply to Richard Lebeaux, whose *Thoreau's Seasons* (University of Massachusetts Press) continues to relate with Eriksonian insight the life he began in his *Young Man Thoreau* (University of Massachusetts, 1977). In the earlier book, Lebeaux treated the pre-Walden years. *Thoreau's Seasons*, a self-contained sequel, covers the period from 1845 to 1862 during which, Lebeaux feels, Thoreau came to regard the seasons and the nature manifested in them as "a means by which to comprehend and characterize his own and human life, and as a medium through which to communicate his thoughts, feelings, moods, and vision."

Lebeaux draws extensively on Thoreau's work to establish his development as man and writer. He also refers constantly to such social psychologists as Daniel Levinson and Erik Erikson, who give his psychobiography its direction, as well as to previous biographers such as Walter Harding.

Lebeaux's title conveys succinctly his thesis. He sees a natural pattern in Thoreau's work whereby the life and thought of the writer follow a parallel to the seasons. With a reasoning which is poetic, exhaustive, and incisive, Lebeaux shows how the springing insights which informed *A Week on the Concord and Merrimack Rivers* began an analogical experience for the maturing man. Thoreau, saddened and guilt-ridden at his brother John's death, saw, in the *naturgefuhl* they had both enjoyed, a reconciliation with a transcending universal purpose. The least interesting parts of Lebeaux's book are these early sections—especially the first chapter, which recapitulates the material of *The Young Thoreau*. This introductory bridge is followed by a discourse on the communion with Nature which Thoreau establishes at Walden; and, then, by a description of Thoreau's life house-sitting Emerson's family during the latter's visit to London. The failure of interest here has partly to do with certain flaws which mar the account throughout, but which are modifed as Lebeaux moves into the later chapters. The Spring season—which should be the most lively—is deadened by the wintry by-products of Lebeaux's psychobiographical method. There are first the conventions and terminology of popshrink. Lebeaux has inherited some stock notions from

Freudians, and post-Freudians, from social psychologists such as Gail Sheehy, and from Erikson and other psychobiographers. The notions involved are frequently valid, but they carry the stale aroma of yesterday's pigeonholes and they are cruelly repeated. Phrases such as "ego ideal," "identity foundations," "midlife crisis," "mentor relationships," and "generativity needs" splatter the page. And these draw attention to the sometimes gawky phrasing which must make Thoreau cough again. The following sentence, for example, describes one of the more incisive decisions in American literary history: "Going to Walden, whatever else it was, was clearly a statement—which the upstanding Citizens of Concord only two miles away could not help hearing—of what he would absolutely not consent to become committed to; it was a steadfast declaration of moratorium in the face of perceived pressures to accept prevailing definitions of personal, social and national identity." Poor Thoreau; stuck in the mud before he sees the clear pond. Many deconstructionists will trudge pitwards with pleasure to see such unrestricted freeplay! Then to make amends, there is the accidental comedy of Lebeaux's jiving observation that in the many drafts of *Walden*, Thoreau was expressing his need to "expand and expound upon his bond with the pond."

It would, perhaps, be trivial to niggle at Lebeaux's phrasing and syntax in this way were the style not to some extent symptomatic. For Lebeaux's doctrine often inclines him to dig for an ulterior motive with a heavy shovel. One of the merits of the book is its courage in evaluating behavior, often persisting in a dubious assertion until it becomes electrically credible. There are times, though, when the reader's headshakes are not likely to be overcome. Such mixed reactions occur more in the early chapters. We are told, for example, of the antagonism which grew between Thoreau and Emerson when the mentor left his disciple in charge of his house and family while he rejoiced in the industry of London. Lebeaux indulges in some adventurous and perceptive analysis of conduct, but mixes it with an unconvincing attribution of motive. One is excited, for example, by Lebeaux's analysis of Thoreau's phallic imagery as he puts down Ellery Channing. He writes to Emerson how his neighbor "will ride a broomstick—though there is nothing to keep him or it up—but a certain centrifugal force of whim which is soon spent—and there lies your stick. . . ." Lebeaux makes Thoreau's malice here undeniable and convincing. On the other hand, the portion of the narrative where

Lebeaux sees in Thoreau's mischievous letters from home some intent to supplant the senior writer as head of the house and master of the bedroom carries a doctrinaire strain. The allegation might have been more convincing had it been left to the end of the chapter where the mounting evidence given for Thoreau's resentment would make Lebeaux's contention more credible. But everyone is put in Freudian boxes packed with the old tissue of ulterior motives. (Consider, for example, Thoreau's disciple Gray Otis Blake, whose family is drawn up in the melodramatic terms of intrafamilial warfare to the point where Blake is accused of having fears of patricide and matrimonial incest.)

The reader is, though, likely to continue reading *Thoreau's Seasons.* The insistence of Lebeaux's thesis carries an integritous force—especially after the fourth chapter. The style begins to catch up with the intensity of the vision. As he assesses the "second Spring," Lebeaux shows how Thoreau, in his *Journal,* resolves "to chart the phenomena of the human life and mind in a manner similar to that employed by naturalists to describe nature." His entries become a "meteorological journal of the mind." Thoreau's first consideration is, of course, propagation. "Nature was becoming a sort of fertility goddess for Thoreau," says Lebeaux—a substitute wife and mother. The reviser of *Walden* was "intent on tilling his seeds in the mind's soil until they yielded a bumper crop." Analyzing the journal to the last image and reported dream, Lebeaux traces a certain digestion and resolve as Thoreau prepares for the second Spring. Much of the renewal has to do with evaluating the contentions with friends such as Emerson and Channing which marred his life up to the end of 1852.

These antagonisms continued in the following years, and were extended to a coolness with Horace Greeley—his most useful publishing contact up to this point. Lebeaux examines Thoreau's relationships with Greeley and other publishers, and with critics as they reflect the movement from the creative Spring through the fruitful Summer and into the waning years of his life. The seasons interacted with each other to good and sad purpose. The revisions of *Walden* became a creative antidote to the autumn and winter.

When *Walden* was finally published in 1854, Thoreau was thirty-six years old. His life and work, says Lebeaux, were in the autumnal and wintry phases. A postcreative remorse hit Thoreau as *Walden* went out of his hands. It was as though he was losing a love or his potency. And his roving lectures seemed to him inadequate. In 1855 he endured a

Dust jacket for the new biography of the Imagist poet Hilda Doolittle

year of the sickness which often slowed his life—a malaise which Lebeaux finds likely to have been partly psychosomatic.

From 1855 on, there were mixtures of misery and reconciliation. There were reinforcements, such as the friendships with Whitman and with the Indian, Polis. And these modified the discouragements: the death of his father, the crucifixion of John Brown and the ensuing civil war, continued leg problems, and ultimate weaknesses of body and soul as the snow flurries of winter presaged impending death from tuberculosis. But Thoreau faced death with the same integrity he led his life. He regarded both as equally meaningful; and, in his last days, he understood problems which had troubled him in his Spring, such as his brother's death, in a way which justified his seasonal philosophy. The cumulating appeal of Lebeaux's book is in the art with which it relates the seasons of a man's life to those of his time and to those which contain an eternal logic which transcends time.

It is pertinent to turn from Lebeaux's full, extensively documented, thesis-dominated book to biographies which avoid both the complexity and the long-windedness found in some definitive biographies. Critics who share Louis Simson's complaint that many biographies today are prolix, dull, thesis-ridden academic rambles may welcome a biographical format exemplified by the Harcourt Brace Jovanovich Album Biographies. The series started this year with lives of Ross Macdonald, Jack Kerouac, James Jones, and Stephen Crane. Edited by Matthew J. Bruccoli, the books aspire to be "compact yet thorough" and to cater to "readers who may not be familiar with the fuller biographies." Those without stamina or desire for the definitive biography, but who want something more exhaustive than the potted biographies found in the *Dictionary of American Biography* or *Twentieth Century Authors* will like these well-illustrated, concise accounts, with their handy opening "Chronology," and selective "Bibliography." The format is, perhaps, most apt for recent American writers who have not yet been extensively treated. This fact probably prompted the editorial choice of subjects—the first two deriving from Canadian families.

The biographies, each written by an authority in the field, vary in length and intent. Bruccoli's life of Kenneth Millar (a.k.a. *Ross Macdonald*) is mainly concerned with his subject's work and with the relationship of that work to the "hard-boiled" novel—that subgenre of detective fiction practiced by writers who owe a little to English detective fiction, more to Poe, but most to the "tough-guy" novels of Chandler and Hammett. This is the shortest book in the series (147 pages), and treats the work rather than the man. It relates the struggles of craft and finances which beset the popular writer, but does not dwell on the problems which sent Macdonald into psychotherapy in 1956. Nor is there any extensive attempt to show the interrelationship of Macdonald's inner life with his art. Bruccoli provides the major facts: the debts and disappointments, which went with the literary successes. He deals more briefly with the intimate worries: Macdonald's daughter's sad, short life; the misogyny which may have prompted the "missing daughter" and "murdering women" motifs in his novels; and the writer's defeat by Alzheimer's disease. But the most thorough analysis is that given Macdonald's deviation from, and contribution to, the detective novel.

Macdonald was—aptly for a writer of private detective fiction and frustratingly for the biographer—a private person. Tom Clark's life of Jean Louis Lebris de Kerouac (*Jack Kerouac*) reads like a French-Canadian rebuttal. Clark's longer book presents the boisterous, tortured Jack Kerouac with as much understanding as possible. The story reads like a Beat-up, hippie soap opera dignified by literary achievements. Clark, like Bruccoli, writes with a brusque pace which modifies any tedium that might result from the catalogue of high disaster. The text runs Kerouac on the road from a mother-loving, football-playing childhood; through his student days; in and psychiatrically out of the navy; along companionships with writers of the caliber of Ginsberg, Burroughs and Creeley; and through alcoholism, breakdown, and the frequent by-products of literary fame. And it requires the memory and description of novels such as *On the Road* and *The Dharma Bums* to elevate the runner. It is a sad story or a mad story. But Clark reminds us of the sense of Burrough's quoted observation that "Kerouac was a writer," that writers "create a universe in which they have lived or would like to live," and that the effect of that creation "is immediate, as if a generation were waiting to be written."

Burroughs's rationale might be applied to James Jones, the subject of the third in the Album Bio Series. George Garrett's *James Jones* shows how far Jones, too, was one of the "Time Ghosts." His life and work reveal the drama of World War II and the postwar years, not from the point of view of a drunken roadrunner, but from that of one who suffered in the trenches during the Pacific war and chronicled that suffering in novels such as *From Here to Eternity, Some Came Running, The Pistol, The Thin Red Line,* and *Whistle*. Garrett is obviously partial toward his subject. In the nicely argued "Reappraisal" which forms an introduction to the life, he asserts that, although *From Here to Eternity* is, as most critics say, Jones's best book, he is no one-book author. He sees the fresh integrity of that novel—written to the tradition of the Illinois country boy who finds experience in the army without losing his innocence—retained with power in much of the later fiction.

In Jones, we see a writer who is more likable than Kerouac—generous (especially in his dealings with younger writers during his short, successful teaching career in Florida), courageous, and with a largesse of soul. He is described as often stubborn, especially in matters of craft; but Garrett obviously finds him principled rather than perverse. This sympathy colors Garrett's treatment at times. His assessment of the critical reception of *Some Came Running*, for example, tends toward special pleading. The rationale of the negative critics is treated in largely general terms. They are described as a non-populist leftist establishment, idealogues who resented Jones's less formulated social credo. This assessment is partially accurate. And Garrett is also correct in summarizing their objections to Jones's craft—such as his radically confused narrative rhetoric. But the rehearsal of their views is conducted largely from Jones's point of view and with little critical detachment.

In general, however, this is an excellent short biography for those who want a concise, reliable, and readable book on Jones and his work. Garrett is thorough. He gives the Handy Artists, and its queen bee mistress, Lowney Handy, adequately humorous treatment; and his coverage of the Pacific war is especially impressive (although Hickam Field is at one point misspelled as "Hickman" and at another as "Hickham," and Wo Fat's Restaurant is woefully reproduced as Wu Fat's).

James B. Colvert's *Stephen Crane*, the latest to date in the HBJ series, has the advantage of dealing with the most prestigious and fascinating writer of the four. It might be possible to write a dull biography of a man who led Crane's adventurous life and who put his experience to such good literary use, but it would demand a very dull writer. Colvert is up to his subject. His story of the New Jersey preacher's kid who crammed into his twenty-nine years an incredible amount of vital literary material is told in a clean prose and with perceptions about both the life and the art of his subject which would have pleased Crane. He is following the way led by John Berryman—an advantage and a challenge.

Crane's journalistic experience certainly gave him the stuff of fiction. He covered passionately the Nebraska drought of 1895, managed to outwit bandits in Mexico, took on the police in New York while covering the tenderloin district, escaped drowning on a filibuster during the Cuban insurrection against Spain, and saw more action than many Greeks in the Greco-Turkish war. But Colvert shows how it was the novelist's apparently inborn gift for profound and witty irony and his forcefully swift style which make novels such as *Maggie* and *The Red Badge*, stories of the caliber of "The Blue Hotel" and "The Open Boat," and a good amount of poetry—an impressive canon for so short a life.

Also crammed into that life were surprisingly full friendships with the writers of his time: Hamlin Garland and William Dean Howells in the States and a host, including Henry James, Joseph Conrad, Ford Madox Ford, and H. G. Wells, in England. There he spent his last, tubercular years. He, and his consort, the fascinating ex-madam, Cora Stewart, were constantly in debt, and Colvert draws

amusing capital from Crane's ironic insistence on playing the Yankee Lord of the Manor on Henry James's doorstep.

These literary, and often social, associates gave some incisive reasons for their excitement over Crane. Colvert includes short, but telling, excerpts by Conrad, Wells, and Edward Garnett, among others, which, with comments by modern critics such as John Berryman and Robert Stallings, convey something of Crane's accomplishments before these were lost in the marshes of Brede, debt, and hackwork. One sentence of Garnett's seems to sum up Crane's special excellence: "The rare thing about Mr. Crane's art is that he keeps closer to the surface than any living writer, and, like the great portrait painters, makes the surface betray the depths." That same quality marks much of Colvert's biography and the best of the writing in this series.

Big brother is watching. The approaching fin de siècle may account for the self-destruction of so many writers. And 1984 should not end without some consideration of George Orwell, whose life proved how a certain measure of self-destruction may be put to a most constructive use. Unfortunately, or fortunately, Bernard Crick anticipated the need for a good Orwell biography two years ago (*George Orwell: A Life*, Little, Brown, 1981). Stephen Wadhams's *Remembering Orwell* (Penguin) does not try to equal Crick's comprehensive and informed work. In his preface, he acknowledges the debt and makes clear that his purpose is less ambitious than, and different from, Crick's.

Remembering Orwell represents biography as oral history in the line of Peter Brazeau's *Parts of a World, Wallace Stevens Remembered* (Random House, 1983). It is a collection of comments on Orwell, by family, friends, and acquaintances, edited down—or up—from a CBC documentary, "George Orwell: A Radio Biography." In his typically pithy and genial introduction, George Woodcock says that Orwell had a gift for making friends—even with people he quarreled with in print. The memoirs are, indeed, multifarious. They include those of immediate family; close friends, childhood and adult; colleagues; ex-pupils; and servants. The danger in such a collection is that it might be repetitive and polyglot. This problem would be less destructive to a radio program, where one cannot dwell and back-check, than to a book, which allows that critical luxury.

The testimony in *Remembering Orwell* is sometimes chatty and occasionally repetitious. The reader also has a feeling of the unacknowledged interlocutor over his shoulder. On the whole, though,

Wadhams has edited adroitly. And the comments of those contributing are given unity by his connecting narrative as he sees Orwell through childhood in Burma and England, schooldays, service in the Burma Police, the early work as a tramp writer, schoolmaster, socialist warrior, and journalist, through to the period of his major works culminating in *1984*. The connecting comments are sometimes flat; they lack the analytical command of Crick's account. But Wadhams's skill in arrangement represents an oblique perceptiveness.

There would seem to be two major reasons for writing a casual, oral biography such as *Remembering Orwell*. The first is obvious: its immediacy. The dramatic pitch of the testifying voices still echoes through the print when, for example, old schoolfellows gossip about the justice or otherwise of Orwell's attack on prep schools like St. Cyprians in "Such Were the Joys," or when those who served with Orwell in Spain recall how he would recklessly expose himself to the fire of the Fascist snipers. The second reason is less palpable, but perhaps more weighty. The radio journalist will sometimes discover details which complement the necessarily filtered evidence of the comprehensive biographer. Crick, for example, in talking with Geoffrey Stevens, an old boy of The Hawthorns, where Orwell taught for an uncomfortable year, elicited the important fact

that Orwell could be very authoritarian—even brutally so when it came to caning time. This trait, which bears interestingly on Orwell's antiauthoritarian fiction, emerges more extensively and dramatically from Stevens's longer discussion in Wadhams's book; but, more important, the creative and humane side of Orwell is shown as the adult Stevens recalls in some detail Orwell's pedagogical skills which made him in the old boy's memory "the best teacher I ever had." This side of Orwell receives only a general treatment in Crick's book. And this is inevitable. The more comprehensive lifewriter cannot dally too long on chatty detail. All this is not to patronize oral biographies by suggesting that they may, if lucky, fill in bits-and-bobs which the definitive biographer might miss or find insignificant—an argument which would be especially weak when comparing, say, Wadhams with Crick, who knows the value of an interview. More profound is the aforementioned merit of immediacy. Books such as Wadhams's suggest the likelihood that biographers—especially those treating contemporary subjects—will follow such programs as the Columbia Oral History Project and use aids such as tape and cassette recorders to achieve an intimacy between reader and writer not conceivable fifty years ago.

The Year in Drama

Howard Kissel

For a long time language has been a little unfashionable in the theater, rather like a once eminent, now slightly dowdy old aunt of whom the family is reluctant to admit it is ashamed. Although the number of plays opening in New York that one can take seriously decreases annually at an alarming rate, an encouraging sign is the increasing importance again being placed on words.

Language, of course, was once considered the cornerstone of the theater and the ability to project language the touchstone of an actor. For many years language was thought to be the thing that made the theater an art superior to film. In the early 1960s, however, movies began to be regarded as a visual rather than a literary art. Visual imagery, the thinking went, was subtler, deeper, more direct

than verbal—a picture is worth how many words?

At the same time the theater itself was losing patience with language. The experiments of Peter Brook and Jerzy Grotowski proceeded on the assumption that the text was somehow not a means of communication but a barrier to it. Even audience members who spoke Polish were unable to understand Grotowski's actors, who twisted the language out of its usual shape. Brook and the English poet Ted Hughes invented a new language for some of his productions. Brook and Grotowski—and their imitators—tried to create a theater in which physical gesture and sounds unrelated to any specific language would transcend national and cultural differences.

On a less intellectual level, the "Method" style

that dominated conventional theater of the period was also hostile to language. The assumption was that authentic emotion had no need of words to make itself felt. Certainly in film and to a lesser degree in the theater it was considered more important for the actor to "feel comfortable" with the dialogue, to mold it to his own needs, than for the audience to hear the playwright's exact words.

Diction was considered an outmoded device. The occasional English play that required such a thing as diction generally arrived with its own English cast, and in some circles the whole thing was seen as an anachronism.

There were divergences from the pattern, but it seems safe to say little of the drama of the past decade will appear worth reading in, say, thirty years. Some of it may continue to be performed, but the texts themselves will hold little interest.

In the past year a change seemed to be in the air, the most obvious instance of which was Tom Stoppard's *The Real Thing*, a play about a writer incapable of dealing—either in his work or his life—with genuine emotion. The play opens with a scene from the writer's current hit, in which a man who knows his wife is having an affair treats her and his plight with brittle, unconvincing humor. There is, of course, great cleverness in the artificiality, but nothing about the writing suggests that Henry, the playwright, is a man of any great depth.

Nor is our impression much changed when we meet him. He is preparing to appear on a radio program in which the guest lists the eight records he associates with turning points in his life. He is trying to remember what music he was listening to when he wrote a play attacking Jean-Paul Sartre. His wife is convinced it was the Crystals singing "Da Doo Ron Ron."

Her suggestion infuriates him: "I'm supposed to be one of your intellectual playwrights," he tells her; "I'm going to look a total prick, aren't I, going on the radio to announce that while I was telling Jean-Paul Sartre that he was essentially superficial I was spending the whole time listening to the Crystals singing 'Da Doo Ron Ron.' " He is no happier to learn that the piece was in fact the Skater's Waltz, which he realizes will also appear "banal."

But if his musical tastes and play-writing style are unimpressive, Henry's conversational skills are quite dazzling. He may not be able to write with the air of a great playwright; nor can he project the public persona such a figure should have. But in private, with no intention of fooling anyone, he is quite brilliant. Here, he keeps rigorous control over his emotional life and his intellect shines—so much

that the person who sees the play is likely to imagine Henry is a significant writer despite the fact his work deteriorates in the course of two acts. By the middle of the play he is forced to do movie sci-fi in order to pay his alimony, and toward the end he is reduced to doctoring the hackwork of Brodie, an ex-convict whose self-righteous cant his mistress has championed.

What one remembers, of course, is Henry's eloquent defense of words when he is explaining why he detests the ex-convict's allegedly heartfelt play. Words, Henry says, are "innocent, neutral, precise, standing for this, deciding that, meaning the other, so if you look after them you can build bridges across incomprehension and chaos. But when they get their corners knocked off, they're no good any more, and Brodie knocks the corners off. I don't think writers are sacred, but words are. They deserve respect. If you get the right ones in the right order, you can nudge the world a little or make a poem which children will speak for you when you're dead."

A few minutes earlier Henry made a similar statement comparing the writer's craft to the art of constructing sound cricket bats. It is the speech people are most likely to remember about the play. It is not worded as eloquently as the "bridge speech," but it makes use of the actor's ability to mime and to use a certain cluck at the back of the mouth to give the illusion of the cricket bat at work; the theatrical effect is quite brilliant.

Just as the play's title is simultaneously the weariest of clichés and the plainest way of talking about "true love," the play is an artful series of parallels between artificial and genuine scenes of love. The opening scene, for example, a segment from Henry's arty play about a woman cheating on her architect husband, is paralleled in the second act by an offstage romance between Henry's former wife, the actress who played the adulterous woman, and an architect, who, we learn, is cheating on her. The actress tells Henry she lost her virginity at the age of seventeen to an actor playing opposite her in "Tis Pity She's A Whore." Henry's mistress, we find, is unfaithful to him with the actor playing opposite her in the same John Ford play, and in a brief scene we hear its elaborate seventeenth-century conceits used as a vehicle for the contemporary actors' passion. What saves the play from its glittering artificiality is—especially interesting in view of its concern with language—its lapses from literary grace. Early in the play Henry's wife notes that if he were ever dealt a real emotional blow his verbal facility would falter. "He'd come apart like a pick-a-stick,"

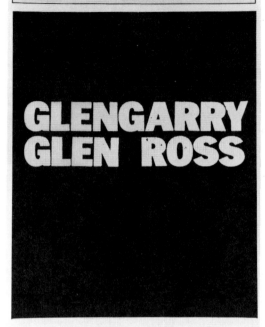

Playbills for a selection of 1984's New York plays

she says. "His sentence structure would go to pot, closely followed by his sphincter." When, late in the play, Henry is indeed hurt by the knowledge his mistress has been unfaithful, his irony and composure fail him. All he can say, when left alone, is "Oh, please, please, please, *don't.*"

Throughout the play Henry's favorite music provides a useful counterpart to the verbal pyrotechnics. Singles such as the Righteous Brothers' "You've Lost That Lovin' Feelin' " and Herman's Hermits' "I'm Into Something Good" are used as transitions between scenes. And the musical accompaniment to Henry's plaintive "Oh, please, please . . . " is Bach's Air on a G String—not in the original, but in the version Henry knows best, an arrangement by Procol Harum. Initially, of course, we are supposed to see Henry's predilection for this kind of music as a symptom of his plebeian tastes. But the songs are undeniably infectious, full of a wonderful innocence and, on their own terms, a certain genuineness of feeling. They stand in healthy contrast not only to the cleverness of Henry and his friends but also to the smug piety of Brodie, the ex-convict whose lack of sophistication is no guarantee of honesty.

Henry is quick to point out that the songs he likes aren't even fashionable in pop circles: "You can have a bit of Pink Floyd shoved in between your symphonies and your Dame Janet Baker—that shows a refreshing breadth of taste or at least a refreshing candor—but *I* like Wayne Fontana and the Mindbenders doing 'Um Um Um Um Um Um.' "

The references and the music itself have a cumulative effect. By the end of the play, when we hear the Monkees singing "Oo, oo, oo, I'm a believer" on the radio while Henry comes to terms with his mistress, we understand his attachment to these songs. In an odd and effortless way, steering clear of either sentimentality or cynicism, they have a direct, emotional, joyful impact. They are "the real thing."

The characters in Stoppard's play, though engaging, seldom make deep claims on our emotions. One is more impressed by Stoppard's recognition of his own weakness in providing emotional subtexts for his witty, intellectual exercises, more impressed by his decision to explore the problem than his ability to solve it. Nevertheless for two and a half hours the viewer finds his mind working continuously and pleasurably. This is the first play in years that fulfills one's notion of "an evening in the theater."

In startling contrast to the formal eloquence and wit of *The Real Thing* is the blunt language of David Mamet's *Glengarry Glen Ross,* a saga of Chicago real estate men who sell property in Florida. The land goes under such highflown names as Glengarry Highlands. We assume there is an irony in the nomenclature since Florida is not generally noted for its resemblance to Scotland. Whether or not the land has any actual value seems not to matter. It is like an imagined point around which the men are perpetually jousting.

Unlike its predecessor, *Death of a Salesman,* in which we see Willy Loman's family, his fantasies, his past, in *Glengarry* we must discern everything by inference. There are only four scenes in the ninety-minute play, in three of which the salesmen fight with one another. In the fourth we see the most imaginative and ruthless of the lot poise himself to attack an innocent customer in a Chinese restaurant.

Mamet's salesmen are in a constant state of turmoil, anxious about their "leads," their commissions, their prizes, their standing vis-à-vis one another. They adopt bullying, blustering postures toward one another, and toward the one hapless customer we see. But these postures, knight's armor though they seem, are barely adequate to cover the nervous, beleaguered egos underneath. Similarly, the language of the play, replete with four-letter words, ultimately comes to seem a poignant kind of bluff. Very quickly the words lose their power to shock. They are weapons blunted with overuse.

The words are proof not of the virility, commercial or otherwise, the men go to such pains to establish but rather of the lives of not so quiet desperation they lead. One is reminded of George Orwell's novel *Coming Up for Air,* in which the narrator, a salesman, observes, "What are the realities of modern life? Well, the chief one is an everlasting, frantic struggle to sell things. With most people it takes the form of selling themselves—that is to say, getting a job and keeping it."

If the words lack the glitter of *The Real Thing,* they share its precision. Here nothing seems artificial, nothing glib or funny just for the sake of being funny. Mamet's speeches are honed to capture the sputtering, barely suppressed anger and pain of his characters. Mamet mimics contemporary speech with painstaking accuracy. "Your mistake, you shoun'a took the lead," one of the men tells another. But Mamet takes this quasi-articulate syntax and builds it into something with a musical sense of momentum. The text emphasizes certain words in italics, as in this speech where one of the salesmen admires a former colleague who has gone off on his own: "Look at Jerry Graff. He's *clean,* he's doing business for *himself,* he's got his, that *list* of his with the *nurses* . . . see? You see? That's *thinking.* Why take ten percent? A ten percent comm . . . why are we giving the rest away? What are we giving ninety per . . . for *nothing.* For some jerk sit in the office tell you, 'Get out there and close.' 'Go win the Cadillac.' Graff. He goes out and *buys.* He pays top dollar for the . . . you see?"

It is not only the long speeches that have a rhythmic cogency. The interchanges between the men have a similar explosive quality, the verbal equivalent of gunfire in a '30s gangster film. Because of the menacing, sometimes enigmatic style of his language, Mamet has often been compared to Harold Pinter. But in *Glengarry* Mamet's work seems closer to another contemporary British playwright, David Storey. In plays like *Home* and *The Changing Room,* Storey created a world in which a representative action gave the impression of occurring constantly, like some cycle in nature. Much the same seems true of the six men in *Glengarry,* whose skirmishes with one another seem part of some ongoing, endless war. The marvel is that the war has intensity, pathos, pain, and yet a powerful underlying comedy, like a canvas by Uccello, in which one senses the thrust of the warriors, the chaos of their encounters, but nevertheless sees them as cartoon figures—brightly, boldly colored, arrestingly shaped.

In the hands of David Rabe the same vulgarity remains inert. In *Hurlyburly* the characters live in Los Angeles, where they devote some of their time to working in television and more to getting high. Much of the dialogue is an attempt to render the spaced-out observations of people on drugs. The speeches may capture this quality but they are not interesting in themselves. Nor do they have the rhythmic tautness of the banalities in *Glengarry Glen Ross.*

It almost doesn't matter which character is speaking, since they all sprinkle their sentences with "you know" and they all have a tendency to drift from one thing to another without much concern for consistency. Here is a sample: "You, you cynical bastard, watch the fine line you are walking between my self-awareness and my habitual trend to violence. 'Cause on the one hand I might appear worried, but on the other I could give a ----, you know, and my urge to annihilate anyone might just fixate on you."

There is an undeniable verisimilitude in such speeches to the diffuse glibness of people whose lives are incoherent even when they are not on

drugs, but three and a half hours of such speeches take us nowhere. At the end of the play the characters know no more about themselves than they did at the beginning. Nor do we. We see them drinking, arguing, philosophizing. Women occasionally appear. The men see them—and they seem to see themselves—as convenient receptacles for sperm. The men tend to share the available women, and every amateur Freudian knows this is an imitation of homosexuality, a link with Rabe's 1976 *Streamers,* another look at men under stress.

The cynicism and vulgarity of the characters seem a facile and unpersuasive form of misanthropy. Nothing they do in the course of the evening persuades us that the human race, even species *Hollywoodensis,* is so pathetically limited and self-hating. Probably the play would have occasioned little notice had it not been directed by Mike Nichols and starred some of Hollywood's most appealing young stars. (A shrewd observer of the Broadway scene found it significant that when Nichols recast *The Real Thing* he just found actors who could play the parts, implying the play would carry them; when he recast *Hurlyburly* he again looked for "names.")

August Wilson's *Ma Rainey's Black Bottom* is, in certain ways, an equally bleak play; but it is written with so much more craft that one accepts its dark vision as genuine, unlike the facile glumness of Rabe's. The play is set in a Chicago recording studio in 1927, where Ma Rainey, a blues singer in the style of Bessie Smith (or, as she puts it, "Bessie What?") is about to cut a record. We watch the members of her band chat and squabble with each other as they wait for her arrival. She is an hour late, a way of irritating the white bosses that also takes its toll on her fellow blacks. Like a good piece of jazz, the play alternates between playfulness, soulfulness, flirting with emotional violence that triumphs at the final cadence.

Unlike many recent pieces of black theater, which are based on street jargon and stock characters, *Ma Rainey,* even when it verges on the conventional, is always redeemed by Wilson's good-natured wit and his ability to invest his characters with a wry, often troubling, always believable humanity.

These excursions into contemporary verbal styles were balanced by a beautiful foray into Edwardian eloquence, Ted Tally's *Terra Nova,* a poignant, imaginatively constructed portrait of the members of Robert Scott's failed attempt to be the first to reach the South Pole. An Englishman imbued with a very stiff upper lip and a rigorous code of ethics and decorum, Scott was beaten to the Pole by the expedient Norwegian Roald Amundsen.

In some cases Tally makes use of the actual language found in journals of Scott's odyssey, as when one of the men, going out into a blizzard to freeze to death lest his feet—so frozen some of his toes have dropped off—impede the progress of the others, tells them, "I am just going outside and may be some time."

Some of his ideas are conventional, but the play has moments of great beauty. One occurs when Scott, who will never see the son he fathered before he left England, has an imaginary talk with his wife about the boy as he cradles in his arms one of his dying men, to whom he has been a solicitous and tender father.

An arresting image of fatherhood lay at the heart of Arthur Kopit's *End of the World*. The central character, a playwright commissioned to write a play about nuclear holocaust, gradually comes to see his own capacity for self-destruction. What makes him aware of the disturbing urges within him is the recollection of a moment when he was carrying his infant son near an open window overlooking Riverside Drive. (From the address we are to know he is a kneejerk liberal.) He has an awful, inexplicable sense of the power it would give him to hurl the boy to the street below. The moment parallels one earlier in the play in which he stood at the window of a skyscraper, aware of the curious drive within him to throw himself out. These authentically felt and described moments of vertigo are presented within the elaborate conceit the playwright presents of himself as an old-fashioned celluloid gumshoe—the archness and coyness of this image tended to attenuate and dilute an otherwise disturbing play.

A modest but affecting effort by Donald Margulies, *Found A Peanut*, presented a tale of cupidity, betrayal, and struggles for power among children ranging in age from five to fourteen, impersonated with uncanny skill by actors in their twenties. The play, believable as a portrait of children, is full of hints of the kind of manipulative adults they will become. We also sense the shadows of the parents who have made them the way they are. What makes the play memorable is the balance Margulies

achieves between the humor he sees in the children's dilemmas and the keen sense of their pain he conveys.

A play that offered promise but virtually no fulfillment was Peter Parnell's *Romance Language*, an attempt to dramatize the aspirations of the major American literary figures of the nineteenth century. The idea was intriguing, the execution entirely campy. Equally disappointing was Peter Ustinov's *Beethoven's Tenth*, which offered the amusing prospect of Beethoven magically coming back to life in the house of a twentieth-century music critic, but the normally inventive Ustinov, playing the composer, seems to have conceived the play mainly as a pretext for shtick and predictable jokes. Beth Henley, who won a Pulitzer Prize for her play *Crimes of the Heart*, continued working the familiar territory of coming of age in the South in *The Miss Firecracker Contest*.

If there is a revived interest in the Word, it would be wrong to suggest that the theatrical innovations of the past twenty years are being abandoned. One of the most important events of the year was a brief run of *La Tempesta*, an Italian version of Shakespeare's *Tempest* directed by Giorgio Strehler, whom Europeans have always ranked with Peter Brook as a stage innovator but whose only work presented in New York for more than a decade was the Paris Opera's production of *The Marriage of Figaro* in 1976.

Strehler is best known for a style of lighting in which the back of the stage is lit, the apron dark, which creates a series of silhouettes that enhance the play's meanings. Strehler used a fairly barren stage for most of the play, which had the effect of lending increased significance to any given prop— a crown, for example—that did appear. He also used elements of classical Italian theater that brought the seventeenth-century play into more familiar territory for Italian audiences and even English-speaking ones.

Such a production is useful—apart from the ways it illuminated the play—in reminding locals, constantly fretting over the state of the theater, how ancient and deep its roots are. However doubtful the health of a given branch, the tree stands firm.

The Year in Poetry

Lewis Turco

Last year there appeared to be some indefinite fits and starts—on the part of some of the younger poets—in the direction of a return to formal writing, something that has been missing in American poetry since the 1950s; but in passing we noted that even more obviously there was a fair number of the "free verse" (that is, *phrased prose*) poets in the U.S. who were writing story poems, or at least poems with some sort of narrative line.

It is important for poets to understand that poems are written for an audience, for other people, and that, in order for readers to continue to read past the first line or two of a poem, something in it must catch and carry their attention. Poets used to know that the "personal poem," what has been known for twenty-five years now as the "confessional" poem, traditionally utilized language music, lyricism, to catch and carry the attention. Nearly all lyric poems are egopoetic in nature, confessional, personal. Not all confessional poems, however, are musical; few are noteworthy beyond their writers' lives because the only interest they have is autobiographical, and there are always new and more topical autobiographies to arrest those who enjoy personal histories rather than literature.

There may or may not be something of a return to formal lyricism in America today—the signals last year appeared to be mixed—but there is little doubt that there has been a movement toward a return to narrative in poetry as a means of interesting the reader in something beyond peculiarities of poets' personality traits and idiosyncratic behavior. In his "Foreword to Kelly's Grandchild," from his book of traditionally formal poems and satires *The Ballad of the Dollar Hotel and Other Poems* (Mountain Laurel), Richard Nason writes, "A few years ago I wandered into the Salmugundi Club on Fifth Avenue in Greenwich Village and heard Nobel Nominee Jorge Luis Borges speak. . . . In the course of [his] talk [Borges] told the American scribes they should pay more attention to the forsaken and neglected poets like Rudyard Kipling and A. E. Housman. Borges meant that poets should bring the narrative line back into American poetry. That's the only way they could reintroduce philosophy to their verse. Needless to say, philosophy embraces aesthetics (beauty), ethics (morality) and metaphysics (spirituality).

"Borges was speaking against the tragic absence of all these qualities in the poetry being written by our laureates today. The Existential poetry of William Carlos Williams, sensible enough perhaps as a reaction to the heavy metaphysical burden of the poetry of Eliot, Pound and, to a lesser degree, Yeats, has in recent decades degenerated to the grudging gibberish of Ashbery and the vacuous, verbless maundering of Ammons. The highly remote, almost indecipherable content of this verse has remained of interest only to those who study it so they may become initiates in the elite academia where it is taught.

"By divesting poetry of all substance and accessible meaning they have alienated the once-vast audience for American poetry. This is a cultural tragedy of the first magnitude. Borges was telling us that it need not be everlasting. That poets can bring back the narrative, reintroduce philosophy, reinvoke in their verse such ancient and efficacious fixtures as common sense, empathy, recall and affectivity; and in the process . . . win back the allegiance of society to the honorable causes of Homer and Shakespeare."

One poet who has always given us a blend of personality and story is the late Richard Hugo. Now, in *Making Certain It Goes On: The Collected Poems of Richard Hugo* (Norton), we are able to see the whole life and life's story of one of America's more interesting contemporary poets. This collection was arranged sequentially by Ripley Hugo and Matthew Hansen.

Richard Eberhart has published his new book, *The Long Reach: New and Uncollected Poems 1948-1984* (New Directions). This is a major event, for Eberhart is an important poet. Eberhart said in the "Foreword" of his *Selected Poems 1930-1965* (1966), "Poetry is like the mystery of the world. . . . It is spiritual and it is sensuous and in its sensuous meshes the spirit is caught as in a thicket. . . ." At its best, Eberhart's poetry achieves this synthesis of mystery and concretion. Although he has been accused by some readers of careless writing in a large production, Eberhart has written some of the finest lyric poems since the great Modernist generation of the early twentieth century.

In many of Eberhart's poems—those written in his middle years particularly—the elements of

Richard Eberhart
THE LONG REACH
New & Uncollected Poems
1948-1984

Cover for the New Directions Eberhart Collection, in which the poet's work achieves a "synthesis of mystery and concretion"

I stood there in the whirling summer,
My hand capped a withered heart,
And thought of China and of Greece,
Of Alexander in his tent;
Of Montaigne in his tower,
Of Saint Theresa in her wild lament.

Eberhart's technique is generally neither traditional nor experimental, but colloquially elegiac. When he writes at the peak of his powers, his poems powerfully confront nature and man's dilemma as a conscious creature caught in the toils of mortality, as in "The Cancer Cells,"

. . . a virulent laughing gang.
They looked like art itself, like the artist's mind,
Powerful shaker, and the taker of new forms.

If the tendency to over-philosophize is Eberhart's main problem, minor ones are an overuse of large words and, on occasion, inexact narrative. As an example of the latter, one might point to "Opposition," the first poem in Eberhart's *Florida Poems* (1981) and collected in this new book. In it he contrasts Florida with New England. The first stanza talks about Florida; the second and concluding stanza says of New England that the Puritans " . . . thought life could be better,/Prayed to God not to do anything wrong,/Held back their passion, aimed to kill,/Burned as witches free life-loving girls." But no witches were ever burned in North America, they were hanged; and it was not the girls who were accused of witchcraft at Salem in 1692, it was the girls who were the accusers of the "witches," most of whom were older women. Anyone who knows these facts will realize that the poem self-destructs through error; not through fictive "lies," but through historical inaccuracy.

Douglas Worth, in his *From Dream, from Circumstance: New & Selected Poems 1963-1983* (Apple-Wood), seems to have developed little if at all. A phrased prose poet of the sort discussed at length here last year, he at first broke his lines at arbitrary, seemingly random places, as in "Maple" (1974): "as if/burning/old love letters//one could empty the heart/of its weight/of yellowed dreams//and sleep/bone clean/and waken green." (The rhyme appears to be accidental.) Though many poems have longer lines now, Worth is still doing the same thing, essentially, ten years later, as in "New Age": "Slowly, the overripe/season's/gold gown, skin//comes rustling/in tattered/majesty to the ground//and the long bone dream/of green/is everywhere." Worth seems more conscious of sound in the later

intellect and rationality tend to govern his work through abstractions that undercut the conflict of the flesh and the spirit, of life and death, which are the central concerns of this poet. One of his most famous poems, "The Fury of Aerial Bombardment," shows clearly this tendency toward over-intellectuality, but in this case the poem turns rhetoric into tragedy by means of a simple catalogue of names of dead soldiers and concrete detail in the last stanza. "The Groundhog" also achieves the synthesis of mystery and reality: "In June, amid the golden fields,/I saw a groundhog lying dead." The poet is shaken, "And mind outshot our naked frailty." The process of decay begins, and the poet returns in autumn " . . . to see/The sap gone out of the groundhog," but the process has not yet been completed. Three years later "There is no sign of the groundhog." The poet is struck at last with the full implications of man's mortality, the fact of eternal mutability, which is the only thing that is unchanging:

poems. The "narratives" throughout are minimal and egopoetic.

David Meltzer is one of those people who believe, evidently, that they are merely instruments of the gods or the muses, by which means poems write themselves. This is the first paragraph of his introduction to *The Name Selected Poetry 1973 1983* (Black Sparrow Press): "I wrote my first poem at eleven. It came through me and out of me, a combination of vision and transmission. Maybe 'trance-mission' would be more accurate. I was in the center of its energy like a glass or lens where words not light come through." Shouldn't we expect that the products of such a visionary experience would be ineffable rather than prosaic, profound rather than cute (like the pun), apocalyptic rather than cryptic? Most of these pieces are in series. Here is the first strophe of *Bolero* (1976):

> It looms up.
> Another word
> larger than a book.
> *Bolero*
> Eyes lit like radio tubes;
> familiar phantom.

Gary Gildner has been a fine storyteller for fifteen years or more. The poems in his *Blue Like the Heavens: New & Selected Poems* (University of Pittsburgh Press) are often autobiographical, but the narrator is an interested yet objective persona who knows how to involve the reader with his characters and incidents. Gildner's voice, too, is that of a practiced raconteur who can use imagery to hold attention and rhythm to move the action forward. This is a book that is enjoyable to read.

Nancy Willard's *In His Country* (1966) was a fine first book. Willard had a mind that liked to tangle disparate but strangely relevant ideas in the skein of language, as in the first stanza of "Picture Puzzles":

> It's because we're broken
>   that we love
>   puzzles, pictures
> cut all askew, fifteen hundred
>   pieces, salvage
> of divine catastrophe.
>   For two dollars my mother
> buys, in good faith,
>   Fra Engelico's Nativity,
> incredibly cracked,
>   sung
> like God's defense
>   on a skeptic tongue.

Then Willard unraveled the strands gracefully in the denouement. Her concerns were religious, having to do with doubt and the possibility of faith in a faithless world, but she was not overwhelmed by philosophy, for she wanted to say something complex, and she knew that she must perform as well as speculate while she tried to save herself and others. She knew that performance is half of art.

Willard's second book, *Skin of Grace* (1967), coming as it did hard on the heels of her first, showed no great development in style, but it did exhibit a deeper involvement with the physical, as distinguished from the spiritual, world. The last stanza of the title poem stood at the very end of the volume, and it summed up the poet's evolving concerns:

> O see the healing, the linnets, the spinning worm,
>   the flash and pivot of creatures living
>   under the skin of grace.

Willard's third book was *19 Masks for the Naked Poet* (1971)—it appeared in a chapbook edition from a small press with illustrations by Regina Shekerjian—and her fourth was *Carpenter of the Sun* (1974). In it there was a change in style, but not a radical one. The poet's earlier books had been relatively formal; now, her work became more colloquial, looser in structure, but not nearly so loose as the poems of many of her contemporaries. Her concerns had changed little, but her emphasis now was overtly upon the things of this world and of the imagination, as "The Church" makes clear:

> If the walls are whitewashed clean, I hope
> that under the show of purity I can find
> a mural of monkeys pressing wine,
> that below the candles on the choir stall
>
> someone has carved a dancing bear or a boy
> riding a wild boar.
> The man who makes the dragon under the
> saint's feet must know the dragon is
>
> beautiful. And therefore, on the altar,
> the Bible will rest on the back of a griffin
> to remind you that the beast is present
> in every birth.
>
> You shall not exclude them from the communion
> of saints and men. If the roof is plain,
> put a cock on the steeple; you shall not
> exclude them from your marriages.

William Blake's Inn: Poems for Innocent and Experienced Travelers won the Newbery Medal for

Dust jacket for the Knopf Poetry Series book of poems, Klappert's second book in 1984

1982. While she was writing her poems Nancy Willard was also becoming well known as the author of books for children. This collection pulled the two strands of her talent together, for it can be enjoyed by readers of any age. *Household Tales of Moon and Water* appeared in 1982, but the reader would have been able to tell that the two volumes were concurrent without reference to their dates, for many of the poems are about Willard's own experience with motherhood and her interest in Blake, as in "Vision and Late Supper" which opens,

Today my son asks me, "What is a vision?"
I say, "Blake saw God in a tree,
and his daddy beat him for telling lies.
That is a vision."

Willard is remarkable in her consistency. Ever the entertainer, ever the craftsman, always the philosopher, the strata of her poems lie one upon the other, the lower layers providing the solid foundation for deep structures of thought and feeling whose surfaces appear as ordinary and as engaging as a meadowland. She is one of those poets who can

be read by anyone enjoyably, simply or profoundly.

Now *19 Masks for the Naked Poet* is reissued in a cloth edition with extra illustrations by Shekerjian (Harcourt Brace Jovanovich). This slim series is an autobiography of the poet, but not necessarily Willard herself, for the third-person viewpoint is used, as in the titles: "The Poet Takes a Photograph of His Heart"; "The Poet Plants a Forest in His Wife's Marimba," and so forth. These are dramatic poems, then, not egopoetic; even so, they constitute an artistic credo and manifesto. Like *William Blake's Inn*, this book can be read and savored either by children or adults, and it will be.

Those who know Norman Friedman's work may be astonished to discover that *The Magic Badge: Poems 1953-1984* (Slough Press) is his first collection of poetry. Those who do not know his work have some fine reading in store. Last year in this space Emily Dickinson was quoted as to how one recognizes a true poem: "If I read a book, and it makes my body so cold no fire can ever warm me, I know *that* is poetry. If I feel physically as if the top of my head were taken off, I know *that* is poetry. These are the only ways I know it. Is there any other way?". That shock of recognition occurs again and again as one turns these pages. For Friedman life is a dream, often a bad one. He writes a controlled verse mode line, and his forms are loosely traditional, but within these structures hallucination occurs, the madness of reality. Here is "The Salmon-Falls, The Mackerel-Crowded Seas":

> Patrolling the breakers with the insistent
> intensity of gulls, all these people jamming
> the beaches seem younger than I, having
> been reproduced at a greater rate, millions
> of assembly-line dolls coarsely made,
> cheaply put together and as quickly falling
> apart, in their shocking clothes and flashy
> talk, swarming over the world, chattering,
> they skim the coastline in flocks, flooding
> the shore, foraging for food, rummaging,
> raging for love, each with a frantic heart
> as dangerous as mine, genitals as hungry,
> genetic package as obsessed, each feeling
> as much emptiness, as much right to ravage
> the planet, they dive for clams or crabs
> to snatch in talon and beak, lift up in
> shocks of air, and let flash on rocks to
> crack and be torn to glut the glutinous
> meat within, scolding and clawing each other,
> then jamming once again to swarm the seas
> on their frenzied search, muttering nearly
> intelligible cries, guttural and mournful in
> my tireless throat, toys against the harsh
> and unheeding scrutiny of the spoiling skies.

Friedman somehow turns people into birds, birds into the planet made flesh and blood, the planet and its hungers into himself. This is some of the best writing of the year, and of the years during which Friedman has been writing.

Selected Poems (University of Arkansas Press) is John Ciardi's first showcase collection since *As If: Poems New and Selected* (1955), and it contains some work from that volume, so this is an extensive look at the production of almost three decades. The new book is divided into several sections: "Tribal Poems," from *39 Poems* (1959), is made up of stories about family: "Aunt Mary died of eating twelve red peppers/after a hard day's work.—Now what shall I pray for gluttonous Aunt Mary/who loved us till we screamed?" The next section is titled from an earlier book, *I Marry You* (1958). These are stories of family again, but the narrator is now the father. "Thickets" is third, a general collection, many having to do with nature, others with the dead: friends, poets. "On the Patio" deals with neighbors and family; "Bang Bang," from *As If*, is about World War II; "Conversations," from *Person to Person* (1964), is made of monologues and dialogues with

people from Leonardo to God, from oneself to outer space. Finally, "Lives of X," from the 1972 book of the same title, is made of long, autobiographical narratives—the book goes in a circle.

But what a circle it is! Though Ciardi follows no chronological order, the poems have been rearranged and new ones added so that the architecture of the whole gives one the feeling, when one has finished reading, that one has come as close to the poet as to an old friend. Ciardi is one of the great storytellers. Reading his work is both an entertainment and an education, a total experience, like life.

Another important book from Arkansas is George Garrett's *Collected Poems*. Garrett has published six volumes of poetry since his first, *The Reverend Ghost*, which appeared in 1957; his *New and Selected Poems* appeared in 1967. The poet is at home in all sorts of forms, from epigrams to aubades, from phrased prose to strict verse. Like Ciardi, he is a fine formal storyteller. Here is "Book Review" in its entirety:

> I am using your pages
> to start wet kindling wood.
> Amazing such pale poems
> can make a bright fire!

Which brings to mind a medieval Irish epigram:

> Not spoken about in Eire
> And among the Scots unmissed,
> If I'd not here dropped his name
> The O'Flynn would not exist.

Some traditions will never die, including the tradition of good writing that grows out of, and has a respect for, history and literature.

Eve Triem's *New As a Wave, A Retrospective 1937-1983* (Dragon Gate), is the 1984 Western States Book Award Winner for Lifetime Achievement. Triem began as a sometimes traditionally lyric poet writing in such forms as the rubai and Italian sonnet, but most often in a standard sort of phrased prose—she managed in some of her earlier poems to sound a good deal like H. D., especially when she invoked the Greek gods, heroes, and heroines.

Darwin's Ark (Indiana University Press) is a volume of poems inspired by Charles Darwin, in whom the author, Philip Appleman, has been interested all his life, as he tells us in a preface. The black and white illustrations are by Rudy Pozzati. These phrased prose poems sometimes remind one of the anthropological, humanist writings of the late Loren Eiseley, one of our finest essayists and con-

Cover for Duncan's first book of poetry in fifteen years, containing further sequences from the ongoing "Structures of Rime" and "Passages" series begun in his earlier books

templators of the long ages. Appleman's poems are meditations on the passage of species and of time, the implications of these passages for mankind. In the title poem Darwin dreams he is Noah ordered to build a boat. This poem is preceded by a series, "Darwin's Bestiary," and it is followed by another series, "Phobias," containing various fears—of ten-year-olds, specialists, fear itself—and, contrarily, "Euphorias." Thus, though the book has a distinctly didactic quality and intent, the method of instruction is the "exemplum" or story. It is entertaining, interesting, and always well written.

In his introduction to *Ground Work* (New Directions), Robert Duncan gives us the requisite neotranscendental essay on soulful poetics, a la Allen Ginsberg and Charles Olson, which sheds no light whatsoever on his practice but lets us know that the Oversoul is on his side, whispering in his ear as he composes: "In *Passages* verses may be articulated into phrases or tesserae of utterances and silences leading to a series of possible sentences. As *Passages* themselves are but passages of a poem beyond that calls itself *Passages* and that is manifest

only in the course of the books in which it appears, even so phrases have both their own meaning and yet belong to the unfolding revelation of a Sentence beyond the work." One assumes that this is the sort of thing that is "taught" at Naropa Institute.

The poems are more interesting, to a degree, than these pseudo-prosodics; unfortunately, Duncan continues his Emersonian pedantry throughout the book, in notes and prefaces, in quotations from and reworkings of the seventeenth-century English poets. Perhaps one could eventually figure out what Duncan is trying to do, but one doesn't have the time, the will, or the inclination to try. This is Duncan's first book in fifteen years.

Once upon a time Lawrence Ferlinghetti had a true, lyric ear. He might have used it to become a fine traditional poet. Instead, he shrugged it off and deliberately wrote bad prose poems, like those of his friend Allen Ginsberg, who never had a lyric ear, yet who is of late years attempting to write rhymed, metered verse like that of his late father, Louis Ginsberg, but having even less success with it. The last time Ferlinghetti's ear for sound manifested itself was in *A Coney Island of the Mind* (1958), not insignificantly his most popular book. Between then and now, in *Over all the Obscene Boundaries: European Poems and Translations* (New Directions), Ferlinghetti has written didactic harangues and speeches that either shout in one's ear or attempt to get a reaction by the use of Pavlovian "cue" words, like Hallmark cards, except that the words are at opposite poles of meaning (like *obscene* in this title). However, in his new book Ferlinghetti has returned to the scenes of his youth, in Paris and elsewhere. In reminiscing, his good ear has returned, reasserted itself. These are enjoyable poems to read, for the most part, with only occasional lapses into the fumigatory.

But no one tells a story quite like Carolyn Kizer, as a slow passage down the pages of her new book, *Yin* (BOA Editions), will demonstrate. A feminist, Kizer remembers how to get and keep the reader's attention without resorting to the sensational or the shocking. In "Semele Recycled," for instance, the poet tells a story out of Greek myth, but she makes it so near, familiar, and compelling, loads it with so much resonance, that the reader wants to keep going and going. Not every poem in the collection measures up to her best standards, but overall, what a fine writer Kizer is and has been for years.

In *Emily's Bread* by Sandra M. Gilbert (Norton), the self is so much more important to the writer than her stories and the characters in them that our attention wanders as we read—unless, perhaps, we are militant "feminists" who enjoy absorbing exempla in the now one-sided Battle of the Sexes.

Drawn by Stones, by Earth, by Things that Have Been in the Fire (Atheneum) by Marvin Bell is a more deeply textured book than his previous collections, more engaged with language, even with narrative. But his nostalgic "I" narrator grates at last, as previously, though perhaps not so quickly. The soul worn too long on the sleeve thins at last to the shade of sentiment.

Marvin Bell selected James Galvin's *God's Mis-*

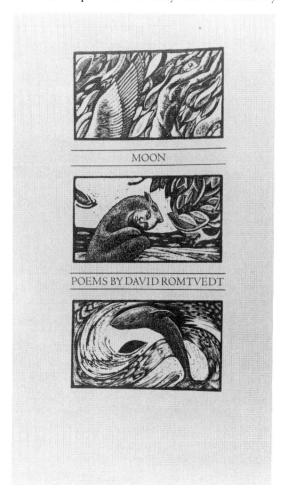

More new books of poetry for 1984

tress (Harper and Row) as the winner in the Open Competition of the National Poetry Series. Here, too, we have the egopoetic narrator maundering on about himself and how sad and poignant everything is that he thinks or says he does. Here is the beginning of "Misericord":

Out at the end of a high promontory
above the dim, oceanic prairie,
we built a little fire for warmth.

Who ever doubted that the earth fell from the sky?
As though it had traveled a great distance to reach us

and still could not reach us,
though we held our hands out to it,
some vague intention, some apprehension
occurred between us.

It happened on the page as well.

Deception Pass by Sue Standing (Alice James Books) is more of the same—the Ego Involved with Itself, Isolated, Insignificant, and Irritating.

Again this year, like last, Robert Wallace is feeling nostalgic in *Girlfriends and Wives* (Carnegie-Mellon University Press); and, like last, he takes us on a trip through his life, only this time we meet all the girls and women he has traveled through and left behind, one of whom is "Irene":

Gerald went with you before I did,
and teased me about how far you went
with him. He's been dead for twenty years.

Holding your hand in hallways or under a blanket
at football games, sometimes I wondered
how you could ever come to look like your mother.

Across the street from the lights of your house,
winter and summer, we parked and necked and
    talked.
I forget now why we stopped going steady.

Eyes pale as air, under leafy streetlamps
you let my hand slip down into your blouse
to touch the warm mice soft in their nests.

The thing about Wallace's story is this: when he's done telling it, we feel as though it's ours he's told.

There are stories, too, in Tess Gallagher's *Willingly* (Graywolf Press)—"Boat Ride" is quite a long one—but narrative is not this poet's strongest suit; song is. The trouble is that Gallagher doesn't exploit her good lyric ear. She writes in a phrased prose mode that looks and sounds too much like many another poet, the language music buried beneath flat syntax. If she were to let herself sing, we would likely find her work remarkable.

Michael Blumenthal enters the lists this year with two books. *Laps* (University of Massachusetts Press) won the 1984 Juniper Prize for its author. This is a series about swimming, which Blumenthal intends to treat symbolically. But the "Prologue" begins with a stiff iambic pentameter quatrain, then dives into imitations of Popean heroic couplets (except for one line, which is short); the second poem begins as a parody of Roethke's "The Waking" before it stops imitating the villanelle and turns into phrased prose. The fourth poem is unrhymed dipods. Finally, Blumenthal settles down into short-lined, phrased prose for the rest of the book.

One of Blumenthal's favorite tropes is the catachrestic mixed metaphor—in one passage he calls the body "the soul's wet suit,/the mind's a cappella/accompaniment, the one note/so often out of tune/in the Vienna Boys' Choir/of the soul." In the next poem he sees some retarded children and ends with the insightful, "I see myself, I say: there/but for the grace of God/go I. And I go on." In the next he says of people watching him swim, "They all complain/about their bulging waists,/their dulling jobs,/expensive tastes./They spend their sleep/in wishing they were slim/like those of us below,/awake, who swim." This is a literature of the unfeeling and the self-righteous, of bathos and shallows.

Blumenthal's second book, *Days We would Rather Know* (Viking/Penguin) is a great deal better, fortunately. It is a collection, not a sequence, and it is both formally and intellectually more consistent, at the same time that it has a greater variety of subjects and approaches. It contains some good writing.

W. D. Ehrhart is another two-volume poet this year, but he is something special, a powerful writer. *To Those Who Have Gone Home Tired: New & Selected Poems* (Thunder's Mouth Press) gathers work from six previous volumes, all published by small houses, and adds a seventh section of new poems. *The Outer Banks & Other Poems* (Adastra Press) is a collection that ends with the title series of ten poems, in which the poet approaches some hard-won tranquility, but the book begins with a straight prose piece, "The Dream," which expresses this poet's obsessive concern with the Vietnam War.

"The Dream" is anything but peaceful, and it will knock your socks off. If its ending is predictable, it is the predictability of dread. You know the worst is coming, but—as in a dream—you are unable to prevent it, and unwilling to stop reading.

Nearly all of Ehrhart's poems are narratives, and his ability to tell a story so that it gets into your mind and stays there is absolute. It is a great pity that a poet this strong has to struggle in the small presses. He deserves a great audience. Perhaps we don't want to hear what he has to say—but we'd better hear it anyway, for our own sakes.

What does one call Peter Klappert's *'52 Pick-Up Scenes from The Conspiracy A Documentary: A Poem in 52 Scenes, 2 Jokers, and an Extra Ace of Spades* (Orchises) that he hasn't already called it himself? A joke, probably. At least these fragments seem to have humor as their object, though it's hard to tell, they're such shards of language:

Male's post-ejaculatory whistle
a message to "take it easy."
Two Princeton University Professors think

Even the shape of the volume is funny. One sighs to think of the tree that died to make this "book." Klappert's second book this year is *The Idiot Princess of the Last Dynasty* (Knopf). This one at least makes sense. It is a long series with a central protagonist, "Doc" Dan Mahoney, an American expatriate of the generation that was "lost." Mahoney is the narrator, and in these monologues cover the period of the Third Republic, September 1939-June 1940. It is an ambitious work, too long and involved to treat here, but it has weight. One wonders how the same poet could have written both books. Perhaps the former was a sort of tailing-off after such a large labor. If so, it should have remained on Klappert's doodle pad.

Stephen Dobyns's *Black Dog, Red Dog* (Holt, Rinehart and Winston), published in the National Poetry Series, reads as easily and as well as a book of short stories. The lines of the verse-mode narratives are an easy iambic pentameter with variations, usually extra unstressed syllables, that reads like prose but subtly provides a strong heartbeat for the images that creep up on you, engross your imagination and attention, and pull you along inexorably to the climax of the story. These are very good poems indeed.

Conrad Hilberry's *The Moon Seen as a Slice of Pineapple* (University of Georgia Press) is made up of three sets of poems. The first, "Housemarks," is about designs from Rudolph Koch's *Book of Signs.* The individual pieces are monologues. The second set is "The Man in the Attic," autobiographical sometimes, but not always—a collection of single items mainly. The final section combines the two

approaches. The designs on which half the "Mexican Poems" are written "are from ancient Mexican clay stamps. . . ." Hilberry writes clearly; his poems often flirt with formality, but they never are stiff, and the stories they tell are engaging and uncomplicated.

Sharon Olds's *The Dead and the Living* (Knopf) is the 1983 Lamont Poetry Selection of the Academy of American Poets. Olds is a teller of compassionate stories. She is generally in command of her narratives, which she seldom allows to become overly sentimental, though sentiment is a large part of this work. One can see no reason whatever for her breaking the lines as she does, however, for these are straight prose pieces, not verse in any way. Olds is not aware at all of complex rhythms or of anything beyond the sensory and ideational levels. Reading too many of these good-hearted little tales at one sitting can be a cloying experience.

In *A Happy Childhood* (Atlantic, Little-Brown) William Matthews sometimes tells a moderately interesting story, but mostly these egopoems are boring. The incessant "I" of the narrator tends to exclude the reader from these celebrations of the self which are unrelieved by lyricism or a strong sensory effect.

Much the same might be said about Dick Allen's *Overnight in the Guest House of the Mystic* (Louisiana State University Press), except that Allen uses so many approaches and is so aware of the various effects available to him on the four levels of poetry—typographical, sonic, sensory, and ideational—that he manages to interest the reader in his nostalgic narratives of the self.

Of this little grouping of egopoets so far, Greg Pape in *Black Branches* (University of Pittsburgh Press) is the most interesting. Although these pieces are autobiographical for the most part, and the viewpoint is author-oriented, first person, single-angle, subjective access narrative, Pape has a way of defining the personalities of the other characters in the poems, of getting us involved, and of summing up or encapsulating his themes climactically, as for instance in these three stanzas from "Stanley":

Where do the failed fathers go
after the jobs are lost
and the money runs out

and tears have dried to salt?
they turn to snow?
They drive blue Fords to Mexico?

We know what the mothers do,
they take us with them
wherever they go.

Len Roberts in *From the Dark* (S.U.N.Y. Press) also tells stories on himself, diving headlong into nostalgia, but, like Pape, he has the ability to make the tales he tells of the good and bad old days of childhood fresh and absorbing.

It has been claimed, and one tends to believe it is true, that there are West Coast poets and East Coast poets. People in the West read their bards, and those in the East read theirs—for the most part. However, West Coast poetry has enclaves in the East, particularly in New York City, whereas East Coast or "establishment" poetry is totally ignored out West, except perhaps in the Northwest.

West Coast poetry since the 1950s has been "experimental," meaning that it follows the prose example of Whitman and the phrased, variably-accentual prosody of William Carlos Williams. Since the 1960s East Coast poets have, to a fair degree, "loosened up"; that is, they gave in, part-way, to the "free-form" folks out West, though they remained more coherent and less *groovy*, like they used to say, less "hip."

Anne Waldman is psychically a West Coast poet—complete with blurb from Allen Ginsberg—who, in her *Makeup on Empty Space* (Toothpaste Press), appears to be reversing the flow of the 1960s, becoming more formal, which is an interesting development.

Howard Moss's twelfth book of poems, *Rules of Sleep* (Atheneum), begins with a pun: "The wrong assumption flirted with the possible:/A grave burst open,/St. Clare's body still in her nightdress/Flying in a vertical rush to Heaven,/Abandoning the stones speechless with sadness." The title of this first poem is "In Umbria," and this portion of the collection discusses Italy intelligently and feelingly, in ruminative, variable blank verse. Later, Moss investigates other subjects in a variety of methods and approaches, some more formal than others, but always beneath his thoughtful evocations there lies the framework of the small tale, the exemplum from the land of the living and the dead. Moss is a pleasure to read.

Copacetic by Yusef Komunyakaa (Wesleyan University Press) is a first full-length collection, and it is full of poems that fascinate for their story, their language art, and the personality of their author, which comes through strongly despite the objective or dramatic viewpoints of many of the poems. The themes range widely over folk material, autobiogra-

phy, social problems, but the ad hoc forms the poet uses to express himself never repeat. The rhythms of many of the best poems are jazz.

The jacket blurb of *Ark 50 Spires 34-50* (Dutton) says that this book "is the second volume of Ronald Johnson's ambitious long American poem, an evolving work-in-progress that has been compared to such masterpieces as Pound's *Cantos*, Zukofsky's *A*, and Williams' *Paterson*." If that's a bit florid, still there is something engaging about these exercises in musical syntax. Here is a section from "Spire on the Death of L. Z.:

> bees purring a
> cappella
> in utter emerald cornfield
> till the cows come
> purple home
> this is paradise
> this is
> happening
> on the surface of a bubble

Cover for the book in which Ferlinghetti returns to the scenes of his youth

The "spires" may not make "sense," but, like music, they can beguile the ear, and like abstract art, intrigue the eye. This volume is a winner of the 1984 National Poetry Series competition.

Another long "American" poem is Alfred Corn's *Notes from a Child in Paradise* (Viking/Penguin). It is all story, an autobiography, in various forms of verse, that tells about the poet's falling in love in the mid-1960s, of his subsequent marriage to Anne and their eventual separation. Corn gives this odyssey a mythic quality by drawing parallels between the couple's physical/spiritual journey and the Lewis and Clark expedition, and by allusions to Dante's *Divine Comedy*. If this sounds ambitious, it is; in large part, amazingly, it works.

The Evolution of the Flightless Bird by Richard Kenney, this year's selection in the Yale Series of Younger Poets (Yale University Press), is a remarkable first book. In his foreword James Merrill says, "With its agreeable eddies of temperament, reflections that braid and shatter only to recompose downstream, this book moves like a river in a country of ponds." Kenney doesn't merely write, he *thinks* as he writes, and he conjures the language to do the many things simultaneously. This is what's so unusual, for such textures are generally the mark of a more mature *makir*, though they are the mark of the very few in these days of the heartful posturing of the self-involved and the other-inflicting.

Edmund Pennant's *Mis apprehensions* (Lintel) is this poet's third book of poems. The first, *I, Too, Jehovah*, appeared in 1962, and his second, *Dream's Navel*, in 1979. Here we have a writer who is able to wrap his fine imagination in original language. This is the whole of "Beginning":

> The first mustard weed
> came back on Hiroshima
> surprisingly golden
> though thin,
>
> and the wild carrot,
> dusky white, the struts
> of the umbels thin.
>
> It would take longer
> for the first iris,
> their petals dangling
> like skin.
>
> We who saw the flash
> and remember no sound in
> the epicenter, soon
>
> will be gone. We pray

> clean rain may purge every seed
> and render it benign, O Lord,
> as in the beginning,
>
> when the lion within the sun
> roared roses, heal-all and violets,
> and wild vervain.

The herbs have their significances: vervain is the key to the gates of Faery; it is sacred because it is used in rites of sacrifice, and it heals many wounds, according to the ancient loresmen. Pennant applies both learning and intelligence to his poems; as a result, they are amplified.

Even if Ron McFarland hadn't said, in the introduction to Dixie Partridge's *Deer in the Haystacks* (Ahsahta Press), that William Stafford had been the author's teacher, one perhaps might have been able to tell—not in this first book's style so much as in its folklore-feeling tales and narratives about the American Northwest. These are plainly prose poems, but the stories are often interesting. Of similar impact and feeling are the poems of David Romtvedt in his first collection, *Moon* (Bieler Press), except that this is a theme book: the poems are evidently intended—according to a forenote—to be read "as expressions of the heart. . . ." in the cause of getting the reader to help "banish all nuclear weapons from the world. And one day to banish all human suffering. Only this."

Ahsahta also published in 1984 *At the Tent of Heaven* by Philip St. Clair, a series of formal monologues by American Indians which, taken as a series, give a poetic history of the tribes and their trials, feelings, concerns. It is very well done. *Jacklight* is by Louise Erdich (Holt, Rinehart and Winston), a young woman who is part Chippewa. Her personal poems and narratives have something of the same feeling as the St. Clair volume, but not the technical competence.

A look, next, at the 1984 crop of small press chapbooks. At the beginning of this essay Richard Nason was quoted on the subject, among other things, of John Ashbery, whom he accused of writing poetry without "meaning"—Ashbery's most recent book, issued in 1984, is *A Wave* (Viking). It appears that there is an Ashbery school of poetry in formation; or perhaps one should say that the "New York School" of poets is going national as the so-called "LANGUAGE poets." The theoretics of this school probably go back to 1958, when the British poet Donald Davie brought out the American edition of his scholarly book *Articulate Energy*. Davie discussed the forms of syntax in English

Jared Carter

Pincushion's Strawberry

Cover for a new book by a poet whose first collection won a Walt Whitman Award

language poetry. Briefly, he said that there were three kinds of syntax traditionally: "subjective" (or *egopoetic*) syntax has the word order following the form of a thought in the mind of a poet (I am in love with darkness); "objective" (or *narrative*) syntax has the word order following the form of an action (John drew his pistol and shot the mad dog); "dramatic" syntax has the word order following the form of a thought in the mind of a persona invented by the poet ("To be or not to be, that is the question" Hamlet says, not Shakespeare).

Davie then spoke about other, nontraditional kinds of syntax, mainly to be found in the twentieth century, especially in such a poet as Wallace Stevens, who wrote in what Davie called "musical" syntax, by analogy with music, which is the most abstract of the arts (that is, there are no "meanings" attached to musical notes, yet they are arranged as "ideas" when a composer composes). However, the syntax might better be called "abstract" syntax, by

analogy with nonrepresentational art, for such art dispensed with recognizable form in an attempt to approach the condition of music.

"Abstract" syntax, then, follows the form of a thought in the mind of the poet, *but without defining that thought.* Thus, the Ashbery school paints abstract word pictures which are not meant to be "understood" or "followed" in the ordinary sense; rather, the reader is to give himself or herself up to the poet just as an audience gives itself up to the sounds of the orchestra. Abstract poetry attempts to follow the dictum of Archibald MacLeish in his "Ars Poetica": "A poem should not mean, but *be*."

Or, to quote a couple of lines from the LANGUAGE poet Lyn Hejinian's chapbook *The Guard* (Tuumba Press), "The chronic idea turns up / a sunny day as an arresting abstract." Here is a bit more than a stanza from this long poem:

Tossed off, serene, Chinese

windmills turn horizontally. The caves cooperate
with factories. Deep
in their mountains they move
spread on lattice, pitched for days
as still as the print on the wall.
The sky was packed
which by appearing endless seems inevitable.

It appears that this new kind of writing is displacing Robert Bly's "deep imagism" as the "avant garde" movement of the 1980s. As the style progresses, it will be interesting to see whether the new poets will be able to approach the mastery of Stevens or Eliot in *The Waste Land*, which, as edited by Pound, was also written largely in abstract syntax. It seems odd that this "new" movement has its roots, like most of the other poetry of post-Modernism, in a particular aspect of Modernism—perhaps the giants of the first quarter of this century really did do it all, and there's nothing left for us to do but nibble their orts.

The beautifully produced chapbook *Tremayne: Four Poems by Donald Justice* comes from the Windhover Press. It adds two fine lyrics to the two of the same title that appeared in the poet's *Selected Poems* (1979). Robert Creeley's annual volume this year is titled *A Calendar*, one poem per month per page on loose leaves in two printed colors, but no publisher listed. Robert Wallace's Bits Press gives us X. J. Kennedy's *Hangover Mass*, short, humorous lyrics done in the poet's usual entertaining style of music and wit. Jack Gilbert's *Kochan*, "with four poems by Michiko Nogami," comes from Tamarack Press, as do Stephen Lewandowski's *Honey and Ashes* and Edward Falco's *Concert in the Park of Culture*. All three are beautifully printed and sewn in wrappers.

The pamphlets issued by Robert L. Barth of work by classically and lyrically formal poets, discussed here at some length last year, continue to appear, and they are important beyond their limited editions. Some of the authors and titles are *The Wide Porch and Other Poems* by John Finlay, *The Cartesian Lawnmower and Other Poems* by Don Stanford, *What the Mind Wants* by Dick Davis, *The Harvesters and Other Poems on Works of Art* by Helen Pinkerton, *Sessions and Surroundings: A Century of Roundels 1883-1983, Part 1* by John S. Anson (despite the title, Anson appears to be sole author of these lyrics written in a form invented by Swinburne which the poet has taken to heart and made the most of), *Nine Poems* by the *excellent* poet Timothy Steele, praised here in 1984, and *Anniversaries, Hours, and Occasions* by Barth himself.

Wiggins Poems by Malcolm Glass (Bucksnort Press) is a series, the protagonist of which is a surreal, Bogart-like character who has various adventures. The mode is verse, the prosody variable accentuals, most of the lines being two-stress (dipodic). The poems are interesting, but the narratives could have been a bit more coherent. *Beau Jest* by Ralph Lowe (Northwoods Press) is a small collection of formal comic poems, well done for the most part.

Finally, Jared Carter brought out two chapbooks, *Pincushion's Strawberry* (Cleveland State University Poetry Center) and *Fugue State* (Barnwood Press). Both are fine collections, the latter consisting of eight poems, all of which are essentially narrative. Carter is a formalist who invents characters and situations, conceives incidents, places his people in believable landscapes and surroundings, and makes them illustrate the human condition, all so skillfully that the reader is unaware of the craft on first reading. Several of the poems have to do with a town that drowns in a rising reservoir, so the chapbook at least approximates a sequence. "The Gleaning," the best poem in the collection, must be compared with the finest of its kind—Robert Frost's "Out, Out . . . ," and Edwin Arlington Robinson's Tilbury Town poems.

In summation, the lyric survives, the narrative is growing stronger; "deep image" surrealism is being supplanted by poems written in abstract syntax. The bare egopoem is still kicking out of the me-first 1970s, but it doesn't appear to be wholly alive—whether this condition is a terminal coma or merely hibernation remains to be seen.

The Year in Fiction

George Garrett
University of Virginia

As everyone, from Henry James to Heisenberg, has been telling us over and over again, for all of this century and a good part of the last one, it all depends on your point of view. *It all depends. . . .* Take a year, not any year, but this most recent year, 1984-1985, directly behind us one and all, at this close proximity, lying there like a great baggy monster, a shapeless sprawling beast breathing its last gasps. When we are this close to it, equally close for now, then it becomes the angle of vision that matters most, and, as the saying goes, everybody has got an angle. Even the dust of last year has not settled, and all the numbers have not been harvested and published yet; so when it comes to the fiction of 1984, the evidence is mostly anecdotal and, as indicated, angular. We can expect publishers and booksellers, critics and reviewers, public and private writers all to see different things and to see the same things somewhat differently from each other; just as we can expect, ever and always, the *readers* of fiction, though much manipulated (and evidently often scorned by many writers, publishers, and reviewers) to have gone their own merry ways, making the final, if sometimes impulsive and whimsical pocketbook choices which, one way and the other, are so often astonishing. Readership is not unlike that other mass of bodies and souls, likewise often manipulated and scorned—the American electorate. If, like myself, you spent 1984 doing your day labor in the groves of academe, depending, for news of the outside, on the *New York Times*, the *Washington Post*, the big news magazines, public tele-

Norman Mailer and George Garrett, with John Aldridge seated in background—Michigan, 1984 (Bob Woodring)

vision, and "All Things Considered," why, then the overwhelming nature of the results of the presidential election, the irrefutable numbers of it, would have to be admitted to be simply astonishing. Which remark, believe me, is not intended to be more than lightly political; but, rather, is meant merely to suggest the *wholeness,* the seamless unity of our society. If, despite the best or worst intentions (depending, reader, on *your* point of view) of a multitude of intellectuals, pundits, classy columnists and venerated sages-in-residence, the electorate went right ahead and reelected the president for a second term, just so, in spite of many well-laid plans and scams, the reading public acted with a considerable independence. Once again the gap between the regions of the heartland and the hot center of the publishing industry in America, the region of . . . what's the opposite of heartland? . . . *New York City,* seemed to be growing wider and more distinctly different. This (shall we call it a) difference of opinion is most obviously evident in the fortunes of the popular fiction of the year. Of course, pop fiction is, by its very definition, a product to be hyped and hustled, to be deftly manipulated. And the fate of

all fiction, especially the most private and "serious," these things which can lay some claim to being classified as literature, depends these days upon the good fortune of pop fiction. A publisher without benefit of blockbuster best-sellers is not going to be around long enough to publish a fair share of anything with literary pretensions. Every publisher in town (in Boston, too) is trying to create solid blockbusters to pay the freight.

Some of the solid successes of popular fiction in 1984—Stephen King's and Peter Straub's *The Talisman,* for instance, or Frederick Forsyth's *The Fourth Protocol*—seem, out of the context of their competition, to be completely predictable. Yet, at least in terms of time served on the best-seller list in 1984, there are others at least equally successful and maybe more surprising. One of these, ". . . *And Ladies of the Club*" by Helen Hooven Santmyer, was surely intended to succeed at the box office and arrived on the scene with a massive dose of hype, with all the power and glory an expensive, indeed ostentatious advertising campaign can generate. Yet this book appeared and faced a veritable lynch mob of negative reviewers. And, to make things worse, the grounds of these negative reviews were much less literary than sociopolitical. The ladies she dealt with in a small Ohio town from 1868 to 1932 did not think, act, or feel as the reviewers felt and thought ladies in a small Ohio town, during the years 1868-1932, ought to. Basically the refrain of most of these negative reviews was that the author's most serious failure lay in her inability or unwillingness to make clear (as many of our more circumspect authors are regularly wont to do) that she, herself, *in person* as it were, did not and does not share any of the benighted traits or attitudes of her characters; and that she, in fact as well as here in fiction, condemns them. That what they were asking for is an example of an intolerably crude form of literary criticism (and would not be tolerated in a freshman theme) goes without saying. And perhaps it did have some effect on sales of the book. But at year's end the novel had been on the *New York Times* best-seller list for over half the year, only rivaled in commercial longevity by another book which, for different reasons, had also received its full share of negative notices—Gore Vidal's *Lincoln*. Again this one arrived behind the full marching band treatment of publisher and book club exploitation. But, then, so do all the big best-sellers; and Vidal, after many years and many honorable performances, is a known quantity as is his particular kind of pop novel. Besides which this pop novel was presented as fourth in a series (Vidal calls it "this chronicle") of novels—*Burr, 1876,* and *Washington, D.C.*—linked together by their concern with the American story and united as well by the adroit use of some recurring fictional characters, especially Charles Schuyler, Emma, and (in Vidal's words) "the vile ubiquitous William de la Touche Clancy." One can only guess what the problems for most of the reviewers must have been. For, in second-guessing the professional book reviewers, one must always keep in mind and view the sheepherding factor; that is, like other insecure souls, most book reviewers of our times tend to play "follow the leader," echoing and revising each other with more intensity than dealing directly with any given book as a discrete experience. Nevertheless it looks as if the problems for Vidal were derived from dashed expectations and (again) from sociopolitical disagreements. Though clearly pop fiction from start to finish, sentence by sentence, *Lincoln* is not overtly campy or cute. It has to be called a serious historical novel about a serious time in our national experience and about some fairly serious, if often inept, people. Certainly Lincoln is treated with high seriousness and with honor. But

here is a Lincoln who is somewhat removed from stereotypical stances. The picture is of a great and ruthless politician, relentlessly obsessed with the preservation of the Union even though that preservation in itself may be unconstitutional and even though the Constitution has to be violated and flouted in other ways to assure survival and victory. This Lincoln is surrounded by hateful and scheming colleagues who are also, fortunately, his inferiors in every way. This Lincoln is largely indifferent to the fate and wishes of the blacks except insofar as they may be used by him to achieve his goals. Yet he is a great and tragic figure. And Mary Lincoln, often treated as a foolish woman, is gently portrayed and shares her husband's tragedy. Of course there is evidence aplenty for Vidal's view of Lincoln and the times, just as there is evidence which may be shaped into the more familiar, sentimental monument. But it does appear that the reviewers were not ready to recommend this slightly altered version of the Great Emancipator to the great American public, perhaps especially in an election year. No matter. At the turn of the year *Lincoln,* too, had been lodged high on the various best-seller lists for more than half of it. Only Robert Ludlum's *The Acquitane Progression* had lasted any longer. Other solid best-sellers at year's end, coming out of the second half of the year, or from the peak Christmas season and intended to carry momentum into spring of 1985, included workmanlike performances like Mario Puzo's *The Sicilian,* John Jakes's *Love and War,* and the indefatigable Arthur Hailey's *Strong Medicine* (an inside look at the pharmaceutical industry, what else?).

A successful commercial book outside the more conventional categories, though well-rooted in a distinct literary tradition, is Dan Jenkins's *Life Its Ownself: The Semi-Tougher Adventures of Billy Clyde Puckett and Them,* building, as the title announces, on the huge success of *Semi-Tough,* Jenkins's earlier account of Billy Clyde Puckett's life and times. The publisher (Simon and Schuster) invokes Mark Twain and Ring Lardner on the book jacket, appropriately summoning up the telling of tall tales and an attitude toward life and art, as well as indicating to the wary reader that more than half the fun to follow will be derived from the language, from the clever exploitation of the living American vernacular as it is presumably preached and practiced in the worlds of Texas, football, television, Hollywood, and many varieties of the American honky-tonk. It is a cheerful, utterly unlikely, satirical, often tasteless and always funny story, skillfully told, and glossed with a happy ending. Its success is earned. I have seen people on airplanes laughing out loud while reading it.

There were also examples of "crossovers," serious writers who have learned enough of the craft, and earned enough readers over time, to find themselves places, briefly or a little longer, in the commercial world of best-seller lists. John Updike's "quirky and charming" (*New York Times Book Review*) and, as ever, very stylish novel, *The Witches of Eastwick*, made its splash. Splashier, and more successful, was Norman Mailer's twenty-second published book, and his first under a multimillion-dollar contract with his brand new publisher, Random House—*Tough Guys Don't Dance*. Which served as a replacement for his even more successful historical novel, *Ancient Evenings*, on the lists. *Tough Guys Don't Dance*, set in Mailer's Provincetown, is at once a salute to and a self-reflexive send-up of the best of the hard-boiled suspense writers, clearly and swiftly executed, rich with energy and riddled with Mailer's particular interests and concerns. It is aptly and honestly described by its publishers as "a stunningly conceived novel that soon transcends its origins as a mystery to become a relentless search into the recesses and buried virtues of the modern American male." Mailer fans must be delighted that its origins as a mystery are soon transcended. Mystery fans must be relieved that it offers no serious competition to the likes of John D. Macdonald or Elmore Leonard.

This was the year, also, that witnessed another serious and important American writer, Joseph Heller, recovering from a long and serious illness, deliver his latest fiction to the best-seller lists. Heller's *God Knows*, something of a Mel Brooks treatment of the life and times of King David, in the King's own words ("King David describes his life in comic and anachronistic style," the *Times* announces), baffled and annoyed some reviewers, pleased others, and evidently pleased a lot of Heller's hip readers who had been waiting for his next move. Described by another novelist (who prefers to remain anonymous) as "Heller's *Portnoy's Complaint*," the novel was something of a surprise, just as each work by Heller since *Catch-22* has been.

Among the many books aimed for much greater things than it achieved was Erica Jong's latest, quasi-autobiographical accounting of the life and times of "gloriously uninhibited" Isadora Wing—*Parachutes & Kisses*. Plenty of sex and plenty of action, including some travels to Russia and elsewhere, as Isadora tries to get her finger on the pulse of the '80s. It is a richly literary book, replete with epigraphs and allusions; a lively, if often briskly synoptic story line; and it is *almost* good fun. Certainly Isadora is funny, whether she means to be or not. Funny in her feelings, as here, typically, when she believes that the Russian airliner is on fire and that she's a goner:

> There was no doubt they were done for. But what did Isadora feel at that moment?—she who had so often imagined death in flight? She knew that if she died on an Aeroflot flight, her death might not even be reported to her next of kin. And yet, all she felt was a terrific sense of lightness, of transparency. All anxiety was gone, somehow, as she prayed to the Goddess to take care of Amanda, take care of Bean, take care of her parents and sisters. So this was her personal Babi Yar! So be it . . .

Plucky middle-aged girl, that Isadora! She also thinks and notices things too: "In Russia everyone craved books, and no one could get them. In America, the best books piled up on the remainder tables while the populace played Pac-Man." Some of the latter, but evidently not enough of them, turned away from Pac-Man, and Ms. Pac-Man too, long enough to enjoy the romance and happy ending, for the time being, of Isadora and her weeping Wasp—Berkeley Sproul III, called "Bean": "All day they loved . . . talked, read poetry, exchanged love letters from Russian, swam, ate wonderful meals in bed, drank wine, and held each other. When twilight came, they ventured out into the city like nocturnal creatures, like the very cats of Venice, like the revelers of the eighteenth century in their astonishing golden masks."

Another book which aroused much expectation in certain circles and received a full measure of attention, earning extensive and more-than-merely-respectful reviews, especially regionally, in and around her home base in New York City, was Renata Adler's second novel—*Pitch Dark*. More than autobiographical, it is a supremely personal, indeed, at times, almost wholly private book, lapidary in style, seismic in delicacy of perception, and stunning in its absolutely confident authority that all or any of this will be of interest to other human beings: *Pitch Dark* nevertheless has a discernible story line, being, as the *Times* described it, "an old-fashioned love story between a journalist and a married man told in the fragmented, 'discontinuous first-person narrative' established in the author's previous novel." *Pitch Dark* seems to have pleased all those who admired *Speedboat*, a small but hardy cult, and to have reached out for others.

Another book for which there were great expectations, perhaps more than could be realized in a popular sense, was Joan Didion's *Democracy*. The subjects—war, global and national politics, love and sex and murder—and the larger claim in the title to depict and examine where we have come, should have guaranteed a considerable popular success. And Didion seemed to be due; a critical consensus had been building for several years in support of her work and her place in the literary pantheon. In my best judgment, *Democracy* is clearly her finest achievement in fiction. Anyone who liked the earlier works, enjoyed the tropes and habits of them, would surely admire this novel where everything was smooth and graceful. Even her bad habits as a writer are under control here. Frankly I was and remain baffled by the harsh and negative reviews the book received. The only reasons I can summon up to account for what happened to *Democracy* are sociopolitical—that author and story together were certainly ambiguous about the validity of some deeply rooted liberal assumptions, pro and con, concerning events and people of our times. And that the most positive character in her story, the real "hero," if you will, happened to be a C.I.A. man. One hates to imagine that on such things the free currency of ideas and the fate of good books may depend. But Solzhenitsyn suggested as much in his controversial 1978 speech at Harvard. He may well be right.

From the commercial point of view, all things considered, it appears to have been a busy, reasonably successful, but basically ho-hum year. Not so in the world of serious fiction. Many things, some of them good things, were happening there. Among the fifteen books selected by the editors of the *New York Times Book Review* under "Editor's Choice: The Best Books of 1984," only one novel by an American was represented—Jayne Anne Phillips's *Machine Dreams*. Which had received wonderful and widespread review coverage and was widely selected, even in places like *People*, at year's end as one of the year's finest. And although the book has not yet, as of this writing, won any of the year's big prizes, its author was just awarded a second National Endowment of the Arts grant honoring her achievement and potential. Essentially a family chronicle novel, telling the story of the Hampsons out of rural West Virginia, from the 1930s through the early 1970s, this book is so adroitly economical and transparent as to mark a significant advance over the ways and means of her other, earlier book, *Black Tickets*, a collection of stories which won her attention and awards. *Machine Dreams* seemed so

assured and skillful that very few reviewers mentioned that it was a first novel.

Of the prizes for serious work in 1984 already announced, the two principal awards for fiction were interestingly, oddly unusual choices. The PEN/Faulkner prize for fiction went to the black writer and former Rhodes Scholar John Edgar Wideman for his novel *Sent for You Yesterday*. Which might well have passed by almost unnoticed, for it was a paperback original, and these are seldom widely reviewed. However, critic Alan Cheuse wrote a rave review of it for the *New York Times Book Review*, and novelist David Bradley, himself a former PEN/Faulkner winner and, as well, a former student of Wideman, pushed it fairly and hard with his fellow judges for the PEN/Faulkner Award. Since the award, Wideman has already had *Brothers & Keepers* published in hardcover, a work which is chiefly factual (though whether it should be called nonfiction is debatable), dealing with his own life and his relationship with his younger brother Rob, now serving a life sentence for felony murder committed during an armed robbery. If the PEN/Faulkner Award for 1984 was something of a surprise, and a happy one, then the American Book Award was, in a slightly different way, even more surprising. The smart money was all betting on Alison Lurie's *Foreign Affairs* to pick up the ABA with ease. But along came *Victory Over Japan*, a collection of fourteen short stories by Ellen Gilchrist. It was unusual, though perhaps appropriate in this amazing year of short stories, to give a major American fiction prize to a story collection. Gilchrist, author of an earlier collection of stories, *In the Land of Dreamy Dreams*, published by the University of Arkansas Press, and *The Annunciation*, a novel, is a native of New Orleans who studied creative writing at Arkansas and writes closely adhering to the conventions of Southern women's fiction. Her publisher (Little, Brown) openly cites "echoes of Flannery O'Connor and Eudora Welty"; and anyone familiar with the evolving genre can see close relationships with the contemporary Southern fiction of, for example, Lee Smith, Bobbie Ann Mason, Lee Zacharias, and Mary Hood, though it must be pointed out that, though Ellen Gilchrist is new on the scene, she is older than any of these other writers and has been writing her stories for as long as or longer than any of them. She has her own voice, her own times, and her own place, chiefly New Orleans. She is, then, part of a literary movement, a lively resurgence of fiction by and about contemporary Southern women. What is interesting, and not a little surprising, is that this movement or "school" has been so successful both in finding places to publish work and in finding readers to read it. And now, as symbolized by Gilchrist's award, as well as by the awards and attention bestowed on the others, winning prizes. This renaissance of serious fiction by the latest generation of Southern women, including many novelists, has not so far been much noted by critics or trend-spotters; but it is already *there,* and Ellen Gilchrist's lively and energetic stories are exemplary of the best of it. The official critical position, echoed in the *Newsweek* piece about the short story today, is that Ann Beattie is the most influential American story writer today, replacing the old king, Donald Barthelme. All of which may or may not be true. What is clearly true is that none of these new Southern writers has been *directly* influenced by either one. These days a young Southern writer is apt to be well aware of everything going on in the literary world. Their aesthetic choices, including those of direct and indirect influence, are made not out of ignorance, but out of the expedient solution of the problem of finding the means to deal with the outward and visible world they know best. That Southern women writers

often sound somewhat alike is more a matter of cultural history than influence. That they do not feel compelled to sound like Ann Beattie or Donald Barthelme or Grace Paley, for instance, signifies that they do not feel that they or their region are by definition inferior to the urban ethnic worlds of the Northeast. That publishers are willing to produce their work at least indicates that publishers are beginning to respond to such basic facts as the major population migration to the Sunbelt.

Something which critics and trend-spotters *have* finally noticed is the sudden burst of new life in the short story. *Newsweek* ("A Silver Age of Short Stories," 14 January 1985) devoted its book section to the subject and barely scratched the surface of it. Nineteen eighty-four saw the publication of a surprising number of short story collections by distinguished American writers. The editors of the *New York Times Book Review* selected two—Saul Bellow's *Him with His Foot in His Mouth And Other Stories* and E. L. Doctorow's *Lives of the Poets: Six Stories and a Novella*—as among the fifteen "Best Books of 1984." And while there might be (indeed already *has been*) some critical debate concerning the quality

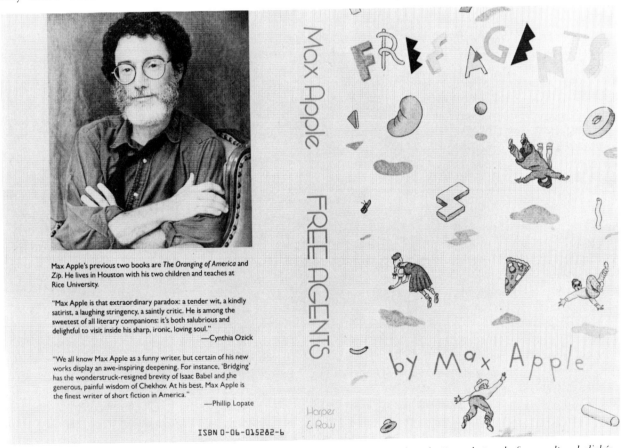

Max Apple's previous two books are *The Oranging of America* and *Zip.* He lives in Houston with his two children and teaches at Rice University.

"Max Apple is that extraordinary paradox: a tender wit, a kindly satirist, a laughing stringency, a saintly critic. He is among the sweetest of all literary companions: it's both salubrious and delightful to visit inside his sharp, ironic, loving soul."
—Cynthia Ozick

"We all know Max Apple as a funny writer, but certain of his new works display an awe-inspiring deepening. For instance, 'Bridging' has the wonderstruck-resigned brevity of Isaac Babel and the generous, painful wisdom of Chekhov. At his best, Max Apple is the finest writer of short fiction in America."
—Phillip Lopate

ISBN 0-06-015282-6

Dust jacket for a collection of stories by an author who can, said Newsweek, *translate the "most battered of our cultural clichés into glittering artifacts"*

of the latter, Bellow's brilliant and award-winning stories seem to stand with his finest work. Of the sixty-eight works listed as "Notable Books of the Year" by the *Times*, fifteen are collections of short stories. In truth, it could, perhaps should have been a separate category. In any case, it was a banner year for the story. Among collections of genuine distinction by established writers are *Free Agents* by Max Apple, *Too Late American Boyhood Blues* by Frederick Busch, *Apples and Pears and Other Stories* by Guy Davenport, *At the Border* by Robert Hemenway, *The Ceremony* by Weldon Kees, *Last Days* by Joyce Carol Oates (who, true to form, also brought out a new novel, *Mysteries of Winterthurn*, in 1984), *A Fanatic Heart* by Edna O'Brien, *Acquainted With the Night and Other Short Stories* by Lynne Sharon Schwartz, *Half Moon Street* by Paul Theroux, and *The Collected Stories* of Dylan Thomas. No two of these collections are really very much alike. The range, the differences, and the variety are enormous. Bellow's five stories, built around the profoundly moving and pertinent prizewinning story "A Silver Dish" (which states its problem with splendid efficiency in the first sentence: "What do you do about death—in this case, the death of an old father?"), are all quite different superficially, yet clearly bloodkin because of a tone and a voice, Bellow's uniquely, which override all differences, giving the collection both dignity and unity. Max Apple's *Free Agents*, his first collection since his celebrated arrival with *The Oranging of America*, adds new beats and directions, mostly personal, to his earlier satirical methods. If Woody Allen were not also a pretty good writer, you could say that Max Apple is the Woody Allen of American literature. He, too, has a constant tone of voice and a basically compassionate if uniformly liberal stance. Yet his stories, constructed out of "ideas" or elaborately exploited and often whimsical gimmicks, are wildly various in both form and content. Frederick Busch is a novelist and, like Apple and others here (even Bellow), a teacher. His book, composed of ten stories, eight of them previously published in literary magazines, is held together by a unity of theme—the persistence of boyhood in American life. Widely reviewed and available, it comes from a relatively small publisher, David R. Godine of Boston. Significantly his book found itself, by and large, on an equal footing in the marketplace with all the others. Guy Davenport's *Apples and Pears* also comes handsomely from a small press, North Point Press. It consists of four stories, one of which, the title story, is itself divided into four titled parts. The stories are illustrated with thirty-two original drawings by the author. There are also poems, journal entries, bits and pieces of other languages. It is all determinedly intellectual and avant-garde, assertively "original." And yet there is great charm to offset any arrogance, and the significant fact is that there is evidently as much an audience for this kind of short fiction as for any other. Robert Hemenway's publisher (Atheneum) urgently intends to emphasize the wholeness of *At the Border*, not calling it exactly a novel, yet naming it as an "eloquent work of fiction . . . in a series of seven long scenes," and quotes the early *Kirkus* review describing the book as composed of "seven story-like sections." The *Kirkus* review, extensively quoted on the jacket, also goes a long way toward describing, perhaps inadvertently, both the character and limitations of a certain kind of *New Yorker* fiction and certainly promising for the reader of Hemenway's stories a special, somewhat rarefied atmosphere: "They describe the course of urban love in too-small New York apartments, around good movies and bargain restaurants and editorial jobs; they convey the palpable sense of *unsureness*, the man and the woman who lose desire at the very peak moments of connection—and whose fragility then becomes their strongest quality. . . . " Not to be confused with *Tough Guys Don't Dance!* So be it. Novel, collection of stories, work of fiction, whatever one chooses to call it, it is (as might be expected from a *New Yorker* editor) subtle, elegant, muted, mostly passive and interior, held together by dint of the central character throughout, John Everett (writer and editor), as well as by some basic recurring images and symbols—borders and limits, paintings, concepts of chivalry, cumulative memories and allusions, and by some central, more or less ineffable concerns. It covers Everett's life in several places (Prospect, Michigan, Chicago, New York City, New Hampshire, Detroit, and Austria close to the Czech border), during the years 1933-1972. It is more often synoptic than scenic, and its essential drama is more a matter of parapsychoanalysis than outward action and reaction. The level of action is perhaps adequately represented by this brief concluding and climactic paragraph, the big moment, the high point of "Polly's Girl": "At the elevators he took both her hands and said good-bye, and then she pulled him to her and kissed him, suddenly and gently, on the lips. To his surprise his throat tightened, his eyes filled, his body trembled at her touch." On the other hand, the writing is uniformly and unassertively stylish. And there are any number of moments of feeling, of discrete personal perception, which are wonderfully realized. For example this moment, in a book, after all, *about* borders, when John Everett suddenly comes upon the Czech border, the Iron Curtain:

> The dirt road went on past the red-and-white barrier through a field and straight up to a chain-link fence topped with several strands of barbed wire. No gate. Well beyond, a wooden watchtower. Beyond that, barracks. A soldier on the tower platform looking down at him. Everett fished his binoculars from the car and looked back up. A boy's round face, a brown uniform, an automatic rifle slung over one shoulder. The iron curtain. Everett had come to think that it was no more now, on most borders, than a figure of speech. But there it was. He felt a shiver of something. Not fear. Recognition.

Hemenway may not be able to give you John Riggins of the Redskins slashing inside tackle on third down, goal to go; but unquestionably he can offer up "a shiver of something" as well as anybody else in the business. Even Updike. Poet Weldon Kees, who disappeared and is believed to be dead, gave up writing in 1945; but *The Ceremony*, a gathering up of uncollected short stories, adds something to his reputation and to our awareness of our past. Joyce Carol Oates's *Last Days* is one of her best collections of stories (I count twelve) so far. No attempt here to "unify" the collection around any other center than that they are top-flight work by one of our most gifted and productive writers. Except for one story which appeared in *Esquire* they are all from large and small literary magazines. Many have won one prize or another over the past few years. Many are quite boldly experimental. One has to admire the bravado of Oates in continuing to explore and exploit the limits of the form when she could so easily rest easy on her habits and laurels. One habit—that of hyping even minor events and incidents to the dramatic limits (and edge of laughter) by a kind of barrage of invisible exclamation points—remains in place. So? So it is by now as much a part of her being (as a writer) as her bone structure. Will not be changed this side of heaven's gate. Take it or leave it.

Edna O'Brien and the late Dylan Thomas are, of course, not strictly eligible for consideration here. Yet, American or not, they were and are influential writers. The two collections were widely reviewed. It is fine and dandy to have Thomas's stories together in one book. He was an admirable and various story writer, gifted and unpretentious. Few poets, in our time, have written short fiction as good as these. O'Brien's selected stories, introduced

by Philip Roth, consist of twenty-nine stories taken from four previously published collections and including four more recent uncollected stories all of which appeared in the *New Yorker*. In his introduction to her work Roth rightly points out that although she is best known for her tales out of rural Ireland and for her steamy sex scenes ("eerily intimate stories relating to sexual love"), there is much more to her work than that. "The worlds depicted are not just those of small farms full of lovelorn women and inebriate men," he writes, "but also the larger world of cities, of resorts, of estrangement, the world of the very rich and careless." The key to where she has come from and where she may be going is most likely to be found in the final four uncollected stories. There is continuity there. They focus directly, often without pity, on the single consciousness of a single woman who is, always, awkwardly in love. She is, as ever, charming in her contradictions and inconsistencies. The powers of aesthetic perception and the assimilation of experience are keen, alert, and exact. Yet these last stories are calmer, easier, quieter, more condensed. They are more easily *interior* stories, propelled by thoughts, memories, feelings. Gentler. More subtle and sophisticated. Still the same voice, but somewhat tamed, without stridency, more apt to self-reflexive comedy. Here she does much the same sort of thing as Renata Adler and, in a different way, Robert Hemenway. She has joined the new *New Yorker* school (where she has been in attendance in various other grades and levels for many years) and moves to the head of the class.

Paul Theroux's latest venture consists of two long stories, or "short novels" as the case may be, essentially united in their concern with what Theroux calls, in the first one, "Doctor Slaughter," "the calculated frolic of a double life." In the first, Lauren Slaughter, Ph.D. and an American in London, doubles her life and pleasure by becoming a successful call girl. She gets in more deeply than she could have imagined and is involved, *used*, in an international murder plot. "Doctor De Marr" is the story of twins in Boston, Gerald and George. George dies and Gerald takes his place in life (they had often switched about, back and forth, as children). George, it turns out, was a fake physician and, in fact, a criminal. What begins, in curiosity, as a kind of adventure, ends with his sordid murder. The stories are told in a skillful and straightforward, no-nonsense manner. Slick, but expertly and neatly done.

It should also be noted that collections of early stories by two of the most praised and discussed writers on the contemporary scene appeared in 1984. These were *Slow Learner* by Thomas Pynchon and *Difficult Loves* by Italo Calvino (translated by the estimable William Weaver). The latter began, as these stories indicate, as a fairly "straight" storyteller, but he has emerged as one of the liveliest and most influential (and, yes, most fashionable) of the new fabulators, a shoo-in, at this stage, to be imitated as much by Americans as, say, were the Latin American writers (who, in turn, were influenced by earlier North American masters) during the past decade.

A number of outstanding first collections of stories were published during the year. Two of the best of these, collections which would stand out in any given year, and against the standards of our most experienced, mature artists, are Andrea Lee's *Sarah Phillips* and Ellen Wilbur's *Wind And Birds And Human Voices*. Andrea Lee captured attention with her 1981 work of nonfiction, *Russian Journal;* and this is her first book of fiction. Again, like some of the other books, it challenges classification. Random House identifies it as a novel. Perhaps so (why not?); but if so, then it is, like some of the others, a novel made up of a sequence of related short stories. It is no great matter in terms of critical appreciation. Lee is a clear and careful stylist, the master of a quiet, steady, middle-style tone of voice. Her prose is dutifully polished and self-edited. But, even amidst the age of the new illiteracy, creators of nice, well-turned sentences are a dime a dozen. It is, in fact, the *content* of her stories which makes them so interesting. Through twelve stories about the almost-autobiographical Sarah Phillips and her family, Lee gives us one of the first, and certainly the most thorough, fictional accountings of the modern black upper-middle class in America. No finger-snapping Afro funk or street jive, none of the familiar tropes of black English or main currents of Afro-American literature. Instead of clichés this is a warm, humane, loving, in-depth picture of blacks who have been leaders, true movers and shakers, not only in their own minority community but also in the larger society as well. What she has to say rings true even as it informs. She does not deal in generalizations, but allows the reader to arrive at them, guided by a meticulous accumulation of accurate details. Ellen Wilbur's much more varied collection is even more masterful and interesting in its dazzling display of fine-tuned prose. One of the first books of a new small press, Stuart Wright Publisher, her handsomely made (surely one of the most elegant hardcover productions of the year) volume arrived with the orches-

Ellen Wilbur, author of Winds and Birds and Human Voices, *a first short story collection (Pam Woodend)*

trated, book-jacket support of the likes of Gail Godwin, Andre Dubus, Rosellen Brown, Richard Yates, and (very rare to see a blurb from this master) Eudora Welty. In each of the ten stories, and especially in the longest, the title story, it is easy to see that she has justly earned her accolades. Ellen Wilbur has arrived on the scene as a genuine talent from whom much can be legitimately expected in the future.

Another first collection of stories which deserves mention is by Gordon Lish, formerly fiction editor at *Esquire* and now working for Knopf. Lish is not (not yet anyway) in the same league, as artist or craftsman, with any of the above-mentioned writers. But his stories are of interest because of his history as an influential editor, working with such acknowledged masters as Raymond Carver, Mary Robison, and Barry Hannah. Characteristic of Lish's editorial influence are a cleverness of construct, a simple structure which is "a good idea," and an extreme understatement which is, in fact, aesthetic minimalism in prose. His work exemplifies these same qualities, but is quite uneven in its successes. Too often cleverness dissolves into cuteness, and all too often minimalism of form is altogether appropriate to the minimal *content* of the story. Still there are a few moments, especially the prizewinning story "For Jerome—with Love and Kisses."

Two prizewinning first collections are Charles Baxter's *Harmony of the World* and Randall Silvis's *The Luckiest Man in the World*. (Does use of the word *world* in your title help win prizes?) Baxter's book won the extremely difficult Associated Writing Programs Award Series, selected as the sixth in that annual series from among several hundred submissions. Baxter's ten stories have been published in the best of the literary magazines and in prize anthologies. Baxter is a "straight" story man, economical though not a minimalist, with a strong sense of character and a good sense of humor. Novelist J. R. Salamanca, praising the "elegance of his invention, the passionate lucidity of his diction, and the dignity and depth of feeling in these stories," calls them "the finest being written in America today." Randall Silvis won himself the Drue Heinz Literature Prize for short fiction, an equally prestigious award. *Publishers Weekly* praised him as "an engaging storyteller," particularly singling out his ability at characterization and his comedic capacities. That two separate prizewinners should be praised for somewhat similar qualities is less surprising than the fact that both qualities go somewhat against the grain of the "mainstream" of the last decade or so. Dimensional characterization has been, until very recently, looked upon as hopelessly conservative, if not overtly reactionary almost in a political sense. Humor, from our most sophisticated and fashionable story writers, has all too often been laughter shared by reader and writer and directed at the clumsy doings of the two-dimensional oafs who populate their fiction and, apparently, the nation at large. That two young and gifted writers, at the outset of their careers, are going in a different direction suggests the times may be achanging. It is also noteworthy that these books were published by university presses—Baxter's by Missouri and Silvis's by Pittsburgh.

The editors for the two most significant annual anthologies of short fiction—John Updike for *The Best American Short Stories 1984* and William Abrahams (longtime regular editor) of *Prize Stories 1984: The O'Henry Awards*—are both aware, and say so, that exciting things are happening with the American short story. There is some overlapping; both anthologies have Cynthia Ozick's "Rosa," and Lee K. Abbott, Jr., is represented, with different stories, in both. But the most interesting thing is how wildly various each of the collections is and how very different they are even though both are excellent. Abraham's choices are, as usual, somewhat less daring, slightly more establishment-oriented. All in all he honestly seems to prefer the local New York

City regional scene to any other. Updike's choices are oddly idiosyncratic. He announces that, among the finalists, he used *endings* as his principal touchstone. And, for example, he simply and flatly refused to admit any stories which, as he judged them, "seemed to be thinly disguised memoirs, even when they were as elegant and illuminating as those by Jamaica Kincaid and Andrea Lee. I asked that something feel invented. . . ." A very subjective call, even for a critic assured of certain certainties. But, as proof in the pudding, his choices are excellent, more wide-ranging than Abraham's with more often a sense of "discovery." It is a pleasure to find good writers like Dianne Benedict, Mary Hood, Madison Smartt Bell, and Jeanne Schinto joining the company of Oates and Ozick, Paul Bowles and Wright Morris; likewise good to see two stories from the excellent *Greensboro Review* and stories from the *Crescent Review* and *Black Warrior Review* right in there with the *New Yorker, Antaeus,* and *Esquire*. Updike has some serious doubts about how well or accurately the newer writers, compared by him with *The Best Short Stories 1934*, reflect and represent the surfaces of American life and times. And he is more than a little dismayed to find that the short story, becoming a fine art, may now follow the way of modern poetry. All of which remains to be seen. It is possible that he is quite wrong on both counts; time will tell. Meantime, however, the two annual prize volumes attest to good health in the writing of short fiction.

It has also been a good year for the first novel. I have no statistics whatsoever, but some strong anecdotal evidence. For the first time in nearly ten years, I was busily and professionally reading first novels, looking for the best I could find for a "New Writers Series" for a group of interested colleges and universities. For this series a limited number of first novelists would be invited to visit campuses. The results of the reading and looking were most interesting. Aside from *Machine Dreams*, which was not really treated by anyone as a first novel, the first book most widely discussed and praised in the conventional media was *Edisto*, by Padgett Powell, "the story of a twelve-year-old South Carolina boy 'dying' into a new life of pubescence. . . ," as the *Times* put it. In context of the other first novels of the year *Edisto* is a pretty good book, a little too cute for its own good, but awake and singing. Not, however, among the very best. Neither were the New York novels which caught the eyes of all the local reviewers there. Among the best of these, and they are each and all good, solid accomplishments (though perhaps not of any great interest to anyone living west of the Hudson or south of the Statue of Liberty) are *Summer in the City* by Mark Stevens, *Elbowing the Seducer* by T. Gertler (this one, a novel of the literary scene, had everyone in the City guessing who in real life was who in the book), *Bright Lights, Big City* by Jay McInerney, and a book described as "weirdly original" by the *Times*—*It Was Gonna Be Like Paris*, by Emily Listfield. My own choices for the best first novels of the year, together with the publishers who deserve some honor for bringing them out into the marketplace: Frederick Barthelme—*Second Marriage* (Simon and Schuster); Elizabeth Cox—*Familiar Ground* (Atheneum); Tish O'Dowd Ezekiel—*Floaters* (Atheneum); Christian Gehman—*Beloved Gravely* (Scribners; this novel won the Maxwell Perkins Award); Denise Giardina—*Good King Harry* (Harper and Row); J. K. Klavans—*It's a Little Too Late for a Love Song* (Morrow); Peter La Salle—*Strange Sunlight* (Texas Monthly Press); Jill McCorkle—*The Cheer Leader* and *July 7* (published simultaneously by Algonquin Books); Nancy Willard—*Things Invisible to See* (Knopf); this last one being the work of an older, much more experienced writer with poetry,

short stories, and children's books behind her, and being in its daring, maybe outrageous shotgun wedding of realism and fantasy, possibly the most astonishing novel of the year.

My personal choice for the finest first novel of 1984, surely a superb novel at any stage of a writer's career, first or last, is *Harvesting Ballads* (Dutton) by Philip Kimball. I have observed this one develop from its first appearances in little magazines, and it has been a long time coming and finding a publisher. In my view it is a triumph worth waiting for. In justice the only appropriate thing I can do is to quote myself, the statement I sent to the publisher after reading the book in galley proof:

> *Harvesting Ballads* is wide awake and all alive, with its string of memorable, intricately related, splendidly told stories; with characters whose jokes and joys, songs and sorrows, brief triumphs and losing battles are things you will want to bet on and can believe in; with a dazzling realization of place, the Plains, with its sad, fabulous history; with a language that sings and crackles with all the wide range

Nancy Willard

ISBN 0-394-54058-1

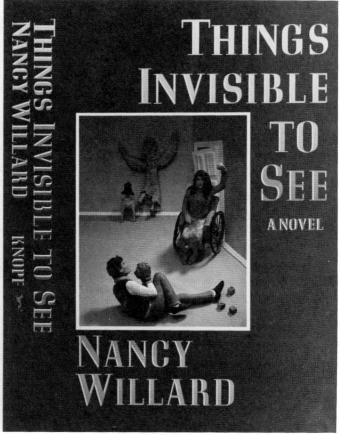

Dust jacket for a first adult novel by the author of three books of short stories, eight books of poetry, and books for children

and poetry of American speech; and with, above all, the potent, powerful controlling imagination of the author, Philip Kimball, a writer who here takes his place, with one wonderful novel, among our very best.

A blurb, to be sure, lost in a world of blurbs. But I will stand by every word of it, and I recommend it to all readers who care.

Kimball's book, by the way, received quite respectable reviews nationally. But in his home country, the Great Plains, *Harvesting Ballads* has been treated lavishly as a major work and an important contribution to the literature of the Plains. The difference in treatment may well be less a matter of local versus national interests than another example, out of 1984, of the failure of the so-called national center to speak to or for the large and populous regions which make up the nation.

At every stage this report grows more personal (you were warned) and more dependent on point of view and angle of vision. Having covered a little of the common history of fiction in a year I am left with a more personal history, an accounting of the books, not best-sellers or prizewinners, some well-reviewed and noted and others ignored, books that I read and admired enough so that they will ever after be associated with the texture and memory of the year they were published. Call it, then, a personal (though no longer private) "Notable Books of 1984" list.

Alice Adams—*Superior Women* (Knopf). By now this form is almost a genre in itself, deriving from Mary McCarthy's *The Group*, Mary Lee Settle's *The Clam Shell*, and a couple, or more, Rona Jaffe novels. Aimed at a larger audience than her earlier fiction, this account of the lives of five women who met at Radcliffe in 1943 proved to be an agreeable, well-executed generational novel.

The Last Good Time (Dial) by Richard Bausch and *The Lives of Riley Chance* (St. Martin's) by Robert Bausch. The Bausch boys, identical twins, are superbly good and gifted and productive young novelists. Though each has his own voice, they are alike in writing strong, straightforward fiction based, usually, on a solid premise. Both mine a deep vein of comedy but are profoundly serious. Richard has received more attention, thanks to the fact that his second novel, *Take Me Back*, was nominated for a PEN/Faulkner Award. Two good novels. Nod goes to *Riley Chance* for its conception ("the harrowing story of a man cursed with immortality") and for the power and detail of the writing, including this, the narrator's description of the pain of dying:

The worst thing about dying is you can't move. Not even an eyelash. And inside, right under the skin, almost at the base of each hair, you've got this raging struggle. Noise so loud you hear it twice, and an odor as foul as any sour or rotten thing you can remember. It's as if somebody stretched your skin over a ferocious dog fight. It's just awful. . . .

Kelly Cherry—*The Lost Traveller's Dream* (Harcourt Brace Jovanovich). Since 1974 Kelly Cherry has produced three collections of poetry and three other novels. None of her fictions are alike save in intelligence, style, invention, and in the fact that she always (in the words of the publisher of this novel) "traverses the cutting edge between serious and absurd, tragic and comic." This story of the lives of three women is first-rate.

Voices from the Moon (Godine) by Andre Dubus. It has been years since Dubus produced a novel. He has been busy as one of the most productive story writers of our time. This one is short and as well-wrought and evocative as any of the stories, all composed with a graceful virtuosity.

Love Medicine (Holt, Rinehart and Winston) by Louise Erdrich. This first novel has won two awards—the $5000 Nelson Algren Award and the National Book Critics Circle Award for the best work of fiction in 1984. Erdrich, a member of the Turtle Mountain Band of the Chippewa, writes of life on a North Dakota Indian reservation from 1934 to 1984.

Sins of Omission (Random House) by Candace Flynt. Her second novel, following the well-received *Chasing Dad* (1980). This one is polished, strongly plotted, with excellent characters and a high professional shine.

Mark Harris—*Lying in Bed* (McGraw-Hill). Among the many and varied works of Mark Harris, one special triumph was *Wake Up, Stupid*, our first contemporary epistolary novel and certainly one of the best and most original examples of the genre of the academic novel. This latest is a sequel, picking up the hero, Lee Youngdahl, years later. It is funny and wise and satirical and *adds to*, if it doesn't top, *Wake Up, Stupid*.

Milan Kundera—*The Unbearable Lightness of Being*. Ever since the splash and excitement of *The Book of Laughter and Forgetting* Kundera has been highly fashionable and instantly influential. Much of this, his first book since *Laughter*, appeared in the *New Yorker*. Kundera is an innovative and exciting eastern European writer with a powerful authority of experience to match his different point of view.

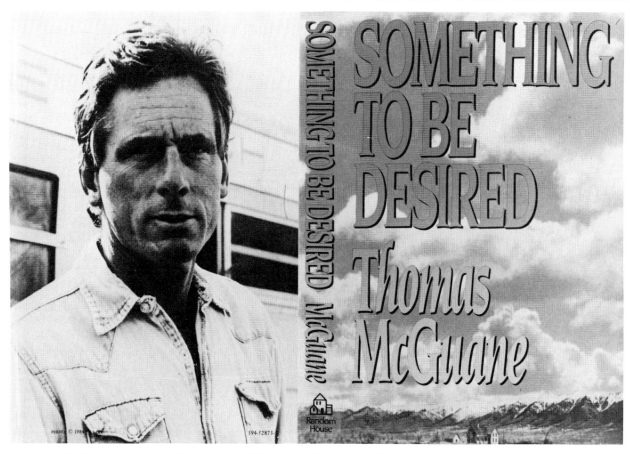

Dust jacket for McGuane's new novel, about "a man blinded by the flaw in himself, yearning not for the best but sometimes for the worst"

Michael Mewshaw—*Year of the Gun* (Atheneum). A high-class thriller about terrorists in Rome, expertly done by this prolific young novelist and nonfiction writer.

Something To Be Desired (Random House)—Thomas McGuane. The new West again. And *all right*, McGuane's heroes and gestures are getting old and stiff, sort of like Joel McCrea and Randolph Scott in *Ride the High Country*. But he keeps the flags and dreams of the 1960s flying in the middle of the shrugging 1980s.

The Foreigner (Atheneum), by David Plante. Something odd and mysterious and a little fancy, a long way away from the fictions of the Francoeur family and with more depth (and less bitchiness) than *Difficult Women*.

David R. Slavitt—*Alice At 80* (Doubleday). A brilliant and successful tour de force essentially about Lewis Carroll and his little girls, by a skilled and experienced novelist (a dozen novels under his own name, an equal number under pseudonyms), poet, translator, editor, and critic. This one received the excellent reviews it deserved.

Smoke Street (Morrow)—Mark Smith. The author of several highly regarded novels, including *The Death of the Detective* and *The Delphinium Girl*, here takes on present-day Central America in a mysterious, surrealist mode.

Slow Fade (Knopf)—Ralph Wurlitzer. I don't know anything about Wurlitzer, but this high-tech Hollywood novel outdoes Don DeLillo at his very best. It is *that* world—chic, slick, sophisticated, bittersweet, a tapestry of bright and clever sentences. Yet, dealing as it does with the curious arena of films and film-making, it is precisely apt. I have seen nothing quite like this since the days of David Stacton.

Richard Yates—*Young Hearts Crying* (Delacorte). Ever since *Eleven Kinds of Loneliness* and *Revolutionary Road* almost everybody who cares about contemporary American fiction has admired the work of Richard Yates. He has a good crowd of well-wishers. Not everyone, however. The *New Yorker* (14 January 1985) joined the negative side this time, mildly sympathetic, though clearly condescending: "Yates is an admired sociorealist who comes down to us by way of Hemingway and O'Hara and James Gould Cozzens. He furnishes his backgrounds, describes and dresses his figures, and attempts to catch the rhythms and sounds and idioms of everyday speech. He keeps his prose out of the way, fashioning colorless, boiled-down sentences that are rarely flavored by metaphors or similes." (If you think that description is complimentary, you haven't been keeping up). He is also attacked for "tired ear" and being humorless — "He gives the impression of wanting to stare his readers down." This latest may not be his best, but it takes large, brave risks, and it gains extra power and resonance from its version of the literary history of a generation and on account of its semiautobiographical elements. Reviews across the country have been generally favorable, another (final) example of the growing split between the City and the Nation.

There is another way a year of our times can make itself known to us, by what it values and wishes to preserve. By what it openly nominates for posterity — or oblivion, as the case may be. Most often this sort of thing is manifest in journalism and in literary criticism, but sometimes the maintenance and revision of literary reputations are to be noticed in the publication or reprinting of primary texts of fiction as well. Indeed, this may represent more important evidence (money over mouth) than critical articles, books, text anthologies, and collections of interviews. My best judgment of the contemporary fiction scene as viewed by its interested gardeners and gatekeepers, the entire critical industry both public and academic, is that it was a transitional year mostly devoted, by themselves as well as others, to the care and maintenance, the preservation of the status quo. Except for the brand new writers there were very few "discoveries" in 1984 and no significant questioning or revising of the received hierarchy. With one exception. In 1983 the publication in hardcover of *LaBrava* by Elmore Leonard led to a significant rise in his reputation, a change confirmed in 1984 by the reprinting and availability of all his previously published thrillers in paperback. Not yet, but scheduled, are reprints of his several Westerns. Leonard was, throughout 1984, the subject of a good deal of attention, culminating in a celebratory feature, "Elmore Leonard's Rogues' Gallery" by Ben Yagoda, in the *New York Times Magazine* (30 December 1984). That Leonard, now in his early sixties, could be found and praised and, simultaneously, more practically rewarded, was a good sign to the crowd of laborers in the literary vineyard as well as to readers looking for new faces

and voices. Similarly, the "discovery" of William Kennedy, whose *Ironweed* took prizes in 1983, was consolidated by the reprinting of his several previous novels during 1984.

Except for these striking exceptions, however, it was an essentially defensive year — critical wagons drawn in a tight circle, but no hostiles yet in sight. But in 1984 there were some odd bits and pieces of primary evidence which can tell us a bit more than the critical accounts choose to. It is too early still, and the angle is too acute, for a real pattern to emerge. But three examples offer some seeds for speculation. The first of these, coming at year's end, represents a slight shift whose full import remains to be seen. For some years now, with several books, there has been a concerted attempt to push the reputation of novelist Don DeLillo beyond the esteem of reviewers and into the hard currency of the marketplace. Nineteen eighty-four found DeLillo in the enviable (and very unusual) position of having all seven of his earlier novels in print in various trade and mass-market paperback editions. Together with this kind of exposure, his name began to crop up more and more in secondary

Dust jacket for the latest book by poet and novelist Slavitt, who has also written as Henry Sutton

sources. It looked to be a solid, careful buildup for his next novel. Then, just before the year's end (and carefully copyrighted for 1984 as well as 1985) the new novel, *White Noise*, appeared in stores in time to partake of the Christmas season and to build interest for the major reviews coming in January. The interesting thing here is that with *White Noise* DeLillo appears under the imprint of a different publisher, Viking, after a good many years with Alfred Knopf. A shift at precisely this point is unusual enough to raise eyebrows in certain circles. When one of the favored few moves, it means something. So far it seems to have meant a lot more than usual attention for *White Noise*.

Not many American writers, no matter how successful, are given occasion or opportunity to restore something long out of print. Most often that possibility is a strictly posthumous one. But 1984 saw the republication of William Manchester's fine 1953 novel, *The City of Anger*. Those who admired the novel in the first place (myself among them) are delighted. In a "Publisher's Note," Little, Brown celebrates the book, though a little defensively: "Whatever its flaws—and like all early work it creaks here and there—*The City of Anger* was im-

mediately recognized as the work of an original mind exploring dark corners of urban ghettos then largely ignored by the press. In those days the births, weddings—even the murders—of blacks went unrecorded." It is sold, this time around, chiefly on the validity of content. But whatever the thoughts of the publisher (even if primarily to keep a successful author happy; who knows?) no American publisher these days sets out to lose money for the sake of any cause or person. Somebody at some point at Little, Brown had to decide that there is (again) an audience out there in America for the book. If so, then that is a sign that *The City of Anger*, with all its weight and depth of cumulative realistic detail, is seen as at least in strong competition with the sophisticated, distanced minimalism which has been "mainstream" for a decade or more. Clearly, this book is intended for a very different American audience than, say DeLillo's work. A sign, then, that at least some publishers in 1984 have not wholly abandoned the hope of somehow reaching Americans who look for a bit more in fiction than verbal texture and technical virtuosity.

Finally, it was a year in which the past laid stronger claims on the present. It might be thought

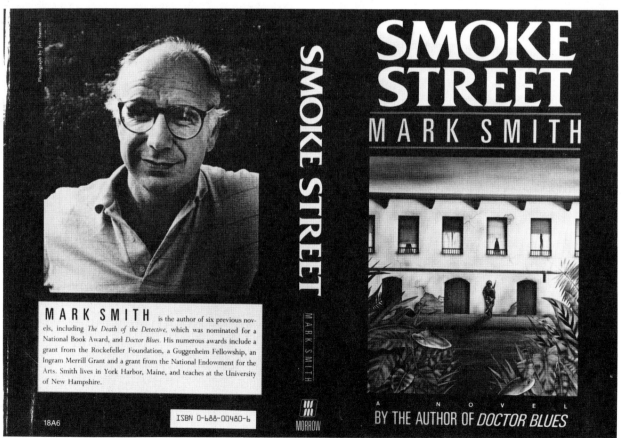

Dust jacket for Smith's surreal story set in a revolution-torn Central American capital

Dust jacket for the eighth book by the author of
Revolutionary Road

(and the thought has, in fact, been expressed by some critics) that the great generation of American twentieth-century masters has at last passed into the realm of the remote past. Not so. This past year it is Faulkner who has asserted his presence. Dismissed by some of the leading contemporaries as irrelevant to postmodern concerns (except insofar as he undeniably influenced so many European and South American writers and, especially, the venerated Gabriel García Márquez), Faulkner's work has nevertheless remained actively, successfully in print, in many forms, since his death. And 1984 witnessed a number of slight changes, *additions to,* that canon. Two of these editions involved fiction. Critic Noel Polk edited a new, corrected text of *The Sound and the Fury* for Random House, an expensive if worthy gesture, indicative of a long-term positive estimate of Faulkner's commercial potential by the fact that Random House also published a handsome edition of the previously unpublished (probably written in 1926) *Father Abraham,* edited by James B. Meriwether. *Father Abraham* represents the earliest surviving Snopes material and, as well, the earliest of Faulkner's writing about Yoknapatawpha County. Its historical value is unquestioned. But, until very recently, previously undiscovered and unpublished Faulkner items were generally relegated to small press and university press publication. In fact, what remains of Faulkner's abandoned second novel, *Elmer,* was published in 1983 by the Seajay Press of Northport, Alabama; and *Father Abraham* was also originally published, in a limited edition, by the Red Ozier Press in 1983. That it was promoted to full commercial status in 1984 stands as yet another sign that, despite much effort and manipulation to the contrary, the living literature of this large nation is, like that nation and its people, too pluralistic, too various and diverse, to be taken for granted, to be subjected to any one rule or set of standards. Mere signs on the horizon, to be sure. There's no literary revolution brewing. The powers-that-be are firmly in place; but, as ever and always, there are enough hints of change in the wind to trouble the repose of all those except the truly serene, writers and readers, who have nothing to lose and everything to gain, come what changes may.

OBITUARIES

John Betjeman

(28 August 1906-19 May 1984)

John Press

See also the Betjeman entry in *DLB 20, British Poets, 1914-1945.*

For many people John Betjeman remains essentially a writer of light verse, a court jester who began his career by cultivating rich aristocrats at Oxford, won a reputation by making it fashionable to admire hideous Victorian buildings, and ended up as a television personality and a court poet. Such misapprehensions should not survive a reading of Philip Larkin's introduction to the American edition of Betjeman's *Collected Poems* (1971) or of those poems; but it is worth saying yet again that he was a serious poet.

In the middle of World War I, when a small boy at Highgate School, he presented a bound collection of his verse, *The Best of Betjeman*, to the American master, Mr. Eliot, who never referred to the matter. At Marlborough, a famous and expensive school, he was a friend of two poets, Louis MacNeice and Bernard Spencer, and of the art historian Anthony Blunt. At Oxford he was delighted when wealthy young men invited him to their magnificent houses in England and in Ireland, but he also made lifelong friendships with W. H. Auden and Evelyn Waugh. His love of pleasure, his ability to move in a variety of worlds, his brilliant frivolity, and his love of the arts were distinguishing marks of his character at Oxford and throughout his life. Betjeman was always a disconcertingly complex character, a virtuoso actor who enjoyed shifting from one role to another. But his devotion to poetry never wavered.

In 1931 there appeared what Betjeman himself called a "precious, hyper-sophisticated book," *Mount Zion*, a slender volume of poems dedicated to Mrs. Arthur Dugdale, hostess to rich, decorative Oxford undergraduates and owner of Sezincote, a country house in Gloucestershire, adorned like the Brighton Pavilion with a dome. The book's typography, its colored pages, the illustration of Sezincote that preceded the poems, and the fact that the book was published by an enormously rich friend of the author's, Edward James (who later married the dancer Tilly Losch), may indicate the nature of Betjeman's first publication. Fifty years ago it was read only by a very small circle of Betjeman's friends, who found its verve irresistible.

His second volume, *Continual Dew*, came out in 1937 and confirmed his reputation as a witty, ingenious contriver of period pieces, a poet who rejoiced in suburbs, railway stations, and macabre anecdotes. Perceptive readers might have detected in *Old Lights for New Chancels* (1940) and in *New Bats in Old Belfries* (1945) a greater seriousness and a deeper lyricism, nowhere more apparent than in "Ireland with Emily":

> There in pinnacled protection,
>> One extinguished family waits
> A Church of Ireland resurrection
>> By the broken, rusty gates.
> Sheepswool, straw and droppings cover
> Graves of spinster, rake and lover,
> Whose fantastic mausoleum
> Sings its own seablown Te Deum,
>> In and out the slipping slates.

And to those volumes also belong the most celebrated of what he called his amatory poems, foreshadowed by "Love in a Valley," from *Continual Dew*, the first of his poems to praise stalwart young women such as Pam, the "great big mountainous sports girl" of "Pot Pourri from a Surrey Garden," Miss J. Hunter Dunn, Myfanwy, "Strong and willowy, strong to pillow me," and the red-haired Amazon who seized him in the licorice fields at Pontefract.

W. H. Auden's selection of Betjeman's verse and prose, *Slick But Not Streamlined* (1947), commended his old friend to an American audience as a serious, original poet. Years later, in 1958, Edmund Wilson declared that, after Auden and Dylan Thomas, Betjeman was the most interesting English poet since T. S. Eliot. Not even in England were his gifts acclaimed until the 1950s. During that decade he published the finest of his architectural writings under the title *First and Last Loves* (1952) and edited *Collins Guide to English Parish Churches* (1958), whose introduction contains Betjeman's strongest and

Dust jacket for a 1984 photographic retrospective of the late Poet Laureate

most evocative piece of prose. His fifth collection of poems, *A Few Late Chrysanthemums* (1954), displays his poetic talents at their richest; while his *Collected Poems* (1958) reputedly sold more copies than any other book of poems published by the firm of John Murray since Byron's *Don Juan*. It is extremely likely that Betjeman owed his immense popularity as a poet to his appearances on TV. He made his name in the 1950s with a series of films on subjects that aroused his enthusiasm: landscapes, gardens, country houses, popular seaside resorts, railway stations, railway lines, nineteenth-century industrial buildings, churches of every period. He wrote beguiling commentaries in verse and in prose that he spoke himself in his slightly hesitant, unmistakably upper-class voice that was so often trembling on the brink of laughter. And he could recreate unforgettably a vanished world, as in *Metro-land,* a film about the now defunct Metropolitan Railway. The villas of St. John's Wood, where prosperous Victorians kept their mistresses, live in his words no less than on the screen:

> What puritan arms have stretched within these rooms
> To touch what tender breasts
> As the cab-horse stamped in the road outside.

Like his prose works, Betjeman's TV films helped

to revolutionize public taste, opening people's eyes not only to the beauty of ancient churches and old buildings but also to the architectural glories of nineteenth-century Britain so often neglected or sneered at by historians.

One of Betjeman's friends, Osbert Lancaster, wrote a book about Greece called *Classical Landscape with Figures.* For Betjeman a landscape needs to be peopled if it is to yield its full significance. One of his most accomplished poems, "Middlesex," opens with a satirical but affectionate portrait of "Fair Elaine the bobby-soxer" as she hurries home from work to suburban Middlesex. Then Betjeman invokes a lost Elysium, the rural Middlesex of his boyhood, before transporting us back still further to the late-Victorian world of the fictional characters drawn by George and Weedon Grossmith in their *Diary of a Nobody* (1892):

> Parish of enormous hayfields
>   Perivale stood all alone,
> And from Greenford scent of mayfields
>   Most enticingly was blown
> Over market gardens tidy,
> Taverns for the bona fide,
> Cockney anglers, cockney shooters,
> Murray Poshes, Lupin Pooters,

Long in Kensal Green and Highgate silent under soot and stone.

Even in that Arcady Death is present. Betjeman acknowledges without affectation or evasiveness his fear of death and damnation implanted by a Calvinist nursemaid and never lost, despite his impassioned attempts to love God. The counterpointing of his zest for life against the terrors of extinction and of eternity endow the music of his verse with an infectious gaiety and a sombre resonance. It is a subtle music, grounded in the intricacy of metrical and stanzaic patterns; and although he confesses that he is a traditionalist in metres and that the rhythms of a dozen poets are generally buzzing about in his brain, his own singing line is enchantingly original. Nowhere is his technical mastery more effectively displayed than in his elegy for an old science don of Pembroke College, Oxford, "I. M. Walter Ramsden." Three Fellows recall the summers of long ago and the rowing men coming back from the river to celebrate the triumphs of the college boat:

> They remember, as the coffin to its final obsequations
>   Leaves the gates,
> Buzz of bees in window boxes on their summer ministrations,
>   Kitchen din,
>   Coming in,
>   From Eights.

Betjeman welcomed the honors lavished on him, including a knighthood and the Poet Laureateship. He relished the fun and glitter of fashionable society, valued the friendship of Princess Margaret, responded gladly to the command of Prince Charles that he should write a poem for his investiture as Prince of Wales, derived pleasure from staying in the splendid houses of the aristocracy. But his deepest loyalties were to friends of all classes and to poetry. He received on his seventy-fifth birthday a beautifully bound and printed book of poems written for him by some of the best living poets, a dozen of whom arrived at his house to present him with the unexpected gift. This tribute probably touched him more deeply than any official marks of favor.

He died in May 1984 at his home in Trebetherick, Cornwall, where he spent so many holidays in boyhood and where he lies buried in the village churchyard not far from the sea that was for him the most potent symbol of eternity.

A TRIBUTE

from ALAN BROWNJOHN

I knew John Betjeman, but only slightly. This means that instead of many recollections of many meetings, which are part of a large and general picture of the man, I have a few very clear memories of meetings and "sightings"—all the more vivid for being few. Here are some of them:

Going to interview him in 1957 for a small (and ultimately rather unsuccessful) magazine of literature and the arts intended for older school pupils. He then still had the flat in Cloth Fair, near Smithfield Meat Market and St. Bartholomew's Hospital. A tiny, cramped place, full of books, windows overlooking a churchyard. Betjeman finished the correction of some proofs for an article in the *Spectator*. "All right, interview me!" he said. Not gruff, not overbearing, rather humorous and reassuring. So we did. Except that the interview turned into two hours' easy conversation about his enthusiasms. He didn't ever, *act* them, but *lived* them. He expounded about architecture, leapt up to quote from volumes of little-known Victorian verse, talked about trains and town planning and hospital visiting. At the end, we thought: we didn't *interview*, we merely talked and listened. There's nothing to write about. But there was plenty.

The Poetry Society was celebrating seventy years of its existence at County Hall in London in 1979, in a large oak-panelled room. The only entrance a large door, where a uniformed dignitary greeted guests. There was a standing microphone, and speeches, and in the middle of one speech, one of the panels *opened* and Betjeman stood revealed, leaning on the arm of a County Hall attendant, alarmed to see that his appearance behind the speaker, as if by magic, through a secret door no one knew existed, had—of course it had—upstaged the speaker. Betjeman was very frail by this time, but very entertaining, and very pleased to be there. And very pleased in the end to have grabbed attention!

The last television recordings, for a series on John Betjeman transmitted in the months before his death. The day of the presentation to Betjeman of a book of twenty poems (by twenty poets) in honor of his seventy-fifth birthday. Sunny morning, TV cameras outside the Chelsea house as we drove up, the poet R. S. Thomas saying, "Are we expected to predict an economic upturn?" as the cameras approached him. Betjeman, very frail now, but wholly delighted, very flattered, very lively in his chair among the books and among the friends (sixteen of the poets in his own sitting room). A last meeting. The TV program contained about sixty seconds of it only.

A TRIBUTE

from CHRISTOPHER FRY

Edith Evans once said in a letter to me that life is long enough but not broad enough—by which she meant that too often good things get crowded out. Certainly it is true of my acquaintanceship with John Betjeman. I have time and again regretted the missed opportunities of getting to know him better.

The first of his letters I can find (he mentions an earlier correspondence) is about the posthumously published sonnet sequence by Christopher Hassall, *Bell Harry:* "It has some beautiful

things in it," he writes. "What a good & kind & entertaining man he was. I hope we'll one day meet and be able to talk of him." But I let time go by without meeting, and then out of the blue came a letter from him, of such sympathetic kindness that it brings him very close: "This letter needs no reply. It is just to tell you how deeply I sympathise with you over your burglary. Pictures & books are like old & trusted friends & to lose them is to lose part of ourself. Still worse the vandalism & malice of the burglary destroys our faith in human nature & goodness. Hold on."

In a letter I wrote to him some time later (alas, I have mislaid his reply and so can't date the time) I said that his *A Ballad of the Investiture 1969* was the best laureate poem that had been written since Tennyson's *Ode on the Death of the Duke of Wellington.* There had been some carping press criticism of some of his other royal-occasion poems, but the Investiture Ballad stands as a model of what such work should be: relaxed, in his own true voice, humorous, recreative of the event, and very moving.

Richard Brautigan

(30 January 1935-? September 1984)

Michael P. Mullen
Indian Hills Community College

On 25 October 1984, the body of Richard Brautigan was discovered, four or five weeks after a single gunshot wound to the head killed him. In an article in *People,* "Author Richard Brautigan Apparently Takes His Own Life, but He Leaves a Rich Legacy" (12 November 1984), James Seymore emphasized one of the most significant aspects of Brautigan's appeal: his humor. Seymore described Brautigan as a "poet-novelist-humorist" with a vision that was "unique, so humorous." A *New York Times* reviewer who made reference to Brautigan's "good humor" is quoted, as is Brautigan's twenty-four-year-old daughter, who said, "He was so funny in the morning."

Brautigan was often compared to Twain and Hemingway, but these influences are not always immediately recognizable. What is more distinctive is Brautigan's bizarre plots and startling figures of

speech. A publisher's note described *The Hawkline Monster: A Gothic Western* (1974) this way: "The time is 1902; the setting, Eastern Oregon. Magic Child, a 15-year-old Indian girl, wanders into the wrong whorehouse looking for the right men to kill the monster that lives in the ice caves under the basement of Miss Hawkline's cold yellow house." In *Trout Fishing in America* (1967), Brautigan's most popular novel, the narrator, in looking for the perfect trout stream, discovers that the Cleveland Wrecking Yard is selling used trout streams for $6.50 a foot. The main character in *A Confederate General from Big Sur* (1965) says, in a chapter titled "The Pork Chop Alligator": "Your alligator looks like a handbag filled with harmonicas."

The playfulness of Brautigan's work attracted readers; his books could be read for pleasure. At the same time, however, his books had substance,

Richard Brautigan (International Portrait Gallery)

which satisfied the critics. In a 29 December 1969 review in *Newsweek*, A. H. Norman wrote of *Trout Fishing in America:* "[Brautigan] combines the surface finality of Hemingway, the straightforwardness of Sherwood Anderson and the synesthetic guile of Baudelaire." More recently, in the March 1984 issue of *American Literature*, William L. Stull discussed at length the allusive quality of Brautigan's books.

John Stickney, in "Gentle Poet of the Young," in *Life* on 14 August 1970, described Brautigan's books as "a gentle carnival to which young people relate easily, a show of laughter, romance, sensation and innocence—an intense identification with nature and all living things. Thoughtful hedonism, it might be called: celebrate the pleasures of life and love on the midway, he advises, because tragedy lurks just outside the gates." In Brautigan's later books, the tragedy tends to prevail. This change in tone is evident in his most recent books, especially *The Tokyo-Montana Express* (1980) and *So the Wind Won't Blow it All Away* (1982). Both contain his characteristic humor; but more than that they are marked by sadness and death and a longing for more peaceful times. Barry Yourgrau, in a review

of *The Tokyo-Montana Express* in the *New York Times Book Review,* wrote:

> He is now a longhair in his mid-40's, and across his habitually wistful good humor there now creeps shadows of ennui and dullness and too easily aroused sadness. The telltales of an uneasy middle-aged soul peep darkly among the cute knickknacks of "The Tokyo-Montana Express"; dead friends, dead strangers in the papers and on the street, ghosts, regrets over wasted years, regrets over women, bad hangovers, loneliness, phone calls long after midnight.

The narrator of Brautigan's last book, *So the Wind Won't Blow it All Away* (1982), was described by a *Publishers Weekly* reviewer as a "melancholy 47-year-old man" (Brautigan's age at the time). The novel is a look backward, as the narrator recalls the fateful year, for him, of 1947, when, as a twelve-year-old boy, he one day had to choose between a hamburger and a box of .22 shells and accidentally killed a friend of his. The narrator, like Brautigan himself, spent his fatherless, impoverished childhood wandering with his mother from town to town in the Pacific Northwest, which led James Seymore to view *So the Wind Won't Blow it All Away* as "Brautigan's final return to his beginnings and the central traumas of his life."

The reviews of *So the Wind* were, as was typical for a Brautigan book, mixed. The *Publishers Weekly* reviewer concluded by saying that the novel was "a flat, listless narrative, enlivened fleetingly by Brautigan's bizarre imagination, but pretentiously self-important and contrived." Also panning the book was the reviewer for the *New Yorker,* who called it "a weary little dirge."

Praising the novel was George L. Ives in *Library Journal,* who said, "Brautigan's latest novel should please both old fans and new readers. His admirers will relish the familiar style—broken chronology and fragmented characterization— which carries the reader on a verbal rollercoaster. But the tighter thematic development in this narrative should widen Brautigan's audience." It didn't; his audience continued to diminish, and this, according to those who knew Brautigan, was one of the things that contributed so much to his unhappiness.

The boom in Brautigan's career came in the late 1960s and early 1970s, when his work first received national attention. Three of his books, *Trout Fishing in America, In Watermelon Sugar* (1968), and *The Pill Versus the Springhill Mine Disaster* (1968), were published in one volume by Seymour Lawrence in 1969 and the success of the collection catapulted Brautigan from a local literary figure to a spokesman for his age.

That the critics were never completely behind Brautigan did not bother him. Helen Brann, the agent who helped engineer the 1970 collection of Brautigan's books with Seymour Lawrence, said that Brautigan didn't care what the critics said about his work: "But what he couldn't bear was losing the readers. He really cared about his audience. The fact that his readership was diminishing was what was breaking his heart." *Trout Fishing in America,* his breakthrough novel, has sold over two million copies. At the time of his death, sales for *So the Wind* totaled approximately fifteen thousand copies. He was still popular in Japan, but that was no longer enough to sustain him.

Both Seymour Lawrence and Thomas McGuane remarked, after Brautigan's death, that he had been unhappy and drinking a lot. Before he left San Francisco to go to his house in Bolinas, California, he borrowed a .44 caliber Smith & Wesson from a friend of his, James Sakata. It was the last anyone heard from him, not unusual since Brautigan often went into isolation when he was working on a novel, and had told people he was going on a hunting trip.

Headlines of the obituaries that appeared after Brautigan's body was found indicate how closely he was still identified with the era whose spokesman he had become: "Richard Brautigan, Novelist, A Literary Idol of the 1960's" (*New York Times*); "Richard Brautigan, 49; offbeat novelist of the '60s" (*Chicago Tribune*); "Brautigan, Literary Guru of the '60s, Dies" (*Los Angeles Times*); and "Author Richard Brautigan, 49: Figure in '60s Counterculture" (*St. Louis Post-Dispatch*).

It wouldn't be fair or necessarily accurate to simply say that, faced by a diminishing audience, Brautigan chose suicide. Don Carpenter, a novelist and friend of Brautigan's, said, "It's not a case of 'hot in the '60s, can't get arrested in the '70s, dead in the '80s.'" Finally, and as is often the case, perhaps it is best to look to the author's works for answers. The narrator in *The Tokyo-Montana Express,* a character very similar to Brautigan, says: "What makes you older is when your bones, muscles and blood wear out, when the heart sinks into oblivion and all the houses you ever lived in are gone. . . ." The critical attention Brautigan's books received during his lifetime indicates that he was more than a voice for a generation, forgotten as that generation gave

way to the one that followed, and the attention given Brautigan after his death should highlight even more the lasting qualities of his work.

A TRIBUTE ——————————————

from HELEN BRANN

Richard Brautigan was a writer I was honored to represent as his literary agent from 1968 on. I think Richard was an American genius, a pure artist, an original voice out of the West from which he came. I believe Richard's work will last, not only because of his brilliant style so individual, spare, and alternately sharp and gentle, but because in books like *Trout Fishing In America, Willard And His Bowling Trophies,* and *The Hawkline Monster* he explored the funny, phony, violent, romantic America he loved enough to see with open-eyed vision. His books, so much shorter in page length than his contemporaries' works, had real size. European publishers and Japanese publishers saw these qualities and all his titles are in print in over twelve countries, including the U.S. editions of all his work.

A personal note about Richard, because he and I became good trusting friends, and that is that he was a consummate professional in his dealings with me and his publishers. I have never had a client so deliberate and knowing about his contracts, so knowledgeable about production problems and design, so fair about what was a reasonable demand and what went over that sometimes fine line. Richard was gentle and kind to me always, funny and acute and great fun to be with whether in New York, San Francisco, or Montana. He spared me his miseries, and now I know how very much he protected me. I loved him very much, and shall miss him always.

A TRIBUTE ——————————————

from KURT VONNEGUT

I never knew Richard Brautigan, except through his writings, which were brought to my attention by my students at Harvard, where I was a lecturer in 1971. He was then published by City Lights. I commended him to my own publisher,

Seymour Lawrence, who subsequently gained him a much wider audience, thanks to the sales force and mass distribution capabilities of Dell. We never met or corresponded or spoke on the telephone.

For what it is worth, which is probably nothing: there was publishing gossip that he entered the world of mass marketing with declarations of not being interested in money, but that he later became a shrewd bargainer.

At this great distance from the man himself, I will guess that he, like so many other good writers, was finally done in by the chemical imbalance we call depression, which does its deadly work regardless of what may really be going on in the sufferer's love life or his adventures, for good or ill, in the heartless marketplace.

Truman Capote
(30 September 1924-25 August 1984)

Kenneth T. Reed
Miami University

See also the Capote entries in *DLB 2, American Novelists since World War II* and *DLB Yearbook: 1980*.

Truman Capote will be remembered as an astonishingly intelligent, inventive master of the American idiom, and as a talented artist tortured by tranquilizers, alcohol, and—worst of all—a fatal addiction to the sweet life denied him as a youth when he was farmed out by his distracted and suicidal mother to board with unlettered kinfolk in rural Louisiana, Mississippi, and Alabama. Considering that he was treated in school as mentally backward, the wonder is how he independently applied himself toward a brilliantly literate style of his own. "Where there is no discipline, there is nothing," he remarked once. But when the discipline went, Capote died as an artist long before his body was discovered in August 1984 at the Bel-Air home of Joanna Carson in Los Angeles.

To himself and to others (who, as Paul Levine rightly remarked, had "a difficult time discerning Capote from his work"), he remained an eccentric spectacle. In *Esquire*, Tom Burke described him as "an exotic-looking faun," "a ruined Puck," and "a tiny, blond Theda Bara." Cynthia Ozick, in her 1973 Capote interview in *New Republic*, marveled over "this tiny-fingered flaccid man, with molasses eyes and eunuch's voice, looking like an old caricature of Aeolus, the puff-cheeked little god of wind." A year later, Capote said in an interview with Gloria Steinem that "I was always sort of a two-headed calf, and was aware of the fact even when I was very young." Later still, he forthrightly announced, "I'm an alcoholic. I'm a drug addict. I'm a homosexual."

He also speculated on the prospect of his reincarnation as a buzzard, a creature that "doesn't have to bother about his appearance or ability to beguile and please; he doesn't have to put on airs. Nobody's going to like him anyway; he is ugly, unwanted, unwelcome everywhere."

Small wonder that his apprenticeship fiction ("A Mink of One's Own," "The Headless Hawk," "Miriam," "Master Misery," "A Tree of Night") was rife with physical and psychological grotesqueness. Small wonder too that when his controversial novel *Other Voices, Other Rooms* appeared amid adverse critical reception in 1948, its landscape was festooned with a four-legged chicken, a two-headed baby, a Duck Boy with webbed fingers, a midget songstress named Miss Wisteria, and a bearded lady. In *The Grass Harp*, his seriocomic 1951 novel, readers were confronted with the "morphodyte" Verena, and in the breezy pages of *Breakfast at Tiffany's* (1958) the delightfully free-spirited Holly Golightly was at the same time a portrait in psychopathology. In 1965 the remarkable nonfiction novel *In Cold Blood* traced the peregrinations of two psychopathic killers, and toward the end of his career, Capote even had the benign, white-haired old lady of "A Lamp in the Window" (from *Music for Chameleons*) reveal her bizarre side by preserving dozens of house cats in her deep freeze.

Still, Capote advanced themes as old as literature itself: the torturous adolescent initiation (as perhaps suggested by his own unhappy experience with "a miserable succession of bugle-blowing prisons, grim reveille-ridden summer camps"), the futile quest to preserve innocence in a fallen world,

Truman Capote (Phyllis Cerf Wagner)

the perplexing search for identity, and the devastating consequences of loneliness and isolation. Although he (and the astute scholar-critic Ihab Hassan) denied it, Capote began literary life as a regionalist in the Southern gothic tradition; and although Capote and his fiction moved from the South to places like Haiti, Hollywood, and Holcomb, Kansas, some of the local colorist in him fortunately persisted. By ingeniously blending fiction with expository writing, he made that fiction (*Music for Chameleons*, for instance) seem very like the most objective of reporting, while his reporting (*In Cold Blood* is the best example) seemed like good gothic fiction. "Perhaps the single constant in his prose is style," Mark Schorer wrote, "and the emphasis he himself places upon the importance of style."

Capote will survive chiefly as a modern master of graceful and evocative prose, rather than for any new and extraordinary wrinkles in theme and idea. No Melville adrift on a sea of metaphysics, no Whitman fired with a vision of America's limitless promise, Capote will queue up somewhere behind his country's major writers. But as a brilliant lyric stylist

turned late-night video quidnunc, this gifted man, who boasted of having registered an I.Q. of 215, seemed surely to have gone wrong in the social funhouse. Architect and underwriter of the 1966 Party of the Decade in New York, Capote toasted five hundred of his "just real friends" (including Roosevelts, Trumans, Kennedys, and Johnsons) at the Plaza, only to end in personal and spiritual isolation a decade later. "So far as I know, I've never betrayed anyone who was kind to me," he protested once.

True enough. Leaving a sordid trail of drunk-driving arrests, shattered friendships, aborted love affairs, incoherent public interviews, hospital sojourns for a variety of serious physical and emotional ailments, Truman Capote was found dead at fifty-nine. This son of Archulus Persons and fifteen-year-old Lillie Mae Faulk, who had taken the surname of his Cuban stepfather Joseph Capote, had treated his language and his literary audiences a great deal better than he had treated himself. "I've got news for you, buddy," he wrote to himself, "you won't have to wait for reincarnation to be treated like a buzzard; plenty of folks are doing it already."

A TRIBUTE *from ROBERT L. BERNSTEIN*

(Remarks spoken at the memorial service for Truman Capote on 25 September 1984.)

It is with a sense of privilege that I welcome you today, as we pause to think for a few special moments about a great American writer, Truman Capote.

Looking back, I realize that we have published Truman for thirty-six years, every step of the way from the very beginning of his career to the very end—an unusual thing in publishing. He had a close and lasting friendship with Bennett and Phyllis Cerf, and it was through that friendship that Truman became more than an author on the Random House list. He became a part of the Random House family, a permanent part.

Everyone who knew Truman for any length of time has at least one story to tell. I have one favorite because it shows Truman at his very best and includes three of his virtues—his graciousness, his thoughtfulness, and his humor.

It happened when I first became president of Random House. Truman was on the phone instant-ly with an invitation, coveted by so many, to the soon-to-be-famous black-and-white masked ball that he and Kay Graham were giving at the Plaza Hotel. He was very emphatic about it, and said that I *must* come.

I felt at that time that I was living very much in Bennett's illustrious shadow, and was moved by Truman's kindness. So, not long afterward, Joe Fox, Truman's friend and editor, and I, together with our wives, found ourselves driving up to the pillared portico of the Plaza in an enormous car we had rented for the occasion. We opened the door, got out, straightened ourselves, and moved past the wooden horses restraining a crowd—in which it seemed that every other person held a camera with flashbulb ready to pop. As we ascended the steps, feeling we'd really arrived, a little boy in the front row looked us over, turned around, and yelled to the crowd, "They're *nobody*!!"

When I told the story to Truman a few minutes later, the Capote grin—that very special one that is known so well—spread across his face and he said, "What do *they* know!"

Truman lived a colorful life, a complicated life, sometimes a turbulent life. But its extraordinary sum is represented in his many friends

---

A TRIBUTE *from JAMES DICKEY*

TO BE DONE IN WINTER BY THOSE SURVIVING TRUMAN CAPOTE

What you hold,
Don't drink it all. Throw what you have left of it
Out, and stand. Where the drink went away
Rejoice that your fingers are burning
Like hammered snow.

He makes no sound: the cold flurries, and he comes all the way
Back into life; in the mind
There is no decay. Imagine him
As to behold him, for if you fail
To remember, he lies without
What his body was.
His short shadow
Is on you. Bring him in, now, with tools
And elements. Behold him

With your arms: encircle him,
Bring him in with the forge and the crystal,

With the spark-pounding cold.

gathered here today. And most especially it can be seen in the books he wrote: *Other Voices, Other Rooms, A Tree of Night, Local Color, The Grass Harp, The Muses Are Heard, Breakfast at Tiffany's, Observations, Selected Writings, In Cold Blood, A Christmas Memory, The Thanksgiving Visitor, The Dogs Bark, Music for Chameleons, One Christmas.*

Truman Capote will be remembered, through these works, as he deserves to be, for a long, long time.

Lillian Hellman
(20 June 1906-30 June 1984)

Richard Layman

See also the Hellman entry in *DLB 7, Twentieth-Century American Dramatists.*

George Jean Nathan called her "the best of our American Women playwrights"; Robert Brustein applauded her for setting intellectual standards in American drama; Harriett Taubman observed that she "did not soften her portraits or observations to please a public unaccustomed to such unyielding truths; such was the measure of her discipline and integrity as an artist."

Martha Gelhorn classified her as a self-serving "apocryphiar"; Sidney Hook accused her of having "duped a generation of critics devoid of historical memory and critical common sense"; Mary McCarthy called her a liar.

Such was the diversity of reactions Lillian Hellman, who died in 1984, provoked during her lifetime. She stood at the forefront of American letters for half-a-century, always outspoken in her opinions and intolerant of those who disagreed with her. She established a reputation for herself as an intellectual, proudly self-taught after dropping out of college in her junior year; and she attracted an almost cultlike following for her radical political stance, even while claiming to be naive about world affairs. She became one of those writers better known for her life than for her works, and still she could claim more plays with Broadway runs of over 325 performances—five—than any other American playwright: Tennessee Williams, Edward Albee, and Thorton Wilder had four; Arthur Miller had three; Robert Sherwood had two; and Eugene O'Neill had one.

Lillian Hellman had two careers. She made her reputation as a playwright and capitalized on it as a memoirist. Her greatest success on the stage

Lillian Hellman (International Portrait Gallery)

was her first play, *The Children's Hour*, produced in 1934. It ran 691 performances on Broadway at a time when Hollywood producers were looking to the theater for writing talent, and within a year Hellman could claim to be the best-paid woman writer in the movies, though she was too independent to last long in an industry for which she had little respect. Over the next twenty-nine years, eleven more of Hellman's plays were produced on Broadway, all but four of them with runs of over one hundred performances. She won two National Drama Critics Circle Awards—for her 1941 anti-Fascist drama *Watch on the Rhine* and for her last original play, *Toys in the Attic* (1960), in which a family learns, as one says, that "On your struggle up the mountain path, you will find that truth is often ugly." In 1964, Hellman was honored by the National Institute of Arts and Letters with their Gold Medal for Drama, awarded only once every five years for extraordinary distinction. She was a popular choice who richly deserved the honor, it was felt.

Lillian Hellman's plays had a common theme—the damage done by the big lie—and she showed herself uncommonly adept at portraying the motivations of self-centered, small-minded people in compromising situations. When she turned from play writing to autobiography in the mid-1960s, some critics claimed that they could see clearly now why Hellman understood duplicity so well. Charges about the cloudiness of her memory, her disregard for historical fact, and the self-serving effect of her distortions spoiled the acclaim Hellman received for her successive volumes of memoirs: *An Unfinished Woman* (1967), *Pentimento* (1973), *Scoundrel Time* (1976), and *Maybe* (1980). She won the National Book Award for *An Unfinished Woman*, and at the time of its publication she was widely praised for her vivid writing style, for what Edward Weeks called her "indignation at meanness," and for a self-portrait that bristled with integrity. More recent appraisals have centered on the fractured version of literary history the book provided.

Pentimento was greeted with intemperate praise that all but overshadowed her previous book. The *Economist* hailed her creation of a "new successful genre . . . [a] superb form of flickering autobiography"; John Leonard in the *New York Times Book Review* called Hellman's prose "as precise as an electron microscope"; Christopher Lehmann-Haupt also in the *New York Times* called the book a "mysteriously exciting and beautiful thing to see." The story "Julia" from *Pentimento* was purchased by Columbia Pictures, and a movie starring Jane Fonda as Hellman and Jason Robards as Dashiell Hammett won three academy awards. Hellman was incensed, complaining that the movie brought her unexpected and unwelcome attention. Though she is a principal character in "Julia," she claimed, disingenuously some thought, to have been surprised

to find herself portrayed in the movie. When she was offered $500,000 for film rights to *An Unfinished Woman*, she refused the money because she could not secure the right of final approval of the production. "My own life, after all, is more important to me than a movie," she exclaimed. "It is a matter of moral responsibility."

That pose took on an ironic twist as literary investigators worked to satisfy the enormous public curiosity generated by the movie about the mysterious anti-Fascist Julia, whom Hellman claimed to have assisted heroically in prewar Germany. It has been shown that Hellman took unusual creative license with the story of Julia, based apparently on the life of Muriel Gardiner. While she never met Dr. Gardiner, Hellman stood by the accuracy of her story despite the remoteness of the possibility, as Gardiner points out, that there was more than one millionaire medical student in Vienna during the late 1930s who married the leader of the resistance and actively participated in his group.

Scoundrel Time, Hellman's account of her political misfortunes in the 1940s and 1950s, was received with greater suspicion and less approval than her previous books. She portrayed herself as a victim of political persecution who stood up to the House Un-American Activities Committee, refusing publicly to "cut her conscience to fit the pattern of this year's fashions." That much was true; but it was suggested that in her recreation of the fearful days of political interrogation in America during the cold war era, she managed, by neglecting them, to denigrate the bravery and honesty and integrity of many other leftist stalwarts who risked far more than she for their ideals. Moreover, she proved simply to be a bad historian, however good she was as a storyteller.

After *Scoundrel Time* was published Hellman became increasingly reclusive. She was very ill, and yet she still demonstrated the feisty courage that had become her trademark. When Mary McCarthy publicly questioned her honesty, Hellman responded with a $2.25 million libel suit, still in litigation at her death.

The final assessment of Lillian Hellman's life and career will not be easy. Her critics cannot ignore the enduring quality of her best plays, and her advocates cannot overlook the ugly implications of her self-satisfying distortions. Questions about the purpose of literature and the relationship between art and truth and fact will be raised again. As a literary figure, she poses the same moral ambiguities as do the characters in her plays. And like them, in her attempt to distort the past she may well have done herself irreparable damage.

A TRIBUTE

from JOHN HERSEY

(Spoken at Lillian Hellman's burial, 3 July 1984.)

I'd like to say a few words about Lillian's anger. Most of us were startled by it from time to time.

Anger was her essence. It was at the center of that passionate temperament. It informed her art: the little foxes snapped at each other, we could see their back hairs bristle, we could smell their foxiness—they were real and alive because of the current of anger that ran through them, as it did through so many of Lillian's characters.

What I want to say is that this voltage of Lillian's was immensely important and valuable to our time. It electrified a mood of protest. The protest was that of every great writer: "Life ought to be better than this!"

This peppery quality took so many dazzling forms in her. You could hear it on the edge of that raucous laugh of hers. It decorated her mischief. I think it even lived in her taste buds—how she loved horseradish, mustard, Portuguese sausage! What a hot woman!

Her inmost fire, though, was not sensual. It was in the mind. It was a rage of the mind against all kinds of injustice—against human injustice and against the unfairness of death. In everything she wrote, and in her daily life, she fought against slander, greed, hypocrisy, cruelty, and everything shabby and second-rate and dangerous in those in power. She was very, very angry at death—and not just at the end. Death became her enemy years ago, when Hammett died, and this enmity made her even more vibrant and alive.

What could calm this anger? Only the sea, and money, and love. Anyone who gave her the slightest flicker of love got in return a radiance of laughter and fun that was unbelievably enjoyable; this was the bright other face of the anger.

Dear Lillian, you are a finished woman, now. I mean "finished" in its better sense. You shone with a high finish of integrity, decency, uprightness. You have given us this anger to remember and to use in a bad world. We thank you, we honor you, and we all say goodbye to you now with a love that should calm that anger of yours forever.

© John Hersey, 1984.

A TRIBUTE

from PATRICIA NEAL

(Spoken at Lillian Hellman's burial, 3 July 1984.)

I will always love Lillian Hellman. She was a very important part of my life, a thread whose fibers were woven into every aspect of my life. At my tender age of twenty she was responsible for my Broadway debut in *Another Part of the Forest*, and a few years later, having come back from Hollywood, I appeared in her play *The Children's Hour*.

In 1952 at a dinner party at Lillian's New York home I met Roald Dahl, who was to be my husband for thirty years. Last month, as ill as she was, she got all dressed up to come to a fabulous party I gave for my youngest daughter, Lucy. She wore a magnificent Russian amethyst necklace. She wanted to know all about my baby Lucy's future plans. She was always very eager to help the next generation. Just last week we discussed having a belated birthday celebration for dear Lillian upon my return to the Vineyard. However, at the airport in Boston I learned of her death from a total stranger.

How sad it is that she has gone. I will remember her with deep love forever and ever.

A TRIBUTE

from RICHARD WILBUR

The musical show *Candide* had its troubles, but collaborating with Lillian Hellman was a delight, and she became a dear friend. She was utterly square and forthright, with a keen and astonished interest in other people which made her a fine conversationalist. She had the dramatist's ear and eye for speech and behavior, and we could talk for hours about why on earth So-and-so had said this or done that. Well aware of the elusiveness of the truth, she was devoted to the pursuit of it in matters small or large. She was decidedly feminine, but she was also a mettlesome and independent woman in no need of the dubious title "Ms." She thought that her best play was *The Autumn Garden*, and so do I.

Alfred A. Knopf

(12 September 1892-11 August 1984)

"We've had a hell of a good time. We've done what we wanted. We've prospered, so what the hell."

It is a truism that nobody ever read a book because of its publisher. This rule can be challenged only in the case of Alfred A. Knopf, whom H. L. Mencken cited as "the perfect publisher." Even if Knopf did not really achieve brand-name status, he nonetheless succeeded better than any other American publisher in making his books recognizable as packages and identifiable as worthwhile reading.

After graduating from Columbia in 1912, Knopf served an apprenticeship with Doubleday and Mitchell Kennerley. In 1915 he established his own imprint with $5000 and his fiancée Blanche Wolfe. His first success was W. H. Hudson's *Green Mansions,* an English novel Knopf republished because he admired it. Before his retirement he published some 5000 books—including the work of sixteen Nobel Prize winners. His list was strong in foreign authors, many of whose books were first published in English by Knopf. American writers included Willa Cather, H. L. Mencken, John Updike, John Hersey, Dashiell Hammett, Raymond Chandler, James M. Cain, Ross Macdonald, John Cheever, Wallace Stevens, Conrad Richter, Joseph Hergesheimer, Conrad Aiken. Mencken's *The American Mercury* was published by Knopf. Music and history, two of the publisher's special interests, were well represented. Knopf sold his firm to Random House in 1966; but his name was maintained, and the imprint continued to operate independently. As long as Alfred A. Knopf was alive, the books were somehow still his.

In a 1983 interview Knopf insisted that his success was largely a matter of good timing: he had started when printing was cheap, credit was easy, authors were tractable, and agents knew their place. But luck had little to do with it. The main factors were taste, style, independence, intelligence, and literacy. A Knopf book was the extension of Alfred Knopf's character. He was an unapologetic aristocrat who published to please himself. In meeting his own standards, he set standards.

Knopf once stated, "I think the bestseller lists ought to be abolished by law. They're just another example of running with the crowd." He ran on his own track. With the passing of Alfred A. Knopf the world of letters becomes more hospitable to mediocrity.

—M. J. B.

A TRIBUTE

from KOBO ABE

It was some fifteen or sixteen years ago. I was in Mr. Harold Strauss's office at the time. I think it was just after *The Woman in the Dunes* was published. Mr. Strauss perspired and laughed a lot, shaking his gigantic figure. However, I was in utter amazement and do not clearly remember our talks then. Anyhow, it was the first professional translation of my work in a foreign country, and because it was a publication from such a well-established publisher as the Knopf Company, I could not fit in with the reality and experienced greater fatigue than joy.

That was when Mr. Knopf dropped by the office. Although I recall little conversation, I felt a warm and sincere personality emanating from his entire body. That was the first and the last time I had ever met him, and therefore, I am not certain if my impression was correct. It could have been an image which I had perceived through Mr. Strauss as a mirror. That Mr. Strauss is now gone. My novels have now been translated into over thirty different langages, and it is no overstatement that it all began with my encounter with the Knopf company. It is not simple to climb over the linguistic barrier of unique language such as Japanese. The impression of that room is deeply imbedded in my memory like a photograph. The name *Knopf* will continue to sparkle as my second birthstone.

A TRIBUTE

from JOHN R. ALDEN

I cannot say I was a Knopf author, since Alfred published only two of my books. Nor can I claim to have been intimate with him. However, my acquaintance with him endured for more than twenty years, and it is a pleasure to express my deep respect for him. Examining the two books of mine that he put forth, *Pioneer America* and *A History of the American Revolution*, I observe again examples of the superior format of his products. He was a stout friend of American historians. Many anecdotes about him will be told. He had a sharp tongue. He said to me once about one of his editors, "He became indispensable within two years. Then, of course, I fired him." Editors were probably as secure in their posts at Alfred A. Knopf, Inc. as they are in most publishing firms. To my personal knowledge Alfred displayed both probity and generosity.

A TRIBUTE
from ROBERT L. BERNSTEIN

I was fortunate enough to know Alfred Knopf as a friend and colleague for many years, and during that time he shared with me one great lesson through his own example. It was that book publishing is more than a business, it is a tremendous responsibility, setting forth in permanent form the ideas of thinking people from around the world. Certainly, the long list of his Nobel Prize winners, and Pulitzer Prize winners, and so many other writers of distinction shows how great was the measure of Alfred's success.

His dedication was leavened by wit. One of the famous stories about him tells of a young editor who asked him to approve signing up a new manuscript. When Alfred asked the editor why he thought it should be published, he said it was a pretty good book. To which Alfred responded: "Would you eat a pretty good egg?"

But basically he remained a man of personal seriousness and conscience. Alfred kept up a large and constant correspondence with writers and publishers and many others, and particularly with public officials. He knew what in his view was right and wrong, and he never hesitated to put his ideas forward; he was in that sense one of the great citizens of our democracy. I recall a letter he once wrote to Spiro Agnew. I am not sure what it said, or whether it touched on his performance as vice-president. But I well remember the healthy skepticism of the signature, which could have come from no one but himself, and which I doubt any vice-president had ever received. It ended: "Disrespectfully yours, Alfred A. Knopf."

Alfred A. Knopf in the 1920s

A TRIBUTE
from AMY CLAMPITT

I never met Alfred Knopf but I seem to have known his name for as long as I can remember, or almost. The first book with the Borzoi emblem that I distinctly remember reading is Willa Cather's *Death Comes for the Archbishop*, which I found at my grandfather's house when I was a child. Though I had dreams of publishing a book at a quite early age, I don't know that I ever consciously aspired to being a Knopf author—and now that I am one, I count myself a very lucky one. The care given to every aspect of my first full-length book, and not least to the design, the choice of the type face, the quality of the paper—as well as to keeping it in print and before the public—are, I am quite sure, a direct legacy from Alfred Knopf himself. There is no one in publishing whom I admire more, or to whom I feel more indebted—as an author, but above all as a reader.

A TRIBUTE

from ROALD DAHL

In 1952 I had got together a collection of short stories and I was looking for a publisher. I was a little-known writer and not many people wanted short stories. At ten in the morning, the phone rang in my New York flat.

"Hello," I said.

The voice at the other end said, "This is Alfred Knopf. I have read one of your stories. I understand you want someone to publish a book of them. I would like to do it."

I said yes on the spot and the reason I did so was this. I have never before (and incidently never since) been telephoned by the head of an important firm *direct*. It is always the secretary who makes the call and says, "Mr. So-and-so wants to talk to you." But not with Alfred.

When I got to know him well, I asked him about this. He said, "I never ask my secretary to ask a writer to hold on while she gets me on the line. I call direct. Why should the writer hold on for me? I would consider it gross bad manners to keep him waiting."

Wasn't that lovely?

Another memory of Alfred goes back to 1953. I was in New York and I was getting married and needed some money for a trip to Europe. He had published just one of my books, a collection of short stories called "Someone Like You." I am sure the sales were comparatively small and I doubt there was more than a thousand dollars in my royalty account.

I phoned him and said, "Do you think I could possibly have an advance?"

"How much?" he asked.

"Well," I said, "I know it sounds rather a lot but what I really need is ten thousand dollars."

"You've got it," he said and rang off.

Ten thousand dollars in those days would be about forty thousand today.

How many publishers would treat a junior writer like that?

A TRIBUTE

from OSCAR DYSTEL

I was truly privileged to have known Alfred Knopf and honored to be in his company, to have shared even a modest amount of his affection and respect.

His advice to me when I left Bantam was wise and totally realistic and it has made the ensuing years much easier for me to handle.

A TRIBUTE

from ROBERT GIROUX

Alfred A. Knopf is *the* towering figure among American book publishers in the 20th century. I knew him for decades as a buyer and admirer of the fine books he published and, in later years, as a friend. Though his death is a loss to the world of books, his son Alfred ("Pat") Knopf, Jr., carries on the family tradition at Atheneum.

A TRIBUTE

from GEORGE V. HIGGINS

My only contact with Alfred Knopf occurred in 1973, I think it was, when the customary administrative foolishness anent the publishing of any book was swirling around *The Digger's Game* and I was summoned by my masters to New York. I met him in the hallway and was introduced to him as the perpetrator of *The Friends of Eddie Coyle*, and he beamed and said that friends of his had taxed him on its publication with so dramatically reversing the practice of the house regarding naughty words. Of course he no longer had a great deal to do with the house, but he and I both pretended that he did, and he told me he had explained that when they finally decided to print coarse language, they did it all at once. I attended his memorial service this month because I thought it an appropriate gesture of respect to a man whose creation had meant a great deal to me, but I don't think I did to him or he did to me, and it would be presumptuous of me to pretend otherwise.

A TRIBUTE

from PAUL HORGAN

Rare is the man or woman whose individual sense of style is so strong, encompassing, and civilized that it changes for the better a whole vein of our culture.

Such a man was Alfred A. Knopf.

As he was born to be a publisher, so he was born to create new standards of excellence in the act of publishing. He found it a vitally necessary component of civilized life, but one showing little interest in a generalized excellence of taste in bookmaking and even in the broadening of editorial adventure. When he founded his own publishing house, with its symbol of the elegant Borzoi—that lean and graceful creature in extended stride—he launched a style of printing, binding, editorial taste, and sophisticated awareness that proposed new standards for all other serious American publishers. All aspects of the making of books advanced from craftsmanship to artistry under his example.

He was, of course, simply expressing in his art and his profession the essentials of his nature. He was a superior judge of the good things of life. The best suited him. He was bold in mind. He was urbane. As with all holding qualified opinions, it was form that interested him most, which probably accounts for his great love of master music. He was courageous in controversy, fastidious in courtesy. His mark is upon our books forever.

A TRIBUTE

from ALVIN M. JOSEPHY, JR.

Alfred A. Knopf was a good friend of historians and often encouraged them to pay more attention to literary style and the skills of good writing. Like Allan Nevins, Samuel Eliot Morison, and others who deplored the poor writing that marred otherwise excellent histories, he sometimes showed little patience with historians who thought they could get by with lazy or sloppy writing.

Great was his horror, therefore, when on one occasion he came on a very poorly written volume on Western American history which he had just published, but which he had not seen before and which had received little, if any, attention from the Knopf editor to whom it had been assigned. Alfred's embarrassment and fury increased when a *William and Mary Quarterly* reviewer lauded the book, but made no mention of its bad syntax, grammar, and other literary deficiencies.

Though it was his own book, and another publisher might have been pleased by the prospect of increased sales resulting from the complimentary review, Alfred barreled off the following letter to the Institute of Early American History &

Culture, which duly obliged by printing it in its September, 1966, *Newsletter:*

"It would be of enormous help to me if people who reviewed books for the W. and M. Quarterly were asked to say something about the author's English prose. I've been fighting a one man fight for decades to try to get American historians to stop writing like pigs. I'm just about ready to give up, having looked at a couple of books that bear my imprint but were not read in manuscript form or edited in any way by me and which will undoubtedly be acclaimed as anything from very good through absolutely first rate up to masterpiece.

"I've had no help whatever from reviewers anywhere and I find that even professionals who read such manuscripts for us, while they are very good in dealing with the author's scholarship, can't recognize or apparently don't want to recognize pig's English when they see it. Remember too that I am not looking for or hoping to find elegance of style. I seek only simple, straightforward prose which conveys unmistakably to the reader exactly what the author is trying to say."

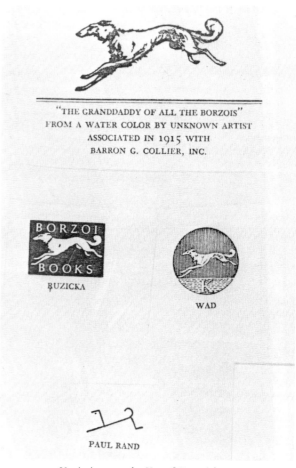

"THE GRANDDADDY OF ALL THE BORZOIS"
FROM A WATER COLOR BY UNKNOWN ARTIST
ASSOCIATED IN 1915 WITH
BARRON G. COLLIER, INC.

Variations on the Knopf Borzoi logo

A TRIBUTE
from DONALD S. KLOPFER

When Bennett Cerf and I came into the publishing business in 1925 we were both smart enough to know that Alfred was already the most important American publisher of the twentieth century. His meticulous taste in his choice of authors as well as his pride in the physical appearance of his books made him an idol to us.

As we got to know him better and see more of him our admiration increased and we became close friends. The greatest piece of luck that happened to Random House after we became a public corporation was when his son Pat left the firm to start Atheneum. We had often kidded about merging but in 1959 we approached Alfred seriously about this matter. Since he was sixty-seven years old he decided to let us buy his business. He was assured of editorial independence and would go on running Knopf as a separate entity and that way we got the most distinguished imprint and a superb backlist. Our relationship became much closer and I'm happy to say that years after Alfred really retired he told me that he felt that AAK under Bob Gottlieb was just as distinguished a publishing house as it had been when he and Blanche were running it.

He was a great man and a great publisher.

A TRIBUTE
from MERIDEL LE SUEUR

Alfred Knopf was a publisher whose like will not be seen again. He had a personal relationship with his writers and created beautiful books out of their creations. He was the only publisher during the infamous McCarthy period who made a public statement of support of his writers and assurance that their work would not in any way be judged or injured by any political criticism or allusion. It is hard to understand how important that was when books were being blacklisted, sold under the counter, the writers besmirched without any opportunity of defending themselves.

For all my generation he was a light, a human and loving editor.

We will not see his like again.

A TRIBUTE
from ELIZABETH LONGFORD

When Bob Gottlieb, guiding star of Alfred A. Knopf, Inc., said he wanted to publish my biography of Wilfrid Scawen Blunt, I was naturally over the moon. Not only because Knopf is a name that reverberates. But because poetic justice would be done. For Blunt's famous *My Diaries*—scandalous according to many people—had originally appeared in the United States under the imprint of Mr. Knopf himself. Without a rare devotion to literature Mr. Knopf and his active wife Blanche would not have taken this risk at a time of hard going.

In 1980 I wrote to thank Mr. Knopf for his "double"—the *Diaries* and *Life*. He replied with a delightful personal letter. "I shall be 88 shortly," he said, "I am very proud and touched really by having your fine biography bear my imprint." I am immensely proud too. He continued: "I have always felt that the diaries were magnificent and that few could surpass the pages, for example, which he devoted to the funeral of Edward VII." Earlier in the same letter Mr. Knopf described how he and Blanche once visited Blunt in his Sussex home, where they were received by their host in Arab robes, met Hilaire Belloc, and gobbled up game from the side board for breakfast next morning.

A few months later Mr. Knopf sent me a present of his best-seller *Little Gloria Happy At Last*, hoping I would enjoy it as much as he had. I felt that someone who could find room in his affections for two such disparate characters as Gloria Vanderbilt and Wilfrid Blunt was a splendid example of the universal man.

A TRIBUTE
from CARLETON MABEE

My most intense memory of Alfred A. Knopf is of a small dinner to which he and his wife Blanche invited me at their home in Westchester County about 1941 when I was young and Knopf was about to publish my first book. I was aware of the Knopfs' high standards in publishing, and was in awe of them, and felt out of place. Observing the Knopfs as hosts, I entered a little into what it was like for them to have the responsibilities of publishers. Before dinner the Knopfs were obliged to listen to one of their guests, the critic H. L. Mencken, whom they had often published, fulminate at length, in his usual negative style, on what was evidently a favorite subject of his, his disappointments with black writers. Then at table, when Mrs. Knopf began to criticize historian Allan Nevins, without knowing that he was my mentor, Mr. Knopf kicked her under the table to make her stop, and in the process kicked me too. Sensing the embarrassments even exalted publishers have to live with, I felt my own embarrassment ebb.

A TRIBUTE
from RUSSEL B. NYE

In 1942 I submitted a chapter of my dissertation (in fact, I submitted two other entries) to the Knopf Fellowship competition. The fellowships were intended to enlist new authors in the Borzoi fold, and I was fortunate enough to receive one. I received a pleasant letter from Mr. Knopf, expressing interest in my topic and encouraging me to proceed, which I did. The book appeared (under wartime restrictions on paper and binding) and was chosen for a Pulitzer Prize in biography. Mr. Knopf wrote me a congratulatory letter, pointing out that although a Pulitzer Prize did not guarantee instant wealth from royalties, it was nevertheless a fine thing to have and that he was naturally pleased that the fellowship had accomplished its purpose. It was not until five years later, at a meeting of the American Historical Association in New York, that I met him in person. He was busy, but took time for a brief conversation. The fellowship, of course, made a great difference in my life, and I remain thankful for Alfred Knopf's encouragement and assistance.

A TRIBUTE
from MARGOT PETERS

At first I was incredulous that Knopf took sixteen months to produce my biography *Mrs. Pat;* then I saw the results. It's a beautiful book, thanks to the high standards set by Alfred A. Knopf. When I later expressed surprise at the very extensive reviews, Bob Gottlieb, my editor, said, "Knopf books *are* reviewed." That says it all, really.

A TRIBUTE
from BARBARA W. TUCHMAN

Alfred's love and admiration for books and even for authors made one feel one belonged to a select and important company—especially if you were one of *his* authors. He was moreover an enthusiast of history and his interest in and appreciation of it was an invaluable encouragement to those of us working in that field. To find a publisher who truly cared for the subject and was proud and happy to publish it gave one confidence through the long struggle to complete a book that was worth more than any prize after it.

A TRIBUTE
from JOHN UPDIKE

I consider myself fortunate in falling into the hands of Alfred A. Knopf early in my career. He resolutely cared about the right things—the creation of texts and the making of books—and wasted little of his own time or of his authors' on peripheral matters. A young man sometimes needs to be told what of the world's business is nonsense and what isn't and this discrimination Alfred was always very willing to make. Though he could be brusque, he also had an Old World sense of occasion and of the good life, which he enjoyed sharing. He gave me, in the matter of book production, what I wanted, and I in turn tried to give him texts whose publication would not, in the long run, lose him money. I will miss him, though his name and aura are all around me here in my study.

Julian Mayfield

(6 June 1928-20 October 1984)

William B. Branch

See also the Mayfield entry in *DLB 33: Afro-American Fiction Writers After 1955*.

In an article published in the *Washington Post* on 20 April 1984, Julian Mayfield scathingly addressed a question that had arisen among some white editorialists in the course of the Rev. Jesse Jackson's presidential campaign.

"Black before American?" he wrote.

"The Washington Post answered this now burning question for me way back in 1944, when I applied for my first serious job. I had just turned 16, received my work permit, and—scrubbed, combed, deodorized and dressed impeccably— presented myself at the newspaper for the job of copy boy. The receptionist, a middle-aged white man, told me straight out: 'We don't hire any colored copy boys.' "

In those days, Mayfield continued, neither custom nor law required businesses to beat around the bush. "The receptionist didn't have to smile, have me fill out useless forms, and tell me The Post would call if a job opened up. And he certainly didn't care whether I was a United States citizen. 'We don't hire any colored boys,' and that was it."

At his death on 20 October 1984, Julian Mayfield—a Washington, D.C., resident—was prominently eulogized in the *Washington Post*, the *New York Times, Jet* magazine, and other publications across the country. The colored boy "untouchable" of 1944 had become—forty years later, at age fifty-six—an important literary and cultural figure worthy of considerable (if final) precious space in the obituary columns of some of our leading journals.

Writer-in-residence for six years in the Department of English at Washington's Howard University when he died, Mayfield's life and career were themselves the stuff from which novels, plays, and films could conceivably be fashioned. Novelist, playwright, journalist, Broadway and Hollywood actor, university teacher, sometime expatriate, adviser to heads of black governments, one-time object of an FBI manhunt—Mayfield began life in modest circumstances as the son of Hudson and Annie Mae Prince Mayfield in Greer, South Caroli-

Julian Mayfield, early 1960s (Roy de Caraba)

na, on 6 June 1928. At age five, he was taken by his parents to Washington, D.C., in search of a better life, and young Julian grew up on the tree-lined streets and attended the segregated public schools of the nation's capital.

Paul Lawrence Dunbar High School—where this writer first encountered him as a fellow speech-class student—is credited by Mayfield with having given him a particular shot in the arm to venture forth and engage life. Though rampant racial discrimination prevailed throughout much of the United States, Dunbar—named after the well-known turn-of-the-century black American poet— regularly posted an unusually high percentage of

181

graduates who went on to higher education, often at some of the most prestigious colleges and universities in the country, and to prominence in later life. Among its alumni were Dr. Charles R. Drew, who pioneered in the field of blood plasma; Dr. Robert C. Weaver, Secretary of Housing and Urban Development under Lyndon B. Johnson and the first black American to serve in the cabinet of a U.S. President; Edward W. Brooke, the first black American since Reconstruction to be elected to the U.S. Senate (from Massachusetts, in 1966; reelected in 1972); Edward Kennedy Ellington, the famous "Duke" of the musical world, and many others.

After graduating with the distinction of winning an American Legion Oratorical Contest, Mayfield served for a time in the U.S. Army, which was also still rigidly segregated. Providently released on a medical discharge, he enrolled at Lincoln University in Pennsylvania but soon left to seek his fortune in New York City. During a succession of the usual unskilled job situations—dishwasher, cab driver, house painter, and the like—Mayfield made contact with other young blacks who were involved in Harlem cultural and intellectual circles. Impressed with his bright and searching mind, they encouraged him to write articles for a variety of short-lived journals, including *Freedom*, a newspaper sponsored by the controversial singer-actor-activist Paul Robeson. In turn, this exposed him to involvement with the political left, of which he soon became a committed part. Its concepts, programs, and discussions opened up to him a vast new world and promised hope for change of the American racial and social ills he knew all too well, as well as linking him to global struggles against racism and imperialism with which he found instant rapport.

Harking back to his high-school speech training, Mayfield also took part in various off-Broadway theatrical ventures, appearing as an actor in *They Shall Not Die*, a protest play about the Scottsboro boys, and starring as the Blessed Martin de Porres in a religious drama about an eighteenth-century black South American who was eventually sanctified by the Vatican. This led to his being cast as Absalom Kumalo in the 1949 Kurt Weill-Maxwell Anderson Broadway musical *Lost In The Stars*, which was based on the novel *Cry, the Beloved Country* by South African author Alan Paton. By this time, Mayfield was all of twenty-one years old.

Mayfield spent a season on Broadway and another on tour with the musical, then returned to New York to scrape by as best he could. There were no "careers" as such for black actors then, and despite his excellent reviews, Mayfield was never again to land a role in a Broadway vehicle. He nonetheless busied himself in Harlem theater ventures, appearing in this writer's *A Medal for Willie* at the Club Baron in 1951, the next year coproducing Ossie Davis's first play, *Alice In Wonder*, and himself becoming a playwright with *417*, a play about the Harlem numbers game, and several one-act pieces, including *World Full of Men* and *The Other Foot*—both written "to fill out the bill" with *Alice In Wonder*.

During this crucial period—the late 1940s and early 1950s—Julian Mayfield was associated with an astonishing array of contemporaries, then or later to become luminaries: Mr. Robeson; actors Todd Duncan, Sidney Poitier, Frank Silvera, Ruby Dee, and William Marshall; writers Langston Hughes, Lorraine Hansberry, Alice Childress, John Henrik Clarke, and John Oliver Killens; directors Paul Mann and Rouben Mamoulian. (Future associations were to include the legendary figures Dr. W. E. B. DuBois and Malcolm X.)

In 1954, Mayfield married a political associate, Dr. Ana Livia Cordero, a physician, and moved with her to her native Puerto Rico. There he devoted himself to sustained literary effort and soon turned out two novels of life in Harlem. The first, *The Hit*, was an expansion of his short play, *417*, about the numbers game. (Mayfield credits writer-actress Alice Childress with suggesting that he turn the play into a novel.)

The Hit, published in 1957 by Vanguard, represented Mayfield's bow to two factors of black American life of which he was not only a keen observer, but in which he was actively involved. One was the aspiration to "make it," to get ahead of the crowd—in short, to move up to, and sustain, a life-style that was decidedly more than minimal. That this essentially bourgeois aspiration appeared to conflict with his acceptance of Marxist philosophy did not seem to trouble him at all. In fact, in conversations, Mayfield often defended this and other deviations from dogmas of the political left with observations to the effect that "these white folks don't know from ---- about being black in America, even if they are Communists!" Thus, in *The Hit*, he very sympathetically portrays fifty-year-old Hubert Cooley, who has tried to "make it" for years as proprietor of two grocery stores, a pool hall, and a dry-cleaning shop—all of which failed, despite all the hard work and sacrifices of Hubert, his wife, Gertrude, and his twenty-six-year-old son, James Lee. Fallen back to being a janitor in a Harlem apartment house, Hubert fails to relate his lack of success to the economic and racial facts of life that have trapped him and most of his fellows in the Harlems of the U.S. The terms "class," "caste," and "institutional racism" would, even if he understood them in an academic sense, be summarily rejected. In the classic pattern of self-group rejection often found among the victims of racism, he took the position that he, Hubert Cooley, was not like "these other niggers." *He* had ambition, drive, and "smarts." He was born to be a leader, an entrepreneur, a success. And the fact that he had not fulfilled his destiny he had finally come to blame on God.

Still, he was giving God one last chance to redeem himself. And this involved factor number two: the numbers game, which Hubert—like millions of his fellows—played virtually every day. If God would only let him hit the numbers big, then he would pack his suitcase and leave this God-forsaken hellhole for good, turning his back on Gertrude, James Lee, and everyone and everything else he had come to believe was holding him back from his true destiny.

When 417, the number Hubert has lovingly crafted and played for seven dollars, does, indeed, hit, Hubert's sense of vindication is quiet but firm. He brings his packed suitcase outside to wait for John Lewis, his number writer, to come to pay him off. His judgment and scorn of his fellows are sharper than ever. Even when, hours later, it has become obvious that John Lewis has absconded with Hubert's winnings, Hubert clings desperately to the thought that this time his time had really come—that he had finally beaten the system. "Come on, John Lewis, come on," he croons, as darkness falls about him.

Though an early work, *The Hit* may still be said to have established Mayfield as an observer, interpreter, and philosopher of the first rank in terms of dealing creatively, colorfully, and tellingly with a limited, but ultimately significant and symbolic, situation. Playwright Lorraine Hansberry later played a variation of the same theme in her first play, the 1959 Broadway hit *A Raisin in the Sun*, when Walter Lee Younger (the son, this time) trusts two neighborhood companions with the proceeds of his father's life insurance check in a scheme aimed at "making it" by securing a license for a liquor store. When one of the young men predictably disappears with the money, Walter Lee is left to grope his way between his dreams and harsh reality—albeit with the considerable help of his matriarch mother.

In his early days in New York, Julian Mayfield was himself an assiduous player of the numbers.

This writer recalls rooming with him in Brooklyn for a time, during which Mayfield announced that he had come up with a foolproof system for beating the "figures." Utilizing the "single action" technique of playing single digits (which paid eight to one) rather than the longer-odds three-digit number (which paid six hundred to one), Mayfield explained that by playing the same single digit repeatedly, and doubling the amount bet each day, when that digit finally "came out," he would recover all he had invested plus a sizable profit. He chose the digit two and proceeded to play. (Fortunately, he was then employed in *Lost in the Stars* on Broadway.) When his one-dollar bets did not pay off the first day, he doubled his play to two dollars a digit the next, four dollars the third day, and so on, and so on. By the seventh day, when his bet was up to $128 a digit, the suspense was unbearable. Every one of the ten digits (which included zero) had appeared, some more than once—except the two. On the eighth day, after Mayfield had begged, borrowed, and all but stolen enough to play the $256-a-digit now due, he was close to exhaustion. Added to the tension was the suspicion that, if he did hit, his Puerto Rican number writer might—like Hubert Cooley's writer later did in *417* and *The Hit*—"split town" with the winnings.

I shall never forget the agonizing suspense of that day. The first digit came out, and word reached us almost immediately: it was not a two. A short while later the second was announced. Again, no two. Sweating and smoking profusely, Mayfield waited for the third. No industry executive awaiting a crucial contract could possibly have suffered more pressure! After the proverbial eternity, the final digit hit the street and reached us by "bush telegraph" in seconds. It was not a two. Mayfield sat on the side of his bed, slowly shaking his head in the realization that this was the end, since there was no possibility he could raise another dime toward the more than $1,600 he would need to continue his scheme for the *next* "just one more day." Predictably, of course, the two "hit" the next day. *Twice!*

In later novels, short stories, and plays, Mayfield greatly expanded the scope of his canvas. The second Harlem novel, *The Long Night*, which Vanguard published in 1958, skillfully tells the story of a young boy's fateful search for his father. *The Grand Parade* (Vanguard, 1961), his most ambitious novel, is an extensive tapestry growing out of the civil rights movement in the U.S. (By then, the Mayfields were back in New York City.) "Black on Black: a Political Love Story," which first appeared in *Black World* (February 1972), grew out of

Mayfield's expatriate days in the West African nation of Ghana, where he served as speech writer and adviser to the recently independent country's president, Kwame Nkrumah. The short story was later reprinted in *Ten Times Black*, a 1972 Bantam Books collection which he also edited.

Fount of the Nation, a full-length play about the troubled head of a black state, which was premiered by the Arena Players of Baltimore in 1978, also owes a part of its inspiration to Mayfield's four years in Ghana during the early 1960s, although a subsequent three-year sojourn in the black-run South American nation of Guyana during the early 1970s undoubtedly provided additional insight. In Guyana, he worked as an advisor to the minister of information, married a local writer, Joan Cambridge, and became senior special assistant to Guyana's Prime Minister Forbes Burnham before health problems forced his return to the U.S. in 1974.

It was as an essayist that Mayfield's fertile mind found perhaps its most fulfilling utilization, however, as he turned out articles, editorials, academic papers, reviews, and other periodical and anthology contributions, from among his earliest writings until just before his death. His last published article, "Is He Really a Scoundrel?," appeared in the 8 July 1984 *Washington Post*, rebutting an attack on the Rev. Jesse Jackson by syndicated columnist Joseph Kraft. In between were some choice, ofttimes *Weltanschauung*, contributions to ongoing debates on a number of issues. "The Cuban Challenge" (*Freedomways*, Summer 1961) reflected his expressed concern for the survival of the Castro revolution in the face of what he saw as hypocritical U.S. government maneuvers—a concern which had led him to defy State Department disapproval of travel there by Americans by visiting Cuba in 1960 in a delegation of black American writers. *The World Without the Bomb: the Papers of the Accra Assembly* (Ghana Government Press, 1963), which he wrote and edited, involved a conference on disarmament called by Ghana in 1962. The *Nation* published his "Legitimacy of Black Revolution" on 22 April 1968 in the aftermath of the assassination of Dr. Martin Luther King, Jr., and the nationwide wave of conflagrations and other protests which followed. "Crisis or Crusade? An Article-Review of Harold Cruse's *Crisis of the Negro Intellectual*" (*Negro Digest*, June 1968) saw Mayfield embroiled in a public debate with a former political ally, to whose latter-day attacks on Paul Robeson and other blacks of the intellectual left Mayfield felt obliged to respond.

Perhaps his most widely read and admired essay, however, is "Into the Mainstream and Oblivion," first published by the American Society of African Culture in *The American Negro Writer and His Roots* (1960), a selection of papers from a conference of black American writers held in New York City in March 1959 under the Society's sponsorship. (It is obligatory to point out here that the Society—or AMSAC, as it was popularly known—was listed by the *New York Times* and CBS News some years later as having been funded by several "foundations" they concluded appeared to be conduits for the CIA. It is doubtful that any of the conference participants—among whom were some of the most prominent black writers of the period—knew of this then, however.)

In his paper, Mayfield prophetically cautioned black American writers—and, by implication, black Americans generally—to pause and reexamine the headlong push of the time for across-the-board integration into the mainstream of American life, literary or otherwise. While applauding efforts to attain full citizenship rights in voting, housing, education, employment, and soon—however belatedly and grudgingly proffered by a white establishment under siege—he demurred that if integration meant "completely identifying the Negro with the American image—that great-power face that the world knows and the Negro knows better—then the writer must not be judged too harshly for balking at the prospect."

Pointing to the black American mother who, having lost a son in the Korean "adventures," remarks: " 'I don't care if the army is integrated; next time I want to know what kind of war my boy is being taken to,' " Mayfield raised searching questions concerning the vaunted American mainstream—a position which presaged that of Dr. King and other civil rights leaders when they finally broke with the national administration in the mid-1960s over what they came to view as a senseless, racist, immoral war in Vietnam.

In the literary milieu, Mayfield argued, "the advantage of the Negro writer, the factor that may keep his work above the vacuity of the American mainstream, is that for him the facade of the American way of life is always transparent. He sings the national anthem *sotto voce* and has trouble reconciling the 'dream' to the reality he knows." And yet, he continued, this very detachment may give him "the insight of the stranger in the house, placing him in a better position to illuminate contemporary American life as few writers of the mainstream can."

It is an arresting and eloquent essay which

fortunately has been reprinted in two currently available anthologies: *Dark Symphony: Negro Literature in America,* edited by James A. Emanuel and Theodore L. Gross (Free Press, 1968); and *Black Literature in America,* edited by Houston A. Baker, Jr. (McGraw-Hill, 1971). It thereby continues to stimulate thought and discussion, especially among those college students, both black and white, who have not yet been victimized by the various efforts in academia to discredit, eviscerate, defund, or outright abolish that embattled category of learning known as black or Afro-American studies. For some years, Mayfield specialized in teaching courses of this genre in a variety of academic posts at American universities: Fellow of the Society for the Humanities (1967-1968) and First W. E. B. DuBois Distinguished Visiting Fellow (1970-1971), both at Cornell; lecturer in the Schweitzer Program in the Humanities at New York University (1969-1970); Visiting Professor at the University of Maryland (1975-1978), and writer-in-residence at Howard University (1978-1984). In addition, he spent the year 1976-1977 lecturing at universities in West Germany, Austria, Denmark, Algeria, and Turkey under a U.S. Fulbright-Hays Fellowship administered by the U.S. Information Service—an association he viewed with some irony, since he had been the object of a federal fugitive dragnet in the previous decade by an agency of that same U.S. government.

This had happened in 1961 when, in a practical extension of his activist philosophy, he became a staunch supporter of a young black man in Monroe, North Carolina, named Robert Williams. Williams headed the local chapter of the NAACP until ousted by National Executive Secretary Roy Wilkins for advocating a policy of countering repeated armed Ku Klux Klan attacks on Monroe's black community by shooting back. (Despite earlier NAACP defenses of the right to protect one's life and property from mob violence, the key word of the civil rights movement of the day was *nonviolence,* and Wilkins appeared sensitive to the prospect of losing white allies if Williams's views were identified with the organization.) When Williams was forced into becoming a fugitive on a dubious charge of kidnapping a white couple who had strayed into a black area under siege, Mayfield was suspected of having spirited him out of Monroe, secreted in the trunk of an automobile. Thereupon, both Williams and Mayfield became objects of a nationwide FBI manhunt. Both fled the country, Mayfield eventually surfacing in Ghana and Williams first in Cuba, later in China. Years later, the kidnapping

charge was dropped, thus clearing the way for both to return.

Having handily filled the role in real life of what was then sometimes called a black militant, it seemed only logical that Mayfield should be called upon to repeat the part on the silver screen. This, too, came to pass. After collaborating with European film director Jules Dassin and actress-writer Ruby Dee on the screenplay of *Uptight!*—a contemporary black version of the old film classic *The Informer*—Mayfield was himself cast in the leading role of Tank, a black activist who is compelled to pay with his life for his betrayal of a fellow conspirator. When the Paramount Pictures production was released in 1969, Mayfield's finely drawn, sensitive performance drew outstanding reviews and even hints of impending Academy Award consideration. He was not nominated, however, and *Uptight!* proved to be both the high point and the end of his Hollywood acting career.

In his last years at Howard, Mayfield worked extensively on an autobiography for Random House and returned to Ghana briefly to research a planned book on black American expatriates in West Africa.

It will no doubt require time for the ultimate impact of Julian Mayfield's career and writings to be critically assessed. Suffice it to say here, however, that he was both black and American; both untiring in assailing injustice and unstinting in defending the rights of those he felt were being wronged; perspicacious in analyzing the world he lived in and prophetic in foretelling certain perils as well as opportunities which lay ahead.

In his youth, he went forth, as he once put it, to "engage the world." And over the course of an extraordinary lifetime, engage it he did.

A TRIBUTE

from MAYA ANGELOU

Julian Mayfield was a fine writer who did not live to see an appreciation of his work commensurate with the quality of his work. Julian Mayfield was a fierce combatant against injustice who did not live to see his battle won. Julian Mayfield was a fine man who, because he was black, did not live to enjoy the fruits of free manhood in the country so sadly crippled by racism. But, Julian Mayfield was a brother, a true, loyal, laughing, supportive brother who, by being, encouraged his brothers and sisters to be more than they thought quite possible.

I must say in love and longing that in the most

profound and important ways, my brother, Julian Mayfield, was a success.

A TRIBUTE ———————————
from GWENDOLYN BROOKS

We have lost, recently, so many of our brilliant black writers: Hoyt Fuller, Larry Neal, Robert Hayden, George Kent—now Julian Mayfield, who was adventurous and vital. I hope his works will be kept alive.

A TRIBUTE ———————————
from KRISTIN HUNTER

The Hit certainly scored a direct one with me. A fine, true, touching book . . . I remember reading it for the first time as if it were yesterday, the memory of it is so fresh, as is the memory of Julian Mayfield, writer, actor, teacher, friend. Enough words. The best possible tribute to Julian Mayfield's memory would be the reissuing of *The Hit* and all his other works, to let them live for old and new readers.

A TRIBUTE ———————————
from JOHN OLIVER KILLENS

My first memory of Julian Mayfield is when he walked out on the stage at the Club Baron in Harlem and began a kind of prologue introduction to William Branch's wonderful play *A Medal For Willie*. This must have been somewhere near the end of the 1940s or the very beginning of the 1950s. Our friendship has continued ever since that time. Though he angered at injustice, he was possessed of an overwhelming sense of humor. He saw the irony and paradoxes of life, especially as it pertained to black people. He was a highly sensitive human being, and his art was consistently committed to the cause of freedom and justice and therefore always found itself aligned on the side of the angels. We were among the original members of the now legendary Harlem Writers Guild. I remember reading a chapter of my first novel-in-progress, *Youngblood*, at his home in upper Manhattan one Sunday afternoon. After I had finished reading the chapter there was a hushed silence in the room, only broken by the enthusiastic applause of my eight-year-old son, Jon Charles (Chuck). Chuck's vigorous applause was belatedly joined by the rest of those in attendance. I had a difficult time explaining to

Chuck the lack of instant applause for *Youngblood*. I tried to explain to him that that was not how these kind of soirees were conducted, an explanation he found hard to reconcile with the quality of his father's writing, as he saw it. I ultimately had to reach far back and forget about humility, as I asked him to remember the quiet following the Gettysburg Address. I am afraid my son's appraisal of the situation left him unimpressed.

Though Julian was often far away (in Ghana, in Guyana) atop some barricade for justice, we always kept in touch. He understood the contradiction every serious artist faces, i.e., the absolute need for solitude vis-à-vis the equally absolute need for the sharing of the human experience. He reconciled this contradiction by becoming an artist/activist.

When I was a writer-in-residence at Fisk University, he came down to Nashville to participate with others like Frank Hercules, Frank Silvera, and me in a Writers Conference. He also followed me as writer-in-residence at Howard University. He will be terribly missed, but his immortality is assured by the legacy of work he has left behind him to inform us of the times in which he lived.

A TRIBUTE ———————————
from E. ETHELBERT MILLER

I knew Julian Mayfield while he worked at Howard University, as a writer-in-residence in the English Department. It would be incorrect to assume that many students as well as faculty members knew the work of Mayfield. While he was employed at Howard, his novels were difficult to obtain. Through a distributor of rare books I was able to acquire copies of *The Hit* and *The Grand Parade*. I remember taking them to Mayfield's office so that he could autograph them. He was amazed that I had copies. Mayfield was an extremely modest man; perhaps this is why he spent time at Howard without receiving the attention he deserved.

There was, however, an article written by Harriet Scarupa for the university's *New Directions* magazine (April 1979). This article was a profile of Mayfield. In it he discussed the years he lived in Ghana (1961-1966) under Kwame Nkrumah's leadership. Mayfield worked for Nkrumah while also editing the *African Review*. In the *New Directions* article Mayfield confessed that he had always been fascinated by black people who wielded power. In one of the last essays he wrote which appeared in the *Washington Post* (8 July 1984), Mayfield came to the defense of Jesse Jackson, a man who was running for one of the most powerful positions in the world. Mayfield made the following statement: "Jackson's basic problem with the opinion makers is that he has driven them to the point of apoplexy because they have been forced to take him seriously. The image of a black man treated on equal terms with foreign leaders is almost as inflammatory as the sight of a black man with a white woman."

Mayfield's remarks reflected the insightfulness and wit one immediately associated with Malcolm X. When one had the opportunity to talk with Mayfield one was always impressed by his humor and political analysis. Many of our encounters together on the campus of Howard University were filled with jokes about one another, as well as laughter which stemmed from our amusement with university policies and procedures.

Five months before he died, Mayfield and I had a chance to sit down and talk about his participation in the Harlem Writers Guild. It was something we had meant to do for almost a year. Finally we found a time and place, taping an interview for the Oral History Division of the Moorland-Spingarn Research Center.

Mayfield provided insights and opinions about the Guild which included among its members such talented writers as John Killens, John Henrik Clarke, and Rosa Guy. Julian Mayfield belonged to an important generation of black people, men and women who came of age under the influence and wisdom of such giants as W. E. B. DuBois and Paul Robeson. They knew these men in their final years and undoubtedly decided to keep their legacy alive through their own writings and political commitments.

At home, in my personal study, there hangs a picture of Malcolm X taken while he was traveling in Africa. The picture was given to my wife and me by Julian Mayfield on our wedding day in 1982.

I like to think that Mayfield was trying to tell me what was important in establishing a new home and family. Along with the new china and silverware—was Malcolm. A reminder that there lived a man who was willing to tell the truth, who forced one to look beneath lies. At Malcolm's funeral Ossie Davis delivered the eulogy. He also spoke at Julian Mayfield's funeral, giving as eloquent a speech as he did years before in Harlem.

Similar things could be said of both Malcolm and Mayfield. Here were men who loved their people. Men who used the gifts God gave them to improve this world.

Liam O'Flaherty

(28 August 1896-7 September 1984)

John Zneimer
Indiana University Northwest

See also the O'Flaherty entry in *DLB 36, British Novelists, 1890-1929: Modernists.*

When Liam O'Flaherty died in September 1984 at the age of eighty-eight he had become an Irish national treasure. This status was late in coming. The Irish had always been uneasy about O'Flaherty—about his political ideas (in his youth he was cofounder of the Irish Communist party) and the image of themselves they saw in his works. But during his last thirty years, lived for the most part in Dublin, his firebrand energies had lain dormant. The uneasiness gave way to recognition. During his years of furious energy he had created an impressive body of work—numerous miscellaneous pieces, fourteen novels, over 150 short stories. He was seen as one of the last links to the Irish literary renaissance, to the tradition of Yeats, Lady Gregory, George Russell, Sean O'Casey, Frank O'Connor. And finally he was awarded the customary honors for a man of literary eminence. In 1974 he was given an honorary doctorate of literature by the National University of Ireland (where he had briefly been a student). In 1979 he was given the Irish Academy of Letters Award for Literature and praised as "one of the greatest names of Irish literature and world literature." In 1983 he was made an honorary life member of the

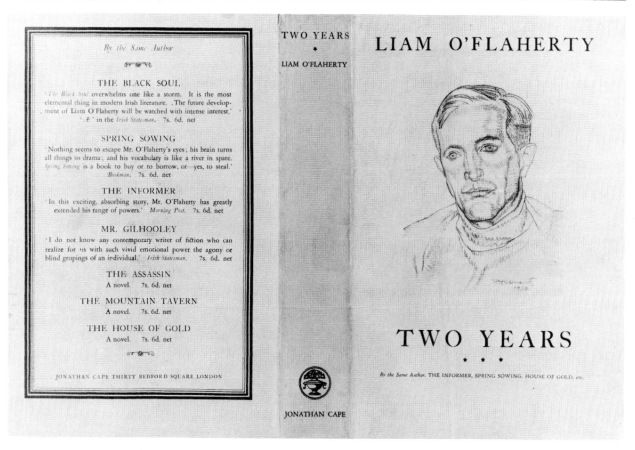

Dust jacket for O'Flaherty's 1930 autobiographical volume, with a drawing by F. A. Coventry

Royal Dublin Society for his writings in Irish and English. When he died, the *Irish Times* accorded him a full page of tributes, and John Broderick called him "the finest Irish novelist of his generation."

O'Flaherty is best known for his novels, especially *The Informer* (1925) because of the award-winning movie based on it. And mostly because of that novel he has been associated with the Irish Civil War of the 1920s and the Irish struggle for independence and unity. Though his most famous, *The Informer* is not considered his best novel. The Irish have tended to prefer *Famine* (1937), a historical novel about the potato blight that decimated the Irish population in the mid-nineteenth century. Broderick, in his obituary tribute, calls it "one of the truly great novels of the 20th century [which] reaches the very soul of a nation in agony." *Skerrett* (1932) is more characteristic of O'Flaherty's genius, however. This novel about the Aran Islands school-teacher hounded to death by the parish priest contains O'Flaherty's greatest themes—the stark life of the Aran Islands and the tragic heroism of a strong and passionate man. According to John Jordan (who said he had this secondhand), O'Flaherty considered this his own favorite among his books.

O'Flaherty never forgot his Aran Islands heritage. "I was born on a storm-swept rock," he said, "and hate the soft growth of sun-baked lands where there is no frost in men's bones." He admired courage and energy and sought to express in his works the beauty of passion. He had little patience for style, calling it "artificial and vulgar," or for "bookish fellows, whose drawing room civilisation obtrudes unpleasantly on the senses." For him art was more a matter of fury than finesse, a "hurricane of genius" in "a beautiful frenzy."

He had a powerful visual imagination, like Fergus O'Connor, a character in his early novel *The Black Soul* (1924), whose brain "had a weird faculty for presenting things to him vividly, as clearly as if they were filmed." Yeats recognized this quality and praised the early novels for their "abounding life," setting O'Flaherty's novels above George Moore's because "he joyously *imagines* when Moore *constructs*." The novels are dashed upon the page, furiously, as if to catch the soul's storm. Though scenes like the murder scene in *The Assassin* (1928) or characters like Gypo Nolan in *The Informer* and

David Skerrett are realized with cinematic vividness, whether it was his subjects or his impatience with craft, the novel was not O'Flaherty's best form. Frank O'Connor said that O'Flaherty's novels could be used as evidence that an Irish novel is impossible.

It is generally agreed that his short stories are O'Flaherty's most enduring achievement, best suited to his lyric gifts. Looking back, in 1979, it was what O'Flaherty himself thought. Edward Garnett, his early literary mentor, had made him "a fervent disciple in the religion of artistic beauty." And when Garnett sent him back to Ireland to write a story about a cow, O'Flaherty said, "I began my communion with the cliffs, the birds, the wild animals, and the sea of my native land." This is the world of the short stories.

He once told Garnett he was not aware of exerting any judgment whatever at the moment of writing, and that the result was a writing that "appears to be unfinished, just like a natural landscape." In his best short stories, such as "The Fairy Goose," "The Cow's Death," "The Rockfish," "Spring Sowing," "The Painted Woman," "Galway Bay," and "Going Into Exile," this is the effect he achieves. They appear to rise out of nature itself, as if the writer had become the speaking part of nature. When O'Flaherty brought what he called his goat's eye or snake's eye or weasel's eye to his native landscape and achieved that "feeling of coldness" for which he strove, all the heat and passion of his creative fury was transmuted into light. Then was revealed in wonder and awe the unthinking life of nature that does not ask a meaning. This is the Liam O'Flaherty that will be remembered.

A TRIBUTE

from ANTHONY C. WEST

I don't know anything about O'Flaherty the man, barring some hairy, and probably apocryphal, legends. I never met him in the flesh. I was only sixteen when *The Informer* came out in 1926 and three years later I was in America, where I went through my so-called formative years; later in London. Then came the war, which took six years off my creative life like many another of my ilk. My destiny didn't lead me into the Dublin fishpond which, in any case, was moribund and provincial, as well as inflicted at that time with an undiscerning Catholic censorship.

But O'Flaherty the writer influenced my own work. By and large he was my kind of artist. His

work helped me by providing an antidote to James Joyce's overweening intellectualism that always seemed to me to endeavour to say the penultimate word, notwithstanding his virtual canonization by many American critics.

A TRIBUTE

from VIVIAN MERCIER

My first meeting with Liam O'Flaherty was also my last, for whenever I caught sight of him again in Dublin I took good care that he didn't see *me*. Though we met forty years ago, I still have vivid memories of the occasion; apparently O'Flaherty had too, since he seems to have borne a grudge against me. It's an old, old story: the natural enmity between author and critic and the vanity of both. Still, I think it's worth retelling, as a warning to young critics and middle-aged writers—in 1945 I was twenty-six and O'Flaherty forty-eight.

We met by accident, in a place unfamiliar to me then, one of Dublin's bigger hotels; I think it must have been the Gresham. There were three or four of us, all of my own age and all short of cash, so I don't know why we went to such an expensive place. Probably we were celebrating either the granting of my Ph.D. or the literary prize that my dissertation had won (thirty-five pounds, which exactly covered the cost of typing it and making enough copies to satisfy the requirements of Trinity College and the "A.E." Memorial Prize Competition, in which I was runner-up). Understandably, I was feeling pretty cocky, quite apart from the drinks we'd been having elsewhere. The only person I'm sure was with me—for reasons that will soon become clear—was my lifelong friend Judy. She and I quickly spotted May Keating, a great friend of Judy's, and noisily hailed her. There was only one man at her table, so we all joined her. She was the mother of our slightly younger friend Paul, and young people enjoyed her witty, gossipy conversation. Alas, both she and Paul are dead some years now.

May introduced the man, who turned out to be Liam O'Flaherty. Nobody was exactly overwhelmed with awe, because Dubliners take writers great and small very much for granted; there are plenty of them around, and O'Flaherty had passed the peak of his Irish reputation by then. I, for one, was already interested in Samuel Beckett because of *Murphy* (1938), though nothing of his had appeared since because he spent the war years in France. I had mentioned him in an introductory chapter of my dissertation on "Realism in Anglo-Irish Fiction 1916-1940," which inevitably included a chapter on O'Flaherty. I hope I wasn't the first at the table to mention one of O'Flaherty's books, but somebody did, and pretty soon I was giving him free criticism and advice, disagreeing with him about which were his best novels, and in general behaving as though I was wet behind the ears—which I was.

Suddenly I became aware that the man across the table was furiously angry with me: he didn't shout, but his words grew more and more emphatic and his eyes (bright blue?) blazed at me under his prominent brows. He was slightly shorter than I, but now he seemed taller, his muscular arms tensed, and the table began to shake. His broad chest was all muscle; it occurred to me that I would be no match for this man of twice my age if it came to a fight. I knew he had played rugby football, perhaps no better than I, but he had also been a sailor, a stoker, a longshoreman, if his autobiographies were to be believed. Complete sobriety fell upon me and I steered the conversation into calmer waters. Before we said goodnight, O'Flaherty practically apologized: "I didn't know ye had been drinking," he said.

But there is no limit to the vanity of youth: having no spare copy of the chapter on O'Flaherty, I left the manuscript for him at the hotel next day. In a day or two, Judy visited him in his room; he showed her my ms., declared that he hadn't read it, and dropped it in the wastebasket before her eyes. She, like a true Dubliner, assumed that he had in fact read it; it is even possible that he took it out of the basket afterwards; anyway, I never saw it again.

Come to think of it, he may not have borne me a grudge then, being satisfied with his fine gesture in Judy's presence. Some ten years later, however, when I was old enough to know better, I committed an offense that was unforgivable. In 1956 the Devin-Adair Company of New York published *The Stories of Liam O'Flaherty*, a big handsome volume of 415 pages. The stories were chosen by the late Devin Garrity, head of the company, and myself: no editor's name was given, but Garrity kindly asked me to write an introduction. In my anxiety to do justice to O'Flaherty, I fumbled the ball again. He was and is one of the great masters of the short story in both Irish (Gaelic) and English: convinced of this, I made a mistake to which academics are prone—I tried to judge him from the perspective of eternity. Worse still, I hedged my bet: the last sentence of the introduction begins, "If Liam O'Flaherty's work survives. . . ." Not having yet written a book into which I could put everything I knew—and my heart and soul as well—I still didn't realize that this is the one thing that must never be said about a living writer. I can't understand why Garrity, usually a quick man with a blue pencil, didn't strike out that sickening "If." It will haunt me until I die. O'Flaherty later gave me material cause for regret, too, by refusing to grant rest-of-the-world copyright for two of his stories, thus vetoing the sale of my anthology *Great Irish Short Stories* in that market. In fact this didn't lose me any royalties, since I had compiled the work for a fee only; still, I'd have liked the anthology to reach Australia and New Zealand, for example; no other contributor had objected. In 1973, when an abridged version of *The Stories* appeared in the Norton Library under the title *The Wounded Cormorant and Other Stories*, the heinous introduction was reprinted, although many of the stories referred to in it were no longer included in the selection. I heard via the Irish grapevine that O'Flaherty was angry and had told W. W. Norton & Company that if the new paperback were reprinted, my introduction must be left out. If Garrity had consulted me, I too would have asked him to leave out the introduction. And so at last O'Flaherty and I had agreed about something, though he never knew of it.

J. B. Priestley

(13 September 1894-14 August 1984)

Stanley Weintraub
Pennsylvania State University

See also the Priestley entry in *DLB 10, Modern British Dramatists, 1900-1945* and *DLB 34, British Novelists, 1890-1929: Traditionalists.*

John Boynton Priestley, who died at his home in Stratford-on-Avon in his ninetieth year, was the last Man of Letters of his generation, the last of that feisty breed of all-purpose writers who served in the Great War of 1914-1918 and rose to literary fame thereafter.

Priestley was self-effacing about his writing, if anyone who has written forty plays and almost as many other books can be said to be unpretentious. In his 1960 best-selling *Literature and Western Man*, which surveyed literature from the Renaissance to the present day, and covered many of his contemporaries of lesser achievement, his own name fails to appear in the index. Yet he had much he could have claimed for himself. Of his seventeen works of fiction, his still readable *The Good Companions* (1929), a warmly Dickensian work now underrated perhaps because it was so popular, was one of the better British novels of the 1920s. His plays had only Noel Coward's as real competition in the 1930s, as Shaw's last works after *Saint Joan* became increasingly rarefied, and the New Wave of dramatists now dominating the stage had not come along until a decade after the Second World War had ended. By then Priestley was turning largely to essays, histories, and memoirs, a third literary career as successful as the earlier two.

While his fiction was effective in a traditional sentimental vein, as befit the middle-class Yorkshireman faithful to his backgrounds, underlying it was a dimension of social criticism which emerged most forcefully in a book of journalistic nonfiction which may be remembered longer than many of his more ambitious works. *English Journey* (1933), a Depression documentary, based on Priestley's travels north as far as his native Bradford, has been described as "plain-man, pipe-in-the-mouth socialism, always more a matter of good companionship than of theory and analysis," but its robust, vivid, opinionated observations stand up well to George

Orwell's *The Road to Wigan Pier* (1937), its only real rival.

Priestley himself thought his most innovative work had come in the theater, where he experimented with time shifts, dramatic language, musiclike abstraction and fantasy. Some of the plays survive their time and succeed in revival, among them *Eden End, Time and the Conways, Dangerous Corner* and —one of the indisputably great English suspense-thrillers—*An Inspector Calls* (1945). But, he admitted, "I think of myself as eighteenth-century. Writers wrote everything then, essays, novels, plays; there was a variety of professionalism." Priestley was the complete professional as writer. Perhaps he might have accomplished more that was lasting had he written less, but writing was a compulsion rather than an economic need for more than a half-century after *The Good Companions*. For him man was "haunted, bedevilled, inspired, by ideas and feelings that often seem new just because they are . . . made out of his literature." He wanted to be part of that process. As he said in his memoir, *Margin Released* (1962), "There was the challenge, time after time, and always I found it irresistible."

Will Priestley be remembered? "The most lasting reputation I have," he wrote disarmingly when he was nearly seventy, "is for an almost ferocious aggressiveness, when in fact I am amiable, indulgent, affectionate, shy and rather timid at heart." The most he would say for his work was that he "debased no civilized values." And there one locates the key in which all his work was written—*civilized values.*

A TRIBUTE

from ALAN SILLITOE

I remember Priestley most for his "Postscripts" which he broadcast during the war. These were very popular, even in my family. We would sit around the wireless whenever he was "on" and revel not only in what he had to say, but at the gruffness

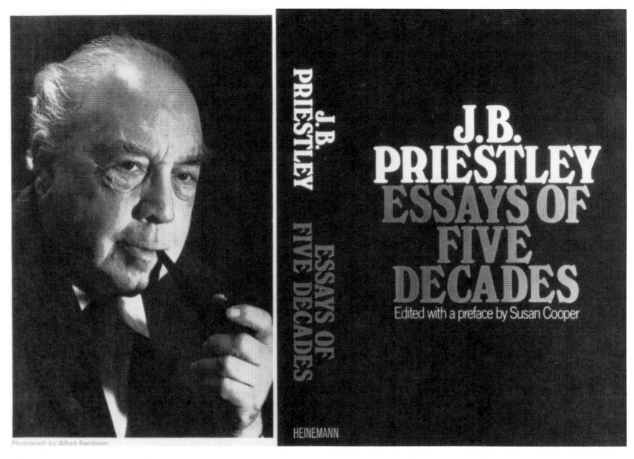

Dust jacket for a collection of Priestley's writings on his family, his recollections of boyhood, and "the encounters and observations of the private man"

and common touch—or human touch, rather—of his voice.

A TRIBUTE

from JOHN WAIN

John Boynton Priestley was one of the last survivors of the generation of English writers and artists whose attitudes were formed before August 1914. Their most deeply shared characteristic was that, though they could see approaching disasters and failures as clearly as anyone else, their pessimism was never really bone-deep. The England in which they grew up was seriously blemished by social injustice, yet there was a sunshine in the air that brought out the color of everyday experience. Although Priestley served in the trenches and later witnessed the effects of unemployment and bad housing in his native region, somewhere inside him lurked a belief that human progress was not, after all, an impossible dream.

It was this belief that made him content to be a popular writer, always glad if he could get his message across to a large audience and not much caring if he was disdained by highbrows. Naturally restless and inventive, he did his share of experimenting, yet never wished his work to be analyzed in the hushed tones that accompanied so much of the officially avant-garde writing of the century.

This is not the place to attempt a final assessment of Priestley's work, though his reputation is bound to settle down in the next ten years or so and will provide a nice problem for the critics as they try to clear a patch for him between Major and Minor, no doubt agreeing in the end on some variant of the Major-Minor or Minor-Major. One thing is certain: in energy and productiveness the man was built on a huge scale, hardly less so than such amiable monsters of fecundity as Dickens and Victor Hugo. Novels, stories, plays, literary and social criticism, metaphysical speculation, autobiography, and decorative belles lettres cascaded incessantly from his pen. After his first smash hit with *The Good Compan-*

ions (1929), which was sentimental picaresque comedy, likeable but a little soft-centered, he took only a year to follow it up with *Angel Pavement,* a solid novel in a tougher, more Bennettian tradition of realism. His plays range all the way from straight domestic drama of conscience like *An Inspector Calls* through the visionary and speculative, as in *Johnson Over Jordan,* to his own brand of shrewd but not cruel satire as in *When We Are Married:* taking in on the way the speculative *Time and the Conways* and the frankly Speakers'-Corner didactic *They Came to a City.* He undertook large tasks in literary history and philosophical speculation (this latter on his almost obsessional subject, time) and also threw off the lightest of trifles, his skill in the gentle, beguiling art of the light essay being most perfectly demonstrated in *Delight* (1949). He was not the kind of writer who works easily in collaboration, being too energetic and positive for harness work, but it is interesting that he twice collaborated successfully with women writers: his wife Jacquetta Hawkes in the masterly *Journey Down a Rainbow* (American society, a standing temptation to writers of all nationalities to produce hysterical drivel, prompted Priestley to some of his finest social commentary) and in helping a best-selling novel to become a long-running play when, with the author, he dramatized Iris Murdoch's *A Severed Head* in 1963. Wherever his reputation finally comes to rest, one feels that at any given moment, until the world takes on an unguessable new shape, a lot of people will be reading him, for a lot of different reasons.

As novelist, playwright, essayist, literary and social critic, propagandist, Priestley lived up to the values he acquired in the Bradford of his boyhood. In part these were the values of Edwardian provincial England generally, when the achievements of high culture had reached a mass public through cheap books, cheap concert tickets, free art galleries, thick and serious newspapers, without yet suffering serious dilution. It was the age of Everyman's Library (which started when Priestley was six), of the Proms and the Queen's Hall, when new orchestral works were rushed out in piano arrangements for four hands so that amateurs could get on to terms with the score before going to hear them in performance. The best in art, literature, and music were there for the taking, but not yet filleted, processed and predigested.

In part, also, his values were those of a definite place. Bradford, in his formative years, was both defiantly local—smaller, and less well served by transport, than its neighbor Leeds—and confidently open to the world. As he recalled, "some of its citizens went regularly to the other side of the globe to buy wool. . . . You used to meet men who did not look as if they had ever been further than York or Morecambe, but who actually knew every continental express."

To some extent this type remained with Priestley all his life as an ideal. The impression he made in the flesh, though never remotely suggesting a man who had never been further than York or Morecambe, was of someone very much at home in provincial northern England. (He once wrote that if given a choice between spending the rest of his life in Capri or Wigan, he would make straight for Wigan.) Not that his exterior was that of a business man or city official. He cultivated a harmless, old-fashioned air of show business; in the 1950s he affected a wide-brimmed black hat that made him look like an Edwardian actor, the kind of player who had enthralled him in boyhood. He was, in fact, a larger-than-life version of the kind of person one meets in artistic circles in provincial cities, enjoying the arts and enjoying the companionship of other people who enjoy the arts: the kind of freemasonry that is lost in a metropolis.

We shall remember him with affection. By preserving his original values so intact, by voicing them so eloquently, and by living so long, he has put all of us in his debt.

A TRIBUTE

from COLIN WILSON

I have always felt that Priestley was one of the great underestimated writers of his time. No, that's not quite true—after admiring him greatly in my teens, I then went through a period—at about the time I was writing my first book, *The Outsider*—when I thought he was just a bumbling, old-fashioned idiot. It was the novelist John Braine who made me look at him again, advising me to read a book of his essays called *Thoughts Out Of Season.* The main thing that impressed me about this was the brilliant intelligence, the sheer liveliness of his perceptions. I then picked up the novel that he'd written for the Festival of Britain, *Festival At Farbridge,* expecting it to be pretty awful. Instead, I found that I couldn't put it down, and read it straight through in about twelve hours.

Why is Priestley so underestimated? The reason is simple. He became famous with *The Good Companions,* which sold three quarters of a million copies *in hardback* within a month or two of publication. He once told a friend of mine that when he went into a literary party, he could actually feel the envy coming at him in waves. Then he went on to write his first play, *Dangerous Corner*—and like his first novel, it was an instant success. So were most of the other plays he wrote in the 1930s. And his second novel, *Angel Pavement*, was equally successful. Writers just thought that it was bloody unfair that one man should have so much success, and the result was that they all assured one another that after all, he was lowbrow and second-rate, and only sold so well because he "wrote down" to an illiterate public. He had a brief period in which the serious

critics changed their minds about him—when he was on the leftist side in the Spanish Civil War. But then, when he achieved a new kind of celebrity at the beginning of the Second World War with his famous "Postscripts" on the BBC, he was once again "too successful," and again nobody had a good word to say for him. And that continued to the end of his life. I was lucky enough to know him—I took the trouble to make his acquaintance because I admired him so much—and never ceased to regard him as one of the major writers of our time. It's enormously sad that he is still so underestimated.

Irwin Shaw

(27 February 1913-16 May 1984)

Walter W. Ross

See also the Shaw entry in *DLB 6, American Novelists Since World War II*, Second Series.

NEW BOOKS: *Bread Upon the Waters* (New York: Delacorte, 1981; London: Weidenfeld & Nicolson, 1981);
Acceptable Losses (New York: Arbor House, 1982; London: New English Library, 1983).

TELEVISION SCRIPTS: "The Top of the Hill," WPIX, New York, 6-7 February 1980;
"The Girls in Their Summer Dresses," "The Man Who Married a French Wife," and "The Monument," adapted by Kenneth Cavender, WNET, New York, 1 June 1981.

OTHER: *Paris/Magnum: Photographs, 1935-1981*, text by Shaw (New York: Harper & Row, 1981).

PERIODICAL PUBLICATIONS: "Another Time, Another Village," *New York*, 14 (6-13 July 1981): 30-32;
"The Conscience of a Heavyweight," *Esquire*, 99 (June 1983): 272-274, 276;
"The Common Man," *Esquire*, 100 (December 1983): 591-595.

Irwin Shaw died of a heart attack at the age of seventy-one in Davos, Switzerland. Although his health had been poor during the past few years, he

had continued to write to the end. He had always maintained that while most people retire, writers never do. From the window in his hospital room, he could see in the distance the mountains he used to ski down when he was younger. On his bedside table were Byron's *Poems* and Mann's *The Magic Mountain*.

Shaw's professional writing career spanned half a century, running from shortly after he graduated from Brooklyn College, when he began selling scripts for radio serials, until the publication of *Acceptable Losses* in 1982. At the time of his death he was well into another novel. His writing credits included short stories, plays, screenplays, and novels.

Since Shaw has never been regarded as a playwright, it is curious that his first serious writing was a play, *Bury the Dead*, which was staged in New York in 1936 at the Ethel Barrymore Theater. This antiwar drama was an immediate success and for a while Shaw considered writing exclusively for the theater. All of his other plays, however, with the possible exception of *The Gentle People* (1939), failed to generate much interest.

During this period Shaw began writing the short stories that many critics regard as his best work. He sold his first story to the *New Republic* for twenty-five dollars in 1937 and soon afterward was appearing regularly in the *New Yorker*. His early stories included "Sailor Off the Bremen," "The Eighty-Yard Run," "The Girls in Their Summer

Irwin Shaw (International Portrait Gallery)

Dresses," and "Main Current of American Thought."

Shaw then turned to the novel, writing *The Young Lions* (1948), which was greeted with warmly favorable reviews. Later novels included *The Troubled Air* (1951), which dealt with the blacklisting of radio broadcasters during the McCarthy era; *Lucy Crown* (1956); and *Two Weeks in Another Town* (1960), which Shaw considered for a long time to be his best book.

During the 1970s, his most prolific period as a novelist, Shaw wrote *Rich Man, Poor Man* (1970), *Evening in Byzantium* (1973), *Nightwork* (1975), *Beggarman, Thief* (1977), and *The Top of the Hill* (1979).

In 1950 Shaw moved to Klosters, Switzerland, where he spent a part of each year. As he said in an interview for the *Los Angeles Times* a few years ago, "America was not a good place to live in then so I found this place (Klosters) while on vacation and settled in." He spent part of the year in the Hamptons, on eastern Long Island, and had a Paris apartment.

In the last five years of his life he wrote a two-part television program, "The Top of the Hill," which was broadcast in February 1980. Three of his short stories, including the classic "The Girls in

Their Summer Dresses," were shown on public television the following year. He also contributed the text for *Paris/Magnum: Photographs, 1935-1981* (1981), a collection of prints by world-famous photographers, and wrote his last two novels, *Bread Upon the Waters* (1981) and *Acceptable Losses*.

Bread Upon the Waters is a novel about the breakdown of a family brought about largely by the unexpected intervention of an outsider. The Strand family appears in every way to be a close and happy one. Allen Strand, the father, has been teaching in the New York public school system for over twenty-seven years. His wife, Leslie, gives music lessons and paints watercolors. They have three children: Jimmy, an aspiring rock performer; Caroline, who is finishing up her senior year in high school; and the oldest, Eleanor, who at twenty-two has found a job in an advertising firm where she earns a larger salary than her father.

The harmony of the Strand family is dramatically and permanently disrupted by an unforeseen incident one late afternoon. After playing a few sets of tennis, Caroline starts to return home through Central Park. On the way she sees a man being attacked by three teenage boys. Immediately she enters the fight, giving one of the boys a nasty gash on the head with her metal tennis racket. Terrified, the boys release their victim and run away. Then Caroline manages to lead the injured man back to her apartment, where the whole family takes care of him.

The real action of the novel begins with the entrance of Russel Hazen, the victim of the mugging. After a while the Strands discover that Hazen is no ordinary person, but a prominent businessman and internationally known philanthropist. Overcome with gratitude for Caroline's help, Hazen is determined to repay her. Everyone in the Strand family is showered with an unending array of gifts beginning with tickets to a concert and followed by an invitation to Hazen's estate on Long Island. Hazen even manages to insinuate himself into the everyday life of the family. He finds a man who signs up rock performers and has Jimmy get in touch with him. Aware that Caroline has promise as a runner, he encourages her to practice daily so that she can win an athletic scholarship to college.

The suspense of Shaw's story rests on the reader's attempt to unravel the motives lying behind Hazen's good deeds. There is the strong feeling throughout that something awful will happen. The climax occurs in a small restaurant in the Loire Valley of France, where Hazen has invited his closest friends, including Leslie and Allen Strand, to a sumptuous dinner. While they are there an unexpected visitor arrives—Hazen's wife. Threatening to scream if anyone tries to leave, she holds the group spellbound while she describes her life with Hazen. He is responsible, she charges, for neglecting their marriage, spoiling their children, and engaging in dishonest business deals. When she finishes, she presents her husband with two options: either he will grant her a divorce with full possession of the Southampton estate, or she will commit suicide and ruin his reputation. Shaw describes the scene with painful clarity; the whole ugly episode is credible because of the earlier hints of impending disaster. The remainder of the story is anticlimactic. A series of unhappy events befalls Hazen and the Strands and explains Shaw's intended biblical quotation in the epigraph: "Cast thy bread upon the waters, for thou shall find it after many days."

Most critics praised Shaw's novel, arguing that it was of higher quality than the novels he had written earlier in the 1970s. Evan Hunter, writing in the *New York Times Book Review* (23 August 1981), was especially enthusiastic: "The blending of a fast-paced story with thoughtful introspection . . . is executed with seeming effortlessness by the author—a sure sign that he has worked long and hard to master his craft. The prose is clean and spare, perfectly suited to the deceivingly plain tale he appears to be telling. The first chapter alone could be taught in creative writing courses across the land as a model of concise exposition."

There is at least one striking resemblance between *Bread Upon the Waters* and *Acceptable Losses,* Shaw's last novel. In each, a single incident determines the course of the action. In the earlier novel it is Caroline's successful endeavor to save Hazen from injury. In *Acceptable Losses,* a phone call in the middle of the night is the starting point of Shaw's tale.

Roger Damon lives with his second wife, Sheila, in New York City. Now in his mid-sixties, he has been working in a literary agency for over twenty years. Very late one Saturday evening when his wife is visiting her mother in Vermont, he is awakened by an ominous telephone call. At first he wonders if it might not be a practical joke played by an old friend visiting the city. It is soon made clear, however, that the call is no joke. Someone who identifies himself as Zalovsky insists that Roger meet him outside his apartment in fifteen minutes. Although Roger remains in his apartment and pretends the call is unimportant, it is obvious that he is deeply shaken.

For the next few weeks Roger's life abruptly changes. At first he tries to keep what has happened a secret. But after manuscripts go unread and arguments flare up with his wife, he finally tells about the phone call. Now in earnest to find out who Zalovsky really is, Roger hires a private detective, who suggests his client draw up a list of possible personal and professional enemies. Much of the novel revolves around Roger's attempt to discover if anyone on his list is in fact out to get him. The story sustains high suspense until the identity of Zalovsky is uncovered.

The critics were not altogether friendly toward *Acceptable Losses.* The majority noted that Shaw seemed to devote an undue amount of attention to symbolism relating to death and disease, to the extent that it became a distraction. They also agreed that the central theme, Roger's search for the real Zalovsky, was often relegated to the background, leaving the reader wondering what the book was really about. John Jay Osborn, Jr., observed in the *New York Times*: "If the extraneous parts of this novel had been deleted by a crafty editor, 'Acceptable Losses' would have been a great short story."

At the time of Shaw's death, many mourned his passing and recalled his generosity to beginning writers. Gay Talese especially remembered the kindness and encouragement he got from Shaw: "He was so giving to young writers all over Europe and in the United States. . . . I met him in 1955, when I was in Paris and just a soldier, and he was as nice to me as he would have been to a John Steinbeck or to a Gary Cooper. I was obscure, unknown. He made you feel that you were on his level, even if you weren't. Generosity is the word. In his house in Switzerland, in his apartment in Paris, along the cafes of the Via Veneto in Rome, in the Hamptons, in the Ritz Hotel in New York, wherever he was, when you were with Irwin Shaw you felt that some of the energy and optimism of that man was infectious."

The consensus among authors concerning Shaw's place in American letters has not altered over the years. He is considered to have held great promise when he was starting out. Many believed that as a short story writer Shaw would one day be viewed as Hemingway's successor. But the publication of *The Young Lions* in 1948 was the great turning point in his writing career. That novel not only brought glowing reviews which compared his work with Norman Mailer's *The Naked and the Dead* and James Jones's *From Here to Eternity,* but it enabled Shaw to rise above a hand-to-mouth existence as a struggling author. The critics argue that Shaw then decided he could earn big money writing best-sellers and traded his integrity as a writer for slick novels and life among the beautiful people.

This remains the consensus today. Shaw did, for the most part, give up the short story and concentrate on the novel during the last forty years of his writing career. But he always worked hard at his craft. At some future date perhaps he will be remembered not as an author who early in life compromised his principles to make a fortune, but as one of America's best storytellers—which he was.

References:

Herbert Mitgang, "Irwin Shaw, Near 70, Adds It Up and Feels 'Right,'" *New York Times*, 17 February 1983: sec. III, p. 21;

Mitgang, "Irwin Shaw, Writer, Is Dead; Acclaimed for Short Stories," *New York Times*, 17 May 1984, pp. 1, 47.

Ross Wetzsteon, "Irwin Shaw: The Conflict Between Bucks and Good Books," *Saturday Review*, 8 (August 1981): 12, 14, 16, 17;

A TRIBUTE

from JOHN W. ALDRIDGE

Although I once wrote a disparaging critique of *The Young Lions* (in *After the Lost Generation*), I've since come to respect Shaw as a first-rate literary craftsman and thoroughgoing professional. He was not a writer of the first class, but as is so often the case with writers who are not, he was able to express the mood and flavor of experience in his time more accurately than many writers of greater talent. I think he was at his best in his short stories, but even in his lesser novels (I think particularly of *Two Weeks in Another Town*) one felt and responded to his skill and sincerity.

A TRIBUTE

from RICHARD HAUER COSTA

Born in 1921, I missed by just a few years Leslie Fiedler's memory from 1936 of seeing Irwin Shaw's first and most powerful play, *Bury the Dead*. "I can remember with embarrassing clarity screaming in ecstasy as the soldiers walked portentously across the stage at the end. It seemed a play written for me and for my friends, our play." And so it was. And so, for many others of us, were stories like "The Eighty-Yard Run," which confirms the para-

dox of Housman's "To an Athlete Dying Young" by dramatizing the plight of a burned-out case named Christian Darling whose future passed when he ran for a touchdown in college, and in practice, fifteen years before; "The Girls in Their Summer Dresses," which may now seem old-fashioned in a time of casual sex but which, in its day, provided vicarious romanticizing for husbands suffering from compulsive fidelity; and "Act of Faith," in which barracks camaraderie rises to heroic stature as a check on anti-Semitism.

He wrote, by his count, eighty-four stories, of which a score are anthologized. Thus he may be even more frequently represented in such collections than other American masters like Hemingway and Faulkner, Katherine Anne Porter and Wilbur Daniel Steele, Flannery O'Connor and J. D. Salinger. Unlike most of them, he continued to write short stories throughout his career—an active half-century. He sold his first to the *New Republic* for $25 in 1937 when he was twenty-three. He quickly cracked the *New Yorker*, which paid him $75, and he continued to publish in that magazine for nearly fifteen years—until 1952, when he quit. "My friends on it, my editors, died, and I didn't like the policy of the new people who came in," he told *Paris Review* interviewers five years ago.

The publication of his long-awaited first novel, *The Young Lions* (1948), changed his life dramatically. A book of 700 pages that is still hard to put down, it lacked the sustained power of Mailer's *The Naked and the Dead* or *From Here to Eternity*, by his close friend James Jones. Nor was it as expert and novelistic as James Gould Cozzens's Pulitzer Prize-winning *Guard of Honor*. It was still the work of a short-story writer, an extension of anecdotal craft. But the proceeds from royalties and the screen sale—Shaw's first big money—convinced him that only in the novel could he find the passport to economic self-sufficiency.

In his second novel, *The Troubled Air* (1951), there are perceptive insights into the workings of the Communist mind and the tactics employed by right-of-center business groups. The flawed large canvass of *The Young Lions* gives way to an intense examination of moral depravity and betrayal in a time of cold war, blacklists, and pseudopatriotism. It deserves to be read as a shrewd anticipation of McCarthyism as *Bury the Dead* was a presage of Hitler's war.

Shortly after the publication of *The Troubled Air* Shaw decided to make his home in Europe, and for the last thirty years of his life he divided his time between his favorite overseas city, Paris, and his chalet in Klosters, Switzerland. He always insisted that he gained rather than lost by deserting his roots; that he broadened himself by living on a continent where the writer is more socially accepted than in America; and "where anybody with $300 in his pocket can come back to the U.S. whenever he wants." His novels as an expatriate—from *Lucy Crown* (1956) to *The Top of the Hill* (1979)—have the same touch of class as everything he wrote, but his plots, according to critical consensus, became more contrived, his style more facile, his characters more cut from soap-opera wholecloth. The big-deal translation of *Rich Man, Poor Man* (1970) and *Beggarman, Thief* (1977) to TV blockbusters was inevitable.

He denied in his novels-for-TV period that he read reviews. But he also said that he was saving the really juicy throat cutting for his memoirs. "You have to expect the raps, when you have achieved popularity, which in high literary circles is proof of venality," he told Willie Morris, adding a remark that can be interpreted as a polite way of saying he cried all the way to the bank.

He was, I believe, the best of the writers who tried to write like Hemingway—one who matured to a professionalism and incandescence that were all his own. The old Brooklyn College quarterback will long be remembered for passages like this one from "The Eighty-Yard Run," which reclaims the pure line of past authenticity from present oblivion:

> Darling half-closed his eyes, almost saw the boy fifteen years ago, on an autumn afternoon, twenty years old and far from death, with the air coming easily into his lungs, and a deep feeling inside him that he could do anything, knock over anybody, outrun whatever had to be outrun.

And, with the spun gold of his style, Irwin Shaw did for a time outrun nearly everybody. Rather than talk of defection from the ranks of the Bellows and Updikes, let us be grateful for the bounty he left us.

A TRIBUTE

from DONALD I. FINE

Irwin Shaw wrote the way he lived—with wit, style, and a dedication to what he believed in. The very facility and ease of his prose for some was a diversion from the deeper meanings of his works. He once said to me, "They think it comes so easy, but I sweat over every word."

Serious writers who have developed narrative skills that bring them popularity and financial success are at risk with the small, often petty and envious literary community that sits in judgment on them. Irwin Shaw was not immune from their green-tipped daggers; in fact, he was more often than not a victim. When his antiwar play, *Bury the Dead,* was first produced in New York's Greenwich Village he was viewed as a promising, struggling new talent (one wonders what the reception would have been if the critics knew that Shaw had been earning a good living writing radio narration since his teens). After the publication of his historic novel of World War II, *The Young Lions,* he became famous, but *his* novel never was taken quite as seriously as the other two great novels to come out of the war, Mailer's *The Naked and the Dead* and Jones's *From Here to Eternity.* Whatever the relative literary merits of these three works, there's little question that Shaw's flowed the most smoothly in the writing, was the most outspoken in its outrage at cruelty, hatred of Nazism and anti-Semitism, and dedication to individual worth—themes that run through all Shaw's work. For some this very openness, this lack of apparent guile was an embarrassment, as it remained for the same people during the rest of his career. *Voices of A Summer's Day,* published in the mid-60s, a lovely evocation of growing up, man and boy, in Brooklyn, was dismissed with a vulgar brush by a front-page review in the book review supplement of the now-defunct *New York Herald Tribune.* The reviewer did not think it was serious enough. How could it be and at the same time be so warm, so effortless in the telling?

Soon thereafter Shaw wrote *Rich Man, Poor Man,* a rich and insightful family novel, especially a story of two brothers in conflict, that brought the author considerable riches for its paperback edition, whose publication was tied in to the successful television series based on the novel. Shaw's reputation among the literary community as a serious writer plummeted. A soap opera, they said, although it is safe to say few if any of them read the book, and fewer would be willing or even able to recognize their own jealousy. Subsequent novels such as *Night Work, Bread Upon the Waters,* and *Acceptable Losses* were given more critical approval and, not incidentally, did less well at the bottom line.

Too much is written about the personal life of famous authors, too little about their writing—especially in this era of television obits and periodicals dedicated to gossip (people-other-people copy, as it used to be known). But a word should be said about Irwin's generosity to other writers, his receptivity to the works of new writers, and his insistence that they get a hearing with his publishers and others in the literary world. He cared about talent, about people who had something to contribute, not only in the arts but also in the world of politics and sports. His legacy is an unparalleled quest for the heart of the matter, the truth beneath the surface. It is one that more writers would do well to consider and carry forward.

As editor in chief of Dell Books and Delacorte Press I was instrumental in bringing Irwin Shaw to Dell from Random House and served with immense pleasure as his editor and publisher while I was in those positions. Later Irwin chose to join me at Arbor House, which I founded and directed until October of 1983. It was during these last days that he wrote his last novel, *Acceptable Losses*, a novel which he told me at the time was about a man facing death, reviewing his life, looking for its meanings. When I founded in December of 1983 my new company, Donald I. Fine, Inc., Irwin and I spoke about his joining me, and he expressed a desire to do so. His death intervened. Irwin Shaw and I were friends. He was always honest with me. I don't know what more a friend can be. I miss him. I believe not only his friends and family but millions of readers will also miss him. But they have an advantage—they do not know the personal loss, and they do have the opportunity to read and reread him. He is one of the few writers whose work yields up fresh pleasures each time it is engaged.

A TRIBUTE

from WILLIE MORRIS

I have many good memories of Irwin—of his loyalty and generosity and sense of fun. Here is one of them.

On the night before the memorial service for our friend James Jones in the Community House in Bridgehampton in 1977, Irwin and William Styron and I went to dinner at a local restaurant. We were accompanied by the best bugler in the U.S. Army, Sergeant Mastroleo. The Sergeant had volunteered to play Taps at Jim's service because he remembered Montgomery Cliff in the movie *From Here to Eternity*. He was based in Washington and had played Taps at the gravesides of three presidents. Bill Styron, Irwin, and I were to give the three

eulogies for Jim the next day, and we decided that evening that one of us would read the moving Taps sequence from the novel before the Sergeant sounded his notes.

As we were leaving the restaurant, Irwin turned to Styron and me: "Absolutely no drinking before the service tomorrow," he said. "We owe that to Jim."

The next morning, about an hour before the service, Irwin showed up in the backyard of my house on Church Lane with the bugler, who was in his dress blues. Irwin caught Styron and me drinking a Bloody Mary. He left in a huff.

As we ascertained later, Irwin parked his car in front of the Volunteer Fire Department adjacent to the Community House. One of the firemen said, "Mr. Shaw, you look like a man who could use a drink." He replied: "You're damned right I can." The firemen led him inside to the soft-drink machine, unlocked it, and brought out a fifth of Old Charter. Irwin, we were informed reliably, had three stiff ones.

Irwin and Jim Jones were brothers. Irwin gave the first eulogy at the service, and when he finished, he sat down again next to Styron and me. "It's tough up there," he said. "I had a drink too."

A TRIBUTE

from GAY TALESE

As a rule, writers are not generous people, particularly toward younger writers. The greatest exception to this, in my experience, was Irwin Shaw. He was the most generous writer I've ever had the honor of knowing, and he influenced me in many ways having to do with style in generosity.

When the young writers that he helped forgot about him, as so many did, Shaw did not seem to resent it; he simply accepted this behavior as the way of the artistic mind and spirit that often form the writer.

He deserved kinder treatment than he got from the book critics, but their resentment of him had less to do with his work than with the way he lived. Irwin Shaw enjoyed living—in a way so few writers do. He was an outdoor man in an indoor sport, and his international fame served to inspire envy and some cruelty in critics. Irwin accepted this, and he left behind a body of work any good writer should envy.

Jesse Stuart
(8 August 1906-17 February 1984)

H. Edward Richardson
University of Louisville

See also the Stuart entry in *DLB 9, American Novelists, 1910-1945.*

NEW BOOKS: *Land of the Honey-Colored Wind,* edited by Jerry A. Herndon (Moorhead, Ky.: Jesse Stuart Foundation, 1982);
The Best-Loved Short Stories of Jesse Stuart, edited by H. Edward Richardson (New York: McGraw-Hill, 1982).

Shortly after meeting Jesse Stuart for the first time in Richmond, Kentucky, my wife and I drove up to W-Hollow from the Bluegrass, where he was then writer-in-residence at Eastern Kentucky University. As we left Grayson and drove north on Kentucky Route 1 entering Greenup County—the Greenwood County of his fiction—we knew we were entering Stuart Country. From Winston High School, Warnock High School in reality, Jesse Stuart had once tried to walk the seventeen miles to W-Hollow near Laurel Ridge, as he renamed his native Seaton Ridge. Six inches of snow lay on the ground when he began his journey, and by nightfall he was lost in a snowstorm. Hard flakes that "felt like grains of corn" blinded him in an "incessant sweep of wind." He survived the subzero weather by carrying eight fodder shocks to one place, improvising from them a snug dwelling, and sharing it with the field mice and the ticking of his watch. This incident, related in *The Thread That Runs So True* (1949), actually took place close to the present site of Greenbo Lake about six miles from fabled W-Hollow.

Stuart was the bardic chronicler of Appalachia—its poet and storyteller. This ancient region of America was peopled with the descendants of "the old people" in landlocked hollows, some of whom yet retain the dialects, handicrafts, and customs of older cultures—those of Scotland, England, and Ireland among them. A poet of power may take materials out of waking fantasies, classic myths, and strange dreams; but often the literary creator uses materials shaped by local legends as

Jesse Stuart, Randall Stewart, and Robert Penn Warren at Vanderbilt University, 1959 (Jesse Stuart Photo Collection)

well. Commencing as a regional writer, Stuart brought to his sources an original, evocative language, at once authentic and stylistically apt and broadly assimilative, because he knew his people from the inside out and was so close to the soil. In time, he successfully transmuted the shadowy figures of local legends into the consciously communicated personae of literary art. *Daughter of the Legend* (1965) makes the point, or a reader may consider any of his innumerable characters—Old 'Op Akers; Grandma Collins; the hunter and imbiber

Warfield Flaugherty; Uglybird Skinner; Cherlie Deer and his brood of beautiful daughters; Uncle Mel Shelton with his mining cap, living (and ready to die, too) for the resurrection; or Peg and Arn Sparks in their hug-me-tight behind their horse Gunpowder on the W-Hollow Road, just *clip-clopping* it along.

On that trip to W-Hollow in the 1960s, the author took me up on top of Seaton Ridge to see his land, nearly 1,000 acres spread out with the Ohio River visible to the north. Though it was a late November afternoon, the sun was bright on the upland meadows, glowing through the trees and giving a yellow cast to the Little Sandy River in the valley below to the west. Driving on a little distance we came to a wide green opening of pasture, in the middle of which was a deserted white clapboard house of simple construction. "I recognize it," I said.

"What is it?" Jesse challenged. "You've never seen it before."

"Why, I saw it in *The Good Spirit of Laurel Ridge*. It's where old Theopolis lived."

Jesse nodded, laughing, enjoying my temporary displacement at being caught between the factual and imaginative worlds over which he was the sole proprietor, and recounted part of the novel. "Old 'Op had to have his music." He told how the old man had strung horsehairs on the walls of his shack and sat listening to the wind crying through his "harps of angels." He spoke of the ghosts old Theopolis heard and saw: the sounds of General John Hunt Morgan and his cavalry riding by and shouting on a raid across the Ohio, and the ghost of another soldier of another time, Ted Newsome. The heritage of the American tall tale, superstition, and rite are richly woven through this curious novel. Still, Theopolis was real enough to have a prototype; and Jesse's tone as he stood before me was that of a chronicler rather than a dreamer.

We got back into that truck and drove over rough winding roads and through the tree shadows. Once we slid down the hill on leaves, the author laughing as he played the brakes against the sliding wheels. We saw the original Stuart homeplace in the distance, which Jesse at the age of fifteen and his Grandfather Hilton had built with the help of a carpenter to hang windows and doors. "You can see the whole fifty acres of my dad's farm there." We got out and walked while Jesse pointed to a yet visible path in places, along which he had walked the five miles to and from Greenup—up this valley, across the long rim of land, and down along Academy Branch—to school each day. He showed me where he wrote beneath "the tough-butted white oaks," and suddenly he ran over to one of them and felt of its rough bark with his palm, rubbing it the way a trainer kneads the withers of a thoroughbred after a good workout. "I wrote some of the sonnets from *Man with a Bull-Tongue Plow* right here." He spoke with enthusiasm and looked directly at me as he talked. It was refreshing to hear an artist tell the truth about his work. Jesse was certainly not the reticent, introverted artist. Nothing of the Salinger, Faulkner, and Cozzens aversions to a curious humanity emanated from him. He talked freely, openly, naturally. "I wrote some of those sonnets on the light underneaths of poplar leaves and copied them when I got home from plowing before the leaves shriveled." He eyed me, chuckled, and then declared with an innocent openness, "A lot of people don't believe me when I tell them that."

Often the first impression of Jesse Stuart's personality was that he was a blend of dynamo and child. He had an artless, ingenuous, spontaneous quality that was sometimes mistaken for naiveté; but there was an unmistakable wisdom, too, that did not go thistle gathering. He had a way of directing a tremendous energy toward people when he talked, and he spoke with a Twain-like innocence—always—whether to an individual or to individuals in a group. His blue eyes lit up in friendly anticipation of his attitudes. Myriad facial expressions punctuated his natural verbal fluency, which abounded in the prefixes and dropped suffixes of his natural, musical, mountain dialect, evident in such words as *a-singin, a-goin*, and *a-runnin*. Sometimes his voice rose in volume, and he gestured vigorously when he was caught up in the fever of an idea. Curiosity radiated from him; he was truly curious about people, and if he liked them, they could feel it. Small wonder Edgar Lee Masters paid Stuart the ultimate compliment, "I have such confidence in him that I would turn him loose in Boston for the rest of his life without fear that Boston would ruin him."

The themes of his work are as wide as it was prolific: the land, the seasons and the cycle of life, love and passion, pride, self-sacrifice, anger and frustration, defeat, death, escape, nature and its flora and fauna, ambition and determination, human conflict, murder and violence, war and weddings, drink and drunkenness, farming and plowing, the lives of soil men and the mountain earth, the local color of the country and town, pioneering and hunting, friendship, betrayal, infidelity and faithfulness, honesty, hunger and harvest, the search for self and the journey motif, loneliness, wind images and work, family and home, music and dancing, courage and fear, Jesse Stuart himself, freedom, Kentucky, America, and the world. No theme in his work appears more frequently than that of home and its manifold meanings, early tempered to profundity by the youthful fire of rebellion—followed, to be sure, by the submission motif. At one point (so he wrote in his personal story *Beyond Dark Hills*, 1938), after the death of his beloved younger brother, he refused, while going to feed the livestock on snowy mornings, to walk in his father's footsteps as he had done before. At another time he told his father, "Fifty acres is not a big enough place to hold me." As he grew into young manhood, he found work away from home—summers in the steel mills of Ashland, three years at Lincoln Memorial University in Harrogate, Tennessee, where he worked his way through college. More than one summer of work at Peabody College in Nashville, Tennessee, and an academic year of graduate work at Vanderbilt followed, then a year as a Guggenheim fellow in Scotland, England, and Europe. Later in life, lecturing often took him away from home for weeks and months at a time. But he always came back, and there in W-Hollow something invariably took hold of him and set him down to write such lines as "Now do not leave me love, for rugged lands" (Poem #128 in *Man with a Bull-Tongue Plow*, 1934).

Despite various offers elsewhere, including Hollywood, where M-G-M had purchased the movie rights to *Taps for Private Tussie* for $50,000, just after World War II Lieutenant Junior Grade Jesse Stuart returned home from naval life in Washington, D.C., and began to farm, write, and lecture again. The year 1946 was hard for him— much work to do on his W-Hollow farm that had lain fallow and in the house that had been empty during the war; but because it was the first year of peace, it was the best of years since 1941. In November 1946 his lecturing commitments took him to the East: New York City, where he spoke at Columbia University; Brooklyn, where he reflected on the correctness of Thomas Wolfe's declaration that only the dead knew that place; and Boston, where he lectured and saw his Harvard friend Henry Lee Shattuck again. After a lecture in Trenton, he wrote in his daily journal, "I was chased by an insane woman." Speaking his way through Pennsylvania, at Easton he followed Randolph Churchill on the podium of the National Dinner Club (14 November 1946). Then it was back to W-Hollow. Returning

moved him deeply; happiness to see home again set him down to write a poem he first called "Heart of America":

> I didn't have any choice as to where I was born,
> But if I had had my choice,
> I would have chosen Kentucky.
> And if I could have chosen wind to breathe,
> I would have chosen a Kentucky wind
> With the scent of cedar, pinetree needles,
> Green tobacco leaves, pawpaw, persimmon and sassa-
> fras.
> I would have chosen too,
> Wind from the sawbriar and greenbriar blossoms.

Later it would be published as "Kentucky Is My Land" in the collection to which it would give its name (1952).

How did the poet-chronicler emerge from mountain shadows to literary fame? He was born in a log cabin atop a high hill overlooking W-Hollow on one side and Shacklerun Valley on the other. The watercourse below on the southern side of the hill away from W-Hollow was recalled as a "lonely spot," a place where one could listen to the sounds of Cedar Riffles Branch traversing "the stony riffles on silent nights" on its way down to the Little Sandy River, but if "the wind is blowing through the pine trees the water cannot be heard." Here, four miles by road from Greenup, Kentucky, on the Ohio River, the oldest son of seven children of Mitchell and Martha Hilton Stuart was born on 8 August 1906, although a mistake made when he was in college has led reference works to report 1907. Counting his birthplace, there were five homes— four of them log—in which Jesse grew up until he and his seventy-year-old grandfather Nathan Hilton built the Mitchell Stuart house on a hill at the head of W-Hollow near the present, widely photographed home where Jesse Stuart's widow still lives.

In 1934 Stuart burst upon the literary scene with *Man with a Bull-Tongue Plow* and was promptly hailed by Mark Van Doren as "a modern American Robert Burns." This early major work was soon followed by two volumes of short stories, then sixteen more collections through the year 1982. Many of the nearly 500 stories remain uncollected. Ruel E. Foster, Benedum Professor of American Literature at West Virginia University, commented in his biocritical study *Jesse Stuart* (1968), "When the definitive history of the American short story is written, Jesse Stuart's name may well be near the top of the list of the best writers in this genre." Stuart also wrote eight novels, eight more volumes of autobiography or autobiographical fiction and biography, eight juvenile books, and eight poetry collections containing around 2,000 poems. His bibliography lists a total of sixty-one separately published works, fifty-five of them book-length.

During more than half a century of publication, commencing with the poetry collection *Harvest of Youth* in 1930, he averaged more than one book, nine stories, forty poems, and five essays or articles a year, exclusive of newspaper pieces. In addition to the continuing demand for his work and the hundreds of reprints of his literary works that have emerged and continue to appear, Stuart kept a vast reservoir of unpublished manuscripts, which he called "my reserve." The year 1984 marks the appearance of an accumulated total of ten books about Stuart's life and work in addition to approximately twenty-two theses and dissertations and more than 275 miscellaneous pieces, most of them in periodicals. By 1980 more than sixty of his works were translated into Arabic, Danish, German, French, Spanish, Japanese, Czechoslovakian, Chinese, Polish, Russian, Bengali, Dutch, Italian, Norwegian, Swedish, West Pakistani, and Telegu.

One problem scholars of American literature have had in evaluating Jesse Stuart's work is its prodigious size. As Donald Davidson commented, *"How do you criticize or teach a flowing river? . . .* [For] it was perfectly clear that Jesse Stuart was a river of poetry—and heaven knew what more." The evaluator would do well to examine the several categories of Stuart's literary contributions, for his attainments in each genre have been not only sizeable, but distinguished. His sonnets and sonnet variations began in the early 1930s to appear in bunches in the *Virginia Quarterly Review, American Mercury,* and Harriet Monroe's *Poetry.* In 1934 Morton Dauwen Zabel, an editor of *Poetry,* announced that Stuart was the recipient of the Jeanette Seawell Davis Prize for that year, with honorable mention going to Ezra Pound, William Carlos Williams, John Gould Fletcher, and Paul Engle. A quarter of a century later, Stuart was awarded the 1960 Fellowship of the Academy of American Poets for "distinguished poetic achievement" for the body of his poetic work. The board that chose him included among its chancellors Robert Nathan, Robert Hillyer, W. H. Auden, Randall Jarrell, and John Hall Wheelock.

Stuart early distinguished himself in the short story by winning the Academy of Arts and Sciences Award for the 1941 volume *Men of the Mountains.* Stephen Vincent Benét presented the award to him in Carnegie Hall in New York City. By 1979 Stuart had had more than 460 stories published in a wide variety of periodicals, ranging from the *Saturday Evening Post* and *Esquire* to *Harper's* and the *Yale Review.* Robert Penn Warren recently pointed to one of his former pupil's most "pervasive effects," so difficult for writers to achieve—"the sense of language speaking off the page, and that is a gift Jesse has, a gift based on years of astute listening and watching. . . . a gift that goes far toward creating a world." The sense of authentic place seems to stamp nearly everything Stuart has written. The place where his characters most often speak is W-Hollow, about which Ruel E. Foster wrote, "He has created a place and wedged it everlastingly in the imagination of America." Later Foster compared that place to Faulkner's Yoknapatawpha County, Elizabeth Madox Roberts's Pigeon River country, and Thomas Wolfe's Altamont. In 1943 the best-selling novel *Taps for Private Tussie* earned Stuart the Thomas Jefferson Southern Memorial Award. In 1974 University of California professor James Woodress, in his *American Fiction, 1900-1950,* listed the Kentuckian as one of the forty-four "most significant producers of fiction during the first half of the 20th century."

Stuart's canon also includes eight works of autobiographical fiction, autobiography and biography, such as *The Thread That Runs So True* (1949), *Beyond Dark Hills* (1938, 1972), and *God's Oddling* (1960, 1968); and eight juvenile books, including *The Beatinest Boy* (1953). Since his first incapacitating stroke in 1978, no fewer than fifteen published works by him or about him and his work have appeared, including those listed at the outset of this essay and a 1983 film based on his most frequently reprinted short story, *Split Cherry Tree* (New York: Learning Corporation of America). *Split Cherry Tree* won an Academy Award in the category of "Best Live Action Short Film" and received the Silver Electra Award from the Birmingham International Educational Film Festival.

Yet Jesse Stuart's literary achievement is only part of a remarkably active life that embraced such other careers as farmer and conservationist, editor, naval officer, teacher and administrator, lecturer, and international man of letters. Much more could be said about his teaching experiences, which provided the background for most of his autobiographical work. Also noteworthy is his journalistic career, during which he wrote a variety of newspaper pieces, more than fifty having to do with his travels in Scotland, England, and twenty-five countries of Europe during his Guggenheim Fellowship in 1937-1938. Later articles dealt with his educational wars in his native Greenup County in 1938, when

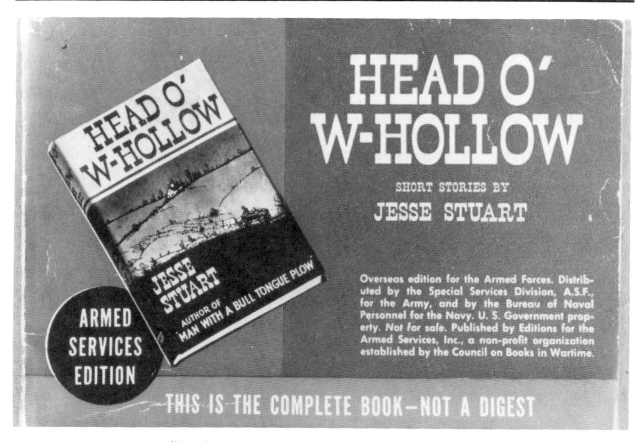

An edition of Stuart's book distributed to servicemen during World War II

he edited the Republican *Greenup County Citizen,* an edition of the *Russell* (Kentucky) *Times,* and for his efforts was blackjacked from behind while having a chocolate milk shake in a local drugstore. Such estrangements between the poet and his people, however, proved to be only transient; by 15 October 1955 he was the incentive for a huge celebration at the Greenup County courthouse—"Jesse Hilton Stuart Day in Kentucky," declared by Governor Lawrence Weatherby. That day his townspeople presented him with a nine-foot Georgia granite monolith topped by a bust of the poet facing southward between two granite pilasters. Cut into the stone in bas-relief was a bull-tongue plow, emblematic of the land and people of whom he sang. Under that his name appears with the words "Poet, Novelist, Educator" and an inscription from Pakenham Beatty:

> By your own soul's law, learn to live,
> And if men thwart you, take no heed,
> If men hate you, have no care;
> Sing your song, dream your dream,
> Hope your hope, and pray your prayer.

During the academic year 1960-1961 he was visiting professor at the American University in Cairo, Egypt, and in 1962-1963 he traveled around the world lecturing for the American Information Service, a branch of the United States State Department. By that time the journalistic habit had become deeply ingrained, and he wrote hundreds of pages about his experiences in and reactions to the countries and people he came to know during his travels. Most of these works, such as his journals of Italy, Lebanon, Africa, India, China, Japan, and Korea, remain uncollected in book form, although his *Dandelion on the Acropolis: A Journal of Greece* (1978) is an exception. The largest of these writings is his unpublished "Egyptian Diary," which he considered so critical of Nasser's Egypt that he smuggled the pages out rather than risk their possible confiscation.

Stuart was a man of public commitment and of philanthropy. He gave half the value of his land to the people in order to establish, before his death, the Jesse Stuart Nature Preserve, thus preserving for all time the old stands of timber and pasturelands, teeming with wildlife—his land "as it was and is." His literary estate is being managed by the Jesse Stuart Foundation, a public, nonprofit organization created in 1979. Having raised more than $1.2 million for the preservation of the poet's physical world of W-Hollow, the Foundation is now striving to increase the visibility of his literary world. Previously unpublished Stuart works will be coming out, along with periodic reprints.

Jesse Stuart died of "intractable heart failure" on 17 February 1984 at the Jo-Lin Health Care Center in Ironton, Ohio, fifteen miles from his beloved W-Hollow. The last thirty years of his life he had suffered no fewer than eight heart attacks and two strokes, the last stroke of 1982 denying him the use of his voice and, according to his doctors, his consciousness. His funeral was held in the same little brick Methodist Church in Greenup where he had been a member since 1952. Governor Martha Lane Collins attended, along with other dignitaries and a large gathering of friends. The Stuarts and their relations filled the whole right half of the church. The Reverend Julian Hammonds, Stuart's minister, led the call to worship, and the congregation sang "A Mighty Fortress Is Our God." Following Beethoven's anthem "Preludio Religioso," Dr. Robert Wood eulogized Jesse in "The Celebration of Triumph," recalling that he was "a warm and outgoing person, and to know him a while was like knowing him a lifetime." Then the Reverend Hammonds spoke. "You people from Greenup who are here," he said, "I hope you'll know what a treasure you had among you." He recalled the poet's "songs of beauty," "What a talent he had!" and how the mountaineer had always been "available and approachable" to people from all walks of life. The minister urged the people to "go out under the trees and read his books again."

Outside, the lowering sky turned pearl gray—the kind Jesse had once described as "February winter shawl-cloud weather"—and the temperature had dropped into the forties. The long procession passed through the eastern end of Greenup and then moved southward past W-Hollow and the site of the old Three Mile way station where Huey the Engineer had throttled his train on the vanished T-rails above the still visible bed of the old Eastern Kentucky Railroad. Then the cortege angled off onto Shacklerun Road, pierced the Plum Grove hills, and climbed the steep hill to the Plum Grove Church. To those who knew the poet's life and work, it was as if he were home again and his prayer had been answered, that the "Creator of the Uni-

verse," as he had once written, would "let me lie back in the heart of it in the end . . . the land that has cradled me."

Now a tablet-shaped gravestone of Vermont granite stands as tall as once did the man it memorializes on the Plum Grove hill. As his land has a voice, so does this stone. One side depicts a carven bull-tongue plow, the symbol of the farmer; the other side a lamp and book, suggesting the teacher and learning; the back of the stone reveals a scene of nature—trees and mountains caught in the setting sun, into which curves a modern highway, dramatizing the possible harmony of conservation and human progress in which the man-artist believed. Under each symbol are related lines from Jesse Stuart's works, and on the front of the stone are the words "The Kingdom of God / Is Within You," a biblical quotation that threads through his last autobiographical work, *The Kingdom Within: A Spiritual Biography* (1979), a curious postmortem published before, yet anticipating, his death with prescient accuracy. Then, below the sculpted pen and scroll of the poet, the stone reads,

JESSE

HILTON STUART

Aug. 8, 1906

Feb. 17, 1984

Below a Latin cross are these lines from *Album of Destiny* (1944):

What is life worth when we're afraid to live,
When we as humans dodge what Nature's given?
What is life worth when we take and don't give,
And when the best in us will not awaken?
What is a lamp without a burning flame?
What is the human brain without insight
To guide us from the night from whence we came
Through paths uncertain to the morning's light?
Do not the flowers look to morning's light
With strength from roots in earth securely fastened?
Should not man look to morning for his light
Before his body fails, his life is wasted?
Life is no more than wind unless we give,
True to our hearts, true to our fellow-men,
That we may in the finish when we leave
Triumph in life that surely comes again.

References:

Ruel E. Foster, Foreword to *Clearing in the Sky and*

Other Stories, by Jesse Stuart (Lexington, Ky.: University Press of Kentucky, 1984);

Foster, *Jesse Stuart* (New York: Twayne, 1968);

J. R. LeMaster, *Jesse Stuart: Kentucky's Chronicler-Poet* (Memphis, Tenn.: Memphis State University Press, 1980);

H. Edward Richardson, *Jesse: The Biography of an American Writer—Jesse Hilton Stuart* (New York: McGraw-Hill, 1984);

Richardson, "Stuart County: The Man-Artist and the Myth," in *Jesse Stuart: Essays on His Work*, edited by J. R. LeMaster and Mary Washington Clarke (Lexington: University Press of Kentucky, 1977);

John Howard Spurlock, *He Sings for Us: A Sociological Analysis of the Appalachian Subculture and of Jesse Stuart as a Major American Author* (Lanham, Md.: University Press of America, 1980);

Jesse Stuart, "Kentucky Is My Land," in *Kentucky Is My Land*, by Jesse Stuart (Ashland, Ky.: Economy Printers, n.d.);

Robert Penn Warren, Foreword to *Head o' W-Hollow*, by Jesse Stuart (Lexington: University Press of Kentucky, 1979);

Hensley C. Woodbridge, *Jesse and Jane Stuart: A Bibliography* (Murray, Ky.: Murray State University Press, 1979);

James Woodress, *American Fiction, 1900-1950*, vol. 1 (Detroit: Gale Research, 1974), pp. xvii, 189-191.

A TRIBUTE

from WADE HALL

Enthusiasm. Passion. Zest. Love of life—all life, human and animal. These are some words that come to mind when I remember Jesse Stuart the man. Although Jesse was no nostalgic sentimentalist and often wrote bitter satire, he loved his Appalachian people and their ways. Hundreds—perhaps thousands—of his readers considered themselves not only his literary fans but his personal friends. Jesse was never too busy to write letters of thanks, to accept total strangers into his home at W-Hollow, or to give words of encouragement to fledgling writers. Jesse Stuart was very much like a character in one of his books—a character based on a larger-than-life man he knew in W-Hollow who, Jesse once told me, he had to "tone down" so that readers would believe him.

Jesse spent so much time with his readers it is incredible that he found time to write more than fifty books, a number of which are already American classics: *The Thread That Runs So True, Taps for Private Tussie, Man with a Bull-Tongue Plow, The Year of My Rebirth, Trees of Heaven*. Although his national vogue in the 1930s as America's plowboy poet lessened in later years as literary tastes changed, Stuart continued to produce some of the most authentic and finely crafted Appalachian fiction and autobiography ever written. His niche in American literature is safeguarded in particular by his fact-based novels and short stories.

A TRIBUTE

from J. R. LEMASTER

I waited twenty-two months for Jesse Stuart to die, and each day was painful. I found myself wishing that he would die and bring to an end my anxiety as well as that of a great number of other people. But I was selfish. When he finally slipped into death, he did it with grace and dignity. In life he was a man of compassion and love; in death he reminds us all that we live in a world where the old "truths of the heart" are daily tested. His fifty or more volumes were about those truths at the time of their writing, over a period of fifty years, and they remain to remind us that the world has not changed for the better. In those volumes Jesse Stuart's memory moves through space and time, as he now moves through space and time, reminding us that the truth is of the earth, in man's relationship to the soil, to wildflowers, to trees, and to one's fellow man, to the baby crying in its mother's arms, to the man in prison for committing a crime, to the preacher in the pulpit preaching the Word, to the farmer making hay, and to the schoolboy making his way home from a day at school. In his fifty or more volumes Jesse Stuart gave us a vision of a world he perceived as a viable alternative to the one in which we live, and that vision remains. Using his beloved W-Hollow as microcosm he spoke to the common lot of humanity all over the world; he never had time for pretense or sham. The greatest proclaimer of democracy in America since Walt Whitman, he left us a legacy no less than that of Walt Whitman. He left us what he often referred to as "the dream."

A TRIBUTE

from RUEL E. FOSTER

I met Jesse Stuart initially in the early summer of 1955 when he was recuperating from his first massive heart attack. He was at home in W-Hollow, carefully guarded by his wife Naomi. Orders from his doctor were that visitors should not stay longer than fifteen minutes. I had stopped by to ask him to write an introduction on a book I had coauthored on Elizabeth Madox Roberts, a Kentucky writer he admired. He couldn't write it because of bad health, but he could talk with a verve and energy that belied his invalid status. I arose dutifully after fifteen minutes and prepared to leave, not wanting to see Jesse topple over in another heart attack. Jesse wouldn't hear of my leaving. He had learned that I had taken my Ph.D from Vanderbilt and had studied under Professor Donald Davidson, Stuart's mentor and great friend. Jesse told me that long ago as a Vanderbilt student he had taken some of his early poems, imitative of the romantics of the day, to Davidson, who returned them with the comment, "Don't be a pretty-boy, Jesse." That was a key moment for Jesse and he never forgot Davidson. Three hours later I did leave, happy to see that Stuart seemed to thrive on athletic talk and appeared no worse for wear after three hours of skipping from Vanderbilt and Davidson to Robert Burns, to Thomas Wolfe to University of Kentucky football and basketball, Shakespeare, O. Henry, Emerson, and a dozen other conversational gambits.

I last saw Jesse when my wife and I paid an overnight visit to his home in W-Hollow. He had just completed his typescript of *The Kingdom Within*, the last novel he was to write. Naomi Stuart, who worried about him, said he had written it under greater compulsion than he had ever showed before, turning it off in about two months. He was immensely pleased with this work and fondled the physical manuscript very lovingly, almost as if he already knew that it would be the last of his galaxy of publications. He would let me read brief snatches of it, then he would take the manuscript back from me. Jesse was tired and a little gray looking. The mail came around noon the next day and among the letters were two from his publisher announcing coming releases of his work. He was pleased and read them aloud to Naomi and to us. As we drove away, Jesse and Naomi were standing in their front yard in the thin March sunlight, their hands raised in a gracious, bright farewell. Three days later Jesse suffered his first crippling stroke. He was never to write again.

I knew Jesse well through the twenty-nine years of our acquaintance. There were visits, meetings and letters—especially letters. Jesse and I exchanged hundreds of letters and never a dull one came from him. I liked and admired him immensely. I have written a book about him. I have talked with many of his friends. Yet I never plumbed the mystery of Jesse Stuart. He was a man who in passing left the most striking vignettes. Once I was driving him to Pittsburgh for a plane. We stopped at a country filling station for gas and I asked Jesse about Muff Henderson, a character in *Foretaste of Glory*, who was a "dancerholic" and had "two-stepped" three of his wives into the grave and had started on a fourth wife. "Was that based on a real man, Jesse?" I asked.

"Sure," he said. "That was ol' J———— W————." Jesse jumped out of the car, cocked his big black cigar in the corner of his mouth, cradled an imaginary seductive partner in his arms; saying "He danced like this," he went two-stepping around the concrete apron of the gas station in a perfect imitation of his fictional character. Jesse's zest and exuberance fascinated the attendant, who was so intrigued that he let the tank run over.

One could not be in his presence for five minutes without being aware of his titanic physical energy. Even after his heart attack, when he carried his nitroglycerine pills with him, Stuart impressed one with his inexhaustible energy. No ordinary physique could have withstood for thirty years the constant battering of heart attacks and two strokes that Jesse suffered. This unusual biochemistry manifested itself in his writing. Jesse loved everything about writing, including the physical act of writing. In making a grocery list, Naomi would write "crackers." Jesse would write "a box of crackers." Poetry he could write only with a pen, but for short stories he always used the typewriter. For years on end he wrote 4,000 letters a year. He was a veritable "Old Faithful" geyser in the sense that writing gushed forth from him in torrents like a great natural force.

In an early autobiographical sonnet, Jesse wrote, "I'm just a dirt-colored man," naming an earthy quality that I soon became aware of. A fine mist of nature blows from each of his books. He talked lovingly of his land, his conservation, his 100,000 trees he had planted. He loved the people of the earth. He was a Thoreau without the brakes on. He created mountain men who remind me of the peasants in the paintings of Brueghel the Elder.

Along with his streak of primitivism Jesse mingled a bit of hardheaded practicality and some of Ben Franklin's pragmatism. He got things done. He had a strong ego; he was a strong man. He made some enemies, and they were mostly in his own county. He did not shrink from them. He was a man of great personal courage and a strong sense of honor. He had friends in each of our fifty states.

Literary critics will not have an easy time with Jesse. He will be hard to pigeonhole. He is like Walt Whitman in this sense. It was natural that Jesse and Thomas Wolfe took to each other so easily when they met in New York. They are a lot alike. Stuart rebounded from the youthful romantic pessimism of *Man with a Bull-Tongue Plow* with a growing confidence and optimism. We see now how much he truly enjoyed life. He was a maker, a poet who said "yes" to life as he matured. He knew sickness, injustice, and death, but he still said "yes" to the bone-deep sweetness and diversity of life. He held off death longer than any man I have ever known. All of his life he avoided literary cliques and coteries. He swam alone. I believe his real and lasting reputation is still ahead of him. I miss him immensely and always will.

Jessamyn West

(18 July 1902-22 February 1984)

Ann Dahlstrom Farmer
Whittier College

See also the West entry in *DLB 6, American Novelists Since World War II*, Second Series.

NEW BOOKS: *Double Discovery* (New York: Harcourt Brace Jovanovich, 1980);
The State of Stony Lonesome (New York: Harcourt Brace Jovanovich, 1984).

PERIODICAL PUBLICATION: Jessamyn West, "Commencement Charge," *Whittier College Bulletin* (October 1956): 7.

Jessamyn West died 22 February 1984 of a massive stroke in Napa, California, at the age of eighty-one. She finished what was to be her last published work, the novel *The State of Stony Lonesome* (1984), in the spring of 1983 while battling the effects of an earlier attack of hepatitis and the onset of arthritis in her hands, the latter being particularly devastating to West because the physical pushing of pen against paper was crucial to her composing.

She was a prolific and varied writer in spite of a comparatively late publishing start at the age of thirty-six: twenty full-length works in eight forms —novel, autobiography, poetry, operetta, essay, science fiction, screenplay, and short story—as well as an anthology of Quaker essays and dozens of additional poems, short stories, and articles over a nearly unbroken forty-four-year span. She received a number of writer's awards and was granted honorary degrees from nine universities and colleges. Her books have been book-club selections and have appeared on the best-seller lists. The film *Friendly Persuasion* (United Artists, 1956), for which she was technical director and wrote a screenplay, won the Gold Palm Award at the Cannes Film Festival and was nominated for an academy award. She was the subject of a documentary film on her writing (*My Hand—My Pen*, Writers on Writing Series, Davidson Films) and of countless magazine and newspaper articles. Her anthology *The Quaker Reader* (1962) inspired Ned Rorem's major composition for the organ, *A Quaker Reader*. She taught classes and gave workshops in creative writing and was a coveted speaker and television talk-show guest. Robert Kirsch, of the *Los Angeles Times*, echoed the feelings of other reviewers when he called her "a treasure of [California's] literature, and, in fact, of the nation's" (18 November 1979). But, as Bill Crider has stated in *Dictionary of Literary Biography*, volume 6, "her work has been mostly neglected by academic critics. This is especially surprising in view of West's vivid, vigorous, and eloquent style and the compassion and humanity with which she treats the serious themes of her work."

It may be, as Crider has said, that academic

Jessamyn West

critics have ignored her *because* of her popularity, or it may be because she has rarely used symbolism. Academicians are fond of analyzing levels of meaning and positing symbolic relationships. West's attempts to provide these levels in *Leafy Rivers* (1967) were not well received. Her strongest tales, like her nonfiction work, involve characters who are complex, not because they represent several ideas but because they are realistic, many-faceted individuals. Perhaps now that her work is complete, it will be recognized for the achievement it is and she will be given her rightful place in American literature.

I do not think that West would ever have finished with storytelling, would have stopped writing, if arthritis in her left hand—her writing hand—and a series of strokes had not made her stop the year before her death. But her last two books were recapitulations, final looks at her own life and its meaning.

Double Discovery (1980) took West on a reexamination—via her letters and her journals—of her journey alone to Europe at twenty-seven. Although the book is a vivid recounting of her physical travels—the places she sees, the people she meets or observes—it is primarily a look into her mind and heart. The discovery she made was double because she found out who she was before she dared admit even to herself that she wanted to be a writer and who she had become some fifty years later.

She went to see England in order to "visit the home of poets and penmen," to "walk where heather and bracken *grew* and nightingales and cuckoos could be *heard*." At a friend's urging, she also visited Paris; she went to Ireland because her mother's ancestors came from there. But it was the unsatisfying Ireland trip that yielded two significant later visits, one to Timahoe with her second cousin Richard Nixon, which enabled her to give the reader a glimpse of the man behind the political offices, and one to Limerick that changed her life when she found by chance the eleven-year-old Irish girl, Ann McCarthy, that she and her husband Max would raise as their own. As Carolyn See said, "Jessamyn West quite gently reminds us that everything is an adventure—hiking through the French countryside with French spinsters, passing up wine in favor of lemon squash; traveling, going away—in order to return, turn back and find yourself" (*Los Angeles Times*, 12 December 1980).

In *The State of Stony Lonesome*, the novel published after her death, she returns to the setting of her own Yorba Linda childhood (here called Valencia). The narrator, Ginerva Chalmers, is more often than not Jessamyn at ages four, twelve and fourteen, sixteen and eighteen, the eldest child who mothers her brother and sister, a person whose fate it has been to be "drawn to the objects and persons and causes enhanced by [her] mother's emotions" and who, because of that, sometimes does not see the strong bond between her parents that underlies the quarrels and the differences. The story centers, however, on Ginerva's uncle Zenith McManus, a ladies' man, a successful Hupmobile dealer, a man who lost his first sweetheart to tuberculosis, his first wife to childbirth, and his second to divorce. In his loneliness and despair at the death of his sweetheart, he forms a special attachment to four-year-old Ginerva, and she to him, which lasts the rest of his life. Their mutual reminiscences, their "walk memories," when he is in one of his own tubercular relapses and she is eighteen, give the story its structure and trace the emotional growth of both of them. The story is written as fiction, but in it West has revisited the southern California landscape she had always considered home, and she has looked again at the relationship of her mother and father and at the bond between herself and her favorite uncle. Julian P. Muller, her Harcourt Brace

Jovanovich editor for over twenty years, considers *The State of Stony Lonesome* a "fitting valedictory."

The retrospective view of *Double Discovery* and *The State of Stony Lonesome* poses the larger question—how did West view herself as a writer? Without qualification, West thought of herself as a writer: not a woman writer or a Quaker writer or a Western writer. Nevertheless, the emphases of the pioneering spirit and the beliefs of the Quakers are apparent in her writing, as are the concerns of Henry David Thoreau, the only author whose influence she acknowledged.

Frederick Jackson Turner defined the Western spirit, which also permeates the literature of the American West, as "a spirit of determination, of endurance, of independence, of ingenuity, of flexibility, of individualism, of optimism." Most of these qualities are also important in Quaker tradition. The beliefs that God is love and that He dwells in every human become, in a logical extension, belief in individual worth and responsibility, in the equality of men and women, and in an optimism about the human condition. The religious view, then, subjugates the possibilities of evil and gives reason for the optimism.

When West "discovered" Thoreau's work during her Berkeley graduate school days, she felt she'd found a kindred spirit. Not only was the transcendentalist an individualist committed to the freedom of the human spirit and a practicer of civil disobedience; he also prized two things that she had long prized, solitude and journal-keeping as enhancers of observation and introspection. These influences have found their way into Jessamyn West's work, although their treatment is always uniquely her own.

One of her contributions—most directly connected to Thoreau's observations of nature—has been her descriptions of first the land and climate of the Midwest and then of southern California. Almost no one else has written of the outlying areas of Los Angeles and Orange counties in the first half of the twentieth century, and certainly no one has done it better. Her feeling for this landscape is fully expressed in *South of the Angels* (1960) where the character Shelby Lewis mirrors her thoughts on the merits of Southwestern landscapes above others: "always been . . . moving west since I was born, toward my rightful home. He felt strangled, remembering all that greenery back East, like a man held down by weeds under water who suddenly breaks free and rises to the surface." West pictures, too, the land's change from virgin hills to cultivated groves: "The land that had been free to voyage

silently under the stars . . . was going to be made to earn its keep like any yoked oxen." And in *The State of Stony Lonesome* that same land at the end of summer: "August heat waves ris[ing] above the foothills like visible exhalations of crouched and panting animals. . . . cactus, sagebrush, and winter's green grass bleached now in August, bone-dry and bone-colored."

In *The Life I Really Lived* (1979), her description of Montebello's outskirts in the 1940s is equally accurate and vivid.

> Our house was peculiar to begin with; the location . . . even more peculiar. The land on the south side of the road, which ran between Los Angeles and the towns of Orange county, had been dairy country. It still was. A big white barn, with its loft and pulley for storing hay, its ground floor with many stalls, stood near us. The dairy herd had diminished. A gas station, a couple of oil derricks, a half-dozen new but ramshackle houses took up the space where cows had once grazed. . . . Our house, a raspberry-pink stucco that in the thirties was called "Spanish," had belonged to the dairy manager. . . . The only tree on the place was a weeping willow, dusty, forlorn, as melancholy to look at as its name.

West believed that the most important search anyone could make is the search for self, to learn what "feelings, beliefs, and convictions" he holds, and once having found them, to have the courage and integrity to be true to them. She asked no less of her characters. They are individuals: none is subservient to a theme or to another character, unless that subservience is part of their nature. West does not ask them to speak for the Society of Friends or for euthanasia, for Indians or for love, but for themselves. They may find themselves in relationships and situations common to all of us, but their ways of dealing with them are their own; their personal problems arise when they deny that individuality.

A number of her women characters confront their own sexuality, particularly Cate Conboy in *The Witch Diggers* (1951) and Leafy in *Leafy Rivers*. Cate's experiences—witnessing the severe and unjust punishment of her younger sister's innocent endeavor to help satisfy the appetites of a peeping tom, seeing her brother's castration of his wife's uncle for his incestuous relations with the wife, learning of her father's adultery, and becoming aware of her own desires for Christian Frazier— lead her to suppress her sexual self as evil, which triggers the story's final tragic events. On the other hand, Leafy, in learning to accept her awakening

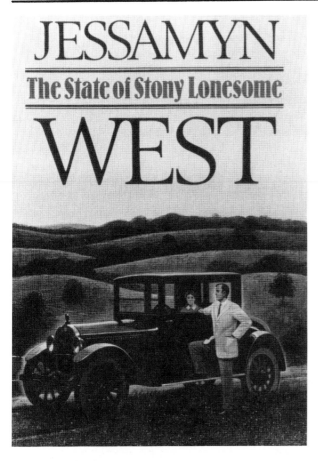

Dust jacket for Jessamyn West's last novel, published posthumously in 1984

sexuality, saves and enriches her marriage.

One of West's most controversial themes was euthanasia, which she first tackled in the fictional *A Matter of Time* (1966), and which received a good deal of criticism. Ten years later she revealed in the autobiography *The Woman Said Yes* (1976) that the alliance of two sisters in ending the cancer-filled life of one of them was identical to the alliance West and her sister Carmen made and carried out. The public outcry was even greater. True to West's belief in the individual, she considered both the fictional and the factual accounting to be about personal choice, not about a general recommendation.

Perhaps West's greatest strength is the sense of reality with which she imbued her characters and her stories. Her desire to make her stories believable, to seem real, was a paramount one. She wanted her readers to "write" with her, to see the several possible endings there could be at any turn just as there are several possible outcomes at any stage in a life. She amended the writing-only-what-you-know advice to include the imagination as the

world best known. Just as Emily Brontë knew no Heathcliff, West did not know the Birdwells of *The Friendly Persuasion* (1945) or the Chases of *The Life I Really Lived*—except in her mind. She was so successful in creating reality in the latter that many readers and a number of critics still feel that it was primarily autobiographical. When she was asked by Nick Williams for the *Los Angeles Times* (13 January 1980) whether or not *The Life I Really Lived* was her life, she answered, "Of course it is. Not that any of it happened to me, but I lived it while I wrote it. All writers do that—they become, as they write, their characters reembodied. They have to feel all of it, suffer all of it, enjoy all of it, or reality won't come out of what they write."

Her ability to do this was enhanced by her use of solitude as a way of looking both outward and inward and by the journals she kept throughout her life where she relived at least part of each day in order to experience it completely. The result is that her two realities—of the world and of the mind—become one reality for her readers. We eat Jess's tangy apples and feel the throb of the organ when his fingers first touched the keys; we hear with Cress the "sullen, hollow suck" of the oil well pumps on Kettle hill; we walk the arroyos with Asa and mark the California seasons with insect habits; we swoop with Lute out toward Ora from the scaffold; cry out with Orpha, "Oh, it was a wonder time!" and know that it was so.

West began her writing life by making the Birdwells and a small section of nineteenth-century southern Indiana real. As she continued to observe, to live, to write, she made not only the Midwest but southern California—indeed, the human condition—real as well. She is the best example of her own words: "Fiction reveals truths that reality obscures."

Reference:

Ann Dahlstrom Farmer, *Jessamyn West*, Western Writers Series, no. 53 (Boise, Idaho: Boise State University, 1982).

Papers:

A collection of Jessamyn West's manuscripts, journals, letters, and other materials is at Whittier College.

A TRIBUTE

from ANN CASH

I had just come back from the store after getting some snuff for two old women and I was sitting with them on the O'Hallerans' steps in front of the Castle Barracks where I lived. I remember feeling it was a good day.

My friend Marie Kerwin came along and asked me if I would go uptown with her. I said I didn't think so. Actually my mother didn't want me to play with her that day. Also I didn't have any money for the bus, so I said no. Somehow Marie talked me into it.

We waited for the bus, I had already figured out a way in my head how I could ride for free. I went to the second level of the double-decker bus, hid under the seat until the conductor went by. It worked.

Marie and I managed to get uptown. But as we were heading towards Woolworth's Marie saw her grandfather. He must have scared her. Next thing I knew she was yelling that she would see me later. I went into Woolworth's and decided to wait for her by the front door. There was a weighing scale just to the right of the door and a woman in a green raincoat with a lot of packages wanted to weigh herself. I asked her if I could hold her packages for her. She gave them to me to hold. I was preoccupied with finding Marie so I quickly gave the woman back her packages and went outside to wait for Marie. There were musicians playing. The lady came up to me and asked me if I would give them the money she had in her hand. I did. She asked me then if I would like to have tea with her. By then Marie had shown up so she took us both for tea. She seemed nice. I liked her. Since my father had died I was something of a street kid and I was used to meeting strangers, especially Americans. It did not seem unusual to me to be going out to tea with a stranger.

At tea, she told us her name was Jessamyn West, that she was a writer and that her husband, Max, was a superintendent of schools. I told her my mother was a widow, that my father died when I was six and left my mother with six children and that she scrubbed floors and earned fifty cents a day.

I met Jessamyn for dinner that night. The next night she had my mother to her hotel for dinner. All the next week I went to Jessamyn's hotel room. I told her Irish stories and sang Irish songs for her. She was magic to me. I loved the freckles on her hands. Her rings—from Mexico, she told me— were unlike the plain wedding bands of Irish women. The stones were so exotic and large. She even smelled wonderful. I was fascinated with her.

My mother told Jessamyn what my life would probably be like if I stayed in Ireland. I would probably end up like my mother, living in one room with at least six kids. My future looked pretty grim.

My mother told me recently that we didn't live just from day to day, that we lived from meal to meal.

The following week after our meeting, Jessamyn had called her husband and told him that she wanted to take me back to Napa Valley to live with them. He thought she had lost her mind. However, he came to Ireland to meet me. Jessamyn got her way and despite enormous obstacles I did go to Napa Valley with my sister to live with Max and Jessamyn.

Jessamyn has since told me that when she gave me the money to give to the musicians she expected me to run away with it. She said I looked like I needed the money more than the ragged musicians. She remembers me wearing a short-sleeved dress on a wintry Irish day and looking blue from the cold.

There are probably reasons I will never know why at that time in Jessamyn's life an eleven-year-old, redheaded Irish girl would have such appeal for her. (She was fifty-six years old and never had any children.) But she fell in love with me and I fell in love with her.

It is now twenty-nine years later, she is gone, and I miss her. I can still feel her hand on my shoulder, guiding me, loving me and taking me out of the cold.

A TRIBUTE

from ALFRED COPPEL

It was a meeting of a group of readers and librarians in a San Francisco high school auditorium. It was also my first time before a group of more than a dozen and I was in a state of nerves. My prepared notes, when I looked at them, seemed to have been written in Sanskrit. When I asked, I was told that I would follow "Miss West" at the podium.

My confidence increased slightly. The nice Quaker lady could warm up the audience. Ready them for my words of wisdom. I had spoken to her briefly. She wanted to know "Are you getting paid?" I said no. "All right, then," she said. "Fair is fair. I'm not either." Right away I liked her.

Then she went to the lectern, flashed a sparkling smile at the audience, and proceeded to knock them out of their chairs with her warmth, her humor and her downright brilliance. She charmed them, captivated them. She had them—and me— eating, as they say, out of her hand.

I got through my own talk somehow. Jessamyn helped. She led the questioning, kept me alive. But I knew that anyone who was there would remember only Jessamyn. I think of her now as she was that night. Bright as a new coin, feminine as Sheba, ageless and delightful.

We became good friends. We seldom spoke about writing, but we talked a great deal about life. That was a subject she knew about. Her wisdom is in her books, along with that gentle, steely realism that makes her work glisten.

She was the only person I know who called me by my true name, Alfredo. She began that after I told her the story of my family's trek from Spain to Mexico to America. She said, "Write about that, Alfredo. It's what novels are made of."

Well, I've done it, but too late to have her read it. Still, her name is on the dedication page. It's a small gift to a great lady.

A TRIBUTE

from JACQUELINE KOENIG

Jessamyn West was the first writer I ever saw. On Sunday, 25 August 1974 I drove one hundred miles to Napa, California, where Jessamyn was the speaker at the dedication of the new Napa City-County Library.

It was the first time I heard her cackling laughter as she chatted animatedly with the Most Reverend Mark J. Hurley, seated next to her on the dais. I wonder if he was laughing later when she said if all the great buildings—church, school, or library—should burn, and you could save one, save the library and the books with all the thoughts on which to build back.

Jessamyn told us they could have asked so many to speak—the mayor, the state librarian, etc.—and they probably should have, but she understood the speaker had been chosen by computer. They fed into the computer such data as the person who had taken out the most books, the person who had kept the books the longest, the person who had had the most overdue books and who had paid the most fines, the person who had requested the most books from the state library, the person who had asked this question and that question by phone, and when the computer spat out its answer, she was the one! The crowd laughed and applauded.

Jessamyn said by the time she was twelve, like Abe Lincoln, she had read everything in the house, including a book on yeast and one on fruits such as gooseberries. Then her little town opened its first library, a closet in the local school, containing fifty donated books, which turned out to be more of the kind she had at home. But she stood barefoot before her father and asked for a dollar for a library card; with four other children requesting money, it was a big request, but he gave her the dollar. She dressed in something more suitable, put on shoes, and walked through the evening to her first library and checked out *The Trail of the Lonesome Pine*.

Following the dedication program, the librarian was presented with the key, opened the door, and everyone went inside the library except Jessamyn, who was again talking to the Reverend (maybe trying to talk her way out of burning churches), and the autograph seekers. Immediately, someone hurried out of the library and asked Jessamyn to join them inside, saying that she was wanted by the people conducting the day. But, not ignoring the line that had gathered on the outside podium for autographs, Jessamyn simply said not until she'd signed all the books. She said there's nothing an author enjoys more than signing her books; that's what it's all about. She did not hurry, either. She thumbed through to find the title page and signed just below the title, above the publisher's name. One of the dearest things to and about Jessamyn was the importance of books. Years later, when I wrote asking if I might mail two last books for signing to complete my signed set, she wrote me, "Agreeable and proud. You are smarter than I am. I haven't a signed First Edition set of my own books."

A man pushed in ahead of me to get his program signed for his wife. He told Jessamyn, "She loves your books." Jessamyn countered, "You don't?" He mumbled something about not being a reader, and Jessamyn demanded, "Why?" He said he had too much work to do. Jessamyn said to me, "I don't see why I should sign for someone who doesn't read my books, do you?" I assured, "Surely, after your fine talk, he will now become a reader." She did sign his program, but my, how she carried on about "*This man doesn't read my books!*" I'm sure the man was sorry he'd ever come near her.

When she did go inside, I admired her wonderful personality. She shook hands and talked to everyone and to their children.

Jessamyn's attire was understatedly elegant. Everything looked like I. Magnin. She was dressed flawlessly appropriate to the occasion in a conservative dress that was just below her knees and revealed a very nice figure without distracting the viewer from her piquant face and what she was saying. Red Skelton, when he was once interviewed by Mike

Douglas, said that before an appearance he always removes all his jewelry so that people's attention is not attracted to it rather than to his expressions and acts. Jessamyn apparently also subscribed to this same sentiment. She wore black patent pumps and carried a lovely summer bag. Her hair was stylishly short and very curly.

Six years and four books later, I returned to Napa to see Jessamyn at Bookends Book Store, where she was signing her new book, *Double Discovery*. She had aged noticeably—even the signing seemed difficult for her—but at seventy-eight, her mind was sharp and her personality bubbly, and she was still telling stories. She was one of the finest storytellers who ever lived.

This being 22 November 1980, people were buying *Double Discovery* for Christmas gifts. Jessamyn was a celebrity in her hometown. Some were buying the book for people who lived away and they wanted to say they'd seen her. One said, "I wanted to meet you; I'm your neighbor." Jessamyn responded to the effect, "Do come and see us. My husband will show you the garden. I am working and can't come out." However, later the same day one lady gave Jessamyn snapshots of Jessamyn in Jessamyn's garden, so apparently she did break from her important work and come out sometimes (perhaps more than she should have).

Barnaby Conrad's neighbor couldn't believe Jessamyn didn't remember her. She said, "But we had dinner together three nights in a row." Jessamyn remembered the visit to the artist's but said she was terrible at remembering people. The lady wouldn't give up, saying, you must remember this? That? And this other thing? "No, no, no," Jessamyn was not to be shaken.

And there were those who came to meet someone who had been on the Dick Cavett show and all they talked about was how she looked. Jessamyn said one lady wrote her, "You won't burn in hell for helping your sister die, but the hairdresser who did your hair for the show will." Jessamyn kept trying for a discussion of the show's content. She objected strongly because Cavett hadn't asked her any questions. She thought if he had her on the show, he should want to know something about her. Instead, she had to do all the talking. I told her I thought that's what Cavett wanted, because she was so good at that. Jessamyn was sure Cavett hadn't read her books and wasn't interested in her. (His staff had contacted Jessamyn and had asked her to come.)

She looked at me and asked, "You read Eudora Welty?" "Oh, yes," I replied. Welty was taped before or after Jessamyn, so they met. Jessamyn had read everything of Welty's and asked if she could send her collection to be signed through a niece who lives near Welty. Jessamyn said she knew Welty didn't want to have to talk to her niece for an hour, so she suggested she mail the collection directly to Welty and have the niece arrange for pickup.

Jessamyn was wearing a most remarkable necklace. She told us she had had her mother's wedding ring, her sister's wedding ring, and her own (which she'd outgrown) as well as a cross which had belonged to her mother. Jessamyn said even though her mother was a Quaker, she liked the cross in jewelry. A welder suggested to Jessamyn one day that these pieces should be enjoyed and used, and he welded the three rings to the ends of the cross and put a chain attachment on the top of the cross. It is a lovely piece.

Jessamyn West is the most remarkable woman I've ever read about, real or fictional. Born just after the turn of the century into somewhat Victorian, unworldly circumstances, she accomplished things when she'd never actually known anyone else who did them. She must have been fearless. In her life and her work, she perfected a combination of intelligence, toughness, determination, compassion, talent, beauty, kindness, and love that is inspirational. She truly lived the life she really wanted.

A TRIBUTE
from EUGENE S. MILLS

When I think of Jessamyn West I recall her intelligence, her strength of character and her playful and humorous ways. She was always a person to be reckoned with, a strong and forceful woman who put herself into life's circumstances with courage and originality. I consider it a rare privilege to have known her personally during the final five years of her life.

A TRIBUTE
from BONNIE NIMS

The first time I saw Jessamyn—one perishing hot day in the summer of 1949—she arrived with my husband at our house in Indiana carrying an armful of day lilies. Their russet and gold petals bore a striking resemblance to Jessamyn's own coloring. "I brought them for you," she said. "I made John stop beside the road so I could pick them. Day lilies—hundreds of them—growing along the ditches!"

She followed me into the kitchen where I rooted around for a very large vase. "I'm putting you to a lot of trouble," she said, "for a bunch of wildflowers. But they seem so wonderful to me. Flowers don't grow like that in the part of California I come from."

I assured her that the flowers were no trouble, that I, too, thought they were wonderful—for I had grown up in Southern California where ditches brimmed with muddy irrigation water and offered no flowers. "But I like it there."

"I do, too," she smiled. "And I like it here."

We soon discovered that we had many things in common besides a California childhood. We both suffered from awe-inspiring migraine headaches as our mothers had before us (they called them "sick headaches"). We found nearly all solemn occasions painfully funny, and all people—even those we didn't like—worthy of attention and study.

We cherished many of the same books. Jessamyn, of course, had read tons more than I. Some books she read over and over again. Especially Thoreau. She liked to copy Thoreau's journals into her own. "Writing down his words helps me feel what he is saying." When she introduced me to the writing of Eudora Welty, she told me, "Sometimes I think God, in His Love, created me to read Eudora Welty."

We agreed about all the important things, but hardly ever about the things that weren't: Campari—Jessamyn thought it tasted the way poison *should* taste. Lying in the sun—either worsened my migraine or started up a fresh one. Crossing bridges—scared Jessamyn. Flying in a plane—scared me. We thoroughly enjoyed our disagreements and the endless, pointless debates that they gave rise to.

When Jessamyn came to visit us shortly after we'd set up housekeeping in Italy, I told her that this was a place where it was perfectly all right to stare. "What a civilized country!" she said. "I have never understood why it is considered polite in America to look the other way as soon as you've found something you really want to see." Later, after Jessamyn had gone and I'd gotten to know the Italians better, I learned that the privilege of staring is reserved only for the natives. Foreigners who did so made a *brutta figura*. But I have no regrets about what I told her. Jessamyn—unaware of public opinion—staring away to her heart's content, enjoyed her visit so much more than she would have without my misinformation.

Jessamyn had a nature that wasn't content with just knowing. She had to feel what she knew, and she did. When our two-year-old son Georgie was dying of cancer, Jessamyn went way beyond sympathizing. She suffered right along with us. It is quite possible that she suffered even more than we did. For we were there and able to act as well as to feel. We had the privilege of being both Martha and Mary. We had no time to feel sorry for ourselves. But Jessamyn, in far-off California, did. She felt sorrow for us all.

And when something good happened, when a new book of John's poems was published, Jessamyn felt that, too. She gloated, she crowed! She was all set to go on the road for a promotion tour. She was brazenly proud. It was deliciously embarrassing.

The wild lilies that Jessamyn brought me gave up the ghost soon after I'd found them a proper vase. But her other gift—her friendship—shines russet and gold, season after season, now and tomorrow. . . .

A TRIBUTE   *from CHRISTINA O'BRIEN*

The moment I found out that I had received a scholarship as an exchange student to a college in California, my decision was made to write my master's thesis on Jessamyn West. I had read *Cress Delahanty* and *Friendly Persuasion* long before I had even made up my mind to major in English and American studies. During my university years I kept reading other books of hers and was fascinated with her compelling style of writing, her deep insight into human relationships, and her depictive portrayal of Southern California.

I arrived in California in the fall, but I did not have the courage to contact her immediately. Not until I had done some thorough groundwork for my thesis did I feel brave enough to ask her for an interview. To my surprise I got a prompt reply with an open invitation to her home in Napa as soon as her busy schedule would permit. Three weeks later I received a luncheon invitation from her, as she was giving a speech in Sacramento which was rather close to the college I attended.

I met Jessamyn West for the first time on 30 March 1967 at 1:00 p.m. at the Senator Hotel in Sacramento. I think there was surprise on both sides. She had envisioned an interview with a blond blue-eyed German girl, maybe even with braids—I must have sounded terribly German in my letters — and I had imagined her to be a rather plain and very bookish-looking older writer. Not at all! Towards me walked a very vivacious, rather tall lady in a bright red coat and some very eye-catching fashion jewelry. She literally bubbled over with questions of this foreign student and finally gave way to telling me about the two girls she had brought over from Ireland. The description of their first days and weeks in California, their different expectations, and Jessamyn's and her husband's adjustment to this new experience was presented to me as an intriguing story. The storyteller was there right in front of me and over her very personal report of those first weeks spent with the two Irish girls (one of them became their daughter, the other returned to Ireland) I forgot to ask her all my very studious questions. Even Jessamyn realized that I hadn't had a chance to ask lots of typical interview questions and invited me again to her home, which in fact materialized a month and a half later.

However, on this March day, riding back to the college in a Greyhound bus, I had plenty of time to evaluate my first encounter with Jessamyn West. I realized that Jessamyn would have been bored if not a little irritated by my scholarly questions and that I took away with me an experience so much more valuable for my future writing and interpretation of her work. She had let me experience her true storytelling ability — a special talent that could turn an everyday event into a good tale.

A TRIBUTE

from PHILIP M. O'BRIEN

From the time of my first introduction to Jessamyn West in 1967 through later visits with her, both at home and in Whittier, my memory of her centers on the times in the course of a conversation when the storyteller emerged. It might be the casual mention of the wind, left-handedness, cats, or family; any of these could prompt a subtle change. She would become animated and a quality would enter her voice which was compelling, giving one a glimpse of the joy of her involvement in the process, making those times memorable. That is not to imply there was a change in personality, only a shift to something more vital to her, for it is my impression she was always very much herself.

Most of my contact with Jessamyn centered around the ultimate transfer of her manuscripts and library to Whittier College. It was clear early on that while deep within she recognized the value of her gift and even wished the project success, she was bothered by the notion it might be viewed as an attempt at self-approbation. Initially only the urging of her husband Harry McPherson persuaded her to make the necessary arrangements.

As a result of the foresight of Harry and Jessamyn and of their acting on that foresight, an unmatched, undispersed record of one writer's life's work resides at Whittier College. Virtually all of the manuscripts, a growing number of letters, and the books from which she drew her inspiration are all there for future generations to consult.

UPDATED ENTRY

James Gould Cozzens

(19 August 1903-9 August 1978)

R. H. W. Dillard
Hollins College

See also the Cozzens entry in *DLB 9, American Novelists, 1910-1945;* and *DLB Documentary Series 2.*

NEW BOOKS: *A Time of War: Air Force Diaries and Pentagon Memos, 1943-45*, edited by Matthew J. Bruccoli (Columbia, S.C. & Bloomfield Hills, Mich.: Bruccoli Clark, 1984);
Selected Notebooks: 1960-1967, edited by Matthew J. Bruccoli (Columbia, S.C. & Bloomfield Hills, Mich.: Bruccoli Clark, 1984).

On Thursday, 22 March 1923, nineteen-year-old James Gould Cozzens noted in his diary that his "boring complaint" concerning the travails of writing his first novel caused his friend Robert Hillyer to say "he's not sure I wouldn't do well to stop writing for awhile and I had to point out it would be easier—and more economical—to stop eating." Whatever other knowledge the young Cozzens may have lacked, he did know that writing was an essential part of his life, perhaps the essential part. He developed the habit of writing every day, and he continued to do so throughout his life until accident and illness cast him into an ever-deepening anhedonia which silenced him in his last years. But prior to that dark time, neither circumstance nor adversity—not even World War II—could keep him from his daily writing. When he could not work on his fiction, he wrote diaries and notebooks, and these two new books are drawn from that writing apart from his fiction: speeches and memos from his time in the Pentagon in the 1940s, diaries from that same time, and notebooks from the 1960s.

Cozzens had at different times considered making books drawn from this material, but, for a variety of reasons detailed in the prefaces to these two volumes and in Matthew J. Bruccoli's biography of Cozzens (*James Gould Cozzens: A Life Apart*, Harcourt Brace Jovanovich, 1983), he never put the books into publishable form. Bruccoli has now done the job for him, shaping the mass of manuscript (the 380-page, single-spaced war diary, the 189 Pentagon memos, and the ten notebooks) into two volumes which, although quite different each from each, are both extraordinarily interesting and valu-

able additions to the body of Cozzens's work.

James Gould Cozzens was the author of ten published novels when he joined the Army Air Forces in 1942, and he was naturally enough assigned first to the Training Literature Section of the Training Arts Directorate and then in October of 1943 to the Office of Special Projects, Office of Technical Information (later the Office of Information Services) at AAF headquarters in the Pentagon. At the OIS, he wrote speeches and articles for the Commanding General (H. H. "Hap" Arnold) and other generals on the Air Staff, and he also came to write a series of memos digesting information from the daily activity reports and the top secret in-and-out log on problems arising anywhere in the AAF that could possibly, by breaking into the news, damage the war effort or the Air Force in any way. "I think it unlikely," Cozzens wrote to General Hume Peabody in 1947, "that any one person in the Air Force was more fully and regularly advised of the scandals, misadventures and dirty deals which here and there enlivened the record." The memos were written for the Chief of the OIS but were also available to the offices of the Chief of Air Staff and the Commanding General, and after the war Cozzens learned that they were also being read by Robert A. Lovett, who was then Assistant Secretary of War for Air and for whom Cozzens had the greatest respect.

A selection of these memos (76 of the 189) has been reproduced in *A Time of War* (1984), interleaved with selections from Cozzens's diaries. Together they present a unique picture of the war, seen from near the top by an outsider, a citizen soldier and professional novelist possessed of the requisite intelligence and integrity to assimilate and make sense of the complex experience which he was lucky enough to be able to observe. Cozzens found in this great body of data the source and substance of his major novel *Guard of Honor* (1948), and it is easy to observe in *A Time of War* his growing awareness of the need for an artistic form of great complexity to enable him to express and interpret the "new acquist of true experience" which he was gaining daily. The complexity of his three postwar novels—*Guard of Honor, By Love Possessed* (1957), and *Morning Noon and Night* (1968)—a complexity of syntax and diction as well as of thought and overall form, may be traced directly to insights he gained during his time of war. And yet the value of this new book extends far beyond its merits as a literary or biographical document, for it offers historians and general readers alike great insight into many of the events of World War II and into the creation of the dangerous world in which we live today.

　　The diary portions of the book tell Cozzens's story, his movement into an unfamiliar situation at the Pentagon, his gaining control of his job, his encounters with the generals who were running the air war, and finally, at the war's end, his job burnout and his great yearning to get back to his real work at home. It also tells the stories of his coworkers, including those of the novelist Edward Newhouse and Miss Johnson, a young secretarial assistant whose almost archetypal Kansas naiveté is transformed by her time in the OIS into an ability to hold her own with the wisecracking men in the office. She roused Cozzens to admit that she was one of only two people he would miss after the war "for an agreeable youthfulness, and what are probably considerable qualities of character, or of essential simplicity and niceness in striking some balance between being everyone's pet and yet never taking the least advantage of it—always equally ready to be teased or kidded or to buckle right down and work as hard as necessary."

　　The diary also contains Cozzens's assessments of his superiors—Generals Arnold and Giles, Anderson, Hood, Eaker and LeMay, Norstad and many others. He is always amazed at Arnold's ability to ruin any well-written sentence while at the same time having the intelligence and skill to run such a massive operation as the AAF with such great success. He observes how Norstad's manner changes after getting his second star, and he describes a snarling, browbeating LeMay. Cozzens's novelist's eye serves him well in his portraits of these complex, capable, and self-contradictory men.

　　The memos are equally fascinating, and Bruccoli's selections allow us to follow certain stories from memo to memo to their end: the complicated history of the gaining of equal rights and privileges for black officers, the struggle for women fliers to gain the recognition that they were as capable as their male counterparts, the history of the poorly designed and even more poorly constructed B-32, the early stages of the American guided missile program which impressed Cozzens as "surely the

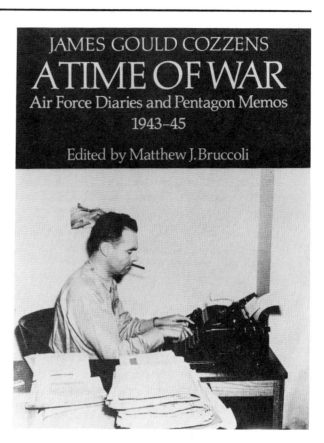

Dust jacket for Cozzens's private and official documents relating to his service at Air Force Headquarters during World War II

end of everything—not this time, but in twenty years or so when we try it again." The black officers' struggle was, of course, the source of *Guard of Honor*, but it stands on its own, with its mix of bigotry, hypocrisy, injustice, and sheer practicality, as a microcosm of the larger civil rights struggle which was to follow the war. That the AAF and the War Department in their own complicated and elephantine way finally moved to assert that the rules apply to all officers equally, regardless of their color or of local conditions, is a victory that should not be ignored in any history of the American quest for social justice. The story is told fully in *A Time of War*, and Cozzens's diary entries allow us to follow the evolution of his own thinking as the situation developed. There is a good deal to be learned from both accounts.

　　Scattered through the memos are also fragments of other important stories: the use of the atomic bomb, the development of jet planes, the gathering of Nazi rocket scientists into the American camp, the preparations for future inevitable confrontations with the Soviet Union, and many others. There is even one chilling note from John

G. Winant, the American ambassador in London, dated 29 September 1944, concerning Polish reports that extermination activities were increasing in German concentration camps; Cozzens's digest of the message (with his parenthetical comment) continues: "Can we bomb extermination chambers and barracks (what's the idea, help the Germans?), or can we warn Hitler some more? (Arnold answers it is up to Spaatz)." Spaatz was the commanding General, U.S. Strategic Air Forces in Europe, and this memo should be of great interest to scholars presently trying to ascertain at just what level of command decisions about not bombing the death camps were made. *A Time of War* should prove a treasure trove of valuable information and insights for historians seeking the clues that make larger history possible.

And yet, despite his almost unique opportunity to observe the goings-on of the Air Force, Cozzens is struck more than once by how little he really knows. On 6 October 1944, he admits that he is always astonished "by the revelation of how big or even enormous the AAF is—I mean that relatively speaking I am in a position to be very well-informed about it—and am—but there are all kinds of activities, all engaging a lot of people and all going on all the time, of which I'm completely ignorant." And on 2 March 1945 he discovers "again how little I really know about anything and how poor is my grasp of the principal preoccupations of the top echelon." These humbling revelations are at the heart of this book; they enable Cozzens to see what he is able to see much more clearly, for he is always aware of the unknowable "Big Picture" to which all the things he does know belong. He never loses his belief that the army was "all right, justly and reasonably run," but it becomes a belief chastened and strengthened by his knowledge of just how much was being done poorly, unjustly, and irrationally. No wonder, then, that Cozzens's wartime experience led directly to the complexities of the later novels.

In May of 1945, while speculating on how unsatisfactory film documentaries of combat are, Cozzens extended his thoughts into general aesthetic questions; the camera, he said, "is fast enough to get the action, and so the action is too fast to register in any real way on a person merely sitting in a projection room or a theatre—I suppose, in fact, it reduces to absurdity the whole 'true to life' theory—it reproduces, but it does not interpret." That sort of speculation on the nature of art, and on realistic art in particular, is the sort of thought which fills and makes Cozzens's notebooks from his

Williamstown period in the 1960s so interesting and valuable. Bruccoli has selected from those notebooks "most of the entries dealing with the practice of literature," and the result is an often cranky, often inconsistent, often brilliant, always challenging set of literary notes by an embattled literary artist, one who is keenly self-aware but extraordinarily sensitive to aesthetic values beyond the self.

The Cozzens of *Selected Notebooks* (1984) is a much older man than the author of *A Time of War*, and he is a man who, despite his protestations to the contrary, has been seriously injured both by the success of *By Love Possessed* and by the firestorm of adverse criticism and publicity which swirled around that success. While he started an abortive novel ("A Skyborn Music"), put his short-story collection (*Children & Others*, 1964) together, and wrote what was to be his last novel (*Morning Noon and Night*), he wrote ten notebooks, taking his frustrations and angers out in them, thinking seriously about serious things in them, observing himself and the world around him, and arguing with himself as well as that world.

The position Cozzens takes in the notebooks is that of a literary realist, yet with a difference. He praises the work of Somerset Maugham, Aldous Huxley, and H. G. Wells; he finds little to praise in the work of Henry James, Virginia Woolf, James Joyce, Henry Miller, or Norman Mailer. He praises the craft of John O'Hara, but not his vision, and one of his comments on O'Hara's work offers an approach to an understanding of Cozzens's idea of what realistic writing should be:

> He has an excellent ear, a good eye, and there's never even a hint of . . . affectation, fakery, and sentimentality in its various dishonest disguises. Yet the truth is, too much of the time he leaves me, let's say, discontented. Even granting that he's right, every one really is a son of a bitch; and his demonstrations are nothing but truth, you (or I) keep feeling they aren't the whole truth. He tells you *what* as well as possible: but left out is, I suppose probably because it doesn't interest him; but possibly because some odd failure of insight keeps him from being able to see, the *why* which alone can make all of this meaningful.

O'Hara, like the documentary camera, reproduces a portion of the truth, but does not interpret, does not see or indicate the larger truth which surrounds that portion.

Throughout these notebooks, Cozzens praises

the realist's craft; he demands surface clarity, without recourse to metaphor, and factual accuracy, but he also demands a complexity of interpretive understanding which goes far beyond that craft. On the one hand he can say that "if any fact is pertinent, state it exactly in plain words," while on the other hand he can say that "if 'simplicity' involves any sacrifice of the truth, of the significance, of a statement, simplicity just isn't worth it." Not simplicity, then, but complexity expressed with clarity, or, as he puts it in a discussion of Dreiser, "If every word isn't explicit and clear—not to be confused with clear-and-simple: in this life the simple may tell some truth but it never tells anything like the whole truth—don't believe a word of it."

What he asks, again and again, from literature is what Milton called a "new acquist of true experience," and that acquist is obtainable only by a clear-eyed intelligence working with clarity of craft, a literature of "adult experience and a grown-up mind." At the same time he knows that his particular judgments of other writers' work (and theirs of his) are highly suspect despite the certainty of his general aesthetic position: "I've long felt that any novelist's estimate of a novel is bound to be so limited and conditioned by the kind of work he finds himself able to do that opinions he may form about another novelist's novel are worthless: and he should always keep them to himself." As was the case in his Air Force diary, Cozzens is never unaware in these notebooks of what he does know and, more importantly, how much he does not know or understand. His position is always balanced by an honest awareness that it is just that—a position. This double vision allows him to be bluntly honest in his opinions, but also in his opinion of those

opinions. His stance is both enlightening and appealing.

Both of these new books throw a great deal of light on Cozzens's life and his personality, but they also remind us of larger values beyond the personal: the wary and the vastness of the human social organism on the one hand, and the work of James Gould Cozzens, the major American novelist, on the other. After speculating in the notebooks on the light that Oscar Wilde's homosexuality, or Maugham's or Waugh's, might throw on their work, Cozzens moves on to a statement that the reader of his diaries and notebooks should constantly remember:

> If the reader's at all perceptive, the work in its plain bias, is telling him what 'knowledge' of the writer's private life could merely confirm. The 'significant light' is thrown on the work by the work. If a book is any good, it's good in itself: and what the author may have been like couldn't matter less.

What the knowledge of Cozzens's life and private thoughts in both *A Time of War* and *Selected Notebooks* confirms is what readers of his novels have known all along, that he is an extraordinarily intelligent and honest writer, able to see the "son of a bitch" in himself and in those around him and still able to go far beyond that narrow sense of self to an art of genuine complexity, compassion, and mature insight. We owe Matthew J. Bruccoli a debt of gratitude for editing and publishing these books; they are of major significance both to American literary history and to American history in general. They both offer us new acquist of true experience.

New Entries

Mary Antin

(13 June 1881-15 May 1949)

Susan Koppelman

BOOKS: *From Plotzk to Boston* (Boston: W. B. Clark,
  1899);

The Promised Land (Boston: Houghton Mifflin,
  1912; London: Heinemann, 1912);

*They Who Knock at Our Gates: A Complete Gospel of
  Immigration* (Boston: Houghton Mifflin,
  1914).

PERIODICAL PUBLICATIONS:

FICTION

"Malinka's Atonement," *Atlantic Monthly,* 108
  (September 1911): 300-319;

"The Amulet," *Atlantic Monthly,* 111 (January
  1913): 177-190;

"The Lie," *Atlantic Monthly,* 112 (August 1913): 177-
  190.

NONFICTION

"First Aid to the Alien," *Outlook,* 101 (29 June
  1912): 481-485;

"How I Wrote 'The Promised Land,' " *New York
  Times,* 30 June 1912, p. 392;

"A Woman to Her Fellow-Citizens," *Outlook,* 102 (2
  November 1912): 482-486;

"His Soul Goes Marching On," *Berkshire Courier*
  (Great Barrington, Mass.), 14 May 1925;

"The Soundless Trumpet," *Atlantic Monthly,* 159
  (May 1937): 560-569;

"House of One Father," *Common Ground,* 1 (Spring
  1941): 36-42.

Mary Antin is the author of *The Promised Land,*
a best-selling autobiography that went through thirty-four editions and sold nearly 84,000 copies before her death. Published in 1912, *The Promised
Land* is a passionate account of a young girl's physical, intellectual, spiritual, and emotional journey
from the medieval Pale of Jewish settlement in Russia where she was born to the early twentieth century in the United States. It was one of the most
popular immigrant autobiographies of all time and
catapulted its author to national fame. For five
years after its publication, Antin traveled from city
to city in the U.S. speaking on behalf of open immigration and patriotism.

Mary Antin was born in Polotzk, Russia, in
June 1881, three months after the assassination of
Czar Alexander II, which triggered a series of pogroms that spread to 160 communities in southern
Russia in the course of one year. The government's
position that the misery of the peasants resulted
from exploitation by the Jews and that the pogroms
were the natural expression of the peasants' anger
led Alexander III, in 1882, to issue the infamous
May Laws which resulted in wholesale expulsion of
Jews from the villages and towns of the Pale. A mass
immigration to America began. Between 1881 and
1914, 2,250,000 Jews, the Antin family among
them, came to the promised land.

Esther Weltman Antin, Antin's mother, had
come from a family unusually prosperous for the
Pale. She provided her daughter with a model of a
woman with intellectual aptitude, ambition, and
energy as well as the competence to earn a living in a
competitive business world. Both Esther Antin and
her mother, who had taught her daughter to write,
were inclined toward study. Antin wrote about her
mother's struggle for an education in *The Promised
Land:* "at the age of ten, [she went] into her father's
business as his chief assistant. . . . My grandfather
was obliged to admit that the little learning she had
stolen was turned to good account, when he saw
how well she could keep his books, and how
smoothly she got along with Russian and Polish
customers. . . . He . . . let her take up lessons
again. . . . at sixteen [she] was . . . unwilling to think
of marriage . . . for already she had everything she
desired, especially since she was permitted to
study."

However, marriage was not a matter about
which Esther had a choice. Based on Israel Antin's
reputation as a scholar and his expected future
development into a distinguished rabbi, a marriage
contract was entered into between the two families.
Israel Antin came from an impoverished family
whose chief pride was his scholarly distinction. In
Antin's words, as a prospective bridegroom he "had
reason to rejoice. . . . He was going into a highly
respectable family, with a name supported by prop-

erty and business standing. The promised dowry was considerable. . . . The bridegroom would have years before him in which he need do nothing but eat free board, wear his new clothes, and study Torah. . . ."

But soon after the marriage the confusion that had made brilliant scholarship and piety appear to be one was clarified, and it became apparent that Israel "was not going to develop into a rav. . . ." He was ordered by his father-in-law to assume support of his family. With no training or experience as a wage earner, he tried and failed at several occupations. Finally, he left Polotzk to spend three years wandering Russia, seeking his fortune. Just as he was about to send for his family, which by now included two daughters, Esther's father died and left her his business, which for a time she managed with great success.

During the three years Israel Antin had been away from home, he had observed and learned much: "the ideal of a modern education was the priceless ware that my father brought back with him. . . . He resolved to live . . . the life of a modern man. And he saw no better place to begin than with the education of the children. . . . My mother was one with my father in all his plans for us. . . ." During these years, two more children were added to the family.

Then both of her parents became seriously ill. There was no money coming in and much money going out for "cures that did not cure." During the years of illness, their business was ruined. When health returned, they were unable to rebuild their business: "everything went wrong, till at last [my father] made a great resolve to begin life all over again. And the way to do that was to start on a new soil. My father determined to emigrate to America."

Israel Antin left Russia in 1891. He was not financially successful in the New World. Three years later, with the aid of a Jewish benevolent society, Esther Antin with her four children under the age of twelve made the 9,000-mile trip from southern Russia to Boston. The family lived in the immigrant slums of Boston, moving many times before settling in the South End. There were several more business failures, and Esther and Israel Antin barely managed to support their children.

Israel had written to his family in Russia repeatedly that in America "Education was free. . . . comprising his chief hope for us children, the essence of American opportunity, the treasure that no thief could touch, not even misfortune or poverty." But poverty could touch that treasure. On the day that Mary and the younger Antin children be-

gan school, the oldest daughter, Fetchke, or Fannie, as she was known in America, went to work in a sweatshop. Mary recalled that morning in *The Promised Land:* "If there was anything in her heart besides sisterly love and pride and good-will, as we parted that morning, it was a sense of loss and a woman's acquiescence in her fate; for we had been close friends, and now our ways would lie apart. Longing she felt, but no envy. She did not grudge me what she was denied." The tender generosity of Fannie Antin toward her sister Mary on this morning characterized her attitude toward Mary all their lives.

Mary Antin was an avid student who learned English quickly and completed the first five grades of school in six months. One of her teachers, Mary S. Dillingham, was responsible for Antin's first publication: she submitted "Snow," a 250-word composition, to *Primary Education* four months after Antin had started school. Fired by seeing her name in print, Antin determined to become a writer.

Within five years, by the time she was eighteen, Antin had her first book in print. She had written letters in Yiddish to her uncle Moses in Polotzk describing the journey from Russia to Boston. There are varying stories describing the events leading up to the 1899 publication of *From Plotzk to Boston.* The translated letters were published first in installments in Philip Cowan's New York-based periodical, the *American Hebrew.* Through the Hebrew Industrial School, which had been founded by wealthy German-Jewish Americans to help children and young girls from immigrant families learn a trade and become self-supporting, Antin had come to the attention of the Hecht family, prominent Boston Jewish philanthropists and social reformers. Lina Hecht, a member of the board of directors of the school and one of the organizers of the Combined Jewish Philanthropies of Boston, and her niece Hattie took a special interest in Antin because of her intelligence and her literary ambitions, which they encouraged. In their home Antin met Solomon Schindler, an eminent Reform Rabbi and social activist who helped her with the translations of the letters. They also introduced her to Mrs. Philip Cowan, who was impressed enough with the girl's work to see that it was published. The Hechts also brought Antin's work to the attention of Israel Zangwill, the distinguished English-Jewish novelist and Zionist, who agreed to write the introduction to *From Plotzk to Boston.* Antin dedicated the volume to Hattie Hecht. The book and the circumstances surrounding its publication brought Antin into intimate contact with some of the most wealthy, cultured, and reform-minded Jewish families on the East Coast.

Benefiting from the example of her mother, the generosity of her sister, the imaginative and dedicated teaching of Mary Dillingham who remained her friend and confidante, and the practical support of Lina and Hattie Hecht, Antin was saved from the sweatshops and elevated to renown. *From Plotzk to Boston* was a volume with two purposes. The proceeds from its sales were destined to keep the girl in school, but the role the book was expected to fill among readers was a propagandistic one. As Israel Zangwill wrote in his introduction: "Mary Antin's . . . debut in letters. . . . happens to possess an extraneous value. For, despite the wave of Russian immigration into the United States, and despite the noble spirit in which the Jews of America have grappled with the invasion, we still know too little of the . . . magic vision of free America that lures them. . . . Mary Antin's vivid description of all she and her dear ones went through, enables us to see almost with our own eyes how the invasion of America appears to the impecunious invader. . . ." The young girl's letters were being used to placate those Americans who felt threatened by the wave of Russian-Jewish immigrants.

Josephine Lazarus, an essayist of note, daughter of a distinguished New York Sephardi family, and the sister of Emma Lazarus, reviewed the book for the *Critic*, commending the "artless narrative" and "peculiar charm, at once childlike and mature" but warning of the danger to the young and gifted writer of forced blooming and "injudicious and indiscriminate praise." She wanted to preserve Antin's unself-conscious youth and save her from being used, even for a noble cause. She was to become Antin's mentor.

Antin was permitted to continue in school and enrolled at Boston Latin School for Girls, the public preparatory school for Radcliffe. It was during those high-school years that Antin became active at the Hale House, the South End settlement house of Edward Everett Hale, well-known man of letters and liberal minister. He invited her to his home to use his library, and Ellen Day Hale, his daughter, a painter, hired Mary to sit for a portrait, thereby enabling her in another way to contribute to the family's perpetually unsolved problem of how to pay the rent.

Antin joined the Natural History Club at Hale House and, along with the other members, enjoyed professionally escorted walks along the Atlantic coast on weekends. One of the lecturers on these occasions was Amadeus William Grabau, a German-

American Lutheran geologist and paleontologist doing graduate work at Harvard. The two fell in love. They were separated for a year, during which Grabau, having completed his doctoral work, taught at Rensselaer Polytechnic Institute. The couple reunited and married in Boston on 5 October 1901. Grabau was then thirty-one years old, and Antin twenty.

The Grabaus moved to New York where Amadeus had been appointed a lecturer at Columbia University. Mary enrolled at Barnard, became a special student because of ill health after the first semester, and after the third semester transferred to Teachers' College but did not complete a degree. Never healthy, she apparently began suffering from severe digestive problems. Such problems were then seen as psychological, and she accepted this diagnosis, describing herself as a "nervous invalid."

During these years, Josephine Lazarus and the Cowans introduced Mary to many distinguished literary and intellectual figures. She continued her education through their mentorship, and Lazarus urged her to write her autobiography. When, on 21 November 1907, the Grabaus' only child was born, Mary named her Josephine Esther after the two most important women in her life: Josephine Lazarus and Esther Weltman Antin.

Josephine Lazarus's death in 1910 spurred Mary Antin Grabau to write. Between September 1911 and April 1912, the *Atlantic Monthly* published five articles that later served as the basis for *The Promised Land* and three short stories in which ethical and religious issues are central.

Mary Antin was a patriot who idolized George Washington and Abraham Lincoln and revered the documents containing the principles upon which her promised land was founded. Her patriotism, idealism, and zeal for assimilation were recognized by many reviewers as similar to the attributes of faith of a devout religious convert. Ultimately, however, her faith had to be measured against the realities of anti-immigration sentiment and racism that were becoming dominant in the United States at that time.

The Promised Land failed to change the exclusionist mood of the country, but it was a literary success that perhaps did ultimately allay some American fears of immigrants. It was widely read and favorably reviewed in many prestigious journals. Antin was compared with the best writers on immigrant life and the best American autobiographers: Benjamin Franklin, Jacob Riis, Carl Schurz, Booker T. Washington, and W. E. B.

Front cover for Antin's autobiographical plea for keeping America open to immigration

DuBois. Her book was praised as a "revelation of the material, intellectual, and spiritual wealth America possesses in her Jewish immigrants," as well as for the "thrill of pride" that any American would feel in the "unstinted tribute" to American democracy.

Lyrical in tone, the book is filled with the dreams of generations of oppressed, poverty-stricken sufferers in other lands and the dreams of generations of liberal and progressive American idealists and social reformers. The first half of the book describes Antin's childhood in Polotzk and the circumstances of that world as she knew it and as she came to understand it through family stories. Aware of the oppressions of superstition and ignorance, of Jews by Gentiles, of women by men, of the poor by the rich, Antin expresses her belief that in the promised land everything will be better. The second half of the book describes life in the promised land. Although she notices many things that

are not improvements, she either attributes them to hangovers from the past or disregards them because in a country with no restrictions imposed on the basis of race or religion or class origin, there exists the possibility of overcoming the social evils attendant upon poverty. Antin was convinced that free education, free libraries, and settlement houses were some of the tools immigrants needed to lift themselves above the remaining social evils; the citizenship that made her and those in her family fellows of George Washington and the friendships extended by the prominent people were others.

But all members of the Antin family did not benefit equally from the promise of the promised land; especially excluded from the new privileges were the two women to whom Antin was closest: her mother and her sister Fannie. She wrote about her mother: "My father gave my mother very little time to adjust herself. He was only three years from the Old World with its settled prejudices. Considering his education, he had thought out a good deal for himself, but his line of thinking had not as yet brought him to include women in the intellectual emancipation for which he himself had been so eager even in Russia. This was still in the day when he was astonished to learn that women had written books—had used their minds, their imaginations, unaided. He still rated the mental capacity of the average woman as only a little above that of the cattle she tended. He felt it to be a wife's duty to follow her husband in all things. He could do all the thinking for the family, he believed. . . . " And her sister's fate might best be described by recalling Antin's description of life in Polotzk. In describing visits to the public baths in the Pale, she remembered: "I always stopped . . . to visit the poor patient horse in the treadmill. I pitied this creature. Round and round his little circle he trod, with head hanging and eyes void of expectation . . . round and round, all solitary, never driven, never checked, never addressed; round and round and round, a walking machine, with eyes that did not flash. . . . How empty the existence of the treadmill horse. . . . As empty and endless and dull as the life of almost any woman in Polotzk, had I had eyes to see the likeness." Fannie's life in America was not much different from the one she would have had in Russia: years in a sweatshop, no education, an arranged marriage, a life of domestic drudgery in which she was allowed to make no decisions about the expenditure of her life's substance.

Perhaps the major difference between the life her mother and sister would have had in Russia and the life they had in the United States was this: Mary

Antin was privileged to benefit from their martyrdom. And, because she was a woman who always saw clearly that their fate might have been her own, her understanding of and gratitude for the good she received was always heartfelt.

Like all traditional Jews, she had been raised with a profound reverence for the Book and the Land. Like many Jews who lose their faith, she retained a sense that the original objects of the faith were still to be revered and considered sacred, but in the secular arena. So, in the worldly milieu, the Holy Book becomes all books; the *chedar* is replaced as a place of sanctity by the public school and the library; the Promised Land becomes not Zion but America. In this sense coming to America was, and for many immigrants still is, a religious experience. This sense of religious pilgrimage is captured in *The Promised Land*.

Most considerations of Antin's work have been from the perspective of the social scientist or historian. However, an autobiography is also a literary creation which shares many of the characteristics of prose fiction. The persona called "I" is a literary character created as much out of the imagination as from the memory of the writer. The voice of the author often speaks independently of the persona's "I." In *The Promised Land* the authorial voice comments on the role her impressions and imagination play in the creation of the work. Sometimes she eschews facts in favor of the impressions an event left on her imagination in order to be faithful to the perceived emotional impact rather than to the past factual reality. She also repeatedly emphasizes that there is a point to this autobiography: America and immigrants are good for each other.

Here, the author comments on her persona: "concerning my dahlias I have been told that they were not dahlias at all, but poppies. As a conscientious historian I am bound to record every rumor, but I retain the right to cling to my own impression. Indeed, I must insist on my dahlias if I am to preserve the garden at all. I have been so long believing in them, that if I try to see *poppies* in those red masses over the wall, the whole garden crumbles away. . . . I have nothing against poppies. It is only that my illusion is more real to me than reality. And so do we often build our world on an error, and cry out that the universe is falling to pieces if any one but lifts a finger to replace the error by truth." The distinction between Mary Antin and the persona "I" can be illustrated by comparing the compositional technique described in "How I Wrote 'The Promised Land,'" an article published in the *New York Times*,

with what is remembered of her habits by those who knew Antin. "I had no plan when I began . . . I put things down just as they came, and so grew the book. When it came to putting these fragments together, I found they fitted wonderfully well, considering their haphazard origin." This method of haphazard composition does not fit the evidence about how Mary Antin wrote and worked at her writing. Her daughter says that she "pored over her writing." Rose McKee, Antin's friend and confidante at Gould Farm in western Massachusetts, remember that Antin was almost obsessive in her attention to detail. Both McKee and Josephine Grabau Ross, in reminiscing about Antin, use the word *perfectionist*.

The *New York Times* article concludes: "A little rearrangement of the loose sheets, an introductory sentence here, a connecting phrase there, and the story fell into chapters that named themselves. . . ." Yet there are numerous letters to Ellery Sedgwick, editor of the *Atlantic Monthly*, in which chapters of *The Promised Land* were first published; judging by the editorial changes, authorial additions and emendations recorded in this correspondence, Antin's chapters hardly seem to have "written themselves."

The pose of spontaneity, insouciance, even, in regard to the art and craft involved in the writing of the book have to do with preserving the impression Antin wished to create with the book. Some of the facts were altered or shaded or "reinterpreted" for the purpose of making conclusions stronger. "I have already shown what a real thing is this American Freedom that we talk about and in what manner a certain class of aliens make use of it" is the essential purpose of the writing.

Modern critics have been quite harsh with Mary Antin. Ludwig Lewisohn described *The Promised Land* as facile and superficial. "To this day," he wrote in 1950, the year after her death, "we are embarrassed and grieved by novels of second-generation American Jews who carry the Mary Antin motif to morbid lengths of self-degradation, raging against their residual Jewishness." *The Promised Land* along with Laura Z. Hobson's *Gentleman's Agreement*, Michael Gold's *Jews Without Money*, and Jo Sinclair's *Wasteland* are all, according to Lewisohn, "quite without literary merit. . . . a frantic escape from Jewishness and Judaism." Another critic, Sarah B. Cohen, complains that the work lacks depth. "In her race for assimilation Mary Antin discarded the garment of Judaism which she refers to in her autobiography as the 'motley rags of formalism.' This religio-cultural strip-tease may have made her more appealing to her Gentile friends, but it certainly left her out in the cold as a profound writer of Jewish-American literature, or for that matter, any kind of literature."

It is true that Mary Antin was ambivalent about Judaism, but not about her identity as a Jew. As a woman and as a Jew, she had been subjected to two kinds of discrimination, and she had developed a dual sense of self with two corresponding sets of loyalties. Clearly she loved and was loyal to and found community with other women. And clearly she did not cease to think of herself as a Jew, especially during those times when it was most threatening to be a Jew. Her daughter and the memoirs of Rabbi Abraham Cronbach, who became her friend during a lecture tour that brought her to South Bend, Indiana, in 1915, testify that the major Jewish holidays were observed in Antin's household. Though she married a Lutheran and explored many forms of religion and religious philosophy, she never abandoned Judaism. But because the two identities were in conflict, she remained ambivalent about Judaism. Curiously, this ambivalence did not carry over to feelings about Christianity, although the two religious leaders in whose discipleship she spent her final years were both men whose spiritual training had been received from women: Meher Baba, whose first perfect master had been Hazrat Babajan, an aged Muslim woman, and Rudolf Steiner, who had studied with Annie Besant.

In *The Promised Land,* Antin frequently indicates an almost excruciating awareness of Judaism as a patriarchal tradition that limited opportunities and options for women. When describing the educational opportunities and privileges available to boys, she wrote, "No wonder he said, in his morning prayer, 'I thank Thee, Lord, for not having created me a female.' It was not much to be a girl, you see."

But as a Jew who had experienced the power and beauty of her tradition, she understood that "No empty forms could have impressed the unborn children of the Pale so deeply that they were prepared for willing martyrdom almost as soon as they were weaned. . . . The flame of the burning bush that had dazzled Moses still lighted the gloomy prison on the Pale. . . . the object of the Jew's adoration has been the face of God."

She might have been describing her own spiritual journey when she wrote: "many times . . . those who escaped from the Pale . . . excited by sudden freedom, thought to rid themselves . . . of every strand of their ancient bonds. Eager to be merged in the better world in which they found themselves the escaped prisoners determined on a change of mind, a change of heart, a change of manner. They rejoiced in their transformation, thinking that every mark of their former slavery was obliterated. And then, one day, caught in the vise of some crucial test, the Jew fixed his alarmed gaze on his inmost soul, and found there the image of his father's God." Mary Antin made a valiant attempt to keep her poppies, insisting they were dahlias. When Ludwig Lewisohn rages and disparages the work of Antin and Sinclair and Hobson, he is dismissing these complexities; he is either choosing to ignore the oppression of women inherent in Jewish history, custom, and religious practice, or he is endorsing it. The questions surrounding assimilation are particularly profound and perplexing for those who are oppressed by their own oppressed group and its traditions, who yet remain self-loving and self-loyal. Perhaps those who have the easiest time with these difficulties are those who do not face them, for whatever reason.

For Mary Antin, the promised land was a world in which these ambivalences might be transcended. For her, the promise of the democratic ideal was the promise of emancipation from all oppressions. She dedicated most of her time during the years between 1912 and 1918 to speaking engagements and political work. Her public lectures were first given under the auspices of the Progressive party, through the personal solicitation of Theodore Roosevelt, and later under private management. Her lectures, delivered throughout the United States, included "The Responsibility of American Citizenship," "How You and I Can Serve Our Country," "The Civic Education of the Immigrant," "The Public School as a Test of American Faith," and some on Jewish subjects as well, "Jewish Life in the Pale: A Lesson for Americans," "The Zionist Movement," "Songs of the Ghetto," and "God and His World."

She campaigned for Theodore Roosevelt in 1912 and Charles Evans Hughes in 1916. An enthusiastic propagandist, she described herself as a radical in "A Woman to Her Fellow-Citizens" (1912) and combined religious and political doctrines in her defense of Progressive politics.

During the years Antin toured the U.S., the Antin-Grabau household was efficiently and comfortably organized and run by Fannie Lasser, sister Fetchke of *The Promised Land,* who had by now divorced the husband to whom she had been matched. It was only because of sister Fannie's domestic competence that Antin was able to travel for months at a time. Antin earned between six and ten thousand dollars annually lecturing on what she termed the "unique spiritual mission of America" and on "reverence for the few who did exemplify prophetic citizenship—such as Jane Addams, Booker T. Washington, Lillian Wald, Jacob Riis." She spoke in temples and in prisons and before audiences from Carnegie Hall to Tuskegee Institute. In addition to lecture fees, she received royalties from her writing. Her husband was still earning the same salary, $2,500 a year, at which he had been hired by Columbia University, although he had been promoted to a full professorship. There is reason to believe that this disparity in financial success discomfited Professor Grabau.

In 1914, Mary Antin's third and last book, *They Who Knock at Our Gates: A Complete Gospel of Immigration*, was published. The book appeals for an immigration policy to "accord with the loftiest interpretation of our duty as Americans." Divided into three sections, the book deals with one of the following questions in each: (1) Has the United States the right to regulate immigration? (2) What is the nature of present immigration? (3) Is immigration good for the nation? In this book, Antin strikes what one reviewer calls "a new note of just criticism of social abuses which are not caused by the immigrant, but of which he is the victim. . . . she . . . shows the exploitation to which the immigrant is submitted and over which he has no control; yet because of which he is so unjustly blamed."

Another reviewer wrote that "this book does for the immigrant what Olive Schreiner has done for woman in *Woman and Labor;* both have expressed with a broad epic touch the inner cry of a group." The book ran in three installments in the *American Magazine*, March through May of 1914, before its publication in book form. In February of 1914, in announcing the upcoming serial, the editors first compared her work with William James's essay on "The Powers of Men" and then claimed, "These articles will make history. To find their equal you have to turn back to the half-century following the American Revolution, when men cared passionately for the Rights of Man and when they wrote with romantic fervor of Liberty, Equality, and Fraternity." Despite the enthusiasm of her publishers and many reviewers and the eloquence and power of the book and despite steady sales, the temper of the times militated against its success. In 1921 Congress restricted the immigration of "undesirable races" and "foreign defective germ plasm."

Meanwhile, the national agony was making itself felt in the Antin-Grabau household in Scarsdale, New York. Josephine Antin Ross recounts, "We fought the World War right in our house in Scarsdale. Mother was for the Allies and Father was for the Germans. . . . They saw what they were doing to me and finally agreed to separate for my sake." Before the United States entered the First World War, Antin was engaged in making speeches for the National Americanization Committee, the National Security League, and the U.S. Government Committee on Public Information. At the same time, wrote Hervey Shimer, a Columbia student of Grabau's, "People ceased studying German and even listening to German music. Doctor Grabau expressed his German sympathies rather forcibly with the result of the severence of his relations with Columbia University in 1919."

By 1918, Antin had become, in her own words, "a Jew, and a Zionist, and a student of Jewish movements." In 1918 she completed a manuscript entitled "The Apostate" which Sedgwick at the *Atlantic Monthly* said was too long to publish as a short story. Houghton Mifflin was interested in an expanded version to be published as a novel. She also wrote to Sedgwick about new stories bobbing around in her mind, ready to be written. However, "The Apostate" was never to see print as either a short story or a novel. And the stories were evidently never written.

Mary Antin suffered a breakdown in health that was to change the course of her life. She ceased her political activities and turned toward a search for health and spiritual direction. Although the ties with her family, especially her sisters, remained strong, she spent the rest of her life in a kind of domestic limbo, going from one rehabilitative facility for nervous invalids to another. For a while she was a resident patient at the Riggs Institute for the treatment of nervous disorders in Stockbridge, Massachusetts. Dr. Riggs was interested in a neighboring facility that had been founded in 1913 by William and Agnes Gould, who believed that through the power of love it was possible to establish the kingdom of heaven on earth. Riggs suggested that Antin visit Gould Farm and meet Will Gould, to see if the work and life there seemed of potential benefit to her. She became deeply attached to Gould and to the Farm and made it her home for many years. She brought her family to Gould Farm with her and shared intimately in all the Farm's concerns. One of Antin's services to the Farm was to introduce there people who "she thought would appreciate and benefit from it, while contributing to it, each in his or her own way."

Motivated to write a book about Will Gould and his work, Antin collected much material; in addition to taking notes on his conversations and sermons, she undertook a pilgrimage, largely on foot with a knapsack on her back, through the section of the Adirondacks where the Goulds had lived. Because she wanted to relate Gould's work to the story of Jesus and to the story of Christian community through the ages, she studied Ernst Renan and other theologians and historians of Christianity. She wrote and sent to Mrs. Gould a first chapter, but the book was never completed.

There were two final publications: a 1937 essay in the *Atlantic Monthly*, "The Soundless Trumpet," in which Antin discusses the nature of the mystical experience; and a 1941 essay in *Common Ground*, "House of One Father," in which she simultaneously reaffirms her solidarity with Jews past, present, and future, and refuses to allow herself to be stampeded by anti-Semitism back into some ghetto of the spirit.

Mary Antin's life is the model for a life of a woman nurtured, encouraged, and supported by a network of women. Women loved Antin, from the time of her fragile girlhood full of promise through the years when the promise seemed fulfilled and she was recognized by an adoring world, on to the years when the promise seemed to have been forgotten. Antin was always grateful and returned what she could, sending her sisters through college, supporting them through times of emotional and financial hardship, never taking lightly what she had been given, because she understood what it meant and knew what it cost. The strength of the supportive sisterhood never diminished, never was shaken by fame and its intrusions or obscurity and its deprivations. In her work Antin leaves a valuable record of this complex network, as well as a record of the immigrant experience, rich with its promises, ambivalences, and complexities.

References:

E. Stuart Bates, *Inside Out: An Introduction to Autobiography* (New York: Sheridan House, 1937), pp. 30-33, 78-80, 109, 251-253;

Annie E. S. Beard, *Our Foreign Born Citizens: What They Have Done for America* (New York: Crowell, 1932), pp. 30-38;

Abraham Cronbach, "Autobiography," *American Jewish Archives* (April 1959): 3-4, 40-43;

Oscar Handlin, Foreword to *The Promised Land* (Boston: Houghton Mifflin, 1969), pp. x-xv;

Ludwig Lewisohn, "A Panorama of a Half-Century of American Jewish Literature," *Jewish Book Annual*, 5711 (1950-1951): 3-10;

Sol Liptzin, *The Jew in American Literature* (New Jersey: Block, 1966), pp. 123-126;

Rose L. McKee, *'Brother Will' and The Founding of Gould Farm* (Great Barrington, Mass.: William Gould Corporation, 1963), pp. 51, 67-68, 73-76;

M. R. Parkman, "The Making of a Patriot: Mary Antin," in Parkman's *Heroines of Service* (New York: Century, 1917), pp. 185-208;

Barbara Miller Solomon, *Pioneers in Service: The History of the Associated Jewish Philanthropies of Boston* (Boston, 1956), pp. 50-52;

Mary H. Wade, *Pilgrims of To-day* (Boston: Little, Brown, 1916), pp. 112-141;

Israel Zangwill, Introduction to *From Plotzk to Boston* (Boston: W. B. Clark, 1899).

The author is grateful to Barry Mehler, Rose L. McKee, and Josephine Grabau Ross for their help in this essay.

Raymond Carver

(25 May 1938-   )

William L. Stull
University of Hartford

BOOKS: *Near Klamath* (Sacramento: English Club of Sacramento State College, 1968);

Winter Insomnia (Santa Cruz: Kayak, 1970);

Put Yourself in My Shoes (Santa Barbara: Capra, 1974);

At Night the Salmon Move (Santa Barbara: Capra, 1976);

Will You Please Be Quiet, Please? (New York: McGraw-Hill, 1976);

Furious Seasons and Other Stories (Santa Barbara: Capra, 1977);

What We Talk About When We Talk About Love (New York: Knopf, 1981; London: Collins, 1982);

Two Poems (Salisbury, Md.: Scarab, 1982);

The Pheasant (Worcester, Mass.: Metacom, 1982);

Fires: Essays, Poems, Stories (Santa Barbara: Capra, 1983; London: Collins, 1985);

Cathedral (New York: Knopf, 1983; London: Collins, 1984);

If It Please You (Northridge, Cal.: Lord John, 1984);

This Water (Concord, N.H.: Ewert, 1985);

Where Water Comes Together with Other Water (New York: Random House, 1985).

OTHER: *Ploughshares*, special fiction issue, vol. 9, no. 4 (1983), edited by Carver;

John Gardner, *On Becoming a Novelist*, edited by Carver (New York: Harper & Row, 1983);

William Kittredge, *We Are Not in This Together*, foreword by Carver (Port Townsend, Wash.: Graywolf, 1984);

"Occasions," in *The Generation of 2000: Contemporary American Poets*, edited by William Heyen (Princeton: Ontario Review Press, 1984).

PERIODICAL PUBLICATIONS:
FICTION

"The Aficionados," as John Vale, *Toyon*, 9 (Spring 1963): 5-9;

"The Hair," *Toyon*, 9 (Spring 1963): 27-30;

"Poseidon and Company," *Toyon*, 9 (Spring 1963): 24-25;

"Bright Red Apples," *Gato Magazine*, 2 (Spring-Summer 1967): 8-13;

Raymond Carver (Kelly Wise)

"*from* The Augustine Notebooks," *Iowa Review*, 10 (Summer 1979): 38-42.

NONFICTION

"Fame Is No Good, Take It from Me," *New York Times Book Review*, 22 April 1984, pp. 6-7;

"My Father's Life," *Esquire* (September 1984): 64-68.

POETRY

"Those Days," *Poet and Critic*, 2 (Spring 1966): 6;

"On the Pampas Tonight," *Levee*, 2 (January 1967): 8;

"The Sunbather, to Herself," *West Coast Review*, 2 (Spring 1967): 23;

"The Sturgeon," *Ball State University Forum*, 8 (Autumn 1967): 9-10;

"No Heroics, Please," *December*, 9, nos. 2-3 (1967): 64;

"Poem on My Birthday, July 2," *Grande Ronde Review*, no. 7 (1967): 7-8;

"Return," *Grande Ronde Review*, no. 7 (1967): 9;

"Sunday Night," *December*, 9, nos. 2-3 (1967): 64;

"My Wife," *New: American and Canadian Poetry*, no. 7 (September 1968): 12;

"Two Worlds," *Midwest Quarterly*, 14 (October 1972): 63;

"In a Greek Orthodox Church Near Daphne," *South Dakota Review*, 10 (Winter 1972-1973): 88.

"I've seen some things," says the narrator in "Mr. Coffee and Mr. Fixit," one of the stories in Raymond Carver's *What We Talk About When We Talk About Love*. Despite his recent billing as "a new, young writer," long before *What We Talk About* thrust fame upon him in March 1981, Raymond Carver had seen some things. At forty-two, he was a recovered alcoholic and the divorced father of two adult children. Since 1960, he had published some 150 stories and poems. His first story collection, *Will You Please Be Quiet, Please?* (1976), had been nominated for a National Book Award in 1977. With Capra Press, he had published a chapbook, *Put Yourself in My Shoes* (1974), and a second book of stories, *Furious Seasons* (1977). Although he insisted he was not a "born poet," he had produced three books of verse: *Near Klamath* (1968), *Winter Insomnia* (1970), and *At Night the Salmon Move* (1976).

Far from being a "new, young writer," then, Raymond Carver is, as the distinguished British critic Frank Kermode wrote in 1981, "a full-grown master." Carver began his literary apprenticeship in the 1950s, studying under the late John Gardner. His journeyman years, the 1960s and 1970s, tempered his art—and nearly wrecked his life. In 1983, he followed *What We Talk About* with a fourth book of stories, *Cathedral*, and *Fires: Essays, Poems, Stories*. That same year, the American Academy and Institute of Arts and Letters granted him one of its first Mildred and Harold Strauss Livings Awards, bringing with it five years of tax-free support. Carver's position as a master craftsman was hard won over twenty-five years.

Like many during the Great Depression, Raymond Carver's father, Clevie Raymond Carver ("C.R."), migrated west from Arkansas. In 1933, he

reached the Columbia River in northeast Washington State and labored on the Grand Coulee Dam. The next year, after returning east and marrying Ella Casey, he moved his family to Clatskanie, a town of 700 in northwestern Oregon. It was there that Raymond Carver was born on 25 May 1938.

Sometime before December 1941 the Carvers moved north, across the Washington border, to Yakima, a hub of the logging industry, where C. R. worked as a saw filer. There, among the Cascade mountains and along the Yakima River, Raymond Carver and his younger brother grew up, duck hunting and trout fishing with their father. "Near Klamath," the title poem of Carver's first book, evokes the rugged tranquillity of the region:

> We stand around the burning oil drum
> and we warm ourselves, our hands
> and faces, in its pure lapping heat.
>
> We raise steaming cups of coffee
> to our lips and we drink it
> with both hands. But we are salmon
>
> fisherman. And now we stamp our feet
> on the snow and rocks and move upstream
> slowly, full of love, toward the still pools.

"It was important for me to be a writer from the West," Carver says of his early career. His imagination was shaped by the landscape of the Pacific Northwest and the expressions of laconic men and women scrabbling to survive in hard country. Stories, oral and written, also shaped his imagination. From his father, he heard about a great-grandfather who fought on both sides of the Civil War. He also read: first the westerns of Zane Gray and the space operas of Edgar Rice Burroughs; later the "men's magazines"—*True, Argosy, Sports Afield,* and *Outdoor Life*. As a teenager, he even took, but never finished, a correspondence course in creative writing, proudly displaying the unearned certificate of completion on his bedroom wall.

In less romantic moments, however, he saw before him an unglamorous future: high-school diploma, then mill work like his father's. Barely nineteen, he married his girl friend, Maryann Burk, on 7 June 1957. Their daughter, Christine, was born on 2 December. A son, Vance, followed on 17 October the next year. In his essay "Fires," Carver describes how the "unrelieved responsibility and permanent distraction" of premature fatherhood constricted his life and art over the next twenty years: "nothing—and, brother, I mean nothing— that ever happened to me on this earth could come anywhere close, could possibly be as important to me, could make as much difference, as the fact that I had two children."

In the fall of 1958, Carver moved his family south to Paradise, in north-central California. Working nights, he enrolled at Chico State College. On 31 October, he published his first piece in the campus newspaper, a letter boldly headed "Where Is Intellect?" It called for a school literary magazine. The next year, Carver founded one, *Selection*, for which he wangled an unpublished poem by his favorite poet, William Carlos Williams. Then, in the fall of 1959, he enrolled in Creative Writing 101 and met his first "real writer," the late John Gardner.

It was a turning point. In both "Fires" and his preface to Gardner's posthumous *On Becoming a Novelist*, Carver pays tribute to this widely respected writer and teacher who died in a 1982 motorcycle accident. Gardner introduced Carver to the little magazines, "where the best fiction in the country was being published, and all of the poetry." More important, he offered "close line-by-line criticism" of his student's work. "He made me see that absolutely everything was important in a short story."

In the fall of 1960, Carver transferred to Humboldt State College in Arcata, California, where he worked in the Georgia-Pacific sawmill. That winter he published his first story, "The Furious Seasons," in *Selection*. It is a lurid tale of incest and murder set in the Pacific Northwest, Faulknerian in structure, with past and present commingling in the stream of consciousness. It abounds with symbolism from its two-word opening, "Rain threatens," to its baroque finale: "The gutter water rushed over his feet, swirled frothing into a great whirlpool at the drain on the corner and rushed down to the center of the earth." Slightly revised, in 1977 it became the title story of Carver's second collection.

The next spring, in Humboldt State's *Toyon*, Carver published a seminal vignette that foreshadows the manner and matter of his later fiction. "The Father" fuses American realism with European surrealism, Hemingway with Kafka. In fewer than five hundred words, most of them unmediated dialogue, it traces a father's existential unraveling. Innocently, his daughter asks about her new baby brother, "But who does he look like, who does he look like?" A second question follows: "Who does Daddy *look* like?" With the conclusion—"Why, nobody!"—the father's doom is sealed: "He had turned around in his chair and his face was white and without expression." As David Boxer and Cassandra Phillips have shown, such dissociation, "a sense of disengagement from one's own identity and life," is among Carver's obsessions.

On a red-letter day in spring 1962, Carver learned that two of his writings, a poem, "The Brass Ring," and a story, "Pastoral," had been accepted for publication in respected quarterlies. "Pastoral" is an homage to Hemingway, "an author whose work I admire greatly," Carver explains, referring to Hemingway's early stories "Big Two-Hearted River," "Cat in the Rain," and "The Three-Day Blow." It introduces a western Nick Adams named Harold, who, estranged from his wife, retreats to a favorite trout stream. Wading in the icy water, he watches a maimed doe stumble across the river. A sinister pack of young hunters follows. Their leader interrogates Harold and takes aim at his stomach— "or else a little lower down." His point made, the boy lowers his rifle. But Harold's pastoral idyll is over: "He stood there staring at the wordless, distorted things around him." Carver has since written, "I like it when there is some feeling of threat or menace in short stories." Both "The Father" and "Pastoral" illustrate what he means.

It was also in the spring of 1962 that Carver took up a third genre, the drama. On 11 May 1962, his one-act play *Carnations* was produced at Humboldt State. The play is student work, modeled on the European absurdists Carver was then reading. But once again, he combines surrealistic motifs with realistic dialogue. Moreover, at the prompting of screen director Michael Cimino (*The Deer Hunter*), Carver has recently returned to play writing. A version of his *Dostoevsky: The Screenplay*, written with his companion Tess Gallagher, appeared in the Spring 1984 *NER/BLQ*. A second script, *Purple Lake*, written with Cimino, is scheduled for production in 1985-1986.

Carver took his bachelor's degree in English from Humboldt State in February 1963. He also edited the Spring 1963 *Toyon*, which includes two of his stories, neither since collected. The first, a classical pastiche entitled "Poseidon and Company," marks a literary dead end. The second, however, introduces another leitmotif: the insidious ways in which minor irritations—here, a hair lodged between the protagonist's teeth—can precipitate spiritual crises. "The Hair" thus anticipates Carver's many stories of "dis-ease," a term he borrows from Camus to describe "a certain terrible kind of domesticity." For example, in "The Student's Wife" (1964), a sleepless night beside her husband drives a young woman to anguish ("Not in pictures she had seen nor in any book she had read had she learned a

Balsa Wood

My dad is at the stove in front of a pan of brains
and eggs. But who has any appetite
this morning? I feel as flimsy as
balsa wood. Something has just been said.
My mom said it. What was it? Something,
something to do with money. I'll do my part
if I don't eat. ~~I'm not hungry anyway.~~ *Dad turns his back to me at the stove.*
~~So upset I've peed my pajamas.~~
~~He turns his back on the pan.~~
"I'm in a hole. Don't dig me no deeper."
Light leaks in from a window. Someone's crying.
The last thing I recall is the smell
of burned ~~eggs~~ *brains* and ~~brains~~ *eggs.* The whole morning
is shoveled into the garbage, and mixed
with other ~~stuff.~~ *things.* Sometime later
~~we~~ *he + I* drive to the dump, ten miles out.
We don't talk. We throw our bags and cartons
onto a mound of ~~paper garbage.~~ *stuff.* Rats screech.
~~and~~ *They* whistle as they come out of rotten sacks,
dragging their bellies. We get back in the car
and watch the smoke and fire. We ~~just~~ sit there.
I ~~can~~ smell the airplane glue on my fingers.
~~My d~~ *Dad* looks at me as I bring my fingers to my nose.
He wants to say something, *better but or wait.*
~~Something for me to remember many years later.~~
~~But he can't.~~ ~~He was~~ a million miles away, ~~and besides,~~ *Someone's crying!*
~~had to learn everything the hard way.~~ *have*
~~But,~~ ~~In~~ fact, we ~~were~~ both a ~~long way from the~~ dump *away*
~~that day.~~ *Even then* I was beginning
to understand ~~how~~ it's possible to be doing something
in one place. ~~that will diminish you.~~
~~And be somewhere else, too.~~

Revised typescript for a Carver poem (the author)

sunrise was so terrible as this"), and in "Preservation" (1983) an out-of-work husband's nerves break down along with his refrigerator. Carver's *Toyon* also included two pieces by a John Vale, who proves to have been himself. To Vale, Carver attributed his much-reprinted poem "Spring, 480 B.C." and a story, "The Aficionados." As its title indicates, "The Aficionados," like "Pastoral," recalls Hemingway. But here Carver rebels against his literary father, exposing the master's belles and bulls as engines of human sacrifice.

Carver's undergraduate years were thus formative ones during which he formulated basic styles, settings, and "obsessions." (He dislikes the word *theme*.) In the fall of 1963, he received a $500 grant for graduate study at the University of Iowa Writers Workshop. It was a small sum for a family of four. Both Carvers worked odd jobs, she as a waitress, he as a clerk in the University library. The strain took its toll. One Saturday afternoon in an Iowa City laundromat Carver had a shattering epiphany. As in a Raymond Carver story, it began with a minor irritation, a woman's beating him to the dryer, thereby preventing him from picking up his children on time. "I realized—what had I been thinking before?—that my life was a small-change thing for the most part, chaotic, and without much light showing through. And at that moment I felt— I knew—that the life I was in was vastly different from the lives of the writers I most admired." Carver failed to finish the academic year.

As Gary L. Fisketjon noted in his review of *Furious Seasons*, Carver's stories present "the terrifying implications of Normal Life." From the mid-1960s to the late 1970s, Carver learned those implications firsthand. Returning to California, he held a series of "crap jobs" in Sacramento—mill hand, delivery boy, even tulip picker. For two years, he worked as a night janitor at Mercy Hospital, stealing writing time by leaving work early. Necessarily, he cultivated short forms.

Between 1965 and 1970, Carver published little fiction. One of the few stories was "Will You Please Be Quiet, Please?" It is a wrenching account of an insecure young husband's coming to terms with his wife's sensuality. Martha Foley, editor of *Best American Short Stories*, included it in her 1967 annual. This was another turning point.

"You are not your characters," Carver says, "but your characters are you." To a considerable degree, his work from these "years of ferocious parenting" reports on the battles he was waging with his family and himself. In "Occasions," he writes, "My poems are of course not literally true—

the events didn't happen, or at least the stuff in the poems didn't happen in the way I say it does. But like most of my fiction, there is an autobiographical element." This element is clear in short poems like "Adultery" and "Bankruptcy" as well as fuller confessional pieces like "Photograph of My Father in His Twenty-Second Year." That poem, along with others like "Drinking While Driving" and "Cheers," reveals that, during his thirties Carver followed his father into alcoholism, "full-time drinking as a serious pursuit."

It was also in 1967 that Carver got his first white-collar job, editing textbooks for Science Research Associates in Palo Alto, California. The next year, his wife received a scholarship to Tel Aviv University. Carver arranged a year's leave, and in spring 1968 the family departed for Israel. But the promised villa on the Mediterranean never materialized, and in less than six months he was back at SRA. Earlier, he had taken a poetry-writing course at Sacramento State College, and in the fall of 1968 the college English Club published twenty-six of his poems as *Near Klamath*, which includes not only regional sketches like "With a Telescope Rod on Cowiche Creek" but also literary studies like "Balzac" and "Antonin Artaud."

In 1970 Carver was fired from SRA. The dismissal coincided with his first major fellowship, a National Endowment for the Arts Discovery Award for Poetry. With fellowship money, severance pay, and unemployment benefits, he could write full-time. Over nine months, he produced most of the stories that make up *Will You Please Be Quiet, Please?* During those same months, George Hitchcock, who had published several of Carver's poems in *Kayak* magazine, brought out a second book of poems, *Winter Insomnia*.

The next year Carver broke into the "slicks"— magazines like *Esquire*, *Harper's Bazaar*, and later *Playgirl*. He had sent a story to Gordon Lish, fiction editor at *Esquire* and formerly the Carvers' neighbor in Palo Alto. Lish rejected the piece, but asked for more. Carver sent everything he had, including "The Neighbors." Lish, whose influence Carver has ranked next to Gardner's, trimmed the title and published "Neighbors" in June 1971. James Dickey, then *Esquire*'s poetry editor, also printed Carver's "Hunter" and "Deschutes River" that same summer.

"Neighbors" is a quintessential Raymond Carver story and has been widely anthologized. Like "The Father," it begins with fairy-tale innocence: "Bill and Arlene Miller were a happy couple." These ordinary people tend the apartment of their neighbors, the peripatetic Stones, whose "fuller and brighter life" the Millers envy. Bill prowls the Stones' apartment, sipping their Scotch, nibbling their cheddar, and modeling their clothes—both Jim's and Harriet's. From this he gets a sexual charge, and his relations with Arlene improve. She, too, goes next door and returns flushed and lusty. "Anything could happen," Bill gushes. Hand in hand, the Millers head for the Stones' apartment— only to discover that Arlene has locked the key inside. Standing in the hallway between their old and new worlds, they feel their identities crumble: "They held each other. They leaned into the door as if against a wind, and braced themselves."

In Freud's terms, "Neighbors" is "uncanny" (*unheimlich*), a disquieting illustration of the return of the repressed. Carver himself notes that "the story has captured an essential sense of mystery or strangeness." Boxer and Phillips define this haunting motif as "a double strand of voyeurism and dissociation." By *voyeurism* they mean not just erotic peeping, which Carver treats openly in "The Idea," but also the Millers' "wistful identification with some distant, unattainable idea of self."

During the early 1970s, Carver held a series of one-year lectureships, beginning in 1971-1972 at the University of California, Santa Cruz, where he founded the magazine *Quarry*. In the spring of 1972 he won the Joseph Henry Jackson award for fiction. In the fall he held simultaneously a University of California lectureship and a Wallace Stegner Creative Writing Fellowship at Stanford. He was writing, but he was also drinking heavily. The extent of his problem became clear in the fall of 1973, when he tried simultaneously to hold a lectureship at U.C.-Santa Cruz and a visiting appointment at the Iowa Writers Workshop. He stayed at the Iowa House, two floors down from John Cheever, then an alcoholic himself. The two "did nothing *but* drink," Carver admits. "I don't think either of us ever took the covers off our typewriters."

Even as Carver's alcoholism worsened during the mid-1970s, his literary standing rose. For three years running, his work appeared in William Abrahams's annual *Prize Stories: The O. Henry Awards*: "What Is It?" (1973), "Put Yourself in My Shoes" (1974), and "Are You a Doctor?" (1975). Several of his poems were reprinted in David Allan Evans's *New Voices in American Poetry* (1973), and in 1974 Capra Press published *Put Yourself in My Shoes* as a chapbook—the first of several Carver limited editions. At the same time, however, Carver's private and professional lives were "completely out of con-

Raymond Carver's caricature of himself, from Self-Portrait: Book People Picture Themselves, *from the collection of Burt Britton (New York: Random House, 1976)*

trol." In the fall of 1975 he began a last one-year appointment, this time at U.C.-Santa Barbara, where he served as advisory editor of *Spectrum*. Again, alcoholism prevented him from finishing out the year. His poem "Cheers," published in the July 1976 *Esquire*, reveals his frame of mind: "Vodka chased with coffee. Each morning/I hang the sign on the door:/OUT TO LUNCH."

In 1976, despite his drinking, Carver published two books. The first, in February, was *At Night the Salmon Move*, a collection of twenty-three poems, nearly all previously published in magazines. The second was *Will You Please Be Quiet, Please?* Published by McGraw-Hill in association with Gordon Lish, this wide-ranging collection of twenty-two stories gathers most of the fiction from Carver's journeyman years, 1963-1975. The earliest story is "The Father" (*Toyon*, 1961); the latest is "Collectors" (*Esquire*, 1975). The book opens with one of the first pieces Carver published in a "slick" magazine, "Fat" (*Harper's Bazaar*, 1971), and closes with the prizewinning title story from *December* (1966).

The major-press imprint assured that the book would get attention, and notices were favorable, especially those by fellow writers. Leonard Michaels wrote, "Raymond Carver's stories are extraordinary in their language, their music and their huge terrifying vision of ordinary human life in this country." Joe David Bellamy described that vision in detail:

> Carver gives new specificity to the plight of "ordinary" people and brings it up to date for a certain familiar class of Americans. Beneath the surface conventionality of his salesmen, waitresses, bookkeepers, or hopeless middle-class "occupants" lies a morass of inarticulated yearnings and unexamined horrors; repressed violence, the creeping certainty that nothing matters, perverse sexual wishes, the inadmissible evidence of inadequacy.

In the words of Boxer and Phillips, Carver's characters are members of "the non-upwardly mobile working and middle classes." Often, as in "Collectors," they are between lives: "I was out of work. But any day I expected to hear from up north. I lay on the sofa and listened to the rain. Now and then I'd lift up and look through the curtain for the mailman." A few are financially as well as spiritually bankrupt, like the husband in "What Is It?" Leo realizes that, at his behest, along with her "big convertible" his wife has sold her body: "He understands he is willing to be dead."

Carver's stories work by implosion, with detonation delayed until just after the closing sentence. Without obvious plotting, details accumulate, then collapse inside or around the central consciousness. For reader and character alike, the shock is subliminal, more felt than understood. Thus, in "Fat" a waitress encounters an affable but ravenous fat man whose "long, thick, creamy fingers" stir her own latent hungers. "My life is going to change. I feel it," she senses.

As the title suggests, the mood of *Will You Please Be Quiet, Please?* is interrogative. Seven of the twenty-two stories have questions for titles, like "What's in Alaska?" There, with a new job pending in Fairbanks, Carl leaves the garage early and buys a pair of comfortable shoes. He and his wife visit friends, with whom they eat popsicles, drink cream soda, and smoke pot. His companions remark, not admiringly, on his footwear. Carl sees, or thinks he sees, his wife embrace his host; his hostess remembers reading about a prehistoric man frozen in a block of Alaskan ice; stoned, the four watch a cat eat a mouse. At home, Carl lies awake beside his sleeping wife:

Just as he started to turn off the lamp, he thought he saw something in the hall. He kept staring and thought he saw it again, a pair of small eyes. His heart turned. He blinked and kept staring. He leaned over to look for something to throw. He picked up one of his shoes. He sat up straight and held the shoe with both hands. He heard her snoring and set his teeth. He waited. He waited for it to move once more, to make the slightest noise.

Whether the eyes belong to a cat, a rat, or a marijuana-induced hallucination, what the reader sees is the emptiness of Carl's life—something the protagonist feels as a growing "dis-ease." For Carver as for Samuel Beckett in *The Unnameable*, existential fear and trembling are unspeaking, unspoken, and unspeakable. The only character who comes close to articulating it is Ralph Wyman, the protagonist in the title story: "Yes, there was a great evil pushing at the world, he thought, and it only need a little slipway, a little opening."

Carver's vision is bleak but never cynical. Counterbalancing the emptiness of the characters' lives is the boundless empathy of the author—and of the reader, whom Carver's style implicates. "Reading is a conjugal act, and in a sense we help write the story," David Dempsey observes of Carver's work. Ann Beattie explains the process: "Stylistically, Carver's short declarative sentences produce a clever effect: his matter-of-factness, his detached observation of events, gains power as the events become increasingly odd and discomfiting." By understatement and outright omission, the author passes the full burden of interpretation to his readers. When the story implodes, the reader feels the void—the emptiness within and around the characters.

In 1977, *Will You Please Be Quiet, Please?* was nominated for a National Book Award. Carver's journeyman years were nearly over. But that same spring he was "in a very grave place." Estranged from his wife and children, he had several times been hospitalized for alcoholism. "I was dying from it, plain and simple, and I'm not exaggerating." Then, on 2 June 1977, shortly after accepting an advance on a still-to-be written novel, Carver stopped drinking. "I'm prouder of that, that I've quit drinking, than I am of anything in my life."

The late 1970s were years of recovery, revision, and spiritual renewal. Asked whether he is a religious man, Carver says, "No, but I have to believe in miracles and the possibility of resurrection."

Late in 1977, Capra Press bought out *Furious Seasons,* a collection of eight stories not included in *Will You Please Be Quiet, Please?* Some, like "Pastoral," were very early, and all but the title story have since been revised and reprinted elsewhere. "Dummy," "Distance," "The Fling," and "Mine" become, respectively, "The Third Thing That Killed My Father Off," "Everything Stuck to Him," "Sacks," and "Popular Mechanics" in *What We Talk About.* There, too, "So Much Water So Close to Home" reappears, albeit much condensed.

Ceaseless rewriting is a hallmark of Carver's work. John Gardner early convinced him that revision, seeing stories and poems anew, was "vital for writers, at whatever stage of their development." In the afterword to *Fires,* Carver explains, "Rewriting for me is not a chore—it's something I like to do. . . . Maybe I revise because it gradually takes me into the heart of what the story is *about.*" For example, "So Much Water So Close to Home" traces a woman's revulsion at the callous handling her husband and his fishing buddies give the nude body

Front cover for Carver's second book of stories

of a young rape victim—the wife's nightmare double. In *Furious Seasons* (as in *Spectrum,* where it first appeared in 1975), the story runs to twenty psychologically explicit pages. In *What We Talk About,* Carver halves the story and radically alters the ending. In *Fires,* he restores the original ending and many of the excised passages but changes the story in still other ways.

In the late 1970s, Carver returned to teaching, first at Goddard College, then at the University of Texas, El Paso. In 1980, he was appointed Professor of English at Syracuse University, where he taught until receiving his Strauss Livings Award in 1983. His separation from his wife became final, and in 1978, he met writer Tess Gallagher. The two now share houses in Syracuse, New York, and Port Angeles, Washington.

With the support of a Guggenheim Fellowship in 1979-1980, Carver prepared the stories that make up *What We Talk About,* which Knopf published in April 1981. Two months earlier, in an essay since titled "On Writing," Carver discussed three quotations that guided his work. The first came from Ezra Pound: "Fundamental accuracy of statement is the ONE sole morality of writing." Carver took the second from a Chekhov story: ". . . and suddenly everything became clear to him." Finally, he trimmed Geoffrey Wolff's injunction, "No cheap tricks," to no tricks at all. "Get in, get out. Don't linger. Go on."

"On Writing" remains the best introduction to *What We Talk About* and to what critics have since termed "American minimalism." As Michael Gorra defines it, minimalism is "a mannerist mode in which the intentional poverty, the anorexia, of the writer's style is mimetic of the spiritual poverty of his or her characters' lives, their disconnection from anything like a traditional community." Although Carver has since moved on to a fuller style, *What We Talk About* remains a minimalist masterpiece. Donald Newlove captured the book's arresting unity of style and subject: "Seventeen tales of Hopelessville, its marriages and alcoholic wreckage, told in a prose as sparingly clear as a fifth of iced Smirnoff."

Carver's triumph in *What We Talk About* was a victory of self-restraint. "What creates tension in a piece of fiction is partly the way the concrete words are linked together to make up the visible action of the story. But it's also the things that are left out, that are implied, the landscape just under the smooth (but sometimes broken and unsettled) surface of things." Gone are the baroque figures of "Furious Seasons" and the lyrical closing cadences of "Will You Please Be Quiet, Please?" In their place is a cool crystalline prose that refracts as much as it reveals, as in the opening lines of "Why Don't You Dance?"

> In the kitchen, he poured another drink and looked at the bedroom suite in his front yard. The mattress was stripped and the candy-striped sheets lay beside two pillows on the chiffonier. Except for that, things looked much the way they had in the bedroom— nightstand and reading lamp on his side of the bed, nightstand and reading lamp on her side.

Alcohol numbs the laconic man's "dis-ease," but the "terrible domesticity" of his situation speaks worlds. A young couple stops by, and the three drink and dance as the neighbors stare. "They thought they'd seen everything over here," the man says. Dancing with her face against his shoulder, the girl pulls him close. "You must be desperate or something," she says. Weeks later, "She kept talking. She told everyone. There was more to it, and she was trying to get it talked out. After a time, she quit trying."

With the last sentence, the story implodes. Here as throughout the collection, what one character calls the "low-rent tragedy" is at once moral and linguistic, a failure of will and words. Like Lewis Carroll's Mad Hatter, Carver shows that we can mean what we say, but we can never say what we mean. The girl cannot "get it talked out" because *it* remains unsayable—a feeling, not a word. Thus, talk and love run at odds throughout the collection, nowhere more than in the title story. "What We Talk About When We Talk About Love" is Carver's wicked send-up of Plato's dialogue on love, *The Symposium*. Drinking gin around a kitchen table, two couples blather on about physical, spiritual, and sentimental love: "it ought to make us feel ashamed when we talk like we know what we're talking about when we talk about love," one opines. As darkness descends, the four drift into alcoholic anesthesia: "I could hear my heart beating. I could hear everyone's heart. I could hear the human noise we sat there making, not one of us moving, not even when the room went dark."

Kind or cruel, the talk in *What We Talk About* remains "human noise" fading out with a dying fall. In "Gazebo," a couple struggles to save a marriage

AT NIGHT THE SALMON MOVE

RAYMOND CARVER

At night the salmon move
out from the river and into town.
They avoid places with names
like Foster's Freeze, A&W, Smiley's,
but swim close to the tract
homes on Wright Avenue where sometimes
in the early morning hours
you can hear them trying doorknobs
or bumping against Cable TV lines.
We wait up for them.
We leave our back windows open
and call out when we hear a splash.
Mornings are a disappointment.

From FIRES, ©1983 by Raymond Carver.

Separate publication of Carver's poem that provided the title for his 1976 collection

"fouled" by adultery. A single word is enough to sound their doom:

> "Duane," Holly goes.
> In this, too, she was right.

Failure of communication is Carver's abiding theme. "Maybe he wanted me to say something," the son concludes in "Sacks" after his father has agonized to explain the affair that wrecked his marriage. In "A Serious Talk," a man visits his ex-wife at Christmas. "There were things he wanted to say to her, grieving things, consoling things, things like that." Unable to say them, he steals her pies, overstokes her fireplace, and cuts her telephone cord. "He hoped he had made something clear." In "One More Thing," the coda to the book, drunken L. D. gropes for a last word. "He said, 'I just want to say one more thing.' But then he could not think what it could possibly be."

What We Talk About was a great critical success, confirming Carver's standing as "a full-grown master." In *New York Magazine* Jayne Anne Phillips declared it "a book of fables for this decade," and in *Time* J. D. Reed concluded, "Carver not only enchants, he convinces." Frank Kermode wrote, "Carver's fiction is so spare in manner that it takes time before one realizes how completely a whole culture and a whole moral condition is represented by even the most seemingly slight sketch."

Only a few dissenters felt that despite its precision and immediacy *What We Talk About* was a narrower book, morally and aesthetically, than Carver's first collection. Doris Grumbach found it "stingy," and James Atlas concluded, "less is less." In his *Paris Review* interview, Carver partly concurred: "For one thing, it's a much more self-conscious book in the sense of how intentional every move was, how calculated." Despite its success— perhaps because of what Robert Houston called its Influence—the book marked a turning point as well as a milestone. "I knew I'd gone as far the other way as I could or wanted to go, cutting everything down to the marrow, not just to the bone."

In "On Writing," Carver set forth the minimalist credo of precision, objectivity, and condensation that guided him in *What We Talk About*. At the same time, however, he voiced serious reservations about dry "formal innovation" in experimental fiction. Some months earlier, in a review of John Yount's *Hardcastle*, he had cast his vote for "fiction that counts" rather than "stories in which people are reduced to nameless or otherwise easily forgettable 'characters'—hapless creatures who have nothing much to do in this life or, even worse, go

about doing unthinking and uncaring things to their own kind." He then defined his version of what his mentor John Gardner had earlier termed "moral fiction":

> In fiction that matters, the significance of the action inside the story translates to the lives of people outside the story. Do we need to remind ourselves of this? In the best novels and short stories, goodness is recognized as such. Loyalty, love, fortitude, courage, integrity may not always be rewarded, but they are recognized as good or noble actions or qualities; and evil or base or simply stupid behavior is seen and held up for what it is: evil, base, or stupid behavior. There *are* a few absolutes in this life, some verities, if you will, and we would do well not to forget them.

For six months after finishing *What We Talk About*, Carver could write nothing. Then came "Cathedral," published in the September 1981 *Atlantic* and two years later the title story of his next major collection. It was, he says, "totally different in conception and execution from any stories that have come before." Critics have since agreed, describing *Cathedral* as "more generous" than Carver's previous work.

In "Cathedral," the narrator is irritable at the news that a blind man, "an old friend of my wife's," is coming to visit. "He was no one I knew. And his being blind bothered me. My idea of blindness came from the movies." But Robert, bearded and booming of voice, upsets his host's preconceptions. With disarming gusto, he eats, drinks, smokes pot, even "watches" television. As the evening winds down, the men watch a program about cathedrals—not the narrator's usual fare. "Do you have any idea what a cathedral is? What they look like?" he asks. When words fail, Robert suggests that they draw a cathedral, his hand piggybacked on his host's. Together, they trace the roof, spires, arches, even the people. Finally, the blind man tells him to draw with his eyes closed. "So we kept on with it. His fingers rode my fingers as my hand went over the paper. It was like nothing else in my life up to now."

In "What We Talk About When We Talk About Love," a character asks, "Do you see what I mean?" Dead silence follows. In "Cathedral," even with his eyes closed the narrator sees exactly what his blind guest means:

> "Well," he said. "Are you looking?"
> My eyes were still closed. I was in my house. I

knew that. But I didn't feel like I was inside anything.

"It's really something," I said.

Thus, in Carver's "more generous" vision sight is capped by insight. As its title and central symbol suggest, "Cathedral" is ultimately a religious story, a story of conversion.

Cathedral remains a transitional book. Only a few of the twelve stories equal the spiritual and aesthetic generosity of the title story. "Feathers" offers three memorable emblems of love—a squawking peacock, a set of plaster snaggleteeth, and a homely baby ("Even calling it ugly does it credit"). In "Fever," an abandoned husband learns the wisdom of his own words: "You've got to work with your mistakes until they look intended." Several stories—"Vitamins," "The Bridle," "Chef's House," "Preservation," and "Careful"—recall the alcoholic and marital wreckage of *What We Talk About*. The titles of others suggest their transitional themes: "Where I'm Calling From," "The Compartment," "The Train." In the last of these, Carver pays homage to John Cheever by continuing his well-known story "The Five-Forty-Eight."

"*Cathedral* shows a gifted writer struggling for a larger scope of reference, a finer touch of nuance," wrote critic Irving Howe. Perhaps the best index of the change in Carver's work is a single story, versions of which appear in both *What We Talk About* and *Cathedral*. In the earlier book, it is titled "The Bath," and under that title in *Columbia* (Spring/Summer 1981) it won the Carlos Fuentes Fiction Award. The next year the story reappeared, revised and expanded, under the title "A Small, Good Thing," in *Ploughshares*. There it took first place in *Prize Stories 1983: The O. Henry Awards* before Carver collected it in *Cathedral*.

As published in *What We Talk About*, "The Bath" is a slice of life in Hopelessville. Anticipating her son's eighth birthday, Ann Weiss goes to the bakery and orders a special cake. Two days later, Scotty is struck by a hit-and-run driver. The cake forgotten, at the hospital Ann and her husband watch over the unconscious child. Each parent goes home briefly to bathe. While there, both receive angry telephone calls alluding to a cake and to Scotty. We—not they—recognize the caller as the baker, enraged at customer's negligence, unaware that Scotty lies near death. "The Bath" exemplifies well the stark existential realism of *What We Talk About*. Detail and characterization are minimal, and the situation is rendered in studiously neutral tones. The narrator, like the baker, offers only "the barest

information." The story ends inconclusively: " 'It is about Scotty,' the voice said. 'It has to do with Scotty, yes.' "

"A Small, Good Thing" is twice again as long as "The Bath," which it not only continues but completes. With added detail, dialogue, and authorial comment, Carver draws us to the parents during their "terrible minutes." Because of "a one-in-a-million circumstance," the child dies. The parents go home, and when the telephone rings, Ann recognizes the voice. Enraged, the parents drive to the bakery. Instead of violence, however, there follows a scene of suffering tempered by forgiveness. The baker acknowledges the enormity of his behavior. He gives the Weisses the only consolation he can offer, his fresh bread: " 'Eating is a small, good thing in a time like this,' he said." The revision thus ends in Christian communion rather than existential isolation. "They talked on into the early morning, the high, pale cast of light in the windows, and they did not think of leaving."

Fires (1983) also offers "more generous" versions of several stories previously published in *What We Talk About*. In addition, it includes two previously uncollected stories, "Harry's Death" and "The Pheasant." The former is oddly hardboiled ("Harry was an operator"), but in the latter a compromised young man undergoes exactly the kind of epiphany Carver admired in Chekhov's stories: "Something became clear to him then." Moreover, in *Fires* Carver reprints fifty of his poems, each slightly or substantially revised. He arranges them in four groups, each encompassing "a constellation of feelings and attitudes." Alcohol is the subject of the first section, from the giddy inebriation of "Drinking While Driving" to the cold sobriety of "Rogue River Jet-Boat Trip." Next comes Carver's long poem "You Don't Know What Love Is," a parody of Charles Bukowski. The third section concerns "foreign travel and personages." With references to Balzac, Mark Twain, *Hamlet*, and Herodotus, it shows the wide range of Carver's reading and testifies to his abiding respect for literary craft. Thus, in "The Blue Stones," he pays tribute to Flaubert's exacting diction—a hallmark of his own best work:

> The smooth stones you pick up and examine
> under the moon's light have been made blue
> from the sea. Next morning when you pull
>   them
> from your trouser pocket, they are still blue.

Last come "things domestic and familiar"—such Carver staples as hunting, fishing, and domestic discord—all of which combine in "Deschutes River": "Far away/another man is raising my children,/ bedding my wife bedding my wife." Here, too, are revised versions of the earlier title poems "Near Klamath," "Winter Insomnia," and "At Night the Salmon Move." At their best, Carver's poems have the virtues of his stories: photographic precision of image, disquieting turns of phrase and event, compelling immediacy, lasting resonance. As a miniature "Raymond Carver Reader," *Fires* is what Shaun O'Connell called it in the *Boston Globe:* "Carver's most revealing book."

In recent interviews, Carver has spoken once again of writing a novel, and he has a new book of poems due out in 1985, *Where Water Comes Together with Other Water.* Although his books have appeared under major imprints, he remains loyal to the small presses. Handsome limited editions of his work continue to appear: the broadside *Distress Sale, Two Poems, The Pheasant, If It Please You,* and the forthcoming *Ten Poems.* In the spring of 1983 he edited a special fiction issue of *Ploughshares,* and more recently he has edited *We Are Not in This Together,* a collection of stories by William Kittredge. William Collins has published British editions of *What We Talk About, Cathedral,* and *Fires,* and Carver's work has been translated into some twenty foreign languages, including Dutch, Arabic, and Japanese.

During his long journeyman years, the man whom Robert Towers calls "one of the true contemporary masters" wrote in short forms because he had to. "The circumstances of my life are much different now," he says, "but now I *choose* to write short stories and poems." It was Joseph Conrad who defined the writer's task as "before all, to make you *see.*" Carver's work—"Viewfinder," "I Could See the Smallest Things," "Cathedral"—demonstrates that sight and insight remain literature's twin concerns. "Good fiction," he says, "is partly a bringing of the news from one world to another."

Interviews:

Cassandra Phillips, "Accolade-Winning Author Returns to Humboldt," *Eureka* (Cal.) *Times-Standard,* 24 June 1977, pp. 1-2;

Mona Simpson, "The Art of Fiction LXXVI," *Paris Review,* 25, no. 88 (Summer 1983): 192-221;

Kay Bonetti, "Ray Carver: Keeping It Short," *Saturday Review* (September-October 1983): 21-23;

Lisa McElhinny, "Raymond Carver Speaking," *Akros Review,* 8/9 (Spring 1984): 103-114.

References:

James Atlas, "Less Is Less," *Atlantic* (June 1981): 96-98;

Ann Beattie, "Carver's *Furious Seasons,*" *Canto,* 2, no. 2 (1978): 178-182;

Joe David Bellamy, "*Will You Please Be Quiet, Please?,*" *Harper's Bookletter,* 26 April 1976;

David Boxer and Cassandra Phillips, "*Will You Please Be Quiet, Please?*: Voyeurism, Dissociation, and the Art of Raymond Carver," *Iowa Review,* 10 (Summer 1979): 75-90;

Bill Burford, "Everything Gone Wrong," *Times Literary Supplement,* 17 February 1984, p. 159;

David Dempsey, "Up, Up and Away with the Short Story," *Antioch Review,* 42 (Spring 1984): 247-255;

Gary Fisketjon, "Normal Nightmares," *Village Voice,* 18 September 1978, pp. 132, 134;

Dean Flower, "Fiction Chronicle," *Hudson Review,* 29 (Summer 1976): 270-272;

Michael Gorra, "Laughter and Bloodshed," *Hudson Review,* 37 (Spring 1984): 151-164;

James W. Grinnell, "*Cathedral,*" *Studies in Short Fiction,* 21 (Winter 1984): 71-72;

Doris Grumbach, "The Extra Skin That Language Can Give," *Georgia Review,* 36 (Fall 1982): 668-674;

Robert Houston, "A Stunning Articulateness," *Nation,* 4 (July 1981): 23-25;

David Kubal, "Fiction Chronicle," *Hudson Review,* 34 (Autumn 1981): 456-466;

Thomas LeClair, "Fiction Chronicle—June 1981," *Contemporary Literature,* 23 (Winter 1982): 83-91;

Susan Lohafer, *Coming to Terms with the Short Story* (Baton Rouge: Louisiana State University Press, 1983), pp. 50, 62-65ff.;

Donald Newlove, "*What We Talk About When We Talk About Love,*" *Saturday Review* (April 1981): 77;

Shaun O'Connell, "Carver's Fires Burn with Magic," *Boston Globe,* 17 July 1983, Sec. A, pp. 55-56;

Jayne Anne Phillips, "The Secret Places of the Heart," *New York* (20 April 1981): 77-78;

James C. Robison, "1969-1980: Experiment and Tradition," in *The American Short Story 1945-1980,* edited by Gordon Weaver (Boston: Twayne, 1983), pp. 78, 86, 100;

Josh Rubins, "Small Expectations," *New York Review of Books,* 24 November 1983, pp. 40-42;

J. I. M. Stewart, "Other Things," *London Review of*

Books, 2-15 February 1984, pp. 16-17;
William L. Stull, "Beyond Hopelessville: Another Side of Raymond Carver," *Philological Quarterly*, 64 (Winter 1985);
Stull, "Visions and Revisions," *Chariton Review*, 10 (Spring 1984): 80-86;

Bruce Weber, "Raymond Carver: A Chronicler of Blue-Collar Despair," *New York Times Magazine*, 24 June 1984, pp. 36-38, 42-46, 48-50;
Geoffrey Wolff, "*Will You Please Be Quiet, Please?*," *New York Times Book Review*, 7 March 1976, pp. 4-5.

James Crumley
(12 October 1939-   )

Robert E. Burkholder
Pennsylvania State University—Wilkes Barre

BOOKS: *One to Count Cadence* (New York: Random House, 1969);
The Wrong Case (New York: Random House, 1975; London: Hart-Davis MacGibbon, 1976);
The Last Good Kiss (New York: Random House, 1978; London: Panther, 1978);
Dancing Bear (New York: Random House, 1983).

James Crumley is a novelist and teacher who, his book jackets almost proudly proclaim, "has worked as an enlisted man in the U.S. Army, a roughneck, a bartender, and a college professor." And while Crumley draws a bit on his extensive experience in academe (he has been a college professor since 1969), it is the raw, uncompromising worlds of the soldier, the roughneck, and the bartender that shape and give tone to his fiction. His first novel, *One to Count Cadence* (1969), was an ambitious effort to capture the absurdity, mixed emotions, and confused values that characterized the Vietnam era. The literary influences upon the creator of this fictional world-at-undeclared-war with itself as much as with a shadowy but real enemy are often too apparent—Joseph Heller, James Jones, and Norman Mailer, with an occasional taste of the most hard-boiled Hemingway thrown in for seasoning. Crumley's second novel, *The Wrong Case* (1975), represents a significant shift in his career toward the genre of detective fiction, which allows him to explore an essentially corrupt world using such devices as a highly structured and suspenseful plot, plenty of action and violence, and a central

character who is uncompromising in his toughness, cynicism, and integrity. This is a formula that Crumley also capitalizes on in his next two novels, *The Last Good Kiss* (1978) and *Dancing Bear* (1983), often standing the genre on its head by creating an antiheroic protagonist plagued by the weakness and vice of the corrupt world in which he lives and works and endowing him, nevertheless, with the sort of noble instincts that motivate him to sift through the scum in order to identify right from wrong. Crumley's detectives are curiously amoral moralists.

Crumley was born in Three Rivers, Texas, on 12 October 1939, to Arthur Roland Crumley, an oil field supervisor, and Ruby (Criswell) Crumley. He was a student at the Georgia Institute of Technology in 1957-1958, but he left college to work at the jobs and gain the experiences that would later inform his fictional world. He served in the army from 1958 to 1961. He later enrolled at Texas A & I University in Kingsville, from which he received a B.A. in 1964. He then continued his education at the Writers' Workshop at the University of Iowa, receiving an M.F.A. in 1966. With a draft of his first novel completed for his Iowa degree, Crumley found employment in two of this country's leading creative writing workshops, at the University of Montana at Missoula (1966-1969) and the University of Arkansas (1969-1970). Crumley has also taught at Colorado State University in Fort Collins (1971-1974) and at Reed College in Portland, Oregon (1976-1977). In recent years he has been a

James Crumley (© Lee Nye)

faculty member at the University of Texas at El Paso, but has continued to spend his summers in Missoula, Montana, the locale that serves as the setting for his last three novels.

One to Count Cadence draws heavily on Crumley's own experiences in the army and is technically very complex. The bulk of the novel is narrated in the first person by the protagonist in a series of flashbacks that are framed by and interspersed with narration that occurs in the present. Most of the time this difficult technique is handled with extraordinary proficiency, but at times the reader can get lost in a confusing transition and not immediately recognize where he is in the novel's complex time scheme. Further, the essential conflict in *One to Count Cadence* is that between the rigidity of military life and the spirit of rebellion in young men of military age. However, Crumley's minor characters are sometimes fuzzy and ill-defined. Even major characters occasionally seem to lack sufficient motivation for their actions, and this blurs the reader's understanding of the conflict that is such an important part of the meaning of the novel.

As the novel begins, we are introduced to its narrator, Jacob Slagstead "Slag" Krummel. There is some suggestion that his physician, Dr. Gallard, has

prescribed writing this story as therapy for Krummel, who is now in a hospital in the Philippines recuperating from wounds received during one of the first skirmishes between U.S. forces and the Vietcong. But it is also apparent that Krummel's wounds are psychic as well as physical. When Gallard sums up the American dream in a story of "the mythic automobile of his youth," Krummel ruminates and concludes, "No longer am I certain if we dream of the power and beauty of the machine or of the stink. Perhaps, and some say for sure, they are the same, but I don't know. I just know the dream is real. Somewhere back in America grown men—doctors, lawyers, corporation chiefs, waste their fluid into the metal, decay and drip, drip, decay and fall, so you and I might dream—and be fooled into a nightmare of death and a cold wind over an open grave." Gallard responds by asking, "Do you see evil everywhere or just reflect it?" It is that sometimes overwhelming sense of his own capacity for evil that has made a cynic of Krummel and that sends his thoughts back to the day he assumed command of a "trick" of ten men in the Operations Section of the 721st Communications Security Detachment at Clark Air Force Base in the summer of 1962.

The rationale for this flashback is that in order

to understand himself, Krummel must understand his relationship with one of the men in his command, Joe Morning. Both Krummel and Morning are college-educated men, and they both share a kind of fierce idealism and capacity for leadership. In Morning, Krummel sees something akin to his own intelligence, intensity, and anger, but he also recognizes that they are inherently different. Crumley goes to great lengths to establish that Krummel is a soldier by virtue of his genetic heritage, tracing the warrior Krummels back to medieval Europe. He also suggests that the nobility and honor that Krummel's ancestors gained from war are not to be had in the modern army. The routine of his command is deathly boring to Krummel, so he and his troops look for an outlet in Philippino bars and whorehouses, or by inventing practical jokes aimed at their superiors, especially the incompetent Lt. Dottlinger.

In most of these adventures, Morning is the ringleader. At one point, Krummel becomes his partner in a black market cigarette scheme, which involves buying American brands at military prices and selling them in Manila for nearly twice the price. When they are caught by corrupt police, who suggest that they might be set free if they are willing to offer a bribe, Krummel envisions the military punishment for their crime and is willing to go along, but Morning refuses. When Krummel asks, "Where do you get off being so damned moral?," Morning responds, "What we're doing is okay; what that bastard is doing is crooked. He's supposed to be a cop." In this sense Morning is the moral center of the novel; the rightness or wrongness of his actions is determined by the role he assigns himself, and since he defines himself as an opponent of both the government and the military, anything he can do to disrupt the system is moral. Unlike Krummel, who was born and bred a soldier, Morning has always been a rebel and defender of unpopular causes. He was thrown out of his Southern college for supporting a demonstration by blacks, who were protesting bad treatment from the white college football players, and he later joined marches and sit-ins in the South for civil rights. Ultimately he had to choose between jail and the army, so he chose the lesser of two evils.

Much of the novel's tension comes from the conflicts within Krummel that are occasioned by Morning's rebellion. Krummel admires Morning because he acts on principle, but he is also Morning's superior who must discipline him or take the blame for his disturbances; therefore, he exhibits the paradoxical behavior of one who wants to be a brotherly friend but has to be an authority figure as well.

When the trick is sent to Vietnam on a secret intelligence mission, they set up their radio equipment on a hill surrounded by jungle. They are soon the target of a Vietcong raid, and both Morning and Krummel distinguish themselves in the fighting. Near the end of the battle Krummel shoots Morning, and he is himself wounded by Lt. Dottlinger. We never know if Krummel has shot Morning intentionally or not. Not even Krummel knows for sure, and that confusion over his own capacity for such an act is a large part of the cause of his despair. While Crumley prefers to leave Krummel's possible motive for the shooting ambiguous, it is clear that Krummel sees Morning as an innocent who strikes out against corruption, thinking that it can somehow be done away with. When Morning shows that he, like Krummel, can channel his rage in order to kill with considerable skill and even enjoyment for the very government he despises, Krummel may want to save him from compromising himself by shooting him before he has time to realize that he has lost his foolish innocence. However, Morning survives and joins the Huks to wage a guerilla war for Philippine independence. He has come to terms with the violence that is a part of his personality, and he is willing to direct it into the service of a revolutionary cause. Krummel, on the other hand, returns to Vietnam to continue to kill the enemy of the government he serves, fulfilling a sort of genetic destiny that he seems not to understand but which he relishes nevertheless.

Reviews of *One to Count Cadence* were generally favorable. In the *New York Times* (21 October 1969) Thomas Lask wrote that it could "easily compete for the awards as one of the best novels of the year" because even though a first novel, it "is as solid as an Egyptian diorite statue"—taut, carefully crafted, and without a fuzzy character or incident. John Reed, a retired army master sergeant writing in the *Saturday Review* (3 January 1970), bemoaned "the incidence of booze, broads, brawls, and bad language," but pointed out that Crumley's "prose is lush and extravagant," and suggested that "he is a story-teller in the old-fashioned sense," who has learned the lessons of Hemingway and James Jones. Like Reed, David Dempsey cited the excess of brawling, drinking, and sex in his review in the *New York Times Book Review* (16 November 1969), but he also found Crumley's strength to be "his ability to overwhelm these faults with a stunning narrative talent." In *Library Journal* (1 September 1969), David E. Lawson applauded Crumley's "keen sense of service absurdities," but he thought the novel as a whole to be generally uneven, incorporating "some first rate service humor with some second rate service philosophy." Only Sarah Blackburn, writing in *Book World* (2 November 1969), thought the novel to be, like "old John Wayne movies," a bit anachronistic: "It's late for this brawling romantic novel about the hell of war, the value of friendship, the difficulties of loving, and how to be a man despite it all."

In a sense, Blackburn's assessment of Crumley's first novel can apply to the next three as well: his work does indeed have the spirit of John Wayne movies; but as he would prove, even the often anachronistic conventions of the hard-boiled detective thriller can be revivified with good writing and solid characterizations. In his next three books Crumley transforms the character of Slag Krummel into a Western private detective, but whether the character is named Milton Chester Milodragovitch III, as he is in *The Wrong Case* and *Dancing Bear*, or Chauncey Wayne Sughrue, as he is in *The Last Good Kiss*, he owes a great deal to the narrator of *One to Count Cadence*. Like Krummel, these detectives are highly educated men who have had considerable experience in the military. Also like Krummel, both Milodragovitch and Sughrue refuse to be moral arbiters of the situations in which they find themselves. They are often nearly as corrupt as the bad men they pursue—they drink to excess, have drug habits, fornicate as frequently as possible, cuss unmercifully, brawl at the slightest hint of insult, and commit crimes ranging from auto theft to murder—and yet, as strange as it may seem, they are always redeemed, perhaps because Crumley does a fine job of making the reader realize that his heroes are dispensers of frontier justice born into an age that considers itself too civilized for them. In any case, the reader has no trouble identifying with these men, who seem always to land on their feet and who, no matter what despicable act they commit, always seem justified in doing it because of the higher principle—call it courage or honor, truth or justice—that they pursue.

Milton "Milo" Milodragovitch in *The Wrong Case* often assumes the role of street philosopher. He tells us that "the people who came to me asking for help convinced me that the world was just as stupid and filthy and cruel and corrupt as I thought it was." Some of this cynicism is the result of his situation in life: his grandfather, who established the family fortune, might have been governor of Montana, but he affected a Cossack uniform. His father was a drunk and a suspected suicide, and his mother was a drunk and a certain suicide who, before she died, arranged that her money be placed in a trust fund until her son reached the age of 53. So Milo, although a rich man, cannot touch his money, and is forced to live from day to day, working as a private detective and stewing in his bitterness and the considerable quantity of whiskey he consumes. He justifies his behavior with a question, "I have neither character nor morals, no religion, no purpose in life, . . . so is it any wonder I drink?"

At the beginning of *The Wrong Case* Milo, who has done a steady business in sleazy divorce investigations, finds that he is essentially out of business when the state passes a no-fault divorce law. As he sits in his office in Meriwether, Montana, feeling sorry for himself, he is visited by a beautiful redhead, Helen Duffy, who asks him to find her brother, Raymond. Milo offers to do so if Helen will spend her nights with him. She pretends not to understand and leaves. Milo later discovers that Helen, an English professor at an Iowa college, has been having an on-and-off affair with Dick Diamond, Milo's friend and an English professor at the local Mountain States University. Milo recants and accepts Helen's job offer, but refuses to take money unless he is successful.

Helen's brother is found overdosed on heroin in the restroom of a bar near the Willomot Indian Reservation. Milo discovers that Raymond was associated with a group of local freaks and homosexuals more or less headed by Lawrence Reese, a huge, mean transvestite. By unraveling the clues, Milo learns that Raymond was murdered because of his involvement with a local drug ring. A sudden increase in hard drugs in Meriwether has led to a dramatic rise in street crime. Milo finds the source of the drugs to be Nickie DeGrumo, owner of the Riverfront Motor Inn and husband to the homely daughter of an East Coast Mafia don. Nickie has gotten into the drug business without the blessings of his father-in-law, and when things begin to sour he begins murdering people to cover his tracks. Milo eventually confronts Nickie in the bar at the Riverfront. He has received tacit approval from Lt. Jamison, of the local police, to kill the person responsible for the influx of drugs and the hike in street crime. But Milo has his own private grudge to settle, since he has also discovered that Nickie murdered his friend Simon, a politically radical old wino who used to be the best criminal lawyer in the mountain West but gave it up because of his disaffection with the system. Confronted by Milo, Nickie has a heart attack and dies instantly.

In the meantime, Milo has become more and

more involved with Helen Duffy, and in the novel's last scene he confronts her mother, whom Helen has represented as a manipulative bitch. What Milo discovers is that Raymond was actually Helen's son, the product of an affair when she was thirteen, that Helen is a pathological liar, and that while she has been living with him, she has continued her affair with Dick Diamond. Milo is unable to bear this last affront to his masculinity, and the novel ends with Helen leaving and Milo settling down to drink a beer and forgive her.

The tension in this novel comes from the confrontation between the old way of life in the West and the new reality of urban street crime. Near the beginning of the novel, Milo says, "Meriwether didn't have much street crime, perhaps because we still suffered from some frontier idea of justice: shoot first, apologize to the survivors." Of course, in many ways, the hard-drinking, hard-boiled Milo is a representative of the old-fashioned frontier brand of justice and Lt. Jamison is a symbol of the new law enforcement officer. As Milo discovers layer after layer of corruption, he learns that society has changed significantly and that in most ways the old justice simply does not work.

Although Greil Marcus of *Rolling Stone* (23 March 1978) cited *The Wrong Case* as "astonishingly sordid," most reviewers agreed that it was a vividly written tale that succeeds because Crumley manages to work within the tradition of Dashiell Hammett, Raymond Chandler, and Ross Macdonald and still be original. In *Publishers Weekly* (14 April 1975), a reviewer claimed that Crumley "purposely fashioned" *The Wrong Case* after Ross Macdonald's California mysteries, yet he applauded Crumley for rivaling his purported model by creating "startlingly real characters." The parallel between Milo and Lew Archer is also pointed out by H. C. Veit in *Library Journal* (1 June 1975), who saw *The Wrong Case* as "one of the existentialist California thrillers, a cut better than most of the competition." Peter S. Prescott of *Newsweek* (23 June 1975) argued that the novel is "a deliberate extension of the by-now-venerable Hammett-Chandler-Macdonald tradition, and an exceptionally good example of the genre." Prescott claimed that Crumley is able to use his predecessors' work while asserting his own tone and creating a style "that imprints itself on the reader's memory." Only the reviewer for the *New York Times Book Review* (14 September 1975) cited Crumley's use of the conventions of detective fiction as a problem: "Crumley has the general idea, but his technique needs refining; and while he handles the situations well enough, a cliché is still a cliché."

It is doubtful that Crumley took such criticism seriously since in *The Last Good Kiss*, his next novel, he used the same "unhappy, . . . near alcoholic, lonesome" private eye with integrity that he did in *The Wrong Case*, only this time he called him Chauncey Wayne Sughrue. Sughrue served three hitches in the army and picked up a master's degree in English literature from Colorado State while on a domestic spying mission there. He was working the sports desk of the Witchita *Eagle-Beacon* when he began doing private detective work for a finance company. As the novel opens, he has settled into private detective work in Meriwether, Montana, at least as a part-time profession. When he is not working on a divorce case or repossessing a car, he is tending bar at a local topless joint, the Red Baron. To Sughrue, the detective work is unromantic and often dirty, but he does it well and has no qualms about any means he has to use to finish a case.

As the story begins, Sughrue is hired to watch over the drunken poet and womanizer Abraham Trahearn by Trahearn's ex-wife, Catherine. After a binge that lasts several weeks and involves stops at most of the sleazy bars in the Western United States, Trahearn gives Sughrue the slip. Sughrue catches up with him at Rosie's Bar in Sonoma, California. The owner of the bar, Rosie Flowers, offers Sughrue her life savings, $87, to find her daughter, Betty Sue, who has been missing for ten years. Sughrue does a little routine checking and becomes intrigued with the disappearance of Betty Sue, once an aspiring actress who became a flower child and was eventually drawn into the corrupt underworld of pornographic films. Trahearn encourages Sughrue in his search, and they travel the West looking for leads. Sughrue comes to recognize Betty Sue as the "eternal victim" whose extraordinary sex appeal is used against her, and his search for her soon becomes an all-consuming quest that leads him to a rehabilitation center for troubled girls operated by Selma Hinds in the mountains outside Fort Collins, Colorado. Selma tells him that Betty Sue, after six months at the center, recovered her innocence and died in peace. Sughrue doubts both assertions, but a check of death certificates at the county courthouse convinces him that Betty Sue is dead, and he sets off on "a black ceremonial wake" that lasts several weeks.

In the meantime, Sughrue has gotten to know Trahearn and his curious domestic situation. He is a World War II marine hero, a successful poet, and the author of three best-selling novels. For nearly twenty years he was married to Catherine, who divorced him because of his penchant for infidelity,

Crumley   Snow   chpt 1 / 1

Chapter One

Those occasional prophets of doom who drank in the Hell-
gate Liquor Store and Lounge began to talk about winter way
before summer began to breathe its last heated breath. As early
as August, the Moon of Burning Grass, they drew an Indian sign
on winter, claiming to read the wind and see the cold, sear
heart of February, the Moon of Children Weeping in the Lodges.
The hornets, these soothsayers said, were building their nests
forty feet off the ground, forecasting a flood of snow, and
the bees were beating their little wings to frazzled wisps
as they hoarded honey against the Montana winter. In the
Valley of the Meriwether River, in spite of the late summer
heat, the horses and cattle sported coats like yaks, and the
wooly worms grew round and fat like hair balls gagged up by
reluctant cats. Ah, the winter coming, they predicted, would
be like a long campaign on the Russian Front.

And who was I to disagree? Unemployed private investigators
who tend bar for a living aren't particularly noted as prognas-
ticators of climatic disasters -- just personal ones. And I
had seen enough Montana winters to know that the worst part

Revised typescript which Crumley explains is "from a novel I never wrote. Somehow the first paragraph became Dancing Bear, *but not for a long time" (the author).*

and who now lives with Trahearn's mother, Edna, who owns a home within shouting distance of her son near Cauldron Springs, Montana. For the past three years, Trahearn has been married to Melinda, a curiously bewitching woman who is a potter. Her pieces usually feature the faces or contorted bodies of women who have been tortured. Melinda is as unfaithful to Trahearn as he is to her, and her infidelity has caused him to suffer so much that he is unable to write.

After his binge, which is brought on by the grief he feels over the death of Betty Sue, Sughrue returns to Meriwether, where he receives a call from Rosie informing him that Betty Sue is still alive, and that her ex-husband, Jimmy Joe, has received a post card from her from Fort Collins. As he drives to Colorado, Sughrue realizes that he has been manipulated by Trahearn, and when he arrives at Selma Hinds's his suspicions are confirmed. Betty Sue Flowers is really Melinda Trahearn, and Sughrue has been encouraged in his search by Trahearn because the jealous husband wanted to dig up every bit of his wife's sleazy past in order to find out about her infidelities to him. What is more, he discovers that because Melinda stole $40,000 from the pornography ring before she left to seek refuge with Selma, they are still looking for her. Before Sughrue can rescue her, she is kidnapped by Mr. Hyland, the head of the ring, who intends to recoup his losses by using Betty Sue in his films and then dumping her down a mine shaft. Sughrue saves her in a bloody raid on Hyland's home. She returns to Sonoma and, while she is gone, Trehearn begins writing what will be his greatest novel, "about love and forgiveness." Unfortunately, when Betty Sue returns to Cauldron Springs, now comfortable with her old identity, Trahearn is once again thrown into a fit of depression; he can't write, and he tries to commit suicide. Betty Sue's body is found floating in a swimming pool with three slugs in her back, set up to look as though she was murdered by Hyland and his men. But only Sughrue knows the truth: she was killed by Catherine Trahearn, who would do anything to protect her ex-husband's fragile talent, and the novel ends with Sughrue vowing to Trahearn that he will get him, although it is also made clear that he never does.

As ironic as it may seem, *The Last Good Kiss*, with its hard-boiled narrator who claims, "I'm not Johnny Quest or the moral arbiter of the Western world. More like a second-rate hired gun or a first-rate saddle tramp," is really a book about women. Through the character of Betty Sue, Crumley is able to explore how women are used by a male-dominated society and forced into the role of eternal victims. In Edna and Catherine Trahearn he depicts woman, not as victim, but as victimizer, for these women, through domineering and misguided mothering, destroy Betty Sue at the very moment she has become reconciled to her past and is prepared to be a victim no longer. Sughrue is uncomfortable traveling in the worlds of these women and that uncomfortableness translates itself into a confusion that permits him to be taken in by the illusions created for his benefit by Trahearn, Melinda, Betty Sue, Edna and Catherine, and Selma Hinds. Despite his mastery in the world of men, in the world of women he is powerless, and ultimately unable to stop the destruction of Betty Sue, even though he senses its approach.

The Last Good Kiss is not only an exceptional genre novel, it is extremely good fiction, and the critics saw its merit. In *Rolling Stone* (5 October 1978) Greil Marcus claimed that *The Last Good Kiss* succeeded as well or better than Robert Stone's *Dog Soldiers* in its portrait of the sordid America of the 1970s, even though the latter work was considered a "real novel" and detective fiction is rarely if ever taken seriously. Marcus argued that because of its exceptional style, dialogue, characterizations, and humor, *The Last Good Kiss* surpassed Ross Macdonald's *The Chill*, and in its treatment of the friendship between two men the novel was at least the equal of Raymond Chandler's *The Long Goodbye*. In the *Virginia Quarterly Review* (Spring 1979) a somewhat puzzled reviewer could not decide whether it was Crumley's style or the novel's milieu that made *The Last Good Kiss* so engaging. Jim Mele, in the *American Book Review* (October 1979), noted the influence of Chandler, Hammett, and Macdonald; applauded the novel's style and dialogue; but ultimately found *The Last Good Kiss* to be "aimless instead of driven, its plot an excuse for showing off a polished hard boiled style instead of a haunting counterbalance for the clipped mannerisms and speech." In *Harper's* (October 1978) a reviewer suggested that no one had told Crumley that he was using genre conventions "as fossilized as the sonnet"—"As long as he writes like this nobody should." And in a similar vein, Bruce Cook, writing in the *Wall Street Journal* (20 October 1978), predicted that with the extinction of the "literary novel," many talented writers would turn their attention to genre fiction: "Crumley's books should resolve any of the lingering doubts that even sniffy academics might have that it is possible to write well and seriously using a form that had its origins in the disreputable pulp paper detective magazines of the Twenties and Thirties."

Dust jacket for Crumley's well-received 1983 novel featuring his character Milo Milodragovitch

To Cook, Crumley's success in both *The Wrong Case* and *The Last Good Kiss* lay in his use of the mystery form to bring characters together and to let his own abilities as a writer shine. In other words, the mystery format is a secondary consideration, and as a method of structuring a literary work it is as valid as "the *Bildungsroman* or the picaresque form or any of the other forms novelists have been using the past few hundred years or so."

In his most recent novel, *Dancing Bear,* Crumley continues his exploration of the mystery form and returns to the character Milo Milodragovitch, who has grown older but no less cynical or tough. As the novel opens, we learn that Milo has abandoned his private agency in favor of a position with Haliburton Security in Meriwether because the steady income helps him support his many vices, which now include a fondness for cocaine. The action begins when Milo receives a certified letter from Sarah Weddington. After driving to the Wedding-

ton home, he discovers that Sarah was one of his father's lovers, that she married rich and inherited a fortune when her husband died, and that she now lives with her grandniece, Gail. Gail has a degree in environmental engineering and has helped her aunt develop an affection for marijuana and radical environmental and political causes. Sarah tells Milo that for the past six weeks a man and woman have met in the small park in front of her home. She asks Milo to find out why.

While he is deciding whether he should take Sarah's case, he manages to foil a convenience-store robbery as part of his Haliburton Security duties. When he threatens to quit the agency, Col. Haliburton offers him a stakeout and a week off, and so he takes it. He arrives at the stakeout disguised as a TV repairman, and his cover is nearly blown when he is accosted by an old man, Abner Haynes, who demands that Milo fix his TV. Eventually Milo sees a woman leave the house he is watching and he follows her, assuming that she is the subject of his surveillance, Cassandra Bogardus. However, he tails her to a bar and discovers that she is really Carolyn Fitzgerald, an environmental attorney from Washington, D.C., interested in buying some wilderness land, part of the Dancing Bear tract, from Milo. He puts her off by claiming that he is too much of a redneck to prohibit jeeps and snowmobiles on his property.

Milo hires Abner to watch the Bogardus house, and he accepts Sarah Weddington's case. After the usual weekly meeting, he follows the man involved in the suspicious meetings in the park to a mountain hideaway outside Elk City, Montana. There the man is murdered with a car bomb. Milo discovers that he was John P. Rideout and that he was carrying a duffle bag loaded with sophisticated weapons, a kilo of marijuana, and several ounces of cocaine. He also finds a matchbook from a Seattle restaurant, so he packs up the guns and drugs and heads for Seattle.

On the way, Milo learns that he is being followed by four men in four different cars. Their skill in tailing him convinces him that they are professionals, but Milo manages to give them the slip in Seattle and make his way to Vashon Island, where he finds Rideout's family. Unfortunately an interview with Rideout's wife proves to be only a sad dead end. As a last resort, Milo calls his Meriwether drug dealer, Raoul, to get the name of someone in the general vicinity of Seattle who will buy the cocaine he is carrying. He sells his drugs to a gang of lesbian dope dealers, and he observes that the gang leader seems to recognize the plastic in which the cocaine is wrapped, but Milo does not pursue his observation and is fortunate to escape with his life.

Back in Meriwether, he finds that two of the men who followed him to Seattle are now camped out in the Bogardus house. When he attempts to break into the house to find out what they are doing there, one of the men commits suicide, and Milo finds the other strangled to death. Later he learns that both were former Seattle policemen working for a Seattle company called Multitechtronics. Through Carolyn he sets up a meeting with Cassandra Bogardus, who tells him that she is a journalist who has uncovered a ring of poachers who are selling grizzly bear and mountain goat skins back East for huge profits. A skeptical Milo continues to pursue his Multitechtronics lead, but he also searches for and finds a Benniwah Indian, Charlie Two Moons, who, Cassandra told him, was involved in the poaching. Through Charlie, Milo finds that poaching is not the problem Cassandra led him to believe it was; through a West Coast lawyer, he discovers that Multitechtronics is a front for a larger, more sinister organization; and almost simultaneously he discovers that Sarah and Gail are missing.

The only alternative Milo has is to return to Seattle to question the leader of the gang of lesbian drug dealers. She tells him that she did recognize the plastic wrapping used for the cocaine, and she gives him a name, Environmental Quality Control Services, a garbage collection conglomerate. Milo finds that the owner of the company is Richard Tewels. Milo and a hired gun from Haliburton Security, Bob Simmons, follow Tewels to a clandestine meeting, and after a bloody shoot-out, Milo learns that he has thwarted a conspiracy among government officials, several international industrialists, and Tewels to cover up a plan to illegally dump toxic wastes. When he returns to Meriwether, he discovers that from the beginning he was the dupe of Sarah, Gail, Cassandra, and Carolyn, who had attempted every legal means to stop Tewels and turned to Milo only as a last resort, knowing that his unconventional methods were the only way to foil Tewels's plan. But Milo, despite being used by these women, has his satisfaction, too: he sees that information the women wanted is traded to the government in return for the cleanup of a dump on

his own property; he sees that land his Cossack-uniformed grandfather had stolen from the Benniwah Indians is returned to them; and he sees that the family of John P. Rideout is taken care of. The entire experience is hardly one to blunt the edge of his cynicism, and he concludes that this was its lesson: "Modern life is warfare without end: take no prisoners, leave no wounded, eat the dead—that's environmentally sound."

Writing in the *New York Times Book Review* (1 May 1983), Jonathan Coleman claimed that *Dancing Bear*, while being "extremely well-written," also "suffers from numbing overkill of action and plot as well as some characters it is hard to care a great deal about." Not only does Coleman not explain how these apparently contradictory views can be reconciled, he also fails to notice Crumley's important statement about the inhumanity of the modern world in *Dancing Bear*. Despite his overt cynicism, Milo is the only protector of humanity in the novel; at a college football game near the end of the novel, he wishes "the boys a better world than their fathers had made." Ostensibly the novel is about protecting the land where the bears danced in Benniwah legend from evil materialists such as Richard Tewels. However, Crumley makes it clear that Milo, too, is a bear, who is made to dance by the environmentalists who manipulate him. In his tough individualism and his concept of frontier justice, Milo is just as much an endangered species as the silver-tipped grizzly, and yet he is used and nearly sacrificed by the very people who would save the bear and his wilderness home. To Milo the environmentalists are essentially the same as the evil materialists in their willingness to abandon values in order to succeed. This is the sort of compromise that Milo's own world view would never permit.

Beginning with his first novel, James Crumley has shown a willingness to explore in his fiction the major issues of our society. Many reviewers, misguided in their concentration on the genre he has chosen for these explorations, have discounted his work because it appears to be pulp fiction. But Crumley is no quitter. He is a writer of exceptional talent who may yet succeed in drawing serious critical attention to high-quality detective fiction that transcends its genre.

Mark Dintenfass
(15 November 1941-   )

Dwight Allen

BOOKS: *Make Yourself an Earthquake* (Boston: Little, Brown, 1969);

The Case Against Org (Boston: Little, Brown, 1970; London: Heinemann, 1971);

Figure 8 (New York: Simon & Schuster, 1974);

Montgomery Street (New York: Harper & Row, 1978);

Old World, New World (New York: William Morrow, 1982).

In 1969, just before the publication of his first novel, Mark Dintenfass told *Library Journal* that he had "always been at some awkward age." He said that he had been "too young to share in the smugness of the 1950s" (the decade of his adolescence, spent in Brooklyn) and "too old to fully trust the revolutions of the 1960s" (years he had spent as a literature student and a writer at universities in New York and Iowa, and as a member of the Peace Corps in Africa). He said that he felt like a "sort of tourist," and that as a writer he had no theme, unless his sense of the "doubleness of things" could be described as such.

The characters in Dintenfass's novels embody the doubleness that he sees at the heart of things. They are New Yorkers, and most of them are intellectuals, or intellectual misfits. They are big, awkward, and consumed by ideas. They spend their lives in single-minded pursuit of ideal states of being. Dintenfass writes about his furious dreamers with ironic sympathy. His prose is exuberant, playful, and copious. None of the astringency or anti-metaphorical minimalism that is present in so much contemporary fiction is to be found in his work. He is in love with the possibilities of language, much as his characters are in love with the possibilities of transforming themselves.

Dintenfass was born in a working-class district of Brooklyn called East New York, the second child of Sidney Dintenfass and Gerri Berger, who were also born and raised in Brooklyn. Their parents, Dintenfass says, "were all born in the old country, in that historic blur where Russia and Poland and the Austro-Hungarian Empire faded into nightmare." Dintenfass's paternal grandfather came to America

Mark Dintenfass

when he was a teenager, and he eventually became the owner of a dry-goods store in Brooklyn. His other grandfather, Dintenfass says, "was a sort of rabbi. He didn't have a congregation, but he seems to have spent a lot of time hanging around the local synagogue. He was not much discussed by my family." Jacob Lieber, the patriarch of the immigrant family in *Old World, New World* (1982), is at least partly based on this grandfather, who, like Jacob, arrived in Brooklyn with four children in tow.

Near the end of the Second World War, the Dintenfasses moved out of East New York to an apartment on Montgomery Street, in the Crown

Heights section of Brooklyn—a neighborhood, he says, that is "notorious now as a battleground for Hasidim and blacks but in those days was a rather genteel working-class district." Dintenfass's father worked in Manhattan garment factories as a "cutter"—that is, as "the guy who ran the machine around piles of fabric to make the pieces that fat Jewish ladies (most of them my aunts) sewed into dresses and suits that thin Jewish ladies (most of them my cousins) bought at Bloomingdale's or the 1940s' equivalent." The garment industry was a seasonal business, and Dintenfass remembers the times when his father came home after being laid off. It was "never a pleasant suppertime scene."

In 1952, Sidney Dintenfass moved the family to Miami Beach in order to help operate a restaurant that one of Dintenfass's aunts had just bought. Within a year, "everything and everyone having gone bust," the Dintenfasses moved back to Brooklyn and rented the bottom half of a two-family house "just around the corner from—and within capgun range of—the Montgomery Street apartment house that is still the only place that . . . I think of as home."

When he was in eighth grade Dintenfass announced that he intended to become a physicist, an ambition that he didn't officially abandon until after he had entered college. As a young boy, he read mainly comic books ("particularly the old ECs, which I generally preferred, being a slightly morbid child, to the more wholesome DCs"), science fiction, and books about rocketry. Later, he says, "I matured in a manner parallel to history by switching from gruesome mythology to gruesome history. I read everything I could find about the Aztecs and the Nazi death camps." Later still, when he was at Brooklyn Technical High School, during the "one single blessed term when I had a good English teacher," he read *Erewhon* ("my first *real* book, I think") and the utopias of Orwell and Huxley and Thoreau.

In 1959, Dintenfass entered Columbia University on a New York State Science Scholarship, which he had chosen to accept instead of a state-funded liberal-arts scholarship—the former paid more of his expenses—and in spite of the fact that he had more or less concluded that he didn't want to pursue physics. Dintenfass says that he came to this conclusion, which he describes as "a romantic rejection of science rather than an embracing of anything else," after reading another utopian, Jean-Jacques Rousseau. After his sophomore year, when he turned to literature, Columbia replaced his state scholarship with a university scholarship. Among

Dintenfass's professors were Moses Hadas and Eric Bentley, but the teacher who meant the most to him was George Nobbe. Dintenfass describes Nobbe as a "three-hundred-pound non-scholar of eighteenth-century literature and the laughing-stock of everyone in the Columbia English Department, except for a handful of us, who would have died for him." Nobbe taught a fiction-writing course as well as eighteenth-century literature. He is one of two teachers to whom Dintenfass dedicated his first novel, and the model for a character in *Figure 8*.

Dintenfass says that he loved Columbia. "It was to Brooklyn what Paris is now to Appleton"—the college town in Wisconsin where he has lived and taught since 1968. After he received his undergraduate degree in 1963, Dintenfass stayed on at Columbia for another year to study dramatic literature under Robert Brustein. (As an undergraduate, Dintenfass had half-seriously entertained the idea of becoming a movie or theater critic. He says he dreamed of replacing the "middle-brow idiots" who wrote for the *New York Times*—"*middle-brow* was very much my favorite word"—and he did write drama reviews for the campus paper, and even managed to make an enemy of a student actor who is now a novelist by suggesting that "his rendition of Richard III was character casting.") Dintenfass didn't find advanced literary study to be inspiring. "Graduate literature programs are where sentimental souls go to die," he says. He wrote his master's thesis on Heinrich von Kleist. It was the last academic paper he would write. He says that the thesis "demonstrated that justice and injustice were used by Kleist as metaphors for order and chaos. The bent was 'existential.' "

In 1962, Dintenfass married Phyllis Schulman, whom he had first met in Brooklyn when he was fifteen. They are distant cousins. As teenagers they had courted each other's friends, and then, Dintenfass says, "One night, with the moon in perfect eclipse, and ruby-red—this is a fact that I wouldn't dare use in a fiction—we got rid of the middlemen."

In 1964, Dintenfass joined the Peace Corps. He was sent to Addis Ababa, where for two years he taught English at Haile Selassie I University. He wrote several stories during his stay, including one that was heavily influenced by his reading of Isaac Singer. (Set in medieval Leipzig, it is about black Jewish magic and is, Dintenfass says, "pure invention.") He sent the story to the Writers' Workshop at the University of Iowa and was admitted to the program.

At Iowa, Dintenfass sat in a class with Gail

Godwin ("I was afraid of her and we never exchanged words") and avoided the seminars taught by such celebrities as Kurt Vonnegut, Robert Coover, and "a Chilean guy who had just published one of his nightmares." In his first year, he taught an introductory literature course for undergraduates, and the following year, having been awarded one of the Workshop's two assistantships, he taught an undergraduate writing class. He was writing a novel called "Leab," after its main character, and Richard Yates, one of the faculty members whose seminars Dintenfass didn't avoid, was so impressed by it that he sent several chapters to his agent. The novel was published in early 1969—as *Make Yourself an Earthquake* and with Yates as one of the two people to whom it was dedicated—by which time Dintenfass had received an M.F.A. from Iowa and had been hired by Lawrence University as an assistant professor of English.

The hero of *Make Yourself an Earthquake* is a retired schoolteacher and widower whose children have put him in a Queens nursing home. A "big, paunchy" man whose "tangle of white hair has a taint of yellow in it like a polar bear's pelt," Leab keeps busy by reading left-wing journals, pulling schoolboy pranks, and taunting an earnest rabbi who would like to teach him the "joy of the Sabbath." He is as unhappy in the nursing home as he was in his loveless marriage, and it is not long before he contrives to escape. Though he has little idea of where he will escape to—certainly not to one of the suburban homes of his children—this detail doesn't much matter to him. What he wants from his adventure—and what he experiences—is "a moment of sheer terror," a moment of unbridled being. An elderly Huck Finn, Leab rides the subway into Manhattan and eventually finds refuge at the apartment of his grandniece, a Barnard student named Suzie Gottlieb. Aside from his brother, Aaron, who has spent most of his life in mental institutions, Suzie is the one relative whom he "cared about at all."

The novel is set in the period when it was written—the late 1960s—and Leab, who is as old as the century, finds himself among some of that era's passionate experimentalists. Suzie lives with a black engineering student grandly named Sainte-Auguste Dupris, who belongs to a West Indian sect that worships an African king called Wamru XI. Augie is mopey and distant, and while Suzie won't leave him, she allows another Columbia student named Conrad Weisman to imagine that she someday will. Brooklyn-born and "trapped," as he puts

it, "in a lout's carcass," Connie is the first of several exuberant eaters to be found in Dintenfass's work. He is also the novel's star intellectual. (He makes a brief appearance, in an academic role, in Dintenfass's third novel.) He lectures to Suzie on "vision" and "existential despair" and to Leab—who has gone into the business of selling fried banana peels in order to finance a trip to Africa with his trio of friends—on the subject of psychedelics and "reality."

Leab's escape from the nursing home, his hectic adventures in upper Manhattan, and his subsequent flight to Africa are all parts of a search for what he calls "concentrated life." In the East African kingdom of Khaffa, the home of Augie's god, Leab discovers a country whose Dionysian rituals can accommodate his long repressed energies. He nibbles on a hallucinogenic herb, dances like a dervish at a festival that reenacts the Wamrugian myth of creation, and has a moment of pleasure ("he hardly felt it") with a middle-aged British woman whose husband, a remnant of the colonial past, is in clumsy pursuit of Suzie. Myth-riddled Khaffa also serves to resolve the tensions among the triangle of Leab's young companions. When Wamru XI is apparently killed in a coup, the fanatical Augie (whose real name, it turns out, is Fred Turner; he is the son of a Chicago preacher and not, as he has claimed, a Haitian) leaves Suzie to his rival ("the fat fool") and sets out to find a replacement for his dead deity. He settles for a native shoeshine boy. Suzie, who has been unable to "feel anything" in Africa, decides that she feels something for Connie which she suspects is love. They return to New York, where they are married, with Leab, who has returned to the nursing home, as a disapproving witness. "Why do they have to make our mistakes?" Leab asks a fellow inmate at the home.

In the *New York Times Book Review*, Harry Roskolenko described *Make Yourself an Earthquake* as a "comedy of student manners, intellectual frippery, sentimental Jewishness, African rituals, and the Columbia-Barnard complex of sex and scholarship. . . . When Jewish folkways and African myths combine, it makes for earthy satire and happy literary mayhem." The novel received other favorable reviews, and the film rights were sold to producer Sidney Glazier. (Glazier produced Mel Brooks's *The Twelve Chairs* and Woody Allen's *Take the Money and Run*.) Dintenfass wrote a screenplay, but the project went no further. He also wrote a screenplay based on his second novel—in collaboration with a Yale University filmmaker, Peter Rosen—but he and

Rosen were unable to find any backing for it.

The thirty-five-year-old divorced narrator of Dintenfass's second novel, *The Case Against Org* (1970), weighs three hundred and twenty-two pounds, lives with his mother in a book-cluttered (*Lolita, Justine, Tilly's Tickler*) apartment in upper Manhattan, and writes and publishes a quarto-sized weekly called the *Orgonon Newsletter*. The contents of the *Newsletter* are loosely based on the psychosexual theories of Wilhelm Reich, and its profits keep this hustler of primal energy, George Nathan Blomberg, or Org, in chocolate cherries and other delicacies.

Org's story takes the form of a diary written over a period of nine months in the late 1960s. Though these confessions are not, he tells us, the great systematic work on the entrapment of the life force that he had intended to write, they will "do" as a record of the "feud between my carcass and my self." Org sets out to describe the events of a climactic week in his "orgonotic" career—and thus to define himself as a revolutionary thinker—but as he tells his story the present intrudes upon his neat recapitulations and forces him to consider the possibility that he is an ordinary fraud.

Org's seminal week begins one summer day as he is returning home from an upper-Broadway grocery. He collapses on the street, perhaps intentionally ("You wouldn't expect a man Org's size to fall so meticulously"), and, in fact, he is smiling when the medics arrive. For, "Here, in my collapse, was the long-awaited warp in the course of fate." He is transported to a hospital and placed in a weight-loss unit known to its inmates as the Pigpen. But Org proves to be an uncooperative patient. The therapy sessions make him laugh. "Hunger made me clear-eyed." And so, one night, buoyed by the riots (Chicago, 1968), which he has seen on television ("fury and chaos, the unformed pureness of the orgone had come bubbling up—and without me!"), he walks out of the hospital into the fearsome world. A worshipper of primal energy, Org quakes in the New York night. "If a man my size may be said to skulk, I skulked.... puffing, nervous, drenched."

In the world outside the hospital—and outside the forum of his *Newsletter*, whose subscribers, he realizes, are "mainly cranks and crackpots"—Org has few allies. Among them are not his "rigid, sanctimonious" Forest Hills relatives, whose daughter, Lila, has been impregnated (with Org's fatherly connivance) by Benny Fried, a Columbia student and Org's editorial assistant. By the time Org escapes from the hospital, unreliable Benny is in Chicago with Lila, having persuaded his former roommate, bony, freckled, carrot-haired Vivian Stein, to take over his editorial duties. Other than his failing mother, whose duties Viv will also eventually assume, Org has only this "lank, unlovely creature." She unblinkingly shepherds his *Newsletter* into print, washes his back, feeds him, and shares her bed with him. Under her influence he comes to understand that while he is a windbag—a "piddling, waddling, comic subversive," whose neo-Reichian theories amount to "gross romanticism"— he is the kind of windbag that will attract a crowd. Viv foresees a career as a lecturer for him. She proposes a cross-country tour, and Org, thinking that immobility rather than fat is his problem ("there is no skinny guy inside me struggling to get out"), weakly assents.

Dintenfass doesn't show us Org on tour, but we do see him in fine rhetorical form at the conclusion of that week which, he believed, would reveal him to be a serious subversive. After eating his way through Manhattan—"never," Paul Theroux wrote in a *Chicago Tribune* review, "has a novel so resembled the menu of an automat"—Org delivers a talk to a liberationist group called the League Against Sexual Harassment. Org is not the virile theoretician that L.A.S.H.'s members expected, and his lecture on "the beauty of the digestive tract" and "the delights of tongue, larynx, and esophagus" disappoints them. Org doesn't quite believe what he says either, and he returns home an "ugly, beaten, formless, self-pitying lump of a man." But then plain, energetic Viv arrives. "She shamed me into activity," Org says, "and so I began to write."

In his *Chicago Tribune* review of *Org*, Paul Theroux went on to write that "one is tempted to say that this [book] is *La Nausée* rewritten by Beckett, but that is too neat. . . . Dintenfass's ventriloquism is his own, his wit is precise, and his learning is considerable." And a reviewer for the *Chicago Sun-Times* wrote: "He is tremendously funny, sometimes sharply so, but never cruel."

In 1970, Dintenfass took a leave of absence from Lawrence. He spent the year in New Haven, where his first son, David, was born (Nathan, his second child, was born in 1975) and where he began work on a novel about twin brothers called "Blues for Robin." The next year, he went to Germany to teach in one of Lawrence's overseas programs. He continued to work on the novel there, but when he returned to Wisconsin, in the summer of 1972, he put it aside and started the book that would become

Figure 8 (1974). Though Dintenfass describes "Blues for Robin" as a "mess" and never tried to publish it, he was able, he says, to use some of its setting (Connecticut) and some of its plot (a murder attempt) in *Figure 8*.

Like his two predecessors, the hero of *Figure 8* burns for an ideal—in this case, the beauty of formal design. He is a silversmith (which also happens to be his name: "he chose the craft to suit his name"), and alone in his upper-Broadway workshop, which doubles as his apartment, he is all concentration. "Blond, bearded, awkwardly tall, Michael Silversmith . . . perched on a stool with his back bent and his knees hooked on a rung so that he curled like a question mark around his bench. The twin black tubes that carried gases to his torch were wound about his arm like the straps of a phylactery; a jeweler's glass sat in the center of his forehead; his eyes, behind yellow safety glasses, were fiercely fixed; and his tongue lolled along his lower lip, pink tip showing, as the moment came when the solder would flow." But Silversmith has lately been unable to finish what he starts. He jettisons imperfect brooches, unwilling to recast them, until one snowy day, he finally decides to seek help from his teacher, a master silversmith called Otti. (Otti is George Nobbe's fictive counterpart.)

Dintenfass's characters tend to have difficulty negotiating the hard, slippery surfaces of the world, and Silversmith, a "big, ungainly gawk," is no exception. Pushing his bicycle along Broadway toward Otti's house, he is hit by a car driven by a poet who is in a hurry to get to a book-signing party. The poet, who was born Geoffrey Holzman and now publishes laconic, second-rate verse under the slick name of Elliot Hopper, has turned up before in Silversmith's life. Eight years earlier, on the Brittany seashore, Hopper seduced Silversmith's gullible (now former) wife, Angela, while "honest, sentimental" Silversmith gave swimming lessons to the poet's prepubescent daughter, Florrie. The present-day Florrie—a Wellesley drop-out who keeps gerbils and marmots in her Manhattan apartment and spends her publishing-house wages on a psychoanalyst—is on hand for Silversmith's second encounter with her mobile father. Though she doesn't recognize Silversmith, she rides with him to a hospital, where his ruined arm is put into a cast.

Dintenfass tells this story of loopy couplings and recouplings from the points of view of the four main characters: Silversmith, Hopper, Florrie, and Angela. (A fifth character, a bookstore owner and Silversmith's landlord, functions as a kind of

chorus, commenting on what to him looks like a farce.) The action that follows the bicycle accident repeats and develops what took place in Brittany. Thus Angela, who is now a dormitory counsellor at a seaside Connecticut college, discovers that her employer has hired her former lover as a poet-in-residence. And Silversmith, who is unable to work and is soon freed from the burden of *having* to work by the death of his revered mentor, Otti, can now apply himself to pursuing the designs of his aggrieved heart. He seeks out Florrie, who is willing to entertain him up to a point; she thinks he may be the sweet, soothing figure that "artful, sleek, trans-Atlantic" Hopper never was, rather like one of the furry animals she keeps as a pet. Their affair climaxes on a Long Island beach, and Silversmith, in love and finally out of his cast, can go back to work.

But the figure eight has only begun to complete itself. Coastal Connecticut, where Florrie takes Silversmith to visit her scheming Dad and his always available mistress, becomes the set for a recurrence of the betrayals and humiliations of the past. Hopper persuades his daughter to ditch Silversmith—"Could I let my little girl marry a man who could lose his wife to someone like me?," he later asks his rival—and cynical Florrie, who has already concluded that honest, dogged Silversmith is "pathetic," complies. Silversmith requires the actual sight of her betrayal—at a party in Connecticut with a beefy blond man, a kind of commercial version of himself—before he can escape from her and the redundancies of his passive, genteel self. Enraged, Silversmith returns to his workshop and contemplates the most lunatic of all designs: he will murder his nemesis. Planning the murder, he feels "the most singular and sanctified passion I have ever had." But when he returns to Connecticut, an adolescent's switchblade in his pocket, and finds Hopper at a party on the beach ("pompous, confident, obscene" in his bathing trunks), he knows the scene will not turn out as he has designed it. Silversmith revises his plans. He lures Hopper into the sea, an element in which he feels safe. The ludicrous struggle that ensues is one of the funniest scenes in Dintenfass's books. Both men emerge from the water, and Silversmith, perhaps finally freed from his furious idealism, is once again able to return to his craft.

Despite the good notices that *Figure 8* received from reviewers such as Michael Mewshaw and Anatole Broyard, the book sold only slightly more than a thousand copies. Dintenfass tends to regard all of his novels but *Old World, New World* (which will be reprinted in paperback) as "children I couldn't afford to decently support. They've ended up in orphanages. The one with the tenderest limbs and the one that lives in the bleakest orphanage and, thus, the one that tears most at my heart is *Figure 8*."

Dintenfass's fourth novel, *Montgomery Street* (1978), is about a filmmaker's search for a story. It is perhaps the most self-consciously "literary" of his books, and it elicited groans from some reviewers. In the *New York Times Book Review*, Herbert Gold said that the novel seemed "tired" and suggested that its form, a journal, had constricted the author's considerable imagination.

The journal-keeper of *Montgomery Street* is Stephen Mandreg, whose one big hit is a "fancy sex comedy" called *Centerpiece*. According to *Time*, "Burly, genial Stephen Mandreg, 33, is perhaps the most inventive and accessible of the new breed of American comic realists." Mandreg is in Cannes when he becomes famous, but he does not stay long; he shyly departs for a village down the coast that reminds him of his home, Brooklyn. Mandreg has decided that in his next movie he will "do Brooklyn in 1960," an idea that is not much encouraged by his producer, "who doesn't know the difference between Brooklyn and Queens."

Mandreg's journal is a record of his creation of a place called Montgomery Street, which, as he tells us in a preface to his "notes," is to be distinguished from the street that can be found on a map of Brooklyn and from the "illusory" street depicted in a movie called *Montgomery Street*. This bookish precursor of the movie is itself a kind of film, being a series of fragments or framed images in which characters slide in and out of view, as if in search of a role. The characters include not only those whom Mandreg creates out of his memories of his Brooklyn adolescence—a love-starved boy named Stevie Feuer; a depressed, middle-aged junk-shop operator named Max Stein—but those screen-world figures, such as his producer and a starlet urged on him by his producer, who influence the shape of his creative work and are, in fact, incorporated into it. Mandreg's problem is to find a story that can accommodate his fictive characters without violating his vision of Montgomery Street in 1960. (While Dintenfass has considerable fun at the expense of the film industry and even occasionally, at the expense of the serious Mandreg—the appended list of his films is hilarious—the book cannot consistently be read as a parody. As Herbert Gold pointed out, Mandreg's voice is too closely identified with the author's.) In the course of his search for a story

Mandreg discovers that what is true about his Montgomery Street is that it is not "story-like"; or, conversely, that what is exhilarating about Montgomery Street is its banality. The dramatic situations that he makes up for his characters all seem false to him. His story ideas seem to him only a little less ridiculous than those that a "script doctor" whom his producer has hired suggests. Narrative is a trap, Mandreg decides. By the end of his journal, he has hit on a simple, nondramatic device for bringing his two main characters, Stevie and Max, together. (Whether this "story" becomes the film is a question that Mandreg doesn't get to.) "A movie," Mandreg says, "is nothing more than a lot of 'bits' of film juxtaposed in an interesting way. The juxtaposition is everything. . . . Not plot but scene is the crux of it. Not story but the hidden weaving of the images." Or, as Dintenfass might say, "No other Montgomery Street but this one—the novel unfolding."

Among the classes that Dintenfass teaches at Lawrence is a film-studies course. He also teaches modern drama and has directed student productions of *You Can't Take It with You* and Tom Stoppard's *Travesties* and *After Magritte*. But his main duties at Lawrence are the courses that he teaches in creative writing and twentieth-century American fiction. Dintenfass is a gifted and popular teacher. Students who have taken his modern American fiction course have said that he taught them how to read. Perhaps one reason that he so strongly affects students is that he teaches individual books—and the durable pleasures that the discovery of their writers' crafts can afford a reader—rather than "texts" that belong to one or another academic category.

Dintenfass's characters aspire to ideal states of being ("concentrated life," aesthetic bliss, intellectual purity), and for that reason they tend to live apart, outside the orbit of the family. The major characters in his first four books are divorced (Org, Silversmith, Mandreg) or widowed (Leab, Hopper), and the worlds that they inhabit are largely empty of children or siblings or parents or grandparents. (Only in *Figure 8*, in the relationship of Hopper and his daughter, does the familial bond exert dramatic pressure.) In these books marriages and families are sketched retrospectively, as institutions from which sane men—or serious romantics—might be expected to flee. In his most recent novel, *Old World, New World*, Dintenfass explores in detail the domestic circles that Leab, Org, and their spiritual brothers have escaped.

Old World, New World is Dintenfass's longest

Come, meet the family.

Imagine, first, the whole crowd of us with all our heat and tumult gathered together in a living room in Brooklyn to celebrate another bris. The time is April, 1942, a rainy Sunday morning, I believe, but as good a place as any to begin. The drinks are on a sideboard, mostly rye and ginger ale and such small kosher wine, and in the little alcove which Esther called a dining room a _____ wood mahogany table is set and waiting with its burden of food. The Seeber women have spent the week preparing the stuff _____ _____ duly suggests to me (_____ _____ _____ _____) _____ and distant and handsome, _____ the beauty of its mother. _____.

_____ _____ _____ _____ platter of deviled eggs was _____ _____

Manuscript of an early draft for Old World, New World

novel, and, in its historical reach and large cast, his most ambitious. His terrain here is mainly Brooklyn, where his subjects, an immigrant family called the Liebers, have settled. The book opens around the turn of the century when Jacob and Sophie Lieber arrive in Brooklyn from a "muddy and ramshackle [Eastern European] village, the very name of which the family would later conspire to forget," and it ends almost eighty years later, when Jacob and Sophie's descendants, having scattered to Manhattan and Great Neck and Miami and California, gather in Brooklyn to sit *shivah* for Jacob's grandchild, a paleoanthropologist who has died in Africa. The events of the intervening decades Dintenfass relates from the points of view of a dozen or so family members. Like a host at a reunion, he moves nimbly among his voluble characters, piecing together from their various stories a history of the family. Several of these characters survive all or most of the novel's eighty years, but none of them proves to be any more (or any less) central to the family's history than a figure such as the pious and melancholy Jacob, who disappears from the book after eighty pages, or Jacob's granddaughter Deanna Himmelfarb, who does not appear until the book reaches its midpoint. (Dintenfass once said that the "saga" from which he learned most when he was writing his own family chronicle was Gabriel García Márquez's *One Hundred Years of Solitude*. "I understood that it was possible to write about a lot of characters over a very long period of time, and that you could move a story along without using much dialogue.") Jacob, who dies in a synagogue, survives in the memories of his descendants, of course, much as his own father, the fanatically religious Moshe, whom Jacob has left behind in Europe, lives on as a "berating ghost" within him. Though many of the Liebers, especially those of the middle generation, seek to banish the past from their lives, or to mythologize it, the old world clings to them; Moshe is said to be the source of the "taint of strangeness," the unworldly fanaticism and self-absorption that almost all the Liebers exhibit in one way or another.

Dintenfass's heroless saga is also essentially plotless. "There are no stories in life," he tells us. "There is only the slow accretion of choices and disappointments, small victories and abrupt endings, an accumulation of time and experience pushing toward change." The Liebers conduct their lives as if there *were* stories in life, as if—as the second-generation capitalist Sam Lieber imagines—the future were "a vulnerable place," pliant and giving. But the stories the Liebers tell themselves and struggle to make come true do not turn out as they expect. Jacob's nine children (five more are born in America, where, according to Sophie, even labor is made luxurious) do not accept their father's Orthodox faith or the rituals that sustain it, and pursue instead what their mother envisions for them: a better life. ("Let them be Americans," Sophie says to Jacob, who regards his sons' ambition—women are reproductive engines, in his view—as "the American sickness.") But while Jacob's children do become "assimilated" Americans, the happiness that they expect their new status to bring eludes them.

Sam's chocolate business ("with nine retail outlets in the best shopping districts of Brooklyn") eventually folds, and in the process precipitates a terrifically rancorous (and funny) family quarrel, during which each of Sam's siblings accurately names the others' sins: selfishness, hypocrisy, jealousy, lust. Sam's sister Molly, a Rubensesque sensualist, has five marriages before retiring, "in a rapture of self-pity," to a hotel. Her sister Evelyn, the family's most ardent aspirant to middle-class respectability, marries the wrong man—a semiprofessional magician who bounces from job to job—and never quite achieves her ambition. (Evelyn's generation tends to make marriages that, when they don't end in divorce, survive largely in order to keep their failures concealed. Of the three major characters of the third generation only one, a Columbia professor, marries; his two cousins are a lesbian and the lover of an African tribesman.) Evelyn's brother Walter, a "small-*c* communist," who is referred to during family discussions as "the delegate from Russia," spends most of his adulthood grooming his daughter, Jeannie, to be an emblem of liberal culture—only to be told by her that the most useful thing her education has taught her is fornication. (Her remark is not quite accurate—she becomes a paleoanthropologist—but it has a liberating effect on her.) Perhaps the least disappointed of the middle generation of Liebers is Deborah, a spinster who spends her life in mystical anticipation of the moment when she will be united with her dead fiancé. Deborah can't be disappointed in this life, anyway, and, as it turns out, this life—or the millions of readers of a book she writes called *Worlds to Come*—rewards her for her faith.

Near the end of the novel, Walter's daughter, wading in an African river, tells herself, "You are like the rest of them, caught up in a delirium of expectations . . . so self-absorbed, so hardened against hurt, that you have lost the capacity to love."

Like all the other dreamers in her family, Jeannie holds herself and her kin to a standard that can't be met. The Liebers are a family who would not be ordinary, who would banish from their lives what Dintenfass calls the "nervous tedium of real time," and while this wildly stubborn capacity for belief is—to the reader, anyway—the source of their charm, it is also the source of their great unhappiness.

In a long and enthusiastic review in the *New York Times Book Review*, Daphne Merkin said that *Old World, New World* was "a saga to do the genre proud." Other reviewers praised the book in much the same terms. Though Dintenfass certainly doesn't regret its commercial success—it has sold around thirteen thousand copies, far more than any of his previous books—he thinks it might have been read differently had it not been billed as a "genre" novel. In the meantime, Dintenfass has had a short story, "Pictures of Em," published in the *Wisconsin Review* and has been at work on a sixth novel, of which he will say only that it is set in Florida and Brooklyn.

Zelda Sayre Fitzgerald

(24 July 1900-10/11 March 1948)

Nancy G. Anderson
Auburn University at Montgomery
and
Richard Anderson
Huntingdon College

See also the F. Scott Fitzgerald entries in *DLB 4, American Writers in Paris, 1920-1939; DLB 9, American Novelists, 1910-1945; DLB Yearbook: 1981*; and *DLB Documentary Series*, volume 1.

BOOKS: *Save Me the Waltz* (New York: Scribners, 1932; London: Grey Walls, 1953);
Bits of Paradise, edited by Scottie Fitzgerald Smith and Matthew J. Bruccoli (London: Bodley Head, 1973; New York: Scribners, 1974);
Scandalabra (Columbia, S.C.: Bruccoli Clark, 1980).

Virtually everything Zelda Sayre Fitzgerald published during her lifetime is now available in some form. Her writing has found the kind of readership she never reached during her lifetime, and a lively critical debate has developed concerning her talent.

At the vortex of this controversy is *Save Me the Waltz* (1932). The novel was long considered the work of a bright, undisciplined amateur, worthy of attention primarily because it had presumably been influenced by the tastes, ideas, and values of her husband. More recently, *Save Me the Waltz* has received attention in its own right, as the deeply felt and carefully crafted expression of a creative, independent spirit seeking aesthetic and personal achievement independent of her husband's influence, assistance, or even of his preference that she not compete in his sphere of professional accomplishment.

Efforts to measure the extent and significance of Zelda Fitzgerald's literary reputation inevitably involve reflections of F. Scott Fitzgerald's life and career. Principal directions of critical and biographical commentary are three. The first sees Zelda Fitzgerald as a brilliant dilettante, whose efforts at writing paralleled her forays into dance and painting—beginning as diversions or distractions, growing into jealous obsessions with matching the achievement of her husband. A second, opposing thrust insists that she was a pioneer in literate and forceful articulation of the dilemma of the modern American woman—how to find value and purpose in life independent of the culturally determined role of homemaker and subordinate helpmeet expected of all women. This second group of interpreters has approached *Save Me the Waltz* as a primary document in feminist fiction and has tended to read Zelda Fitzgerald's other writing in the light of her struggle to gain spiritual and artistic autonomy despite the often overprotective, sometimes

Zelda Fitzgerald in the early 1920s

jealously competitive opposition of her husband. A third position is found by most assessments, including that of Nancy Milford in *Zelda: A Biography,* in some degree of balance between the first two positions. From this perspective, Zelda Fitzgerald's writing is considered and assessed in its own terms: as the work of a woman of exceptional energy and ability whose slow maturity into the richness of *Save Me the Waltz* was won by victory over the opposing forces within herself—self-doubt, lack of discipline, uncertainty of identity—as much as it was won over external opposition. It was a costly battle, because the struggle was often one growing from, as well as causing loss of, family identity, loss of early values, loss of the security of marriage and love. The cost was indeed so high that, as she approached mature achievement, Zelda Fitzgerald also approached physical and psychological exhaustion. Thus *Save Me the Waltz,* a culmination, is also the record of disintegration; following its 1932 publication, Zelda Fitzgerald was never again able to mount the concentration and discipline necessary

to build upon and surpass its promise. Nevertheless, that novel alone has earned her a position in the world of twentieth-century American fiction. Whether she would have come to write that book had she never moved in the brilliant, sad world of F. Scott Fitzgerald is impossible to say—and beside the point. Her life with him was *her* life, and it led to *Save Me the Waltz,* just as his life with her led to *The Great Gatsby* and *Tender Is the Night.* What each might have done without the other is moot—and unknowable.

The Zelda Fitzgerald who would become the author of *Save Me the Waltz,* as well as a ballerina of some promise and a highly creative painter, was not the creation of F. Scott Fitzgerald. Seeds of her personality, her proclivities, her creativity, preexisted their marriage, in the girl who was born into staid Mongomery, Alabama, with the dawn of the twentieth century. Zelda Sayre's parentage was at once traditional and iconoclastic; her father, Anthony Dickinson Sayre, was a highly respected figure both for his family background and for his own achievements. His forebears had been important in Montgomery civic and political life since pioneer days. By the year of Zelda's birth he had forged an important career, first in law, then in the Alabama legislature, and finally in the judiciary. He ultimately was appointed, and continuously reelected, to the State Supreme Court, where his judicial opinions became models of clarity and probity. They are still widely admired, respected, and used as points of reference in Alabama legal circles. Zelda's mother, Minnie Machen Sayre, came from a family of equal Old South distinction. Her father had been both a member of the Confederate establishment in Kentucky and a U.S. senator of that state. He was a successful entrepreneur during the postwar railroad boom, and thus Mrs. Sayre had had some taste of luxury before marrying the austere and frugal A. D. Sayre, whose social standing had little to do with money.

Zelda Sayre came late in her parents' childbearing lives. She was the youngest of five children—four of them female—and was in some ways her mother's darling. Judge Sayre, always preoccupied with the weight of worldly affairs as well as with supporting a large household on a limited, if respectable, income, seemed to all his children—the youngest most of all—distant and imposing. Minnie Sayre, in contrast, sought outlets from the Victorian staidness of her domestic role by being alternately indulgent and demanding. She seems especially to have encouraged creative independence in Zelda, although she would come to be a harsh judge of her daughter's most unconventional social behavior.

Zelda Sayre, then, early became both independent and self-assured—perhaps absorbing her father's sense of position—and self-indulgent. Biographers conventionalize her as a typical Southern belle. Perhaps she was, in her desire to be a center of attention among men. But her most salient characteristics—a wild abandon bordering on tomboy recklessness, a mischievous sense of humor (she delighted in shocking conventional sensibilities by wearing a skintight and skintoned swimsuit)—are far more individual than socially determined in the mold of the usual belle, interested primarily in social advantage and sex-role gratification of ego. In fact, the legends which coalesced around the young Zelda Sayre in her late teens, tales of daring at college weekends and country club dances with young soldiers from nearby Camp Sheridan, seem rather to be calculated tests of the limits of acceptable behavior for a Southern girl of good background. She was, even before meeting Scott Fitzgerald in the summer of 1918 at one of those country club dances, truly more a creature of the post-Edwardian experimentation than she was a subdued belle. Certainly, her character was shaped by implicit rebellion against the conventions represented by her father; more important, however, were individual personality traits of exuberance, humor, creativity, and at times willfulness. The teenager who danced in the ballet recital of 1916 was already seeking outlets for social and aesthetic activity not available in Montgomery. The young lady fresh out of high school who allowed herself to fall in love with Fitzgerald and his dream of metropolitan glamour, success, and fame was on her way to finding them.

Marriage in St. Patrick's Vestry on Fifth Avenue; adulation as the flapper wife (and supposed model for characters) of the brash young author of *This Side of Paradise*; collaboration in her husband's willing acceptance of the roles of archetypes of the new Jazz Age Golden Youth—Zelda Fitzgerald's marriage seemed fulfillment of all her wishes. Even after her daughter was born, in October 1921, and family responsibilities began to intrude, life still seemed uncomplicated, delightful, a constant source of amusement. Only when Fitzgerald's search for literary success began to turn toward a struggle for artistic achievement—in the works which would become *The Great Gatsby* and *Tender Is the Night;* only when the delights of success began to be tempered with the difficulties of mature life did the glamour begin to fade. The consequent bittersweetness of their lives together is, in fact, much of the stuff of his mature fiction and is central to *Save Me the Waltz.* Her growing restiveness and restlessness, his developing dependence on alcohol, the bouts of marital tension alternating with waves of affection and mutual indulgence have been well explored and documented in Fitzgerald studies. Zelda Fitzgerald's affair with French aviator Edouard Jozan, in the summer of 1924 amid the pines and palms of the Riviera, may have been a relatively innocent flirtation, or perhaps retaliation for some real or imagined marital slight on Scott Fitzgerald's part. It may have been a deeply felt effort to recapture life's romance and excitement. Whatever its original nature, it became a crystallized moment in their lives from which neither would fully recover. She returned to the role of mother and wife, and he completed *Gatsby,* but the marriage never fully healed itself. Beset by self-doubt, he struggled for almost a decade to finish another novel, and she plunged into an ever more frenetic search for outlets for emotional and creative energy.

By 1930, Zelda Fitzgerald's increasing despair had become severe emotional trauma. The rest of her life was a war against mental and emotional disintegration. Her internal struggle was worsened by Fitzgerald's own inability to find artistic or personal stability. Throughout the rest of his life, he strained to write while battling alcoholism, the depletion of energy he termed "emotional bankruptcy," the financial burdens associated with Zelda Fitzgerald's treatments and their daughter's schooling, as well as his own indulgent life pattern. When he died in December 1940, Zelda Fitzgerald had not really lived with him for a decade; she was to live without him for another eight years. Roughly one-quarter of her adult life had been happy and rewarding. Yet throughout it she maintained, despite the awful tensions and agonies of the 1930s, a love for her husband and a respect for his talent. Even when she seems most to have needed to free herself, as Milford's biography shows, she was also deeply aware that what she was had grown from their shared goals and experiences.

From the happiest days into the deepest despair of disorder, Zelda Fitzgerald had sought, perhaps inspired by her husband's example, to add to the meaning (or to combat the meaninglessness) of her life through artistic expression. The pattern of her life helped determine the form and substance of her efforts.

The kinds of artistic activity might be divided into three stages. The first is the happy, exuberant self-expression of her early writing, 1922-1924 Next, during the years between 1927 and 1930, she turned to dance, painting, and increasingly competent fiction, partly to establish a sense of self independent of her husband's identity, partly to escape the difficulties of his own frustrations as he struggled to write his fourth novel. After her breakdown, her most mature work—and at the same time, her most disturbing—emerged insistently in her painting and her fiction, culminating in *Save Me the Waltz.* Partly therapeutic, it was *her* work, not an extension of her life as Mrs. Fitzgerald, not even a rebellion against boredom; it was a struggle to find meaning in form, language, idea, to lose herself in *work* in the best sense of artistic creativity: not for escape, but for truth.

As she moved toward that final commitment, Zelda Fitzgerald moved back and forth among forms of art. As a girl, she had toyed with dance; she would take it up again, seriously, at age twenty-seven. Like most bright youngsters, she had written some verse; as a young married woman, she would turn to writing again, first in light sketches and essays, then in fiction as well. She tried her hand at drawing, too, in those early years of marriage—including a proposed dust jacket for Fitzgerald's *The Beautiful and Damned,* of a nude in a glass of champagne. Later, she would move back and forth among writing (both nonfiction and fiction), painting, and (until 1930) dancing. For ease of examination of her writing, however, it is desirable to treat it in categories, rather than entirely chronologically, since for the most part, the three periods of her writing are identified, first with nonfiction, then with short fiction, and third with *Save Me the Waltz.* While some parallel activity is involved, there is, overall, a pattern of stages. Only after the novel did she return to nonfiction and try drama.

Whatever form is under examination, and whatever the seriousness of style, purpose, or subject matter—even in the deepest agonies of self-discovery in *Save Me the Waltz*—Zelda Fitzgerald was often an artist of charm, wit, and delight. Like Emily Dickinson, she loved words for their own sake—for the surprise they could offer, for their textures, and for their capacity to be put together in ever-new combinations. Her earliest writings are almost entirely celebrations of wit—jeux d'esprit. In 1922, caught up in a spirit of jubilation occasioned by her husband's success and the public adoration they were receiving, she embarked, with almost accidental casualness, upon her writing career, in a series of journalistic articles and sketches.

Dust jacket for Zelda Fitzgerald's 1932 novel, which openly treats her marriage

One of these was a mock review of *The Beautiful and Damned,* which appeared in the 2 April 1922 *New York Tribune,* under both her maiden and married names. Her tone is one of surprised delight that the book has magically appeared, as a vehicle for providing her with cute cloth of gold dresses and platinum rings. She describes it facetiously, as a "manual of etiquette," and a guide to how to dispose of one's husband's old shoes. Even when she turns more seriously to the work of a critic, she maintains a playful, insouciant attitude:

> It seems to me that on one page I recognized a portion of an old diary of mine which mysteriously disappeared shortly after my marriage, and also scraps of letters which, though considerably edited, sound to me vaguely familiar. In fact, Mr. Fitzgerald—I believe that is how he spells his name—seems to believe that plagiarism begins at home.

Much has been made of this early indication of Zelda Fitzgerald's discomfort with her husband's use of her experience—and evidence exists that he had persuaded her to give him access to the diary even before they were married. There certainly is a note of wry teasing here, but it seems aimed more at catching him in a slightly embarrassing situation than at protest. A few lines later, she delights in pointing out a more serious literary gaffe—confusion over the birth date of his major female character. What predominates in the review—really a kind of publicity piece—is her pleasure in writing it, a pleasure of a piece with her easy acceptance of the role of intelligent and articulate partner of the darling of the Jazz Age. A note of discomfort with that position is sounded, but it is not clearly recognized as such by its author.

This same mood of playful delight produced three brief journalistic pieces in 1922: "The Super-Flapper," sold but never published and apparently now lost; "Eulogy on the Flapper," published in *Metropolitan* magazine, June 1922; and "Does a Moment of Revolt Come to Every Married Man?," published in the March 1924 *McCall's* magazine as a brief piece accompanying one on the same topic by her husband. Together with the later *McCall's* piece "What Became of Our Flappers and Sheiks?" (October 1925), these 1922 articles portray Zelda Fitzgerald as conscious of herself as a focus of popular demand for a spokeswoman for the liberated playgirl the "flapper" was supposed to be. They also exhibit her awareness that she was popularly supposed to be a model for such characters in her husband's fiction. She plays toward these assumptions: " 'Out with inhibitions,' gleefully shouts the Flapper, and elopes with the Arrow-collar boy that she had been thinking, for a week or two, might make a charming companion" ("Eulogy"). And "The flapper springs full-grown, like Minerva, from the head of her once declassé father, Jazz, upon whom she lavishes affection and reverence, and deepest filial regard" ("Flappers and Sheiks"). But just as notably, as Milford has observed, Zelda Fitzgerald sees the flapper not as a brainless hedonist, bent on trivial social rebellion, but as a new kind of young American woman, seeking "the right to experiment with herself as a transient, poignant figure who will be dead tomorrow," despite the obvious experience that nine out of ten self-dramatizing young women live to grow into maturity ("Eulogy"). "The best flapper is reticent emotionally and courageous morally. You always know what she thinks, but she does all her feeling alone" ("Flappers and Sheiks"). Thus, even in her light-hearted journalism, Zelda Fitzgerald was developing a judicious ability to differentiate between cliché

and actuality, and was moving toward writing as an exploration of purpose, as well as a form of expression.

For the five years following 1922, Zelda Fitzgerald was absorbed in her increasingly difficult life as spouse to a famous but artistically unsatisfied author. Social and marital pressures grew, first in New York, then in France. *The Great Gatsby* was completed; Mrs. Fitzgerald's liaison with Edouard Jozan took place; Fitzgerald drank more heavily and friction grew. In accordance with a pattern developed early, the response of the Fitzgeralds was to look for a fresh start, geographically as well as socially. In 1927, they returned to the United States and attempted to settle down at Ellerslie, an estate near Wilmington, Delaware. There, Zelda Fitzgerald's energies became more and more strongly focused on finding interests beyond her marriage. She turned to ballet, taking formal lessons; her interest in drawing blossomed into half-serious efforts at art—creation of decorative lampshades and an elaborate dollhouse for her daughter. And she returned to writing.

As with the dance, and with the decorative drawing and painting, Zelda Fitzgerald seemed to be, with her reawakened interest in writing, going beyond her earlier efforts at diversion toward creativity as a combination of release and escape. In all her interests, Scott Fitzgerald encouraged her, without taking her efforts fully seriously—an attitude she may have, at least superficially, shared.

In her writing, she initially returned to the popular journalism with which she had experimented before. Four articles were published, all in slick magazines. All bore, jointly or entirely, her husband's byline, though he acknowledged in personal records that she had written them. "The Changing Beauty of Park Avenue" appeared in *Harper's Bazaar*, January 1928. "Looking Back Eight Years" (June 1928) and "Who Can Fall In Love After Thirty?" (October 1928) were published by *College Humor*. The fourth piece, first sold to *Photoplay* as "Editorial on Youth," was ultimately published in *Smart Set*, May 1929, as "Paint and Powder."

As the titles might suggest, the emphasis in these pieces was on transience. In "The Changing Beauty of Park Avenue," Zelda Fitzgerald concentrated on descriptive imagery of the splendor and color of that center of American success: "where one may buy an apple with as much ritual as if it were the Ottoman Empire, or a limousine as carelessly as if it were a postage stamp." *College Humor*, a magazine which capitalized on identity with the Jazz Age, featured "Looking Back Eight Years," with drawings of both Fitzgeralds by the well-known illustrator James Montgomery Flagg. Its focus is on the changing social scene after the World War. Not nostalgic, it traces flappers and sheiks who have grown into the mainstream. Zelda Fitzgerald develops ideas from her earlier articles: these young people were not merely frivolous; they were willing to face issues, even with the consequence of social unrest. In this unlikely vehicle, she approaches an essay on mores. Still, she exercises her characteristic flair for the unusual trope, the slightly disconcerting wit:

So that now the nuances and gradations of society in general seem of the same importance as the overtones of society in particular; sauce and trimmings make better eating than meat. And we predict a frightful pandemonium to eat it in unless indeed every generation has gone through the same difficulties of adjustment.

The sense of the strained metaphor and the buried pun—eating from a *pan*demonium—foreshadow the increasingly tense and distorted nature of much of Zelda Fitzgerald's later work: her obsession with dancing, beyond the limits of physical pain; her expressionistic paintings of human figures with oversized limbs and feet, and strained musculature. Even at her most serious, however, there is frequently a grim sense of the relationship between grotesquerie and humor.

Pleased with the articles, which they apparently thought were primarily Scott Fitzgerald's work, the editors of *College Humor* approached him to write a series of sketches or articles on different types of girls. *College Humor* did not pay the high fees to which he was accustomed, and he was not really interested. On the other hand, if Zelda Fitzgerald could write them with some guidance and polishing from her husband, they would provide both easy revenue and a focus for her creative restlessness. In order to command the best prices the magazine could offer, and to keep the editors interested, Zelda Fitzgerald agreed that they should be signed jointly. As with her earlier articles, these sketches were rendered more immediately marketable under his cachet. The series ultimately included six titles, composed between April 1929 and March 1930, while the Fitzgeralds were living, once again, in Paris: "The Original Follies Girl," "Poor Working Girl," "The Southern Girl," "The Girl the Prince Liked," "The Girl with Talent," and "A Mil-

lionaire's Girl." The first five were published, as agreed, in *College Humor*, between July 1929 and January 1931. "A Millionaire's Girl," at the end of the series, was so well done that the Fitzgeralds' agent, Harold Ober, submitted it, under Fitzgerald's name alone, to the *Saturday Evening Post*, where it appeared in the 17 May 1930 issue. Ober apparently made an honest mistake. The result earned $4000 for Zelda Fitzgerald, albeit at the cost of losing public credit for her achievement.

Almost from the beginning, she seems to have recognized that she could turn the planned sequence of light sketches into fiction. It was not her first attempt. In 1923, while they were living in Great Neck, Long Island, she had, with Fitzgerald's encouragement and help, written a story entitled "Our Own Movie Queen," which had been published under his name in the *Chicago Sunday Tribune* of 7 June 1925. A surviving typescript shows extensive revision in his hand, and he wrote in personal records that the story was about one-third his, including the conclusion. But the essential tone— glibly facetious, tinged with sophisticated wit—is that of Zelda Fitzgerald's journalistic pieces of the period. She adopts a consistently superior tone, verging on condescension, toward the humorously named heroine, Gracie Axelrod, a poor girl who wreaks a plebeian's revenge on the snobbish Blue Ribbon family. Yet, despite the uncertain attitude toward Gracie, her creator endowed her with a capacity to fend for herself in the world, through resourceful use of her physical attractiveness, and a certain self-protective predatoriness.

"Our Own Movie Queen" was slight, but it gave Zelda Fitzgerald a start toward fiction, and it contained gleams of the kind of female protagonist—tough, humorous, self-sufficient if self-absorbed—who would appear again and again in her writing, culminating in Alabama Beggs of *Save Me the Waltz*. When six years later Zelda Fitzgerald turned to the "Girl" series for *College Humor*, she had a precedent for moving beyond essayistic sketches toward the development of character in action of full-fledged fiction.

The "Girl" series is a study in that development. It was a hesitant progress, but almost from the first, as the surviving typescripts indicate, it was her own show. The earlier pieces bear corrections and suggestions in Fitzgerald's hand, as well as in hers, but they were neither substantive nor consistent throughout the series. He may have assisted or guided her in earlier stages of organization and composition for each piece, but existing evidence suggests that Zelda Fitzgerald's own craft and revision shaped the pieces, from the short, sketchlike "Poor Working Girl" to the heavily revised typescript of "A Millionaire's Girl," more than a third of which was rewritten in the typescript stage.

The first two of the series do little more than portray undeveloped characters in intriguingly described surroundings, though Eloise of "Poor Working Girl" has some of the toughness of the earlier "Our Own Movie Queen." Harriet, the "Southern Girl" of the third sketch, received more sympathy and attention. While her story retains some of the air of the mood piece, designed to create sympathy for the disciplined, self-sufficient belle fallen upon straitened circumstances (images of decay, failure, or loss dominate Zelda Fitzgerald's fiction), a basic plot is added. It traces the complications of separate romances between Harriet and a pair of young men from Ohio, permitting exploration of a theme of incompatibility between north and south perhaps reminiscent of Scott Fitzgerald's "The Ice Palace." The ending is tritely sweet, but the story was a decided advance beyond the sketchlike qualities of the first two pieces. Descriptive passages are both hauntingly evocative and concretely precise:

> Wistaria meets over the warm asphalt in summer, and the young people swim in the luke warm creeks. The drug stores are bright at night with the organdie balloons of girls' dresses under the big electric fans. . . .Telephones ring, and the lacy blackness under the trees disgorges young girls in white and pink. . . .

"The Girl the Prince Liked" and "The Girl with Talent" were more ambitious efforts, as though their author had gained confidence and begun to hit her stride. They were longer, and each followed its heroine through a sustained and complex plot, as the two women—"girl" was no longer applicable—fought to find excitement and happiness outside the confines of conventional, if affluent, marriages. Zelda Fitzgerald sought release by continuing her dancing studies in Paris with a teacher of acknowledged reputation, Madame Egorova. She sought a concomitant artistic release through her writing; she had come to term both dance and writing her "work," rather than seeing them as diversions. Her heroines, less responsible (or inhibited), abandoned families and respectability to find glamour and adventure.

Zelda Fitzgerald was also developing technical competence worthy of these more ambitious

Acrobats (Montgomery Museum of Art)

efforts. Most striking was her achievement of a point of view, a narrative perspective, which permitted her to create both a sense of involved immediacy with her characters and a level of detached objectivity. Early in her series, it was little more than an unidentified narrator, a first-person voice unidentified by gender or personality: a presence in the environment. In "Southern Girl," the voice became communal: a "we" narrator spoke for the town, though a singular "I" departed Jeffersonville, the initial setting, to follow Harriet to New York. In "The Girl the Prince Liked" and "The Girl with Talent," the narrative consciousness began to take part—sometimes conspiratorially, sometimes disapprovingly— in the action, contributing to complications and outcomes. By the end of the series, in "A Millionaire's Girl," there is almost a complete fusion between narrator and protagonist, as though the narrative identity were a self-questioning element of the protagonist's psyche.

Another well-developed technical trait came to be the extensive use of descriptive setting as suggestion of mood and tone. Both the narrator-protagonist fusion and this use of concrete, if romanticized, detail were elements of an increasing proficiency in manipulation of personal experience. This emergence of a communicated sense of deeply felt personal struggle lifted the last of the "Girl" series beyond the limits of an amateur mood sketch. In her protagonists, Zelda Fitzgerald was more and more acutely objectifying her own inner struggles for identity and achievement. Thematically, she had begun to weigh the consequences of talent subordinated to marriage, and the equally foreboding consequences of a life in which love and romance are sacrificed to the search for individual freedom. The "Girl" stories remained too brief and glib—tinged with "happy" reversals and sophisticated cynicism—to permit full realization of these techniques and ideas, but they were significant transitional pieces in the movement from flapper articles to *Save Me the Waltz*.

Unhappily, even before the last of them had seen publication, Zelda Fitzgerald's own inner struggles had led to physical and nervous exhaustion—the first of the breakdowns which would force her to spend most of the rest of her life in hospitals or sanitaria, under the care of psychiatrists. Following her collapse in the spring of 1930, as she began to recuperate in a Swiss clinic, she continued to write. Forced to abandon dancing, which her doctors thought destructive, she concentrated on fiction, and later on painting, for both therapy and self-development. As early as 8 June 1930, she had completed the first of a series of as many as thirteen stories, written between that date and 1932, only two of which survive. Titles of three—"A Workman," "The Drouth and the Flood," and "The House"—are mentioned in correspondence among the Fitzgeralds, their literary agent, and the Scribners editor Maxwell Perkins. Brief synopses of eight others survive in the Ober Agency files: "All About the Downs Case," "Cotton Belt," "Duck Supper," "Getting Away From It All," "God and Little Fishes," "One And, Two And," "The Story Thus Far," and "Sweet Chariot." By November 1930, Scott Fitzgerald, seeing the success of the stories as therapeutic, was urging Ober to find magazine publication for some of these under the blanket title "Stories from a Swiss Clinique." Though both Ober and Perkins found some of the stories powerful and parts of others well done, none of these were published.

Two of the stories she wrote during that flurry

of energetic application were successful. "Miss Bessie," completed at Prangins clinic in the fall of 1930, was accepted by *Scribner's Magazine*. Zelda Fitzgerald agreed to revise what Perkins termed her more "remote" and "too numerous" similes and metaphors, and the surviving typescript bears heavy revisions in her hand. The story, which appeared as "Miss Ella" in the December 1931 *Scribner's*, evidences strong continuity with the "Girl" series. Point of view is again that of a peripheral observer-participant, a young relative or friend of the old-maid protagonist. Age and sex of the narrator remain unspecified, though the sensibility seems feminine. The strong sense of sympathy, of identity, between narrator and Miss Ella is pivotal to the story's success. Although the central actions take place in the past of the story, long before the narrator's birth, both narrator and reader seem present as events are recalled through some unidentified source of knowledge of the narrator. The story is Southern Gothic, turning on Miss Ella's steadfast commitment to the memory of a rejected suitor whose suicide had ended her chance for a happy marriage. The atmosphere is one of repressed, self-punishing fury—psychological tension effectively, if unrealistically, symbolized by the suicide weapon deliberately allowed to remain as a *memento mori* in the summerhouse, an innocent enough location, though somehow tinged with foreboding by Zelda Fitzgerald's use of description.

> No one but us ever went near the playhouse, not even the grand-nieces of Aunt Ella [the aunt of the protagonist] when they came occasionally to visit. Almost buried in a tangle of jonquils and hyacinths dried brown from the summer heat, its roof strewn with the bruised purple bells of a hibiscus overhanging its tiny gables, the house stood like a forgotten sarcophagus, guarding with the reticent dignity that lies in all abandoned things a paintless, rusty shotgun.

Even the semitropical flora seem brutalized and tinged with spiritual and actual death. This descriptive morbidity was an exploration, in yet another form, of a feminine psyche struggling unsuccessfully for mature fulfillment. "Miss Ella," however, achieved deeper resonance and integrity through its more consistent sounding of the note of ruin and waste which had sometimes surfaced in the "Girl" stories.

The other surviving story, her last published short fiction, was "A Couple of Nuts," which appeared in the August 1932 *Scribner's Magazine*. It is usually seen as her most accomplished short work, one in which she was fully in control of her talent. It offers no major departures in technique: point of view is channeled through an unnamed narrator-participant, who moves in the same decadent world of European café society as the protagonists, Larry and Lola. The narrator, unlike the young innocents, is an established habitué of the salons, clubs, and villas of Paris and the Riviera; Larry and Lola are naive but adventurous nightclub entertainers, attempting to parlay talent, youth, and charm into success and acceptance. The narrator follows them through a negative metamorphosis from a kind of worldly innocence which accepted life, including marriage, as a grand romantic venture to dissipation and dissolution. They cease to have adventures, and become mere adventurers.

Jeff Daugherty, a new character in Zelda Fitzgerald's range of choices, precipitates that decay. He is charming, wealthy, but thoroughly amoral. He toys with their transparent ambitions in idle amusement while carrying on a passing liaison with Lola. Almost an allegorical personification of superficial glamour masking meaningless and unproductive destructiveness, he—and his equally predatory ex-wife—exude ruin. Yet he is not alone in responsibility; the narrator stands inactive, allowing Daugherty to destroy the couple's dreams—perhaps from lassitude, perhaps from class loyalty. The story is suffused with an ominous tone of loss and destruction. As Larry and Lola depart the Riviera, for example, before returning to the States and final destruction, Zelda Fitzgerald's description of the gay beach's sudden loss of charm offers an objective correlative for the moral decay beneath the surface of their lives: "The ocean turned muddy and our bathing clothes didn't dry from one brisk swim to another; we grew irritable with the unspent tang of the sea." "A Couple of Nuts" also displayed Zelda Fitzgerald's mastery of irony as a device for control, avoiding the mawkishness of some of the "Girl" stories. The narrator, with self-deprecating wit, analyzes her unwillingness to act to save the youngsters. Most ironically, Lola ends the story by describing the Daughertys as "a couple of nuts," the same phrase with which Daugherty had earlier dismissed Larry and Lola from his consideration. Her use of the expression betrays Lola's almost total lack of comprehension of the enormity of the evil which has crushed her fragile dreams.

The final paragraph of "A Couple of Nuts" captures both Lola's fragile innocence and the dark mood of the story. The world-weary narrator speaks of aid provided to Lola, following Larry's death by drowning.

> Lola and Larry! No, they never saved anything. Well, I sent her the money and I suppose she'll be all right for another five years. She'll be pretty that long, anyway. It takes time a good thirty years to batter down a woman's looks and crumple the charm she acquires from moving in a world she finds rich in that fantastic quality. Poor kids! Their Paris address turned up just the other day when I was looking for my trunk keys, along with some dirty post-cards and a torn fifty-franc note and an expired passport. I remembered the night Larry gave it to me: I had promised to send them some songs from home—songs about love and success and beauty.

Zelda Fitzgerald's tender yet tough dying-fall ending, as succinct and understated as that of the later *Tender Is the Night*, both epitomizes this story and bears witness to the success with which she had absorbed the tutelage in writing her husband and his work had to offer.

From early magazine humor to polished short fiction, Zelda Fitzgerald's writing had grown from divertissement to serious effort to explore theme through adequate aesthetic form. There had been a steady progression. As she seemingly recuperated from her illness, she grew more and more confident of her writing. Publication of "Miss Ella" and acceptance of "A Couple of Nuts" spurred her on to attempt more challenging fiction: sometime in the fall or winter of 1931-1932, she began planning a novel, an impressionistic study of female character, grounded in her own experience growing up in the traditional South, marrying a successful and charming artist, enjoying youth and vitality in New York and France—then experiencing growing dissatisfaction, loss of identity, and marital friction. Her protagonist, Alabama Beggs, is a more substantially drawn version of the restless, courageous women of her earlier fiction, seeking self-sufficiency even at the cost of loss of security and possible failure. Like her creator, Alabama turns to ballet—rather more fruitfully—to forge her own aesthetic career, as a way of separating her identity from that of her husband.

Unlike her creator, Alabama was not beset with the possibilities of psychic disintegration. Just as Zelda Fitzgerald was beginning the novel, she experienced a second major collapse; Fitzgerald, recently returned from a film-writing project in

Hollywood, moved her to Baltimore for treatment at the Phipps Clinic, associated with Johns Hopkins University hospital. It was the beginning of sixteen years spent in and out of hospitals and clinics in Baltimore, New York, and Asheville, North Carolina.

At Phipps, her doctors encouraged, with her husband's agreement, her work on the novel. By early March, writing feverishly, she had completed a typescript, which she rushed off to Maxwell Perkins at Scribners. Learning after the fact that the novel had been submitted without his review, Scott Fitzgerald was furious; his irritation was apparently surprising to the doctors and to Perkins, though her actions would indicate Zelda Fitzgerald herself may not have found them entirely unexpected. He soon received a copy in Montgomery, where he was preparing to move the family to Maryland. However, the damage was done. He had been wrestling with material similar to much of the autobiographical experience Zelda Fitzgerald had used, trying to incorporate it into the fourth novel he had been working on without satisfactory results for years. He felt used and betrayed. Nevertheless, he turned his attention to aiding his wife in revising and editing the manuscript. Because the early typescripts have not been found, the exact nature and extent of his suggestions and revision are unknown. External evidence, in correspondence and in transcripts of Zelda Fitzgerald's psychiatric therapy sessions, indicates that the Fitzgeralds worked to tone down autobiographical references, such as the use of the name "Amory Blaine" for her major male character. That name was, of course, taken from that of the hero-protagonist of Fitzgerald's *This Side of Paradise.*

After revision, Fitzgerald came to support publication of *Save Me the Waltz* and attempted to promote its success, though whether he recognized intrinsic merit in the novel or simply saw its publication as therapeutic is not clear. His support did exact a stiff price. In 1933 in a major confrontation during a joint conversation with her doctor, he insisted that her "lesser" talent never infringe again on their common life experience. If she were to continue to write, it would have to be on his terms. Apparently, she acquiesced, abandoning a new novel on psychiatry to turn her creative attention more heavily toward painting. Her finished writing, from 1933 until her death, would never encompass serious fiction. Instead, she would return to the nonfiction essays and try her pen at light, farcical drama.

Some of these torments and tensions had already surfaced in the published novel Zelda Fitzgerald presented to the world on 2 October 1932. Entitled *Save Me the Waltz,* from a phrase she is said to have spotted in a phonograph record catalogue, it is the capstone of her writing career and the center of interest in her as an artist. Divided into four sections, the novel tells the story of Alabama Beggs, almost exclusively from the perspective of the protagonist herself, although not in first person: her childhood and youth in the South just before and during World War I; her marriage to artist David Knight and their life in New York and Paris and on the Riviera after the war; her belated career as a ballet dancer; and her rejoining her husband and daughter to return to her childhood home because of the illness and death of her father.

In Part 1, Alabama Beggs, youngest daughter of Judge Austin Beggs and Millie Beggs, copies the wiles of her older sisters Joan and Dixie, who turn to their mother for help against their authoritarian father. Alabama sees the Judge as "a living fortress" who "loved Millie's children with . . . detached tenderness and introspection," the distance perhaps a direct result of the death of their only son. To Alabama's discerning eye, her mother Millie, "moving through the sorrows of life with the beatific mournfulness of a Greek chorus . . . , by the time she was forty-five, had become an emotional anarchist . . . her way of proving to herself her individual necessity of survival." Extending her mother's attitude and rebelling against the Judge's restrictions, Alabama becomes part of the social life of her town, which includes the officers stationed nearby. Alabama, to the dismay of the Judge, becomes " the wildest one of the Beggs, but . . . a thoroughbred." After a season of flirting with officers—married and unmarried—Alabama falls in love with "a blond lieutenant," David Knight, an aspiring artist whose career has been interrupted by the war. The war ends before David can be shipped overseas. After convincing the skeptical Judge and a hesitant Alabama of his ability to support a wife, David makes wedding arrangements, and Alabama marries him in New York.

The Knights' married life, the focus of Part 2 of *Save Me the Waltz,* lacks stability from the beginning, because of the self-absorption of the two and their increasing competitiveness. David Knight is immediately a successful artist, and the couple, living first in New York and then Connecticut, enjoy the concomitant notoriety and social license. Two major disruptions are Alabama's pregnancy and a visit from Judge and Mrs. Beggs, a disastrous event resulting in estrangement because of the parents' disapproval of the behavior they witness. After the birth of the Knights' daughter, Bonnie, David and Alabama take a ship to Europe, in hopes that a new environment will stimulate David's painting. Renting a villa at St-Raphael, they try to bring order to their lives, but fail: David is painting, Alabama is bored, and they meet new friends with whom to party, including a group of French aviators. Alabama falls in love with one of them, Jacques Chevre-Feuille, and her brief affair with him nearly destroys her marriage. Jacques is transferred, and in 1927 the Knights move to Paris, where their lives are again a continuous party: "Nobody knew whose party it was. It had been going on for weeks."

With a studio on the Left Bank David again becomes successful, and the Knights are again in demand. David meets dancer Gabrielle Gibbs and becomes infatuated with her. Meanwhile Alabama is growing steadily discontented with her life, and after attending a performance at the ballet, she turns an earlier interest in dance into an obsession fully developed in Part 3 of the novel.

Alabama becomes a student of ballet under the tutelage of Madame, a retired member of the Russian ballet. Despite the physical and emotional pain and rigors of training and the strain on, and neglect of, her family, Alabama persists:

> It seemed to Alabama that, reaching her goal, she would drive the devils that had driven her—that, in proving herself, she would achieve that peace which she imagined went only in surety of one's self—that she would be able, through the medium of the dance, to command her emotions, to summon love or pity or happiness at will, having provided a channel through which they might flow. She drove herself mercilessly. . . .

Her friends and her life itself are at the studio. The competitiveness between Alabama and David becomes more obvious, with neither understanding the art of the other and each resenting any imposition on life or work: "David and Alabama passed each other in the musty corridors hastily and ate distantly facing each other with the air of enemies awaiting some gesture of hostility." Alabama's hard work culminates in an offer for "a solo début in the opera *Faust* with the San Carlos Opera of Naples." Against David's wishes, Alabama cancels their planned trip to visit their aging parents and accepts the offer.

The last section of *Save Me the Waltz* covers Alabama's life in Naples, the end of her ballet career, the tentative reconciliation of the Knight family, their return to the South because of the illness and death of Judge Beggs, and David and Alabama's uneasy plan to settle in a new home. Initially, Alabama moves to Naples, leaving David and Bonnie in Paris. The work in Naples is hard: the company is second-rate, and her living conditions are unpleasant—a balcony with no floor and a room with an iron bed, a maple wardrobe, and a lavabo. Alabama has a successful debut:

> They [the clippings from the paper] were agreed that the ballet was a success, and that the new addition [Alabama] to Madame Sirgeva's corps was a competent dancer. She had promise and should be given a bigger rôle, the papers said. Italians like blondes; they said Alabama was as ethereal as a Fra Angelico angel because she was thinner than the others.

However, a visit from Bonnie is almost as disastrous as the Beggses' visit to New York: Bonnie does not like Italy and stares "incredulously" at her mother's "pink boarding house." She quickly returns to the more gracious ambience of life with her father, now in Switzerland.

A short while later David receives a telegram from Millie Beggs about the Judge's serious illness. When David tries to notify Alabama, he learns she is in the hospital, delirious from blood poisoning that developed from a blister on her foot. To save her foot, the doctors have to cut the tendons; though she can walk, she will never dance again. The Knights go to Alabama's home, where she tries to achieve a reconciliation with her father before his death in November 1931. Before they leave there to settle in a new home, they give a farewell party after which "they sat in the pleasant gloom of late afternoon, staring at each other through the remains of the party. . . ."

Save Me the Waltz was not a financial or critical success: 1392 copies of the 3010 printed were sold, and Zelda Fitzgerald received only $120.73, because of extensive revision of galleys. The critical reception was somewhat superficial, but there were three consistent comments in the reviews: a novel by the wife of a successful and famous novelist, problems with language, and lack of proofreading. Naturally there were the inevitable comparisons with the works of F. Scott Fitzgerald with one headline proclaiming: "Mrs. Fitzgerald's First Novel Places Her on Scott's Level." Generally, however, the reviewers attacked the distorted or invented language and the poor proofreading. The assessments of language ranged from "ludicrous lushness of writing" and "exaggerated images" to "[Zelda Fitzgerald] created for herself almost another language and when this does prove intelligible, its effect is devastating." The denunciation for poor proofreading was almost unanimous. In contrast, however, one contemporary and personal evaluation of *Save Me the Waltz* seems to foreshadow the later more favorable critical analysis of the work. On 22 May 1933, Malcolm Cowley wrote Scott Fitzgerald:

> "It moves me a lot: she has something there that nobody got into words before. The women who write novels are usually the sort who live spiritually in Beloit, Wisconsin, even when they are getting drunk at the Select. Zelda has a different story to tell."

Similarly, a 1953 Grey Walls edition of the novel received a favorable reception in Britain with the *Times Literary Supplement* praising the novel for "powerful and memorable" writing and "qualities of earthiness and force."

From the beginning, biographers of both F. Scott Fitzgerald and Zelda Sayre Fitzgerald have turned to *Save Me the Waltz* for illustration, description, and verification of important events in, and influences on the two lives; they further use it as evidence for interpretations of controversies about the two lives. The earlier biographers of F. Scott Fitzgerald—Arthur Mizener and Andrew Turnbull—made less use of it than the later ones—Matthew J. Bruccoli, André Le Vot, and James R. Mellow; Henry Dan Piper also devotes considerable attention to the novel in *F. Scott Fitzgerald: A Critical Portrait*. Zelda Fitzgerald's biographers, Nancy Milford and Sara Mayfield, cite it even more extensively. All of these writers have analyzed the novel to try to understand the competition between Zelda and Scott Fitzgerald over the subject matter of their writings. In varying degrees in these studies, *Save Me the Waltz* has also been used to describe the importance of Judge Sayre in his daughter's life, the courtship and marriage of the Fitzgeralds, and Zelda Fitzgerald's devotion to ballet.

Just as Judge Beggs holds a place of significance in the novel with a description of him at the beginning and his death at the end, so Judge Sayre was an influential force in Zelda Fitzgerald's life. Le Vot describes this relationship:

> His [Judge Sayre's] was the only authority for which she had any respect, even if she did make a game of disobeying his orders, of defying him and pitting her will against his. . . . Throughout her life Zelda would regret the lost orderliness, the reassuring stability her father's authority provided.

The Judge is intrinsic to the atmosphere of Zelda's (and Alabama's) childhood and youth, and biographers and critics refer to the novel for their study of it because of Zelda Fitzgerald's detailed portrayal of Judge Beggs.

Save Me the Waltz has been carefully studied for its coverage of the Fitzgeralds' love and marriage. The critics frequently begin with the description of David Knight:

> There seemed to be some heavenly support beneath his shoulder blades that lifted his feet from the ground in ecstatic suspension, as if he secretly enjoyed the ability to fly but was walking as a compromise to convention. Green gold under the moon, his hair lay in Cellinian frescos and fashionable porticoes over his dented brow.

Then they turn to Zelda Fitzgerald's description of Alabama in love with David:

Self-portrait (collection of Scottie Fitzgerald Smith)

So much she loved the man, so close and closer she felt herself that he became distorted in her vision, like pressing her nose upon a mirror and gazing into her own eyes. . . . She felt the essence of herself pulled finer and smaller like those streams of spun glass that pull and stretch till there remains but a glimmering illusion.

The novel has further been used in debates over relationships that marred this marriage: with Edouard Jozan as Jacques Chevre-Feuille and Lois Moran as Gabrielle Gibbs. Gradually, of course, the love of Alabama and David is stretched too far, and irreparable damage is done. From the almost fairy-tale beginning through the strained marriage, as Scottie Fitzgerald Smith—the Fitzgeralds' daughter—summarizes in her foreword to *Bits of Paradise*, "*Save Me the Waltz* . . . tells the story of their romance better than anything else which has been written. . . ."

Certainly, this novel is important for biographical and autobiographical studies, perhaps even more in the earlier, now destroyed, drafts than in the revised, published, and posthumously edited versions. As noted above, there were also episodes taken from the Fitzgeralds' lives that were excised, either at Fitzgerald's insistence or as a result of the joint revision by Scott and Zelda Fitzgerald. However important the novel is to the study of the lives of these two, there is a caveat inherent in the observation of Zelda Fitzgerald's sister Rosalind Sayre Smith, quoted by Sara Mayfield:

" 'Save Me the Waltz' is autobiography highly seasoned with fiction and some exaggeration. . . . Much of what she writes is invention but much is also true."

Save Me the Waltz has more value than simply a record of the life of its author and her perception of her marriage, family, and art. Recent studies have praised elements in the novel that were suggested or misrepresented—even misunderstood—in the initial reviews and early biographies. Specifically, scholars are studying *Save Me the Waltz* for its perceptive insight into post-World War I life with all of its restlessness and lack of purpose, its sensitive study of a woman's search for identity, and its excellent description of the world of a ballet dancer.

Henry Dan Piper describes *Save Me the Waltz* as "one of the authentic literary documents of the post-World War I decade." After her slow, easy life in the South, complicated only by her own escapades and conflicts with her father, Alabama enters New York of the 1920s. David had already written her enthusiastic and fantastic descriptions of the city:

"City of glittering hypotheses. . . . chaff from a fairy mill, suspended in penetrating blue! Humanity clings to the streets like flies upon a treacle stream. The tops of the buildings shine like crowns of gold-leaf kings in conference. . . ."

Seen firsthand as the Knights go from hotel to hotel, party to party, New York gradually becomes less magical to Alabama: "The streets of New York smelled acrid and sweet like drippings from the mechanics of a metallic night-blooming garden." But David and Alabama leave New York searching for a fresher, more stimulating environment, eventually settling in Paris after a sojourn on the Mediterranean coast: "They hadn't much faith in travel nor a great belief in a change of scene as a panacea for spiritual ills; they were simply glad to be going."

Initially the spirit of Paris has some of the same magic that New York first had: "The pink flare from the street lights tinted the canopy scalloping of the trees to liquid bronze: those lights are one of the reasons why the hearts of Americans bump spasmodically at the mention of France; they are identical with the circus flares of our youth." (Some of the impressionistic and somewhat whimsical descriptions of New York and Paris are related to Zelda Fitzgerald's paintings of these scenes.) But, as they feared, Paris is no panacea, for

The post-war extravagance which had sent David and Alabama and some sixty thousand other Americans wandering over the face of Europe in a game of hare without hounds achieved its apex. The sword of Damocles, forged from the high hope of getting something for nothing and the demoralizing expectation of getting nothing for something, was almost hung by the third of May.

The magic and illusion about the settings disappear as their happiness continues to dissipate.

The theme of the search for identity parallels Zelda Fitzgerald's portrayal of the search for happiness and stability after the disillusioning war. This search is complicated, even aggravated, by the conflict between wife and husband and the competition between artists, both striving for success. With the developing popularity of women's studies, the novel is receiving more and more attention for its demonstration, as Piper worded it, of "the price the women of her [Zelda Fitzgerald's] generation paid for their boundless sense of freedom." Jacqueline Tavernier-Courbin expresses this theme as "the desire of a woman to free herself from her subordinate position in a man's world and her need to discover herself, to go to the end of herself, through the artistic expression of emotion." Alabama first tries to find her model in her mother:

> "Tell me about myself when I was little," the youngest girl [Alabama] insists. She presses against her mother in an effort to realize some proper relationship.
> ....
> The girl had been filled with no interpretation of herself. . . . She wants to be told what she is like. . . .

Alabama cannot understand her mother's acceptance of a subordinate role in the Beggs household, but, ironically, she tries to replace the Judge in her own life with someone of equal strength: David fails to meet her criteria. At the beginning of their romance he carves their names in the doorpost of the clubhouse as "David, David, David, Knight, Knight, Knight, and Miss Alabama Nobody." From New York he writes to her as his "princess" whom he will "shut forever in an ivory tower for [his] private delectation." Alabama objects to both of these descriptions. When they move to Europe, Alabama further proclaims her searching: "I am only really myself when I'm somebody else whom I have endowed with these wonderful qualities from my imagination." Gradually coming to almost despise "the unrest of David" as inadequate for her and yet so like her, she attempts to get some meaning for her life from the Judge even as he is dying: "Why do we spend years using up our bodies to nurture our minds with experience and find our minds turning then to our exhausted bodies for solace? Why, Daddy?" Her confession to David, at the end of the novel, expresses the failure of her search for meaning and identity thus far: "I just lump everything in a great heap which I have labelled 'the past,' and, having thus emptied this deep reservoir that was once myself, I am ready to continue." Meredith Cary summarizes Zelda Fitzgerald's treatment of Alabama's search for identity:

> Zelda Fitzgerald avoided the polemic common in representations of the female version of defeat. The function of the novel is to trace the causes of Alabama's downfall, but

the pattern of causation is so intricate and diversified and the responsibility so inadvertent that no villain is produced. Rather than assigning blame, Zelda Fitzgerald fleshes forth a situation and its results.

The failure to find her identity and appropriate role in her parents or with David drives Alabama to ballet. She hopes the "cathedral" of ballet will replace the "living fortress" of the Judge. The depiction of Alabama's obsession with success as a ballet dancer is a significant achievement of the novel: Piper says, "It was one of the first and still is one of the best stories that has been written by an American about the career of a ballerina." Zelda Fitzgerald's descriptions of the drudgery and pain of training are unrelenting:

> Alabama rubbed her legs with Elizabeth Arden muscle oil night after night. There were blue bruises inside above the knee where the muscles were torn. Her throat was so dry that at first she thought she had fever and took her temperature and was disappointed to find that she had none. . . . She was always stiff, and she clutched the gilt flowers [of the sofa] in pain. She fastened her feet through the bars of the iron bed and slept with her toes glued outwards for weeks. Her lessons were agony.
> ....
> Miles and miles of pas de bourrée, her toes picking the floor like beaks of many feeding hens, and after ten thousand miles you got to advance without shaking your breasts. . . .
> Alabama finally taught herself what it felt like to move the upper part of her body along as if it were a bust on wheels.
>
> ....
> By springtime, she was gladly, savagely proud of the strength of her Negroid hips, convex as boats in a wood carving.

(As with the descriptions of New York and Paris, these passages also describe paintings of ballet dancers Zelda Fitzgerald created.) The characterization of Madame, like that of Judge Beggs, is quite effective in the novel as Zelda Fitzgerald presents the demanding but sensitive, aging ballet mistress:

> The Russian face was white and prismatic as a dim sun on a block of crystal. There were blue veins in her forehead like a person with heart trouble, but she was not sick except from much abstraction. She lived a hard life.

Despite David's lack of understanding of her ballet—and similarly hers of his painting—and the growing alienation between them when he explains the difference between "the amateur and the professional in the arts," Alabama seems to be nearing an end to her search for meaning with Madame as an admirable and sympathetic guide. However successful her debut as a ballet dancer in Naples might be, the achievement is short-lived—and without glamour except for a beautiful basket of calla lilies wired from David. But in this segment of the novel that is completely fictional (Zelda Fitzgerald never accepted an offer to perform), the author keeps a clear perspective on the fantasy: the success is hollow because of the low caliber of the company. Furthermore, Zelda Fitzgerald adds a note of ironic humor by undercutting the floral gift: the lilies are tied with a ridiculous "white tulle bow" and, thanks to the Italian florist, the card reads: From your two "sweat-hearts." Alabama does not achieve fulfillment through self-expression in art.

Zelda Fitzgerald adds one further note of irony to Alabama's search for identity and meaningful expression: the characterization of the Knights' daughter, Bonnie. In essential defiance of her mother's concerns, Bonnie rejects ballet completely—her mother's training and her own. She resents her mother's total absorption in her lessons and practice. When her mother is working hardest and staying at the studio for long hours, Bonnie draws a picture of two people holding hands "gingerly" with the caption: "This is when my Mother and Father go out walking. . . . C'est trés chic, mes parents ensemble!" She gives up her ballet lessons as soon as her mother moves to Naples. Alabama is further rejected when Bonnie is scornful of her mother's life in Naples; she prefers her father's world, where she is treated like his "royal visitor," unlike her mother, who rejected David's "tower." Bonnie's escape to her father in Switzerland is the novel's only shift away from the narrative perspective of Alabama, as if to emphasize this difference between daughter and mother. Ironically in the earlier days on the Mediterranean, Alabama had voiced the same sentiment: "Because, my daughter, I am so outrageously clever that I believe I could be a whole world to myself if I didn't like living in Daddy's better." The final irony is their visit back to the South where Bonnie plays house with her grandmother as "an agreeable little girl," as if fully accepting the stereotypical family role. Again Zelda Fitzgerald adds the notes of irony: in these games Bonnie is "the head of the family" and plans to "be as Mummy was." Alabama can only comment, "Con-

sciousness . . . is an ultimate betrayal, I suppose."

Not only has *Save Me the Waltz* been reevaluated for Zelda Fitzgerald's perceptive treatment of themes and characters, but her style is also receiving more careful analysis. No longer is the language completely denounced as problematical. Linda Wagner, in her "assessment of craft," traces the development of style from its "adolescent flightiness" to a "somber, spare, direct" style for the death of the Judge, a change that effectively complements the changes in character and mood in the novel. Several scholars have analyzed the imagery to show the significance of flowers from the white flowers of the South and Alabama's first orchid to the "nasturtiums of leather and rubber and wax gardenias" of Paris to the calla lilies of Alabama's debut. Equally important to characterizations is the use of sun-moon imagery with the moon associated with David and the sun with Jacques and Madame. And not to be forgotten is Zelda Fitzgerald's humor, so evident in the earlier short works, underlying the novel despite its more tragic concerns. The wit is in the dialogue (humorous exchanges between Alabama and various servants in Connecticut and Europe); in the whimsical descriptions and the playing with words ("the family hatched into girls"; "heavy impregnated mops"; "hair . . . like nacre cornucopias"; "a ruching of girls"); in several events such as the Beggses' visit to New York and Bonnie's visit to Naples, where she is bitten at a party by a monkey; and ultimately in the ironic perspective with which Zelda Fitzgerald is able to look at her subjects, regardless of how serious—and even painful and tragic—they are.

Thus, with the advantage of retrospection, Zelda Fitzgerald is now being credited with greater achievement in *Save Me the Waltz* than she initially received. Certainly the novel is important for its insights into the lives of the Fitzgeralds, and more specifically, Zelda Fitzgerald's own personal struggles, but it is also worthy of literary analysis, and of a much wider readership than it has yet received.

As noted above, Zelda Fitzgerald abandoned serious fiction following *Save Me the Waltz*, at least until her husband's death in 1940. She turned instead to an attempt at witty stage comedy, and to nostalgic essays, occasionally tinged with traces of her earlier clever playfulness, although of a dryer, darker tone than the essays of the 1920s.

Much of her creative energy, for the rest of her life, went into her painting. Though it is not possible to date her artwork with any certainty, most of those which survive seem to have been painted in the early 1930s and toward the end of her life in the 1940s. A typical painting from the years in Baltimore might be of a heavy-limbed athlete, or a dancer, expressionistically exaggerated in certain proportions—particularly in the legs and feet—as if to stress the strain of life and of art. Her Paris years had given her knowledge of modernistic French and German cityscapes. Some of her most delightful paintings are of impressionistic city scenes: streets, parks, upturned faces, even occasional animal figures. These paintings, frequently in pastel or watercolor, seem full of light, movement, and whimsy. Still more imaginative are fantasies such as "The Lobster Quadrille," an illustration of Lewis Carroll's *Alice in Wonderland,* painted toward the end of her life. Its background is of a cityscape, parklike trees, and many-windowed buildings. Central to the humor of this painting is its focus, almost as though they were at home on boulevards and promenades, on a group of figures including crustaceans, fish, and a human female, all in light airy colors and poses.

Flowers were frequent subjects, sometimes partaking of both the lushness and strangeness of her descriptive passages in Part 1 of *Save Me the Waltz.* A little later, she became intensely religious, and paintings of the late 1930s and 1940s suggest religious allegory, though even these frequently incorporate bodily sensuosity and whimsicality of face and figure. Her paintings have received public display: in 1934 at the New York Gallery of the Fitzgeralds' friend Cary Ross; in 1974 in a retrospective at the Montgomery Museum of Fine Arts; and in

smaller, informal showings in Asheville and Montgomery during her lifetime. Some of those described during her lifetime have disappeared or were destroyed following her death. Others, now prized by Fitzgerald collectors, seem not to have meant a great deal to her. Her daughter writes of the cityscape series:

> I kept trying to persuade her to continue [in 1946] with the series of glorious water colors of New York and Paris which she made for me. . . . She would faithfully promise to produce more, but when a package would arrive at last, I'd find a set of paper dolls of Goldilocks and the Three Bears, or a Bible Illustration. . . .

Zelda Fitzgerald had begun by painting a dollhouse; at the end she still turned to paper dolls—always a fascination of hers—as often as to more serious pieces. Perhaps that same instinct toward the less demanding, the less serious, helped direct her toward *Scandalabra,* the "farce Fantasy" which she began writing shortly after publication of *Save Me the Waltz.* It was selected for performance in the initial season of the Junior Vagabond Players, an offshoot of the Baltimore community theater, the Vagabond Players. It ran from 26 June-3 July 1933. Zelda Fitzgerald's approach is in the tradition of Oscar Wilde, updated through Noel Coward—an airy sex farce, dependent for humor on clever reversal of expectation, both in action and in dia-

The Lobster Quadrille from Alice in Wonderland *(collection of Arlyn Bruccoli)*

logue. The plot follows the misadventures of a serious and moral couple, Andrew and Flower Messogony, who, in order to qualify for a legacy, must engage in a life of libertine hedonism. They are guided in their attempts (innocent, ultimately, of any true misbehavior) by a comic butler variously called Bounds or Baffles. The plot's complications entail a series of apparent liaisons with another, worldlier couple, Anaconda and Peter Consequential, and much opportunity for Wildean banter:

> DOCTOR: Just say to yourself "All life is a play." I had a patient who believed that so nicely before they took him off to Bloomingdale.
> BAFFLES: Mr. Andrew *will* confuse life with reality, sir.

The fey quality—there is even a leprechaun in the cast—does not quite come off, and the wit is not always sprightly, but, after some revision by Scott Fitzgerald, the play ran to the satisfaction of cast and author. Its whimsy masks the treatment of familiar themes. It is an ironic reversal of the plot of *The Beautiful and Damned,* and one commentator sees its apparent adultery reiterating Part 2 of *Save Me the Waltz.* But *Scandalabra,* the lightness of which is evident in the names of the major characters, is social satire of a world where modest behavior is not to be desired. It was a way of using *her* material safely.

In 1931, in the midst of her burst of fictive creativity, Zelda Fitzgerald had found time to compose a brief sketch, "The Continental Angle," an exercise in gustatorial nostalgia. It provided a sequence of memories of meals and restaurants from "the Ducoed chairs of Southern tearooms" to the Plaza Hotel and the Paris Ritz. It was published in the 4 June 1932 issue of the *New Yorker.* Melancholic and nostalgic, especially in its evocations of sensory memory, it was in the descriptive vein of her earlier "The Changing Beauty of Park Avenue." Its publication suggested further exploration of this approach. Her last two published efforts were longer, more detailed articles in a nostalgic, lightly humorous tone, which appeared in the new magazine *Esquire* in 1934 under, once again, a joint byline with her husband, whose name the magazine was seeking. Though the pieces were indeed Zelda Fitzgerald's, they would subsequently find publication in *The Crack-Up,* the 1945 collection of Fitzgerald's essays and notebooks edited by his friend Edmund Wilson. "Show Mr. and Mrs. F. to Number----" appeared in the May and June 1934 issues of *Es-*

Untitled dancers (collection of Matthew J. Bruccoli)

quire. In a series of vignettelike scenes, it describes through impressionistic memories places the Fitzgeralds had lived, from the Biltmore Hotel in 1920 to the Algonquin in 1933. "In the Hôtel O'Connor [on the Riviera, 1925] old ladies in white lace rocked their pasts to circumspection with the lullabyic motion of the hotel chairs. But they were serving blue twilights at the cafés along the Promenade des Anglais for the price of a porto, and we danced their tangos and watched girls shiver in the appropriate clothes for the Côte d'Azur." The mood is more restrained, almost elegiac, but the detached amusement, the distanced observation, are the hallmarks of Zelda Fitzgerald's earlier delight in the movements and colors of life. The distorted diction—"lullabyic"—and displaced grammar—"serving blue twilights"—are echoes of her Dickinsonian delight in the possibilities of words.

"Auction—Model 1934" was printed the following month, July 1934. Its thrust is similar: description of the contents of a metaphorical packing case full of artifacts associated with memories from the Fitzgeralds' past. "These socks made us late for a dinner with Galsworthy while the twilight turned purple and Turneresque over the Thames. These socks have wrinkled above the parquets of Lady Randolph Churchill's London and waltzed in a sad Savoy Hotel to the envy of women in black at twenty-one, because a lot of men had forgot to come home." Eventually, each item is sold, or consigned to the attic of memory.

These two pieces have been placed among her best writing on the basis of their mixture of controlled memory and humorous style. But they are also full of loss, regret, and—above all—transience. They speak of goodbye to her happier days, and perhaps they are appropriate final publications.

Zelda Fitzgerald lived much of the rest of her life in Highland Hospital, Asheville, North Carolina, though she occasionally took trips with her husband and daughter, or visited her mother's home in Montgomery. Ironically, in May 1940, a few months before Scott Fitzgerald's death in Los Angeles, where he was living while writing for the film industry and working on his fifth novel, she became sufficiently well to begin living for long periods in Montgomery. During this fourteen-year span, 1934-1948, she continued to paint, and in the last few years of her life, she turned again to composing a novel, ultimately entitled "Caesar's Things." Only a few chapters and fragmentary alternative versions exist, in manuscript at Princeton University. They combine almost impenetrable religious allegory with a plot involving an artistic married couple, Janno and Jacob, so beautiful and so much alike they seem golden twins, who encounter another, similar figure, named Jacques. Janno's flight into the romantic release Jacques offers brings guilt and suffering. Where the fragment would have gone is unknowable. That Zelda Fitzgerald, at the end, was still working out her life through literature is evident. Another, shorter typescript, "Other Names for Roses," more coherently reworks themes of love and betrayal, with a young married couple in France, dancers as significant figures, nostalgia and sadness over ruin.

In March 1948, the hospital wing in which Zelda Fitzgerald was living burned. Her remains were buried in Rockville, Maryland, with those of her husband.

Bibliography:

Matthew J. Bruccoli, *F. Scott Fitzgerald: A Descriptive Bibliography* (Pittsburgh: University of Pittsburgh Press, 1972; supplement, Pittsburgh: University of Pittsburgh Press, 1980)—includes section on Zelda Fitzgerald.

Biographies:

Arthur Mizener, *The Far Side of Paradise: A Biography of F. Scott Fitzgerald* (Boston: Houghton Mifflin, 1951);

Andrew Turnbull, *Scott Fitzgerald* (New York: Scribners, 1962);

Nancy Milford, *Zelda: A Biography* (New York: Harper & Row, 1970);

Sara Mayfield, *Exiles from Paradise: Zelda and Scott Fitzgerald* (New York: Delacorte Press, 1971);

Matthew J. Bruccoli, Scottie Fitzgerald Smith, and Joan P. Kerr, eds., *The Romantic Egoists: A Pictorial Autobiography* (New York: Scribners, 1974);

Bruccoli, *Some Sort of Epic Grandeur: The Life of F. Scott Fitzgerald* (New York: Harcourt Brace Jovanovich, 1981);

André Le Vot, *F. Scott Fitzgerald: A Biography*, translated by William Byron (Garden City: Doubleday, 1983);

James R. Mellow, *Invented Lives: F. Scott and Zelda Fitzgerald* (Boston: Houghton Mifflin, 1984).

References:

W. R. Anderson, "Rivalry and Partnership: The Short Fiction of Zelda Sayre Fitzgerald," *Fitzgerald/Hemingway Annual 1977* (Detroit: Bruccoli Clark/Gale Research, 1977), pp. 19-42;

Matthew J. Bruccoli, "Zelda Fitzgerald's Lost Stories," *Fitzgerald/Hemingway Annual 1979* (Detroit: Bruccoli Clark/Gale Research, 1980), pp. 123-126;

Meredith Cary, "*Save Me the Waltz* As a Novel," *Fitzgerald/Hemingway Annual 1976* (Englewood, Colo.: Bruccoli Clark/Information Handling Services, 1978), pp. 65-78;

Anna Valdine Clemens, "Zelda Fitzgerald: An Unromantic Revision," *Dalhousie Review*, 62 (Summer 1982): 196-211;

Douglas Marshall Cooper, "Form and Function: The Writing Style of Zelda Sayre Fitzgerald," unpublished dissertation, University of Delaware, 1979;

F. Scott Fitzgerald, *As Ever, Scott Fitz Letters Between F. Scott Fitzgerald and His Literary Agent Harold Ober 1919-1940*, edited by Bruccoli (Philadelphia & New York: Lippincott, 1972);

Fitzgerald, *Dear Scott/Dear Max: The Fitzgerald-Perkins Correspondence*, edited by John Kuehl and Jackson R. Bryer (New York: Scribners, 1971);

Henry Dan Piper, *F. Scott Fitzgerald: A Critical Portrait* (New York: Holt, Rinehart & Winston, 1965);

Victoria Sullivan, "An American Dream Destroyed: Zelda Fitzgerald," *CEA Critic*, 41 (1979): 33-39;

Jacqueline Tavernier-Courbin, "Art as Woman's Response and Search: Zelda Fitzgerald's *Save Me the Waltz*," *Southern Literary Journal*, 11 (1979): 22-42;

Linda Wagner, "Note on Zelda Fitzgerald's *Scandalabra*," *Notes on Contemporary Literature*, 12 (May 1982): 4-5;

Wagner, "*Save Me the Waltz*: An Assessment in Craft," *Journal of Narrative Technique*, 12 (Fall 1982): 201-209;

Ray Lewis White, "Zelda Fitzgerald's *Save Me the Waltz*: A Collection of Reviews from 1932-1933," *Fitzgerald/Hemingway Annual 1979* (Detroit: Bruccoli Clark/Gale Research, 1980), pp. 163-168;

Zelda: Zelda Sayre Fitzgerald Retrospective, foreword by Scottie Fitzgerald Smith (Montgomery, Ala.: Museum of Fine Arts, 1974).

Papers:
Zelda Sayre Fitzgerald papers are in the Firestone Library at Princeton University.

Rose Franken
(28 December 1895?-)

Yvonne Shafer
Florida State University

BOOKS: *Pattern* (New York: Scribners, 1925);

Another Language (New York, Los Angeles & London: French, 1932; London: Rich & Cowan, 1933);

Mr. Dooley Jr.: A Comedy for Children, by Franken and Jane Lewin (New York & Los Angeles: French, 1932);

Twice Born (New York: Scribners, 1935; revised edition, London: Allen, 1969);

Of Great Riches (New York & Toronto: Longmans, Green, 1937); republished as *Gold Pennies: The Story of a Marriage* (London: Constable, 1938);

Claudia: The Story of a Marriage (New York & Toronto: Farrar & Rinehart, 1939; London: Allen, 1946);

Claudia and David (New York & Toronto: Farrar & Rinehart, 1940; London: Allen, 1946);

Claudia: A Comedy Drama in Three Acts (New York & Toronto: Farrar & Rinehart, 1941; London: French, 1945);

Another Claudia (New York & Toronto: Farrar & Rinehart, 1943; London: Allen, 1946);

Outrageous Fortune (New York & Los Angeles: French, 1944);

Soldier's Wife: A Comedy in Three Acts (New York & Los Angeles: French, 1945);

Young Claudia (New York & Toronto: Rinehart, 1946; London: Allen, 1947);

The Marriage of Claudia (New York: Rinehart, 1948; London: Allen, 1948);

The Hallams (New York: French, 1948);

From Claudia to David (London: Allen, 1949; New York: Harper, 1950);

Claudia: The Story of a Marriage (Garden City: Doubleday, 1951); republished as *The Book of Claudia: The Story of a Marriage* (London: Allen, 1951)—first six Claudia novels, revised; *The New Book of Claudia* (London: Allen, 1958); republished as *Claudia Omnibus* (Garden City: Doubleday, 1958)—first seven Claudia novels, revised; *The Complete Book of Claudia* (London: Allen, 1962; Garden City: Doubleday, 1963)—all eight Claudia novels, revised;

The Fragile Years (Garden City: Doubleday, 1952); republished as *Those Fragile Years* (London: Allen, 1952);

The Quiet Heart (London: Allen, 1954);

Rendezvous (Garden City: Doubleday, 1954);

Intimate Story (Garden City: Doubleday, 1955);

The Antic Years (Garden City: Doubleday, 1958);

When All Is Said and Done: An Autobiography (London: Allen, 1962; Garden City: Doubleday, 1963);

You're Well Out of the Hospital (Garden City: Doubleday, 1966; London: Allen, 1966).

Rose Franken (Billy Rose Theatre Collection, New York Public Library at Lincoln Center)

PLAYS: *Another Language*, New York, Booth Theatre, 25 April 1932; London, Lyric Theatre, 1 December 1932;

Claudia, New York, Booth Theatre, 12 February 1941; London, St. Martin's Theatre, 17 September 1942;

Outrageous Fortune, New York, 48th Street Theatre, 3 November 1943;

Doctors Disagree, New York, Bijou Theatre, 28 December 1943;

Soldier's Wife, New York, Golden Theatre, 4 October 1944; London, Duchess Theatre, 27 August 1946;

The Hallams, New York, Booth Theatre, 4 March 1948.

SCREENPLAYS: *Beloved Enemy*, by Franken, John Balderston, and William Brown Meloney, United Artists, 1936;

Claudia and David, by Franken and Meloney, 20th Century-Fox, 1946;

The Secret Heart, screen story by Franken and Meloney, M-G-M, 1946.

OTHER: "An Author's Slings and Arrows," *New York Times*, 21 November 1943, II:1.

Rose Franken was born Rose Lewin in Gainesville, Texas, to Hannah Younker Lewin and Michael Lewin. When she was quite young, her mother left her father and took her to New York City, where, living with her mother's family, she attended the Ethical Culture School. Her mother wanted her to attend Barnard College, but, just as she was supposed to enter that school, on 1 September 1915 she married Dr. Sigmund Franken, by whom she had three sons. She has lived most of her life in the New York area, where her plays are set.

Following her overnight success with her first Broadway play, *Another Language* (produced in 1932), Franken liked to give interviews in which she presented herself as a featherbrained, impractical housewife who only started writing because her husband bought her a typewriter and she thought she ought to do something with it. In reality she had a very practical approach to life and her career. She successfully balanced the activities of playwriting and writing novels, and she was an immensely popular and prolific short-story writer. She not only wrote plays; she also directed and produced them. Her plays reveal intelligence, education, and a strong interest in serious social questions.

In 1925 Franken produced a novel called *Pattern*, which was successful enough to encourage her to follow a career as a writer in spite of her busy domestic life. Partly autobiographical (as are most of her novels), the novel is the story of a young girl who grows to womanhood and marries but finds her great love for her mother an obstacle to complete maturity and to fulfillment in her marriage. The basic problem appears again in the characterization of Franken's most popular heroine, Claudia. Reviewers noted that Franken had great promise and commented on her observation and humor. These qualities were also noted in her short stories, which were published in *Redbook*, *Good Housekeeping*, and other women's magazines. Although she became one of the highest-paid modern short-story writers, critics characterized her short stories, as well as her novels, as "sentimental," "light," and "candidly feminine." Franken, who wrote her short stories very quickly and did very little rewriting, explained her stories' point of view by saying, "In a love story it is always the woman's relationship to the man that is the more interesting, that makes the story."

The year after *Patterns* was published, Franken became interested in writing for the theater and wrote a play, "Fortnight," which was never published or produced. Next, she and Jane Lewin wrote a children's play, *Mr. Dooley Jr.*, which was also not produced but was published in 1932. After Franken's play *The Hallam Wives* was, she claimed, rejected by almost every producer in New York, it was successfully produced at a summer theater in Greenwich, Connecticut, in 1929. After its run in Greenwich, she made revisions and changed the title to *Another Language*, which was produced in New York in 1932. Reviewers gave the work lavish praise. Robert Coleman in the *New York Mirror* described Franken as, "The most amazing figure to flash across the theatrical horizon this season—or any other season for that matter." The play, which was selected by Burns Mantle for inclusion in *The Best Plays of 1932-33*, enjoyed a long run in New York and was successfully produced in London.

Although *Another Language* was usually described as a comedy, Franken had written with a serious purpose and was angered by people who saw only humor, when she had intended to write a play which would upset people and make them think. Certainly her point of view is clear to the present-day reader. Following in the steps of Sidney Howard in *The Silver Cord* (1926), Franken launches a broad attack on tyrannical mothers and proceeds to question the value system of the typical American family. The play begins with preparations for the Hallams' regular Tuesday-night family dinner at the grandparents' home in Manhattan. The usual crowd of the three older sons and their submissive wives (comic characters in the play) appear, and there is speculation that two seldom seen family figures may also attend: Stella, the wife of the youngest son, Victor, and Jerry, a grandson who troubles the family by his artistic interests and his wish to be an architect. When Stella and Jerry meet, it is apparent that they speak "another language" from the rest of the family and that they are drawn together not only intellectually but sexually. In her excitement Stella puts aside her aversion to the family and invites everyone to dine with her and Victor the next week.

In the second act there is a darker mood and the family dinner, not surprisingly, turns into a disaster. Jerry arrives early and tells Stella he loves her. In contrast, Victor is highly critical of Stella's clothes, the apartment, the dinner, and her insistence that Jerry should study architecture. Victor is capable of change, but he is so involved with the traditional Hallam view that he cannot respond to Stella's attempts to draw him into a broader outlook on life and a more liberal attitude toward the relations between a man and a wife. The Hallams believe that wives should have children, cook, and take care of their husbands—and, incidentally, bow

before Grandmother Hallam's every wish. When the family arrives, there is considerable tension because of the atmosphere of confrontation regarding Jerry's career and the involvement of Stella in "the family's business." As the conflict intensifies, Grandmother Hallam feigns illness out of pique; the family leaves; and Victor, although given the opportunity to stand up for his wife, goes with them.

In the final act, when Victor discovers that Jerry has spent the night with Stella, he behaves with unexpected dignity. The shock jars him into an awareness of his need for Stella and his past insensitivity. Whether or not he can save his marriage and what will happen to Jerry are questions which are left open. The play made a strong statement about the insularity, provincialism, and intolerance of the middle-class family, and challenged the accepted view of the role of women in American society. *Another Language* is important both in terms of its popular and critical success and because it is an expression of the views Franken continued to explore throughout her career in the theater.

Nine years elapsed before Franken followed up this major success with another play. In 1933, after the death of her husband, she went to Hollywood and collaborated with other writers on movie scripts, receiving screen credit with John Balderston and William Brown Meloney for the script *Beloved Enemy* (1936). She married Meloney on 27 April 1937. While in Hollywood Franken continued to earn large sums for her short stories, including a series of ten short stories about a young woman named Claudia, which were published in *Redbook*. These ten vignettes about the marriage of Claudia and David, which move chronologically from the wedding night to the birth of their second child, were published together as a novel, *Claudia*, in 1939. Franken stated that *Claudia* reflected "the loveliness of my own young marriage," and she also remarked that if she had known she would write seven more novels about Claudia, she would not have killed off Claudia's mother in the first one. All of the novels focus on ordinary domestic situations: births, deaths, weddings, illnesses, problems of parents and children, moving from one home to another, and the problems of growing old. David figures in the novels, but the focus is on Claudia. The books were so popular that they were published in "omnibus" editions, for which Franken revised the novels to make a single narrative, in 1951 (first six novels), 1958 (first seven novels), and 1962 (all eight novels). The character of Claudia became familiar to readers in this country as well as abroad. The first novel (actually the collected stories about Claudia) reveals Franken's virtues as a writer as well as her faults. The *Saturday Review of Literature* described *Claudia* as "sentimental and amusing, silly and very good fun." Other critics noted wisdom beneath the comedy and praised the dramatic quality of the dialogue. Readers did not object to the sentiment and eagerly read the novel along with its sequels. In 1941 Franken capitalized on the success of her first Claudia novel by writing, casting, and directing a play version. After auditioning more than two-hundred actresses, she cast the then-unknown Dorothy McGuire in the leading role. McGuire achieved stardom as the rather daring and naughty child-wife who does not want to behave like or assume responsibilities of an adult, but has a strong curiosity about sex. Despite the serious undertones of the play, it is essentially comic, and audiences responded enthusiastically. Claudia and David Naughton lead a pleasant life, but their relationship is unfulfilled because of her immaturity and her dependence on her mother. As the play progresses, Claudia's behavior is explained by the fact that both her husband and mother have made life so easy for her that she has never had to face any difficulties and does not want to. In the end an awakening sense of sexuality, the revelation of her mother's imminent death, and her own pregnancy lead her toward a more mature approach to life.

The critics rejoiced that Rose Franken had returned to Broadway. Many critics, including the exacting George Jean Nathan, called *Claudia* the best play of the season, and several felt it should receive a Pulitzer Prize. Richard Watts, in the *New York Herald Tribune*, expressed the attitude of the majority of the critics, praising the play for its "subtlety of characterization and honesty of emotion" and calling it "a drama of distinction and depth." He was also impressed by the direction, saying, "Miss Franken's direction is as good as her playwriting which is high praise."

The success of *Claudia* heightened Franken's interest in theater, and she and William Brown Meloney acted as coproducers for the remaining plays she wrote. When Meloney read her next play, *Outrageous Fortune*, he exclaimed, "Good God, Rosie, this is damned censorable stuff!" The play was presented in 1943 despite many difficulties but did not receive the acclaim accorded Franken's first two plays. In fact, it received so many negative or mixed reviews after the Boston tryout that the original producer pulled out. While many of the critics praised the production and the acting, particularly

Elsie Ferguson as Crystal Grainger in Outrageous Fortune, *1943*

the performances of Maria Ouspenskaya and Elsie Ferguson, whom Franken had lured back to the theater, some were offended by its sympathetic treatment of a woman with a past, its open analysis of homosexuality, its attack on anti-Semitism, and its frank discussion of male and female sexuality. Franken, however, was determined that her outspoken attack on intolerance would open in New York.

Outrageous Fortune shows the disturbing effects of artistic and sensual impulses in a proper bourgeois home. Set in the home of a successful Jewish businessman and his wife, it involves their relatives, friends, and weekend guests. The arrival of a beautiful and worldly woman disturbs the placid surface of their life and reveals a variety of tensions, repressions, and secrets. By the end of the play none of the problems is really solved, but there is an increased level of tolerance and understanding. Several New York critics felt the play was confusing and had too many themes, but the play was highly praised by a few critics for its courageous subject matter and the high quality of the playwriting. George Jean Nathan felt it was her best play, the only intellectually stimulating play in the early season, and "a credit to the American drama." Although the play ran only seventy-seven performances, it was selected by Burns Mantle (against opposition) as one of the best plays of the year, and he stated, "The most controversial, and the most intelligently written of the early season plays was Rose Franken's *Outrageous Fortune*. . . . Even those reviewers who could not generously approve of it admitted its interest-exciting qualities and the excellence of the performance given to it." The chief objection to the play was its thoughtful treatment of homosexuality, and in 1974 Franken commented, "It was indeed quite a little ahead of its time."

In 1943 Franken also directed her play *Doctors Disagree*. The first of her plays not to appear in Mantle's annual best plays collection, it ran only twenty-three performances. The plot and characterization struck some critics as clichéd and lightweight, and even Franken's staunch supporter Nathan wrote, "It was written originally as a serial for a popular women's magazine and it betrays its geniture." The *New Yorker*'s Wolcott Gibbs dismissed it, satirically referring to the difficulty of a woman faced with the task of darning her husband's socks "after a hard day in the abdominal cavity." However, the play was significant in that it seriously examined the situation of a woman doctor in competition with male doctors.

Franken continued her exploration of the change in the position of women in American society in *Soldier's Wife*, produced in 1944. Less challenging than *Outrageous Fortune*, the play appealed to audiences and most critics, and was selected for *Best Plays of 1944-1945* (1945). In contrast to many plays written in the atmosphere of war, *Soldier's Wife* was humorous and light, in the vein of *Claudia*. Despite the tone, Franken was exploring a real problem—the readjustments necessary between a man and wife after the husband has been away at war and the wife has developed independence and a career. Retreating from her earlier position championing the right of women to careers and the necessity for maturity and independence, Franken presents another child-wife (quite similar to Claudia) who starts to develop independence to the extent of repairing electric plugs and publishing as a book the letters she wrote to her husband when he was overseas. The book is successful; she receives offers from film companies, and is asked to write a newspaper column. Although her husband says he has no right to ask her to stop, he is clearly relieved when the electric plug she has mended fails to work, she declines the offer of the job, and informs him that she wants to have another baby.

With her last play, *The Hallams*, Franken returned to the family she created in her first success, *Another Language*. In this sequel, Victor becomes the hero. The audience learns that following Stella's death, which may have been suicide, Victor moved away from the family, and he seems to have spent the intervening years in contemplation of his values and those of Grandmother Hallam, who is still running the family. He has turned against the narrow view that success (including profit from the war), Protestantism, and family loyalty are the guiding forces in life. Once again the discontented (and often amusing) wives and their materialistic husbands come together for the weekly dinner, and there is concern about Jerry, the would-be architect, who has been forced to leave the family business and enter a tuberculosis sanatorium. As the play develops it is revealed that he has left the sanatorium and married a young woman completely unknown to the family. When Jerry and his wife, Kendrick, unexpectedly appear, it is clear that she is an independent woman with strong attitudes about her career and her rights as a human being. She is like Stella in the earlier play but has a greater ability to stand up for herself against the Hallams. By the end of the play the family's interference has caused Jerry's death. Juxtaposed with his death is the awakening of life in Victor as he perceives Kendrick as a recreation of Stella. At the play's end Grandfather Hallam challenges his wife's domination and intolerance and tells her that if Victor brings Kendrick back to the family as his wife, she must be accepted. The play is another examination of family life in America and of the complexities of marriage and a career for women. Unfortunately, because it appeared too long after *Another Language* and had too little humor, it pleased neither critics nor audiences and closed after twelve performances.

Following *The Hallams* Franken did not write or direct any more plays, continuing her immensely successful career as a short-story writer and novelist. Reviewing her popular autobiography, *When All Is Said and Done* (1962), Brooks Atkinson remarked, "She is not committed to any medium that does not pay her well. . . . Broadway does not qualify." Lack of financial remuneration from *Outrageous Fortune*, *Doctors Disagree*, and *The Hallams* may well have been a factor in her exit from the theater, but she had made large sums of money on the other plays, particularly *Claudia*, for which she earned $1,000 a week in royalties plus film and radio rights. She was an astute businesswoman and highly concerned with her profits, but disappointment over the response to a play which expressed her deep concerns was the chief factor in her decision to stop writing plays.

Although there were rumors for many years that Rose Franken was about to return to the theater, she chose instead to write novels which were popular with the reading public. Although her reviews were generally positive, the critics did not treat her as a novelist of stature. Critics spoke of *Rendezvous* (1954) as engaging and amusing, but superficial. C. L., writing in the *New York Times*, commented, "Miss Franken writes with warmth and delicacy. . . . The severely critical will dismiss *Rendezvous* as being an overly arranged story of sentimentalized trivia." Again, the novel focused on a woman, this time a young French girl who is torn between the urge to see the world and the needs of her family. Critics commented on the "self-sacrificing ending" and the tender characterization of the heroine, Josephine. In *Intimate Story* (1955) Franken depicted another familiar situation: Mrs. Gerry, a middle-aged widow, must learn to accept the independence of her children, overcome loneliness, and find new activities which will bring her happiness. M. B. Snyder, writing in the *Chicago Sunday Tribune*, said "The novel is a delightful study and complicated story of feminine emotions and relations." *The Antic Years* (1958) was a return to the character Claudia, and the last novel in this series. In it Claudia, her husband, and two children travel to Europe, and Claudia is exposed to the sophistication of foreign travel, exotic drinks, seasickness, jealousy of a glamorous woman, and homesickness. At the end of the novel the family resists the temptation to remain in France and returns to America. The novel was described as "light reading," "delightful," "entertaining," and "for feminine readers." Although the critics frequently took a rather condescending tone in reviewing Franken's books, they often noted their pleasing qualities and the great popularity Franken enjoyed. This popularity was demonstrated by the three "omnibus" editions.

Franken's autobiography, *When All Is Said and Done*, was followed by a humorous book, *You're Well Out of the Hospital* (1966), which was written when she was seventy-one years old.

It is ironic that Rose Franken wrote fewer plays than short stories and novels because the critics generally perceived a seriousness and intensity in the plays which was missing in the novels. Her career in the theater was remarkable. Without any formal theatrical training and with no apprenticeship in the theater, she had a career as a playwright and director which spanned sixteen years. Her plays successfully toured the United States and England; at one point she was involved in casting three road companies for *Claudia*. The critical response to her plays was largely favorable, and she drew praise from George Jean Nathan, Richard Watts, Burns Mantle, Ward Morehouse, and Brooks Atkinson. Nathan had great hopes for her and wrote of *Soldier's Wife*, which he did not like, "Miss Franken has talent and even when she deliberately sacrifices it to the box office, as in this case, it can not entirely resist her." Her plays are notable for their frank examination of problems in American society and unpopular subject matter. Particularly in *Outrageous Fortune* she revealed a courageous, unconventional attitude and a strong technique. Her dialogue is sharp and theatrically effective, and her plays range from broad comedy to intense drama. Although her novels continue to be reprinted, there have been no revivals of her plays.

References:

Judith Olauson, *The American Woman Playwright: A view of Criticism and Characterization* (Troy, N.Y.: Whitston, 1981), pp. 24-57;

Yvonne Shafer, "Rose Franken's *Outrageous Fortune*," *Exchange*, 4 (Spring-Summer 1978): 8-15.

Ella Leffland

(25 November 1931-   )

Paul Skenazy

BOOKS: *Mrs. Munck* (Boston: Houghton Mifflin, 1970; London: Hamish Hamilton, 1971); *Love Out of Season* (New York: Atheneum, 1974); *Rumors of Peace* (New York: Harper & Row, 1979); *Last Courtesies and Other Stories* (New York: Harper & Row, 1980).

Ella Leffland is a short-story writer, novelist, and painter. Born in Martinez, California, a small industrial community northeast of San Francisco, she is the daughter of Sven William and Emma Jensen Leffland, emigrants from Denmark who met and married in San Francisco. Leffland's father was an auto painter and, like the father in *Rumors of Peace*, he transferred to wartime work (in the shipyards) during World War II.

Leffland has always lived and worked in the northern California area, though she travels extensively and has spent extended periods of time in Europe. Her family retains close bonds to Denmark, and she visits there frequently: "When I grew up I always thought I was here on a short vacation. Denmark was home and here was some sort of interim place. So I grew up with either a double or a no sense of belonging, I don't know which."

Leffland majored in art as an undergraduate, receiving her B.A. degree from San Jose State College in 1953. From childhood, she always wanted to be both a painter and a writer: "I sent out my first short story to the *New Yorker* when I was 14. I printed it in longhand since I didn't have a typewriter." Almost twenty years later her first published fiction, "Eino," appeared in the *New Yorker*: "I came back from my second trip to Europe and sent 'Eino' off and they accepted it. Since I'd been bombarding them with stories for years, this was really the climax of a long siege."

Leffland's stories elusively reflect her experiences, environments, and family antecedents without being autobiographical mirrors. Martinez, for example, appears under its own name in *Mrs. Munck*, and in only slightly disguised form as Mendoza in *Rumors of Peace*. Port Carquinez of *Mrs. Munck* is modeled on Port Costa, a small community

Ella Leffland

near Martinez. Her European sojourns provide the setting, if not all of the substance, of her stories of wandering youths, hopeful artists, and idealistic dreamers traveling through Spain, France, and Germany, and on a steamer from England to America. Leffland finds both theme and argument in her Danish background. America is complexly related to a more traditional world in her works. Her concern for the past produces her haunting stories of European life and generates the contrasts of past and present which occur in her novels, in which an older order of civility and grace stands in mute rebuke to our own.

In Leffland's novels, the characters live out their lives against the changing historic and geographic landscape of the San Francisco Bay Area. In *Mrs. Munck* (1970), Leffland parallels the title character's personal experiences with the transformation of Port Carquinez, once an Italian and Portuguese fishing village, into a resort and motel complex. In *Love Out of Season* (1974), the time is the 1960s world of Haight-Ashbury, drugs, black and flower power, war protest, and feminism in San Francisco. And in *Rumors of Peace* (1979), the setting is small-town California during World War II, from the Japanese attack on Pearl Harbor to the dropping of the atomic bomb on Hiroshima.

Within these circumstances, the protagonists face their own emergence from periods of withdrawal or stasis, as in *Mrs. Munck*, perhaps the most intense and focused of all Leffland's works. The story moves backward and forward in time from a "Prologue" in which Rose Munck begins a new life at her husband's death by dedicating her widowhood to the care and persecution of Mr. Leary, her uncle-in-law. Leary is a seventy-year-old invalid, who, years before when he was her boss, seduced and betrayed her, and was perhaps responsible for her baby daughter's death. Now, their positions reversed, he is under her control. Leffland has said that in *Mrs. Munck* "I wanted to show how someone who was really unstamped by convention . . . and who was getting ready to flower and go off in her own direction whatever that was, was mutated by the dictates and the mores of society. I'm sure this happens to men too, but not quite as frequently as to women, like Rose." Rose's independence is suggested in her life as a farm child who grew up (in Leffland's words) "way up there in the middle of nowhere," her self-education, her early separation from her parents, and the dreams of traveling around the world, which carry her to San Francisco and her fateful meeting with Leary. As her married name implies, she has spent the last twenty-five years living "like a nun . . . a priest," in the hermitage provided by her hatred and her sense of victimhood. Solitary walks and endless reading have insulated her from her husband, her neighbors, her community, and her own body. As Leffland has noted: "Mrs. Munck sacrificed everything that was meaningful to her, in her, in order to instinctively fulfill her sense of hatred."

Leary's presence—his name, too, suggests his essential character—re-ignites not only her passion for revenge but with it her memory, and her self-interest. Her plans to destroy Leary preoccupy her less and less as she starts to see herself once again.

Leary's eyes serve as the first of many mirrors in which she views her past and begins to recreate her self-image. She buys new clothes and a car; she begins to converse with her neighbors; she confronts the startling changes in her hometown; and she becomes involved with Husar, the broker for the resort company that wants to remake Port Carquinez. Mrs. Munck is the last holdout: the last home owner who hadn't sold, the only woman bound more firmly to her past than her present.

Her attraction to Husar, however, also suggests her vulnerability to the new forces of change that will, despite her, transform her world from its static, unsightly state as a lost backwater of the past. Husar is a defeated dreamer himself, a failed husband, a sexually agile lover. In an image symbolic of his role with Mrs. Munck, he lives in half the former town jail, which he has remodeled into a modern apartment. As broker for the resort company, he literally sells transformation.

The tension of past and present, the known and unfamiliar, the security of hatred and the fears of love and sexual desire climax for Mrs. Munck when Leary discovers her packing to start a new life as Husar's wife. As the two struggle and she almost strangles him, she remembers their earlier fight and realizes that it is she who inadvertently killed her daughter; to kill Leary would only bind her permanently to the "circle of the dead." At the same time, she also rejects the future Husar offers as another false hermitage. Port Carquinez, with its grotesque outcroppings, its faded citizenry, and its hidden natural wonders is like Rose's own craggy, broken surface of personality, and Husar can only see both as opportunities for cosmetic surgery.

In the end, Rose returns to the farm of her childhood and to an unexpected confrontation with her mother. For it is not only through the males of her world that she has been victimized but also in the self-denial that she has seen modeled in her mother's life. In the strange reversals of the last pages, Rose's twice-widowed mother adopts and succors Mr. Leary, enchaining him, as she had her husbands, in her care (and martyrdom). With this new aggrandizement, she delivers Rose from herself: delivers her from the need to live through her dream of revenge, and from her own self-image, based on resistance to her mother's life as the long-suffering female attendant, expressing affection but feeling contempt for an ungiving failure of a man. Her mother's power is in her patience; she outlasts her men by assuming the traditional care-taking role. Rose realizes that her vision of revenge on Leary was only an unconscious repetition of her mother's whole pattern of life-denying relationships with men which turned them into confined and bedridden children.

Mrs. Munck received more brief notices than full-length reviews. Critics commented on the novel's technical strength and thought it an impressive literary debut. The book was read primarily as a study of revenge, and little was said of Mrs. Munck's reemergence into the community, her love affair, or the story of the changes in Port Carquinez. Reactions to the novel seem indicative of an uneasiness with such a study of rage coming from, to quote *America*, "a young lady." The *New York Times Book Review* and *Saturday Review* relegated the novel to their detective story columns. And even Christopher Lehmann-Haupt's quite enthusiastic commentary in the daily *New York Times* began by contextualizing the novel in terms of Kate Millett before pronouncing it a "powerful dramatization of an oppressed woman's plight and revenges" in the tradition of the Brontës and Thomas Hardy. Asked about the novel's feminist stance, Leffland herself says that though the book was written "just before the feminist movement got going, I thought: How very nice to know I wasn't alone all this time."

There were some critical reservations in each review: Lehmann-Haupt felt the novel had "excessively wooden moments," *Saturday Review* said the tale went on so long "that somewhere in the middle impatience replaces suspense," and *Kirkus Reviews* found the story only "restrictively successful" because of its "disfigured view of life . . . sometimes bordering on the malevolent." But for the most part, reviewers tended to agree with the *New Statesman*'s assessment of *Mrs. Munck* as "an assured study of calculated revenge, both chilling and moving . . . a most accomplished and unusual first novel."

Like Rose, Johanna Kaulbach in *Love Out of Season* (1974) grows up in northern California and is a child of nature and of art who loves more deeply than wisely. Born as Fayette Coombs, the child of Okie parents, Johanna is raised by her teacher and that woman's father-in-law, from whom she adopts her name. These educated German immigrants bequeath her their faith in ideals, their passion for moral action, an unsettling assumption of the need for perfection, a deep knowledge of literature and love of art, and their heavy, dark German furniture. From them Johanna learns to "hold steady a sense of beauty, a sense of order, and a sense of honor." From her intimacy with the woods, she learns about the "restorative and soothing" soil, the "self-contained earth," so different from "the beings who must find their place on it."

Armed with little else but the pride inherent in such beliefs, Johanna is another of Leffland's extremists, ill-adapted to the realities of her environment, but attractive, self-contained, and single-minded in her devotion to her life as an artist, to her friends, and to her refusal to accept less than total fulfillment from her world. Within the frame provided by two peace marches in 1965 and 1968, the novel follows Johanna through her relationship to Morris Levinsky. The two meet in a laundromat and, despite themselves, become possessed by each other in a circling, confused, painful, and self-destructive love. Johanna's selfhood is consumed by Morris's ravenous ego. Gradually she sacrifices her artistic discipline, intimacy with friends, and aesthetic principles. Eventually, she agrees to sell the canvases she has been painting but withholding from display; the commercialization of her art suggests the destructive, ravaging revelation of her private vision to public knowledge.

For his part, Morris aches for the clarity and dignity, the pleasure and sanity, of life with Johanna yet feels her furniture and past as a "weight" which threatens him and which, since he is forty, unmistakably reminds him of his age, the limits of his future, and his distance from the promising world of youth he sees around him. His inner resources are undeveloped and limited, though he too maintains memories of his childhood and preserves his patrimony in the form of a thimble his father used in his work as a tailor. He evades Johanna through lies, finally squandering their future in an orgy of gambling.

Each finally drifts out of the relationship into alternatives offered by the times: the aimless street world of drugs and random partners, the well-meaning, upper-middle-class dropout life of Esalen. Both find their way back to their initial careers, each scarred by the memory of the pain and by the brief possibility their love offered of something more fulfilling than dedication to work. Each remains incomplete, finding only limited compensations in routine, in art, in new relationships.

Leffland spares her central characters nothing in their frustrated lives. The city they live in is slowly changing; its neighborhoods are being demolished. The historical events of the period, from the Vietnam War to the beginnings of feminism, are used to highlight the inner dislocation of the characters. Within such cataclysmic changes and such vain hopes for immediate solutions to the unsolvable problems of finding meaning in oneself and one's world, private relationships like that of Johanna and Morris stretch the personality to the point of breakage and destruction, until all ego is lost.

By the end, Johanna is faced with a seemingly irreconcilable choice between, as Yeats put it, "perfection of the life or of the work." In choosing her work, Johanna chooses no sacred calling, no saving vocation. Her art is reduced to merely a consoling passion that leaves her not so much happy as sane and balanced. The last scene has Morris banging at the "vulnerable" doors of a bus while, inside, Johanna rides away from him, herself contained in the "clamourous, swaying crowd." She stands "hemmed in, immobile," enclosed in the "terrible thought" that the time that would, eventually, heal the "bright red terrifying wound" of her desire would also obliterate hers and Morris's bodily presences into a "collective cry" in which they "won't be anything at all."

Johanna's final engulfment is a sign both of her new understanding and her lost uniqueness, her vulnerability to the common woes, the common fears, the common consequences. Like Mrs. Munck and almost all of Leffland's protagonists, Johanna resists joining the ranks of the everyday, the solemn and unheroic survivors. Art, nature, self-focus, idealism, pride, suffering: the badges of uniqueness vary in the novels and stories. But Leffland's characters attempt to shield themselves behind such vanities of dispensation, protecting themselves from their inevitable confrontations with human limit, with time, and with their commonality.

At the same time, the novel also speaks of the individual torments and meaning of these particular lives, and the need to retain memory of the past and to preserve certain parts of one's individual heritage and the culture's story from the intruding knowledge, and eradicating kindness, of those who would turn everything into a bland, equalized whole. Johanna, for example, must finally learn how to arrange that German furniture inside her apartment so that it can become integrated with her contemporary life and tastes. And Morris also comes to discover the need to preserve, as he realizes that "those secret soul-battering memories were man's natural condition, they constituted whatever muddled richness he possessed, and he was being dispossessed of it by a well-meaning world of good works."

Like *Mrs. Munck*, *Love Out of Season* received little critical notice. *Choice* praised Leffland for her "mature and critical vision" of the world of the 1960s and her ability to create "characters of timeless individuality." Patricia S. Caplan in the *National Observer* spoke of the book's "superb craftsmanship"

and Leffland's ability to "weave the characters' lives into the social fabric of the drug scene, the encounter movement, the late-'60s 'revolution.'" Lehmann-Haupt, on the other hand, liked the book less than its predecessor. While noting that both novels worked a similar vein—"impoverished childhood, changed identity, upward striving and disappointed hopes"—he found *Love Out of Season* "more slag than metal" because Leffland failed to establish a connection between the world of San Francisco and the story of her lovers.

The novel's dual ambitions—to trace an era and record the meeting of these two particular individuals—do sometimes conflict. Occasionally, the novel summarizes too much material, or reunites figures arbitrarily. Such scenes turn the book into a record of its time, breaking down the structure of the personal stories and dissipating the force. But what is remarkable is how little strain one feels through most of the novel between character, historical moment, and idea. And within the powerful chronicle of these two lives and the echoing experiences of their friends, Leffland writes scenes of haunting brilliance, including some startling descriptions of Johanna at work. And Leffland meditates convincingly, if darkly, on the false salvations offered by this particular historical moment, dedicated as it was to the transcendence of time. *Love Out of Season* is a bigger canvas than *Mrs. Munck* in its concerns with history and character and in its density of thought, and it is handled with great skill.

Rumors of Peace (1979) seems a departure for Leffland from her austere and extreme characters. Instead of the marginal and psychologically unstable protagonists of the stories and earlier novels, the center of this retrospective first-person memoir is Suse, a young girl growing up in California during World War II. Suse ages from eleven to fifteen, from tomboy pride to the bittersweet disillusionments that accompany the end of an idealized romance, and from a fearful, paranoid vision of the threat of enemies in her midst to a still darker, because realistic and historically encompassing, understanding of a world given to violence, hatred, and war. At once elegiac and discomforting, *Rumors of Peace* challenges easy categorization or any simple, soft-hearted efforts to memorialize a heroic or patriotic period of personal, or national, past.

The novel has a quality of dailiness that is life-affirming. The reader sees not only Suse but her brother and sister, her parents, her friends. One is drawn into minor incidents and mundane crises, from Frank Sinatra to first love and first dresses. Suse learns to swim, wanders the creek edges of her community, and moves in gradually enlarged circles beyond her home. These experiences establish the environment for Suse's rapidly changing self-perception.

Suse is a child indifferent to social praise, social place, and the social arrangements that dominate the thinking of most of those her age. She swims until her hair turns green from the chlorine, isolates herself from her classmates, and is so uninterested in school that she is placed with the "poor workers" and "fools." Eventually, her world begins to alter. She feels her first stirrings of sexuality, an irritating and uncontrollable itching which develops near certain men and which oddly, and delightfully, results in her initial intellectual progress. She starts to read classics like *Madame Bovary*, and she grows more and more intimate with the older, comically snobbish Helen Maria, who introduces Suse to other parts of the world of the past, and of the mind. Dazzled by knowledge at first, Suse slowly realizes that in isolation learning is merely another compromise with reality, offering no substantial answers to the deepest problems which plague her.

Suse's personal development is inextricably bound to her deep involvement with the process of the war. Overcome by the possibility of invasion or bombing, Suse is caught up in the war psychology of shelters, fear of imminent attack, and the internment of Japanese-Americans. She obsessively tries to understand the war, but only finds herself more and more frustrated by new, contradictory stories, by conversations with adults, and particularly by her meeting with Egon, a German-Jewish man on whom Suse develops a mindless, overpowering crush.

Her budding sexual desires again lead Suse to books: to days in the library reading about the Jews, communism, Rosa Luxemborg, persecution. Leffland provides a beautiful, penetrating vision of what it means to find one's way into a subject for the first time as Suse learns how questions are asked, encounters the mind-numbing difficulties of confusing words and inexplicable ideas, discovers how to abstract from material to a view of the whole, and succumbs to the humbling moment when resistant facts dispel her initial conclusions and the process begins again.

For Suse this study confirms her intuitive sense that life is not the fulfilling, affirming experience others tell her it is. She finds evidence for her belief in forces beyond understanding and control. She also discovers that learning, instead of being what was joyously described to her as a rapture in which subjects unfold, parts interrelate, and understanding produces a beautiful and confirming symmetry, is a poetic blossom leaved by conflict and endless argument:

> Each century was the same; history was the same record played over and over. War was war, and peace was preparation for war; it was as if man were crazy, had always been, would always be, and the people on the street were man in his daily and abiding craziness. . . . It was the pure form of senselessness that was history.

Suse faces several realizations like this one: about her pipe dreams and projections of love, about the impossibility of clear and reassuring truths, about the mixed motives of her own country in the war, and about the need to exist within such dark terrors and still find ways to live and to relish the pleasures that are available. Egon takes her to an open window and forces her to stare out at the beauty of a clear day, echoing an earlier recognition on her part that "even if life was a black tunnel with no happy endings, there were bright moments here and there. And you had to take them. You had to take them or you would have nothing at all at the end."

Yet Suse remains unconvinced by such brief, compromising illuminations. To the end of the novel she remains, like all of Leffland's protagonists, too greedy—or experience, perhaps, remains too penurious for such passionate feeling. She still wants everything: "peace, glory, love, life everlasting," and has only been granted, in answer, "a window, a summer day," as memory and palliative.

Reviewers were almost unanimously delighted with this novel. *Kirkus Reviews* remained Leffland's harshest critic, finding the book "bland, too insistent, and overdone." But others were quite lavish in their praise. Although Rosellen Brown, writing in *New York*, felt the novel went on too long and began to sentimentalize characters toward the end, she said it was "a book of acute insight and delicious humor, its evocation of a time and place moving in its precision." *West Coast Review of Books* called it a "stunning novel, a rare book, a delicious recalling"; Daphne Merkin in *The New York Times Book Review* thought it "like stepping into a Norman Rockwell painting" and praised its "sure grasp of living detail," and Harriet Rosenstein in *Ms.* praised Leffland's ability to render Suse's inner life and her "anthropologist's sensitivity to the conversation and ritual behavior of adolescent groups."

A conflict of cultures and times is also appar-

-597-

I ~~gave a~~ shrug, not wanting her to know how I felt, tightened

up and sick inside, with a light, airy trembling feeling in my

arms and legs. How (could) she smoke? How could ~~she~~ keep her hand

from shaking?

"Anyway," she said, ~~squinting in the sunlight,~~ "I suppose that's

it. The end of the war."

~~Maybe. The~~ end of everything, ~~Maybe the whole world will blows~~
~~up.~~

"I doubt ~~that.~~"

The basic power of the universe. Why didn't they leave it

alone?"

"I don't know, ~~I~~ ~~she said, shaking her head reflectively.~~ "But

maybe we should think of what the alternative might   have

been. Probably a long costly invasion - "

"Money."

"I'm not talking about money. I'm talking about lives."

"What about the people in that city? A whole city?"
~~There's no point getting angry at me. I didn't do it.~~
A whole city ceasing to exist, and who had done it?
No, they did it. ~~The ones who held the reins now, who we~~

were supposed to have faith in; who talked ~~about~~ of constructive

thought, creativeness, cooperation, ~~an~~ drawing the good out of

pwople. ~~They didn't even have any good in themselves.~~ They were
~~a bunch of bastards.~~ I felt my throat ache; the sky ~~suddenly~~

blurred and sparkled. I closed my eyes so she couldn't see them,

Revised typescript for a work in progress (the author)

ent in all the fictions in *Last Courtesies and Other Stories* (1980), a collection that includes all of Leffland's published short works of the past twenty years and three previously unpublished stories. The stories have appeared in such journals as the *New Yorker, Cosmopolitan, Harper's, Epoch*, and *Quarterly Review of Literature*, and several have been chosen for inclusion in the annual *Best American Stories* and *O. Henry Prize Short Stories* volumes; the title story won the O. Henry Prize as the best short story of 1977.

All fourteen tales describe situations of disorientation and discomfort. Characters live, or travel, within environments foreign to them. This is literally the case in the several stories written early in Leffland's career, about young American travelers wandering through Europe and elsewhere, like "Vienna, City of My Dreams," "Eino," "Monsieur Scream," "Glad Offerings," "Water Music," and "The Famous Toboggan of Love." But the foreign territories extend to America, as in "Gorm," about Danes displaced to the United States and settling briefly in the Philippines and India, or "Last Courtesies," with its San Francisco community of Russian-Americans. The foreign country is also temporal, as in "The Linden Tree," about a gay man facing the death of his companion, or "The Queen of Ivsira," in which an aging maid on a ship must accept a new loss of status. Often the foreignness is complicated by generational conflicts, in which young and old collide, their different moralities and ideals rubbing bruisingly against each other.

The most extreme of the foreign countries, however, is interior, consisting of the unknown and dissatisfied, unconscious longings that condition the lives of Leffland's protagonists. The characters are least at home with, and in, themselves. Whether alone or with others, they share an uncomfortable privacy. In some cases, this separation from themselves results in communion with objects, as in "The House of Angels," in which an unwanted brother invests his love in the figure of an angel adorning the outside of a building about to be demolished. Or they might fill their loneliness with ghosts, as in "Conclusion," where a simpleminded German servant, her loveless world contained by the biblical injunctions she quotes as answer to all confusion and change, is physically ravaged by a phantom, a photograph of a German film star she invests with her suppressed longings and needs.

But such overt ghosts are only more agile, or personified, metaphors. In almost all the stories, characters displace themselves onto the environ-

ment and into other people, unknown belief systems, imagined traditions, or ideals of the past. The hopeful young artist of "Monsieur Scream" travels to the village where his father once lived in his bohemian days, trying to paint his way into adequacy and parental recognition, and instead developing a debilitating fear of a legendary apparition he imagines stalking the musty attic over his bed. The young woman of "Vienna, City of My Dreams" begs and bribes the commonest form of notice—the saying of her name—from the couple who run her pension. In "Inside," a woman is convinced that people who "stare" at her in museums and parks know the secret of her life and soul, a secret her father died without revealing to her.

Many of these displaced individuals are young, financially secure, and wandering from parents who have ignored them or discouraged their hopes. The recognition these young protagonists seek in others suggests that their vulnerability is a bitter aftertaste of childhood rejection and emotional frigidity which have left them without the security of personal belief and without faith in a world commensurate to their desires.

But such psychological understanding also seems to miss some deeper point. One must talk also of failed cultural parenting. Although a symbol of wealth, America is absent as a source of values for Leffland's wandering expatriates who, as titles of the stories suggest, invest themselves in "dreams" of a Vienna, or "glad offerings" to idealized visions of a traditional system of social decorum in Spain. The American travelers are desperate and greedy, anxious to become absorbed in some imagined Europe of courtesies, decorum, taste, beauty, and time-honored relations among people, and between people and the sanctities of culture. Instead, they meet real European families and couples: aged citizens who disregard their entreaties or misunderstand their requests; poor workers trapped in the wearing despair of their mundane and petty habits. Against American imaginative projections, the Europeans offer only silent dinners of unappetizing food, gossipy tales of love for an ugly old cat, the petty squabbles of two brothers and a tired mother cooking in the kitchen, the financial advantages a family acquires from its status as proprietor of the town hostel. The Europeans have no time or energy to dream, or to fulfill the dreams and expectations of these visitors. Their daily lives are their stories, the exactments of poverty their culture.

The youths fail from their intense needs and their intense self-focus. They are deranged, but that derangement is the register both of their despair and of their wisdom. The adolescent of "Water Music" annoys an older woman passenger and acquires the unspoken admiration of the ship's captain for his bouts of cacophonous piano music, in which he tries to articulate the immense power he feels in his relationship with the sea. The music is vain, self-serving, and self-defeating. But the young man's attempts to make art of his feelings amount to the youth's refusal to abide within the mundane middle ground of acceptance and levity of the talkative old woman, who is bothered by loud noises and interested only in good social conversation over dinner. One-armed Mayo, in "The Famous Toboggan of Love," parlays obnoxious behavior, her stump of flesh, and one precious, if grotesque, memory of love in Spain into a demand for recognition from those who would blanket her in the self-satisfying comforts of pity.

There is a resistance to normality in the single-minded, obsessive lives of Leffland's characters. They deny their commonality with the confused and weary, surviving each day as an end in itself. But they also abjure the pieties and compromises offered by liberalism and embedded in the life-denying comforts and securities of marriage, family, and the distinct ease obtainable in our contemporary world. To the couple in "Conclusion," their maidservant is a "project." In both "Gorm" and "The House of Angels" a sister finds uneasy release from responsibility for her brother in marriage. Sentimental visions of "last courtesies" cost the opera-loving protagonist of that story her life. Only perhaps in "The Linden Tree" does one find an accommodation which is not a defeat. The approach of death offers no vain comforts. But at least there is a community of shared feeling in this story between two men, a feeling that has weathered their passions, rounding out the corners and soothing the raw fibers of desire with the balm of shared days, shared frustrations and pleasures, shared tastes.

Two limits to the stories in *Last Courtesies* might be noted. First, read in sequence, there is a sameness of atmosphere, of despair, of failure and disaster unavailable to palliatives. A gloom washes over the action, like the rain and fog that seem almost invariably to darken the landscapes inside the stories themselves. The darkness is lightened by Leffland's mastery of detail and delight in the surprising grotesque wonders of the world, but the brooding sense of misery tends to lump the stories together in one's memory.

Second, the stories all turn on themselves in their endings. At times, the surprise or revelation is only the final shock of a recognition that has been building throughout, as in the narrator's understanding in "The Famous Toboggan of Love," or the last lines of "Inside." Stories like "Water Music" and "Glad Offerings" shift our point of view to force a reevaluation of our emotional relationships and judgment. But in other fictions, the end seems excessive or even sentimental; "The House of Angels" pushes its point home too firmly. Finally, some plot turns, like that of "Last Courtesies," seem arbitrary, unfair to both reader and character, and a product of a plan which has not accommodated itself to the changing, internally consistent structure of the fiction itself.

But the stories in *Last Courtesies* are all written with grace and skill. The later pieces, like "The Linden Tree," possess an intricate patience with time's alterations absent from the earlier fiction, but each story is notable for its precise language and Leffland's sure control of scene. As John Romano noted in the *New York Times Book Review* of this collection: "There is not a contemporary writer of short stories from whom truth of feeling, splendidness of insight, and a human beauty both aching and real can more confidently be expected."

Leffland lives with her cat in San Francisco, and she supports herself by her writing. Though a respected member of the city's literary community, she does not teach on a regular basis and seldom gives public readings. She does occasional book reviews for *Harper's*, the *New York Times*, and *New York* magazine, though she says she doesn't like writing (or reading) reviews. "I always feel that mine is a personal opinion, a personal reaction, and it might not be a valid reaction. I think it's so difficult to paraphrase everything that's taken years to be put into a book. . . . To me it is a horrible agony." She is presently working on a novel which "is different from the other books in that it is historical. It's not my home ground this time."

Whatever the landscape, however, one expects Leffland to continue to describe an unaccommodating world, peopled by creatures uncomfortable with each other, often robbed even of the privilege of self-intimacy. A clash of cultures—temporal, spatial, sexual—is central to her work, though it is rarely simple or one-sided. The past is often idealistic, but as often idealized; confirming, but also a convenient retreat from present circumstance. Personal and social history echo each other within her protagonists, who both fear and desire the change that inevitably occupies their lives and surrounds them in their environments. It is in a person's reactions to new experiences that Leffland finds the motive energy for her plots: the way her characters retreat, submerge themselves in loneliness, fantasy, art, culture, or madness to avoid the alterations, and begrudgingly come to accept their transformed circumstances. Ella Leffland is an artist who writes knowingly and deeply of that shared private ground of loneliness called selfhood and of the circumstances of time and place which have helped shape this personal terrain.

Jack Lindsay
(20 October 1900-   )

Orin Anderson

SELECTED BOOKS: *Fauns and Ladies* (Kirribilli, Sydney: J. T. Kirtley, 1923);

Marino Faliero: A Verse Play (London: Fanfrolico Press, 1927);

William Blake: Creative Will and the Poetic Image (London: Fanfrolico Press, 1927);

Helen Comes of Age: Three Plays in Verse (London: Fanfrolico Press, 1927);

Dionysus. Nietzsche Contra Nietzsche: An Essay in Lyrical Philosophy (London: Fanfrolico Press, 1928);

The Passionate Neatherd (London: Fanfrolico Press, 1929);

Hereward, a Verse Play, book by Lindsay and music by John Gough (London: Fanfrolico Press, 1930);

Rome For Sale (London: Mathews & Marrot, 1934; New York & London: Harper, 1934);

Caesar Is Dead (London: Nicholson & Watson, 1934);

Last Days With Cleopatra (London: Nicholson & Watson, 1935);

Despoiling Venus (London: Nicholson & Watson, 1935);

Come Home at Last and Other Stories (London: Nicholson & Watson, 1936);

Mark Antony: His World and His Contemporaries (London: Routledge, 1936; New York: Dutton, 1937);

The Wanderings of Wenamen: 1115-1114 B.C. (London: Nicholson & Watson, 1936);

Who Are the English (London: Left Review, circa 1936);

Shadow and Flame, as Richard Preston (London: Cape, 1937);

John Bunyan: Maker of Myths (London: Methuen, 1937);

Anatomy of Spirit (London: Methuen, 1937);

1649: A Novel of a Year (London: Methuen, 1938);

To Arms: A Story of Ancient Gaul (London: Oxford University Press, 1938);

Brief Light: A Novel of Catullus (London: Methuen, 1939);

England, My England, Key Books, no. 2 (London: Fore, 1939);

Lost Birthright (London: Methuen, 1939);

A Short History of Culture (London: Gollancz, 1939);

Into Action: The Battle of Dieppe (London: Dakers, 1942);

We Shall Return (London: Dakers, 1942);

Second Front (London: Dakers, 1942);

Beyond Terror (London: Dakers, 1943);

British Achievement in Art and Music (London: Pilot Press, 1945);

Hullo Stranger (London: Dakers, 1945);

Men of Forty-Eight (London: Methuen, 1948);

Mulk Raj Anand: A Critical Essay (Bombay, Kitabs, 1948); republished as *The Lotus and the Elephant* (Bombay: Kutub Popular Press, 1954);

Clue of Darkness (London: Dakers, 1949);

Marxism and Contemporary Science; or, the Fulness of Life (London: Dobson, 1949);

Charles Dickens: A Biographical and Critical Study (London: Dakers, 1950; New York: Philosophical Library, 1950);

A World Ahead: Journal of a Soviet Journey (London: Fore, 1950);

Three Letters to Nikolai Tikhonov (London: Fore, 1950);

The Passionate Pastoral (London: Bodley Head, 1951);

Byzantium Into Europe (London: Bodley Head, 1952);

Betrayed Spring: A Novel of the British Way (London: Bodley Head, 1953);

Rising Tide (London: Bodley Head, 1953);

Tristan Tzara, Jack Lindsay, and an unidentified American sculptress in Paris (Isak Grunberg)

Rumanian Summer: a View of the Rumanian People's Republic, by Lindsay and Michael Cornforth (London: Lawrence & Wishart, 1953);

Civil War in England: The Cromwellian Revolution (London: Muller, 1954; New York: Barnes & Noble, 1967);

The Moment of Choice. A Novel of the British Way (London: Bodley Head, 1955);

After the 'Thirties: The Novel in Britain and Its Future (London: Lawrence & Wishart, 1956);

George Meredith: His Life and Work (London: Bodley Head, 1956);

The Romans Were Here: The Roman Period in Britain and its Place in Our History (London: Muller, 1956);

Three Elegies (Twinstead, Essex: Myriad Press, 1957);

Life Rarely Tells: An Autobiographical Account Ending in the Year 1921 and Situated Mostly in Brisbane, Queensland (London: Bodley Head, 1958); republished as volume 1 of *Life Rarely Tells*, 3 volumes (1982);

Arthur and His Times: Britain in the Dark Ages (London: Muller, 1958; New York: Barnes & Noble, 1966);

The Discovery of Britain: A Guide to Archeology (London: Merlin Press, 1958);

1764: The Hurly Burly of Daily Life Exemplified in One Year of the Eighteenth Century (London: Muller, 1959);

The Revolt of the Sons (London: Muller, 1960);

The Roaring Twenties: Literary Life in Sydney, New South Wales, in the Years 1921-26 (London: Bodley Head, 1960); republished as volume 2 of *Life Rarely Tells*, 3 volumes (1982);

The Writing on the Wall: An Account of Pompeii in its Last Days (London: Muller, 1960);

All on the Never-Never: A Novel of the British Way of Life (London: Muller, 1961);

William Morris: Writer (London: William Morris Society, 1961);

The Death of the Hero: French Painting from David to Delacroix (London: Studio Books, 1961);

Fanfrolico and After (London: Bodley Head, 1962); republished as volume 3 of *Life Rarely Tells*, 3 volumes (1982);

A Short History of Culture From Prehistory to the Renaissance (London: Studio Books, 1962; New York: Citadel Press, 1963);

The Way the Ball Bounces (London: Muller, 1962);

Daily Life in Roman Egypt (London: Muller, 1963; New York: Barnes & Noble, 1964);

Masks and Faces (London: Muller, 1963);

Choice of Times (London: Muller, 1964);

Nine Days' Hero: Wat Tyler (London: Dobson, 1964);

Leisure and Pleasure in Roman Egypt (London: Muller, 1965; New York: Barnes & Noble, 1966);

Our Anglo-Saxon Heritage (London: Weidenfeld & Nicolson, 1965);

The Clashing Rocks: A Study of Early Greek Religion and Culture, and the Origins of Drama (London: Chapman & Hall, 1965);

J. M. W. Turner: His Life and Work: A Critical Biography (London: Evelyn, Adams & MacKay,

1966; Greenwich, Conn.: New York Graphic Society, 1966);

Our Roman Heritage (London: Weidenfeld & Nicolson, 1967);

The Ancient World: Manners and Morals (London: Weidenfeld & Nicolson, 1968; New York: Putnam's, 1968);

Meetings With Poets: Memories of Dylan Thomas, Edith Sitwell, Louis Aragon, Paul Eluard, Tristan Tzara (London: Muller, 1968; New York: Ungar, 1969);

Men and Gods on the Roman Nile (London: Muller, 1968; New York: Barnes & Noble, 1968);

Cezanne: His Life and Art (London: Evelyn, Adams & MacKay, 1969; Greenwich, Conn.: New York Graphic Society, 1969);

The Origins of Alchemy in Graeco-Roman Egypt (London: Muller, 1970);

Cleopatra (London: Constable, 1971; New York: Coward McCann & Geoghegan, 1971);

The Origins of Astrology (London: Muller, 1971; New York: Barnes & Noble, 1971);

Gustave Courbet: His Life and Work (London: Bath, Adams & Dart, 1972; New York: Harper & Row, 1972);

Faces and Places (Toronto: Basilike, 1974);

Helen of Troy: Woman and Goddess (London: Constable, 1974; Totowa, N.J.: Rowan & Littlefield, 1974);

Blast Power and Ballistics: Concepts of Force and Energy in the Ancient World (London: Muller, 1974; New York: Barnes & Noble, 1974);

Death of a Spartan King, and Two Other Stories of the Ancient World (London: Inca Books, 1974);

William Morris: His Life and Work (London: Constable, 1975; New York: Taplinger, 1979);

The Troubadours and Their World of the Twelfth and Thirteenth Centuries (London: Muller, 1976);

Decay and Renewal: Critical Essays on Twentieth Century Writing (Sydney: Wild & Woolley, 1976; London: Lawrence & Wishart, 1976);

Hogarth: His Art and His World (London: Hart-Davis MacGibbon, 1977; New York: Taplinger, 1979);

The Monster City: Defoe's London 1688-1730 (London: Hart-Davis MacGibbon, 1978; New York: St. Martin's Press, 1978);

William Blake: His Life and Work (London: Constable, 1978; New York: Braziller, 1979);

The Crisis in Marxism (London: Moonraker Press, 1981; New York: Barnes & Noble Imports, 1981);

Thomas Gainsborough: His Life and Art (London, Toronto, Sydney & New York: Granada,

1981; New York: Universe, 1981);

Collected Poems, edited by J. M. W. Borg (Chicago: Chiron Press, 1982);

Life Rarely Tells, 3 volumes (Sydney, London & New York: Penguin, 1982);

PLAYS: *The Whole Armour of God*, London, Pilgrim Players, 1944;

Robin of England, London, Unity Theatre, 1945;

Face of Coal, by Lindsay and B. Coombes, London, Scala Theatre, 1946;

Iphigeneia in Aulis, Adaptation of a Play by Euripides, London, Mermaid Theatre, 1967;

Supper With Socrates, London, Mermaid Theatre, 1981.

OTHER: *Poetry in Australia*, edited by Lindsay and Kenneth Slessor (Sydney: Vision Press, 1923);

John Harington, *The Metamorphosis of Ajax*, edited by Lindsay and Peter Warlock (London: Fanfrolico Press, 1927; New York: McKee, 1928);

Delighted Earth. A Selection from Herrick's Hesperides, edited, with a foreword, by Lindsay as Peter Meadows (London: Fanfrolico Press, 1927);

Loving Mad Tom: Bedlamite Verse of the XVI and XVII Centuries, edited by Lindsay (London: Fanfrolico Press, 1928);

Satyrs and Sunlight, Being the Collected Poetry of Hugh McCrae, edited by Lindsay (London: Fanfrolico Press, 1928);

Fanfrolicana, edited by Lindsay (London: Fanfrolico Press, 1928);

The Tunning of Elynour Rumming, by John Skelton, edited by Lindsay (London: Fanfrolico Press, 1928);

A Handbook of Freedom, edited by Lindsay (New York: International Publishers, 1939); republished as *Spokesmen for Liberty* (London: Lawrence & Wishart, 1941);

Giuliano the Magnificent, Adapted From a Work by D. Johnson, edited by Lindsay (London: Dakers, 1940);

Anthology: New Lyrical Ballads, edited by Lindsay, Maurice Carpenter, and Honor Arundel (London: Editions Poetry, 1945);

Anvil: Life and the Arts: A Miscellany, edited by Lindsay (London: Meridian, 1947; New York: Universal Distributors, 1947);

New Developments Series, edited by Lindsay (London: Lane, 1947-1948);

Poems by Herrick, edited by Lindsay (London: Grey Walls Press, 1948);

Selected Poems of William Morris, edited by Lindsay

(London: Grey Walls Press, 1948);

Key Poets, edited by Lindsay and R. Swingler (London: Fore, 1950).

TRANSLATIONS: *Lysistrata* (Sydney: J. Kirtley, 1925; London: Fanfrolico Press, 1926);

The Complete Works of Gaius Petronius (London: Fanfrolico Press, 1927);

Propertius in Love (London: Fanfrolico Press, 1927);

Homage to Sappho (London: Fanfrolico Press, 1928);

Aristophanes, *Women in Parliament* (London: Fanfrolico Press, 1929);

The Complete Poems of Theocritos (London: Fanfrolico Press, 1929);

The Complete Poetry of Gaius Catullus (London: Fanfrolico Press, 1929);

Homer's Hymns to Aphrodite (London: Fanfrolico Press, 1930);

Mimiambs of Herondas (London: Fanfrolico Press, 1930);

Decimus Ausonius, *Patchwork Quilt* (London: Fanfrolico Press, 1930);

Sulpicia's Garland: Roman Poems (New York: McKee, 1930);

The Golden Ass by Apuleius (New York: Limited Editions Club, 1932; new translation, London: Elek, 1960);

Daphnis and Chloe by Longus (London: Daimon Press, 1948);

Vitezslav Nezval, *Song of Peace*, translated by Lindsay and S. Jolly (London: Fore, 1951);

Adam Miekiewicz, *Poems* (London: Sylvan Press, 1957; New York: Transatlantic Arts, 1957);

Modern Russian Poetry (London: Vista, 1960);

Ribaldry of Rome (London: Elek, 1961); republished as *Ribaldry of Ancient Rome* (New York: Ungar, 1965);

Ribaldry of Greece (London: Elek, 1961); republished as *Ribaldry of Ancient Greece* (New York: Ungar, 1965);

Giordano Bruno, *Cause, Principle and Unity: Five Dialogues* (London: Daimon Press, 1962; New York: International Publishers, 1964);

Elenore Bille-de-Mot, *The Age of Akhenaten* (London: Adams & MacKay, 1967; New York: McGraw-Hill, 1968);

Teferos Anthias, *Greece, I Keep My Vigil For You* (London: Anthias Publications, 1968).

A profound analyst and a fiery poet, Jack Lindsay is an extraordinary polymath who, in a career which has spanned this century, has published well over 250 major works, anticipating, adding to, or reflecting most of its important intel-

lectual influences from early existentialism and Nietzscheanism to post-cold war Marxism.

Aldous Huxley, D. H. Lawrence, Liam O'Flaherty, and Robert Graves found him a focal point for action and reaction in the days of Bloomsbury in the 1920s. From the 1920s into the 1950s, Sigmund Freud, W. E. B. DuBois, Jean-Paul Sartre, Bertolt Brecht, and William Butler Yeats variously held lengthy talks or correspondence with him. T. F. and Llewelyn Powys, Edith Sitwell, Tristan Tzara, Elio Vittorini, Kenneth Slessor, Nikolai Tikhonov, Krishna Menon, Dylan Thomas, and Bernard Miles are numbered among his coworkers and friends from the early 1940s into the 1980s.

Lindsay has been a Fellow of the Royal Society of Literature in the United Kingdom since 1946; in 1982, he became a Fellow of the Australian Academy of Humanities. He holds the Gold Medal of the Australian Society of Literature (1960); the Soviet Order of Merit (*Znak Pocheta*, 1968); an honorary doctor of letters from the University of Queensland (1972); and the Order of Australia (1982).

In a world of increasing philosophical polarization, Lindsay has from time to time suffered critical neglect, even abuse, for his steadfast practice of his art in the face of political, critical, or economic expediency; but, writing in his ninth decade, he is beginning to gain a grudging respect in the United Kingdom, honors in his native Australia, and a reawakening of interest among socialist countries, many of which have treated him officially as a "nonperson" for the last decade and a half.

Jack Lindsay was born 20 October 1900 at Melbourne, Australia, into a family with a legacy of talented artists and writers including: Percy, landscape painter and illustrator; Sir Daryl, director of the National Gallery at Victoria; illustrator Ruby, wife of cartoonist Will Dyson; Sir Lionel, etcher, wood engraver, watercolorist, journalist, and art critic; and prolific, controversial Norman Lindsay, the artist H. L. Mencken lauded as Rubens's only equal. Jack Lindsay was the first son of Norman and Catherine Parkinson Lindsay. Shortly after Jack Lindsay's birth, his father moved the family to Sydney and quickly became a national figure with his weekly cartooning for the *Bulletin*. The rest of Norman Lindsay's time was filled with work for himself: creating watercolors, pen-and-inks, etchings, oils, ship models, and sculpture; and novels, while presiding over a studio awash with a tide of professional boxers and horsemen, other writers and artists, and numerous models. To his son Jack, Norman Lindsay bequeathed an intense vigor, artistic fecundity of uniform high quality, and a vitality visible in the work, which Edith Sitwell was later to call "an amazing and unchained energy."

In his Australian youth, Jack Lindsay became possessed by the written word, beginning at the age of five, when he taught himself to read in order to interpret his father's political cartoons. Thus began a lifelong commitment to the creative process, and by the time he was seventeen, Lindsay had read virtually every major published poet in the English language, up to the end of the last century. At the University of Queensland, where his closest friends included Jim Quinton (an American who was a former member of the I.W.W.) and Gordon Childe, who became the first Abercromby Professor of Prehistoric Archeology at the University of Edinburgh, Lindsay took an honors degree in classics at twenty-one.

He then moved to Sydney, joining his father and poets Hugh McCrae and Kenneth Slessor in the *Vision* experiment. With Norman Lindsay's manifesto *Creative Effort* (1920) and *Vision* magazine as their standard, they sought "a genuine Australian literature" based upon Nietzschean concepts, an elevated life and art which harked to the Hellenic Golden Age, despised the narrow prudishness of a society which "limited the vitality" of Australian art, and blasted the course of European modernism for its nihilistic failure to rebuild a civilization perverted by World War I. Lindsay found himself in the midst of Sydney literary life with its pub chairman, Christopher Brennan, and its legends and firebrands—Slessor, McCrae, R. D. Fitzgerald, Henry Lawson, and A. G. Stephens.

Jack Lindsay lived the life of the world-despising, starving artist in a crumbling attic in Wooloomooloo, married Janet Beaton, the granddaughter of Australia's first Privy Councillor, and visited Springwood, his father's Olympus in the Blue Mountains, where the satiric Ishmael Club and the "*Vision*-aries" provided counterpoint to the comings and goings of Gruner, Nellie Melba, Arthur Benjamin, and the like. Lindsay gave his father's new universe a joyous, Rabelaisian expostulation of Nietzsche. At the same time, Lindsay wrote criticism, poetry, and classical translations for the *Bulletin, Art in Australia,* and *Vision* and published his first book, *Fauns and Ladies* (1923), in what he later called "all-too-faithful admiration of Hugh McCrae's work," specifically *Satyrs and Sunlight.* With musician Adolph Beutler, Lindsay worked out a system of music composition using harmonies and sight-and-sound patterns on player-piano rolls. But

it was his translation of Aristophanes which determined his future.

Published in Sydney by John Kirtley in 1925, Lindsay's translation of *Lysistrata*, with Norman Lindsay's illustrations, was well received in England (and pirated in the United States), prompting Lindsay's traveling to England the following year to found Fanfrolico Press, the prestigious fine press that was a "worthy successor to William Morris' Kelmscott Press" and the vanguard of the Australian "cultural invasion" of Europe and its modernism. Lindsay's renaissance-type abilities came to the fore at Fanfrolico: he found and edited manuscripts such as John Eliot's *Parlement of Prattlers* (1928); translated many works from the Graeco-Roman world beginning with an extensive revision of *Lysistrata* (1926), *The Complete Works of Gaius Petronius* (1927), *Propertius in Love* (1927), and *Homer's Hymns to Aphrodite* (1930); published English Renaissance poetry, including John Harington's *Metamorphosis of Ajax* (1927) and John Skelton's *The Tunning of Elynour Rumming* (1928); and produced works by Slessor, McCrae, Norman Lindsay, William Morris, and his younger brothers Ray and Philip (Ray remained in Australia, but Philip joined Lindsay in England).

The Fanfrolico Press offices were originally at 5 Bloomsbury Square, and the energetic Australians soon caught the eye of bohemian and literary London. Lindsay was the prototype for Willy Weaver in Aldous Huxley's novel *Point Counter Point* (1928), "a little man perpetually smiling . . . bubbling with good humor and an inexhaustible verbiage." And Lindsay's predilection for entanglements with exotic women such as Elza Craig, who had an explosive impact on his life, and Betty May, former wife of Aleister Crowley's "Ideal pupil and magical heir" Raoul, got him caricatured in Edith Young's *Lisa* (1930) as the narrator-lover of Lisa (Elza Craig), a girl who "creates about herself an atmosphere of legend," and lampooned in Roy Campbell's *The Georgiad* (1933): "The living image of a country lover, in wooly underpants, a sort of Faun/Who seems to wish he never had been drawn. . . ."

Kirtley left Fanfrolico Press after a year, and his place was filled by P. R. Stephenson (P. R. S.), whom Lindsay had known in Brisbane at the University of Queensland. Stephenson was a Rhodes Scholar and proved a strong ally for Lindsay practically until the end of Fanfrolico. The press operated until 1930, publishing thirty-seven titles (twenty-nine illustrated) of 325-500 copies each, setting a standard in fine press publishing and providing a platform for the *London Aphrodite* magazine.

There were only six numbers of the *London Aphrodite* (July 1928-July 1929). The contents of the first issue were contributed by Slessor, McCrae, Robert Nichols, P. R. Stephenson, Lindsay, and Liam O'Flaherty. The first number did well, although the critics ignored or jeered the "Nietzschean" Olympians. Staunch supporters included Gordon Bottomley, the Hon. Evan Morgan, and A. P. Sachs (an American businessman who wrote them an essay on Heisenbergian Indeterminacy). There were Fanfrolico-*Aphrodite* meetings at the Tour Eiffel restaurant with Augustus John, Matthew Smith, and Aldous Huxley, who corresponded regularly with Lindsay. (*Do What You Will*, 1929, which Huxley wrote after he had read Lindsay's *Dionysus. Nietzsche Contra Nietzsche*, 1928, contains material which appeared previously in letters to Lindsay). Among other friends and contributors to *Aphrodite* were T. F. and Llewelyn Powys, Rhys Davies, Sacheverell Sitwell, Norman Douglas, and Edgell Rickword.

As an offshoot of the *London Aphrodite*, Lindsay and Stephenson printed 3,500 copies of Lindsay's *The Passionate Neatherd* (which was also published by Fanfrolico in 1929). There was even a defender among the ranks of previously outraged critics. A long review in the *New Age* welcomed "the work of adult verse in a world of beastly adolescents."

Another offshoot of *Aphrodite* signalled the parting of Lindsay and P. R. Stephenson: the Mandrake Press, a non-Fanfrolicon entity conceived by Lindsay to be solely under Stephenson's control and to publish a book to accompany an exhibition of D. H. Lawrence's paintings, a project which did not conform with Norman Lindsay's *Vision* universe. By the time negotiations were complete and Mandrake Press had brought out the book, strained relations between Stephenson and Lindsay had ended their Fanfrolico association. Lawrence was not pleased with the results of Stephenson's solo effort (in one of his letters he wrote, "Oh that Mandrake—vegetable of ill omen!"), but he continued to carry on a correspondence of some length with Lindsay, bursting out once with "Give up all this muck about love. . . . You're right in what you hate. Stick to that and you'll get somewhere. Stop the love slush. Stick to your hate. That's what's real and good and creative in you."

The cause of Lawrence's remarks was akin to that of the Stephenson-Lindsay disharmony. The

Lindsays lived their artistic theories, and the metaphysical romanticism of Australian Olympus had propelled Jack Lindsay into a disastrous entanglement with Elza Craig. It was shortly after his arrival in London, while Lindsay was being introduced around by Nina Hamnett, paying courtesy calls on his father's behalf to Walter de la Mare, Ralph Strauss, and Holbrook Jackson and going to pubs and parties with Peter Warlock (Philip Heseltine), D. B. Wyndham Lewis, Augustus John, and Liam O'Flaherty, that P. R. Stephenson's fiancée Winifred Edwards introduced Lindsay to the Chelsea group in which Elza Craig, whose "serene, stricken silence" and long, draping clothes, as though she had stepped from "some unknown pre-Raphaelite painting," was something of a cult figure. Lindsay's association with Elza as she sank from Pre-Raphaelite myth through self-centered possessiveness into dementia and, finally, died from cancer brought about the end of Fanfrolico Press, the alienation of family, friends, and associates, and the disruption of his life and art.

One such casualty was Lindsay's relationship with Robert Graves, which began well enough with the Fanfrolico edition of sixteenth- and seventeenth-century Bedlamite verse, *Loving Mad Tom* (1928), edited by Lindsay, with foreword by Graves, musical transcriptions by Warlock, and illustrations by Norman Lindsay. Graves offered Jack and Elza the use of his house in Wales, and once he "turned up in a taxi with a pleasant old table" for them. Then Lindsay took exception to Graves's dismissal of Yeats's work as "sentimentally soft" and implied that Graves's friend Laura Riding was to blame for an "intellectualizing" which was exercising undue influence over Graves. A break occurred between the two men. A further clash came in the 1930s when Graves and Lindsay were asked by *Bookfellow* to review each other's fictional Roman best-sellers, Graves's *I, Claudius* (1934) and Lindsay's *Caesar Is Dead* (1934), and a brief correspondence between them continued the caviling.

Lindsay's friendship with Yeats died of neglect rather than of any conflict. Yeats made first contact in July 1929, at the end of the *London Aphrodite*, and initial discussions, which included ideas about a theater for verse drama, were lost in the frustrations surrounding the ending of Fanfrolico Press. Also about that time Lindsay was involved in correspondence with Sigmund Freud over *Dionysus. Nietzsche Contra Nietzsche* and a proposed Fanfrolico edition of Nietzsche's *Thus Spake Zarathustra*. The book never materialized, partly because of Freud's

6

Also turn from novels because of work in two different lines.
At request of manager at Mullers who liked my history writing I
did varioys hist. works, <u>Civil War in England</u>, <u>1764</u> - I turned to
Graeco-Roman Egypt where papyri had lomg interested me - <u>Daily Life</u>
<u>in RE</u>, <u>Leis ure and Pleasure</u>, Men and Gods on Ri Nile - then via that
to ancient sceince, <u>Origins of Alchemy</u>, <u>Astrology</u>, Blastpower.

ALSO via Tony Adams to art-themes. Did Death of Hero for him while he
was at Studio (also rewrote Short <u>History of C.</u> for him there). He
knew I had been struck by a show of David at the Orangerie soon after
the war. Then (via a book on Turner's poems commissioned by a small
press through Tony), I started on Turner (having looked through his
sketch books etc at BM and finding them full of his notes).
Led to Cezanne, Courbet, Hogarth.

at same tome Constable had asked me for Life of Cleo. - led to one
cf Helen of Troy, then Morris and Blake.   Troubadours, Mullers.
    Gainsborough in press for Hart+ Davis

I don't think much of this very useful. But pattern since 1959-61, barth
of the children, has been very much stay-at-home here, with (a)
completion of arc of the Britush Way (2) series on GR Egypt moving
into one on ancient sceience (3) attempt to develop Marxist aesthetics
via Lives of painters. *Interactn of persnl, socil, aesthetic elemts.*

ask me to elaborate any points if necessary ——

   . . .

Guiding principle: Hegel's comment that the educated man is the one
who can do anything. Dialectics as the philosophy of development. If
one truly graps it one can deal with any aspect of human movement and
development. Not simply by applying principles of cpurse. One must
know the field, its material etc. But the dialectical prinples help there
too, since they act as guides in grasping the significant aspects, etc.

Hence my attempts to deal with so many different fields. How well? not
for me to say.

all of which intrst me a great deal   *Jack L*

Lindsay's notes for Orin Anderson's biographical work on him reluctance to comment critically upon Nietzsche in an introduction to the edition, partly because Elza was beginning to claim more and more of Lindsay's time.

With Stephenson's exit, Lindsay moved to a large house in Woodchurch Road, Hampstead. Brian Penton, another Brisbane man, took over Stephenson's work; Penton and his wife Olga shared the Woodchurch Road house with Lindsay, Elza, and Lindsay's brother Philip. Despite the success of the enterprise—*The Passionate Neatherd;* Lindsay's verse play *Hereward* (1930); *Mimiambs of Herondas* (1930); poems by Ausonius, *Patchwork Quilt* (1930)—the Pentons departed for Australia.

As she became more unstable, Elza Craig made life increasingly difficult for Lindsay. He found it harder and harder to run the press and sold it to Simpkin-Marshall. There followed a tortuous period in which Lindsay went to extremes in order to reach through his companion's madness, wandering with her over much of southern England, living in isolation and extreme poverty, barely above the level of starvation.

Lindsay emerged from this time with a new understanding of what had occurred in the *Vision* experiment and Fanfrolico Press: in place of an Olympus shored up by metaphysics, he saw the creative process as an essential humanizing force which had carried him from metaphysical abstraction to the concrete.

To his translations, poems, and essays, he added a formidable talent as novelist, turning first to his familiar classical world in what proved to be a popular trilogy, *Rome For Sale* (1934), *Caesar Is Dead,* and *Last Days With Cleopatra* (1935). *Rome For Sale* centered upon the poet Catullus and the period of revolutionary crisis under Caesar. Against Catalina are set Cicero "the professional compromiser and falsifier" and Caesar "the supple schemer who bided his time, making the possible always his limit." *Rome For Sale* quickly went into a second British edition and a first American edition, a sign that Lindsay's breadth of vision and regained independence did not go unnoticed. *Caesar Is Dead* extends Lindsay's drive to "objectify the world of Catullus' poems." His new composition technique was "to compose from the mass-effect to the particular," and this second book of the trilogy opens with a long, multiangled account of the assassination day that does not present Caesar himself directly. *Last Days With Cleopatra* continues the Caesarian revolution in the same spirit, but in straightforward narrative. Lindsay's different method of approach to character in each book expresses each different historical phase. *Rome For Sale* divides accounts of ritual and ordinary life to point up contrasts between the unified but passing religious life of the old fertility cults with the awkward, unsettled nature of contemporary society. The sharp, broken, rapidly changing patterns of *Caesar Is Dead* show the explosive revolutionary forces growing from the opposing elements of society in the first book. *Last Days With Cleopatra* uses the narrative of two "minor" characters who live on the fringe of what is usually considered the major historical action. From their tangential perspective, the reader observes the contradictions of Antonius, the imperial theocratic drive of Cleopatra, and the beginning of a new epoch in history. Of course the major events of history do occur on the periphery of vision for most people, and the main characters can rarely be sure of the historical importance of their actions. Lindsay's historical fiction is above the popular connotations of "historical novel" and, as with his other work, is not content with filling a polite literary corner, but surges to a world view. The Roman trilogy eventually supported two pendant works, *Despoiling Venus* (1935), about Clodia and Caelius Rufus, and *Brief Light* (1939), about Catullus, whose poems set *Rome For Sale* in Lindsay's mind originally.

Despite the disjointed nature of life with Elza, by 1936 Lindsay had produced more than thirty books: translations, poetry, plays, novels. In 1936, with the rise of fascism, Lindsay turned his attention to that which Huxley termed "all the iniquitous things that had been done in the name of Progress and National Prosperity." From Nietzsche and Freud, Lindsay began a revaluation of Plato and Blake. In the process, he read Hegel, which led him to the main works of Marx and Engels. Lindsay's work all along had been concerned with the life-and-death cycle of regeneration, which he now found reflected in the Marxian principles of conflict and the unity of opposites. When, in February 1936, he read a newspaper report that "shock-troops in Spain had disobeyed Franco's officers and joined the mob," he wrote a rough poem, which anticipated the civil war by six months, and sent it to Lawrence and Wishart's trade journal, the *Eye.* In its unpolished but prophetic state, it became the first published work on what would become the great literary cause of the Spanish civil war. The young man who had gone without food in an attic in Wooloomooloo rather than have dealings with the trappings of a perverse world, suddenly, in England, became alight with the immediacy of politics—that same spark intermittent in Auden, Spender, and Day Lewis.

No longer was the pursuit of the poetic image a matter of contending with philistine commercialism or challenging the errors of modernism. For Lindsay, fascism implied direct suppression of the creative impulse, and in 1936 Marxism alone opposed Hitler and his imitators.

A declamatory poem, *Who Are the English?*, submitted by Lindsay to the *Left Review*, was successful enough to be reprinted in pamphlet form and produced in mime-dance by the newly formed Unity Theatre. Its popularity prompted Edgell Rickword to write to Lindsay, asking him to create another. Lindsay responded with *On Guard For Spain*, which was produced by Unity Theatre. In this form, it served as the basis for rallies in support of the Spanish Republic presented across England by Victor Gollancz, Harry Pollit, and the duchess of Athol. Lindsay was working fourteen hours a day, his incredible energy enabling him to stick to any job day or night without a break, "using pen or typewriter twelve hours at a time."

Methuen published its first Lindsay work in 1937, *Anatomy of Spirit*, a collection of essays intended as part of a larger work on Giordano Bruno. The same year they requested and published a biography of John Bunyan. Edgell Rickword asked him to review novels for *Left Review* and to compile an anthology, *A Handbook of Freedom* (1939). The Left Book Club asked him to chair the poetry section and to coedit their monthly; Lindsay also suggested and edited verse broadsheets. In addition, he finished his novel *1649* (1938), "taking afresh the cycle of a year," the first of a British historical trilogy with the weight of his Roman one. All of these activities took place through the mail; living away from London, Lindsay worked up to fourteen hours a day in addition to taking care of Elza.

Lindsay continued to work at his extraordinary pace after Chamberlain announced that Britain was at war with Germany, and in the "bitter days of the phony war, with the feeling that at any moment all hell would let loose," Lindsay wrote another part of his British historical trilogy: *Men of Forty-Eight* (1948), with its background of European revolution and British Chartism, is the centerpiece of his fiction. Methuen delayed publication until 1948, and the book's anti-Fascist nature caused it to be largely ignored by a war-weary England, despite its being acclaimed by French poet Louis Aragon and by Edith Sitwell, who proclaimed, "I am overwhelmed by *Men of Forty-Eight*. It is a book on such a

scale, and written with blood and fire. It is *tremendous*."

Lindsay was called up the day Germany invaded the Soviet Union; he was assigned to Signals Interception at Trowbridge, Wiltshire, and, later, on the Isle of Man. At Trowbridge, he joined the Communist party (living his theories) and met Tony Adams, a young artist and publications designer home on leave from the RAF, who was the original organizer of the party branch at Trowbridge and destined to become a coworker and a publisher of several of Lindsay's important works.

Elza Craig, whose gradual deterioration alternated between spates of violence and of insolent lethargy, when faced by the forced separation, voluntarily checked into a mental home near Dorchester, almost immediately checked out, and went to Bristol where, shortly, she died. Lindsay continued to write with amazing energy, completing, in addition to his army duties, a long poem on Dieppe, *Into Action* (1942), and *We Shall Return* (1942) and *Beyond Terror* (1943), novels partly using tales by friends who had been at Dunkirk and Crete.

A detailed discussion of the synthesis which took place in the logical succession of Lindsay's work from Plato and Blake to Kierkegaard and Nietzche, to Hegel, and to Marx and Engels appears in *After the 'Thirties* (1956), a general outline of its effects in "Towards a Marxist Aesthetic," *Decay and Renewal* (1976), and the manner and conditions under which it occurred in *Fanfrolico and After* (1962), the final part of Lindsay's autobiographical trilogy. *Fanfrolico and After* ends in 1941 with Elza Craig's death and Lindsay's call-up. By that time he had written, edited, or translated more than seventy-five books, edited three major magazines, and had numerous articles and poems published in periodicals. Yet, in a sense, he was just beginning.

On the Isle of Man, Lindsay wrote a selection of army poems, *Second Front* (1942), and began *Hullo Stranger* (1945), a novel on women in the war industry. Lindsay's control of the contemporary novel had been building in *We Shall Return* and *Beyond Terror*, and it is well exhibited in the subtle focus of this study of the role and plight of women in modern war.

In the midst of writing *Hullo Stranger*, Lindsay was posted to the War Office in London. An earlier interview (which he had reluctantly attended in the middle of a leave spent indulging in pubs and poetry with his brother Philip and Dylan Thomas) had resulted in Lindsay's being chosen as script writer for the Army Bureau of Current Affairs Theatre. He was the only private in the War Office, and he spent most of his time at Eaton Square working on documentaries, doing the work of a captain, and causing considerable protocol headaches (to get around some of the rank problems, the Royal Army designated him "Professor" Lindsay).

Most of Lindsay's off-duty time was spent in the company of Dylan and Caitlin Thomas and Philip Lindsay, who had married Isobel Day and was living in Earls Court. And Jack Lindsay met Ann Davies, Unity Theatre's talented actress who played the Principal Boy in Unity's pantomime satire *Babes in the Woods*. Ann Davies, who attended the Tabernacle Welsh Baptist Church regularly, where she helped to conduct its Sunday school, was also a gentle and devoted Communist. Besides being a well-known actress, playing bomb shelters in Unity's Mobile Theatre during the Blitz, she was secretary of Fore Publications, automatically making her secretary, general manager, advertising manager, and "Lord High Everything Else" of *Our Time* (15,000 circulation), *Seven* (almost 37,000 circulation), and *Theatre Today* (approximately 20,000 circulation). Montagu Slater, who took over the editor's position of *Our Time* when Randall Swingler went into the army, recalled meeting Lindsay at that time: "We had been prepared for a quick thinker but not for a jet, and Jack in his supersonic style in no time at all was busy on ABCA living newspapers, on several novels and poems of different shapes and sizes, and all being written at once, while in his spare time he wrote a play for Unity, *Robin of England*, became a director of Fore Publications and married Ann. Energy can be catching. Jack and Ann became for me at any rate twin symbols of the idea of getting-things-done."

Lindsay was working at his usual rate to his usual exacting standards. He had done *The Whole Armour of God* (1944) for Martin Browne and Pilgrim Players. It was performed across England in churches and parish halls and was well received as a thought-provoking documentary on Christian resistance to fascism in Europe. Now he did a full-length documentary with B. L. Coombs, *Face of Coal* (1946), performed at Scala Theatre by Bernard Miles's *Theatre 46*. It got a good reception and much publicity.

In addition to his army and theater work, Lindsay was working closely with Krishna Menon and Tony Adams in Meridian Press and with the SCR Writers Group, PEN, and the CP Writers Group (joining in the large meetings held in the Salisbury Pub in St. Martins Lane). The Lindsays took a large house in St. Johns Wood, where they hosted L. L. Whyte's philosophy/science meetings;

eighteen years after the invasion of Europe Lindsay had come full circle to reside again in the same district of London in which he and Kirtley had begun before setting up in Bloomsbury Square.

Lindsay did not begin his long friendship with Edith Sitwell until 1948, when she wrote to him of his review in *Our Time* of her *Shadow of Cain*: "You might almost have timed this essay to the exact moment when it would be of greatest help to me. . . . this profound and wide understanding of all the implications in the poem . . . has made me wish to write again." She continued to acknowledge her debt to Lindsay for "renewing" her poetry when she was sixty, and for the rest of her life she kept her interest in the Australian's work.

From early postwar times, Lindsay and Ann Davies had often been in Paris, where they met and joined in café talks with many of their fellow spirits: Konstantin Simonov, Aleksandr Fadeyev, Alberto Giacometti, Elio Vittorini, and Pablo Neruda. They also met and held talks with W. E. B. DuBois (introduced by Howard Fast). By 1949, they counted among their friends and acquaintances Louis Aragon, Tristan Tzara, Paul Eluard (introduced by Nancy Cunard), and other poets of the Resistance. *Meetings With Poets* (1968) provides an incisive account of Lindsay's memories of the Resistance poets, as well as reminiscences of Edith Sitwell and Dylan Thomas.

In 1948, Lindsay saw the organization supposedly devoted to unifying humanity turn contrary to its purpose. He fast became a "heretic," primarily because he disliked and attacked the Zhdanov disquisitions. Lindsay's stands, though given much support by the younger members, were unpopular with Emile Burns and other party functionaries. Paloczi-Horvath recorded that on his return to Hungary in 1948, the Stalinist secret police interrogated him at some length about English "traitors" to be liquidated "after the heroic British working-class had taken power." One of these "traitors" to the party was Jack Lindsay; they feared that his deep intellect and exceptional perception could not be contained politically. Against all threats and censure, and while practically all other English intellectuals were fleeing from the Cold, Lindsay stuck to his humanity-centered socialist position, defending the creative aspects of Marxism in the face of those who pushed for Zhdanovistic authoritarianism.

Lindsay, in effect, took over Fore Publications, with Swingler's agreement, after the war. *Our Time* was dead, victim to the resurgence of the entertainment industry, and Lindsay worked toward bringing out *Arena* magazine, with the support of his wife Ann and Edith Sitwell. The periodical was conceived to be a platform for the "advanced writing from the Resistance groups, plus the best of Soviet work." The first issue of *Arena* appeared in 1949. Lindsay was joined by Tony Adams, Randall Swingler, and John Davenport in the endeavor. The magazine's contents represented a broad spectrum: Edith Sitwell's "Street Acrobat," five of Jean Cassou's "Sonnets Composed in Secret," Eluard's "From the Horizon of One Man to the Horizon of All," Camus's "Archives of the Plague," essays by Tzara on the dialectics of poetry, Pasternak on Shakespeare's imagery and rhythm, Alick West on Shaw, Lindsay on Catullus, stories by Tikhonov and Endre Illes, poems by Malcolm Lowry and Hugh MacDiarmid. *Arena* number one fell flat. No bookshop would take it; the only review was in the *Daily Worker*—a damning attack on Lindsay's editorial note, because he had asserted that the task of *Arena* magazine was "neither to label our culture as 'decadent' nor to acclaim it as securely progressive," that conflict existed and therefore presented an occasion for renewal through dialogue (an unforgivable heresy in 1949).

The crux of Lindsay's heresy was *Marxism and Contemporary Science* (1949), sharply criticized by Emile Burns and nearly the cause of Lindsay's expulsion from the party, although today its analyses are commonplaces of the Marxist world. To further complicate matters, Lindsay's *Byzantium Into Europe* (1952), a working-man's history published by Bodley Head, proved too unorthodox for the London literary scene. It was roundly and thoroughly damned, so quickly and emphatically, in fact, that it became obvious that some of the reviewers had not bothered to read the book. Serious academics were scandalized and embarrassed when an anonymous reviewer used the sacrosanct *Times Literary Supplement* to conduct a "political witch-hunt" instead of writing about *Byzantium Into Europe*, the subject of the "supposed review." The resulting furor made critics and publishers wary of someone who could excite such "unprofessional passions," and the literary world turned its back on Lindsay, for the moment.

Lindsay and Ann were forced by degrees from London to Penshurst, then to a forester's hut, Quarry Cottage. Conditions were harsh, and when, in 1951, Ann developed breast cancer, they had to move, living first with the Swinglers near Halstead in Essex. Lindsay learned of an old farm building down the road, and when he heard the name, Bang-

Dust jacket for Lindsay's 1952 book that proved too politically unorthodox for the London literary scene

slappers, he had to see it. He and Ann moved in late that year.

In between *Marxism and Contemporary Science* and *Byzantium Into Europe*, Lindsay produced an "exceptional psychological biography," *Charles Dickens* (1950); his well-received translation of Stancu's *Barefoot* (1950); poems written at Quarry Cottage, *Three Letters to Nikolai Tikhonov* (1950); two novels and a journal of his and Ann's trip to the Soviet Union, *A World Ahead* (1950), among others. Lindsay and Ann continued to work daily on their many projects; she was at work on her translation of Zola's *La Terra* the day she died, in 1954.

Lindsay was distracted. He spent most of the year traveling throughout Europe and the Soviet Union. He spoke at the Fielding Celebrations and was asked to stay on for the Second Writers Conference, which kept on being postponed. During three months at the end of 1954 he worked on Russian poetry, visited Georgia and Abkhasia, and became friends with Russian writers.

At the Amsterdam peace meeting shortly after Ann's death, Lindsay met Meta Waterdrinker, who as a Communist had lived through the Nazi occupation of the Netherlands. In Amsterdam, as Lindsay attended the Peace Conference meetings and refreshed his acquaintance with Brecht, he sensed an ally in Meta, the quiet potter who as a young girl delivered anti-Nazi pamphlets door-to-door at the height of the Fascist control of Amsterdam. Becoming Lindsay's touchstone in the middle of a polarized world, Meta gradually became closer to Lindsay, and on 30 June 1958 she became his wife. They have two children, Philip Jan (born 1959) and Helen Marietta (born 1961). Meta and Jack Lindsay lived at Bangslappers until the end of 1984, when they moved to a house on Clarendon Road in Cambridge.

When Jack Lindsay first met Bertolt Brecht, they both were staying in the Bristol Hotel in Warsaw. After a day of talks in the bombed-out city, Lindsay's belief in the constant rebuilding of human unity was strengthened by the sight of a couple dancing in a space cleared in the rubble across the street from the hotel. The dance was as important as anything Brecht or he had said: Lindsay's renewal through points of destruction is reflected in Marx, not institutionalized Marxism, and the penalty he has had to pay has been one of constantly being made the odd man out. However, time and his refusal to stand still intellectually are beginning to vindicate his dedication to the creative process.

After 1965 he wrote no more novels, concentrating instead on biographies of artists, originally suggested and published by Tony Adams, particularly *J. M. W. Turner* (1966). Also, his cultural and scientific studies led to the profound *Blast Power and Ballistics* (1974).

As ever, Lindsay continues to write poetry and nonfiction, to translate, and to explore philosophy. His *The Crisis in Marxism* (1981), published by Moonraker Press just before the untimely death of its director, Tony Adams, appears to be as ahead of its time as were *Marxism and Contemporary Science* and *Byzantium Into Europe*, although it has so far been ignored rather than attacked.

Perhaps Lindsay could have avoided the mud, censure, and resulting disregard had he chosen the politically expedient line, or followed fashion away from Marxism in the cause of self-preservation. Forced to fight on two fronts, especially in the face of his grief over the death of Ann Davies, bits of polarized dogma found their ways into Lindsay's work at the end of the 1950s. But he soon shook off the uncharacteristic heavyhanded buzz words ("cash-nexus," "bourgeoisie") and avoided stylized vernacular except when appropriately addressing the literary Left. As always, once he had worked his way through the points of decay, his almost kinetic perception led him to a renewal of the creative process.

Lindsay's power, control, breadth of vision, and poetic force are the hallmarks of his work, whether it is prematurely termed "jargon"; whether it is "revelation" to the young radical who discovers that Lindsay over three decades ago put forth terms in concrete relationships that are only lately beginning to surface in academic communities as abstractions ("Structure in Dominance," "Art as Productive Activity"); or whether it is, as so many have seen in his work, in Edith Sitwell's words: "what all great art does—what Beethoven does—and what sounds in all great art. . . . I hope the reviewers will realise what they are reading. I don't see how they could help it." It has taken time, but Sitwell's wish for Lindsay's all-encompassing intellect and literary ability is being realized.

Bibliography:

J. M. W. Borg, ed., *Handlist of Works by Jack Lindsay* (Lake Forest, Ill.: Chiron Press, 1982).

References:

Lin Bloomfield, ed., *The World of Norman Lindsay* (Melbourne: Macmillan of Australia, Prty, 1979);

Harry F. Chaplin, ed., *The Fanfrolico Press. A Survey* (Sydney: Wentworth Press, 1976);

Doris Lessing, Edgell Rickword, and others, *A Garland For Jack Lindsay* (London: Piccolo Press, 1980);

Edgell Rickword, ed., *Nothing is Lost: Ann Lindsay 1914-1954* (London: The Writers Group of the Communist Party, 1954);

Bernard Smith, ed., *Culture and History: Essays Presented to Jack Lindsay* (Sydney: Hale & Iremonger, 1984);

Alick West, *The Mountain in the Sunlight. Studies in Conflict and Unity* (London: Lawrence & Wishart, 1958), pp. 195-199;

Judith Wright, *Preoccupations in Australian Poetry* (London: Oxford University Press, 1965).

Papers:

The bulk of Lindsay's papers from 1931 to 1968 are

in the University of Queensland Library, Brisbane, Australia.

AN INTERVIEW

with JACK LINDSAY

DLB: You seem to have attracted an inordinate number of attacks alternating with neglect, measured against your accomplishments over the many decades of your work. How have you continued to write under such circumstances?

LINDSAY: Certainly there is some indigestible Australian component in us Lindsays which the English-speaking establishment can't swallow. In my case it has been exacerbated by my persisting in belonging to every possible "anti-" movement (often one-man movements); I think I can claim to have been a premature anti-Fascist all along the line, so that even when something I've taken up ends by getting accepted, I've long past moved on to something else.

I have been able to carry on with my work with continual starts or movements into new spheres of material because there has been for me the stimulus of an unending quest. Naturally I have been pleased when some kindred spirit responded, but the general neglect of my work has never held me back for a moment. In fact, it has helped to make me feel that I am indeed breaking new ground, uncovering new aspects of reality. Perhaps if I had halted at one particular point and kept on expanding or restating my position from there, I might have eventually drawn more of the literary/academic community to an understanding of what I was after. But it has always been the quest which mattered, the feeling that I was continuing the search for an ever fuller truth, a deeper consciousness of what goes to make humanity.

DLB: Your personal aesthetic has caused you to move from issue to issue, even from genre to genre. . . .

LINDSAY: I have never wanted to limit myself to one mode or range of expression—the novel, the historical study, the biography of creative artists, philosophic or literary analysis, and so on. I have felt the need to master various modes in terms of my quest, then, as a new aspect of reality arose which required (it seemed to me) a fuller working-out, I turned to it. I have always prepared thor-

oughly for any work. I don't mean that I had every detail irrevocably planned and worked out beforehand. On the contrary. I wanted to be able to give as free a play to imagination or analysis as possible. For instance, I have always held that unless the characters essentially take control of the movement of a novel from the start, it is dead.

Literary, artistic, and philosophic issues have been with me since childhood in Australia, and anthropological and scientific questions could hardly fail to become part of my search, helped by various acquaintances such as my early friendship with Gordon Childe which continued in England, my meeting with Lancelot Whyte just as I was seeking a more adequate concept of dialectics.

DLB: How have you reconciled publishers' wishes with your own pursuits?

LINDSAY: There have been problems with publishing, since so often after building up a market in one field, I have changed to another. Also, "Marx-

Dust jacket for Lindsay's 1976 collection of essays

ists" have disliked my work; "non-Marxists" have looked the other way. But, the books have sold well enough to make publishers consider them.

I have had the good fortune to encounter now and then a publisher who became genuinely interested in my work and was ready to back me when I turned in new directions. Jim Reynolds (of Mullers, then of Weidenfeld and Nicolson, then of Granada) and Tony Adams (first in Studio Vista, and then in his own firms) are the outstanding examples.

DLB: What is the origin of such a driving search?

LINDSAY: I began as a poet, and in a sense have been that all my life, for I saw poetry as creative exploration and construction from the outset (influence of Keats, Coleridge, Blake). So, I early discovered Plato and tried to write philosophic dialogues as a natural extension of my obsession with poetry, with the creative Image. From there I kept on finding thinkers who dealt with issues that were coming up in my mind—Bergson, Croce, Gentile, Nietzsche, Hegel, Bruno, Goethe, Marx. . . .

DLB: Marx?

LINDSAY: When I speak of Marx or Marxism, I am of course speaking of the philosophic tradition that starts with Herakleitos and Plato and goes on through Bruno, Spinoza, Kant, Hegel, to Marx. And, then to whatever new definitions of development and qualitative change emerge as going beyond Marx into fuller comprehensions of the way that one level or stage of reality moves through its own inner conflicts and contradictions to a new and higher level (unless it breaks down, presenting elements for renewal). And, of course, I should add a number of poets to the tradition I am sketching here: Shakespeare, Donne, and Blake, for example.

DLB: Why have you chosen to remain not only a Marxist but a member of the Communist party?

LINDSAY: Why a Communist? My notions of brotherhood, of utopian community, were an inevitable aspect of my views of poetry: Plato, Blake, Shelley, Morris. Plus a tragic sense from Dostoevski. Then, in 1936, reading Marx for the first time, with the Spanish civil war starting and the antifascist movement, I felt a great enthusiasm for the Soviet Union.

Although when I later visited (1949, 1954) the apparent lack of understanding of Marxism there began to worry me, I kept my enthusiasm until 1956 and the Khrushchev relevations. Since then, though my experiences have shown that there are genuine socialist elements among quite large sections of the people, I have been thoroughly aware of the dire limitations of the major "communist" governments. But, it has seemed to me that the point is not to give up the ghost, but to understand as well as possible what went wrong, and how, and to find ways forward without the old distortions. Thinkers like Gramsci, though not perfect, do show the effort to start off again in new directions. That is, despite the terrible distortions that have occurred, I feel that one must find ways of moving to a genuinely free, equal, fraternal society.

Marx's analyses of the *contradictions* of capitalism are shown daily to be valid (in *Grundrisse* Marx argued that the end of capitalism would come through the full implementation of *automation*). Yet, if he were alive today, he would repudiate the Soviet Union as a socialist society on its way to communism—though he would not simply denounce it, but would seek to unravel the historical reasons and the faulty positions behind its failure in socialist democracy.

I have always set out my positions: ready to be thrown out of the CP, but ready to stay in while I could put forward what seem to be genuinely dialectical and democratic positions.

DLB: What about future work? New directions?

LINDSAY: Now in my eighty-third year, I do not own the restless energies I had til recently. But, I will keep on working to the end. After the Penguin edition of my first three autobiographical works, I feel that my main task is to carry on the story after 1941. Thus, I will be able to clarify, I hope, what I have called my "quest"—and to make further contributions to the breaking down of the distortions in dialectical thought: Marx I see as a great turning point in the line of thought that begins with Herakleitos, but one that needs to be increasingly gone into for weaknesses and distortions (mechanizations).

—*Orin Anderson*

Marsha Norman

(21 September 1947-   )

Mary Ellen Miller
Western Kentucky University

BOOKS: *Getting Out* (New York: Dramatists Play Service, 1979);

'night, Mother (New York: Hill & Wang, 1983).

PLAYS: *Getting Out*, Louisville, Ky., Actors Theatre, 1977; Los Angeles, Mark Taper Forum, February 1978; New York, Marrymount Manhattan Theater, October 1978; New York, Theatre De Lys, May 1979;

Third and Oak, Louisville, Actors Theatre, 1978;

Circus Valentine, Louisville, Actors Theatre, 1979;

The Holdup, San Francisco, American Conservatory Theatre, 1983;

'night, Mother, Boston, Robert Brustein American Repertory Theatre, 1983; New York, Golden Theatre, 31 March 1983; New York, Westside Arts Theater, 18 April 1984;

The Shakers, Louisville, Kentucky Center for the Arts, 19 November 1983;

Traveler in the Dark, Cambridge, Mass., American Repertory Theatre, February 1984.

Writers and other artists who seem to the general public to be overnight successes are fond of pointing to the many years of struggle that preceded the limelight. Marsha Norman's spectacular success with her first play, *Getting Out*, makes her something of an exception. She wrote the play in 1976 when she was twenty-nine years old. It was staged by Jon Jory of Actors Theatre in Louisville, Kentucky, in 1977 at the Festival of New Plays, and it was cowinner of the Festival first prize. Her *'night, Mother*, first staged at the Robert Brustein American Repertory Theater in Boston, won the Pulitzer Prize in 1983. With two exceptions, *Circus Valentine* (1979) and *Traveler in the Dark* (1984), anything of Norman's that has reached the stage has been well received.

Norman's world is one in which rather ordinary people confront extraordinary circumstances, or, as she told Elizabeth Stone for *Ms.*, "It is possible for me to claim center stage at the John Golden Theatre for a mother and daughter in Nowhere, U.S.A., who are struggling with desperate philo-sophical issues." Her basic theme was explored in her prizewinning high school essay, "Why Do Good Men Suffer?" She says of that subject now, "I'm still writing the same thing. . . . What else is there to know in the world?" (Mel Gussow, *New York Times Magazine*). Or, as she told *Contemporary Authors:* "I always write about the same thing: people having the nerve to go on. The people I care about are those folks you wouldn't even notice in life—two women in a laundromat late at night as you drive by, a thin woman in an ugly scarf standing over the luncheon meat at the grocery, a tiny gray lady buying a big sack of chocolate-covered raisins and a carton of Kools. Someday I'd love to write a piece about people who can talk. The problem is I know so few of them."

Critics have been nearly unanimous in praising her work, especially the quality of her dialogue. Listening, she says, is her greatest talent, and the poignant realism of her dialogue reflects that. In *Getting Out*, Carl, the pimp who wants to keep Arlene working for him, describes the life she will have as a dishwasher, "An you git maybe 75 a week. 75 for standin over a sink full of greasy gray water, fishin out blobs of bread and lettuce. People putting pieces of chewed up meat in their napkins and you gotta pick it out. 8 hours a day, 6 days a week, to make 75 lousy pictures of Big Daddy George. Now, how long it'll take you to make 75 working for me?"

Though Norman's parents stressed the importance of scholastic achievement, nothing in her background foreshadows her career as a dramatist. She was born Marsha Williams, 21 September 1947, in Louisville, Kentucky, the first of four children born to Billie and Bertha Williams. Her father was a salesman, and both parents were strict fundamentalists—so strict, in fact, that Norman's mother did not like for her to associate with other children for fear she would encounter ideas the parents did not approve of. For company she turned to books, to piano, and to an imaginary playmate, Bettering.

Norman has spoken frequently of her sense of isolation as a child and of her rejection of her parents' religion: "I felt terribly out of place, isolated,

308

Marsha Norman with Tom Moore, director of 'night, Mother *(Courier-Journal and* Louisville Times*)*

violently opposed to almost everything I saw," she told Amy Gross in *Vogue*. Kate Stout (*Saturday Review*) credits the childhood revelation that things can't be black and white for what she sees in Norman's plays as "instinctive resistance to emotional manipulation, an unshakeable reliance on her own mind, an aversion to judgment, and an almost pathological need for the privacy to store such volative secrets."

At Durrett High School in Louisville Norman was a good student, active on the newspaper and yearbook staffs. It was here that her essay on the suffering of Job won first prize in a local writing contest. It was subsequently published in the *Kentucky English Bulletin*. After high school, she went to Agnes Scott College in Decatur, Georgia, on a scholarship. This small liberal arts college did not have a creative writing department, so Norman majored in philosophy, working part-time as a volunteer in the pediatric burn unit at General Hospital in nearby Atlanta. She graduated in 1969 and returned to Louisville, where she married her former English teacher, Michael Norman. For the next two years

she took graduate courses at the University of Louisville, earning her M.A. in 1971. (She has since completed most of the requirements for a second M.A. at the Center for Understanding Media in New York City.) During the Louisville years she taught disturbed adolescents at Kentucky Central State Hospital. In 1973 she joined the staff of the Brown School for gifted children, where she taught filmmaking to adolescent children and drew up a humanities curriculum for children of middle-school age. At this point she had not considered writing as a career, but she had submitted occasional pieces to newspapers and had written a musical for children.

In an interview with Lillian Hellman in *American Theatre* (May 1984), Norman spoke of her lack of a role model for writing: "I was a kid who didn't really know it was possible to write for a living. I grew up in a religious fundamentalist family in Kentucky, and mother hoped I would work for the airlines for a few years and then marry a doctor. But all through high school, there were teachers who put your [Hellman's] plays in my hands. And finally there was a moment during my first marriage, when I had begun to refer to my first husband as 'the keeper,' when Martha Ellison, a dear friend and former teacher, gave me *An Unfinished Woman* and said, 'Lillian Hellman said this better than anybody has ever said it,' and she was referring to your line about the driving desire to be alone when you want to be and not alone when you don't want to be."

By 1976 Norman was writing full-time, contributing articles and book reviews to the *Louisville Times*, for which she also created the weekend children's supplement, "The Jelly Bean Journal." She met with Jon Jory, artistic director of Actors Theatre of Louisville, about a program she was developing for local young people, and Jory encouraged her to write a play. *Getting Out,* based on a violent young woman she had known at Kentucky Central State Hospital, was the result.

From this point on things moved rapidly. Norman was named playwright-in-residence at Actors Theatre. She met and married Dann Byck, Jr., a founder and the first president of Actors Theatre. (She was divorced from Norman in 1974.) Her next plays, *Third and Oak* (1978), *Circus Valentine* (1979), and *The Holdup* (1983), did not match the spectacular success of *Getting Out* (*Circus Valentine* was unfavorably reviewed), but *Third and Oak* was generally well received. During these years (1978-1980), Norman also worked with the resident company at the Mark Taper Forum on a Rockefeller playwright-in-residence grant. She wrote teleplays—*It's the Willingness* for PBS, *In Trouble at Fifteen* for NBC—and screenplays—*The Children with Emerald Eyes* for Columbia, *Thy Neighbor's Wife* for United Artists, and *The Bridge* for Joseph E. Levine.

The mind behind *Getting Out* and *'night, Mother* is mature and educated, and the artist's hand is accomplished. Both plays are about choices, choices by women. The choice in both cases—a life of dishwashing in *Getting Out* and suicide in *'night, Mother*—is not ostensibly attractive but both women make the "better" choice: Arlene to stay outside prison and Jessie to end her meaningless life. By returning to her former trade, prostitution, Arlene can have money, clothes, a nice place to sleep, and good food to eat; but there is the danger of being sent back to prison. Washing dishes, the only job open to her, she can have almost nothing—a slum apartment and long hours of work—but she can keep, as her friend Ruby tells her, *all* her money. She has killed her former self, Arlie, the hateful, rebellious self who got her into trouble. Both selves appear in the play, played by different actresses,

and Norman has been criticized for what some critics have called a tired theatrical convention. The play works so well that this criticism seems pointless.

More typical and more accurate responses to *Getting Out* are judgments like Kate Stout's: "In it are Marsha Norman's trademarks: powerful language that draws on not only dialect (of Eastern Kentucky in this case) but the lyricism of the commonplace; a fearless commitment to honesty, even if the truth reaches to the unpleasant; and dry, always perfectly timed humor. Like *'night, Mother,* it is emotionally grueling, yet free of emotional puppetry." The two settings, Arlie in prison and Arlene in the slum apartment, are beautifully balanced and the first so convincingly realized that Norman has been asked (one of her favorite responses) how much time *she* has done in prison.

In *Getting Out* (as in all her work) Norman shuns no subject. Arlie's world is one of incestuous abuse, neglect, and poverty, heartbreakingly depicted. This is the world Arlene (she changes her name to accommodate her changed perspective) rejects, but at the play's resolution the two selves are reconciled and Arlene salvages enough of Arlie—her humor, resistance, spirit—to make the new self convincing. It is this reconciliation that argues against Stanley Kauffmann's charge that there is "no connection between the two people."

In addition to the Festival prize at Actors Theatre in Louisville, *Getting Out* was voted the best new play produced in a regional theater by the American Theater Critics Association and was published in *The Best Plays of 1977-78*. After its Louisville opening, it ran at the Mark Taper Forum in Los Angeles and then moved to New York City, where it opened at the Phoenix Theater's off-Broadway season at the Marrymount Manhattan Theater, October 1978. Of the critical response to the New York production, John Simon's is typical: "No gesture is arbitrary, no syllable rings false. The language is the play's greatest asset: course-grained, unvarnished, often hateful, sometimes fumbling for tenderness, funny yet beyond laughter (except the hysterical kind), heartbreaking yet a stranger to tears. And always frighteningly true." Norman says of Arlie, "That person locked up was me. My whole life I felt locked up. I felt in isolation. . . . I think the writing of *Getting Out* for me was my own opening of the door." (Judy Klemensoud, *New York Times*).

Norman's next three plays, *Third and Oak* (1978), *Circus Valentine* (1979), and *The Holdup* (1983), were written while she was playwright-in-residence at Actors Theatre in Louisville. *Third and Oak* (premiered at Actors Theatre in 1978) consists of two one-act plays, "The Laundromat" and "The Pool Room." Neither has the power of *Getting Out* but both show Norman's ability to dramatize the ordinary in extraordinary fashion: two women in a laundromat, two men in a poolroom, brought together out of loneliness.

Circus Valentine (staged at Actors Theatre in 1979) is about a traveling circus on the small-town circuit. Norman spoke with Allan Wallack of *Newsday* about its negative critical reception: "It was devastating. It took me about two years to recover from it and regain my confidence.... But the most wonderful result of failure was that ultimately I felt strengthened by it—that they [the critics] had hated the play and I survived. That they had said everything awful that could be said. And I *still* wanted to write."

The Holdup was not produced by Actors Theatre except as a workshop production, but a revision of it had a successful opening in San Francisco at the American Conservatory Theatre, spring 1983. The play is a western comedy based on tales her grandfather told her.

'night, Mother, Norman's fifth play, was written in the summer of 1981, after Norman and her husband had moved to New York, where they now live. After its first staging at the Robert Brustein American Repertory Theater in Boston in January 1983 it opened at Broadway's Golden Theatre on 31 March 1983, with Kathy Bates as Jessie and Anne Pitoniak as Thelma. It ran for ten months and, with the original cast, reopened at the off-Broadway Westside Arts Theater on 18 April 1984.

Two characters appear in the play, Jessie and her mother, Thelma, but an important part of Norman's dramatic gift lies in her ability to characterize people who do not appear: Jessie's father, who is dead; her brother Dawson and his wife Loretta; Jessie's son Ricky. Each is fully realized; each has played a part in the decision which Jessie has made, the decision on which the play is built: to end her own life. "I'm going to kill myself, Mama," she announces early in the play. Although she is relatively young, she has looked at her life and found it wanting. Her husband has left her; her son has turned out bad; because of her illness (epilepsy) she cannot hold a job. Her mother has tried to help by taking her in; her brother and his wife are good people, but Dawson is insensitive enough to give her nothing but Christmas and birthday presents of bedroom slippers in his wife's size.

Jessie tells her mother: "Anyway, after Christmas, after I decided to do this, I would wonder, sometimes, what might keep me here, what might

be worth staying for, and you know what it was? It was maybe if there was something I really liked, like maybe if I really liked rice pudding or cornflakes for breakfast or something, that might be enough."

Step by slow step Thelma is brought to the horrifying realization that Jessie means what she says and that she is powerless to prevent it. Jessie moves calmly and deliberately through her schedule for the evening: cleaning the gun, filling her mother's candy dishes, posting the numbers for grocery delivery and repairmen.

To say that *'night, Mother* is about suicide would be misleading; it is about choice, about Jessie's decision to "get off the bus," because it is going nowhere she wants to be. It was not Norman's intention to judge the act of suicide in philosophical, religious, or societal terms. What she wanted to do, she told Kate Stout, was "to get as close to the line of thought that produces an action like Jessie's and try to understand how she might have felt.... We are generally cheated of any firsthand knowledge of how suicides feel. And in a sense that is something of what I think I can contribute as a writer."

Norman's sixth play, *Traveler in the Dark*, opened at Harvard University's American Repertory Theatre in February 1984. This play has a male protagonist, a surgeon, whose frustration at his powerlessness to save someone he cares about leads him to question the meaning of his entire life. Reviews were generally negative. Jack Knoll wrote in *Newsweek* that "the action seems whipped up under the lash of Norman's urgent need to dramatize a crisis of faith." But even its harshest critics made a genuine effort not to undersell a disappointing play, "The play seeks to debate science and faith, love and self-knowledge, the rage to grow and the resistance to change. Norman writes candidly and capably about God, reason and honor. And those topics do count more than cocoa and marshmallows [a reference to *'night, Mother*]." A scene from her most recent work, *The Shakers*, a musical based on a religious sect of the nineteenth century, was performed at the opening of the Kentucky Center for the Arts.

Though *Getting Out* and *'night, Mother* remain her major dramatic accomplishments, she is still in the process of making what is certain to be a major contribution to American drama. She "feels blessed," she has said, "with talent, energy, curiosity, and wonderful educational opportunities." A final assessment cannot be written at this point in Norman's career, but remarks like those of Amy Gross are not exaggerated: "She writes plays that have the moral texture of the great dramas and the penetration of the great tragedies."

What playwrights do, Norman has said, "is to offer candidates for inclusion in the archives of personal history." She has given at least two candidates to those archives already, Arlene in *Getting Out* and Jessie in *'night, Mother*. Kauffmann and a few others may be right to be alert to a certain moral earnestness, at least when "moral earnestness" endangers dramatized "personal history." On the other hand, Norman's central concern (expressed in "Why Do Good Men Suffer?") is never out of fashion, and her gift for suspense and her brilliant handling of dialogue and dialect are the soul of major drama.

References:

Marsha Norman, "Articles of Faith: A Conversation with Lillian Hellman," *American Theatre* (May 1984): 11-15;

Linda Stahl, "The Storyteller," Louisville (Kentucky) *Courier-Journal Magazine*, 20 May 1984;

Elizabeth Stone, "An Optimist Writes about Suicide, Confinement, and Despair," *Ms.*, 12 (July 1983);

Kate Stout, "Writing for the 'Least of Our Brethren,'" *Saturday Review* (September-October 1983);

Allan Wallack, *Newsday* (8 May 1983).

Helen Hooven Santmyer

(25 November 1895-   )

Judith S. Baughman

BOOKS: *Herbs and Apples* (Boston & New York: Houghton Mifflin, 1925);

The Fierce Dispute (Boston & New York: Houghton Mifflin, 1929);

Ohio Town: A Portrait of Xenia (Columbus: Ohio State University Press, 1962; republished, New York: Harper & Row, 1984);

"*. . . And Ladies of the Club*" (Columbus: Ohio State University Press, 1982; republished, New York: Putnam's, 1984).

Helen Hooven Santmyer's "*. . . And Ladies of the Club*" may or may not be great fiction. However, the story of this novel's movement from anonymity to the best-seller lists undeniably contains the stuff of great fiction, or at least of great romance. An 88-year-old woman confined to a Xenia, Ohio, nursing home by emphysema, arthritis, and partial blindness suddenly finds the fourth of her largely ignored books—and her only novel in more than fifty years—hailed as the literary sensation of 1984. The book, which had sold poorly when it was originally published by a university press in 1982, is reissued by a large New York publisher in a first printing of 175,000 copies. A major book club lavishly announces the novel as its main selection for June. A second New York publisher acquires paperback rights for $396,000, and television producers discuss a possible miniseries. Widely reviewed, the novel—a 1,176-page chronicle of middle-class life through four generations of an Ohio town—receives extravagant praise and equally extravagant attacks. It makes the best-seller lists before its official trade publication date. Its author becomes the subject of television, magazine, and newspaper feature stories and is proclaimed, in the words of *Life* magazine, "champion of the small town and of late bloomers everywhere." The writer enjoys her celebrity, but she also clearly understands its power to overshadow her actual achievement in the novel, to make knowing the story of the book's success more important than reading the book itself. To a "MacNeil/Lehrer Report" interviewer who suggests that "*. . . And Ladies of the Club*" is a great American novel, Santmyer wryly says, "After this blows over, nobody's going to read it. It's too much of an undertaking."

The most publicized author of 1984 was born in Cincinnati on 25 November 1895, the oldest of three children of Joseph Wright and Bertha Hooven Santmyer. The family were longtime residents of Xenia, a southwestern Ohio town fifteen miles east of Dayton. Xenia is clearly the model for the small Ohio towns that provide the primary settings for all three of Santmyer's novels; it is the declared subject of *Ohio Town*, her volume of essays first published in 1962.

Like Xenia, the Hooven/Santmyer family his-

Helen Hooven Santmyer in her late thirties

tory richly fuels the books, particularly " . . . *And Ladies of the Club.*" Both of Santmyer's grandfathers were Civil War veterans whose military experiences are reflected in those of the novel's two primary male figures, physician John Gordon and rope manufacturer Ludwig Rausch. Details of Gordon's and Rausch's professions are also drawn from real life. At least one member of Santmyer's family was a doctor, and both the Hoovens and the Santmyers were involved in the cordage industry: the novelist's maternal great-uncle founded the Hooven and Allison rope plant in Xenia, and her father managed the smaller R. A. Kelly factory for many years. Like the majority of the novel's characters, the Santmyers were quite affluent, relentlessly Republican (politics was a staple of dinnertime conversation), and staunchly Presbyterian, though of the liberal branch that allowed dancing, card playing, amateur theatricals, and other frivolities. And, of course, Santmyer's mother, whom the novelist describes as "spirited," was a member of the Woman's Club of Xenia, the prototype for the organization that Anne Alexander Gordon and Sally Cochran Rausch help

found in the fictional Waynesboro. For the *Life* feature story Santmyer related her childhood impressions of the Woman's Club: "We always stopped whatever noisy games we were playing when we saw the ladies beginning to assemble. . . . We had great respect for them; they had a reputation for being very well educated, very full of ideas. They were an example to me."

Inspired by these literary women, by her very supportive parents, and by her voracious reading in the Xenia Public Library (the founding of which is a central subject for both " . . . *And Ladies of the Club*" and *Ohio Town*), Santmyer decided early on that she wanted to be a writer. Following her 1914 graduation from the local high school, she left Ohio for Wellesley College where she joined a faculty-supported student writing group called the Scribblers. Graduating in 1918 with a B.A. in English, she was one of ten members of her class elected to the yearbook's Hall of Fame. From Wellesley she traveled to New York to find a job in publishing. Between 1919 and 1921 she worked as a secretary to Robert Bridges, the editor of *Scribner's Magazine;* at *Scribner's,* according to a *Chicago Daily News* report, she met F. Scott Fitzgerald, whose drinking and outrageous conduct seemed to her the marks of "a spoiled Princeton boy." Weary of New York, Santmyer returned to Xenia where she taught English in the public high school during the 1921-1922 academic year; she then spent two years— 1922 through 1924—as a teaching assistant in the English department of her alma mater, Wellesley. During this period she also worked on her first novel.

Herbs and Apples (1925) traces the life of Derrick Thornton between 1907 and the early 1920s. Surrounded by affectionate parents, lively siblings, and much extended family in her small Ohio town of Tecumseh, Derrick decides at the age of eleven that she wants to be a writer, wants to attain immortality. (Her decision is confirmed when she reads *The Life, Letters, and Journals of Louisa May Alcott*, and Santmyer has repeatedly cited the importance of Alcott to her own work.) Derrick forges a network of male and female friends during her childhood, then attends an unidentified northeastern women's college where she forms close friendships with five classmates, all of whom aspire to lead uncommon lives. Following Derrick's graduation, she moves with two of these young women to New York, where she works as a secretary to a magazine editor. Finally she returns home to Tecumseh to care for her father and younger siblings following the death of her mother; there she becomes a high school English teacher and gives up her dreams of laurel for the herbs and apples of ordinary experience.

Beyond the autobiographical insights that it obviously provides, this first novel introduces two elements that recur throughout Santmyer's work. The first is a profusion of social details fixing time and place: the homes, the meals, the family and community relationships in Tecumseh; the train rides and dorm rooms and late night discussions of World War I-era college life; the streets and apartments and young bohemians in New York following the war. Like many later critics of "... *And Ladies of the Club*," reviewers for both the *New Republic* and the *New York Times* felt that *Herbs and Apples* was overburdened by these details. Yet these reviewers also recognized a seriousness of theme in the novelist's treatment of the desire for immortality, the second of the elements that reappear in her later work. The child Derrick firmly believes in her own inevitable fame, a youthful conviction that Santmyer both celebrates and gently teases in all her books. As she writes in *Ohio Town*, "So long as these streets which briefly hold him are friendly and kind, a child moves in them happily; he is indifferent to ugliness; he is blind even to such elements of the picturesque as may exist, since it does not any of it concern him—the *real* him, whom the world will some day know." In *Herbs and Apples,* as later, it is ordinariness, the merging of the individual with the larger community, that finally triumphs.

During the four years following the publication of *Herbs and Apples,* Santmyer worked on a second novel and, with the financial support of her father, attended Oxford University where she wrote a thesis on eighteenth-century English Gothic novelist Clara Reeve and earned a Bachelor of Literature degree in 1927. In that year she also met Mildred Sandoe, a Xenia librarian, who became her lifelong friend. (In 1957, when both were, in Sandoe's words, "rattling around" in their own houses, they decided to live together in Santmyer's family home; today Sandoe, who is some four and one-half years younger than Santmyer, has her own room in the same Xenia nursing home, Hospitality Home East.) Santmyer became a member of the Woman's Club of Xenia in 1928, and in 1929 her second novel, *The Fierce Dispute,* was published.

Drawing its title from John Keats's lines "... the fierce dispute/Betwixt damnation and impassion'd clay" ("On Sitting Down to Read *King Lear* Once Again"), the novel focuses upon a child named Lucy Anne who lives in a decaying mansion on the edge of an unnamed Ohio town with her widowed mother, Hilary, and her maternal grand-

mother, Margaret Baird. The three figures endure self-imposed isolation as Lucy Anne's mother and grandmother struggle for the soul of the child. Hilary, through her disastrous marriage to an unstable but brilliant Italian musician, represents both the lure and the danger of art; Mrs. Baird, through her ancient family lines, her wealth, and her devotion to propriety, represents both the stability and the narrowness of conventional upper-middle-class life. Lucy Anne, who has musical talent but who also desires the activities of ordinary life denied her by her isolation, is torn between her mother and grandmother. The fierce dispute waged in the novel thus contains both personal and philosophical elements.

Reviewers in the *New York Times*, the *New York Herald Tribune,* and *Saturday Review of Literature* praised Santmyer's characterization, particularly of the child, and her ability to suggest the influence of the past upon the present and future. Indeed, some of the most affecting passages in the novel treat Civil War-era letters which Lucy Anne rescues from an old trunk and which suggest to the child the inevitability of both human sorrow and endurance. Yet critics also justly attacked the novel's resolution for its improbability. Perhaps influenced by her study of Clara Reeve, Santmyer surprisingly injects elements of the supernatural to bring about the novel's climax. Of all her books, *The Fierce Dispute* is the least satisfying.

Following the publication of this second novel, Santmyer settled permanently in Xenia. Her parents built a studio for her in the attic of the family home, and she joined the staff of nearby Cedarville College. Between 1936 and 1953, she served as head of the English department and Dean of Women at Cedarville. In 1953 she began yet another career as a reference librarian at the Dayton and Montgomery County Public Library, a position she held until her retirement in 1960. Between 1929 and 1960 Santmyer did little writing; the early newspaper claims that "... *And Ladies of the Club*" was fifty years in the making are apocryphal. Yet in her mid-sixties she once again resumed her literary career, producing the fine essays collected in *Ohio Town.*

Originally published by Ohio State University Press in 1962 and reissued by Harper and Row in 1984, *Ohio Town* is an affectionate, often humorous, and always fascinating portrait of Xenia. In each of its thirteen chapters, Santmyer treats one element of the town's landscape and institutions: its fine homes which have preserved various architectural styles—and family characters—since 1803; its public library which, like the library in "... *And Ladies of the Club*," was founded and operated during the 1870s by the Woman's Club and which through its several catalogues reflects the tastes of each generation; its churches which in their austerity or lavishness capture the natures of their individual congregations; the cemetery, the death lists of which record the scourges of each era—consumption, cholera, scarlet fever, childbirth, Shiloh and Vicksburg. The history, the sociology, the psychology of the town are defined by its venerable landmarks.

Ohio Town is undeniably nostalgic in tone, and yet its real point is not that much has been lost—the old-fashioned family doctor, the once majestic elms, the railroad as a primary symbol of escape and return. Its theme is, instead, that much continues, that the past merges with the present and future, that the essentially immutable landscape of homes and libraries and churches and cemeteries suggests "the inexhaustible richness and complication of ordinary daily life." Xenia is portrayed, then, as a microcosm of human experience that is as "unchanged in its essentials as earth and sky since the days of Theocritus," a living lesson for a new generation of children: "If they live long enough they will learn that everything has happened here, and may happen again. The town is Winesburg and Spoon River, it is Highbury and Cranford, it is even Illyria and Elsinore. Little that mankind knows and endures but has been here known and endured. . . ." *Ohio Town*, which won the Hood Memorial Award of the Ohioana Library Association in 1964, is a remarkable achievement.

In one of its passages *Ohio Town* is also ironically predictive of the work to come: "But however many of the old houses stand today, to remind us of another time, no one can ever write a book based on the lives that have been spent under their roofs. To know about those lives you must be child, grandchild, great-grandchild of the town; and to tell about them you must betray kin or friends of your mother, your grandmother, your great-grandmother. . . . Nor would invention serve the native who is familiar with the pattern of events: your tale might be so unbelievable as to make you feel safe, yet someone would surely point to a door, a parlor window, a side porch, and say: 'How did you know? I thought everyone was dead who might have remembered. . . .'"

The "book based on the lives that have been spent under their roofs" was begun shortly after the publication of *Ohio Town*. Originally written in longhand in bookkeepers' ledgers, the manuscript of "... *And Ladies of the Club*" was sent to Ohio State

Newspaper ad (New York Times Book Review, *24 June 1984*)

University Press in 1976. The press director, who liked the book but feared its length (over 500,000 words long, it filled eleven mailing boxes), asked Santmyer to trim it. Although her editing was slowed by increasingly poor health, she was able to complete the task with Mildred Sandoe's help, and in 1982 Ohio State published 1,500 copies, of which only about 200 were sold, primarily to libraries.

Here the story might have ended, except for a series of improbable events that have become the staple of press coverage. During a visit to the Shaker Heights, Ohio, public library, Mrs. Grace Sindell overheard another woman praise "... *And Ladies of the Club*" as the best book she had ever read. Mrs. Sindell checked it out and then shared her excitement about it with her son, Gerald Sindell, a Hollywood television producer, who passed it on to yet another Los Angeles producer, Stanley Corwin, a former publishing executive. Corwin and Sindell bought all rights to the novel from Ohio State University Press, then contacted a friend, Owen Laster, an agent with the William Morris Agency, who sold the book to Phyllis Grann, president of Putnam's. Putnam's issued a huge first printing of the novel and also sold the paperback rights to Berkley

Books. Enthusiasm for "... *And Ladies of the Club*" increased at every stage of its journey; but media coverage of the phenomenon truly began when the Book of the Month Club announced in early January 1984 that it had chosen the novel as its main selection for June and when on 12 January the *New York Times* ran a front-page story headlined "Happy End for Novelist's 50-Year Effort." Although the *Times* erred in calling the book a product of a half-century's work and in labeling it Santmyer's answer to Sinclair Lewis's *Main Street*, the account stimulated interest in "... *And Ladies of the Club*" and its author. The elderly novelist was featured on all the network news programs and became the subject of stories in *Life*, *Newsweek*, and *People*. Eight days before its official trade publication date, "... *And Ladies of the Club*" made the *New York Times Book Review* best-seller list (number 14 on 17 June); the following week it was number 2; two weeks later it reached number 1, where it remained for seven weeks; and at the end of the year it was still on the *Times* list.

The novel itself is a sprawling account of life in an Ohio town between 1868 and 1932. Told from an omniscient-author point of view, it focuses upon two women, Anne Alexander Gordon and Sally Cochran Rausch, from their college graduation and their becoming the youngest charter members of the Waynesboro Woman's Club to the death of Anne, the last of the founders. During the sixty-four years covered by the novel, the two women marry (the stoic Anne chooses a brooding doctor; the ebullient Sally finds an energetic rope manufacturer), they have children and grandchildren and great-grandchildren, they tend their houses and engage in community affairs. Sharing their joys and sorrows, their pleasures and responsibilities, they lead quite ordinary middle-class existences.

The true structuring device for their lives, however, is the Woman's Club, where each meeting begins with the statement "Madam President and Ladies of the Club." Through the Club Anne and Sally involve themselves with other women who have social or intellectual influence in Waynesboro: the suffragette wife and daughters of a judge, the formidable spouse of a retired general, the wives of local ministers and seminarians, spinster schoolteachers, ancient ladies from a distinguished but declining family. Strong or weak, rich or poor, these women deliver original essays at their meetings, perform such community service as founding a subscription library and organizing public lecture series, and lead the social life of Waynesboro with their amateur theatricals and fairs. And because each member has numerous relatives or other connections, these characters, too, are figuratively brought into Club meetings. Thus the reader observes almost every aspect of the middle-class life of the town.

Just as the Club provides structure for Anne's and Sally's experiences, so too does it dictate the structure and dominant tone of the novel. Through the Club membership rolls and headnotes that preface each chapter, the reader is apprised of marriages, reminded of those members who have died or left town, and prepared for events to come. The membership list for 1884-1885, for example, boasts fifteen active members, shows three names in the "In Memoriam" column, and begins with the headnote "*Waynesboro was shocked by the loss of its most distinguished citizen*. . . ." Moreover, because the sensibilities, the proprieties, of the Woman's Club dominate the novel, certain scandalous goings-on—possible homosexuality, adultery, suicide, drug addiction—are merely hinted at, not openly discussed. Such treatment seems absolutely consistent with the values of the Club members. Thus structure and tone converge in this massive book.

The reviews of the novel have been very mixed. Such admirers as Vance Bourjaily in the *New York Times Book Review* and Cynthia Grenier in *The American Spectator* have focused upon its scrupulous rendering of social details: houses, clothes, manners, all of which evolve as the novel progresses through its sixty-four years. They cite, too, its quiet but effective treatment of certain of its scenes and characters—the death, perhaps suicide, of a laudanum-addicted, forcibly retired schoolteacher whose reduced means can no longer support her habit; the resolve of yet another spinster teacher in rejecting a prominent suitor in order to pursue her own austere, scholarly life. Attackers of "... *And Ladies of the Club*," such as Gene Lyons in *Newsweek* and Michael Malone in *The Nation*, accuse it of propagandizing for white, middle-class, Republican values of the narrowest sort. These critics claim that blacks and other minority groups are ignored or patronized, labor unions are deplored, and the seven Ohio Republicans who served as U.S. Presidents during the period covered by the novel are endlessly discussed and very nearly deified. The truth lies, of course, somewhere in the middle ground: the details are impressive, but they also clearly slow the action of the book; the moving scenes are all too often supplanted by flat exposition; illiberal attitudes are expressed by many of the characters, but they accurately reflect, after all, standards of class, area, and historical period. Despite violent disagreements with one another, the reviewers all concur that the novel is worthy of attention, for whatever reason.

"...And Ladies of the Club" is clearly the sensation of the year, earning its author membership in the Ohio Hall of Fame, an honorary Doctor of Humanities degree from Dayton's Wright State University, and a richly deserved national celebrity. Whether its success results from its inherent worth as fiction or from the dramatic story of its creation, discovery, and promotion, the very real achievement of Helen Hooven Santmyer in writing this, the last of her four admirable books, can hardly be debated.

References:

"Ambition Compromises," *New York Times Book Review*, 13 September 1925, pp. 17, 19;

Vance Bourjaily, "The Other Side of 'Main Street,'" *New York Times Book Review*, 24 June 1984, p. 7;

Paul Galloway, "An Octogenarian Star Is Born,"

Chicago Daily News: Leisure, 17 June 1984, pp. 3, 20;

Cynthia Grenier, "...And Ladies of the Club," *American Spectator*, 17 (November 1984): 46-47;

Ernest P. Horowitz, "Herbs and Apples, by Helen Hooven Santmyer," *New Republic*, 45 (6 January 1926): 198;

Jane Howard, "Portrait: Helen Hooven Santmyer," *Life*, 7 (June 1984): 31, 34, 36;

Gene Lyons and Tracy Robinson, "Xenia's Literary Lady," *Newsweek*, 103 (18 June 1984): 93;

Gene Lyons, "Sunny Side of the Street," *Newsweek*, 103 (18 June 1984): 93;

"MacNeil/Lehrer Report," PBS, 5 July 1984;

Michael Malone, "...And Ladies of the G.O.P.," *Nation*, 239 (21-28 July 1984): 52-54;

Edwin McDowell, "Happy End for Novelist's 50-Year Effort," *New York Times*, 12 January 984, A1, C28;

New York Herald Tribune: Books, 28 April 1929, p. 25;

Saturday Review of Literature, 6 (10 August 1929): 41;

"Women at War," *New York Times Book Review*, 5 May 1929, p. 7.

Frederick Lewis Seidel

(19 February 1936-   )

Stephen Whited
Georgia State University

Final Solutions (New York: Random House, 1963);

Sunrise (New York: Viking Press, 1980);

Men and Women: New and Selected Poems (London: Chatto & Windus, The Hogarth Press, 1984).

Frederick Seidel, born in St. Louis, Missouri, to Jerome Jay and Thelma Seidel, attended Harvard College, taking an A.B. in 1957. As an undergraduate, he had his work published in the *Harvard Advocate*. He married Phyllis Munro Ferguson in June 1960 and they had two children, Felicity and Samuel. The Seidels were divorced in 1969. Seidel lives in New York, but he also spends much time in England, where he collaborates on screenplays with Marc Paploe.

Seidel was the Paris editor for *Paris Review* (1961) when he interviewed Robert Lowell for the *Paris Review* craft interviews, and he has continued

to serve as advisory editor since 1962. He has lectured at Rutgers University and published poems in the *American Poetry Review*, *Evergreen*, the *New York Review of Books*, *Partisan Review*, *Paris Review*, and *Poetry*. Seidel has published three books of poetry: *Final Solutions* (1963), *Sunrise* (1980), and *Men and Women: New and Selected Poems* (1984).

Final Solutions exhibits Seidel's remarkable ability for carefully delineated characters and images. *Sunrise* demonstrates the efforts of a more mature writer seeking meaning and answers presented within a larger social context. *Men and Women: New and Selected Poems* further demonstrates Seidel's poetic wit, irony, and acute sensitivity to detail of previous work. Although *Final Solutions* is marked by despair and outrage, *Sunrise* and *Men and Women* are less indignant and more concerned with the interrelatedness of time, action, and

Frederick Lewis Seidel (Susan Rowland)

metaphor. The world Seidel presents is strained and intensely disaffected, but there is a sympathetic element in the poetry that results from his vision of human resiliency and sensitivity.

The manuscript of *Final Solutions* was awarded the Helen Burlin Memorial Award sponsored by the YM-WHA Poetry Center (92nd Street, New York). As part of the award the poems were to be printed by Antheneum; however, attorneys for the Poetry Center and George Frankenthaler, President of the Y and former State Supreme Court Judge, decided that "competent legal opinion confirms the presence of libel in one of the poems." Seidel refused to delete the poem in question, "Americans in Rome", and the award was withdrawn. Antheneum refused publication, and the jury, comprised of Louise Bogan, Stanley Kunitz, and Robert Lowell, resigned in protest. Random House finally published the book, all poems intact, under the editorship of Jason Epstein.

Reviewers made favorable comparisons with T. S. Eliot, Robert Lowell, and John Berryman.

R. W. Flint announced to *Commentary* (August 1963) readers that Seidel "has decided to publish a piece of ventriloquism of great virtuosity. The poet 'imitated' is Robert Lowell, one of the jury that passed on the manuscript." Lowell provided a glowing book jacket endorsement, and Louise Bogan said in the *New Yorker* (12 October 1963) that "he does not miss an effect.... He is a master of metaphor.... Whether or not Seidel's talent will come into the full power it now suggests it is impossible to predict. But how extraordinary if it should." Although Bogan's hopefulness is somewhat guarded, her acknowledgment of Seidel's abilities recognizes an experimental poetic nature influenced by Lowell yet very much different in intention.

The fifteen poems of the book reflect upon visions of public and private existence. The problematic experiences of such lives as those exhibited in "The Widower," "The Coalman," "Americans in Rome," "Dayley Island," and "Thanksgiving Day" carry the weight of a fragmented society growing ever more alienated. Personal pretensions and social structures break down (. . . the penitents'/Blue knees carved to an altar rail/In stone Trastevere, where rents/Split with indulgences, where love hangs on its nail./I turn the light out . . . I am sure/ Of nothing . . ."); social injustice is exposed as an exploitative evil ("The Mine Workers' huge Santa Claus/Made of coal derivatives beams/His headlamp on their new all-glass office"); and a war weary society faces the meaninglessness of battle and destruction, its sacrifice and struggle ("I was the only child,/And a first boyfriend's brother,/Dead—in a shell-shocked truck/Crash, I think—in Sweden,/ Couldn't make the war matter"). Through these voices of public anguish, the poet is a distant observer providing the characters a confessional mode that displays the outrage and pain of various socioeconomic views, confessional views felt and understood by the poet while not necessarily a part of his own experience.

"Wanting to Live in Harlem," the first poem of the collection, introduces in the private voice many of the subjects and views that appear throughout the book: the illusion of cultural security ("Pictures of violins in the Wurlitzer collection/ Were my bedroom's one decoration"); the troublesome question of class distinction ("Backs, bellies and scrolls,/Stradivarius, Guarnerius, Amati,/Colored like a calabash-and-meerschaum pipe bowl's/ Warmed, matured body—//The color of the young light-skinned colored girl we had then"); a confused social and ethnic identity ("I was thirteen, had just been bar mitzvah./My hero, once I'd read about him,/Was the Emperor Hadrian; my villain, Bar Kochba,/The Jew Hadrian had crushed out at Jerusalem"); and a mother's slow death ("Even then, in '49, my mother was dying"). The trauma of such experiences reveals a social fabric which has failed and is unraveling. In this poem, the traditions of culture and religion offer little comfort, for even the inspiring music of Bach contains elements of fragmentation since his

> ... Lutheran fingerings had helped pluck
> The tonsured monks like toadstools from their lawns,
> And now riddled the armor I would have to shuck ....

What is left to the living when all sacred meanings have themselves become the basis for the profane nature of a "riddled . . . armor"?

> I had given up violin and left St. Louis,
> I had given up being Jewish,
> To be at Harvard just another
> Greek nose in street clothes in Harvard Yard.
> Mother went on half dying.
> I wanted to live in Harlem. I was almost unarmored . . .
> Almost alone . . . .

The syntax and rhymes of these lines make the intention clear. Giving up heritage and past "to be at Harvard" is presented in frightful, jingling rhymes that contrast sharply with the stark pacing of unarmored loneliness in the last three lines.

Of course, Seidel is not totally alone, for as he expresses in other poems there is a shared community of suffering in a fragmented society. Such poems as "Heart Attack," "Americans in Rome," "Wanting to Live in Harlem," "The Beast Is in Chains," and "The Sickness" share thematic concerns that focus upon the personal suffering presented in "Wanting to Live in Harlem" and act as a sequential discourse on ethical values, past and present experience, race, class, aging, and death. The poems are prophetic in their anticipation of the searching of the 1960s.

> Ten years! I had been trying to find a room ten years,
> It seemed that day, and been turned down again and again.

In the twenty years separating the publication of *Final Solutions* and *Sunrise*, Seidel's poetic voice shifts to attend more closely to the effect of time and to the accoutrement of "a room" so desperately necessary in a climate of political upheaval, institutionalized death, and insensate popular culture.

The critical reception of *Sunrise* (Lamont Poetry Prize, Academy of American Poets, 1980; award for poetry, National Book Critics Circle, 1981; poetry prize, *American Poetry Review*, 1981) has borne out Louise Bogan's early optimism for Seidel's work. The book reveals the full power of a mature poetic voice, a mastery of metaphor, and a depth of interpretive insight clearly evolving from the promise of the first book. "Wanting to Live in Harlem" reappears in the collection to serve as an interpretive link to the early poems, and to provide background for the central focus of the book, the title poem, "Sunrise."

"Sunrise" provides a contrapuntal expression for the accompanying poems with their swirl of images and emotions filtered through the unconscious. Awakened by the alarm, a sleepy mind revels in a surrealistic juxtaposition of images. Ironically, the essential pattern of the poem is formal, a Spenserian stanza and modified rhyme scheme; however, the poem derives its energy from the sweep of motion and expanse of imagery, at once physical and spiritual. Yet through all this vigorous turmoil of activity, time is still.

> The gold watch that retired free will was constant dawn.
> Constant sunrise. But then it was dawn. Christ rose,
> White-faced gold bulging the horizon
> Like too much honey in a spoon, an instant
> Stretching forever that would not spill . . . .

In forty stanzas, Seidel stretches reality as image and compresses reality as time into a Bergsonian vision of existence, passing yet ever present. Through free association and a montage of disturbing perceptions, the poet analyzes various subjects against the serious injury of a child, the mad dash across half the planet to the child's bedside, and the countdown of seconds before the final awakening. He concerns himself with the desperate search through the quotidian for value and meaning in what Wallace Stevens called "the things we suggest or believe or desire, the summation of our actions." His intent is not simply to present another "Wasteland"; the hopeless landscape of Seidel's world reflects how pitifully little our society with its abundance and prosperity suggests, believes, or desires. Seidel looks carefully within the metaphor for renewal, but he finds little hope beyond the endurance of the sensitive, individual spirit.

I wake beneath my hypnopompic erection,
Forty stanzas, forty Easters of life,
And smile, eyes full of tears, shaking with rage.

There are no answers; only rage remains among a "heap of broken images."

Among the stoney rubble picked through in "Sunrise," politics reflects only waste and death; echoes of "Wasteland" are not incidental, for during "Bicentennial April . . ./Spread out on the ceiling like a groundcloth," all symbols of renewal and leadership are etherized.

Find life on Mars. Find Jesus. "You are a failya,"
The President of the United States said.
He was killed, and she became Bob's. His head,
Robert Kennedy's, lay as if removed
In the lap of a Puerto Rican boy praying.

The sentiment of these lines also appears in "1968," where the political fundraiser is a "rock superstar."

Fifty or so of the original
Four hundred
At the fundraiser,
Robert Kennedy for President, the remnants, lie
Exposed as snails around the swimming pools, stretched
Out on the paths, and in the gardens, and the drive.

Thus hope is reduced to "the oyster glow/Of dawn dope and fog in L.A.'s/Bel Air." The irony in "1968" is all the more poignant in light of Kennedy's death, which results in the "failya" of "the campaign year—/And the beginning of a new day." However, this "new day" brings only a

. . . John the Baptist,
At least, come
To say someone else is coming.
He hikes up his shoulder holster
Self-consciously, meeting their gaze.
That is as sensitive as the future gets.

Yet it is not future time that is indicted here; for example, in "To Robert Lowell and Osip Mandelstam," the power of misinterpretation to influence our perception of time is clearly stated.

Of course the future always is,
Like someone just back from England
Stepping off the curb, I'll look the wrong way and be nothing.

The fearful extent to which we have been distracted and misguided is revealed by our lack of meaningful connections with the past. The difficulty of regaining such connections is presented in "Sunrise."

To speak the name of the dead is to make them live
Again. O pilgrim, restore the breath of life
To him who has vanished. But the names they give.
No one can pronounce the hieroglyphs.
Then they have vowels to breathe with their bare midriffs,
Yes which? Which one's known how to vocalize
The consonants. The kings don't recognize
Their names, don't recognize our names for them;
The soft parts that could not be embalmed are life.

As William Carlos Williams said of poetry, "men die miserably every day/for lack/of what is found there," for that special essence of life cannot be embalmed and viewed; it must be used and understood to be of value. However, the society pictured in "Sunrise" has no rich, present sensibility. Its past is reduced to staring "at the stared-at./Ramesses II in an exhibit case." Its future has become simply "A bulbously gloved hand [that]

Frees the faulty door. Thrown open. Into
The countdown, and counting. —9. When you
Are no longer what you were. Thrown open.
—8. O let me out nor in.

The poem ironically conveys the absurdity of passing hopefully through a door opened by a hand gloved like that of a cartoon character. Yet the ambiguity of the line "let me out nor in" allows neither escape from nor acceptance of this ambiguity, for there is in this active participation with life's countdown a figurative awakening in "Sunrise" when one's humanity bursts forth to "smile, eyes full of tears, shaking with rage." These are human emotional responses, deeply felt expressions of humane sensitivity, the savoring of which offers hope and knowledge.

Seidel's most recent publication, *Men and Women: New and Selected Poems*, is his first collection to appear in England. The book offers most of the poems of *Sunrise*, "Wanting to Live in Harlem" from *Final Solutions*, and nine new poems. Among the new poems, one hears Seidel's familiar themes; the presentations are typically formal, brilliantly pictured, and full of self-referential echoes.

In "Scotland" the superficiality of the modern experience is juxtaposed with archetypal traditions and long-felt emotions, which are, so to speak, under the gun.

The windows were wide-open through which I
Could flee to nowhere--nowhere meaning how
The past is portable, and ~~also~~ why
The future of the past was always now.

Typescript with metrical schemes for a poem (the author)

A stag lifts his nostrils to the morning
In the crosshairs of the scope of love,
And smells what the gun calls Scotland and falls.

This death is followed by a rich display of historical
and mythic connections played out as a film pro-
jected in fast motion. Death is viewed from on high
as

The black speck of the coffin trailing a thread,
Lost in the savage green, an ocean of thawed
Endlessness and a spermatozoon.

Seidel also uses an aerial view in "The New
Cosmology" to convey the insignificance and superficiality of a temporal mythic consciousness based
solely on a popular culture. Any transcendent vision of existence has been reduced to a confusion of
totems: "the Ark," "kryptonite," "Superpowers,"
great spiritual power alongside the comic and the
illusory. Thus no longer can we, with Whitman,
imagine continuity in the leaves of grass, for contemporary life appears to have lost its transcendent
vision.

We turn a page of *Life,*
Lying open in the grass.

Our insignificance and helplessness are as profound in the age of the "radio telescope / Discoloring an inch of mountainside in Chile" as in the days of the "tribes of Israel in their tents" because we have lost our connections with the past.

For Seidel, an endless moment of memory, reevaluated again and again, contains the essential motive of one's salvation. As a self-psychoanalysis, the poem probes deeper and deeper into the recurring images and metaphors for answers. Despite the intensely despairing nature of these poems, humor and optimism are displayed in the act of wonder and in the pleasure of irony. For example, childhood is pictured in "A Dimple Cloud" as a "portrait of the autist / Asleep in the arms of his armchair, age thirteen . . . ." The pun is developed further as metaphor:

All he has to do to sleep is open
A book; but the wet dream is new, as if
The pressure of *De Bello Gallico*
And Willa Cather face down on his fly,
Spread wide, one clasping the other from behind,
Had added confusion to confusion, like looking
For your glasses with your glasses on . . . .

Here art appears to breed stupor and confusion, and in light of such poems as "Sunrise," "What One Must Contend With," and "Homage to Cicero," the portrait is of the artist as "autist" reduced to a state of innocence, a "staring at the stared-at."

The sadistic eye of the autist shapes the world
Into a sort of, call it innocence,
Ready to be wronged, ready to
Be tortured into power and beauty, into
Words his phonographic memory
Will store on silence like particles of oil
On water—the rainbow of polarity

Which made this poem. I put my glasses on,
And shut my eyes. O adolescence, sing!

The irony here is bitter. As the poem points out, the portrait of the artistic young man may be "a breeze almost too sweet / To bear," for such innocence is mocked by the face of poverty, loneliness, depression, insanity—the world the innocent must finally experience.

In a companion piece to "Wanting to Live in Harlem," "The Blue-Eyed Doe," Seidel turns again to a childhood in St. Louis and to the horror of witnessing a mother's insanity.

Childhood is your mother even if
Your mother is in hospitals for years
And then lobotomized, like mine. A whiff
Of her perfume; behind her veil, her tears.

The child (as well as the adult and poet) finally finds protection in the guise of experience, but the poem creates great psychological tension by turning the image around to reflect "childhood [as] your mother," which translates into experience based on pain and emotion (I am often old / Enough to leave my childhood, but I stay").

The real world vanishes behind the fawn
That leaps to safety while the doe is skinned.

Yet as an adult, the poet is doomed to examine the skinning in minute detail.

How easily I can erase an error,
The typos my recalling this will cause,
But no correcting key erases terror.

Indeed, such terror hangs on the "almost unarmored" consciousness in a timeless manner, described in "Sunrise" as

. . . too much honey in a spoon, an instant
Stretching forever that would not spill . . . .

"The Blue-Eyed Doe" ends with an image of time that also echoes important phrases from other poems ("we're no longer what we were," "staring at the stared-at," or "confusion, like looking / For your glasses with your glasses on . . ."):

Blue eyes that will need glasses in a year—
I'm here and disappear, the boy I was . . . .

Although Seidel's poetry exhibits much frustration at the apparent powerlessness of the poetic vocation, his stance is not Audenesque—poems can alter life. Poetry provides meaningful patterns with which one orders knowledge and experience, and Seidel's continued poetic efforts attest to his faith in the medium. His genius for rhyme, formal pattern, vivid imagery, and surrealistic juxtaposition are evidence of much careful attention to the possibilities of the poetic form and the power words impart.

Peter Straub

(2 March 1943-   )

Patricia L. Skarda
Smith College

BOOKS: *Ishmael* (Dublin: Irish University Press, 1972; New York: Underwood Miller, 1983);

Open Air (Dublin: Irish University Press, 1972);

Marriages (London: Deutsch, 1973; New York: Coward, McCann & Geoghegan, 1973);

Julia (London: Cape, 1975; New York: Coward, McCann & Geoghegan, 1975); republished as *Full Circle* (London: Corgi, 1977);

If You Could See Me Now (London: Cape, 1977; New York: Coward, McCann & Geoghegan, 1977);

Ghost Story (New York: Coward, McCann & Geoghegan, 1979; London: Futura, 1980);

Shadow Land (New York: Coward, McCann & Geoghegan, 1980; London: Collins, 1981);

Floating Dragon (New York: Coward, McCann & Geoghegan, 1983; London: Collins, 1983);

Leeson Park and Belsize Square (New York: Underwood Miller, 1983);

The Talisman, with Stephen King (New York: Viking, 1984);

Wild Animals: Three Novels (New York: Coward, McCann & Geoghegan, 1984).

Peter Straub (Kirby McCauley)

In *The Talisman* (1984), Peter Straub sacrificed some of his narrative authority for the privilege of working with Stephen King, his friend and coauthor. Within a month of publication, the collaboration put *The Talisman* at the top of the *New York Times* bestseller list, where King feels somewhat more at home than Straub does. For Straub, *The Talisman* may be true to its title. On the strength of it, Book-of-the-Month Club has picked up *Wild Animals: Three Novels* (1984, containing *Under Venus*, the first printing of his second novel; *Julia*, 1975; and *If You could See Me Now*, 1977). Straub has also had a number of interview opportunities, written and televised, to announce his forthcoming novella *Blue Rose and Koko*, a generational novel about Vietnam veterans. He says he is moving away from supernatural material toward increasing complexity, broader scope, and international settings, but his best work to date focuses on private experiences on the margin where nature and supernature meet, where reality converges with dream, where writing leaves off and the imagination takes over.

Straub's career as a writer began with poetry and academic literary criticism. His training as a reader of literature came from the University of Wisconsin (B.A., 1965) and Columbia University (M.A., 1966), where he wrote a thesis on William Carlos Williams. For three years he taught at his own high school, Milwaukee Country Day, a conservative model for the prep school in *Shadow Land* (1980). He married Susan Bitker in 1966, and in 1969 they moved to Dublin, where Straub studied with Denis Donoghue at University College. Poetry was then "ninety percent" of what he read and wrote; two sequences of poems, *Ishmael* and *Open Air*, were published in 1972. He began a dissertation on Victorian fiction and D. H. Lawrence, but he gave it up after repeated disagreements with Donoghue. Some of his thinking about the relative merits of creative and critical writing runs as a leit-motif throughout *If You Could See Me Now*. In the summer of 1972 he took time off to write *Marriages*, a first-person rendering of an extramarital affair set on the Continent. When it was bought and published by André Deutsch in 1973, Straub and his wife moved to London so that Susan Straub could get training as a counselor at the Tavistock Institute and Straub could write fiction in what Straub calls "a bigger world."

His second novel, "Under Venus," failed to find a publisher, despite a number of complete revisions of point of view; Straub even cast one version as a letter to F. Scott Fitzgerald. Impressed by the successful suspense of a futile chase of ghosts in *Marriages*, his English literary agent suggested that he write a Gothic novel. Straub, with a scholar's enthusiasm, began to read Mary Stewart and other historical Gothic novels while he supported himself by writing short stories for British women's magazines. Those that failed to please were "too literary," but *Julia* and *If You Could See Me Now* were not.

Julia and *If You Could See Me Now* established Straub's primary fictional pattern of depicting the horrors of guilt in characters who explore the past to understand the present. In the first, Julia Lofting solves a twenty-five-year-old murder that leads to her admission of guilt in the death of her own daughter. Julia, who inadvertently killed her choking child by a clumsy tracheotomy, proves to be as much a child-murderer as is the ghost of Julia's Kensington home—Olivia Rudge, a child herself, who mutilated and murdered an innocent boy. In *If You Could See Me Now*, Miles Teagarden, the implied author and the first of Straub's many fictionalized selves, proves his innocence of the twenty-year-old rape and murder of his cousin Alison Greening. The past literally haunts the present in both novels, and characters frequently articulate why: "Those who believe in the past are condemned to live in it," someone says to Julia, who responds with Straub's perspective, "The past has everything to do with my present." Miles defines eternal recurrence as a tenet of faith: "I have always held to the past, I thought that it could, would, should be repeated indefinitely, that it was the breathing life in the heart of the present." In *Julia* the past breathes death, for Julia cannot live with guilt; she finally commits suicide as the ghost of Olivia Rudge bids her do. But in *If You Could See Me Now*, Miles not only escapes death but also clears his name and saves his young cousin Alison Updahl from the vengeful ghost of her aunt Alison Greening.

Throughout *Julia*, Straub creates terror in claustrophobic images appropriate to the haunted house in Kensington where the child murderer of the past lived and where Julia, the child murderer of the present, now lives. The house is "a great structure, a huge form, which hedged [Julia] out and kept her at bay: It would resist her impositions, it would not yield to her." The house is alive, obstinately defiant of Julia's attempt to turn off the heat or to find quiet in rooms where an improbable "elbow of noise seemed to pulse from the walls." Julia's claustrophobia transfers to other "horribly small" places and exemplifies her mental state: "[Julia] felt, more than ever, that she was living inside a comprehensive error, the mistake that her life had become; bigger forces lay without, waiting." For Julia Lofting and for Peter Straub, the bigger force is evil, the absence of good, the inherent depravity of humankind.

The embodiment of evil is first the ghost of Olivia Rudge and second Julia's unforgiving and unforgiven husband Magnus Lofting, the father of Julia's child and of Olivia Rudge herself. Magnus haunts Julia, "wrapping her in a blanket of deception," and literally driving her to suicide to protect his own reputation. Olivia haunts Julia too, but her disposition is more sinister. Olivia's own mother explains her dead daughter's behavior simply:

> Olivia was evil. She was an evil person. Evil isn't like ordinary people. It can't be got rid of. It gets revenge. Revenge is what it wants, and it gets it. . . . What she was was worse than what she did. Ordinary people can't touch it.

The halting prose of this indictment limits its effectiveness but not its effect in the fiction. Only evil incarnate kills a little boy for no cause other than for being "partially German." And only evil explains Magnus's delight in psychological tortures. His duplicity terrifies more than any description of Olivia's bloody knives in the sand, shattered mirrors in the house, or mutilations in the past.

Murder, here as elsewhere in Straub's writing, is "the greatest crime against the soul. . . . an eternal crime." As such, murder results from evil; the magnitude of the cause matches its effect. After the horrors of messages in blood, flying vases, house break-ins and break-downs, Julia's suicide completes the apparent collaboration of Magnus and Olivia. An initial seance, enigmatic intuitions, and telepathic communications pale next to the selfish lies that kill dreams first and dreamer second. *Julia* was republished in London as *Full Circle*, also the title of Peter Fetterman's English film version, released in America as *The Haunting of Julia*, starring Mia Farrow. The haunted-house motif and the psychological traumas brought only moderate box-office success.

The relative success of *Julia* encouraged Straub to develop a short story plot into full-length fiction in *If You Could See Me Now*. The pattern of guilt remains the same, but Straub experimented with point of view and with his prose. The story is simple, but the execution complicated. When Miles Teagarden, a thirty-three-year-old English professor, returns to his grandmother's house near Arden, Wisconsin, to finish his dissertation on D. H. Lawrence, he quickly discovers that the Valley people have added the murder of three young girls to his real adolescent sins of petty thievery and love of his California cousin Alison Greening, who died twenty years ago. Alison haunts Miles in real and hallucinatory appearances as shadows, memories, intensified atmosphere, rustling noises, and wet leaves and sticks. In defense, Miles abandons literary criticism to write out his memories, discovering as he writes that the reason for his return to the family home is the promised reunion with Alison Greening. When writing of real events, his once literary experiences, "brewed up out of Jack London and Hawthorne and Cooper and Disney cartoons and Shakespeare and the brothers Grimm," become real malevolence, actual hostility, and eventually Miles's "primitive apprehension of evil." Like *Julia*, Miles senses that he is "on the verge of being crushed by immense forces, by forces of huge and impersonal evil." Only his writing keeps him sane. "Evil is," Straub writes through Miles, "what we call the force we can discover when we send our minds as far as they can go: when the mind crumbles before something bigger, harder than itself, unknowable and hostile." By writing of his dead cousin, Miles could feel "her hatred and jealousy"; he could know that her "spirit was rancid with jealousy of life."

Miles writes because his own life is at stake, and the intensity of Miles's lived experience gives Straub far greater control over all aspects of his fiction than he had in *Julia*. Almost playfully, Straub includes italicized statements from Valley people to broaden the seriousness of Miles's actions and conversations. Repeatedly, Miles's anger strikes others as cause for suspicion or proof of guilt for the recent murders of Gwen Olson (twelve), Jenny Strand (thirteen), Candace Michalski (seventeen), and for the past murder of Alison Greening (fourteen), whom all the others resemble.

Straub tightens his metaphors as if bridging the gap between his fiction and poetry. Miles's "old sins" are "permanently pinned to [his] jacket"; his life is "bent and altered by sexual disappointment"; old pioneer women, like his wise Auntie Rinn, "seem weightless, transparencies held together by wrinkles." Sensory details accumulate as Straub defines and describes present circumstances. Some devices are more humorous than clairvoyant, such as Miles's "olfactory hallucinations"—his ability to smell people on the other end of the telephone. Smell, the most difficult sense to express, supplies a pattern for Miles's sensitivity. The surly waitress smelling of baby oil and tooth decay, "mostly the latter," reveals Straub's humor and Miles's academic prejudice in an unnecessary decorative description. But the recognition of Alison's ghost in the smell of the quarry where she died prepares for Miles's realization that "another world, a world of Spirit" not only exists but also threatens him.

When Alison Greening takes her revenge on her rapist and murderer, Miles comes to see her as his incisive Auntie Rinn describes her: "corrupt," "calculating," "destructive." Miles exposes evil in the selfish lies and excuses of the police chief who believes that "rape isn't perverted. . . . it's almost a normal thing." He finds evil in the homophobia of the Valley community. And he sees evil in his cousin Duane Updahl, who beats his daughter Alison because he "hated women." Miles thinks Duane murdered and mutilated the girls who resembled Alison Greening because she spurned him twenty years ago. Miles is wrong; the ghost of Alison Greening herself murders her modern look-alikes.

Alison Greening's ghostly return, like Miles Teagarden's return to his grandmother's house, is ultimately an imaginative act, more symbolic than literal but tortuously traumatic nonetheless. As Miles burns his dead cousin's shadow and the Updahl home, he purges himself of his past, replacing childhood dreams with adult realities. If Alison were to return again, Miles says finally to his young cousin Alison Updahl, she might come back "as us," rather than as the rattling stones, screeching air, and circles of grass in a leafstorm. Alison Greening is an imaginative construct of Straub's early version of the inevitable imperfection in the psychology of Miles Teagarden and his one-time friends and family. Her haunting is self-inflicted and, in the fiction, almost enjoyed by each of the repressed characters in turn.

Shortly after completing *If You Could See Me Now*, Straub met Stephen King in London. He had been "enormously" impressed by King's work in *Carrie* and *Salem's Lot* as well as by the income each earned from publishers and film studios. Stephen King's discipline and his "imagination that never stopped" spurred Straub to work even harder. For *Ghost Story* (1979), Straub studied the complex ambiguities of language and method of gothic classics, especially Henry James's *Turn of the Screw*, and he wrote with a clearer sense of his own language, structure, and theme. He worked then as now from 10:00-12:00 and 2:00-6:00, using mornings for drafting directions and characters and the afternoon for the working versions of narrative. With jazz recordings in the background, Straub contemplates his whole, completing one motif when another has taken hold. His method, he says, is "like playing across the bar line in music, ending a phrase four or five bars into the next chorus." With *Ghost Story*, Straub learned to time his climaxes, alternating passages of low intensity with surprising effects of high intensity. The suspense never flags.

The setting of *Ghost Story*—Milburn, New York—returned Straub and his ghosts to the Northeast, a more traditional place for his guilt-ridden characters and conventional hauntings than was Wisconsin. The success of the book—a Book-of-the-Month Club full selection and a movie by Universal—enabled Straub and his family to return to New England, to Fairfield County, Connecticut, which was later the setting for *Floating Dragon* (1983), his second best-seller. *Ghost Story*, with "smart and passionate" jacket blurbs by Stephen King, linked Straub with King in ways readers could understand and endorse. But *Ghost Story* succeeds artistically as few if any of King's fictions do. Here Straub matches violence with appropriate causes, elaborating on evil in a narrative structure as complicated as its subject.

Ghost Story builds on the conventions of horror fiction with ghosts, possessions, demonic bargains, werewolves, vampires, clairvoyance, telepathy, and literally murderous guilt. Between familiar shape-shifting manifestations of evil—lynx, bird, wasp, or any number of human forms, most of them female—Straub articulates his imaginative purpose through an implied author, one Don Wanderley, who controls the novel by excusing temporal lapses and revealing crucial theories behind the fiction. Evil and its incarnations, he says, are "the originals of everything that frightens us in the supernatural. . . . in stories we make them manageable." Straub's stories in general, and *Ghost Story* in particular, show that destruction of deep fears can be managed by an imaginative confrontation more powerful than our fears. Here and in his later fiction, evil manifests itself through death and de-

struction as past terrors are transformed into present horrors. The intuitive author learns that evil can be found "in the places of your imagination. In the places of your dreams." The images of evil can, Straub proves in *Ghost Story*, "frighten you to death." The cliché takes on fresh meaning in a novel full of death and dreadful scares.

Death comes in grisly ways: arms cut off by a thresher, slit throats, stranglings, shootings, hypnotic suggestions of suicide. More gruesome still are the deaths of the malevolent sources:

> Peter brought the knife down into Fenny's chest. Something white and foul exploded upward, a reeking geyser, from Fenny's ribcage. . . . Small white worms swam across the white skin. . . . Don hurriedly raised the axe over his head and brought the sharpened blade down into Bate's neck, cutting down deeply into the chest. With the next blow he severed his head.

Death, protracted and vivid, counterbalances the fear of evil. The novel ends with the possibility that other fears will have to be killed, but, in the context of *Ghost Story*, such evils are destroyed as surely as imaginative man could do it.

In part, *Ghost Story* is built around the guilt of five pillars of Milburn society. Fifty years ago five young men killed Eva Galli, a mysterious, wealthy, aristocratic, young girl of their dreams, who transformed herself into a succubus. The murder was not intentional, but murder was done. To save themselves from public embarrassment and possible imprisonment, the five men hid the body in a borrowed car and pushed it into a deep pond. When the car sank, Eva Galli resurrected herself to peer at her murderers through the back window. As the car sank, she vanished; across the pond a lynx stared knowingly at the guilty men, and then it too vanished. The men had killed one dream only to be haunted forever by another.

For fifty years guilt and fear possessed the five men who formed the Chowder Society, a group of friendly raconteurs who met biweekly to frighten each other with ghost stories, though never with more than a mention of the murder of Eva Galli. Her return in various shapes and disguises throughout fifty years testifies to the individual and collective fears of the Chowder Society. When their fears reach the point of frightening them to death, when they believe St. Augustine's truth that "fear itself is an evil thing," an author arrives to initiate their quest for the source of fear, the source of the evil that has surrounded and stifled them. Belief in evil's reality, and its power, persuasion, and presence, is the principal weapon against the embodiment of evil. *Ghost Story* tells the story of the courageous men who battle evil with the weapon of belief. Their persistence restrains the horrors from being merely ghoulish. The Chowder Society learns Augustine's truth that "by evil the heart is driven and tormented for no cause." It sees, ultimately, the truth of Eva Galli's mystery of evil: "I am you."

Amid the defeat of the ghosts of fear and evil, Straub does what he set out to do: "To take the classic elements of the horror novel as far as they could go." He abridges and modernizes *The Turn of the Screw*, several short stories by Hawthorne, as well as images and motifs from Irving, Poe, and Dickens. But the whole is much more than a pastiche of parts. Through hallucinations and dreams and morbid psychology, Straub disproves the theory that "nothing is, in fact, what it seems to be." The fiction becomes facts that require not merely a willing suspension of disbelief but belief. An elderly lawyer explains the theory behind the fiction by saying:

> We're all frightened. . . . when all of us were joined by Don, the forces, whatever you want to call them, we increased. . . . we invoked them. We by our stories, Don in his book and in his imagination. We see things, but we don't believe them; we feel things—people watching us, sinister things following us— but we dismiss them as fantasies. We dream horrors, but try to forget them. And in the meantime, three people have died.

By the novel's end, over twenty people die, but the number doesn't matter. What does matter is that archetypal evil, like that found in the first garden of the biblical Eden, has answered Straub's invocation to manifest itself. Evil reveals itself in the horrors of the worst blizzard in the history of Milburn and in the terrors buried deep in the hearts of guilty men; mutilation and murder match the cause. At the end of the novel, the implied author explains the sinister prologue by killing (or at least wounding) a wasp that just before was Dr. Rabbitfoot, a character in his own novel; his own created character proves to be the haunting friend of his dead brother and of his one-time lover; all these ghosts are provoked by the persona's kidnapping of a friendless nine-year-old girl in a park, a child controlled by another woman and another author—Peter Straub himself. The levels of evil, like those of this imaginative fiction, require several readings, more than most

casual readers would give, but here at least Peter Straub was more interested in his art than in his readership. *Ghost Story* may be his greatest credit.

Back in Connecticut, Straub rushed to finish *Shadow Land* (1980), which his eager publisher advertised before it was completed. *Ghost Story* predicted a continuing stream of popular best-sellers, but *Shadow Land* disappointed the publisher and confused an audience expecting ghoulish ghosts. From successful dabbling in evil in *Ghost Story*, Straub turned to the mysteries of magic and fairy tales in a land of shadows, where "everything is a lie. . . . just because you saw it doesn't mean it really happened." *Shadow Land* is a tale of "radical illusions—the speeding of time, the transformations and sudden dislocations of space." The story is presumably told in the Zanzibar, a Los Angeles nightclub on Sunset Strip, by Tom Flanagan to a nameless novelist, obviously Peter Straub himself. Tom recounts a year at an Arizona prep school and a summer at a magician's Vermont home, both shadowy confusions of fairy tales, mental gymnastics, magic, sadism, and madness. Many of the mysteries resolve themselves in the master magician's evil, "that flabby jealous devil of the second-rate." Coleman Collins's repeated magic became "so warped by hate and greed" that he would "steal and kill, cheat and tyrannize anyone less powerful." In effect, Coleman Collins, once a famous magician, murdered the parents of his nephew Del Nightingale for money and for the possession of Del, Tom Flanagan's best friend. Later, Tom, with powers greater than either Collins's or Del's, saves himself and his friend from the mad magician and from torments only magic or fairy tales could perpetrate.

The novel seems more nightmare than reality despite concrete references to masters of horrors— Scott, Irving, Lewis, Shelley, or Poe—and to the Brothers Grimm, who admit that they have shown the world "a terror full of wonder," a particular kind of unreal reality. Prophecy and telepathy, use and misuse of sleights of hand and mind convert a strange Arizona prep school and a Vermont home into a platonic inversion where every shadow seems substance. The real magician is, of course, Straub himself, the novelist who, like a magician, "is a general with an army full of deserters and traitors. To keep their loyalty, he must inspire and entertain, frighten and cajole, baffle and command. And when he has done that, he can lead them." Straub has some difficulty leading readers through the horrors of crucifixion of a teenage boy or the hideousness of dogs chasing badgers to bloody death, but the shadows are still more terrifying than the reality, and that is what Straub intended to prove.

His critics note, usually with dismay, a proliferation of flashbacks and anticipations of narrative adventure, unspeakable horrors, and a taste for blood. Many remark that the model provided by Stephen King leads Straub away from story into merely ghoulish effects. But Christopher Lehmann-Haupt of the *New York Times* speaks wisely when he says that the story of "a boy doing battle with a powerful king" keeps Straub from failure. Here Straub creates and dissolves illusions, fulfilling the promise of his poem "Wolf's Litany": "I honor the harshness of evening and the blunt curtain of shadow."

More shadows follow *Shadow Land* in *Floating Dragon*, a novel set near Straub's Connecticut home, where he admits that he and his wife became depressed by suburbia "like repressed, rebellious children." As if in retaliation to the stultifying atmosphere around him, Straub learned the history of Fairfield County and created a compendium of horrors designed to punish the shallow housewives, adulterers, corporate tycoons, and even the children in a commuter community with a history of periodic terrors.

The novel tells of two dragons over and in Hampstead, Connecticut: one is natural, the lethal DRG-16, a chemical warfare gas that stuns some victims and kills others; the other is supernatural, an actual dragon, the devil that has periodically scourged the area with death or destruction. Graham Williams, the implied author, joins forces with three of the most improbable and imaginative of heroes to fulfill the promise of Revelation 20:2, the last words of the novel: "And he laid hold on the dragon, that old serpent, which is the devil, and bound him a thousand years." Countless incarnations of devils with protean and tireless wiles have held the people of Hampstead in bondage since Patchin County was settled three hundred years ago. The heroes reconstruct the roster of evil names and deeds from memory and official histories of the county as they build their faith and telepathic strength to battle the unbelievable source of Patchin's terrors.

By Straub's own admission, the terrors challenge readers' imaginations. From the natural dragon distributing itself across the landscape, people die of unforeseen heart attacks and leaking skin. Some people are murdered by a psychopathic doctor or their own bad memory of thoughtless unkindness. The weak succumb to suicide: a policeman "pushed the barrel into his mouth and bit

down on the front sight. Then he pulled the trigger and the back of his head exploded over the rear window and the top of the car." At least seven children drown themselves near the beach and appear as cold ghosts at their bereft mothers' bedsides. An executive of the chemical company responsible for the natural dragon dies an unseemly death as a leaker in a New York tenement where his last sight is illicit sex: "White froth scattered across the room like blown suds. . . . the frothy white substance poured out of the wrecked bandages. In ten minutes Leo Friedgood was an arrangement of wet clothes, shiny bone, and a damp spaghetti of bandages in a pool of slime." The four heroes gifted with second sight and kinesthesia, intuition and imagination, strong minds and morals witness theft, adultery, sadism, and vandalism; see physical evils of suffering, death, and disease; and decide that they must conquer metaphysical evil.

The causes of death become deliberately confused as horrors multiply in number and kind. The dread becomes phantasmal, part of a grave disorder of reality. Ghosts lure the living into death's safety and relative health. The minds of ordinary people lurch into the future or lunge into the past as hate becomes love and love becomes hate. Dreams become reality and reality dreams as fires scourge homes, maps, memory, and as mad dogs, bats, and flies attack even the heroes. The crescendo of horrors builds to an explosive pitch at an increasingly rapid pace; only cosmic and otherworldly "realms of existence, realms of being" beyond anything known before can match the terror.

Then in a stunning climax the shape-shifting devil appears and attacks. A "dark form" with long ears, hooked nose, thick chin, and goat legs takes on a massive tail, long jaw, spiked snout, and "malevolent eyes encased in bone." The dragon roars from the depths of its cave, and, after an amalgamation of religious and psychic forces, finally succumbs to the magic, the myths, and the religious sword of salvation hefted by an improbable human hero. Graham Williams tries repeatedly to explain the whole of the mystery, but all he can do is describe the horrors. Instead of theorizing, he records what he and the other heroes saw, felt, and thought. The result is compelling, haunting, and every bit convincing for the reader capable of the willing suspension of disbelief.

In *Floating Dragon*, Peter Straub speaks of the unspeakable, matching a complexity of form with a complexity of substance in an extension of the rich traditions of horror fiction. His critics may not understand his responsible merging of psychic and

religious responses to cosmic evil and its many horrifying effects, but his readers can and do. Both
readers and critics hear echoes of King in the chem-
ical-industrial disaster (*The Stand*), mad dog (*Cujo*),
psychological evil (*The Shining*), precognition (*The
Dead Zone*), and psychokinesis (*Firestarter*), but
Straub's prose style and historical structure distinguish him from Stephen King.

    The Talisman, already bought by Stephen
Spielberg, contains more inside jokes between Peter
Straub and Stephen King than thoughtful organization or economical prose. They define the novel
as fantasy rather than horror fiction, and they
admit that the tone "is a little bit delirious and sort
of crack-brained." Within the picaresque story,
Straub and King borrow characters, devices, and
settings from a host of contemporary novelists, children's stories, and fairy tales. Playfully chiding
other writers, Straub and King name a sadistic
evangelist Sunlight Gardener and an evil employer
Smokey Updike; in honor of John Irving the novel
begins at a New Hampshire hotel. The protagonist,
a twelve-year-old called Jack Sawyer, mixes measures of Tom Sawyer and Jack of beanstalk fame
with Dorothy from *The Wizard of Oz*. Jack Sawyer's
purpose is to save his mother from death by lung
cancer by finding and bringing back the Talisman,
an object strange and magical, pulsing with healing
powers in an abandoned California hotel. The journey from New Hampshire to California is facilitated
by fanciful flipping from modern America and its
unintelligible burdens to "The Territories," a condensed medieval world peopled by monomaniacs
and werewolves and a dying queen markedly like
Jack's mother. The journey takes hitchhiking Jack
through the trials and tribulations of most adolescent boys as well as through the "blasted lands" of
nuclear holocaust. He spends considerable time at a
perverse school for boys where evangelization
works by sadism, and where a werewolf from "The
Territories," a kind of cowardly lion from Oz, dies
saving Jack. An old black traveling jazz musician
named Speedy Parker resembles the scarecrow in
Oz, and the Tin Woodman is a rational young boy
named Richard Sloat.

    The exchanges between Richard and Jack
might have been between King and Straub. Jack
asks his childhood friend, "Don't you want just a
little magic, Richard?" And Richard responds as
King might to Straub, "You know, sometimes I
think you just want chaos. . . . I think you're making fun of me. If you want magic, you completely
wreck everything I believe in. In fact you wreck
reality." Jack's counter provides the heart of the

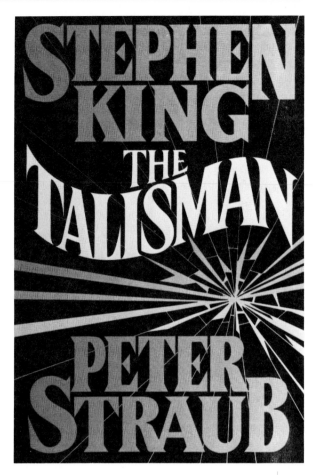

*Dust jacket for Peter Straub's bestselling 1984 collaboration with
Stephen King*

fiction: "Maybe there isn't just one reality." There is
so little reality in this fiction that *The Talisman* seems
more nearly a jeu d'esprit than a novel at all.

    Jack gradually realizes the truth of his father's
victimization and murder by his partner Morgan
Sloat, a "blight spirit," Richard's greedy, evil father.
Richard eventually understands the difficult truth
himself, but not without suffering from his father's
wiles. Only the magic of the Talisman can heal the
rational son who is maimed by adolescent acne and
worse:

> Blood was running from his nose. When he
> got closer he saw that some of those hard red
> bumps had split open and white bugs were
> working their way out of Richard's flesh and
> crawling sluggishly over Richard's cheeks. As
> [Jack] watched, one birthed itself from
> Richard's nose. . . . His shirt humped and
> writhed with the things.

Later there is a stench "as the bugs beneath the

Talisman fried away." Without the Talisman, a judge commits suicide rather than go to jail for killing boys committed to the Sunlight Home. The act is an afterthought:

> He had remained as cheerful as possible under the circumstances, but now, as he sat cleaning his fingernails with the long blade of his pocket-knife in his study at home, a great gray wave of depression crashed over him. Suddenly he pulled the knife away from his thick nails, looked at it thoughtfully for a moment, and then inserted the tip of the blade into his right nostril. He held it there for a moment and then whispered, "Oh shit, Why not?" He jerked his fist upward, sending the six-inch blade on a short, lethal trip, skewering first his sinuses and then his brain.

The healing of the good and the punishment of the bad is the Talisman's business. Jack Sawyer survives cruelties more grim than any in Straub's earlier fiction, and he possesses more courage and love than Dorothy ever had. But the imbalance between his goodness and valor and the grisly horrors he endures or witnesses gives violence its own patterns, gratuitous ones. The werewolf does not merely save Jack, he punishes with vengeance:

> Wolf twisted Sonny's arm. There was a ripping sound, the sound of a turkey drumstick being torn from the cooked bird by an over-enthusiastic child. Suddenly Sonny's arm was in Wolf's big paw. Sonny staggered away, blood jetting from his shoulder. Jack saw a wet white knob of bone. He turned away and was violently sick.

The reader is too after a siege of bloody hands, smashed heads, clawed backs exposing the spine "like a bloody extension cord." Gore splashed on walls from humans and wolf alike in a bloody war of worlds that oppose one another for little or no reason. Imaginative goodness does eventually heal the mother for whom the search for the Talisman began, but even her appearance violates the sense of necessary realism. Jack finds her

> crumpled like a candy wrapper under the window. Thin and lank, her hair trailed on the room's dirty carpet. Her hands seemed like tiny animal paws, pale and scrabbling. . . . Her hair puddled on the grimy carpet, her small knotty hands. . . . Her hair felt full of sand and her head was burning. . . . Through her flimsy nightgown her hip felt as hot as the door of a stove. Against his other palm, her left shoulderblade pulsed with an equal warmth. She had no comfortable pads of flesh over her bones—for a mad second of stopped time it was as though she were a small dirty child somehow left ill and alone. . . . One of her arms dangles before him like a reed meant to be cut in half by a scythe.

The images of death may be real, but the comparisons to animal paws, the door of a stove, and a reed ready for cutting diminish the pathos with dirt, grime, sand, and the forced repetitions of language pushing beyond ability. The moment of healing, protracted by insensibility rather than emotion, resolves itself by Jack's mother becoming the Talisman itself for a moment before it vanishes. Lily Cavanaugh, a grade-B actress, is magically restored by the Talisman in "the gray-golden cloud" that lengthens itself over the mother's body, "coating her in a translucent but slightly opaque, delicate moving membrane. . . . from an opening in the Talisman. . . . like a vagina." Being literally reborn may be the intent, but the Talisman is too vague, too confusing, and too improbable to counter the real horrors of sickness, death, and evil.

The Talisman itself is "a crystal globe perhaps three feet in circumference," a size easily carried by car from California to New Hampshire. But it is also described as *the world—ALL worlds—in microcosm. More; it is the axis of all possible worlds.* Its power defies definition by words; artificial emphases of full caps and italics cannot describe it either. Although the Talisman sings, turns, and blazes with "clear white radiance that was all colors—sunrise colors, sunset colors, *rainbow* colors," it remains unrealized. Perhaps if Straub had had his more metaphysical way with the surrealism, the Talisman would have had philosophical or historical or religious parallels that would do it justice. But in the fantastic world of *The Talisman* the object of the quest seems a bit silly. For good reason, the Talisman vanishes at the novel's end; the Queen of the Territories opens her eyes; Mark Twain gives the epilogue; Peter Straub and Stephen King have had their fun. When Straub reclaims his narrative authority, his next fiction will continue to fulfill his artistic promise; he will then have more than the magic sales of *The Talisman*.

References:
Andree Hickok, "Peter Straub: Master of Horror," (Bridgeport, Conn.), *Sunday Post,* 24 April 1983, E1, E8;

Anna Shapiro, review of *The Talisman,* in *New York Times Book Review,* 28 October 1984, p. 28;
Stanley Wiater, "Titans of Terror," *Valley Advocate,* 31 October 1984, pp. 1, A9-10.

Lewis Turco
(2 May 1934-   )

Mary Doll

BOOKS: *First Poems* (Francestown, N.H.: Golden Quill, 1960);

The Sketches of Lewis Turco and Livevil: A Mask (Cleveland: American Weave Press, 1962);

Awaken, Bells Falling: Poems 1959-1967 (Columbia: University of Missouri Press, 1968);

The Book of Forms: A Handbook of Poetics (New York: Dutton, 1968);

The Inhabitant (Northampton, Mass.: Despa Press, 1970);

The Literature of New York: A Selective Bibliography of Colonial and Native New York State Authors (Oneonta, N.Y.: New York State English Council, 1970);

Pocoangelini: A Fantography and Other Poems (Northampton, Mass.: Despa, 1971);

Poetry: An Introduction Through Writing (Reston, Va.: Reston Publishing Company, 1973);

The Weed Garden (Orangeburg, S.C.: Peaceweed Press, 1973);

Seasons of the Blood (Rochester, N.Y.: Mammoth Press, 1980);

American Still Lifes (Oswego, N.Y.: Mathom, 1981);

The Compleat Melancholick (Minneapolis: Bieler Press, 1985).

PLAYS: *Dreams of Stone and Sun,* May 1959, Harriet Jorgensen Little Theater, Storrs, Conn.;

The Elections Last Fall, December 1969, Experimental Theater, State University of New York at Oswego.

PERIODICAL PUBLICATIONS:
FICTION
"The Man in the Booth," *Ploughshares,* 10 (Special 1984 issue).

NONFICTION
"The Hillsdale Epistles," *Carleton Miscellany,* 7 (Summer 1966): 17-32;

"*The Wasteland* Reconsidered," *Sewanee Review,* 87 (Spring 1979): 289-295.

POETRY
"At Home," *Sewanee Review,* 67 (1959): 638;

"An Open Letter to Leroi Jones," *New York Times Magazine,* 25 May 1969, pp. 118;

"The Day the Shed Came Apart," *Yale Review,* 37 (January 1984): 307;

"Memory," *Nation,* 238 (21 April 1984): 490;

"Recollections XI," *Hudson Review,* 37 (Spring 1984): 86.

Lewis Putnam Turco was born in Buffalo, New York, to Luigi and May (Putnam) Turco and raised in Meriden, Connecticut, where he attended public schools and Suffield Academy. After graduation he joined the navy world cruise of the aircraft carrier *Hornet* and, at the age of nineteen, began his career as a poet. One of his earliest critics, in advising the young poet against the confessional mode, shaped two characteristics of his work: experimentation with poetry as craft, and the development of poetic voice.

After his honorable discharge from the service, Turco attended the University of Connecticut, studying under John Malcolm Brinnin, and went on to receive his Master's from the University of Iowa, where he studied with Paul Engle and Donald Justice. Since 1965 he has taught at the State University College of New York at Oswego, where he is Professor of English and Director of the Program in Writing Arts.

As a teaching writer, Turco has had his work recognized with residencies in both poetry and fic-

Lewis Turco (Mary Jo O'Shea)

tion at Yaddo, as a poetry fellow at Bread Loaf Writers' Conference, with research grants from the SUNY research foundation, with a Book Club for Poetry selection, a chapbook award, and, most recently, with his selection as a faculty exchange scholar throughout the university system of New York State. He and his wife Jean have two children, Melora Ann and Christopher Cameron.

Those familiar with Turco's writing agree that it presents a world both like and not like our own. Its fascination lies in its ambiguity, true to the promptings of inner life. Ray Bradbury has said, "Everything he writes about in *The Inhabitant* is part of my own real or remembered world." The poet Philip Booth has commented, " 'The Ferry' crosses me over to wherever it is that all true poems tug and pull." And the American literary critic Hyatt H. Waggoner has compared Turco's worlds to Emerson's "forms," saying that "he is really, it seems to me, doing what Emerson meant by 'sharing the circuit of things through forms,' making the forms . . . translucid so the light can shine through."

Critics of Turco's earlier work, however, focused less on its presentment of psychological truths than on its preoccupation with technique.

For some, Turco's experiments with language and form got in the way of the poem itself, making the work seem marked by "easy virtuosity." For others, Turco's world was too static. As Henry Carlile put it, "Turco has a fondness for negative declarations which tend almost to negate themselves in the process. . . . one might ask: if nothing is happening, why write about it?"

These criticisms stem, in part, from Turco's interest in language as substance, to be molded so as to produce layers of sensory impressions. With a keen ear for language and a delight in old words, he was in many instances producing poems that were, as William Heyen said, "too stiff, metrically, or too pretty, or too ingenious, or too heavily moral and wise." Perhaps in response to these comments, Lewis Turco created an alter ego, "Wesli Court," an anagram of his own name. As a traditional versifier, Court could publish as many metrically "correct," formalistically clever works as Turco desired. One book of poems, two chapbooks, and one children's story have been published to Wesli Court's credit.

But the other area of concern to critics—Turco's still worlds—relates to his new and different sensibility. This is a sensibility that reveals not human subjects and ego consciousness so much as a live quality in objects and nature. In his best work, Turco shows what it is to "see through a glass, darkly" from the other side. The critic who is firmly planted in Aristotelian poetics will have difficulty adjusting to this nonmimetic, nonexpressive universe. And yet, as Bradbury, Booth, and Waggoner among others have noted, this "other" world brings us closer to our own psychic depths in a way akin to Emerson or to the Zen poet. In defining the Zen poet in his college text *Poetry: An Introduction, Through Writing* (1973) Turco could well be offering a definition of his own poetic voice. The Zen poet, he writes, "is attempting to put himself into the place of the thing perceived—he is empathizing with the object; more, he is trying to *become* one with the object."

First Poems (1960), a selection of the Book Club for Poetry, contains pieces that were written during Turco's navy and undergraduate years and reveals his musical ear for language. As Donald Justice, in his foreword, comments: "reading this book is a little like listening to a gifted musician practicing scales, arpeggios, and the sonatas of Clementi."

Divided into three sections with a total of thirty-eight poems, the book shows a range of technique and imagination that marks the later work as well. "Dirge à la Dylan" is a clear illustration of Turco's fondness for the sound of words. His ear for Dylan Thomas's sensual playfulness can be heard in the opening stanza: "When I was a curled boy, short and long-/shadowed beneath an apple moon,/I peeled my dreams out of cider skies/and toasted them crisp each fiery noon."

A less derivative poem is "Chant of Seasons," which allows the singing voice to emerge with sadness. The stanza on the season of fall is remarkable for its compactness of sound and theme:

> What of the time when fall's returned—
>   When fall's returned?
> Then listen to the wind and leaves
> During the night: the day deceives.
>   Beyond the frosts there is discerned
>   The womb's within which death conceives,
>   When fall's returned.

Here is Turco's most meditated-upon season, fall, with all of its amplified meanings. The theme of cyclical time as opposed to linear time sets up a Romantic dichotomy between nature and man, eternity and mortality. Imbedded in "Fall" is also the Judeo-Christian idea of Adam's fall through Eve: of the burden man must bear because of

woman's womb "within which death conceives." Even in this early chant of the seasons, Turco shows signs of attempting to breach the gap of traditional oppositions posed by a Romantic imagination. By going beyond fall to winter, with its "bold immensity of snow," he allows his poetic imagination to play with cold, to "grant bone a glimpse of the abstruse/*Finis* that it must undergo. . . ."

Aside from its pivotal effect on human time, fall also connotes to Turco the pivot point between intellect and imagination, as in the beginning of academic life each fall semester. In "Poems for an Old Professor," a series of four poems which Richard Eberhart said showed Turco's profundity, the poet again sets up categorical oppositions. Here, the old, dry life of an academic professor who teaches Milton is juxtaposed against the imagined chance for a new life offered from Milton's text by Eve. The old professor represents routine: all that which can be delegated to keeping meaning clear, explicated within the bounds of written texts. But Eve represents ritual. Her "deplorable behavior" is the text of lived experience—the poetry of life that lies between the lines. The professor, in his quest for clarity, is in a sense deconstructed by the very text he manipulates. What is, in the classroom and for the professor, an academic search for intellectual meaning becomes, in the poem, an opportunity to search for the lost paradise of male consciousness.

One theme in *First Poems* has been consistent throughout all of Turco's work, the theme of seeing. Mirrors, glass, pools, water, eyes are frequent images; and the myth of Narcissus, with its motif of seeing the reflected self, is a recurring myth. Talking about his own convictions in what could be a gloss of this theme, Turco said in a recent interview: "I believe it is only possible for a person to define himself in terms of others, and one sees oneself reflected in the eyes and actions of others. I believe that one sees oneself most clearly mirrored in the people and things that surround one."

"Street Meeting" exemplifies this credo perfectly. Two people meet after years of separation. While their words are platitudes, their eyes are pools for self-understanding. By seeing loneliness and loss in another's eyes, the narrator transcends ego consciousness to glimpse something of the existential depths of the human psyche: "We departed knowing/Till next we met our prisons would keep growing."

In what remains the most perceptive critical comment to date of Turco's work, Stanley Romaine Hopper praised "Street Meeting" for the release of what he called "poetical meaning." He said that "subordinating the persons to the deeper meaning of events, and by fusing the contradictory elements in the language . . . the 'poetical' meaning of the encounter is made to emerge." Hopper recognized early on in Turco's work what has become perhaps its unique poetic quality: the elevation of psychological over personal truths.

In *Awaken, Bells Falling* (1968), Turco's second collection, a trend toward an ever-deepening psychological vision is evident. John Ciardi praised Turco's "gift of seeing things"; Richard Eberhart commented on his "shrewd eye on the world"; and Mary Oliver had this to say: "In building his poems Mr. Turco has a gift for the exciting image—a way of combining objects from different existences that helps us to see sharply and freshly."

These observations about seeing and objects suggest that by the late 1960s Turco had found the theme and images necessary for the poetic voice he was developing. Some poems, however, still evidenced an infatuation with verbal dance, as in "The Forest of My Seasons." A sestina, with six end-words of the first stanza repeated in particular order for the next five stanzas, it uses as basic building blocks important Turco words: *snow, wind, horns, woods, can,* and *shade*. But because sonics and puns are allowed to overtake meaning, the poem seems more the work of Wesli Court mocking poetic formalistic tradition.

Not so "The Professor and the Sphinx," originally published in *Northwest Review* and reprinted in *The Best Poems of 1965: Borestone Mountain Poetry Awards* (Palo Alto: Pacific Books, 1966). Here Turco's paradoxical imagination is felt. He ponders again the dilemma of the professor who has a poet's soul ("a phoenix nesting in my skull") whose work with words seems lifeless. This he contrasts with a forgotten power within language, known by our ancestors, by Oriental art, and by poetry: "I know the poems on my shelves speak with/one another in an/ancient language I have somehow forgotten." For a poet-professor caught in the desert of academe, the challenge is to unlock language's hidden magic. Turco's extended metaphor of Egypt illuminates the richness of the idea of silent speakings.

"The Old Professor and the Sphinx" marks a turning point in Turco's development as a poet. By moving away from form toward a concentrated use of touchstone words, Turco permits the words themselves to release what Hopper referred to as "poetic meaning," fusing sound, form, and idea. In the juxtaposition of *professor* with *sphinx*, Turco is

really suggesting that his function as a poet is like that of the archeologist, digging down beneath surfaces, exhuming meaning from hidden depths. In such a way, the professor discovers what the poet knows: the hermetic roots of language.

Integral to such a shift toward word-conjuring is the development of voice. Increasingly, what speaks in a Turco poem is a consciousness of objects and nature. *Awaken, Bells Falling* is a hauntingly distanced work where the *It* rather than the *I* is evoked. As William Heyen remarked, "The sensibility behind these poems is willing to allow its subjects to Be rather than constantly Become." "School Drawing" and "Mice in the Sunday Walls" are two fine examples. In the former, the poet meditates on his daughter's crayoned drawing. He sees a surrealistic world containing only a road, a windmill, and a crayoned sun. There is no connection among the objects; they just are. But by using his poet's imagination to see through images, to find meaning *only* in images, he allows the power of imagistic statement to emerge: "It is burning/and there is no wind."

"Mice in the Sunday Walls" also focuses on the nonhuman world. Again, a paradox of speaking-silence presents itself. The situation juxtaposes human noncommunication with nonhuman speech: "Sunday's trap is set for us to trigger/The doorbell. The door. The whole hall hungry/its yellow stairs snapping at our laces." The poet's duty-call on Sundays reveals a strong sense of nothingness: "nowhere to go, nothing to see, little to do/here in childhood's hall of mirrors." And yet, as in a Frost poem, the bleakness of such blank horizons where one reflects neither "too deeply. Nor far" provokes insight. The point is that silence prompts the *things* of the world to present themselves to the eye of the beholder.

Although *The Inhabitant* (1970) was Turco's next published work, *Pocoangelini: A Fantography and Other Poems* (1971) was written first. In tone, the Poco poems represent a departure from the objective perspective discussed above. Through the guise of a madcap trickster figure named Pocoangelini, these poems show Turco's earlier Romantic themes from an upside-down point of view. Such serious ideas as death, time, darkness, and silence are turned into comic songs. Poco allows Turco to imagine his dark themes differently.

One manifestation of this difference is the arrangement of poems into series. Forty-two separate poems, with a prologue and epilogue, constitute the work, suggesting that the voice of Poco is not unilateral, but various and that truth has many

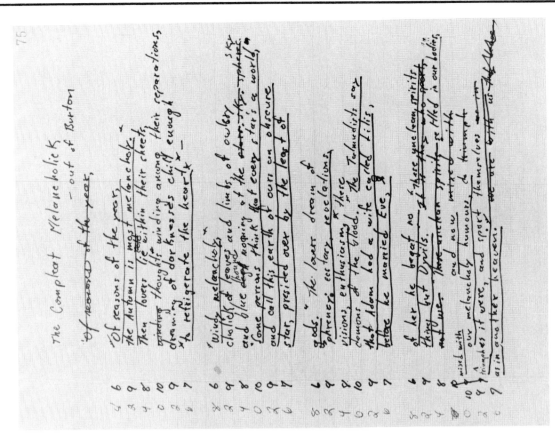

Lewis Turco's notes for a book and working manuscript for a poem (the author)

voices. The effect this has on the reader's understanding of character is profound. For what Turco shows is a non-Aristotelian character type who resists the demands of plot and linear development. As in the tradition of the fool or the trickster, Poco's character can never fully be revealed: that is his triumph over time.

Turco's delight in the imagination is evident in the Poco poems by the breadth of adventures, dialogues, and soliloquies of his character. In #28, for example, Poco assumes the voice of Pan: musical, sensual, natural: "If my song wears an old blanket/it hides young fleas./My hoof plucks no mandolin./Listen to this tune, hairy as a donkey." He is nature and nature is he: "spearing/the grottoes between his toes" (#25). Imagination can, just as equally, picture winter as Pan—"that old man with hooves" who can be seen "goring the white air," and "tearing shreds/out of the moon" (#29). To be able to imagine coldness with precision is a feat of such psychological triumph that Poco can "thrust his tongue" at it and all it connotes.

These flights of fancy give wing, as well, to the dark themes. Poco is not grounded in literal reality, like some flatfoot cop (#10) or like a Western male hero—Adam, say, or Mars, or Odysseus, or the unnamed male quester, a conglomerate of all three, who, in #21, is a victim of his own tunnel vision, unable to see deeply or to find the hidden treasures of language. This antihero, Poco sees, uses language as a weapon: "Glib/rolled words in his hand—a journal/held like a gun," hoping thus to kill off the monsters of darkness. But Pocoangelini, as trickster, fool, or angel, is charactered from the imagination, which can both "see" the dark and "hear" the silence:

Pocoangelini's house has wings
 lining its walls,
dark eyes that see in the dark—
 darts, feathering calls
 in the pine halls;
grass and the smell of seed,
 the spider's net
stretched from shadow to shade
 to catch the owl's saw-whet
 voice in a sunset
tangle of silk. The night
 is a great falcon
circling the weathervane,
 ears tuned to the unbroken
 silence, the word unspoken.

With *Pocoangelini*, and certainly with the other

series poems in that collection—*The Sketches* and *Bordello*—Turco was working with voice. The various speakers are Others: Guido the ice-house man, Uncle Larry, Miss Mary Belle. They are Hank Fedder or Lafe Grat. They are not the poet. By donning a mask of the Other, in the manner of E. A. Robinson or Edgar Lee Masters, Turco was developing the voices of America, finding in them a more general expression of the human condition than that afforded by any narrow personal idiom.

The Inhabitant continues and deepens this search for voice. Here Turco finds a symbolic structure, the house, entirely consistent with what was becoming a poetics of the psyche. For Freud and Jung alike, the house is symbolic of the self with its arrangement of upper and lower floors corresponding to conscious and unconscious layers of the psyche. Turco makes use of this symbol in *The Inhabitant* in order to show that his unnamed quester inhabits a structure, himself, that is multilayered, mysterious, yet capable of transformation.

In this series of poems, the title refers to the self's search for home in a house where each room makes its appeal. As he moves through doors the Inhabitant journeys deeper into his own secret places, discovering "mathoms" (useless treasures) in the attic and monsters in the basement. He is a listener and a watcher—a stranger inside his own habitation. But because he wanders, listens, and sees, the Inhabitant is able to discover how to dwell with darkness. The seven-part concluding poem called "The Dwelling House" reworks the Genesis story with the suggestion that, through sensory awakening, man can be molded anew.

That Turco intended his vision to be psychological is clear. "Poetry is capable," he said recently, "of touching the deepest portions of the human psyche. . . . We are still after our deeper selves, and poetry, . . . has always been capable of getting into these levels of existence, of being, and making them conscious." *The Inhabitant*, a conscious creation of the psychological dimension of poetry, is also a poetic conjuring of the first order.

Nor is it accidental that *The Inhabitant* is illustrated. Fourteen prints by the artist Thomas Seawell accompany the poems. Visual and verbal image combine to draw the reader's eye ever more into focus on the things of life. Through focusing on the objective image, imagination awakens and the soul is born.

"The Kitchen" is one example of how life's particulars speak to the male psyche. The Inhabitant, in the kitchen with his wife and daughter, is the only one who tunes into the sounds of the dishwasher's "hum and bite." Its cycle suggests to his ears the cycle of life:

> Each cup has its voice, each saucer its ear, and
>   the thin chant planes between the shelves,
>   touching the timbres of glass and crystal
>   as it passes. The gentleman listens, is
>   touched to the bone by this plainsong—
>   he feels his response in the marrow's keening.

For Turco, men—not women—feel their mortality: in the ear, in the bone. Their senses are "keener," but as in the pun, this only makes them mourn their fate. Women, progenitors of the human life cycle, are oblivious to sound's sense: "But the women do not—either the elder nor the child—sense the music their things make." And fate is literally in the hands of women who, like their mythic counterparts, are spinners and weavers of the threads of life, in whose web the human condition is caught. The poem's circular ending—there is a return to the sound of the dishwasher—fuses form with theme in a subtly interesting way. The poet shows that even the closed cycle of life can have its musical dance.

Other poems in the series bring out the psychomythic undertone of The Inhabitant's searchings, making them, as Conrad Aiken remarked, a poetry of "whole meaning." The Inhabitant's descent down the basement stairs to retrieve his daughter's doll becomes a descent into "silence spinning." In his search for lost treasure the Inhabitant is like Orpheus, whose visit to retrieve Eurydice from Hades reveals myth's fear of sight's power. "Turning to look" is prohibited. The Inhabitant's mission is fraught with this dread importance: "do not glance back nor at the ragged doll or she shall be left at the stairhead beneath the writhing mop, and the wheel will begin to spin, its voice to whine—the webs will net dust in the billowing corners when night goes out." The treasures one puts one's eyes on are both life-sustaining and life-threatening, equally.

Turco's concentration in "The Looking-Glass" is also on the eye as window to the soul. Invoking Narcissus and the phoenix, he provides an arresting image of eye preening in its vision. The image suggests an insight into the Narcissus myth: that to fall in love with one's reflected vision is not the same thing as to fall in love with one's face. Rather, one loves image. To preen *thus* is to be transported to another place of being and so, transformed:

> and there lying in
>   its circle
>
> of smooth things the
>   eye preens
>
> in its own vision
>   before it
>
> rakes the wind again
>   and rises
>
> into the sun the
>   fierce air.

The mythic spiritualism of *The Inhabitant*, which Conrad Aiken described enthusiastically as "the best new poem I've read in something like thirty years," is carried even deeper in *American Still Lifes* (1981). What emerges is an increasingly translucent vision, where the eye is in all things. As William Heyen noted, Turco was moving his poetry into "the stillpoint." Hyatt H. Waggoner, in commenting on Emerson's notion of the true poet, implied that Turco's insights were guided by a true poet's sense of imagination, which "does not come by study, but by the intellect being where and what it sees."

Both Heyen's and Waggoner's remarks were made in reference to a chapbook, *The Weed Garden*, (1973), whose title poem was reprinted in *Best Poems of 1971: Borestone Mountain Poetry Awards* (Palo Alto: Pacific Books, 1972). Both it and another chapbook, *Seasons of the Blood* (1980), can be considered preparing ground for *American Still Lifes*. In *Seasons*, particularly, the poet's use of Japanese forms—the mondo, katauta, sedoka, haiku, and senryu among others—encouraged a dialectical Western mind to ponder the virtues of Eastern paradox. The Japanese basic unit of three lines was the perfect vehicle for Turco, who was building his poetry more and more around imagery and sensory impression.

American Still Lifes contains three sections: "Twelve Moons," "Still Lifes," and "Autumn's Tales." Together they provide a kind of Eastern response to the West's problem with time as history or mortality. In their celebration of imagination's eternity, the poems represent an artistic and personal triumph for Turco, whose struggle with the theme of death finds reconciliation here in a timelessness of the senses trained to listen to stillness. All of nature becomes Turco's reflecting pool: darkness "sings" and silence "is hanging fire behind the moon." Nature's world creates strong sensory impressions in flame, wind, and the whickering of horses. Against these particulars human life is stilled, made to become but a part of larger cyclical patterns.

"Twelve Moons," for example, sets a tone of biding or waiting. The theme retells the idea of the Fall of Man; but Turco, in playing with the theme, opens the idea out to reveal its rich substructures. Fall is lived, experienced, sensed, not just understood as a doctrine of sin and redemption. Almost every poem, indeed, employs the word *fall*. Light falls, shadows fall, fish and seagulls fall; a chestnut falls. There is snowfall and footfall. Evening falls. Such concentration invites us to bide time with a basic Judeo-Christian motif, so as to hear in its soundings a newness.

"Still Lifes" and "Autumn Tales" also play with our senses. In both, Turco uses language to reawaken our eyes so that we may see in a still life canvas or in the frame of a camera many other images. The poems resonate so deeply because Turco's trope, *fall*, is explored with completeness and yet restraint. By turning doctrine into poetry, Turco shows that language is, at root, metaphor: capable of carrying us over into new awarenesses.

"Still Lifes," a series of twenty-nine poems, presents a history of the New World from Colonial to modern times. Without explicit time connections, history becomes poeticized. Time is really memory, a deeper collective history of the human race. Images inhabit such structures from our past as a tollhouse, a covered bridge, and a trestle. That these old structures are visited by ghosts or by an unnamed consciousness of the poem suggests a psychological truth Turco had been developing since *The Inhabitant*. Old forms are containers for living images. Their appeal lies in what Suzanne Langer calls "semblance," or "likeness": they are truths of a different order. As Langer puts it, "The function of 'semblance' is to give forms a new embodiment in purely qualitative, unreal instances, setting them free from their normal embodiment in real things so that they may be recognized in their own right. . . ." Turco's achievement is in bringing an Eastern prosody of the senses to bear on the familiar themes and things of Western culture. In so doing he petitions us to let go of our traditional responses.

The final poem of "Autumn's Tales," "The Vista" is an example of Turco's fusion of form, idea, image, and sound to create "semblance." The other eight poems in the series are about Fall capture, as in a camera's frozen moment, the coming of a storm. In the last poem nature is trapped by a blizzard; but although the sense of being devoured by snow is strong, Turco maintains a tone of calm detachment. The descent into the earth's maw is simply seasonal:

> The cars are trapped in frost fire;
> the eye of a pond witnesses what it can
> before the cataract steals its sight.
> Houses settle into their yards,
> farms into their fields and fences.
> The hills rise over the valley,
> and the river is lost.

Yeats once said that poetry is what a man writes out of his quarrel with himself. Throughout his poetic career Turco has dared venture into his own fears and silences, into the idea of death, and into America's lost past. In *First Poems* a Romantic imagination was seeking ways to overcome the splits between mortality and eternity, mind and spirit, literalism and metaphor, comedy and tragedy. Exploring the traditional forms and genres of Western poetry—everything from narratives and satires to accentual syllabics and sestinas—he demonstrated his command over language. His Wesli Court poems were part of that demonstration. But he never forgot the advice of his first critic to drop the confessional I. Out of this quarrel he found other voices from which his themes were distilled. In the forms of Eastern culture Turco's poetry reached a new level: not *his* command, but language's depths were plumbed, and archetypes surfaced.

From the beginning Turco's themes have remained consistent: darkness, winter, silence, fall. Writing with the cold eye of the Zen poet, he has provided a stunning response to Western pessimism, as seen in the tradition of the Fall; and Western egoism, as seen in traditional interpretations of Narcissism. His poetry uncovers grace in the void and the images with which to see that grace. His words petition modern Western consciousness to look more deeply into the depth dimension. And if Turco's world is fantastical and still, this is because of his reverence for imagination, without which our world is not fleshed. Through him we come to see what lies just behind all things, even if the vista is but a blanket of white snow.

References:

Donald J. Masterson, "Making the Language Dance and Go Deep: An Interview with Lewis Turco," *Cream City Review*, 8, nos. 1 & 2 (1983): 108-117;

Marianne Moore, Howard Nemerov, Alan Swallow, eds., *Riverside Poetry 3*, Introduction by Stanley Romaine Hopper (New York: Twayne, 1958).

Literary Awards and Honors Announced in 1984

ACADEMY OF AMERICAN POETS AWARD

James Schuyler, Philip Booth.

LAMONT SELECTION
Sharon Olds, for *The Dead and the Living* (Knopf).

IVAN YOUNGER POETS AWARD
Edward Hirsch, Brad Leithauser, Gjertrud Schnackernberg.

WHITMAN AWARD
Eric Pankey, for *For the New Year* (Atheneum).

AMERICAN ACADEMY AND INSTITUTE OF ARTS AND LETTERS AWARDS

AWARDS IN LITERATURE
Amy Clampitt, Don DeLillo, Sanford Friedman, Robert Haas, Lincoln Kirstein, Romulus Linney, Bobbie Ann Mason, Craig Nova.

E. M. FORSTER AWARD
Humphrey Carpenter.

GOLD MEDAL FOR HISTORY
George F. Kennan.

HAROLD D. VURSELL MEMORIAL AWARD
W. M. Spackman.

JEAN STEIN AWARD
Andrea Lee.

MORTON DAUWEN ZABEL AWARD
Jamaica Kincaid.

RICHARD AND HINDA ROSENTHAL FOUNDATION AWARD
Danny Santiago.

ROME FELLOWSHIP IN LITERATURE
David St. John.

SUE KAUFMAN PRIZE FOR FIRST FICTION
Denis Johnson.

WITTER BYNNER PRIZE FOR POETRY
Henry Taylor.

AMERICAN BOOK AWARDS

FICTION

Ellen Gilchrist, for *Victory Over Japan* (Little, Brown).

NONFICTION
Robert V. Remini, for *Andrew Jackson and the Course of American Democracy, 1833-1845, Volume III* (Harper & Row).

FIRST FICTION
Harriet Doerr, for *Stones of Ibarra* (Viking).

BANCROFT PRIZES IN HISTORY

Louis R. Harlan, for *Booker T. Washington* (Oxford University Press); Paul Starr, for *The Social Transformation of American Medicine* (Basic).

BAY AREA BOOK REVIEWERS ASSOCIATION AWARDS

FICTION
Ron Loewinsohn, for *Magnetic Field(s)* (Knopf).

NONFICTION
Bruno Bettelheim, for *Freud and Man's Soul* (Knopf), and Todd Gitlin, for *Inside Prime Time* (Random House).

POETRY
Jack Marshall, for *Arriving on the Playing Fields of Paradise* (Jazz Press).

BRUCE CATTON PRIZE

Dumas Malone.

CALDECOTT MEDAL

Alice and Martin Provensen, for *The Glorious Flight: Across the Channel with Louis Bleriot* (Viking).

CAREY-THOMAS PUBLISHING AWARD

Farrar, Straus & Giroux, for *A Vanished World*, by Roman Vishniac.

COMMON WEALTH AWARD FOR LITERATURE

Eudora Welty.

DELMORE SCHWARTZ MEMORIAL POETRY AWARD

Ruth Stone.

DRUE HEINZ LITERATURE PRIZE

Randall Silvis, for *The Luckiest Man in the World* (University of Pittsburgh Press).

EDGAR ALLAN POE AWARDS

NOVEL
Elmore Leonard, for *La Brava* (Arbor).

FIRST NOVEL
Will Harriss, for *The Bay Psalm Book Murder* (Walker).

FACT CRIME
Shana Alexander, for *Very Much a Lady* (Little, Brown).

CRITICAL/BIOGRAPHICAL STUDY
Donald Spoto, for *The Dark Side of Genius: The Life of Alfred Hitchcock* (Little, Brown).

PAPERBACK ORIGINAL
Margaret Tracy, for *Mrs. White* (Dell).

JUVENILE
Cynthia Voigt, for *The Callendar Papers* (Atheneum).

SHORT STORY
Ruth Rendell, for "The New Girlfriend," in *Ellery Queen's Mystery Magazine*, August 1983.

GRAND MASTER AWARD
John Le Carré.

SPECIAL EDGAR
Richard Lancelyn Green and John Michael Gibson, for *A Bibliography of A. Conan Doyle* (Oxford University Press).

ERNEST HEMINGWAY FOUNDATION AWARD

Joan Chase, for *During the Reign of the Queen of Persia* (Harper & Row).

SPECIAL CITATIONS
Denis Johnson, for *Angels* (Knopf), and Chuck Wachtel, for *Joe the Engineer* (Morrow).

FRANCIS PARKMAN PRIZE

William Cronon, for *Changes in the Land* (Hill & Wang).

JANET HEIDINGER KAFKA PRIZE FOR FICTION

Joan Chase, for *During the Reign of the Queen of Persia* (Harper & Row).

INGERSOLL PRIZES

T. S. ELIOT AWARD FOR CREATIVE WRITING
Anthony Dymoke Powell.

RICHARD M. WEAVER AWARD FOR SCHOLARLY LETTERS
Russell Kirk.

IOWA SCHOOL OF LETTERS AWARD FOR SHORT FICTION

Ivy Goodman, for *Heart Failure* (University of Iowa Press).

IRITA VAN DOREN AWARD

G. Royce Smith.

IRMA SIMONTON BLACK AWARD

Mavis Jukes, for *No One Is Going to Nashville* (Knopf).

MEDAL OF HONOR FOR LITERATURE

John Updike.

NATIONAL BOOK CRITICS CIRCLE AWARDS

FICTION
William Kennedy, for *Ironweed* (Viking).

GENERAL NONFICTION
Seymour M. Hersch, for *The Price of Power: Kissinger in the Nixon White House* (Summit).

POETRY
James Merrill, for *The Changing Light at Sandover* (Atheneum).

CRITICISM
John Updike, for *Hugging the Shore: Essays in Criticism* (Knopf).

BIOGRAPHY/AUTOBIOGRAPHY
Joyce Johnson, for *Minor Characters* (Houghton Mifflin).

NATIONAL JEWISH BOOK AWARDS

BIOGRAPHY
Dan Kurzman, for *Ben-Gurion: Prophet of Fire* (Simon & Schuster).

CHILDREN'S LITERATURE
Chaya M. Burstein, for *The Jewish Kids Catalog* (Jewish Publication Society of America).

FICTION
Arthur A. Cohen, for *An Admirable Woman* (Godine).

HOLOCAUST
Marguerite Dorian, for *The Quality of Witness: A Rumanian Diary 1937-44* (Jewish Publication Society of America).

ISRAEL
Peter Grose, for *Israel in the Mind of America* (Knopf).

JEWISH HISTORY
Michael Stanislawski, for *Tsar Nicholas I and the Jews* (Jewish Publication Society of America).

JEWISH THOUGHT
Steven T. Katz, for *The Post-Holocaust Dialogues: Critical Studies in Modern Jewish Thought* (New York University Press).

SCHOLARSHIP
S. D. Goiten, for *A Mediterranean Society* (University of California Press).

VISUAL ARTS
Roman Vishniac, for *A Vanished World* (Farrar, Straus & Giroux).

YIDDISH LITERATURE
Chaim Leib Fox, for *Tsu Di Himlen Arof* (To the Heavens Above) (CYCO).

NATIONAL MEDAL FOR LITERATURE

Mary McCarthy.

NEBULA AWARDS

NOVEL
David Brin, for *Star Tide Rising* (Bantam).

NOVELLA
Greg Bear, for *Hardfought*, in *Isaac Asimov's Science Fiction Magazine*.

NOVELETTE
Greg Bear, for *Bloodmusic*, in *Analog*.

SHORT STORY
Gardner Dozois, for "Peacemaker," in *Isaac Asimov's Science Fiction*.

NEWBERY MEDAL

Beverly Cleary, for *Dear Mr. Henshaw* (Morrow).

NOBEL PRIZE FOR LITERATURE

Jaroslav Seifert.

PEN AWARDS

PEN/FAULKNER AWARD
John Edgar Wideman, for *Sent for You Yesterday* (Avon).

HEMINGWAY AWARD FOR
FIRST FICTION
Joan Chase, for *During the Reign of the Queen of Persia* (Harper & Row).

POGGIOLI TRANSLATION AWARD FOR
A WORK IN PROGRESS
Stephen Sartarelli, for *Horrcynus Orca* by Stefano D'Arrigo.

TRANSLATION PRIZE
William Weaver, for *The Name of the Rose* by Umberto Eco (Harcourt Brace Jovanovich).

ALGREN FICTION AWARD FOR
WORK IN PROGRESS
Chris Mazza, Martha Miyatake.

PEN/ROGER KLEIN AWARD
FOR EDITING
Jonathan Galassi, Random House.

PHILIP K. DICK
MEMORIAL AWARD

Tim Powers, for *The Anubis Gates* (Ace).

PRESENT TENSE AWARDS

FICTION
Aharon Appelfeld, for *Tzili* (Dutton).

SOCIAL AND POLITICAL ANALYSIS
Peter Grose, for *Israel in the Mind of America* (Knopf).

HISTORY
Salo W. Baron, for *A Social and Religious History of the Jews, Vol. 18* (Columbia University Press).

BIOGRAPHY
Ruth Jordan, for *Daughter of the Waves* (Taplinger).

JUVENILE
Barbara Pomerantz, for *Bubby, Me and Memories* (UAHC).

RELIGIOUS THOUGHT
Rabbi Eliezer Berkovitz, for *Not in Heaven* (Ktav).

TRANSLATION
Grace Schulman, for *At the Stone of Losses* by T. Carmi (Jewish Publications).

NONFICTION
David Altshuler, for *The Precious Legacy* (Summit).

PULITZER PRIZES

FICTION
William Kennedy, for *Ironweed* (Viking).

BIOGRAPHY
Louis R. Harlan, for *Booker T. Washington* (Oxford University Press).

GENERAL NONFICTION
Paul Starr, for *The Social Transformation of American Medicine* (Basic).

POETRY
Mary Oliver, for *American Primitive* (Atlantic-Little, Brown).

DRAMA
David Mamet, for *Glengarry Glen Ross* (Grove).

REGINA MEDAL

Madeleine L'Engle.

SCOTT O'DELL AWARD FOR
HISTORICAL FICTION

Elizabeth George Speare, for *The Sign of the Beaver* (Houghton Mifflin).

WESTERN STATES BOOK AWARDS

FICTION
Alberto Alvaro "Tito" Rios, for *The Iguana Killer* (Blue Moon Press).

POETRY
Nancy Mairs, for *In All the Rooms of the Yellow House* (Blue Moon Press).

CREATIVE NONFICTION
Clyde Rice, *A Heaven in the Eye* (Breitenbush Publication).

LIFETIME ACHIEVEMENT
Eve Triem.

Checklist: Contributions to Literary History and Biography, 1984

This checklist is a selection of new books on various aspects and periods of literary and cultural history; biographies, memoirs, and correspondence of literary people and their associates; and primary bibliographies. Not included are volumes in general reference series, literary criticism, and bibliographies of criticism.

Abel, Lionel. *The Intellectual Follies: A Memoir of the Literary Venture in New York and Paris.* New York: Norton, 1984.

Anderson, Sherwood. *Selected Letters.* Edited by Charles E. Modlin. Knoxville: University of Tennessee Press, 1984.

Annan, Noel. *Leslie Stephen: The Godless Victorian.* New York: Random House, 1984.

Baldwin, Neil. *To All Gentleness: William Carlos Williams the Doctor-Poet.* New York: Atheneum, 1984.

Baraka, Amiri. *The Autobiography of LeRoi Jones.* New York: Freundlich, 1984.

Barnard, Mary. *Assault on Mount Helicon: A Literary Memoir.* Berkeley: University of California Press, 1984.

Bellamy, Joe David. *American Poetry Observed: Poets on Their Work.* Champaign: University of Illinois Press, 1984.

Benson, Jackson J. *The True Adventures of John Steinbeck, Writer.* New York: Viking, 1984.

Berges, Marshall. *The Life and Times of Los Angeles: A Newspaper, a Family and a City.* New York: Atheneum, 1984.

Bergreen, Laurence. *James Agee.* New York: Dutton, 1984.

Berthold, Dennis, and Kenneth M. Price, eds. *Dear Brother Walt: The Letters of Thomas Jefferson Whitman.* Kent, Ohio: Kent State University, 1984.

Blotner, Joseph. *Faulkner: A Biography.* New York: Random House, 1984.

Borges, Jorge Luis. *Evaristo Carriego.* Translated by Norman T. di Giovanni. New York: Dutton, 1984.

Brady, Frank. *James Boswell: The Later Years, 1769-1795.* New York: McGraw-Hill, 1984.

Brink, André. *Writing in a State of Siege: Essays on Politics and Literature.* New York: Summit, 1984.

Brodsky, Louis Daniel, and Robert W. Hamblin, eds. *Faulkner: A Comprehensive Guide to The Brodsky Collection: Volume II, The Letters.* Jackson: University Press of Mississippi, 1984.

Bruccoli, Matthew J. *Ross MacDonald/Kenneth Millar.* New York & San Diego: Harcourt Brace Jovanovich, 1984.

Bush, Ronald. *T. S. Eliot: A Study in Character and Style.* New York: Oxford University Press, 1984.

Cagin, Seth, and Philip Dray. *Hollywood Films of the Seventies: Sex, Drugs, Violence, Rock 'n' Roll & Politics.* New York: Harper & Row, 1984.

Carr, Virginia Spencer. *Dos Passos: A Life.* Garden City: Doubleday, 1984.

Carter, Paul A. *Another Part of the Fifties.* New York: Columbia University Press, 1984.

Cheever, Susan. *Home Before Dark: A Biographical Memoir of John Cheever.* Boston: Houghton Mifflin, 1984.

Clark, Tom. *Jack Kerouac.* New York & San Diego: Harcourt Brace Jovanovich, 1984.

Colvert, James B. *Stephen Crane.* New York & San Diego: Harcourt Brace Jovanovich, 1984.

Connelly, Thomas L., and Louis D. Rubin, Jr., Madison Jones, Harold Bloom, and James Dickey. *A Southern Renascence Man: Views of Robert Penn Warren.* Edited by Walter B. Edgar. Baton Rouge: Louisiana State University, 1984.

Conrad, Peter. *The Art of the City: Views and Versions of New York.* New York: Oxford University Press, 1984.

Crist, Judith. *Take 22: Moviemakers on Moviemaking.* New York: Viking, 1984.

Dahl-Wolfe, Louise. *Louise Dahl-Wolfe: A Photographer's Scrapbook.* New York: St. Martin's/Marek, 1984.

Davies, Stevie. *Emily Brontë: The Artist as a Free Woman.* New York: Carcanet, 1984.

Davis, Kenneth C. *Two-Bit Culture: The Paperbacking of America.* Boston: Houghton Mifflin, 1984.

de Beauvoir, Simone. *Adieux: A Farewell to Sartre.* Translated by Patrick O'Brian. New York: Pantheon, 1984.

Delany, Sheila. *Writing Woman: Women Writers and Women in Literature, Medieval to Modern.* New York: Schocken, 1984.

Edel, Leon. *The Letters of Henry James, Vol. IV, 1895-1916.* Cambridge, Mass.: Harvard University Press, 1984.

Elledge, Scott. *E. B. White: A Biography.* New York: Norton, 1984.

Evans, Harold. *Good Times, Bad Times.* New York: Atheneum, 1984.

Farber, Stephen, and Marc Green. *Hollywood Dynasties.* New York: Delilah/Putnam, 1984.

Farnan, D. J. *Auden in Love.* New York: Simon & Schuster, 1984.

Fitzgerald, Penelope. *Charlotte Mew and Her Friends.* London: Collins, 1984.

Frame, Janet. *An Angel at My Table: An Autobiography, Volume Two.* New York: Braziller, 1984.

Friedman, Maurice. *Martin Buber's Life and Work: The Later Years, 1945-1965.* New York: Dutton, 1984.

Fuentes, Norberto. *Hemingway in Cuba.* Secaucus, N.J.: Lyle Stuart, 1984.

Gardner, John. *The Art of Fiction: Notes on Craft for Young Writers.* New York: Knopf, 1984.

Goldberg, Anatol. *Ilya Ehrenburg: Writing, Politics, and the Art of Survival.* New York: Viking, 1984.

Goodwin, John, ed. *Peter Hall's Diaries: The Story of a Dramatic Battle*. New York: Harper & Row, 1984.

Guest, Barbara. *Herself Defined: The Poet H. D. and Her World*. Garden City: Doubleday, 1984.

Halperin, John. *The Life of Jane Austen*. Baltimore: Johns Hopkins University Press, 1984.

Hemingway, Ernest. *Ernest Hemingway on Writing*. Edited by Larry W. Phillips. New York: Scribners, 1984.

Hill, Christopher. *The Experience of Defeat: Milton and Some Contemporaries*. New York: Viking, 1984.

Kael, Pauline. *Taking It All In*. New York: Holt, Rinehart & Winston, 1984.

Kazin, Alfred. *An American Procession: The Major American Writers from 1830 to 1930, the Crucial Century*. New York: Knopf, 1984.

Kelvin, Norman, ed. *The Collected Letters of William Morris. Volume One: 1848-1880*. Princeton, N.J.: Princeton University Press, 1984.

Kohfeldt, Mary Lou. *Lady Gregory: The Woman Behind the Irish Renaissance*. New York: Atheneum, 1984.

Lahr, John. *Automatic Vaudeville: Essays and Star Turns*. New York: Knopf, 1984.

Langer, Elinor. *Josephine Herbst*. Boston: Atlantic/Little, Brown, 1984.

Lebeaux, Richard. *Thoreau's Seasons*. Amherst: University of Massachusetts Press, 1984.

Lee, Lawrence, and Barry Gifford. *Saroyan: A Biography*. New York: Harper & Row, 1984.

Lehmann, John. *Three Literary Friendships*. New York: Holt, Rinehart & Winston, 1984.

Leppmann, Wolfgang. *Rilke: A Life*. New York: Fromm, 1984.

Levy, Alan. *Vladimir Nabokov: The Velvet Butterfly*. Photographs by Horst Tappe. Sag Harbor, N.Y.: Permanent Press, 1984.

Lewis, Robert. *Slings and Arrows: Theater in My Life*. Briarcliff Manor, N.Y.: Stein & Day, 1984.

Malina, Judith. *The Diaries of Judith Malina 1947-1957*. New York: Grove, 1984.

Marshall, Peter. *William Godwin*. New Haven: Yale University Press, 1984.

Martin, Wendy. *An American Triptych: Anne Bradstreet, Emily Dickinson, Adrienne Rich*. Chapel Hill: University of North Carolina Press, 1984.

Matich, Olga, and Michael Heim, eds. *The Third Wave: Russian Literature in Emigration*. Ann Arbor, Mich.: Ardis, 1984.

McAleer, John. *Ralph Waldo Emerson: Days of Encounter*. Boston: Little, Brown, 1984.

Mehta, Ved. *The Ledge Between the Streams*. New York: Norton, 1984.

Mellow, James R. *Invented Lives*. Boston: Houghton Mifflin, 1984.

Mikes, George. *Arthur Koestler: The Story of a Friendship*. London: Deutsch, 1984.

Miller, Arthur. Salesman *in Beijing*. New York: Viking, 1984.

Miller, James. *Rousseau: Dreamer of Democracy*. New Haven, Conn.: Yale University Press, 1984.

Nadel, Ira Bruce. *Biography: Fiction, Fact and Form*. New York: St. Martin's, 1984.

O'Sullivan, Vincent, and Margaret Scott, eds. *The Collected Letters of Katherine Mansfield: Volume One, 1888-1917*. New York: Oxford University Press, 1984.

Parris, Leslie, ed. *The Pre-Raphaelite Papers*. New York: Allen Lane Books/Viking, 1984.

Parris, ed. *The Pre-Raphaelites*. New York: Allen Lane Books/Viking, 1984.

Pawel, Ernst. *The Nightmare of Reason: A Life of Franz Kafka*. New York: Farrar, Straus & Giroux, 1984.

Perry, George. *Life of Python*. Boston: Little, Brown, 1984.

Peters, Margot. *Mrs. Pat: The Life of Mrs. Patrick Campbell*. New York: Knopf, 1984.

Phillips, Larry W., ed. *Ernest Hemingway on Writing*. New York: Scribners, 1984.

Plimpton, George, ed. *Writers at Work: The Paris Review Interviews, Sixth Series*. New York: Viking, 1984.

Pottle, Frederick A. *James Boswell: The Earlier Years, 1740-1769*. New York: McGraw-Hill, 1984.

Pound, Omar, and A. Walton Litz, eds. *Ezra Pound and Dorothy Shakespear: Their Letters 1909-1914*. New York: New Directions, 1984.

Prenshaw, Peggy Whitman, ed. *Conversations With Eudora Welty*. Jackson: University Press of Mississippi, 1984.

Pritchard, William H. *Frost: A Literary Life Reconsidered*. New York: Oxford University Press, 1984.

Pym, Barbara. *A Very Private Eye: An Autobiography in Diaries and Letters*. Edited by Hazel Holt and Hilary Pym. New York: Dutton, 1984.

Quennell, Peter, ed. *The Selected Essays of Cyril Connolly*. New York: Persea, 1984.

Raeburn, John. *Fame Became of Him: Hemingway as Public Writer*. Bloomington: Indiana University Press, 1984.

Ransom, John Crowe. *Selected Essays of John Crowe Ransom*. Edited by Thomas Daniel Young and John Hindle. Baton Rouge: Louisiana State University Press, 1984.

Rhys, Jean. *The Letters of Jean Rhys*. Edited by Francis Wyndham and Diana Melly. New York: Viking, 1984.

Richardson, H. Edward. *Jesse: The Biography of an American Writer—Jesse Hilton Stuart*. New York: McGraw-Hill, 1984.

Richardson, Joanna. *Colette*. New York: Watts, 1984.

Ronda, Bruce A., ed. *The Letters of Elizabeth Palmer Peabody: American Renaissance Woman*. Middletown, Conn.: Wesleyan University Press, 1984.

Rovere, Richard. *Final Reports: Personal Reflections on Politics and History in Our Time.* Garden City: Doubleday, 1984.

Rudnick, Lois Palken. *Mabel Dodge Luhan: New Woman, New Worlds.* Albuquerque: University of New Mexico Press, 1984.

Samuelson, Arnold. *With Hemingway: A Year in Cuba.* New York: Random House, 1984.

Sarton, May. *At Seventy: A Journal.* New York: Norton, 1984.

Scammell, Michael. *Solzhenitsyn.* New York: Norton, 1984.

Schickel, Richard. *D. W. Griffith: An American Life.* New York: Simon & Schuster, 1984.

Schwed, Peter. *Turning the Pages: An Insider's Story of Simon & Schuster, 1924-1984.* New York: Macmillan, 1984.

Shirer, William L. *Twentieth Century Journey: A Memoir of a Life and the Times; Volume II, The Nightmare Years, 1930-1940.* Boston: Little, Brown, 1984.

Silverman, Kenneth. *The Life and Times of Cotton Mather.* New York: Harper & Row, 1984.

Simenon, Georges. *Intimate Memories.* Translated by Harold J. Salemson. New York & San Diego: Harcourt Brace Jovanovich, 1984.

Sokolov, Raymond. *Wayward Reporter: The Life of A. J. Liebling.* Berkeley, Calif.: Creative Arts, 1984.

Spurling, Hilary. *Ivy: The Life of I. Compton-Burnett.* New York: Knopf, 1984.

Stallworthy, Jon, ed. *Wilfred Owen: The Complete Poems and Fragments.* New York: Norton, 1984.

Thorpe, Edward. *Chandlertown: The Los Angeles of Philip Marlowe.* New York: St. Martin's, 1984.

Tolkien, J. R. R. *The Monsters and the Critics: And Other Essays.* Edited by Christopher Tolkien. Boston: Houghton Mifflin, 1984.

Trevor, William. *A Writer's Ireland: Landscape in Literature.* New York: Viking, 1984.

Wadham, Stephen. *Remembering Orwell.* New York: Penguin, 1984.

Waugh, Evelyn. *A Little Learning.* Boston: Little, Brown, 1984.

Waugh. *When the Going Was Good.* Boston: Little, Brown, 1984.

Weaver, William. *Duse.* New York & San Diego: Harcourt Brace Jovanovich, 1984.

Welty, Eudora. *One Writer's Beginnings.* Cambridge, Mass.: Harvard University Press, 1984.

West, Anthony. *H. G. Wells: Aspects of a Life.* New York: Random House, 1984.

Wilson, A. N. *Hilaire Belloc.* New York: Atheneum, 1984.

Wood, Sally, ed. *The Southern Mandarins: Letters of Caroline Gordon to Sally Wood, 1924-1937.* Baton Rouge: Louisiana State University Press, 1984.

Woods, Oliver, and James Bishop. *The Story of the* Times. Salem, N.H.: Michael Joseph, 1984.

Woolf, Virginia. *The Diary of Virginia Woolf: Volume Five, 1936-1941*. Edited by Anne Olivier Bell, assisted by Andrew McNeillie. New York & San Diego: Harcourt Brace Jovanovich, 1984.

Zweig, Paul. *Walt Whitman: The Making of a Poet*. New York: Basic Books, 1984.

Necrology

Ansel Adams—22 April 1984
David H. Appel—1 July 1984
Sylvia Ashton-Warner—28 April 1984
Brooks Atkinson—13 January 1984
Luigi Barzini—30 March 1984
Sir John Betjeman—19 May 1984
Ursula Bloom—29 October 1984
Paul Darcy Boles—4 May 1984
Helen Dore Boylston—30 September 1984
Van Allen Bradley—25 December 1984
Richard Brautigan—? September 1984
George P. Brett, Jr.—11 February 1984
Gustav J. Breuer—22 January 1985
Peter Bull—20 May 1984
Ben Lucien Burman—12 November 1984
Truman Capote—25 August 1984
Julio Cortázar—12 February 1984
Ursula Reilly Curtiss—10 October 1984
William Empson—15 April 1984
Samuel G. Engel—7 April 1984
Charles G. Finney—16 April 1984
Carl Foreman—26 June 1984
Frances Goodrich—29 January 1984
Norbert Guterman—20 September 1984
Albert Halper—19 January 1984
Lillian Hellman—30 June 1984
Chester Himes—12 November 1984
Denis Johnston—8 August 1984
Harnett T. Kane—4 September 1984
Henia Karmel-Wolfe—9 July 1984
Roland Kibbee—5 August 1984
Alfred A. Knopf—11 August 1984
Stephen E. Koss—25 October 1984
Nora Kramer—4 July 1984
Norman Krasna—1 November 1984
Richard Lattimore—26 February 1984

LeRoy Leatherman—9 April 1984
J. Ben Lieberman—19 September 1984
John Lee Mahin—18 April 1984
Alfred Mayer—27 October 1984
Julian Mayfield—20 October 1984
Liam O'Flaherty—7 September 1984
George Oppen—7 July 1984
James Reid Parker—27 January 1984
Sam Peckinpah—28 December 1984
Roland Penrose—22 April 1984
J. B. Priestley—14 August 1984
Carl Proffer—24 September 1984
Ellen Raskin—8 August 1984
Leo Robin—29 December 1984
Joseph Schrank—23 March 1984
Arthur Schwartz—3 September 1984
Irwin Shaw—16 May 1984
Mikhail A. Sholokov—21 February 1984
George A. Spater—14 June 1984
Manès Sperber—5 February 1984
Jess Stein—23 June 1984
Philip Van Doren Stern—31 July 1984
Margaret Bingham Stillwell—22 April 1984
Jesse Stuart—17 February 1984
Gerald Sykes—15 July 1984
Harold C. Syrett—29 July 1984
Walter Tevis—8 August 1984
Ernest R. Tidyman—14 July 1984
Agness Underwood—3 July 1984
R. G. Vliet—11 May 1984
Jessamyn West—23 February 1984
Meredith Willson—15 June 1984
Louis B. Wright—26 February 1984
Ben David Zevin—27 December 1984
Paul Zweig—29 August 1984

Contributors

Dwight Allen .... *Ossining, New York*
Nancy G. Anderson.. *Auburn University at Montgomery*
Orin Anderson ....*Myrtle Beach, South Carolina*
Richard Anderson...*Huntingdon College*
Judith Appelbaum...*New York, New York*
David Haward Bain...*Brooklyn, New York*
Judith S. Baughman..*Columbia, South Carolina*
William B. Branch...*New Rochelle, New York*
Robert E. Burkholder ....*Pennsylvania State University-Wilkes Barre*
Bryce J. Christensen...*The Rockford Institute*
John P. Dessauer..*Center for Book Research*
R. H. W. Dillard ....*Hollins College*
Mary Doll..*Fulton, New York*
Ann Dahlstrom Farmer ....*Whittier College*
Anthony M. Friedson...*University of Hawaii*
George Garrett...*University of Virginia*
George Gibian ....*Cornell University*
Howard Kissel ....*New York, New York*
Susan Koppelman ....*St. Louis, Missouri*
S. Lillian Kremer...*Manhattan, Kansas*
Richard Layman...*Columbia, South Carolina*
Mary Ellen Miller ....*Western Kentucky University*
Michael P. Mullen ....*Indian Hills Community College*
Ira B. Nadel ....*University of British Columbia*
John Press...*Frome, Somerset, England*
Kenneth T. Reed...*Miami University*
H. Edward Richardson ....*University of Louisville*
Jean W. Ross ....*Columbia, South Carolina*
Walter W. Ross ....*Columbia, South Carolina*
Yvonne Shafer...*Florida State\University*
Carl R. Shirley..*University of South Carolina*
English Showalter...*Modern Language Association*
Patricia L. Skarda ....*Smith College*
Paul Skenazy...*Santa Cruz, California*
Peter Stansky ....*Stanford University*
William L. Stull ....*University of Hartford*
Lewis Turco..*State University of New York at Oswego*
David Warrington ....*Indiana University*
Stanley Weintraub..*Pennsylvania State University*
Stephen Whited...*Georgia State University*
Jonathan C. Williams ....*Jargon Society*
John Zneimer ....*Indiana University Northeast*

Yearbook Index: 1980-1984

6232

BROTHERS & KEEPERS

JOHN EDGAR WIDEMAN

GIRLFRIENDS AND WIVES

Robert Wallace

THE LIVES OF
Riley Chance
A NOVEL

Robert Bausch

NEW AS A WAVE
A RETROSPECTIVE: 1937–1983

1984
Winner
WESTERN STATES BOOK AWARDS

EVE TRIEN